T0094216

ROUTLEDGE HANDBOOK OF SOUTH ASIAN CRIMINOLOGY

Although the literature and cultural practices of the South Asian region demonstrate a rich understanding of criminology, this handbook is the first to focus on crime, criminal justice, and victimization in Afghanistan, Bangladesh, Bhutan, India, Maldives, Nepal, Pakistan, and Sri Lanka.

South Asia's rapid growth in population and economy continues to introduce transformations in social behaviors, including those related to criminality and victimization. Readers of this handbook will gain a comprehensive look at criminology, criminal justice, and victimology in the South Asian region, including processes, historical perspectives, politics, policies, and victimization. This collection of chapters penned by scholars from all eight of the South Asian nations, as well as the US, UK, Australia, and Belgium, will advance the study and practice of criminology in the South Asian region and carry implications for other regions.

The *Routledge Handbook of South Asian Criminology* provides a wealth of information on criminological issues and their effect on the countries and governments' efforts to mitigate them. It is essential reading for students and scholars of South Asian criminology, criminal justice, and politics.

K. Jaishankar is presently the Professor of Criminology and Head of the Department of Criminology at the Raksha Shakti University (Police and Internal Security University), Gandhinagar, Gujarat, India. Prior to this present position, he served as a faculty member at the Department of Criminology and Criminal Justice, Manonmaniam Sundaranar University, Tirunelveli, Tamil Nadu, India. He is the recipient of the prestigious National Academy of Sciences, India (NASI) SCOPUS Young Scientist Award 2012—Social Sciences and ISC—S.S. Srivastava Award for Excellence in Teaching and Research in Criminology. He was a Commonwealth Fellow (2009–2010) at the Centre for Criminal Justice Studies, School of Law, University of Leeds, UK. He is the founding editor-in-chief of the *International Journal of Cyber Criminology* (www.cybercrime-journal.com) and editor-in-chief of *International Journal of Criminal Justice Sciences* (www.ijcjs.com). He is the founding president of the South Asian Society of Criminology and Victimology (SASCV) (www.sascv.org) and founding executive director (honorary) of the Centre for Cyber Victim Counselling (CCVC) (www.cybervictims.org). He was a discussant in the "Opening discussion: Focusing on victims of crime—comparing crime patterns and improving practice. Researchers' advice to policy" of the Stockholm Criminology Symposium held during June 11–13, 2012, in Stockholm, Sweden, and responded to the questions of Beatrice Ask, the Swedish minister for justice, and Paula Teixeria da Cruz, the Portuguese minister for justice. He was a Keynote Speaker at the 15th World Society of Victimology Symposium held in July 2015 at Perth, Australia, and at the 14th World Society of Victimology Symposium held in May 2012 at The Hague, the Netherlands. He was appointed as an International Ambassador of the British Society of Criminology (BSC). He is the founding father of the academic discipline cyber criminology (2007) and is the proponent of the space transition theory of cybercrimes (2008). His areas of academic competence are cyber criminology, victimology, crime mapping, GIS, communal violence, policing, and crime prevention. Visit www.jaishankar.org for more information.

ROUTLEDGE HANDBOOK OF SOUTH ASIAN CRIMINOLOGY

Edited by K. Jaishankar

Routledge
Taylor & Francis Group

NEW YORK AND LONDON

First published 2020
by Routledge
52 Vanderbilt Avenue, New York, NY 10017

and by Routledge
2 Park Square, Milton Park, Abingdon, Oxon, OX14 4RN

Routledge is an imprint of the Taylor & Francis Group, an informa business

© 2020 Taylor & Francis

Library of Congress Cataloging-in-Publication Data
Names: Jaishankar, K., author.
Title: Routledge handbook of South Asian criminology / K. Jaishankar.
Description: 1 Edition. | New York : Routledge, 2020.
Identifiers: LCCN 2019015181 (print) | LCCN 2019016889
(ebook) | ISBN 9780429320118 (Ebook) | ISBN 9781482260458
(hardback) | ISBN 9780429320118 (ebk)
Subjects: LCSH: Criminology—South Asia—History.
Classification: LCC HV6022.S64 (ebook) | LCC HV6022.S64 J35 2019
(print) | DDC 364.954—dc23
LC record available at https://lccn.loc.gov/2019015181

ISBN: 978-1-4822-6045-8 (hbk)
ISBN: 978-0-429-32011-8 (ebk)

Typeset in Bembo
by Apex CoVantage, LLC

Printed and bound in Great Britain by TJ International Ltd, Padstow, Cornwall

To my Sister K. Jayabharathi and my Brother K. Jaikumar who significantly sacrificed for my School and Higher Education

CONTENTS

Contents

CONTRIBUTORS

Zahid Shahab Ahmed is an Alfred Deakin Postdoctoral Research Fellow at Alfred Deakin Institute for Citizenship and Globalization, Deakin University, Australia. He is the author of *Regionalism and Regional Security in South Asia: The Case of SAARC* (Routledge, 2013). He specializes in peace and conflict studies, Asian regionalism, and foreign policy relations of South Asian countries.

Sally Atkinson-Sheppard is a criminologist and strategist from the UK. She was awarded her PhD from King's College London in 2015 after completing an ethnographic study into street children's involvement in organized crime in Dhaka, Bangladesh. She began her career as a researcher for the Metropolitan Police Service (MPS) in London, where she worked with young offenders engaged in violent offending, developed the MPS first Gangs Manual and represented the MPS in a collaborative study with the British Prison Service that explored the psychology of gang related violence. She went on to advise on a variety of criminal justice reform projects in Bangladesh, including leading the Bangladesh Prison Directorate and the Bangladesh Anti-Corruption Commission through the development of their first strategic plans. She has recently returned to the UK after living and working in Beijing for 3 years, where she led the first study into migrant children's involvement in gangs and organized crime in China. She lectures at King's College London and Bath Spa University.

Subrata Banarjee is working as an Assistant Professor of the Department of Criminology and Police Science at Mawlana Bhashani Science and Technology University, Santosh, Tangail, Bangladesh. Before that he worked in Bangladesh Institute of Labour Studies, Dhaka, as a research associate. He has completed his graduation and master's in criminology and police science and worked as an intern in Terrorism Prevention Branch, United Nations Office on Drug and Crime Prevention (UNODC), UN; Vienna, Austria. His areas of interest are issues of terrorism, female criminality, child rights, penology, and victimization.

Roshi Bhandaree is a government attorney and has done a master's degree in criminal law and justice and LLB from Kathmandu School of Law. Currently, she is working on a project titled Young Women for Change organized by Midwifery Society of Nepal (MIDSON) and supported by International Women's Health Coalition (IWHC) working on the key issues of young women addressing adolescents and youth on sexual and reproductive health. Prior to this, she worked as an intern at the Office of the Attorney General, Kathmandu, Nepal. Following this, she worked as a legal assistant at D.R. Khanal and Co. and at Sharma and Law Associates after completion of a bachelor's degree. She is a diploma holder on 7th ESDR Residential School on Economic, Social and Development Rights, and Good Governance with Special reference to Law and Development, 4th Dec.–24th Dec. 2011 organized by Kathmandu School of Law.

Dalbir Bharti is a former IPS (Indian Police Service) officer. He took voluntary retirement from the IPS in 2011, and presently, he is a Delhi NCR–based Legal Consultant. He did his M.A. (Political Science) from Kurukshetra University and later he did LL.B. from Dr. Babasaheb Ambedkar Marathwada University, Aurangabad, and received a doctorate from University of Mumbai. He served in the State of Maharashtra and under the government of India in various capacities such as Superintendent of Police in Jalna and Sindhudurg districts; Deputy Commissioner of Police in Aurangabad and Mumbai cities; Additional Commissioner of Police in Nagpur city; Deputy Inspector-General of Police, CRPF; Inspector-General of Police, Amravati Range, and Director of Maharashtra Intelligence Academy, Pune. His published books are: (1) *The Constitution and Criminal Justice Administration*; (2) *Police and People*; (3) *Women and the Law*, and (4) *Social Harmony: A Remedy to Intolerance*. The Hindi version of his book *Police and People* has been awarded Pt. Govind Vallabh Pant Purashkar in 2011 by the government of India.

John Braithwaite is a Distinguished Professor at the Australian National University (ANU). He is currently the Research Council Federation Fellow at the Australian National University. In 2001, he established Regnet (Regulatory Institutions Network), a worldwide network of institutions, practitioners, and academics researching the key domain of regulation with an eye toward human rights, justice, and sustainable environmental policy. He is universally considered one of the most renowned contemporary criminologists, partly due to his decisive role in the development of the right of redress. His powerful and striking theories and vision have positioned him as a world-leading social scientist. He is the recipient of a number of international awards and prizes for his work, including an honorary doctorate at KU Leuven (2008), Stockholm Prize in Criminology (2006), the University of Louisville Grawemeyer Award with Peter Drahos for Ideas Improving World Order (2004), and the Prix Emile Durkheim, International Society of Criminology, for lifetime contributions to criminology (2005).

R. Rochin Chandra is presently the director of the Centre for Criminology & Public Policy at Udaipur, Rajasthan, India. He received his MPhil Degree in criminology from the Raksha Shakti University, Ahmedabad, Gujarat, India, and master's degree in criminology and criminal justice science from Manonmaniam Sundaranar University, Tirunelveli, Tamil Nadu, India. In his master's degree, he received the prestigious Prof. Stanley Yeldell Gold Medal and he was recognized as a Young Change Maker in India. He also serves as an editorial assistant of the *International Journal of Criminal Justice Sciences*.

Lham Dorji is the deputy chief research officer and the head of the Socio-Economic Analysis and Research Division of National Statistics Bureau, Bhutan. He worked with the Centre for Bhutan Studies & GNH Research as a multidisciplinary researcher for about 10 years.

Fasihuddin is the founder of Pakistan Society of Criminology and editor-in-chief of *Pakistan Journal of Criminology*. He is MBBS, LLB, and MA in political science with Gold Medal. He is a senior officer of Police Service of Pakistan (PSP) and the author of *Expanding Criminology to Pakistan*. He presented his field experiences in many international conferences and seminars and visited many countries including USA, UK, Canada, Germany, Italy, Norway, Sweden, Denmark, Turkey, Thailand, Nepal, China, and Japan and has published a number of international papers. He is respected as a pioneer of criminological studies in his country, where he is constantly engaged through the forum of Pakistan Society of Criminology to bring academics and practitioners of his country to one place and organize the individual efforts of Pakistani researchers and law-enforcement officials into an academically viable whole. He is a member of many international societies of criminology and police forums around the world. His special interests are police reforms, children's and women's rights, and policing in Pakistan.

Sonam Gyeltshen is a Research Officer in the Socio-Economic Analysis and Research Division, National Statistics Bureau (NSB), Royal Kingdom of Bhutan.

Debarati Halder is presently the Professor of Legal Studies and Head, Centre for Research on Policy and Law (CRPL), Unitedworld School of Law (UWSL), Karnavati University, Ahmedabad, Gujarat; Managing Director of the Centre for Cyber Victim Counselling (CCVC), India (www.cybervictims.org). She received her LLB from the University of Calcutta and her master's degree in international and constitutional law from the University of Madras. She holds a PhD degree from the National Law School of India University (NLSIU), Bangalore, India. She has authored three books, titled *Child Sexual Abuse Laws in India* (Sage, 2018), *Cyber Crime against Women in India* (Sage, 2016, with K. Jaishankar), and *Cyber Crime and the Victimization of Women: Laws, Rights and Regulations* (IGI Global, 2011, with K. Jaishankar), and has co-edited a book titled *Therapeutic Jurisprudence and Overcoming Violence against Women* (IGI Global, 2017, with K. Jaishankar). She has published many articles in peer-reviewed journals and chapters in peer-reviewed books.

Md. Shakhawat Hossain is currently working as a Lecturer in the Department of Criminology and Police Science at Chittagong University, Chittagong, Bangladesh. Before that, he worked in Police Staff College Bangladesh (an apex training center of Bangladesh Police). He completed his graduation and postgraduation from the Department of Criminology and Police Science at Mawlana Bhashani Science and Technology University, Santosh, Tangail, Bangladesh. He has attended several national and international conferences on contemporary issues of the criminological arena. His areas of interests are terrorism, political crime, domestic violence, investigation, police, and victimization.

Aminath Shifaya Ibrahim is an attorney and a mediator in the Maldives. She was a Law Lecturer at Faculty of Shariáh and Law, Maldives National University (previously known as Maldives College for Higher Education) until her appointment as the Deputy Attorney General in 2009 and later on served as the Deputy Minister for Labor Relations. She is a member of the Charted Institute of Arbitrators (CIArb). She received her LLB (Hons) from United Kingdom and completed her masters in Comparative Law (MCL) with a distinction from Malaysia. Her research interests include employment and labor law, criminal law, and alternative dispute resolution.

International Crisis Group is an independent organization working to prevent wars and shape policies that will build a more peaceful world. Crisis Group was founded in 1995 as an international nongovernmental organization by a group of prominent statesmen who despaired at the international community's failure to anticipate and respond effectively to the tragedies of Somalia, Rwanda, and Bosnia. The group was led by Morton Abramowitz (former U.S. Ambassador to Turkey and Thailand, then president of the Carnegie Endowment for International Peace), Mark Malloch-Brown (former head of the UN Development Programme, then UN Deputy Secretary-General and UK Minister), and its first Chairman, U.S. Senator George Mitchell. The idea was to create a new organization with a highly professional staff to serve as the world's eyes and ears for impending conflicts and with a highly influential board that could mobilize effective action from global policymakers. Crisis Group sounds the alarm to prevent deadly conflict. They build support for the good governance and inclusive politics that enable societies to flourish. They engage directly with a range of conflict actors to seek and share information and to encourage intelligent action for peace. In this more polarized, fragmented, and dangerous world, Crisis Group's work points a way forward. War is not inevitable; it is a man-made disaster. Crisis Group today is generally regarded as the world's leading source of information, analysis, and policy advice to prevent and resolve deadly conflict.

Mohammed Jahirul Islam is an Assistant Professor and Chairman of Criminology and Police Science, School of Life Science, Mawlana Bhasani Science and Technology University (MBSTU) at Tangail, Bangladesh. Before joining the MBSTU faculty, he was employed as a research officer at Bangladesh Institute of Development Studies (BIDS) and a guest lecturer of Sociology at Bangladesh Open University. He received his M.S.S degree in sociology from Shahjalal University of Science and Technology (SUST) in 2009. He has written a number of research articles on theoretical and historical criminology, philosophy of science, punishment, female criminality, gender issues, terrorism, and fundamentalism.

Kirthi Jayakumar is an activist, artist, and writer from Chennai, India. She is the founder and director of the Red Elephant Foundation, a civilian peace-building initiative that works for gender equality through storytelling, advocacy, and digital interventions. She is a member of the Youth Working Group for Gender Equality under the UNIANYD. She is the recipient of the U.S. Presidential Services Medal (2012) for her services as a volunteer to Delta Women NGO and the two-time recipient of the UN Online Volunteer of the Year Award (2012, 2013). Her second book, *The Dove's Lament*, made it to the final shortlist for the Muse India Young Writers' Literary Award. Kirthi was recently invited to the United States of Women Summit at the White House in Washington, DC, as a nominated change maker. Kirthi is the recipient of the 2016 Orange Flower Award from Women's Web, the 2016 World Pulse Impact Leader Award, and the 2017 Empowerment Leader Award from the Dais Foundation.

Mohammed Bin Kashem is currently an Associate Professor of Sociology and Dean (Acting) Curriculum Development & Evaluation, National University, Bangladesh. Earlier he was an Associate Professor of Sociology at the University of Chittagong, Bangladesh. He holds a master's degree in criminal justice from University of Baltimore, USA. His research interests include crime prevention effectiveness and comparative policing.

Mahfuzul I. Khondaker is a professor of criminal justice at Kutztown University of Pennsylvania, United States of America. He has taught in Bangladesh, Indiana University of Pennsylvania, and Fayetteville State University before joining Kutztown University. He has authored many articles and book reviews and presented papers in numerous national and international conferences. He has published several articles and book reviews and presented in numerous conferences. Currently he is an editorial board member of the *Prison Journal*, published by Sage. He is also a board member of BCPS, a nonprofit organization that assists individuals and families involved in the criminal and juvenile justice systems. He has received a number of awards for teaching and community service. He teaches courses on criminology theory, research methodology, juvenile justice, introduction to criminal justice, crime prevention, and comparative justice systems. His research interests include crime and justice issues in Bangladesh, juvenile delinquency, crime and delinquency prevention, crime and perceptions of crime among the South Asian immigrants, women and victimization, and crime in the Third World countries.

S. Manikandan is currently a Research Assistant at the Centre for Criminology and Victimology, National Law University, Delhi, India. He holds master's (MA) and research degrees (MPhil) in criminology from University of Madras, Chennai, Tamil Nadu, and Raksha Shakti University,

Ahmedabad, Gujarat. He has completed a research study by collaborating on victimology and refugee studies titled "Victimization Narratives of Rohingyas: A Qualitative Study at Bangladesh Refugee Camps" and topped the MPhil batch of 2017–18. His primary research interests are victimology, crime prevention, and corrections.

Thomas Minten obtained a master's degree in business engineering from KU Leuven (Belgium) and a master's degree in economics from Pompeu Fabra University in Spain. He is currently pursuing a PhD in economics at the London School of Economics. His main fields of interest are public economics and health economics. In 2015, he worked at the National Statistics Bureau in Bhutan, where his research mostly revolved around the Bhutanese youth. He co-authored papers involving crime and mental health issues of young Bhutanese people and on the insights from a multidimensional child poverty index of poor Bhutanese children. He was also involved in holding several trainings of statistical software during his stay in Bhutan.

Tony Murphy is a Senior Lecturer in Criminology at Sheffield Hallam University (the Helena Kennedy Centre for International Justice) and an Associate Lecturer in the Social Sciences at the Open University, UK. He has also worked at the University of Westminster, Manchester Metropolitan University (MMU), and the London School of Economics (LSE). He has studied at the London School of Economics, the Open University, and the University of Oxford. He has researched and published across a range of social policy and criminology areas.

Aishath Ali Naz is a founder and consultant at Clinical Psychologist of Maldives Institute for Psychological Services, Training and Research. Previously she worked as the Deputy Director, National Narcotics Control Board (2000 to 2005); was a member of the first Human Rights Commission of the Maldives (2003 to 2005); and was a member of the Parole Board, Maldives (2012–2014). She holds a PhD in clinical psychology (2010), University of Manchester, U.K.; MPhil in clinical psychology, NIMHANS, India (1999); MSc in psychology, India (1996); and in the 16th International Gang Specialist Training Conference, Chicago, USA, 2013, she was certified as an international gang specialist trainer. She won the national award in recognition for developing mental health services in the Maldives (2012). She has travelled to 12 atolls of Maldives and conducted trainings to a target population of 14,000 participants on the topics of preventing gang, domestic, sexual, and drug-related violence; parenting, communication, and life skills; understanding mental illness; and preventing drug abuse (1999–2014). She has presented papers and chaired sessions in conferences and seminars held in USA, UK, Nepal, India, Malaysia, Sri Lanka, Thailand, Indonesia, China, and the Maldives. She was the Local Consultant to the Ministry of Islamic Affairs on the Leaders of Influence Program under Asia Foundation.

Sugata Nandi specializes in the history of urban crime in colonial India and is currently an assistant professor of history at the West Bengal State University, Kolkata, India. Previous to this position he was a Lecturer at the Presidency College, Kolkata. His doctoral thesis is a study of the Calcutta goondas in the context of city politics and police surveillance during 1918–47. He has presented papers on related themes in a number of international and national seminars/conferences. Educated in Kolkata and New Delhi, Nandi has been a Fulbright Fellow at the University of Washington, Seattle, USA, and has taken part in a summer school at the Leiden University, the Netherlands. He has done research projects sponsored by the University Grants Commission, India, and the Centre for Studies in Developing Societies, New Delhi.

Ummey Qulsum Nipun holds an MSc in victimology and criminal justice from the Tilburg University, The Netherlands. Her research interests are on female victimization, child abuse, and child development. A victimologist and development specialist, she has worked in the humanitarian and development sector for the last 9 years in renowned INGOs like UNICEF, Save the Children, IRW, and Child Helpline International. She has been working to serve the destitute children of Bangladesh for Save the Children and to reduce child abuse with Child Helpline International in Amsterdam and recently completed her mission in Somalia, being based in Mogadishu while supporting the Internally Displaced Children affected in long-term war and political turmoil. Currently she is servicing as a United Nations staff for the welfare of destitute children and mothers living in Tea Garden areas of Bangladesh. As an emergency officer of UNICEF, she has been working to support newborn children and their mothers and adolescents who are in deep need of basic human rights, life skill–based supports, etc.

Jeeva Niriella is currently a Professor of Law and the Head of the Department—Public and International Law, Faculty of Law, University of Colombo, Sri Lanka. She is an attorney at law and the founding president of Srilankan Society of Criminology (2015). She is a member of the Presidium of the Asian Criminological Society (ACS) and vice president (Sri Lanka) (co-opted) of the South Asian Society of Criminology and Victimology (SASCV). She is appointed by the government of Sri Lanka as a member of the National Authority for the protection of victims of crimes and witnesses, Sri Lanka (2015–17). She is also the government-appointed director of Columbo Stock Exchange, Sri Lanka. She is a member of several bodies such as National Research Committee, National Science Foundation, Sri Lanka; Asia Crime Prevention Foundation, Sri Lanka; Advisory Panel, *International Journal of Contemporary Laws*; International Economic and Development Research Foundation India; and International Bar Association.

Binita Pandey is a human rights lawyer and has done LLM in human rights and gender justice from Kathmandu School of Law, Nepal. Currently, she is working as a program officer—legal support at Women's Rehabilitation Center, Lalitpur. She is the first Asian winner of Lex-Lead essay competition in 2015. Earlier, she had worked as a teaching assistant at Kathmandu School of Law and a researcher at its Policy and Legal Research Centre. She is a graduate of Purbanchal University, Nepal, holding a bachelor's degree in law. She is one of the founding members of Acting Servitor Together for Human Rights Implementation (SARTHI), which is a nonprofit organization working for human rights in Nepal. She loves travelling and reading novels. For academic purposes, she has been to India, China, Japan, Germany, and Poland. Her areas of interest include doing research on social issues, the issues of women and children, law and development, and good governance.

Pramila Pantha has done LLM in criminal law and justice and LLB from Kathmandu School of Law, Nepal. She has been working as a legal assistant at Janata Law Firm, Nepal. Prior to this, she worked as an intern at the Legal Aid and Consultancy Center, Nepal (LACC). She is one of the founding members of Acting Servitor Together for Human Rights Implementation (SARTHI), which is a nonprofit organization working for human rights in Nepal.

E. Enanalap Periyar is presently an Assistant Professor in the Department of Criminology and Criminal Justice, Manonmaniam Sundaranar University, Tirunelveli, India. Earlier, he was an Indian Council for Social Sciences Research (ICSSR) Fellow in the same department. He was formerly a lecturer in police science and criminology at APA College of Arts and Science, Nanguneri, Tirunelveli District, India. He is the Treasurer of the South Asian Society of Criminology and Victimology (SASCV). He holds a master of science degree in criminology and PhD in criminology from Manonmaniam Sundaranar University on homicide and victim–offender relationships.

Mohammad Azizur Rahman is an associate professor of Criminology and Police Science at Mawlana Bhashani Science and Technology University, Bangladesh, holding honors and three masters' degrees in sociology, regional development planning, and criminology. He has long been engaged in multidisciplinary research, teaching, and human development work at home and abroad. His research interests include the socio-spatial analysis of crime and policing, victim surveys, crime prevention, Islamist terrorism, and anti-Muslim hate crime. Some of his studies include the factors affecting public views of the police, the state of prisons and the integration of released prisoners, Islamist terrorism, socio-sexual behavioral characteristics of brothel sex workers, and the location and quality of life in informal settlements.

Manisha Rajak is a human rights lawyer at Kathmandu, Nepal. She pursued her Master's in human rights and democratization (Asia Pacific) from University of Sydney, Australia in 2015. She has completed her LLB from Kathmandu School of Law, Nepal. Currently she is working as a legal translator/interpreter and case documentation officer at Advocacy Forum, Nepal. Previously, she was involved in the project Prevention of Torture, and now she has been engaged in the project Rights of Migrant Workers in Nepal. Prior to this, she worked as an intern at the Office of the Attorney General, Kathmandu, Nepal. Following this, she joined Advocacy Forum Nepal as an intern, where she worked in the conflict period cases of Nepal. She has worked as a student lawyer (paralegal) through the Clinical Legal Education Program (CLEP) organized by Kathmandu School of Law on 2009. She is one of the founding members of Acting Servitor Together for Human Rights Implementation (SARTHI), which is a nonprofit organization working for human rights in Nepal.

Imran Ahmad Sajid conducted his PhD research on the juvenile justice system in Pakistan. He has contributed to various subject matters of criminology in Pakistan. He worked as managing editor of *Pakistan Journal of Criminology* from 2012 to 2016. He joined the Institute of Peace and Conflict Studies, University of Peshawar, Pakistan, as Lecturer late in 2016. He has multiple publications in national and international journals. Currently, he is managing editor of *Pakistan Journal of Peace and Conflict Studies*.

Mandira Sharma is one of Nepal's civil society leaders. She founded the Advocacy Forum, a human rights organization, which conducted investigations and filed cases on behalf of thousands victims of Nepal's 10-year civil war, which began in the mid-1990s. Her innovative grassroots work linking to the national and international human rights mechanisms has a far-reaching impact on rule of law and human rights in the country. For her courage and tenacity, she was awarded the Human Rights Watch prestigious Human Rights Defender Award (2006), one of the most prestigious honors in the field of human rights. She received her BA in law from Tribhuwan University in Kathmandu and her LLM degree in international human rights from the Law University of Essex in Colchester, England.

Sandhya Basini Sitoula is a Program Coordinator at the Center for Legal Research and Resource Development (CeLRRd), a leading NGO in Kathmandu, Nepal. Her responsibilities include coordinating all field activities related to the Combating Trafficking of Persons Project. In addition, she is responsible for conducting research to raise awareness of trafficking issues and leading training sessions for organizational field staff. She received a LLB in jurisprudence and human rights law and master's of law in human rights and gender justice from the Kathmandu School of Law, Nepal. She has been the editor of multiple annual reports for the Center for Legal Research and Resource Development and is an executive member of the Human Rights Committee of the Kathmandu District Court Bar Associations. She was granted a Humphrey Fulbright Fellowship at USA (2013–14), where she explored best practices for combating human trafficking with particular attention to the areas of law enforcement and prosecution, specifically strategies and mechanisms for victim and witness protection.

Asha P. Soman is presently working as Assistant Professor at School of Law, Alliance University, Bangalore. She received BA LLB (Hons) from Mahatma Gandhi University, Kerala, and toped LLM (commercial law and human rights) from Cochin University of Science and Technology, Kerala, and she received a doctorate (outer space law) from National Law School of India University, Bangalore. She is the recipient of the K.C. Menon Memorial Endowment, 2013, and Merit Award from Sarada Krishna Satgamaya Foundation for Law and Justice (formerly Justice V.R. Krishna Iyer Foundation for Law and Justice), Ernakulam, for securing highest marks in LLM examination 2013 of the Cochin University of Science and Technology, Kerala. She was also a best intern at the Summer Internship Programme (SIP-2012) conducted by the National Human Rights Commission, New Delhi. She has authored and presented many papers in international and national conferences on various socio-legal, socio-legal-science, and socio-enviro-legal issues. She has acted as a resource person, organized many workshops, and done field studies. Her areas of interest are outer space law, jurisprudence, company law, human rights, socio-legal studies, enviro-legal studies, and multidisciplinary studies.

D.B. Subedi is currently a Lecturer at the School of Government, Development and International Affairs, the University of the South Pacific Fiji Islands. Before joining the University of the South Pacific Fiji Islands, D.B. Subedi worked as a Lecturer in the University of New England, Australia. He has an interdisciplinary academic background, specializing in peace and conflict, security, and political and international affairs. He received a PhD degree from the University of New England, Australia (2014), where his PhD thesis studied the politics of postconflict peace building in Nepal with a primary focus on reintegration of Maoist ex-combatants. His work experience in the Asia Pacific comes from Sri Lanka, Nepal, Myanmar, Philippines, and Australia. His research interest focuses on the nexus between conflict, security and development, and its implications for peace building and state building, development, social cohesion, and security in the Asia Pacific region.

P. Madhava Soma Sundaram is a Professor at the Department of Criminology and Criminal Justice, Manonmaniam Sundaranar University, Tirunelveli, Tamil Nadu, India. He holds master's and PhD degrees in criminology from the University of Madras. Earlier he has worked for the government of India to develop its policies on juvenile delinquency and substance abuse prevention by implementing its laws through national-, regional-, and state-level consultations; worked with national-/state-level NGOs by creating a network among themselves for urban crime prevention; and designed, implemented, and evaluated capacity-building programs for criminal justice professionals and civil society. Starting his career as a lecturer in criminology in 1992, he has authored many books, articles, and monographs. In his long career in criminology, he has picked up a few awards, like the ISC-Prof. S. S. Srivastava Award for Excellence in Teaching and Research in Criminology (2009) and Fellow of the Indian Society of Criminology (FISC). His areas of academic proficiency are juvenile justice, criminal justice studies, victimology, and crime prevention.

Amit Thakre is presently working as an Assistant Professor, LNJN National Institute of Criminology and Forensic Science, New Delhi, India. Prior to this present position, he served as a trained criminologist in the Department of Criminology, Raksha Shakti University, Ahmedabad, Gujarat, India, and research consultant at the National Human Rights Commission of India, New Delhi, India. He holds PhD in criminology from Manonmaniam Sundaranar University (MSU), Tamil Nadu, and a master's in criminology from Gurugobind Singh Indraprastha University, New Delhi. Earlier to joining the doctoral program at MSU, he was a lecturer in Institute of Forensic Science, Nagpur University, and Guest Faculty in Bihar Judicial Academy. His research interests are crime prevention, policing, and innovative interventions.

Ali Wardak is a professor of criminology at the University of South Wales and a Fellow of UK's Higher Education Academy. He obtained his PhD from the University of Edinburgh in Scotland. His main teaching and research interests focus on comparative and transnational crime and justice, rule of law, and the relationships between state and nonstate justice systems. From 2006 to 2008, he worked for the United Nations Development Programme (UNDP) in Kabul and co-authored the 2007 *Afghanistan Human Development Report*, where a hybrid model for post-Taliban justice system in Afghanistan is proposed. He has published widely, and his publications include three books: *Social Control and Deviance: A South Asian Community in Scotland* (2000, Aldershot: Ashgate), *Transnational and Comparative Criminology* (2005, London: Cavendish), and *Race and Probation* (2006, London: Willan). He is the joint winner (with John Braithwaite) of the 2013 Radzinowicz Memorial Prize for the best article published in the *British Journal of Criminology*. He is a vice president (representing Afghanistan) of the South Asian Society of Criminology and Victimology (SASCV) and has been an invited speaker at major conferences/forums in Africa, Asia, Australia, Europe, and the United States.

James Windle is currently a lecturer in criminology at University College Cork, UK, and he received his PhD from Loughborough University. His research focuses on illicit drug markets, illicit enterprise, and organized crime. He is author of *Suppressing Illicit Opium Production: Successful Intervention in Asia and the Middle East* (IB Taurus, 2016) and co-editor of *Historical Perspectives on Organized Crime and Terrorism* (Routledge, 2018). He has published in journals including the *European Journal of Criminology, Asian Journal of Criminology, International Journal of Drug Policy,* and *Third World Quarterly.* In 2008 he served as a research intern at UNODC, and in 2015 he contributed to the Brookings Institute project Improving Global Drug Policy: Comparative Perspectives and UNGASS 2016.

FOREWORD

South Asia is a vast geographic area that inhabits almost a quarter of the world's population. With the rapid growth of its population and economy, its significant growth as well, and this region is impacting globally. Its nations, belonging to the developing world, are experiencing quick advancement of modernization that includes all life aspects: the entrance of modern technology into less developed areas, economical changes that impacts the societies' class systems, breaking of old traditions, growing secularity and tolerance, and adaptation to Western norms with stronger individualism and personal liberty, besides growing materialism and personal competitions and more. These transformations indicate changes in individual, group, and social behaviors; while some old inter- and intrapersonal issues are less significant; however, new ones have showed up. Furthermore, with their appearance, criminality and victimization also undertook some new transformations.

Do the new transformations of criminality and victimization represent the same old ones, or are they entirely new? One may claim, for example, that chain snatching, a traditional offense where the target victims might be adult women who can almost do nothing against the quick running or motor cycle–driven young male(s), is not much different than the victim of internet fraud of the same adult population, less familiar with technology, and this naiveté is abused by younger computer crooks. However, is it? The picture is even more complicated, since the old crimes still exist despite the appearance of the new ones. While, for example, the internet is intensively abused in the performance of modern forms of sexual harassment and offences. Children, women, and to a lesser extent also men, are still being sexually harassed, abused, and assaulted. In rapidly changing societies, old and new forms of criminality mix and challenge the criminologists and criminal justice researchers.

Criminology is highly influenced by social changes and cultural transitions that are typical to the contemporary globalized era. Hence, it is necessary for criminology to adapt itself to the changing social world, to the mixing of sets of values and norms of behavior. At present, criminology finds itself standing in between two poles. The first is the strong global aspect of criminological knowledge created by worldwide scholars and researchers—where knowledge created in one location can be easily adapted into another. The other pole is that of localization of knowledge; accordingly, criminological knowledge reflects a certain society with its typical norms and social problems. Each pole has its significance for enriching state-of-the-art criminology. It is better for criminology not to lose any of the insights of these poles and to be prepared to apply its knowledge according to the certain needs.

Having this in mind, the *Routledge Handbook of South Asian Criminology* seems to hold the stick of knowledge by both sides. First, its intensive list of topics reflects many other international handbooks of criminology that present issues on crime and criminal justice, politics of criminal justice, and current issues of victimology. From this angle, this book is relevant and enriches other global works on criminology. Second, the topics and subtopics of different chapters present a localized knowledge. They cover criminological discussions related to all the South Asian nations: Afghanistan, Bangladesh, Bhutan, India, Nepal, Maldives, Pakistan, and Sri Lanka. Each chapter brings forward its own unique contribution, which reflects its local position. Altogether, however, they create a whole greater than its parts, that is, a cutting-edge, accumulated regional criminology that stands in between the two aforementioned poles.

Therefore, one can but congratulate the editor's (Professor K. Jaishankar) initiative of providing a comprehensive handbook related to criminology, criminal justice, and victimology in the South Asia region. The *Routledge Handbook of South Asian Criminology* is timely; it can advance the study and practice of criminology in the South Asian region and can carry implications for other regions.

Professor Natti Ronel,
Department of Criminology,
Bar Illan University
Israel

ACKNOWLEDGMENTS

My ardent thanks are due to *Gerhard Boomgaarden*, Senior Publisher, Routledge, Taylor and Francis Group, who initially reached me with the possibility of such a great book titled *Routledge Handbook of South Asian Criminology*. Also, I sincerely thank *Tom Sutton*, Publisher, Routledge, for his help with the initial book proposal.

Due to some unforeseen circumstances, the book proposal did not materialize with Routledge, and I took it to CRC Press, which is also a part of Taylor and Francis Group. *Carolyn Spence*, the then acquisitions editor of criminal justice books at CRC Press, benevolently observed merit in this work and accepted my book proposal titled *Handbook of South Asian Criminology*. There are no words to express gratitude toward *Carolyn*, and without her this book would not have appeared. I am profoundly obligated to her. Additionally, I thank Editorial Assistant *Ashley Weinstein* of CRC Press for her assistance in the initial book production work.

In 2018, I was informed by *Ellen S. Boyne*, Editor, Routledge, that the CRC Press Criminology and Criminal Justice books were unified with the Routledge imprint and the *Handbook of South Asian Criminology* will be published under Routledge. *Ellen* was greatly supportive, and I thank her from the bottom of my heart.

Additionally, *Kate Taylor*, editorial assistant, Criminal Justice and Criminology, Routledge effectively coordinated with me in conveying this production to reality, and my earnest thanks are due to her. Also, she reported that this book will be renamed *Routledge Handbook of South Asian Criminology*. By this the book returned to its original idea.

Professor Natti Ronel, Bar Illan University, Israel, has composed a convincing foreword, and I sincerely express gratitude toward him for the devoted help he gives all my scholarly endeavors. Despite the fact that we are miles separated, he is dependably with me scholastically, socially and spiritually.

A. Ravisankar designed the text work of the cover page of this book on the Image by Naturals, available at www.pixabay.com, which is released into the public domain under Creative Commons CC0. I sincerely thank him for dedication, patience and passion.

My heartfelt thanks are due to *Rashmi Choudhury*, my MPhil student, who significantly assisted me in the editorial work. She is dedicated and is greatly supportive.

My past and present employing establishments, the Manonmaniam Sundaranar University, Tirunelveli, Tamil Nadu, India, and the Raksha Shakti University, Ahmedabad, Gujarat, India, provided an excellent working environment which enabled me to put my full energy in to this publication, and my cordial thanks are due to them.

I genuinely thank the peer reviewers of this book; some of them are additionally writers of this book. Without these individuals the quality of the book would not have been guaranteed.

Getting chapters from South Asian countries was a challenging assignment, as the field of criminology is still in nascent stages in some regions of South Asia. Hence, I had to utilize the services of some of my own contacts in India, and they graciously accepted to write chapters. Also, it was necessary to get permission from some authors/institutions/journals for republication of their works, and I thank them from my bottom of my heart.

In spite of different unexpected conditions through which this book got fundamentally postponed, be that as it may, the authors of this book had confidence in me and remained with me. Without their patience and assistance, it would not have been conceivable draw out this publication. I will forever remain grateful to them.

Last but not least, my family members were dependably with me, encouraging this publication, and I will be ever grateful to them.

INTRODUCTION

Towards a South Asian Criminology

K. Jaishankar

South Asia is a region that is rich in traditions and culture. Literature, religion and cultural practices of this region demonstrate a traditionally rich understanding of criminology, criminal justice and victimology. South Asian literature is replete with stories of victim justice and restorative practices. Reminiscences of crime and justice can be found in ancient texts like *Manusmriti* (for more details see Chapter 9 of this book), *Arthashastra* and *Thirukkural* (for more details see Chapter 11 of this book), which are more than 2000 or more years old. Hinduism, Buddhism, Jainism, Islam and various tribal religions played a great role with regard to the concept of justice and nonviolence at both individual and community levels.

The colonial period introduced a new and formal centralized criminal justice system dismantling the then-existing idea of justice. The 20th century saw the establishment of new states where ethnic, religious, linguistic, caste, communal, tribal and other identities played a role in the institution of constitutions and in the legal sphere of criminal and victim justice. Today, South Asian countries face acute problems of corruption, criminal violence, terrorism, extremism, poverty, environmental degradation, white-collar/cybercrimes, violations of human rights, state-sponsored terrorism, crimes against humanity and individual and collective victimization. There is a need to assess the status of such issues from a holistic perspective, and in this direction I developed the concept of South Asian criminology and I founded the South Asian Society of Criminology and Victimology (SASCV— www.sascv.org) in 2009. The *Routledge Handbook of South Asian Criminology* will be a treasure trove taking the concept of South Asian criminology to a worldwide audience.

The *Routledge Handbook of South Asian Criminology* is a comprehensive collection of chapters focusing on crime, criminology, criminal justice and victimization in South Asia. The book is intended to be a key resource for readers interested in the criminological, criminal justice and victimological aspects of the South Asian region consisting of nations such as Afghanistan, Bangladesh, Bhutan, India, Pakistan, Maldives, Nepal and Sri Lanka. Each chapter in the book addresses single or multiple topics across the region. Each chapter provides a comprehensive review of the issues, focusing on how crime and victimization are affecting the South Asian region and the efforts taken by the governments to mitigate them. Contributors are from all over the world, but the focus of the chapter(s) is South Asia.

This book is divided in to five parts. Part I. Crime and Criminal Justice Processes, Part II. Historical Perspectives of Crime and Justice, Part III. Politics of Crime and Justice, Part IV. Crime and Justice Policies and Part V. Victims and Victimization. All the chapters focus on various criminological issues of the South Asian region and have contributors from all the countries of South Asian region, the U.S., the UK and Australia.

Part I, Crime and Criminal Justice Processes, starts with Chapter 1. Chapter 1 highlights the state- and non–state-oriented criminal justice systems of Afghanistan. Afghanistan has always been in the limelight around the world for its increasing instability due to extremist groups and warlordism. The post-Taliban administration has paved the way for the need to rebuild the Afghan state-oriented criminal justice system. However, the progress to rebuild is still facing serious problems. The author hence highlights the need for alliance between state and nonstate criminal justice systems in Afghanistan. The current criminal justice system is ineffective and dysfunctional. The establishment of inter institution coordination and communication can pave the way for the renewal of the existing culture of abuses in the Afghan society. The author has proposed an integrated multidimensional model of a postwar criminal justice system in Afghanistan. The author believes that the rich legal culture of Afghanistan can be a boon to the development of an effective and accessible criminal justice system.

Chapter 2 focuses on Bangladesh's criminal justice system and discusses the issues of the criminal justice system. The authors start with highlighting the three main components of the system: the police, courts and corrections. The authors then give an overview of the structure and functioning of each of these subsystems, providing a detailed and comprehensive picture of the various agents of the law enforcement, judiciary and correctional systems. In addition to that, they discuss the various issues and the major concerns in Bangladesh over the last few decades such as the dissatisfaction of the general public with the police, severe overcrowding in the prisons, lack of judicial intervention, rise of domestic violence and several other issues. The chapter concludes by briefly talking about some of the law and policy initiatives in the country to mitigate the growing crime trends and their not-so-effective implementation.

Chapter 3 focused on the efficiency of the Bhutanese criminal justice system and its lack of proper reporting of crimes and national database of crime records, for which the author suggests the creation of university study centres to spread knowledge of criminology. As the author points out, crimes in Bhutan are facing a growing trend of sex trafficking and drugs abuse, mainly due to Westernization and globalization. The chapter describes the Bhutanese legal system and its influence from Buddhist ideologies, because of which the penal code divides crimes into four classifications: felony, misdemeanor, petty misdemeanor and violation (notably, the crime typologies are similar to those in the United States). The chapter also states what the Bhutan penal code criminalizes: crimes against women and children, prostitution, corruption, and damaging reputation of a person more seriously. The author emphasizes that the Bhutan penal code has been one of the first worldwide laws to deal with cybercrimes. The author then describes the Bhutanese legal system as a unique system which does not fall within the category of common law system or the continental civil law system. The chapter then focuses on the process of prosecution, which is entirely guided by the Bhutan civil and Criminal Procedure Code, Bhutanese Penal Code and the constitution, which ensure both the victim and the accused get justice and appeal. Furthermore, the Bhutanese constitution also ensures that underprivileged citizens should get free legal aid from the courts. Lastly, the author describes the role the Royal Bhutan Police, which is the main policing agency in Bhutan; the Bhutan Penal Code provides numerous provisions for effective policing, and the government has taken measures to check corruption in every field of governance including policing.

Chapter 4 draws special attention to the evolution of the criminal justice system in India. The author highlights the different techniques and methods that were used by rulers to establish law and order during ancient times. The chapter starts with the huge importance that was prevalent in the Indian civilization, i.e., dharma, which is the principles of righteousness. This chapter has covered the evolution of India's criminal justice system from three periods, which are Ancient India, Medieval India and Modern India. The author has shown the distinction that occurred in the establishment of police, courts and jails and punishment during Ancient and Medieval India. Modern India saw renewed criminal justice system due to the British Rule. The present-day criminal justice system of India has hence welcomed many new reforms and developments to its existing system. The various components of the present system are still products from the British Rule, but there has been gradual shift from its retributive nature to a more reformative and rehabilitative nature of punishment.

Chapter 5 provides a brief overview of the crime situation in Maldives and the various components of criminal justice system of Maldives. Over the last years, Maldives experienced an increase in the reported levels of assault, illicit drug use, theft, domestic violence and increase of homicides; this last point has been mainly linked to criminal gangs. Furthermore, prostitution and abuse of illicit drugs are on the rise. The author describes changes that occurred after the introduction of the new Penal Code of the Maldives, which restructured criminal offences and their punishments. The authors give a flow chart representing the sequence of criminal proceedings for an adult and a juvenile who is charged as an adult. The authors examine the steps that lead to the creation of the Maldives Police Service (MPS), discussing its role and authority, and to the consequent reforms that lead to change of the presidential agenda and to the Maldives Police Act (2008). Then the authors describe the Maldivian judiciary system and the Maldivian court structure, prison administration in Maldives and changes into prison, police, human rights and political reform that occurred since the brutal murder of a young inmate in 2003. Lastly, the authors give recommendations to police and prison management and to establish effective restorative justice programs.

Chapter 6 outlines the functioning of the criminal justice system in Nepal and emphasizes the need for reform of both structural and legal frameworks. The author describes the institutions in the criminal justice system viz., the police and its various units, government attorneys and their administrative components as well as the structure and responsibilities of the judiciary and an overview of the correctional system. The author concludes by discussing the current issues in policing such as internal problem of accountability, crime investigation with respect to lack of evidence as well as issues in the trial process, defence and legal aid. The author also proposes solutions to the significant problems to form a stable foundation in the criminal justice system of Nepal.

Chapter 7 discusses the criminal justice system of Pakistan in the first part and, in part two, discusses the issues of the crime situation, policing, judiciary and prisons in Pakistan. The author beautifully illustrates the criminal justice processes (such as criminal law-making, the police structure and police functions, as well as the responsibilities of the judiciary and the prison administration). The author also briefly discusses the current crime situation in Pakistan as well as the police structure and issues in police administration highlighting the issue of gender disparity and lack of modernization in the system. The author concludes by focusing on the contemporary issues in the judiciary and the prisons by painting a grim picture of Pakistan's criminal justice system while also talking about some of the constructive steps taken so far by all the stakeholders of the system.

Chapter 8 discusses Sri Lanka's criminal justice system, focusing particularly on how the Sri Lankan constitution and other relevant statutes regulate the main agencies in Sri Lanka. Throughout the chapter the author describes rights guaranteed by the constitution of Sri Lanka and procedural laws relating to controlling the actions of the law enforcement agencies. The author describes how the Sri Lankan constitution governs police and law enforcement, pointing out different kinds of law enforcement regulated by the Sri Lankan constitution and the permissions given to the law enforcement officers. The author also describes rights that the Sri Lankan constitution recognizes to the accused. The author further describes the Sri Lankan judicial process, mainly focusing on the rights guaranteed by the constitution to the accused during the period of the trial and how these rights are ensured by the constitution. According to the Sri Lankan constitution, the presumption of innocence lies at the heart of the criminal law and protects the liberty and dignity of the accused. Lastly, the author describes how the constitution and the main laws regulate prison management in Sri Lanka.

Part II, Historical Perspectives of Crime and Justice, starts with Chapter 9. Chapter 9 addresses a critical assessment of the *Manusmriti*, which is considered by many a definitive work on ancient

Hindu law. The authors highlight the criminal justice tenets found in *Manusmriti* and present a critical analysis of the same. In the first section, the authors discuss the tenets of administration of justice. The authors have highlighted in this chapter how the *Manusmriti* characterized the organization of lawful justice and infliction of punishment according to the order of the castes, i.e., the Varna. This chapter also critically evaluates how the higher castes had privileges in Manu's notion of crime and punishment. In the chapter, the authors have also highlighted how the British colonial rule fitted well with the *Manusmriti*. The authors have also emphasized how the making of the Indian constitution eradicated the unjust and discriminatory laws of the *Manusmriti*. Finally, the authors portray how still the *Manusmriti* is indirectly prevalent in village justice system of India.

Chapter 10 focuses on the crime of witchcraft accusation and victimization in Nepal, describing some main findings of a study done by the author. The author first describes the Witchcraft Accusation Act, enacted in 2015 by the Nepalese government, and following laws that the Nepalese government has enacted in order to resolve the problem of witchcraft accusation, which, however, did not bring the expected results. The author describes the methodology of the research conducted and then describes, through tables and charts, the main results. Among the main findings, the author describes age and sex of victims, violence against them and interaction between victims and the Nepal criminal justice system. The author further describes difficulties that police face whenever they have to deal with the perpetrators and the role of the local community in supporting them. Furthermore, the author describes that the police are often influenced by the local community to file cases and save the perpetrators, stating the need of the police for more power to resolve disputes on local level. The author concludes that there is a clear failure of the Nepalese criminal justice system to control witchcraft accusation crimes.

Chapter 11 looks into the major contributions of classic Tamil literature from ancient south India (Sangam Age) such as *Thirukkural* and *Silappadikaram* into the justice and administration of the traditional Tamil society. The authors divide the chapter into two parts. The first part focuses on the history, literature and justice administration during the Sangam Age. The authors elegantly capture and peep into the ancient literature to describe the courts of justice and their functioning. The second part of the chapter focuses on the crime and justice in Tamil literature to throw some light on the various nuances of criminal jurisprudence, specifically focusing on crime prevention, forensic science, policing, penology and corrections as well as victimology and victim justice. The authors conclude by emphasizing the importance of the Tamil literature to the fields of criminology, criminal jurisprudence and criminal justice.

Chapter 12 is divided into four sections. In the first section, the author traces the genesis of the Goondas and captures a detailed history of how the Goondas Act impacted the majority of the gangsters and how it changed Calcutta by taking some typical cases. The author also talks about how the history of Calcutta was linked with communal riots and institutional politics and how the Goondas evolved as a different community compared to the previous years. The author concludes the chapter by saying that till today, because of the matrix of the politics, the Goondas still pose a serious threat in independent India.

Chapter 13 provides an introduction to the size and scope of opium production in three South Asian nations (India, Pakistan and Afghanistan) and how it was different during the colonial times. The author discusses how these nations have taken up counter-measures to prevent the diversion of opium from the state monopoly. The author also draws interesting insights from two criminological perspectives: situational crime prevention and a routine activity approach to help identify the efforts and risks of diverting opium in those three countries.

Chapter 14 discusses the evolution of the concept of homicide in India till today. The authors divided the chapter into four sections. The first section deals with ancient Hindu codes regarding homicide, the responses to homicide and related punishments; the second section deals with the concept of homicide in the medieval period; the third section deals with a British colonial understanding of homicide in India; and the last section deals with the contemporary understanding of homicide in post-independence and contemporary India. Lastly, the authors conclude that the level of punishment in ancient India for homicide varied between various Varnas and that further studies are needed in order to understand patterns in homicide throughout Indian history.

Part III, Politics of Crime and Justice, starts with Chapter 15. Chapter 15 discusses the practical application the routine activity theory to better understand terrorism and trafficking. The author first discusses terrorism in South Asia and its main reasons. Through a chart, the author shows terrorism incidents in South Asia since 1970, discussing the main reasons behind these acts, particularly religious reasons. The author then describes the phenomena of drugs and human traffic in South Asia, pointing out the reasons for people to initiate these activities. The author also compares South Asia's traffic activities with Africa and the Middle East and gives definitions of the traffic phenomena overall. The author then exploits the routine activity theory in order to provide a better understanding of the terrorism and traffic activities in South Asia and why people decides to join such activities.

Chapter 16 is divided into two parts. The first part of the chapter is fully focused on developing a Hobbesian analysis of the rise of the Taliban in Afghanistan. The author then discusses main conclusions in part two, affirming that the Afghanistan tragedy is a product of decades of policies that have been altogether too Hobbesian and insufficiently Jeffersonian. The authors discuss reasons for several Islamic tyrannies and civil wars associated with them. Lastly, the authors propose an alternative a kind of rural village republicanism supported by a democratic state.

Chapter 17 shows a detailed overview of the criminal organizations in Dhaka by exploring the mastaans as well as a variety of other criminal groups, including organized crime groups which are distinct from the mastaans, 'rich or upper-class' gangs, 'student groups' and then finally extremist groups and the ways in which terrorism is conceptualized in Bangladesh. The author discusses the nature of these groups and the associations they have with one another. Lastly, the author discusses the complexity of criminal groups in Dhaka and their implications for global understanding of crime and violence.

Chapter 18 provides a summary of the war crimes in Sri Lanka based on the studies done by the International Crisis Group. The author begins providing an overview of the political and military facts and the effects that the war had on Sri Lankan civilians. The chapter discusses the violence that civilians suffered from after the war. The chapter then discusses the possibilities that Sri Lankan security forces committed war crimes, among those attacks on civilians, hospitals and humanitarian operations, and gives a neutral overview of the war crimes committed by the LTTE and its leadership. Lastly, the chapter emphasizes the importance of investigating war crimes and prosecutes who is responsible for them.

Chapter 19 tries to explore the association between Madaris and suicide terrorism in Pakistan. The authors have made an effort to discuss a few questions, out of which the most fundamental question is the involvement of the Madaris in producing suicide bombers. The authors firstly present the historical background of Madaris, explore the relationship between Pakistan and Madaris and then extensively examine the association between Madaris and suicide terrorism through various research findings. The authors then point out through research findings the myth of emergence of suicide terrorists from Islamic fundamentalism due to the biases of media and present identical patterns and similar phenomena in the involvement of foreign occupation in triggering religious suicide terrorism. The authors conclude the chapter by highlighting the need for reforms in Madaris and also reconsideration of the policies of media.

Chapter 20 explores the trends, dynamics and drivers of post-conflict crime and violence in Nepal. The chapter is established through multiple fieldworks done by the author between 2008 and 2014 in Nepal. The author also throws light to the major types of post-conflict crime and violence issues that have occurred in Nepal. The author then presents various approaches to analyzing post-conflict crime and violence. In this chapter, the author has taken into consideration three dimensions—the socio-economic, institutional and political and social dimensions—to analyze and understand the causes of post-conflict crime and violence in Nepal. The author presents his own analytical framework based on literature review and fieldwork to understand post-conflict crime and violence. The author concludes the chapter by describing the challenging and complex nature of post-conflict crime and violence in Nepal.

Chapter 21 presents the patterns, trends and causes of religious terrorism in Bangladesh. The authors draw attention to the relationship between religious militancy and terrorism. The authors then highlight the causes for growing terrorism and how it has flourished. The authors have analyzed the terrorist incidents from 1991 to 2001 through a content analysis of secondary sources of data and present a historical background of the emergence of religious terrorism in Bangladesh. The authors showcase the different types of terrorist attacks that occurred every year. The authors also throw light on the factors that have been identified as major causes for religious terrorism in Bangladesh. Finally, the authors conclude by suggesting certain measures and recommendations that can be utilized for counterterrorism.

Part IV, Crime and Justice Policies, starts with Chapter 22. Chapter 22 draws attention to the regional cooperation and responses to human trafficking in South Asia. The author kicks off by showing data on where the victims of trafficking from South Asia end up being exploited. The author then highlights how the lobbying of some NGOs has led SAARC to take up the issue of human trafficking in its agenda and further draws attention to the various other transnational crimes where the SAARC has engaged at various levels. The author also points out the limited role of NGOs in the task force and presents a picture of the slow cooperation among SAARC that has happened on issue of trafficking, unlike other issues on which there has been steady progress. The author then explains the need to integrate the dialogues on human trafficking from security and legal perspectives. Finally, the author concludes by presenting recommendations that could be of significant utility.

Chapter 23 draws attention to the religious, societal reflection and rights of transgender people in India. The author firstly presents the picture of neglect and trauma faced by transgender people in India. The author also points to the violations of several fundamental rights and the inadequacy of the government in tackling such sensitive issues and throws light on the various kinds of encroachments faced by transgender over their rights and institutionalized exploitation. The author also highlights the need for the existence of transgender rights in Indian society and goes onto to describe various other pressing issues that the transgender community has to face on a daily basis. Finally, the author concludes by bringing forth some notable proactive steps taken by various state governments and organizations to address the issues of the transgender community. The author also suggests various recommendations and implementations to bring the transgender community into the mainstream of the society.

Chapter 24 focuses on the transitional justice processes in Bangladesh. The main focus of this chapter is to explore whether transitional justice could be an option in re-establishing human rights and ensuring their enforcement in Bangladesh. The author firstly presents the transitional justice mechanism in Bangladesh and its effects. Secondly, the author explores the consequences of applying transitional justice mechanisms in Bangladesh in comparison with other countries in which similar situations have occurred. Finally, the author questions the delay of 40 years to start a trial process against the main perpetrators in the Bangladesh case and concludes by offering some recommendations and implementations to better serve justice to the war victim community in Bangladesh.

Chapter 25 presents a situational analysis of the Nirbhaya incident and juvenile justice policies in India. The author has made an effort to understand and investigate the new concepts and amendments brought into the laws governing juvenile delinquency in India. The author starts the chapter by highlighting how the new juvenile legislation defines heinous offences, which was lacking before, and then focuses attention on the introduction of a new legal proviso called the judicial waiver system. Further, the author makes an effort to understand juvenile delinquent behavior through various debates that arose during the Nirbhaya incident and draws attention to the psycho-social maturity of juveniles and how it could be a reason for committing crimes. The author then focuses on how the influence of peers can have a detrimental effect on decision-making and judgement during adolescence. The author concludes the chapter by explaining the need to examine the changing philosophies of the juvenile justice system.

Chapter 26 draws attention to the trends, factors and determinants of crime among young offenders in Bhutan. The authors firstly present a descriptive analysis of crime data (of young Bhutanese people), sourced from the Royal Bhutan Police (RBP). Then secondly the authors outline a complementary discussion on the outcome of a qualitative research with 44 young convicts and further present an analysis of the broad categories of crime among the youths of Bhutan. The main focus of the analysis is on understanding the many facets of crime, which include nature of offences, seasonality of crimes, socio-demographic and demographic characteristics and crime trends across gender, age and regions. The authors also highlight the reasons for criminal deviance among young people, which would help establish better crime managing tools in the country. Finally, the authors end the chapter by focusing attention on the young convicts and establishing a common ground to understand the most probable reasons for them to resort to criminal acts.

Chapter 27 emphasizes women victims of war and crime in Afghanistan. The author explores the current situation of women in Afghanistan, from the Taliban rule to the present day. The author also tries to understand why women are easy targets in Afghanistan and presents a criminological examination of violence against women and elaborates on various factors that could be potential causes for the atrocities against women in Afghanistan. The author further examines how the profound demonstration of the ideas of patriarchy took the shape of active violence against women in Afghanistan and points out how cultural practices have given rise to crimes against women. The author also explores the role of the social practice of masculinity as a potential cause for violence against women and then highlights how the limited legal standing of women in Afghanistan is also a potential cause for violence against them. Finally, the author mentions the need to involve people at every level as a solution to give the women of its country a better status.

Chapter 28 presents a victimological perspective of human trafficking in Nepal. Firstly, the author presents the current situation of human trafficking of Nepal. Secondly, the author draws attention to the laws and policies regarding counter-trafficking in Nepal. The author then presents a valid point as to how important it is to consider protecting and restoring the rights of the trafficked persons along with imposing trafficking policies and laws. Further, the author describes the special needs and rights for the protection and support of trafficking victims and witnesses. Also, the author advocates the implementation of certain packages of services like physical and psychological security of victim, right to privacy of victim, victims' participation in court proceedings, right to information, timely advice and assistance, right to compensation, victims' right to rehabilitation and reintegration and no penalization of trafficked persons. The chapter ends by bringing attention to the well-being of the trafficked persons in order to give them justice.

Chapter 29 presents political crime victimization in Bangladesh. The author first portrays the historical background of political crime in Bangladesh. Secondly, the author outlines an emphasis on political crime and victimization after the independence of Bangladesh by providing a contrasting image during two different governments. The chapter outlines political clashes, civil disobedience, terrorism, hate crime and political assassination, illegal surveillance, torture and deadly force as the major forms of political crimes in Bangladesh. The author then draws special attention to individual cases of victimization and points out the increasing rate of political crime due to the criminalization of politics and the politicization of criminals in the country. The author also provides various causes for the political crime and outlines the social consequences of political crime. Finally, the author ends the chapter by addressing how to eradicate political crimes in Bangladesh. The involvement of the government, civil society and the conscious people is a necessary and crucial step.

Chapter 30 delineates the traditional practices and victimization of women in Nepal through the narratives of Chhaupadi (practice of secluding women during menstruation). The authors have highlighted how certain cultural practices are still prevalent in Nepal that disregard basic human rights. In the chapter, the authors provide a detailed discussion of the evil practice of Chhaupadi in Nepal and its repercussions, with findings of a content analysis. Through this chapter, the authors have shown how prevalent Chhaupadi still is in Nepal and how often there have been incidences of Chhaupadi-related violence every year. The authors have also found the Chhaupadi-affected areas in Nepal and portrayed the details regarding violence against women during this cultural practice. Violence against women has been divided into socio-cultural violence, sexual and reproductive violence and physical violence. The authors then highlight the physical, psychological, educational, sexual and reproductive and social effects of the practice of Chhaupadi on women. Finally, the authors end the chapter by drawing attention to some positive initiatives taken by government of Nepal in eradicating this rampant practice of Chhaupadi.

The last chapter of the book, Chapter 31, provides an examination of collective and secondary victimization of Rohingyas in Myanmar and Bangladesh. The author points out extensively the atrocities faced by the Rohingyas at the hands of Myanmar armed forces. The author also urges study of the collective victimization and victims of abuses by criminologists and victimologists from international perspectives. The chapter has been divided into three parts in which the author firstly introduces the Rohingya Muslims and their historical background. Secondly, the author describes the secondary victimization faced by them as refugees in Bangladesh. And thirdly, the author examines the phases of Rohingyas' victimization in Myanmar and Bangladesh. In the chapter, the author has also suggested short-term and long-term policy recommendations to solve the Rohingya refugee crisis.

PART I

Crime and Criminal Justice Processes

1

AFGHANISTAN

State and Non–State-Oriented Criminal Justice Systems[1]

Ali Wardak

Introduction

Afghanistan is a land-locked country that lies at the crossroad between South and Central Asia. To the north and northwest of the country lie the former Soviet republics of Uzbekistan, Tajikistan and Turkmenistan; to the South and East is Pakistan; to the West of Afghanistan lies Iran, and to its north-east is China. It is this strategic geo-political location of Afghanistan that has made it both a crossroad between civilizations and a battlefield between competing global and regional powers (Wardak, 2004).

The total population of Afghanistan is estimated to be between 20 and 25 million, composed of various ethnic and tribal groups, most of whom have lived together in the country for centuries. These include: Pashtun, Tajik, Hazara, Uzbek, Turkmen, Aimaq, Baluch, Brahui, Nuristani, Pashaie, Pamiri, Kirghiz, Qizilbash, Mongols, Arabs, Gujars, Kohistanis, Wakhis and Jats. Among these, the Pashtuns constitute the largest ethnic group (estimated around 50% of the total Afghan population), followed by Tajiks, Hazras and Uzbeks (Dupree, 1980; Canfield, 1996; Glatzer, 1998; Wardak, 2004).

Although these various Afghan groups are generally distinguishable from one another by their members' distinct language (or accent) and ethnic origin, for generations trade and commerce, universities/colleges, government institutions and cross-regional employment opportunities have pulled thousands of Afghans from different ethnic/tribal backgrounds to live and work side by side. Furthermore, inter-marriages, service in the national army and police, and participation in shared cultural, religious and social activities have strengthened citizenship at the expense of ethnic/tribal affiliations in urban centers and cities. This interaction among Pashtuns, Tajiks, Hazaras, Uzbeks, Turkmens and other Afghan ethnic and tribal groups has resulted in a cultural fusion among various Afghan ethnic and tribal cultural traditions at the national level. The richness of Afghan national culture owes much to this centuries-old multi-cultural fusion (Wardak, 2004).

However, since the Soviet military intervention in Afghanistan in 1979, the country has been used as a battlefield between competing global and regional powers and groups—a battlefield between the former Communist USSR and the capitalist West (mainly the USA) in the 1980s; in the 1990s a battlefield between Pakistan, the Arab Gulf countries on the one hand and Iran and Russia on the other; and a battlefield between foreign Muslim extremist groups and a right-wing U.S. administration. In this process of rivalry, Afghanistan's main immediate neighbors infiltrated deep into Afghan politics. With competing interests in the country, they created their client factions/warlords and sponsored them militarily, financially and politically. The factions gradually became so dependent

11

on their foreign sponsors that they saw Afghanistan's interests through the eyes of these foreigners. These neighbors also exploited Afghanistan's existing ethnic and religious composition and justified their interventions on the grounds that they had common religious and ethnic ties with their clients. Thus the armed conflict (which continued for several years even after the defeat of the former Red Army) resulted in the extensive destruction of Afghanistan's economic, political and social infrastructure. The Western world, particularly the USA, which lured the Soviets to invade Afghanistan, and strongly supported the Afghan *mujahedin*—Islamic warriors—almost completely, abandoned the ruined country after the Red Army was defeated (Wardak, 2004).

The destruction of the country's economic infrastructure, particularly, provided opportunities for foreign players and their client Afghan warring factions to exploit the situation, seeking their strategic goals and sectarian interests at the expense of the Afghan population. The almost total collapse of the Afghan pre-war economy gradually resulted in the emergence of a "war economy" (Rubin, 1999; Goodhand, 2003)—economic conditions that mainly centered on the manufacturing, repair, use and smuggling of weapons and ammunition, on the one hand, and on the smuggling (and production) of illicit drugs and national treasure on the other. The nearly a quarter-of-a-century-long conflict also resulted in a generation of young people who were largely deprived of the opportunity of gaining educational qualifications and other useful skills. This "war generation" of thousands of young people has been deeply traumatized by the war—many lost their parents, relatives and homes. The various factions were able to recruit their fighters from amongst this war generation so that the conflict in which they had a stake continued. Fighting for one or other warlord provided these young men with a source of income, social status and a way of channeling their energies. More importantly, this situation provided the opportunity for foreign Muslim extremist groups—mainly *Al-Qaeda*—to use Afghan soil as headquarters for terrorist activities against other nations. There now exists an increasingly convincing body of evidence which links the Afghanistan-based *Al-Qaeda* to the 9/11 terrorist attacks on New York's Twin Towers and on other targets in the United States.

In the wake of the US-led military campaign in Afghanistan that resulted in the collapse of the Taliban regime, the Bonn Agreement of December 2001 was signed among the representatives of Northern Alliance warlords, pro-Zahir Shah (former king of Afghanistan) technocrats/intellectuals, and two other small Afghan groups that were mainly based in Pakistan and Iran. Although the four anti-Taliban groups did not consult (or represent) the people of Afghanistan, the Bonn Agreement, which was signed in a rush, did open the possibility of a new participatory political order for Afghanistan. It provided a framework of state formation processes that aimed at the eventual creation of a "broad-based, multi-ethnic and fully representative" government by 2004. The agreement, which resulted in the establishment of the Afghan Interim Administration in December 2001, raised hopes among many Afghans that there was an opportunity to end warlordism in Afghanistan and to rebuild the country's social, political and economic institutions.

However, the reinstatement of most warlords as key political and military leaders in the post-Taliban administration and the US government's emphasis on the "war against terrorism" rather than on rebuilding Afghanistan has spread disillusion among many Afghans about the prospects of lasting peace. The US's military and financial support for warlords, who may cooperate in hunting down remnants of the Taliban and *Al-Qaeda*, continues to be a major obstacle to the development of national participatory institutions in Afghanistan and therefore a major source of increasing instability in the country. Central to political stabilization and to the re-building of social and political order in Afghanistan is the establishment of an effective system of justice in the country. This chapter assesses the rebuilding of the criminal justice system in Afghanistan from the perspectives of both the state-oriented criminal justice system and the non–state-oriented criminal justice system (the historical and cultural system) and proposes a synergy of the two systems.

Criminal Justice System in Afghanistan

1. State-Oriented Criminal Justice System

Although it is difficult to draw a clear dividing line between state- and non–state-oriented criminal justice systems in Afghanistan, the former generally refers to positive law that functions through legal codes and state institutions, such as the courts, prosecutors, police, the prison service and the bar of law. Thus, in the context of Afghanistan, key state justice and judicial institutions include the Supreme Court (*stara mahkama*), the Attorney General's Office (*loy saranwali*), the police (*sarandoi*), the Ministry of Justice (*wezarate-e-adelia*) and the prison service. Although these institutions are supposed to be closely interconnected, in reality there exists little organic chain-like interaction among them, and therefore they hardly operate as a system (Wardak, 2009). Nevertheless, the totality of these generally justice institutions has historically been referred to as a *nezam-e-adlee wa qazaiee* (justice and judicial order/system), which was central to the maintenance of social and political order in pre-war Afghanistan (Wardak, 2013).

While progress in rebuilding the Afghan state criminal justice system during the past 10years has been slow and patchy, it has nevertheless been noticeable: significant work has been done on legislation; several hundred judges, prosecutors and prison wardens and thousands of police personnel have been trained; some criminal justice institutions have been refurbished; and several new ones have been built from scratch (UNDP, 2007). Progress has also been made with regard to building administrative capacity within the existing justice institutions and the publication and distribution of a large body of law to legal professionals (UNDP, 2007). Progress in rebuilding Afghanistan's state criminal justice system has included the establishment of the Independent Bar Association of Afghanistan, legal aid departments in Kabul and in three provinces, the Independent National Legal Training Centre (INLTC) in Kabul and a committee for the simplification of judicial bureaucracy (UNDP, 2007, p. 33). Moreover, there has been an agreement between the Attorney General and Ministry of Interior on the development and implementation of measures to improve prosecution processes and the introduction of common telephone numbers for use by the public to register complaints (UNDP, 2007, p. 33) (Wardak, 2013).

However, despite the above-mentioned achievements, the post-Taliban state criminal justice system is far from delivering justice to the Afghan people and faces serious problems. The nature and severity of these problems appear to have heavily overshadowed what has been achieved thus far. These problems include endemic corruption, high levels of professional incompetence, inadequacy of physical infrastructure such as courtrooms and detention/correctional facilities, very low levels of public trust and the provision of minimal international funding for the rebuilding of justice and rule-of-law institutions in post-Taliban Afghanistan (Carter & Clark, 2010; Wyler & Katzman, 2010). Due to the United States' overemphasis on the War on Terror in Afghanistan, the issue of rebuilding justice and rule-of-law institutions has, until recent years, been largely neglected (Wardak, 2013).

Some of the problems that Afghanistan's criminal justice system currently faces, particularly the lack of sufficient professional, human and legal resources, inadequacy of physical infrastructure and low salaries for justice officials, could be directly traced to the very low level of investment in this sector. Other than insufficient investment in the justice sector, national and international efforts have primarily focused on strengthening the pre-war state justice institutions in Afghanistan—they have mainly focused on patchy legal engineering and quick fixes and on meeting targets and the technical aspects of reform at the expense of its normative dimensions (Carter & Clark, 2010; Wardak, 2004. Different donor countries concentrated on different aspects of the justice sector without effective coordination among them and with the Afghan state institutions (UNDP, 2007; Wardak, 2009). This situation also seems to have resulted in the continued absence of a coherent vision for rebuilding and reforming the justice sector in Afghanistan. The outcome has been a fragmented justice system, the key components of which (the judiciary, police, prosecution and prison service) do not operate as a system at all (Johnson, Maley, & Wardak, 2003; Wardak, 2009). All these problems, combined with a growing insurgency and persistent institutionalized corruption, have further complicated the task of rebuilding an effective criminal justice system in post-Taliban Afghanistan (Wardak, 2013).

2. Non–State-Oriented Criminal Justice System

The role of the Afghan central government and its formal institutions of criminal justice (courts, police, corrections etc.) in maintaining social order in Afghan society has always been limited (Wardak, 2002a; ICG, 2003). This particularly applies to rural Afghanistan, where it is estimated that more than80% of the Afghan population live. In some southern and eastern parts of the country, formal institutions of criminal justice have no (or just nominal) existence, and yet there exist a reasonable degree of social order in these areas.

A great many potentially serious disputes, relating to domestic violence, divorce, inheritance and marriage, are normally settled within the "private" sphere of the Afghan extended family without the involvement of local/tribal or state institutions (Wardak, 2002a). They are dealt with on the spot before becoming a "public" problem and a burden on other societal institutions. However, those disputes that are considered "public" are resolved by public institutions at local and tribal levels. The main institution that has traditionally operated as a mechanism of dispute settlement (at village and tribe levels) is *jirga/maraka*[2] among the Pashtuns and its approximate equivalent—*shura*[3]—among the non-Pashtuns of Afghanistan (Carter & Connor, 1989; Farhadi, 2000; Gletzer, 1998; Hashemi, 2000; Malekyar, 2000; Wardak, 2004).

The particular form and composition of a *jirga* or *shura* are determined by the nature of a dispute at hand, but typically by a body of respected *marakachian* or *rishsafidan* (local elders and leaders) who refer to customary laws in order to reach a settlement that is acceptable to disputants and to the community. *Jirga* and *shura* address issues ranging from minor bodily harm and agricultural land boundaries to serious and sometimes violent conflicts concerning communal lands and murder (Wardak, 2013).

Jirga in every day practice refers to a local/tribal institution of decision-making and dispute settlement that incorporates the prevalent local customary law, institutionalised rituals, and a body of village elders whose collective decision about the resolution of a dispute (or local problem) is binding on the parties involved (Wardak, 2002b). Those on the *jirga* combine "traditional authority" (based on personal qualities, social status and leadership skills) and "competent authority" (based on the individual's recognized expertise and skills), which play a central part in achieving a *prikra* (ruling) that is satisfactory to both parties (Wardak, 2004).

One important form of tribal *jirga* is *nanawate*, which means seeking forgiveness/pardon and the obligatory acceptance of a truce offer. This happens when the tribal *jirga* makes a *prikra* (decision) that relatives of the *par* (guilty party) send a "delegation" to the victim's house. This consists of a group of people that include elders, a female relative of the offender holding a copy of the holy Quran, and a *mullah* (Muslim priest), alongside the offender's other close relatives (and sometimes the offender himself), who bring a sheep and flour to the victim's house. The sheep is often slaughtered at the door of the victim's house. Once inside the house, the delegation seeks pardon on behalf of the offender. As it is against the tribal code of behavior to reject a *nanawate*, the victim's relatives pardon the offender, and the two parties are reconciled. This reconciliation is called *rogha*. Thus unlike formal state justice, which often labels offenders as different and evil and excludes them from the community, *nanawate* reintegrates them into the community. Existing criminological knowledge suggests that reintegrative social control is, by and large, more effective in reducing crime than disintegrative social control, normally exercised by formal state institutions (Braithwaite, 1989; Wardak, 2004).

The processes, rituals and outcome of *jirga* as a traditional tribal/local Afghan institution resemble closely the spirit, values and principles of "restorative justice"—one of the most recent paradigms in modern criminology and criminal justice. Although the phrase "restorative justice" is defined differently in different social contexts, it proposes a community based model of justice that places special emphasis on the restoration of dignity, peace and relationships between offenders and victims; it provides restitution to victims and promotes the reintegration of offenders into the community (Braithwaite, 2002a; Braithwaite, 2002b; Braithwaite, 2003; Bottoms, 2003; Hudson, 2003; Johnston, 2001; Van Ness, 2003; Wardak, 2004).

Jirgas and *shuras* place strong emphasis on reconciliation and making peace among disputants. Thus, unlike the state justice system, which creates losers and winners, *jirgas* and *shuras* reach community-led decisions that promote restorative justice (as opposed to retributive justice), and help to restore peace and dignity among the victims, offenders and the community (Coburn & Dempsey, 2010). These local Afghan institutions also aim to reintegrate offenders back into the community after holding them accountable for a wrongdoing (Coburn & Dempsey, 2010). As a form of alternative dispute resolution, these practices can also reduce strain on a capacity-deficient state-oriented criminal justice system (Coburn & Dempsey, 2010, pp. 2–3). In addition, *jirgas* and *shuras* are shown to be more accessible, more efficient (in terms of time and money), perceived as less corrupt and more trusted by Afghans compared to formal state courts (Asia Foundation, 2010; Wardak, 2013).

The main reasons that Afghan people have preferred *jirga/shura* to formal criminal justice is because the former is conducted by respected elders with established social status and the reputation for piety and fairness. In many cases, the disputants personally know the local elders and trust them. In addition, in the context of *jirga/shura*, elders reach decisions in accordance with accepted local traditions/values (customary law) that are deeply ingrained in the collective conscience of the village/tribe—they have a profound existence in the collective mind of the village and in the minds of its individual members. Also, unlike state courts, *jirga/shura* settles disputes without long delays and without financial costs. Illiteracy plays an important role in discouraging people from using the formal courts—the overwhelming majority of Afghans are unable to make applications, read/understand the laws or complete the paperwork (Wardak, 2004).

However, *jirga/shura* has its own problems: in some cases of murder, *jirga* may recommend *badal* (direct vengeance) or the marriage of a woman from the *par's* tribe to the victim's close relative. Although these practices have become increasingly rare in recent years (Johnson et al., 2003), the first punishment is in direct conflict with Afghan state laws, and the second one is a clear violation of fundamental human rights. In addition, *jirga/shura* is generally a male-only institution; it can also be excessively influenced sometimes by powerful elders. More importantly, in areas where warlords exercise direct control over the population, *jirga/shura* decisions are influenced (or undermined) by those with guns and money (Wardak, 2004).

Interim Legal Framework and the Current Criminal Justice System

The Afghan Interim Administration (AIA) that was established as a result of the Bonn Agreement in December 2001 inherited a criminal justice system devastated by the 25-year-long civil conflict in Afghanistan. However, under the Bonn Agreement, the 1964 Afghan constitution and "existing law" were reinstated with some important modifications. In effect, this constitution and the "existing laws" currently provide an interim legal framework for Afghanistan. This "framework" represents a mixture of *shari'a* and positive laws that were enforced until the Military coup in 1978 (Wardak, 2004).

Despite the formal reactivation of the formal Afghan criminal justice "system" through-out the country, it is far from prepared to deliver justice. It is a hugely devastated institution. The devastation not only includes extensive damage to buildings, office furniture, official records, and essential office equipment but also includes the lack of qualified judges and other justice personnel. Importantly, it is highly fragmented, with little or no interaction among the judiciary, the police, the prosecution and the prison/correction service (Amnesty International, 2003a; Johnson et al., 2003). One of the main reasons for the lack of co-operation between the judiciary and the police is that the latter consist predominantly of Northern Alliance militia who are highly dependent on and more loyal to their factional patrons than to the national Afghan Interim Administration. The police, in many ways, are merely an extension of the Northern Alliance's militia, who mainly represents Afghan Tajiks; they have no (or little) basic understanding of policing, and most of the people they police have no trust in them (Amnesty International, 2003a; Johnson et al., 2003; Wardak, 2004).

In addition, corrective regimes and rehabilitative programmes for both adult and young offenders do not currently exist in Afghanistan. Although *dar-al-ta'adeeb* (juvenile correctional institution) is nominally functioning in Kabul, the institution has neither the necessary facilities nor the profes-sional personnel to deal with the serious personal and social problems that young Afghan rule-breakers face today. Thus, the current fragmented Afghan justice "system" is highly ineffective and dysfunctional; it does not operate as a system at all (Wardak, 2004).

Similarly, the Afghan prison/correction "service" has only a very basic existence in the main urban centers; it has no existence at all in many rural districts and some provincial centers (Amnesty International, 2003b; Johnson et al., 2003). Although the prison service in Kabul was recently trans-ferred from the Ministry of the Interior to the Ministry of Justice, its personnel have not changed. Many of the inmates are political prisoners who live in very over-crowded conditions and are fed by their relatives and friends. The situation in the prisons is particularly serious in Sheberghan and Herat (Amnesty International, 2003b; Physicians for Human Rights, Report, January 28, 2002). The sources report that these prisoners are treated in in humane ways, and many of them suffer from illnesses related to malnutrition and overcrowding; dozens have died since their surrender to the US-led Northern Alliance forces in November 2001 (Wardak, 2004).

However, Afghanistan has a large body of codified laws including the Afghan Civil Code (1975), the Criminal Codes (1976), the amended Law of Criminal Procedure (1973) and the Law of Police (1973). Although these laws are currently implemented, they need some important modifications. In addition, as stipulated in the 1964 constitution, in areas where no law existed the *hanafi*[4] school of *shari'a* is considered applicable. These various laws, which currently provide the interim legal frame-work, are to be used as an important element of the post-war criminal justice system in Afghanistan (Wardak, 2004).

Call for Synergy Between State- and Non–State-Oriented Criminal Justice Systems

The examination of the key elements of post-war criminal justice in Afghanistan shows that a rein-stated pre-war Afghan criminal justice system (or a superficially reformed one) will not have the capacity to face the challenges of the post-war situation and meet the demands of the 21st century. It points to the need for the development of a new post-war model of justice—an integrated multi-dimensional model that represents Afghan cultural traditions, religious values and legal norms and at the same time has the capacity to draw on human rights principles. Thus, an experimental model is proposed, which is illustrated in Figure 1.1 (Wardak, 2004).

The post-war justice model (Figure 1.1) proposes the establishment of *jirga/shura* and a genuinely independent human rights unit alongside the existing court of justice (based on *shari'a* and positive law) and their integration into the overall system of justice at district level. The *jirga/shura* unit would be staffed by one or two full-time paid coordinators based in a fully equipped local office with a *jirga* hall. These local officers would replace *amer -e- hoquq* (law officer) who is closely connected with the formal justice system and has a reputation for corruption. *Jirga/shura* would be conducted by around

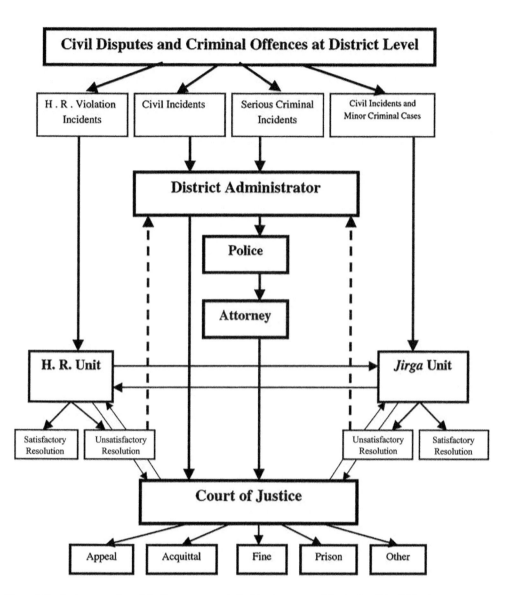

Figure 1.1 An integrated model of a post-war criminal justice system (district level) in Afghanistan.

half a dozen elected local elders with expertise in traditional dispute settlement and/or legitimate social influence. The elders would be paid only an honorarium (in the form of consultancy fees) and travel expenses; the expenses of hosting *jirga/shura* would also be paid from the public purse. Although not illustrated in Figure 1.1, *jirga/shura* would also advise the district administrator in issues relating to local governance (Wardak, 2004).

As Figure 1.1 illustrates, the *jirga/shura* unit would mainly deal with minor criminal and all types of civil incidents at district level. In the case of civil incidents, people would have the choice to start their cases with either *jirga/shura* or the district court of formal justice. However, all serious criminal cases would be dealt with exclusively by the district court of justice, and those cases that *jirga/shura* fail to resolve satisfactorily would be referred back to the formal process of the district criminal justice system. The referral would be based on a joint decision by *jirga/shura*, district judge and the district administrator. While paperwork and official procedures must be kept to the minimum, the final *prikra* (ruling) should be communicated to both the district court of justice and the human rights unit to ensure that it is in line with national legal norms and with accepted principles of human rights. In this way, *jirga/shura* would not only significantly reduce the workload of the court of justice; more importantly, the use of this traditional local/tribal institution of dispute settlement would empower ordinary people to have ownership of the criminal justice processes (Wardak, 2004).

Figure 1.1 further illustrates complex interrelationships between the district court of justice, *jirga/shura* and human rights units: as mentioned earlier, while the final *prikra* (ruling) of *jirga/shura* should be reported to both the district court of justice and to the human rights unit, the latter two would consult the former for its mediatory role in cases that need diversion from the formal justice processes. Likewise, *jirga/maraka* and human rights units would consult the court of justice about cases that may need to be dealt with in more strictly legalistic ways within the criminal justice system. A positive and constructive interaction between the state and local civil society institutions would provide an integrated inter-agency justice system that is effective, accessible and humane. However, such a system of justice is part and parcel of the processes of democratization, institutional reform (and building), disarmament and the establishment of the rule of law in post-war Afghanistan. It can only, therefore, successfully operate in a social and political environment where the rule of law prevails, not the rule of gun and money (Wardak, 2004).

Conclusion

What has been discussed in this chapter shows that despite the historical fragmentation and the current devastated state of the Afghan criminal justice system, Afghanistan has a rich legal culture that could partly be used as a basis for rebuilding a new post-war criminal justice system. This legal culture also provides important lessons for Afghans to avoid repeating the mistakes of past rulers of the country who mainly used their systems of justice as an instrument of state control. An unfortunate consequence of this has been the development of criminal justice systems that have been elitist, inaccessible and corrupt, which alienated ordinary people from the state and its formal institutions of justice. This further resulted in the huge lack of communication between the Afghan state and ordinary people, which further widened the "culture gap" between cities and rural areas in Afghanistan. Thus, it has not been a coincidence that ordinary people, especially in rural Afghanistan, have traditionally preferred not to use formal criminal justice institutions for the resolution of their disputes (Wardak, 2004).

The proposed integrated model of post-war criminal justice system in Afghanistan proposes inter-institutional co-ordination between the Afghan formal criminal justice system, informal criminal justice, educational and human rights institutions. It is argued that the incorporation of *jirga/shura* into the formal criminal justice system would not only simplify the justice process for ordinary people; more importantly, it would enable them to have its ownership. This, it is maintained, would make the criminal justice system more widely accessible, cost-effective and expeditious. Likewise, addressing issues relating to the vast violation of human rights during the several years of brutal war and challenging the existing "culture of human rights abuses" effectively need inter-institutional co-ordination. The creation of a truly independent human rights unit and its incorporation into the criminal justice system is an effective way of creating awareness about human rights, accounting for past crimes and preventing future violations of human rights (Wardak, 2004).

More importantly, this inter-institutional interaction between the local justice, executive, educational and civil society institutions would provide an important channel of communication between the state and ordinary Afghan citizens. This would gradually result in the inclusion of women and those without guns and money into the political, economic and cultural life of the Afghan society.

These processes would further pave the way for the gradual replacement of a "culture of human rights abuses" in Afghan society by a culture of respect for human rights and the rule of law. Indeed, communication plays an important role in social integration (Habermas, 1984) and in strengthening social solidarity (Durkheim, 1964) that Afghanistan badly needs today. However, in order to test the applicability of this model in the real world, it first needs to be thoroughly discussed among Afghan and international legal experts and ordinary people, at grassroots level, and then piloted in selected districts in Afghanistan (Wardak, 2004).

Notes

1 This chapter is a revised version of two previous articles of the author: 1. Wardak, A. (2004). Building a post-war justice system in Afghanistan. *Crime, Law & Social Change, 41*, 319–341; 2. Wardak, A. (2013). State and non-state justice systems in Afghanistan: The need for synergy. *University of Pennsylvania Journal of International Law, 32*(5), 1305–1324. Republished with permission.

2 *Jirga* and *maraka* involve very similar processes, and the main constituent elements of the two are not fundamentally different from one another. Therefore, the concepts are often used interchangeably. However, the fact that *jirga* deals with serious and important conflicts within the tribe (or between tribes) such as murder, disputes over land, mountain, jangle/woods and the fact that it operates at a higher level of tribal formation, its social organization is more structured. *Maraka*, on the other hand, mostly deals with civil and relatively less serious criminal matters at local village (or inter-village) level, and therefore, it is loosely structured and its related rituals are not as elaborate as those of a tribal *jirga* are. The term *"jirga"* according to the *Pashto Descriptive Dictionary* (1978, p. 1272) is an original Pashto word, which in its common usage refers to the gathering of a few or a large number of people; it also means consultation according to this source. The word *jirga* is also used in Persian/Dari. According to Ghyathul-Lughat (1998 [1871], p. 119) it is derived from *jirg*, which means a "wrestling ring", or "circle", but is commonly used to refer to a gathering of people. Other scholars believe that the word *jirga* originates from Turkish, where it has a very similar meaning (Faiz-zad, 1989, p. 5; Wardak, 2004).

3 Carter and Connor (1989, p. 9) operationally define shura in this way: "A shura is a group of individuals which meets only in response to a specific need in order to decide how to meet the need. In most cases, this need is to resolve a conflict between individuals, families, groups of families, or whole tribes". This description would seem to indicate that shura and jirga are fundamentally very similar Afghan informal (non-state) mechanisms of conflict resolution that operate in varying social and tribal contexts.

4 This version of the *shari'a* existed in symbiotic relationships with Afghan customary laws and with *sunni* "folk Islam" that generally reflected the cultural, social and economic realities of everyday life of the overwhelming majority of the people of Afghanistan. *Ulama* (Islamic scholars) interpreted this version of Islam and the *shari'a* and also worked as *qadi* (judge) in state courts (Olesen, 1995). However, in order to have control over the *ulama* and over their interpretation of Islam and *shari'a*, the government established the official institution of *jami'at -al- ulama* (society of Islamic scholars/jurists) and the state-funded Islamic madrasas of *dar -al- o'lume arabi* and *abu hanifa* in Kabul.

References

Amnesty International. (2003a). *Afghanistan: Police reconstruction essential for protection of human rights*, 12 March Report. London: AI.

Amnesty International. (2003b). *Afghanistan: Crumbling prison system desperately in need of repair*, 1st July Report. London: AI.

Asia Foundation. (2010). *Afghanistan in 2010: A survey of the Afghan people*, 134. Retrieved from http://asiafoundation.org/resources/ pdfs/Afghanistanin2010survey.pdf.

The Bonn Agreement. (2001). Agreement on provisional arrangements in Afghanistan pending the re-establishment of permanent government institutions. Bonn.

Bottoms, A. (2003). Some sociological reflections on restorative justice. In A. Hirsch, J. Roberts, A. Bottoms, K. Roach, & M. Schiff (Eds.), *Restorative justice and criminal justice* (pp. 79–114). Oxford: Hart Publishing.

Braithwaite, J. (1989). *Crime, shame and reintegration*. Cambridge: Cambridge University Press.

Braithwaite, J. (2002a). Setting standards for restorative justice. *British Journal of Criminology, 42*(3), 563–577.

Braithwaite, J. (2002b). *Restorative justice and restorative regulation*. New York: Oxford University Press.

Braithwaite, J. (2003). Principles of restorative justice. In A. Hirsch, J. Roberts, A. Bottoms, K. Roach, & M. Schiff (Eds.), *Restorative justice and criminal justice* (pp. 1–20). Oxford: Hart Publishing.

Canfield, R. (1996). Ethnic, regional, and sectarian alignments in Afghanistan. In A. Banuazizi & M. Weiner (Eds.), *The state, religion and ethnic politics: Afghanistan, Iran, Pakistan* (pp. 75–103). New York: Syracuse University Press.

Carter, L., & Connor, K. (1989). *A preliminary investigation of contemporary Afghan Councils.* Peshawar: ACBAR.

Carter, S., & Clark, K. (2010). No shortcut to stability: Justice, politics, and insurgency in Afghanistan. Retrieved from www.chathamhouse.org/sites/default/files/public/Research/Asia/1210pr_afghanjustice.pdf.

Coburn, N., & Dempsey, J. (2010). Informal dispute resolution in Afghanistan, 3–4. U.S. Institute of Peace. Retrieved from www.usip.org/files/ resources/sr247_0.pdf.

Dupree, L. (1980). *Afghanistan.* Princeton: Princeton University Press.

Durkheim, E. (1964). *The division of labour in Society.* New York: Free Press.

Faiz-zad, M. (1989). *Jirga Haie Bozorge Milie Afghanistan.* Lahore: NFD.

Farhadi, R. (2000). Tajikane Afghanistan wa Qadamhaie Ashti Bain Aishan. In *Qadamhaie Ashti wa Masauliate ma Afghanistan.* Falls Church, VA: Kabultec.

Ghyathul-Lughat. (Ed.) (1998). *Maulana Gheyathoddin.* Kanpur Press: New Delhi. First Edition 1871.

Glatzer, B. (1998). Is Afghanistan on the brink of ethnic and tribal disintegration? In W. Maley (Ed.), *Fundamentalism reborn? Afghanistan and the Taliban* (pp. 167–181). New York: St. Martins.

Goodhand, J. (2003). From war economy to peace economy? *Paper presented at a symposium on state reconstruction and international engagement in Afghanistan,* May 30–June 1, Bonn.

Habermas, J. (1984). *The theory of communicative action, vol. 1, reason and rationalisation of society.* Boston: Beacon Press.

Hashemi, M. (2000). Qadamhaie Asshti Baine Uzbakan. In *Qadamhaie Ashti wa Masauliate ma Afghanha.* Falls Church, VA: Kabultec.

Hudson, B. (2003). Victims and offenders. In A. Hirsch, J. Roberts, A. Bottoms, K. Roach, & M. Schiff (Eds.), *Restorative justice and criminal justice* (pp. 177–194). Oxford: Hart Publishing.

ICG (Asia Report No 64, 2003b). Peacebuilding in Afghanistan, Brussels. Retrieved from www.crisisgroup.org/file/2828/download?token=qIcYygFu.

Johnson, C. W., Maley, A. T., & Wardak, A. (2003). *Afghanistan's political and constitutional development.* London: ODI.

Johnston, G., (2001). *Restorative justice: Ideas, values, debates.* Cullompton: Willan.

Malekyar, S. (2000). Qadamhaie Ashti wa Solh dar Ananaie Hazarahaie Afghanistan. In *Qadam-haie Asshti wa Masauliate ma Afghanha.* Falls Church, VA: Kabultec.

Olesen, A. (1995). *Islam and politics in Afghanistan.* Curzon: Surrey.

Pashto Descriptive Dictionary. (1978). Kabul: The Academy of Sciences of Afghanistan.

Physicians for Human Rights. (2002, January 16). *Report on conditions at Sheberghan Prison, Northern Afghanistan.* Retrieved from http://physiciansforhumanrights.org/issues/mass-atrocities/afghanistan-war-crime/dasht-e-leili-photos.html.

Rubin, B. (1999). The political economy of war and peace in Afghanistan. *Paper presented at the meeting of the Afghanistan Support Group,* Stockholm, Sweden.

UNDP. (2007). *Afghanistan human development report, bridging modernity and tradition: Rule of law and the search for justice,* 4. UNDP: Centre for Policy & Human Development. Retrieved from http://hdr.undp.org/en/reports/nationalreports/ asiathepacific/afghanistan/nhdr2007.pdf.

Van Ness, D. (2003). Proposed basic principles on the use of restorative justice: Recognising the aims and limits of restorative Justice. In A. Hirsch, J. Roberts, A. Bottoms, K. Roach, & M. Schiff (Eds.), *Restorative justice and criminal justice* (pp. 157–176). Oxford: Hart Publishing.

Wardak, A. (2002a). Structures of authority and establishing the rule of law in post-war Afghanistan. *Paper presented at establishing the rule of law and governance in post conflict societies,* Conference Organised by Harvard University, the United Nations Association—USA, and Koç University, Istanbul, July 11–14, 2002.

Wardak, A. (2002b). Jirga: Power and traditional conflict resolution in Afghanistan. In J. Strawson (Ed.), *Law after ground zero* (pp. 187–204). London: Cavendish.

Wardak, A. (2004). Building a post-war justice system in Afghanistan. *Crime, Law & Social Change, 41,* 319–341.

Wardak, A. (2009). Rule of law in Afghanistan: An overview. In W. Danspeckgruber (Ed.), *Petersberg papers on Afghanistan and the Region* (p. 47). Liechtenstein Colloquium Report Vol. IV. Princeton, NJ: Liechtenstein Institute on Self-Determination, Princeton University.

Wardak, A. (2013). State and non-state justice systems in Afghanistan: The need for synergy. *University of Pennsylvania Journal of International Law, 32*(5), 1305–1324.

Wyler, L. S., & Katzman, K. (2010). Afghanistan: U.S. Rule of law and justice sector assistance. *Congressional Research Service,* R 41484.

2

BANGLADESH

Issues and Introspections on Crime and Criminal Justice

*Mahfuzul I. Khondaker, Mohammed Bin Kashem,
and Mohammad Azizur Rahman*

Introduction

The South Asian nation of Bangladesh, with an estimated population of more than 168 million people, is the world's eighth most densely populated country. The population of Bangladesh is ethnically homogeneous, with 98% being Bengali, as well as being largely Muslim, young, poor, and rural (World Factbook, 2012). Bangladesh has a long, rich cultural history dating back thousands of years. In the middle 1700s, the area became part of British India (Banglapedia, 2011). In 1947, when the British left India, the subcontinent was divided in to two nations—India and Pakistan (which included Bangladesh, then called East Pakistan) (World Factbook, 2012). Bangladesh gained its independence from Pakistan in 1971 and is currently a democratic nation with a secular unicameral parliamentary form of government (Banglapedia, 2011). It is governed by two major political parties, the Bangladesh Awami League and the Bangladesh Nationalist Party (D'Costa, 2012). Its capital is Dhaka, and itis divided into seven administrative divisions (i.e., states) (World Factbook, 2012). Bangladesh's legal system clearly displays its British legacy; many current laws were originally enacted by the colonial British. The Parliament is responsible for enacting secular laws in Bangladesh; however, Islamic and other religious family laws are applied through the court system, particularly in the Family Courts.

Like any other formal criminal justice system, Bangladesh's criminal justice system is divided into three subsystems: police, courts, and corrections. Bangladesh has a national police force that can trace its roots back to the Colonial Police Act of 1861 and is the main police force (Islam & Ali, 2008). The national police are divided into five regional administrative units which are further broken down into 64 districts. There are a total of over 125,000 police officers assigned to more than 500 police stations across Bangladesh (Bangladesh Police, 2012). This translates to a rate of approximately 85 officers per 100,000 citizens.

Bangladesh's court or judiciary system is divided into two parts: the Supreme Judiciary and the Sub-ordinate Judiciary. The highest court in Bangladesh is the Supreme Court, and Supreme Court Justices are appointed by the president (World Factbook, 2012). The president can appoint any number of Justices to the Supreme Court as he/she deems necessary.

The correctional system is national and can trace its roots back to the Prison Act of 1894(Das & Palmiotto, 2006). There are more than 80,000 inmates, which is an incarceration rate of about 51 per 100,000 (Walmsley, 2010). There are 68 correctional facilities, which hold both those awaiting trial and those who have been sentenced (ICPS, 2008). A very high number of those incarcerated are detainees awaiting court hearings since the courts are backlogged. The living conditions in Bangladeshi correctional facilities are poor, and the facilities are generally out of date. Overcrowding is a problem, with the correctional facilities being estimated to be between 250 to 300% overcapacity. Recently, there has been a dramatic increase in the number of inmates. Both prisons and police are under the Ministry of Home Affairs. As with the police, correctional staff are often viewed as corrupt and brutal (Khondaker & Lambert, 2009).

Before British colonization, Bangladesh had an informal justice system which was based in the local community. The village leaders tried to find an amicable solution for the disputant parties in both criminal and civil matters. This informal justice system, *Shalish* or sometimes called *Panchayat*, has been in place in Bangladesh from the time of antiquity. The remnants of *Shalish* can still be seen in rural Bangladesh as a form of adjudicating disputes (Khondaker & Lambert, 2009). As the vast majority of citizens in Bangladesh are of the Muslim faith, religion plays a role in informal crime control. In some areas, informal *Sharia* systems are used in conjunction with or in place of the formal criminal justice system. This religious system tends to deal with more minor crimes, while the official government system deals with more serious, violent crimes (Banglapedia, 2011). As Bangladesh becomes more economically developed and urban, many of the past informal social crime control mechanisms are losing their power, and there is greater reliance on formal government agencies to deal with crime (Khondaker & Lambert, 2009).

This chapter provides a description of the criminal justice system in Bangladesh, discusses the issues of the criminal justice system, and concludes by highlighting the recent trends in crime. The authors focus on the structures and functions of three subsystems, namely police, courts, and corrections.

Criminal Justice System in Bangladesh

1. Police and Other Law Enforcement Agencies

The Bangladesh Police is the main law enforcement agency of Bangladesh. The Bangladesh Police is a centralized national organization functioning since independence in 1971 with slogans of 'discipline', 'security', and 'progress' (www.police.gov.bd). The Police Act of 1861 governs its administration, and the Police Regulation of Bengal (PRB), 1943 guides its operational aspects provided that the controlling authority—the Ministry of Home Affairs (MoHA) has the power to issue administrative regulations on personnel and police operations. Bangladesh Police has its administrative set up in urban and rural areas. The Bangladesh Police, having its headquarters based in Dhaka, consists of a number of branches and units that mainly include: Range Police and Metropolitan Police, Traffic Police, Armed Police Battalion (APBN), Criminal Investigation Department (CID), Special Branch (SB), Rapid Action Battalion (RAB), and training institutions, such as Police Staff College, Police Academy, and Police Training Centers. The 'Range' and 'Metropolitan' police are again subdivided into districts, circles, police stations, and outposts. Apart from these units, there are Railway Police, Court Police, and Marine Police. In recent years, Industrial Police, Highway Police, Tourist Police, and Police Investigation Bureau (PIB) were also created. While metropolitan police stations (*thanas*) are guided by metropolitan police acts, other police stations at district and *upazillas* (sub-districts) are guided by the PRB and the Police Act of 1861.

Bangladesh has a total of 139,546 police members (including 4,804 female police) with 629 *thanas* (police stations). Its police population ratio is 1:1073, which is lower than other South Asian nations and two times lower than the UN recommended ratio of 1:450. The police force has 16 ranks from constable to Inspector General of Police (Bangladesh Police Website). The category of gazetted officers (Assistant Superintendent of Police (ASP), Senior ASP, Additional Superintendent of Police, SP, Additional Deputy Inspector General of Police (DIG), Additional Inspector General of

Police (IGP), and IGP) and non-gazetted (Constable, Naik, Head Constable, Assistant Sub Inspector (ASI), Sergeant, TSI, SI, Inspector) is roughly analogous to commissioned and non-commissioned officers in the military.

The paramilitary Rapid Action Battalion (RAB) is considered a separate entity even though it is formed as a unit within the police under the same legal provision. Rapid Action Battalion was created as a composite force, drawing its personnel from the police, paramilitary forces, and the various branches of the armed forces under the Armed Police Battalions (Amendment) Act, 2003. Since 2004, RAB got wider acceptance for its significant performance in crime control, confiscation of illegal arms, arrest of wanted criminals, controlling woman and child trafficking, and money laundering. The Border Guard Bangladesh (BGB), the erstwhile Bangladesh Rifles (BDR), is the oldest paramilitary force of the country. It is organized into a central headquarters and various sectors, battalions, and border outposts mainly along the bordering areas of Bangladesh. Two main functions of BGB are border protection and prevention of smuggling in the border areas. But in cases of deteriorating law-and-order situations, they also assist police. The Coast Guard was established in 1995 under the Coast Guard Act 1994. It is mainly responsible for counter-smuggling, illegal immigration, and other sea crime activities in Bangladeshi sea territory. The Coast Guard executes its function in coordination with the Bangladesh Navy.

There are also Chaukidars and Dafadars, Ansar and VDP, BGB, and Coast Guard, and they are also engaged in law-and-order maintenance (Rahman, 2010, forthcoming; Saferworld, 2010). Chowkidars (village police) and Dafadars (higher ranked village police) are the Ministry of Local Government employees responsible for maintaining law and order in rural areas. They are required to provide information to the Officer-in-Charge (OC) of the police station about the incidence of crime in the area and movement of criminals. These village police are involved in prosecutorial function of the village court under the Village Court Ordinance. *Ansar* and Village Defense Party (VDP) are responsible for the protection of villages, persons, and property in rural Bangladesh, and additionally, they assist police in maintaining law and order. In April 2006, the government has formed a female unit of the Ansar.

2. Judiciary

The judiciary administers the criminal courts and sentencing. There are two levels in the court system of Bangladesh—subordinate courts and the Supreme Court. Subordinate courts are divided into civil courts and criminal courts. Civil courts are created under the Civil Courts Act of 1887, and there are five tiers of civil courts to try all suits of civil nature. There are two classes of criminal courts—Courts of Session and Courts of Magistrate. There are four tiers of judicial magistrates—chief metropolitan magistrate in metropolitan areas and chief judicial magistrate in other areas, and magistrate of first, second, and third class.

The Supreme Court is divided into two sections—the High Court and the Appellate Court. While the High Court hears the original cases and assesses cases from lower courts, the Appellate Court has jurisdiction to hear appeals of judgments, decrees, orders, or sentences of the high court or of any other body. Verdicts of the Appellate Court are binding on all other courts. The High Court may proclaim any law incompatible with fundamental rights as null and void. The Supreme Court is not only autonomous but also acts as the keeper of the constitution. In addition to interpreting laws, the Supreme Court can enforce fundamental rights of the citizens. Additionally, there are administrative tribunals to decide service disputes of public servants and some special courts and tribunals such as family court, money loan court to decide money claims of the banks and other financial institutions, and women and children repression prevention court to decide cases of crimes committed against women and children. In 2007, the interim Caretaker Government implemented the Supreme Court's 12-point directive for the separating judiciary from the executive as granted by the constitution, and accordingly all magistrates at subordinate courts started exercising their functions under the Supreme Court, and the Criminal Procedure Code (1898) was revised (Kashem, 2010). In an effort to combat crime and terrorism, special tribunals have also been created. The judges in these courts are appointed by the president. The president may also remove sitting judges with advice from the Supreme Judicial Council (the Chief Justice and two senior judges).

The guilt of a defendant is determined by a judge and not a jury (Das & Palmiotto, 2006). Plea-bargaining does not exist in the court system of Bangladesh. Thus, in the face of the judicial system's million-case backlog, the government has been experimenting with alternative dispute resolution (ADR).

3. Corrections

The nomenclature in Bangladesh makes no distinction between jails and prisons. All institutions are referred to as jails in Bangladesh. Therefore, in this chapter, the words 'prisons' and 'jails' will be used interchangeably. The prison system of Bangladesh had its inception in the legislation of the Prison Act of 1894, which was basically derived from the England Prison Act of 1877. The jail administration is governed by the Bengal Jail Code 1864. Presently there are 68 jails divided into three categories: high security, central, and district. The jails are the only correctional institution in Bangladesh which combines the function of jail and prison. Jails hold people awaiting trial as well as those presently undergoing trial, persons under protective custody, and sentenced prisoners. There is one separate institution for women (see Kashem, 1996, 1999, for more discussion on types of jails).

According to the Prison Directorate as of March 31, 2014, the prison population was 65,662 (male 63,451 and female 2,211) against the rated capacity of 34,167. The rate of prison population is 42 (per 100,000 of the total national population). Of the total prison population 69% are under-trial prisoners (Prison's Directorate, 2014). The prison population of Bangladesh has increased almost 100% between 1990 and 2014. Presently most prisons are operating above design capacity. "Most experts argue that a prison is crowded when more than 85 percent of its cells are occupied" (Toch, 1985, p. 64). Data show that Bangladeshi prisons are operating at over 92% of their current capacity. For example, as of March 31, 2014, the prison population of the country's largest jail, Dhaka Central Jail, is around 9,000 against the rated capacity of 2,682.

The Bangladeshi prison administrators follow the control model, which concentrates authority in the prison administration. In the control model, administrators believe that "inflexible, strict controls should permeate all aspects of prison life" (Craig, 2004, p. 100). In managing jails the administrators adopt a number of strategies in order to achieve total control over the inmates. First: prisoners are divided into gangs consisting of 21 to 24 prisoners. According to the Jail Code every prisoner has to maintain a membership in a gang throughout the whole period of their imprisonment. Gang membership cannot be changed without the order of the competent authority. They eat, sleep, and work together. Prison activities are thus organized in groups and always under continuous surveillance that clearly helps the administrator to reinforce extensive rules of conduct (Kashem, 1996). Second: the use of convict officers in supervising the inmates is another strategy of prison administrators in achieving total control over the inmates. There are three types of convict officers in Bangladeshi prisons: convict watchmen, convict overseers, and convict warders (Personal Interview, November, 2014). The prison guards and convict officers very often use physical force in order to gain compliance from the inmates (Kashem, 1996).

Discussion

1. Issues in Policing

The police play a vital role in the adjudication process governed by the Code of Criminal Procedure and Special Powers Act (SPA) of the land (Police Reform Program, 2010). The police have been found to abuse their authority in registering first information reports (FIR) or making general diaries (GD) entries, by falsely involving innocent persons in an FIR, letting the accused go free, and conducting baseless investigations (Shahjahan, 2006). The police use of discretionary powers often causes serious miscarriages of justice. In the court of first instance (magistrate court), police officers (without professional training or legal expertise) perform prosecutorial functions, and the court system does not have administrative control over police prosecutors. Police interrogation does not require the presence of a defense attorney as in the US system. The same officials being assigned with investigation, law and order and prosecution duties become unaccountable and inefficient (Shahjahan, 2006). For example, because of the weaknesses in the Evidence Act (1872) the present practice of torture in police custody remains very common. Amendments of these legal provisions are required to rectify existing weaknesses in investigative practices (UNDP, Human Security Report, 2003).

A police cell or custody is the most insecure place, and the custodial deaths and extra-judicial killings by law enforcement personnel raise huge concerns over the human rights and human security of the arrested in Bangladesh (Rahman, forthcoming). Due to the culture of immunity along with politicization of the police force and bribery practices, police torture in custody is common. Use of the police force to torture opposition party leaders, threat, false report, and erroneous investigation for getting bribes or being influenced by the influential and rich people, release of offenders from police cells, and a number of recent killing cases of ordinary people by the police are linked to police abuse of power and human rights abuse (Rahman, 2010, forthcoming). The apex court, the media, national and international human rights organizations, and civil society have seriously pointed to this problem of extrajudicial execution in the form of crossfire, encounter, gunfights, and the recently added disappearance replacing crossfire (Sultana, Rahman, & Roshni, 2014).

In addition to the above issue, Bangladesh has been experiencing an alarming increase of extrajudicial killing and torture by law enforcement over the last few years, particularly since 2009 by the newly created elite force—Rapid Action Battalion (RAB). Despite its good work, the RAB has been in public debate for its extra-judicial executions. Local and international human rights groups, National Human Rights Commission, civil society leaders, and politicians have blamed RAB for the disappearance of suspects and human rights abuse. In 2010, the RAB admitted the killing of more than 600 people since 2004, and more than 54 were killed by RAB just in 2011, which were not investigated or judged by the government of Bangladesh (Sultana et al., 2014). In 2010, out of 127 victims of extra-judicial killings, 68 were killed by RAB, 43 by police, 9 were jointly killed by RAB and police, 3 by the joint operation of RAB and Coast Guard, 3 by the joint operation of RAB, Police, and Coast Guard, and 1 by BGB (Sultana et al., 2014).

It is important to note that under-reporting of crime is common in Bangladesh, particularly for property crimes. Victims are not willing to report crime to the police in Bangladesh for various reasons, and only one-third of crime victims go to the police for reporting. The police is considered one of the most corrupt institutions in Bangladesh (Transparency International Bangladesh, 2004, 2005, 2008; Rahman, 2010; Kashem, 2002, 2003; Shahjahan, 2006; Huda, 2009). Several studies suggest that police take bribes in registering FIR or GD at police stations, rarely use fair procedure in arresting, investigating, interrogating, or prosecuting criminals, harass innocent victims because of political or external interference, and discriminate against poor and vulnerable people in their treatment (Rahman, 2010). To many, the police are dishonest and impolite. Hence, the level of public confidence in police is low in the country (Rahman, 2010, forthcoming; Kashem, 2002, 2003; UNDP Bangladesh, 2007; Saferworld, 2010). Given the low confidence in the police and the understanding that the police cannot be of much help, people do not go to the police. In many cases, incidents of violence are not reported because of inadequate support services in the police stations and negative police attitudes (UNDP, 2002, 2007).

A very few descriptive and exploratory studies indicate that the general public is dissatisfied with the quality of police work, believe that the police are not doing a good job, and rate police service as extremely poor, indicating that the police are impolite, dishonest, corrupt, and not dedicated (Rahman, 2010, 2011; Kashem, 2001, 2002; Saferworld, 2008, 2010; Huda, 2009; Khondaker & Lambert, 2009; UNDP Bangladesh, 2002, 2003, 2007). According to a baseline public attitude survey conducted by the UNDP in 2006, more than 70% of respondents were dissatisfied with police behavior, and police attitudes were particularly bad toward poor and vulnerable people (UNDP Bangladesh, 2007). Bribery, negligence of duty, bad behavior with less powerful citizens, external interference in police work, and corruption are the key obstacles to obtaining justice in Bangladesh (UNDP Bangladesh, 2007).

2. Issues in Prisons

Considering the deterrent effects of punishment, the 'get tough' approach is predominant in the correctional philosophy of Bangladesh, and the aim of prison is retributive punishment. In assessing the state of jails in Bangladesh, the German Society for International Cooperation (GIZ) observed: "the country's prisons are severely overcrowded. Even the Prison Directorate explicitly states that it is unable to adhere to the minimum standards for prisons as required by the United Nations—namely the provision of sufficient light, ventilation, space and privacy" (GIZ, 2012). According to a senior former jail official, in recent years rated capacities in many jails have been raised without ensuring required facilities like water supply and sanitation for the additional number of inmates. As a result, water and sewerage arrangements come under severe strain due to the excess number of inmates (Personal Interview, November 2014).

Judicial intervention forced many American prisons to pursue legal, humane custody, and control more diligently. Alternatively, the court systems of Bangladesh have been following the 'hands-off' policy with regard to prison operation and management. That is, they rarely interfere with the internal management, administrative, and disciplinary practices of prisons. In reality they are "outside the law" (Kashem, 1996). In fact, prisons are essentially human warehouses where harsh discipline is the salient feature of prison life in Bangladesh. Without any standard-setting bodies (for example, ACA in the USA) to correct many deficiencies of jails, inmates in Bangladesh are forced to reside at an extreme level of crowding. For instance, it was found that inmates were provided with per-capita floor space of 10square feet in Chittagong District jail (Kashem, 1996). Overcrowding affects the living conditions, and evidence suggests that due to the shortage of floor space, prisoners of many jails had to sleep in shifts (Kashem, 1996).

In Bangladesh the current sentencing policies are not designed to promote rehabilitation. Even the existing rehabilitation efforts do not carry some reasonable prospect for success. The Inspector General of Prisons (Head of Prisons) recently at a conference argued that "a significant number of prisoners re-engage in criminal activities after they are released due to a lack of proper rehabilitation facilities and failure to reintegrate into the society" (*The Daily Star*, May 2014). A 1998 Maryland Report concluded that rehabilitation programs can effectively change offenders (Sherman et al., 1997). Over-reliance on incarceration in punishing offenders in the end are associated with higher rates of recidivism and reduced public safety (Lawrence, 1991). Given the present level of crowding, the prison system could consider using alternatives to imprisonment such as community-based sanctions for non-violent offenders. As Lawrence (1991, p. 457) points out, "the key element in community correction emphasizes reintegration—the transition process from correctional institutions back into the community". Also, early release of elderly inmates (over 60) serving life imprisonment could be an alternative, as these prisoners no longer pose a threat to society (Ornduff, 1996).

Conclusion

Crime has been a major concern in Bangladesh since its independence in 1971. In the past 20 years, there has been an increase in crime, especially violent crime, and a breakdown of law and order in

Bangladesh. For example, between 2000 and 2010 the number of homicides increased by over 17%. Most importantly, the patterns of murders have changed significantly in terms of premeditation and brutality over the years. The use of firearms in committing crimes, especially murder, has increased in the past decade as well. In 2010, over 162,000 crimes were reported to the police, a rate of 110 per 100,000 citizens, even though the number is much higher, as underreporting of crime is common in Bangladesh, particularly for property crimes (Bangladesh Police, 2012). In the 10 years between 1996 and 2006, crimes reported to the police increased from 93,000 to 130,000 (i.e., an increase in the rate from 78 to 87 crimes per 100,000 citizens) (Bangladesh Police, 2012). Just four years later, by 2010, over 162,000 crimes were reported to the police, a rate of 110 per 100,000 citizens (Bangladesh Police, 2012).

Besides police statistics, the nature and trend of crime can be explored from the limited available studies conducted by some international development agencies, donor organizations, local NGOs, human rights groups, and institutional and individual researchers. According to the US Department of State Report, homicides, sexual assaults, personal robberies, and residential break-ins are common forms of crimes but do not exceed average levels of major cities in the US (US Department of State, 2014). Financial scams, vehicle thefts, and petty drug crimes comprise the majority of criminal activity in major cities. Targeted kidnappings and kidnapping plots (local businessmen, known criminals, and some politicians) represent a small amount of the overall crime environment. In addition, Bangladesh has experienced local, regional, and international terrorism threats, which are becoming major concerns for Bangladesh's government (Rahman & Kashem, 2011).

In Bangladesh, there are no such initiatives like Uniform Crime Reports (UCR) or victimization surveys, which are common to many Western and developed countries. However, in recent years the Bangladesh Police started generating crime statistics at national aggregate level and comparing them between different years. In 2013, 179,199 crimes were reported to the police, even though the number is much higher, as under-reporting of crime is common in Bangladesh due to various factors that were discussed earlier. Based on police administered crime statistics of Bangladesh, total number of crimes reported by the police rose from 108,938 in 2000 to 127,616 in 2002. It is found that the number of cases recorded by the police has decreased from 2002 to 2004, and afterwards the number has increased again. In 2004, the number of crime has slightly decreased (5%) as compared to the previous year, and it is claimed that this decline could be due to the introduction of Rapid Action Battalion in controlling crime (Jahan & Kashem, 2006). However, some crimes have increased: the number of murders was 3,400, 3,902, and 4,219, and violence against women was 10,535, 12,815, and 12,904 in the years 2000, 2004, and 2009, respectively (Rahman, 2011).

Violence against women (VAW) has become a critical socioeconomic issue for Bangladesh due to the rise of domestic violence, dowry-related violence, acid violence, murder, rape, sexual harassment, workplace violence, eve-teasing, and trafficking (Akter & Rahman, 2015). Despite various laws and policy measures, crimes against women have been rising. According to a Bangladesh Bureau of Statistics Survey (BBS, 2013), 87% of women reported being victims of physical violence, 80% of psychological violence, and 26% of sexual violence which were committed by their husbands and partners in 2011.

Police statistics include only the registered cases of common crimes—dacoity, robbery, murder, riot, burglary, theft, arms, woman and child oppression, arms, explosives, and smuggling (Bangladesh Police, 2014). The comparative police statistics show that all crimes have increased since 2002 except for the crimes of murder, woman and child repression, and police assault (Bangladesh Police, 2014). If we calculate the trends over 12 years (2002–2013), it is noticed that murder has increased by over 25%, woman and child repression by over 3%, drug crime by 297%, and smuggling over 35%.

Additionally, there has been an increase in terrorist activity by militant Islamic groups in Bangladesh, leading to hundreds of deaths (Uddin, 2009). For example, on August 17, 2005, 450 bombs aimed at government buildings were set off by Jamaatul Mujahideen, an Islamist extremist terrorist group (National Counterterrorism Center, 2011). Crime also has a political nature in Bangladesh, as many violent crimes—especially torture, assault, and murder—are patronized by political leaders, and criminals of many of such crimes are affiliated with different political parties.

Also, there are some laws enacted after independence by the successive governments mainly aimed at oppressing political opponents. The enactment of additional special laws—such as the Special Powers Act (1974), Antiterrorism Act (1992), Public Safety Act (2000), Speedy Trial Act (2002)—has increased the punitiveness of the system (UNDP, 2002) and helped the ruling elites to act against opposition political leaders (Rahman, 2010). At the same time, the criminal justice system is under-funded, painfully slow, and inefficient. The state—especially the leaders of the ruling political party—exercises strong control over police agencies. Unless a total reform is done on the criminal justice system of Bangladesh, it would be difficult to mitigate the growing crime rate and new crimes like cybercrimes.

References

Akter, M., & Rahman, M. A. (2015). Underlying issues for the rise of violence against women in Bangladesh. *Presentation at the ACJS conference* held on March 5–7, 2015, Florida, USA.

Banglapedia. (2011). *Bangladesh.* Retrieved from http://search.com.bd/banglapedia/.

Bangladesh Police. (2012). *Bangladeshi police.* Retrieved from www.police.gov.bd/.

Bangladesh Police. (2014). *Comparative crime statistics: 2002–2013.* Retrieved from www.police.gov.bd/Crime-Statistics-comparative.php?id=208.

BBS. (2013). *Report on Violence Against Women (VAW) survey 2011.* Dhaka: BBS.

Bengal Jail Code. (1864). *Rules for the superintendence and magistrate of jails in Bengal.* Calcutta: Inspector-General of Prisons, Bengal Presidency.

Craig, S. (2004). Rehabilitation versus control: An organizational theory of prison management. *The Prison Journal, 84*(4), 92s–114s.

The Daily Star. (2014, May 7). Lack of rehabilitation creates repeat offenders. Retrieved from www.thedailystar. net.

Das, D., & Palmiotto, M. (2006). *World police Encyclopedia.* New York: Routledge.

D'Costa, B. (2012). Bangladesh in 2011: Weak state building and different foreign policy. *Asian Survey, 52,* 147–156.

GIZ (Deutsche Gesellschaft für Internationale Zusammenarbeit). (2012). *Justice and prison reform for promoting human rights and preventing corruption.* Bangladesh: GIZ.

Huda, M. N. (2009). *Bangladesh police: Issues and challenges.* Dhaka: The University Press Limited.

ICPS. (2008). *World prison brief—Bangladesh.* Retrieved from www.kcl.ac.uk/depsta/law/research/icps/world brief/wpb_country_print.php?country=87.

Islam, N., & Ali, M. (2008). A study on service quality of the Bangladesh police. *Global Journal of Business Excellence, 1*(1), 1–8.

Jahan, F., & Kashem, M. B. (2006). Law and order administration in Bangladesh. Working paper, Dhaka, Bangladesh: Center for Governance Studies, BRAC University.

Kashem, M. B. (1996). Jails in Bangladesh. *International Journal of Comparative and Applied Criminal Justice, 20*(1), 31–40.

Kashem, M. B. (2001). *Public confidence in the police.* Center for Criminological Research. Bangladesh: Department of Sociology, University of Chittagong.

Kashem, M. B. (2002). Public attitudes toward crime and sentencing in Bangladesh. Center for Criminological Research, Bangladesh. Unpublished Report. Department of Sociology. University of Chittagong, Bangladesh.

Kashem, M. B. (2003). Preventing crime: Police and crime control in Bangladesh. *Asian Policing, Journal of Asian Association of Police Studies, 1*(1) 70–90.

Kashem, M. B. (2010). Crime and punishment in Bangladesh. In G. Newman (Ed.), *Crime and punishment around the world Asia/Pacific Volume.* Santa Barbara, CA: ABC-CLIO Publishers.

Khondaker, M., & Lambert, E. (2009). Views toward crime, criminals, treatment, and punishment among Bangladeshi and U.S. college students. *Asia Pacific Journal Police and Criminal Justice, 7*(1), 1–20.

Lawrence, R. (1991). Reexamining community corrections models. *Crime & Delinquency, 37*(4), 449–464.

National Counterterrorism Center. (2011). *2010 report on terrorism.* Washington, DC: Office of the Director of National Intelligence.

Ornduff, J. S. (1996). Releasing the elderly inmates: A solution to prison overcrowding. *The Elder Law Journal, 4*, 173–200.

Rahman, M. A. (2010). *Factors affecting public attitude toward the police in Bangladesh.* Unpublished manuscript (MA criminology research paper submitted to the University of Toronto).

Rahman, M. A. (Forthcoming). Model police station and satisfaction with police service in Bangladesh: The case of Dhaka Metropolitan Police. Accepted for publication in the *Asia Pacific Journal of Policing and Criminal Justice.*

Rahman, M. A., & Kashem, M. B. (2011). *Understanding religious militancy and terrorism in Bangladesh.* Dhaka, Bangladesh: Institute of Cultural Affairs (ICA) Bangladesh. (Unpublished study report of the ICA Bangladesh supported by the institutional research grant of Social Science Research Council (SSRC), Bangladesh.

Saferworld. (2008). *Human security in Bangladesh.* Retrieved from www.saferworld.org.uk/downloads/pubdocs/Bangladesh_HS_report.pdf.

Saferworld. (2010). *Security provision in Bangladesh: A public perceptions survey.* Retrieved from www.saferworld.org.uk/downloads/pubdocs/Security%20 provision%20in%20Bangladesh%20exec%20sum%20English.pdf.

Shahjahan, A. S. M. (2006). Police reforms in Bangladesh. In *Strengthening the criminal justice system.* Dhaka: Asian Development Bank. Retrieved from www.adb.org/Documents/Books/Strengthening-Criminal-Justice-system/strengthening-criminal-justice-system.pdf.

Sherman, L. W., Gottfredson, D., MacKenzie, D., Eck, J., Reuter, P., & Bushway, S. (1997). *Preventing crime: What works, what doesn't, what's promising.* A report to the United States Congress. Washington, DC: National Institute of Justice, US Department of Justice.

Sultana, S., Rahman, M. A., & Roshni, M. R. (2014). The state of extra-judicial execution by the law enforcement in Bangladesh. *Presentation in the ACJS conference* held on March 5–7, 2015, Florida, USA.

Toch, H. (1985). Social climate and prison violence. In M. Braswall, S. Dillingham, & R. Montgomery (Eds.), *Prison violence in America* (pp. 37–46). Cincinnati, OH: Anderson Publishing.

Uddin, M. (2009). Security sector reform in Bangladesh. *South Asia Survey, 16*, 209–230.

UNDP Bangladesh. (2002). Human security in Bangladesh. In *Search of justice and dignity.* Dhaka: UNDP. Retrieved from www.undp.org.bd/info/hsr/index.htm

UNDP Bangladesh. (2003). *Towards police reform in Bangladesh: Need assessment report 2003.* Dhaka: UNDP Bangladesh. Retrieved from www.prp.org.bd/Menudownloads.htm

UNDP Bangladesh. (2007). *Public attitude baseline survey—2006 final report on public attitude baseline survey for the police reform program—BGD/04/001.* Dhaka: UNDP Bangladesh. Retrieved from www.prp.org.bd/Menu downloads.htm

UNDP Bangladesh. (2014). *Police reform program.* Retrieved from www.undp.org.org.bd.

US Department of State. (2014). *Bangladesh 2014 crime and safety report.* Retrieved from www.osac.gov/pages/ContentReportDetails.aspx?cid=15389.

Walmsley, R. (2010). *World prison population list* (7th ed.). London: Kings College London, International Centre for Prison Studies. Retrieved from www.kcl.ac.uk/depsta/law/research/icps/downloads/world-prison-pop-seventh.pdf.

World Factbook. (2012). *Bangladesh.* Retrieved from www.cia.gov/library/publications/the-world-factbook/geos.

3

BHUTAN

Penal Laws, Crimes and Criminal Justice Processes

Debarati Halder

Introduction

The Himalayan Kingdom of Bhutan had remained isolated for many years from the rest of the world. It was only after the 1970s that the fourth king of Bhutan, King Jigme Singye Wangchuck, took progressive steps to bring people-oriented developmental goals, and the world came to know about Bhutanese ideology of Gross National Happiness. Bhutan is well known as a favourite tourist destination, especially from India and South Asian countries, and also from Korea, Singapore, Malaysia, Europe, the USA, Australia etc. Even though Bhutan is a preferred destination for tourists, ironically, Bhutan has been also a chosen destination for drug peddlers (Chua, 2008) due to its geographic location, which helps to yield more crops to be used for narcotics. Similarly, Bhutan is also affected by migration of women and children for sex trafficking, especially to the eastern regions of India, and they are prone to dreadful sexually transmitted diseases like HIV/AIDS (Sarkar et al., 2008).

It is interesting to note that due to rapid urbanisation of the society in Bhutan, the Bhutanese youth are adhering to Western cultures. Sadly, urbanisation and Western influence has also brought many negative impacts including breaking of nuclear families, driving the youth to be more addicted to technology, which is reducing the scope of physical socialisation with families and peers as was the tradition of Bhutan (Chua, 2008). These may lead to growth of crime rates especially for cases like sexual harassment, drug abuse, domestic violence and privacy infringement through information and digital technology.

There are very few surveys (L. Dorji et al., 2015) depicting the rate of crimes such as the survey on gender violence in Bhutan, which was carried out by National Commission for Women and Children in Bhutan (2012). As per this survey, it could be seen that there was 6.1% prevalence of physical violence on married women; in 2.1% cases, sexual violence by intimate partners was noted; 6.3% cases were noted where women suffered physical violence by non-partners; and 3.5% cases were noted where women suffered psychological violence by non-partners. However, this report did not give any details regarding the types of psychological or physical violence.

There is a need to understand the patterns and trends of crimes in Bhutan as well as the functioning of the criminal justice system in Bhutan. In the present chapter, an effort is taken in that direction. Notably, there has rarely been any socio-criminological-legal research conducted on the issue of crimes and the criminal justice system in Bhutan. There is no proper source or literature on crime rates, trends and usage of penal laws for prevention of crimes in Bhutan. The limited research that is available on the crime situation of Bhutan primarily investigates crime and mental health (L. Dorji et al., 2015), violence against women (T. Dorji, 2015), drug and alcohol addiction among the youth (Chua, 2008; L. Dorji, 2012), corruption and related issues (Namygel, 2009), Bhutanese refugees in Nepal (Laxminarayan & Pemberton, 2012) and legal aid in Bhutan (Sherab, 2014). Apart from the said resources there were no resources dealing with other trends of crimes that may be prevalent in Bhutan. One of the main reasons for such limited resources available on crime and the criminal justice system in Bhutan may be because of non-reporting behavior due to the family-oriented traditional culture; reporting crimes to the criminal justice administration may be seen as a shameful act (Chua, 2008).

Even though there is a lack of literature regarding trends of crimes or crime patterns in Bhutan, the criminal law-making process or policing, this chapter will rely on the Bhutan Penal Code and the constitution to understand the above-mentioned issues. This chapter will basically delve into the constitution of Bhutan, which was formally introduced on 18 July, 2008,[1] and the very progressive Penal Code of Bhutan, which came into effect on 11 August, 2004, to build an overview of crime and criminal justice system of Bhutan. Following the introduction, this chapter is divided into two parts: 1. Penal Laws and Crimes in Bhutan and 2. Criminal Justice Processes in Bhutan, and it will conclude with some suggestions.

I. Penal Laws and Crimes in Bhutan

The Bhutanese constitution is divided into 35 Articles, which are further divided into separate sections dealing with matters including the three divisions of governance, viz., executive, legislature, judiciary; institution of monarchy; fundamental rights and duties; trade and commerce; environmental rights and duty; spiritual heritage; provisions regarding emergency; amendments etc. It may be interesting to note that the Bhutanese legal system is framed upon seven core Buddhist ideologies including proper decorum, legality, freedom from duress, decision through majority, grounds of a judicial decision resolution through rebuttal and plead guilty.

While the constitution is the source of all laws, formation of governmental departments, and rules and policies, it also provides an overview of rights and wrongs which are governed by the Penal Code of Bhutan. The Bhutan Penal Code is divided into seven parts which are further divided into 35 chapters. These chapters deal with the types of offences, restitution of justice in different ways for such offences, forms of sentencing etc.

A brief overview of the Penal Code of Bhutan illustrates that crimes are divided into the following types:

1. Crimes against the nation, which may include terrorism, illegal immigration, sedition etc.;
2. Economic crimes including cheating, money laundering, tax evasion, corruption-related crimes etc.;
3. Crimes targeting women and children including sexual crimes like rape, molestation, woman and child trafficking, prostitution; general crimes against children including forceful child labour, discrimination in regard to education etc.; domestic violence-related crimes targeting women including wife abuse, marital rape etc.;
4. Crimes targeting property including theft, burglary, trespassing etc.;
5. Cybercrime-related issues including hacking, cyber stalking etc.;
6. Crimes targeting the body of the person including bodily harm, homicide, motivational murders, defamation, etc.;
7. Religious crimes etc.;
8. Other social crimes like substance abuse including drug and alcohol abuse etc.

As has been discussed earlier, s.3 of the Bhutan Penal Code divides crimes into four classifications: felony (any crime which is awarded an imprisonment term for a minimum period of three years or more), misdemeanour (for crimes which are awarded a maximum term of three years imprisonment to minimum one year imprisonment), petty misdemeanour (for crimes which are awarded with imprisonment for term of less than one year maximum and a minimum of one month) and violation (when the crime is awarded with a fine of the daily minimum national wage rate up to a maximum of 90days).[2] Felonies can further be divided into four categories, namely, felony of first, second, third and fourth degree.[3]

As could be seen from the existing literature, not all of these crimes are analysed extensively in surveys conducted either by the government or any other non-governmental organisations (NGOs). However, it needs to be noted that the Bhutan Penal Code has taken serious note of crimes against women and children whereby it has criminalised corporal punishment on children by teachers, caregivers or parents, only when such use of force causes substantial damage to the body of the person or causes death to the person to whom such force is used in the name of discipline or controlling.[4] The penal code recognizes no criminal liability of a juvenile if the child is below 10 years of age.[5] But at the same time, it provides opportunity for correctional institutions when the juvenile is above 10 years of age.[6] The penal code criminalises illegal abortions under s.146. Apart from criminalising trafficking of persons including children under s.154, the penal Code also criminalises kidnapping (s.162), abduction (s.165) and criminal elopement (s.169), thus creating clear categories of criminal liabilities in cases of forceful removals of a person from his/her secured place. Further, the penal code also criminalises abandonment of children by parents or caregivers, child abuse, abuse and abandonment of mentally challenged children, paedophilia and child trafficking under Chapter 15 of the Code.

The penal code further criminalizes rape of any individual under s.177 irrespective of his/her gender or sexual orientation, rapes of married persons (s.179), of children below 12 years of age (S.183), of pregnant women (s.185), gang rape (s.187), gang rape on married persons, children below 12 years and above 12 years and statutory rape (S.181). The uniqueness of Bhutan penal laws regarding rape lies in the fact that it recognises marital rape (s.199) irrespective of the gender. Social crimes including crimes against women and children also include criminalising indecent exposure (s.209), sexual harassment (s.205), child molestation (s.203) etc. Further, it may be noted that the penal code also criminalises prostitution under Chapter 26 of the Penal code; it also criminalises several offences against privacy including eves dropping (Chapter 30), harassment etc. While some researchers and reports have thrown light on trafficking (Sarkar et al., 2008), violence against women (T. Dorji, 2015) and child abuse (United Nations, 2008), there is not much literature available about the current status of sexual offences including marital rape in Bhutan.

Notably, substance abuse and alcohol abuse among the youth of Bhutan have attracted the attention of many stakeholders such as the government, the NGOs and the civil society (L. Dorji, 2012; UNODC, 2012). While drug and alcohol abuse is an issue of concern with regard to Bhutanese youth including school children, there are several government agencies, such as the Bhutan Narcotics Control Agency, that are responsible for monitoring the situation (UNODC, 2012). The Bhutan Penal Code has successfully targeted the root cause of substance abuse in Bhutan by criminalising environment-related issues which may generate crimes including substance abuse like narcotic and drug abuse under Chapter 33 of the penal code. Also, it has criminalised several social behavioural problems of youth such as public intoxication, illegal sale of tobacco, illegal sale of alcohol, gambling, environmental crimes like motivational destruction of environment and the like under Chapter 27.

Corruption, money laundering and fraudulent activities are also highlighted by the Bhutan criminal justice system, especially the Penal Code under Chapter 34. It may be necessary to point out that the Bhutanese constitution embraces the philosophy of equality and equal distribution of wealth. Since Bhutan is a landlocked country, there is an inflow and outflow of illegal money to and from neighbouring countries such as India, Nepal, and Bangladesh, and the possibility of the use of Bhutan for smuggling goods between other countries has not been ruled out by the lawmakers and police.

Bhutan has also made homicide, murder, manslaughter, assault etc. penal offences under Chapter 11 of the Penal Code. It is interesting to note that this particular chapter differentiates between different types of dreadful attacks on persons, thus making it easier for the criminal justice system as a whole to ensure speedy justice to the victim as well as the perpetrator. Bhutan needs to be secured from external terrorist attacks as well as internal civil unrest, which may be motivated by various reasons including bad governance. While the later possible phenomenon is monitored by government agencies by means of laws, especially Chapter 20 of the Penal code which deals with embezzlement and bribery, the earlier possibilities are kept in check by means of laws meant for national security, as has been stated in Chapter 23, which deals with treason, terrorism, related offences etc. It must be noted that due to the progressive outlook of the fourth king, Bhutan became a democratic monarchy, giving prime importance regarding law-making and rights and duties of the citizens including the royal family members to the constitution; and this to a certain extent reduced the risk of internal civil unrest, as had happened in Nepal immediately after the royal massacre of Nepal (Bearak, 2001) in which the then-King Birendra was killed.

The Bhutan Penal Code also indicates a strong note against damaging the reputation of a person irrespective of gender. Chapter 22 of the penal code criminalises defamation, libel, blackmail and false advertisements for maligning the name of the person. This is particularly in line with the constitutional right to human dignity to all. Also, Bhutan is one of the few countries which has developed penal laws to deal with cybercrimes. Even though the penal law does not include crimes like cyberstalking or revenge pornography or cyberbullying, Chapter 31 of the Penal code criminalises tampering with computer materials, pornography and illegal possession of computer materials.

Further, Bhutan considers illegal handling of stuffs of national and cultural heritage as criminal activities under Chapter 24 of the Penal Code. It needs to be mentioned here due to their ancient background that Bhutanese antiquities may be in high demand in foreign markets like India and China. The Bhutanese government is presently taking precautionary measures to develop foreign policies with neighbours like India, China, Nepal etc. to prevent illegal export of the antiquities and also hazardous narcotics objects.

II. Criminal Justice Processes in Bhutan

1. Judiciary

The Bhutanese legal system is a unique system and on a close examination it reveals features of various legal systems but it neither falls within the category of common law system (adversarial system) nor the continental civil law system (inquisitorial system). In 1953, His Majesty the third Druk Gyalpo Jigme Dorji Wangchuck established the legislative branch called the Tshogdu. The Tshogdu comprised 150 members of which 106 members were elected representatives of the people of 20 Dzongkhags (districts); 10 from the Zhung Dratshang (clergy); and 24 nominated representatives of the government. The Tshogdu as the legislative arm of the Government adopted the Thrimzhung Chhenmo, the Supreme Law of Bhutan in 1959. The Thrimzhung Chhenmo had comprehensive provisions dealing with legal principles and procedure both for the civil and criminal cases. The enactment of Thrimzhung Chhenmo marked the beginning of the modern law making process in Bhutan.

(Sherab, 2014, p. 8)

The appointment of judges (Drangpons) in the districts started in the 1960s and the High Court as a court of appeal was established in 1968. Since then the judiciary has evolved over the years. The formal justice system is safeguarded, upheld and administered fairly and independently without fear or favour by the Judiciary.[7] The judicial authority is vested with the Royal Courts of Justice comprising of the Supreme Court, High Court, Dzongkhag Court and Dungkhag Court (Divisional Court).[8] The Supreme Court (with 5 Justices including the Chief Justice) is the highest appellate court in the country. Next in line is the High Court (with 9 Justices including the Chief Justice), which exercises appellate jurisdiction over Dzongkhag Courts. There are 20 Dzongkhag Courts (one in each district) which act as the appellate court for the Dungkhag Courts and is the court of first instance where there is no Dungkhag Courts. Dungkhag Courts were established essentially to enhance access to justice for the rural masses. Currently, there are 15 Dungkhag Courts of first instance. Both the Dzongkhag Courts and the Dungkhag Courts act as trial court, depending on the hierarchical set up. While all the courts exercise general jurisdiction, the High Court is the court of first instance on constitutional matters. Additionally, the constitution also provides for the establishment of 'such other Courts and Tribunals'4 as may be necessary.

(Sherab, 2014, p. 8)

The process of prosecution is entirely guided by Bhutan civil and criminal procedure Code, Bhutanese Penal Code and constitutional rights. Both the victim and the accused have right to get justice and appeal. It may be necessary to point out that while the Bhutanese constitution ensures that victims of crimes are entitled to get help from the criminal justice machinery including government lawyers in the prosecution stage, the Bhutanese constitution through various laws also ensures that underprivileged citizens should get free legal aid from the courts (Norbu, n.d.; Sherab, 2014). The Bhutanese judiciary created a huge example of welfare governance by creating a national system of legal aid without state funds (Norbu, n.d.; Sherab, 2014). This has helped many Bhutanese citizens to access justice irrespective of their financial, social or educational background.

2. Police

The Bhutanese government has given due importance to construct a proper policing system by forming the Royal Bhutan Police, which is the main policing agency in Bhutan. The Civil and Criminal Procedure Code (Wangdi, Tashi, & Dorji, 2014) of Bhutan and the Royal Bhutan Police Act provide statutory guidelines for policing, investigation etc. The Bhutan Penal Code provides numerous provisions for effective policing by way of laying down exceptions to the crimes through provisions such as Chapter 7, which deals with justification of affirmative defence. Also, the Civil and Criminal Procedure Code (2011) and the Royal Bhutan Police act laydown strict rules which, if violated, may result in suspension of the duties of the concerned police officer or disciplinary actions against the police officer concerned (Wangdi, 2014).

Bhutan is no exception in giving due preference to the rights of the accused (Wangdi, 2014; Article 7, Fundamental rights under Bhutanese constitution); but at the same time, the Bhutanese constitution also ensures the right against arbitrary arrest and detention, human rights violation in any form by police officers or any other civilians and the right to fair trial.[9] The accused is thus given right to consult his/her lawyer to defend him/herself. Similarly, as the Royal Bhutan Police Act and the civil and criminal procedure code laydown, the police must show compassionateness to the victim and should avoid victim blaming while interacting with the victim (Wangdi, 2014). The recent researches also showed that the Bhutanese government and the police organisation are also encouraging for community policing and encouraging youth to participate in community policing (Zangpo & Kamnuansilpa, 2013). It is noteworthy that the Bhutanese government has taken measures to check corruption in every field of governance including policing. To check corruption Bhutan has established an Anticorruption Commission and introduced public welfare laws like the Anti-corruption Act of Bhutan, 2006, Bhutanese Penal code, which deals with corruption under Part Four, especially Chapter 20 (Namygel, 2009).

The police are responsible for reporting crimes, investigating offences, helping victims to reach the courts and connecting them with government prosecutors, especially when the crime is cognizable in nature (Wangdi, 2014).

3. Sentencing Processes

The Bhutan Penal Code further ensures speedy and effective means of justice by classifying crimes according to the harms created by them to the affected parties and the sentencing classification for each categories of crimes recognised by the Bhutan Penal Code. Bhutan does not have capital punishment; sentences for felony of first degree may include life imprisonment or a minimum imprisonment of 15 years. Felony of first degree shall include grievous offences like murder, terrorism, offences against Ku Sung, Thuk Ten, Zung, creation of weapons for mass destruction etc. Felonies of second degree include offences which are awarded a term of imprisonment for not less than 9 years and not more than 15 years.[10] Felonies of third degree include crimes which are awarded imprisonment for a term not less than five years and not more nine years. And felonies of fourth degree shall include offences for which sentences are awarded for imprisonment for a term not less than three years and not more than five years.[11] Further, the sentencing for crimes in the nature of misdemeanours has been fixed with imprisonment for a term which shall not be more than three years and not less than one year; for crimes in the nature of petty misdemeanours, the sentencing is fixed for imprisonment for a term of not less than one month and not more than one year.[12] The Penal Code also states that in case of next conviction for the same offence, a convicted person shall be liable for enhanced punishment, which includes upgrading of petty misdemeanour to misdemeanour, felonies of fourth, third and second degrees to next degrees and to first degree finally.[13]

Sentencing in Bhutan also includes value-based sentencing. S.18 of the Bhutan penal Code explains this by stating that the offence graded as value based under this code shall be a felony of the third degree if the value or the amounts involved in the crime exceeds the total amount of the daily minimum national wage rate at the time of the crime for a period of 30 years or more; it shall be a felony of fourth degree if the item of the crime is not described in the earlier subsection and the value and crimes involved in it exceeds the total amount of the daily minimum national wage rate at the time of committing the crime less than 30 years and for a period of 15 years and more; it shall be a misdemeanour if the item of the crime is not described in the earlier subsections and the amount involved in the crime exceeds the total amount of the daily wage rate at the time of the committing of the crime for a period less than 15 years and not less than 7 years or more; and it shall be a petty misdemeanour if the crime is not described in earlier sections and the amount involved is less than the total amount of the daily wage rate at the time of committing of crime for a period less than 7years. As the Penal Code suggests, the court should also consider forfeiting the property, paying the damages etc. for restitution, recovery etc.; the court may also consider removing the offender from official designation in cases of value-based sentencing.[14]

Though there is no literature on the correctional systems of Bhutan, the Bhutanese judiciary and the Penal Code ensure correctional administration for the prison inmates to rectify their mistakes and take a positive attitude to life.

Conclusion

A brief overview of the Bhutanese penal code, the legal system, the provisions for legal aid and the existing literature on trends of crimes in Bhutan as discussed above may show that Bhutan may have excellent crime-prevention policies, but it lacks proper execution in certain respects, especially in cases of encouraging reporting of the crimes and creation of a national database of crime records. It needs to be remembered that the Bhutanese criminal justice system is based on the ancient Buddhist ideologies, which give preference to equality, proper and fair justice to all and mediation. While there are some reported cases of domestic violence, the existing literature shows a gradual growth of crime rates among youth especially by way of substance addiction. It is noteworthy that Bhutan has taken many positive steps to restrict the growth of substance abuse by way of alcohol and drug abuse, but there are not many studies to show how far the rate of substance abuse has come down or grown. Bhutan, being an ancient monarchical kingdom which has adopted a newly democratic governmental system, needs more infrastructure to properly execute the laws and policy guidelines.

Bhutan presently does not have many law universities or university departments providing education on law or[15] social sciences including behavioural sciences, police sciences, criminology and victimology. Interested stake holders therefore have to travel to neighbouring countries like India (Sherab, 2014), China etc. to gain knowledge in these subjects. However, it needs to be understood that each nation has its own heritage and culture, depending upon which the customary laws in the civil and criminal procedure codes are enacted. During the British colonisation, Bhutan resisted the penetration of the British legal principles in its own legal framework. This has helped Bhutan to maintain its own uniqueness in lawmaking as well as in framing up a modern constitution, the Penal Code, the judicial system the civil laws etc., which are highly influenced by ancient Buddhist ideologies, modern understanding of judicial sentencing etc. It is understandable that this had been possible due to the very progressive king's efforts to merge ancient ideologies with modern criminal justice sciences. Unfortunately, as the existing literature suggests, only a few of the judicial officers, police officers and government officials including university professors could have been trained to execute this unique blend of ancient and modern laws and policy guidelines. Even though it has been shown that Bhutan has an increasing number of internet users, it is unfortunate that not all police officers, judicial officers and lawyers are well connected with the worldwide criminal justice fraternity. This is evident from the lack of research on the issue from Bhutan by Bhutanese stakeholders.

Further, it has been noted by this author that many government agencies like National commission for Women and Child, Royal Bhutan Police etc. have their own websites, but they do not have up-to-date information about new trends of crimes, crime rates, new laws etc. While the print, television and electronic media may speak about Bhutan's involvement with its neighbours like India, China etc. in building up joint military actions to resist terrorism, there are far fewer reports about modern Bhutan's movements against woman abuse, child abuse, human right abuse etc. There is also little research on Bhutanese mass movement to awaken youth to report social and domestic crimes as well. Given the fact that Bhutanese youth are driving fast towards communication technology, there are also no reports on the government or any other stakeholder formulating any strategy to tackle possible abuse of human rights in the digital and internet communication systems.

Further, it can be seen that the Bhutanese Penal Code has not recognised several other types of crimes related to digital technology, prison violence, school violence etc. The Bhutanese government can consider encouraging setting up NGOs or inviting foreign experts for imparting training to police officers to deal with such offences. Bhutan must also create more university-level study centres to impart knowledge on criminology, criminal justice sciences, law, behavioural sciences etc. and must encourage judicial officers, police officers and academicians and students to take part in national and international seminars on criminal justice sciences, restorative justice, digital communication technology and cybersecurity issues, good governance etc.

Bhutan must also ratify UN treaties and conventions dealing with cross-border human right violations, cybercrimes, child rights violations, domestic abuse etc. It is expected that by taking up measures such as these, Bhutan may not only encourage its own officials and civil citizens to take a combined effort to prevent crimes, it may also showcase to the world its own unique constitutional rights and duties for safeguarding citizens as well as the environment, penal laws which stand apart from the rest of the world due on its progressive outlook to several issues including marital rape, sexual offences etc. and the uniqueness of judicial process which is influenced by ancient and modern ideologies.

Notes

1 See the preamble of the Constitution of Bhutan.
2 See s.3 of the Bhutan Penal Code.
3 See s.4 of the Bhutan Penal Code.
4 See s.109 of the Bhutan Penal Code, which speaks about use of force for care, discipline or safety of another.
5 See s.114 of the Bhutan Penal Code.
6 See s.116 of the Bhutan Penal Code.
7 Constitution of the Kingdom of Bhutan, art. 21, § 1.
8 Ibid.
9 See Article 7 of the Bhutanese constitution.
10 See s.9 of the Bhutan Penal Code.
11 See ss.10 and 11 of the Bhutan Penal Code.
12 See ss.12 and 13 of the Bhutan Penal Code.
13 See s.15 of the Bhutan Penal Code.
14 See ss. 19–22 of the Penal Code; also see Chapter 5 of the Penal Code.

15 Currently, Bhutan does not have a law school to provide law degree and all aspiring lawyers pursue their law degree in India and other countries. However, a one-year course (Post Graduate Diploma in National Law) on the national legal system and national laws is a must for every lawyer who wishes to practice law in Bhutan. As of now, there are approximately 112 lawyers (As per the list maintained with the Office of the Attorney General of Bhutan) in the country which is inclusive of judges, prosecutors, government attorneys and a few private practitioners. It may be noted that at the moment there is no standard rules and regulations regarding to the issuing of license to practice law. However, a person with a law degree and who has successfully completed the diploma in national law can practice law.

(Sherab, 2014, p. 9).

References

Bearak, B. (2001, June 8). *A witness to massacre in Nepal tells gory details.* Retrieved from www.nytimes.com/2001/06/08/world/a-witness-to-massacre-in-nepal-tells-gory-details.html.

Chua, M. (2008). *The pursuit of happiness: Issues facing Bhutanese youths and the challenges posed to gross national happiness.* Retrieved from http://sonamdorji505.blogspot.com/2011/11/pursuit-of-happiness-issues-facing.html.

Dorji, L. (2012). *Alcohol use and abuse in Bhutan.* Thimphu, Bhutan: National Statistics Bureau. Retrieved from www.nsb.gov.bt/publication/download.php?id=208.

Dorji, T. (2015). *Domestic violence cases on the rise.* Retrieved from https://thebhutanese.bt/domestic-violence-cases-on-the-rise.

Dorji, L., Gyeltshen, S., Jamtsho, C., Minten, T., Dorjee, T., Namgay, P., & Wangchuk, T. (2015). *Crime and mental health issues among the young Bhutanese people.* Thimphu, Bhutan: National Statistics Bureau. Retrieved from http://bhutan.unfpa.org/sites/default/files/pub-pdf/CRIME%20AND%20MENTAL%20HEALTH.pdf.

Laxminarayan, M., & Pemberton, A. (2012). Victims justice preferences in a collectivist, informal setting: The case of Bhutanese refugees in Nepal. *International Journal of Law, Crime and Justice, 40*(3), 255–269.

Namygel, T. (2009). Effective legal and practical measures in combating corruption. In UNAFEI (Ed.), *Resource material series no. 79* (pp. 153–159). UNAFEI: Fuchu, Tokyo. Retrieved from www.unafei.or.jp/english/pdf/RS_No79/No79_00All.pdf.

National Commission for Women and Children in Bhutan. (2012). *Study on violence against women in Bhutan*. Retrieved from www.ncwc.gov.bt/files/publication/Study%20on%20Situation%20of%20Violence%20against%20Women%20in%20Bhutan.pdf.

Norbu, J. (n.d.). *Specific justice needs of under-privileged people: Legal services and legal aid interventions: Bhutanese perspective*. Retrieved from www.saarclaw.org/uploads-saarc/publications-images/1018-FILE.pdf.

Sarkar, K., Bal, B., Mukherjee, R., Chakraborty, S., Saha, S., Ghosh, A., Parsons, S. (2008). Sex-trafficking, violence, negotiating skill, and HIV infection in brothel-based sex workers of Eastern India, Adjoining Nepal, Bhutan, and Bangladesh. *Journal of Health, Population and Nutrition, 26*(2), 223–31.

Sherab, J. (2014). *Report on legal aid symposium held at Terma Linca, Bhutan*, October 27–28, 2014, Thimphu, Bhutan. Retrieved from http://docplayer.net/42852968-Report-on-legal-aid-symposium.html.

United Nations. (2008). *Committee on the rights of the child forty-ninth session, consideration of reports submitted by states parties under article 44 of the convention concluding observations*. Bhutan. Retrieved from http://www2.ohchr.org/english/bodies/crc/docs/AdvanceVersions/CRC.C.BTN.CO.2.pdf.

UNODC (United Nations Office of Drugs and Crime). (2012). *Bhutan: Safeguarding youth from the perils of drug use*. Retrieved from www.unodc.org/southasia//frontpage/2012/May/bhutan_-safeguarding-youth-from-the-perils-of-drug-use.html.

Wangdi, K. (2014). Investigation of criminal offences in Bhutan. In UNAFEI (Ed.), *Resource material series no. 92* (pp. 44–51). UNAFEI: Fuchu, Tokyo. Retrieved from www.unafei.or.jp/english/pdf/RS_No92/No92_00All.pdf.

Wangdi, K., Tashi, S., & Dorji, T. (2014). Criminal procedure in Bhutan. In UNAFEI (Ed.), *Resource material series no. 92* (pp. 52–57). UNAFEI: Fuchu, Tokyo. Retrieved from www.unafei.or.jp/english/pdf/RS_No92/No92_00All.pdf.

Zangpo, N., & Kamnuansilpa, P. (2013). Attitudes of Royal Bhutan police officers towards community policing in Bhutan. *Journal of African & Asian Local Government Studies, 2*(3), 119–130.

4

INDIA

A Historical Perspective of the Criminal Justice System[1]

Dalbir Bharti

Introduction

Socio-economic and political conditions prevailing during different phases of history influenced the evolution of the Indian criminal justice system. The objectives of the criminal justice system and methods of its administration changed from time to time and from one period of history to another. To suit the changing circumstances the rulers introduced new methods and techniques to enforce law and administer justice. In early society the victim had himself (as there was no state or other authority) to punish the offender through retaliatory and revengeful methods; this was, naturally, governed by chance and personal passion (Choudhuri, 1995). Gradually, individual revenge gave way to group revenge, as man could not have grown and survived in complete isolation, and for his very survival and existence it was necessary to live in groups. Group life necessitated consensus on ideals and the formulation of rules of behavior to be followed by its members. These rules defined appropriate behavior and the action that was to be taken when members did not obey the rules (Choudhuri, 1995). This code of conduct, which governed the affairs of the people, came to be known as *Dharma* or law (Bharti, 2002).

In the very early period of the Indian civilization great importance was attached to *Dharma*. Everyone was acting according to *Dharma*, and there was no necessity of any authority to compel obedience to the law. The society was free from the evils arising from selfishness and exploitation by the individual (Jois, 1984). Each member of the society scrupulously respected the rights of his fellow members, and infraction of such rights rarely or never took place (Choudhuri, 1995). However, the ideal stateless society did not last long. While faith in the efficacy and utility of *Dharma*, belief in God and the God-fearing attitude of people continued to dominate the society, the actual state of affairs gradually deteriorated. A situation arose when some persons began to exploit and torment the weaker sections of society for their selfish ends. Tyranny of the strong over the weak reigned unabated. This situation forced the law-abiding people to search for a remedy. This resulted in the discovery of the institution of the king and establishment of his authority over the society, which came to be known as the state (Choudhuri, 1995). As the very purpose of establishing the state and the authority of the king was the protection of person and property of the people, the king organized a criminal justice system to enforce the law and punish those who violated it (Bharti, 2002).

Although the Indus Valley civilization suggests that an organized society existed during the pre-*Vedic* period in India, traces of the criminal justice system can only be found during the *Vedic* period, when well-defined laws had come into existence. The oldest literature available to explain the code of conduct of the people and the rules to be followed by the king are *Vedas*. In this chapter, the evolution of the criminal justice system in India is covered from the *Vedic* period onwards, dividing it into three periods—Ancient India (c. 1000 B.C. to A.D. 1000), Medieval India (A.D. 1000 to 1757) and Modern India (A.D. 1757 to 1947). Also, in this chapter, a glimpse of the contemporary criminal justice system is also provided.

I. Ancient India (c. 1000 B.C. to A.D. 1000)

This period of Indian history is also known as the Hindu period because of the prevalence and dominance of Hindu law. The elements of state administration signifying rule by a king with the help of his advisers or assistants may be traced back to the early *Vedic* period. In the *Rig-Veda* the king is called *Gopa janasya* or protector of the people. This implies that he was charged with the maintenance of law and order (Chopra, 1913). According to the *Dharma sutras* and the *Arthashastra*, it was the duty of the king to ensure the security and welfare of his subjects. Violation of criminal laws was considered an offence against the state. Any member of the public could bring the violation to the notice of the king, and the king was under a duty to apprehend and punish the offender. It was provided that the king should take cognizance on his own, with or without any complaint by a private party, of criminal offences (Jois, 1984). The information or complaint about the offence committed by any individual could be made by any citizen and not necessarily by the person injured or his relatives. The person, who on his own accord detected commission of offences and reported to the king, was known as *stobhaka*, i.e., informant. He was entitled to remuneration from the king for giving first information (Jois, 1984; Bharti, 2002).

Notably, the beginning of a regular system of state judicial administration may be traced to the pre-Mauryan age. The Mauryan period (c. 326–185 B.C.) fills a gap between two great epochs of administration of criminal justice in ancient India, namely, that as mentioned in the *Dharma sutra* on the one hand and that of Manu's code on the other (Jois, 1984). The few references in Megasthenes' *Indica* to the penalties for offences current in Chandragupta's time breathe the spirit of the penal law of the preceding period (Jois, 1984). From Pillar Edict IV of Ashoka, we learn that even after his conversion to Buddhism he continued the death penalty for crimes, only softening its rigour by giving the convicts three days' respite before execution. The system of justice of the preceding period appears to have been continued by the Mauryas (Chopra, 1913). The old division of urban and rural judiciary was continued in Ashoka's reign. The few references in the records of Mauryas point to the continuance of the state police of the preceding period. The jail administration of the earlier times appears to have been continued (Chopra, 1913; Bharti, 2002).

The Guptas (c. A.D. 320–550) created afresh a system of administration on imperial lines after the downfall of the Mauryan empire. After the Guptas, in Northern India, King Harshvardhana (A.D. 606–47) created a sound and efficient administration. The contemporary Chinese Buddhist pilgrim Hiuen Tsang gives high praise to Harshvardhana for his love of justice, his unremitting industry in the discharge of his duties and his piety and popularity (Smith, 1998). However, on the other hand, the penal law was marked by a certain degree of harshness, in strong contrast to exceptional mildness under the Imperial Guptas (Smith, 1998). In the Deccan, the administration of the Imperial Chalukyas of Vatapi (A.D. 540–753) was marked by the usual characteristics (Smith, 1998). The administration of Rajput states of Northern India was of the bureaucratic type (Bharti, 2002).

The salient features of the criminal justice system as evolved and prevailed during Ancient India are described below.

1. Police

The first institution of state police may be traced to the pre-Mauryan period. Its full development is recorded in Kautilya's *Arthashastra*. It mentions that the police during Ancient India was divided in two wings, namely, the regular police and the secret police. The regular police consisted of three tiers of officials: the *Pradesta* (rural) or the *Nagaraka* (urban) at the top, the rural and urban *Sthanikas* in the middle and the rural and urban *Gopas* at the bottom. In the course of his description of the *Pradesta's* duties, Kautilya tells how an inquest was held in case of sudden death. This involved a post-mortem examination of the body as well as thorough police investigation. In Kautilya's work the secret police is divided into two categories, namely the peripatetic and the stationary (Jois, 1984). The *Manu Smriti* prescribed instructions for the king to detect offences with the help of soldiers and spies. The *Katyayana Smriti* mentions informants and investigating officers. This suggests that an agency like modern police existed during that period to assist the king in administration of justice (Jois, 1984).

A person who was appointed by the king to detect commission of offences was called *Suchaka*, i.e. Investigation Officer (Jois, 1984). The special responsibility of the king in the matter of controlling crimes, detection of crimes and punishing the offenders was stressed in the *Manu Smriti*[2] that contained the following guidelines for the king (Bharti, 2002):

- Persons who commit offences or who conspire to commit offences are generally found in assembly houses, hotels, brothels, gambling houses, etc.;
- The king must post soldiers and spies for patrolling such places and in order to keep away thieves and antisocial elements; and
- He should appoint reformed thieves who were formerly associated with such doubtful elements, and through them, offenders must be detected and punished (Jois, 1984).

2. King and Courts

Administration of justice, according to the *Smritis*, was one of the most important functions of the king. The King's Court was the highest court of appeal as well as an original court in cases of vital importance to the state. In the King's Court, the king was advised by the Chief Justice and other judges, ministers and elders and representatives of the trading community. Next to the King's Court was the Court of Chief Justice, which consisted of a board of judges to assist him. In towns and districts the courts were presided over by the state officers, under the authority of the king, to administer justice (Chopra, 1913).

The criminal justice system of Ancient India was so organized that every villager had easy and convenient access to a judicial forum. In *Vedic* society the village Samitis and *Sabhas* were two important instruments of Indian polity. The village councils, similar to modern *Panchayats*, consisted of a board of five or more members to dispense justice to villagers (Chopra, 1913). The administration of justice was largely the work of these village assemblies or other popular or communal bodies. Village headmen had the authority to levy fines on offenders. There were several village committees, including a justice committee, appointed by the people's vote (Jois, 1984). Village council dealt with simple civil and criminal cases. Other criminal cases were presented before the central court or the courts in towns and district headquarters presided over by the government officers under the royal authority to administer justice (Jois, 1984).

3. Jails and Punishment

Like the institution of the state police, that of the state jail also begins with the pre-Mauryan period. It was provided that a jail should be constructed in the capital providing separate accommodation for men and women, and it should be guarded. It was also prescribed that the prisoners should be employed in useful work. The policy of taking a sympathetic view, as regards persons found guilty of offences and punished with imprisonment imposed on them, was also laid down in the Ancient Indian law (Jois, 1984).

The *dandaniti*, i.e. punishment policy, is one of the elaborately dwelt-upon subjects in Ancient India, as it was intimately connected with the administration of the state. Manu emphasized the importance and utility of punishment, saying, "Punishment alone governs all created beings, it protects them and it watches over them while they are asleep" (Jois, 1984, p. 324). As per Manu, Yajnavalkya and Brihaspati, there were four kinds or methods of punishment during Ancient India, namely, admonition, censure, fine and corporal punishment (Kulshreshtha, 1968). The nature and types of punishments were very cruel, inhumane and barbarous (Jois, 1984).

Kautilya lays down that awarding of punishment must be regulated by a consideration of the motive and nature of the offence, time and place, strength, age, conduct, learning and monetary position of the offender and whether the offence is repeated (Jois, 1984). An old man over eighty, a boy below sixteen, women and persons suffering from diseases were to be given half the punishment; a child less than five committed no offence and was not to suffer any punishment (notably, this principle is resonated in the ideals of the neo-classical school of criminology) (Jois, 1984). In certain cases, the court was empowered to grant compensation to the aggrieved party in addition to the punishment given to the offender (Jois, 1984).

From the above discussion, it is seen that the institutions of criminal justice administration had taken their roots during the *Vedic* period in India. The system gradually developed, and during the Mauryan period a well-defined criminal justice system had come into existence as described in the *Arthashashtra* (Bharti, 2002).

II. Medieval India (A.D. 1206–1757)

Towards the end of the eleventh century, the downfall of the Hindu rule began. Local Hindu rulers were attacked and defeated by foreign invaders of Turkish race. Gradually, old Hindu kingdoms began to disintegrate (Kulshreshtha, 1968). The numerous raids of Mahmud Ghazni during A.D. 1000 to 1026 had revealed that India was vulnerable and fabulously rich (Chopra, 1913). After successive invasions by Ghazni, Mohammad Ghori attacked India, defeated Prithvi Raj, a Rajput king, in the year 1192 and occupied Delhi. After the death of Ghori in 1206, Qutub-ud-din-Aibak established the Slave dynasty and became the first Muslim king to rule from Delhi (Jois, 1984). Subsequently, the Khiljis (A.D. 1290–1320); the Tughluqs (A.D. 1320–1414); the Syeds (A.D. 1414–50); and the Lodhis (A.D. 1451–1526) ruled India as Sultans of the Delhi Sultanate. Babur defeated Ibrahim Lodhi in the famous First Battle of Panipat in A.D. 1526 and established the Mughal empire. The Mughal Emperors ruled India effectively up to A.D. 1707 except the period A.D. 1540–55, when the Suri dynasty established by Sher Shah Suri was in power. After the death of Aurangzeb in 1707, the Mughal empire started declining. Bahadurshah II was the last Muslim ruler. The Muslim rule in India came to an end formally in 1858 when the British took over the control of Indian affairs from the East India Company (Bharti, 2002).

The Muslim rulers emphasized the importance of administration of criminal justice and introduced reforms to improve the judicial machinery. For the first time in the country, the Chief Judge was appointed by Qutub-ud-din-Aibak. Balban introduced the system of espionage to find the truth about the criminals. Sikandar Lodhi initiated several reforms in the criminal justice system. The judicial reforms of Sher Shah Suri formed a bridge between the Sultanate period and the Mughal period. He reformed the judicial machinery. Sher Shah Suri was of the opinion that stability of the government depended on justice and that it would be his greatest care not to violate it either by oppressing the weak or by permitting the strong to infringe the laws with impunity. Heads of the Village Councils were recognized. They were ordered to prevent theft and robberies. In case of robberies, they were made to pay for the loss sustained by the victim. However, he did not disturb the village autonomy. Police regulations were drawn up for the first time in India. The judicial officers below the Chief Provincial *Qazi* were transferred after every two or three years (Bharti, 2002).

During the Mughal period, Akbar introduced many reforms in the administration of justice. He created common citizenship and a unanimous system of justice for all. Besides, he prohibited slavery, repealed the death penalty clause for criticizing Islam or the Prophet Mohammad, and prohibited the forcible practice of *sati*. Jahangir abolished the cruel and barbarous punishments and decentralized the power of the courts. Shahjahan established the regular system of appeal (Singh, 1994). Aurangzeb entrusted the preparation of a comprehensive digest of Muslim criminal law to eminent Muslim theologians. The digest so prepared was entitled *Fatwa-i-Alamgiri* (Jois, 1984).

When the Sultans ruled most of the parts of India from Delhi, a few Hindu kingdoms also existed in some parts of the country. Among these, the Vijyanagar empire, from A.D. 1336 to 1646, was the most famous. Krishnadevaraya was the greatest of the rulers of this dynasty. He reigned from 1509 to 1529 (Smith, 1998). The example of Vijyanagar and their system of adjudication of criminal justice indicate the functioning of full-fledged judicial system (Jois, 1984). But during the medieval period of Indian history, the criminal justice system of India was highly influenced by the Muslim rulers, and therefore, the period is generally known as the Muslim period (Bharti, 2002).

Salient features of the evolution of the criminal justice system during the Muslim rule in India are discussed below.

1. Police

Policing of the cities and towns was entrusted to *Kotwals* and of the countryside to *Faujdars*. The judiciary and police were placed under the *Chief Sadr* and *Chief Qazi* both offices being held usually by the same person (Chopra, 1913). The Mughals had established the *kotwali* system in the cities and the *chowkidari* system in the villages. The Court of *Fauzdar* tried petty criminal cases concerning security and suspected criminals. *Kotwals* were also authorized to decide petty criminal cases (Kulshreshtha, 1968).

2. King and Courts

The administration of justice was one of the primary functions of the king. The monarch was the head of the judicial organization (Choudhuri, 1995). According to Islamic jurisprudence, as was the position under the Hindu jurisprudence, the ruler constituted the highest court of justice (Choudhuri, 1995). To maintain and enforce the criminal code was one of the important functions of the king. Being head of the state, he was the supreme authority to administer justice in his kingdom (Bharti, 2002).

Different courts were established to deal with different kinds of cases. Courts were constituted at the central capital and at the headquarters of a province, district and *parganah*. During the Sultanate period the Court of *Diwan-e-mulzim* was the highest court of criminal appeal. To deal with the cases of criminal prosecutions of rebels and those charged with high treason, a separate court, *Diwan-e-siyasat*, was constituted. The judiciary and police were placed under the *Chief Sadr* and *Chief Qazi*, both offices being held usually by the same person. In due course a hierarchy of *Qazis* was established to dispose of cases of civil disputes and criminal complaints (Chopra, 1913). At each provincial headquarters, *Adalat Qazi-e-subah* was empowered to try civil and criminal cases of any description and to hear appeals from the district courts. Similarly, there were courts at the district and *parganah* headquarters. Appeals were filed before the district court from the judgements of the *Parganah Qazis, Kotwals* and village *Panchayats* (Choudhuri, 1995). Petty criminal cases were filed before the *Kotwal*, who was the principal executive officer in towns (Bharti, 2002).

During the Mughal rule a separate department of justice (*mahukma-e-adalat*) was created to regulate and see that justice was administered properly. Justice was administered by means of a hierarchy of courts rising from the Village Council (*Panchayat*) to the *parganah, sarkar* and provincial courts and finally to the *Chief Sadr-cum-Qazi* and the emperor himself (Chopra, 1913). The Emperor's Court had jurisdiction to hear original and criminal cases. In criminal cases the *Mohtasib-e-Mumalik* or the Chief *Mohtasib*, like the Attorney General of India today, assisted the emperor. In order to hear an appeal, the emperor presided over a bench consisting of the Chief Justice and *Qazis* of the Chief Justice's Court. The public was allowed to make representations and appeals to the Emperor's Court in order to obtain his impartial judgement (Kulshreshtha, 1968). The second important court of the empire was the court of the Chief Justice (*Qazi-ul-qazat*). This had original civil and criminal jurisdiction and also heard appeals. It was required to supervise the working of the provincial courts (Kulshreshtha, 1968). At each provincial headquarters, the Provincial Chief Appellate Court, presided over by the *Qazi-e-subah*, besides hearing appeals, also had the original civil and criminal jurisdiction. In each district, chief civil and criminal court of the district was presided over by the *Qazi-e-sarkar*, who was the principal judicial officer of the district. *Qazi-e-parganah* presided over the *Adalat-e-parganah* that had to deal with all civil and criminal cases arising within the jurisdiction of the *parganah*, including the villages (Kulshreshtha, 1968).

During the Muslim rule in India, the village continued to be the smallest administrative unit of the government. Each *parganah* consisted of a group of villages. For each group of villages there was a village *Panchayat*, a body of five leading men, elected by the villagers. The head of the *Panchayat* was known as *Sarpanch* (Choudhuri, 1995). From ancient times the Village Councils (*Panchayats*) were authorized to administer justice in all petty civil and criminal matters (Kulshreshtha, 1968). The institution of *Panchayat* as it existed during the Hindu period remained untouched during the Muslim rule in India. The authority of *Panchayat* was recognized, and it continued to decide both civil and criminal cases of purely local character during the Muslim period. Village *Panchayats* were mostly governed by their customary law. Though the decisions given by *Panchayats* were based on local customs and were not strictly according to the law of the kingdom, there was no interference in the working of *Panchayats*. As a general rule, the decision of *Panchayat* was binding upon the parties, and no appeal was allowed from its decision (Chopra, 1913). Mostly these *Panchayats* decided cases between Hindus, who formed the bulk of the population. Consequently, administration of justice under Muslim rulers did not cover about three-fourths of their subjects (Jois, 1984).

3. Punishments and Jails

The punishments for various offences were classified into four broad categories, viz., (a) *kisa*, i.e. retaliation, which meant in principle, life for life and limb for limb; (b) *diya* meant bloodmoney being awarded to the victim or his heirs; (c) *hadd* inflicted on persons who committed offences against God; (d) *tazeer*, i.e. punishment for the cases not falling under *hadd* and *kisa*. The punishment which fell in this category consisted of imprisonment, corporal punishment and exile or any other humiliating treatment (Jois, 1984). The type and quantum of penalty to be imposed was entirely within the discretion of the judge. In criminal cases, a great deal of discretion was allowed to them, and they took a variety of factors into account in awarding punishment (Chopra, 1913). Punishments prescribed were very cruel. Mutilation of the body was one of the types of punishment which resulted in great suffering and gradual death (Jois, 1984).

A special feature of the punishments was that of *diya* i.e. bloodmoney. This applied to cases of certain offences including those falling under *kisa*. Bloodmoney was awarded to the victim or the heirs of the victim in a fixed scale. In the cases falling under *kisa* also, the person entitled to inflict injury on the wrong doer could forego his right by accepting *diya*. If one of the heirs accepted *kisa* and gave pardon, the other heirs had no other alternative than to accept their share of bloodmoney. According to a *fatwa* delivered in March 1791, one man named Mongol Das murdered his wife and one of her heirs gave pardon, and therefore no death sentence could be inflicted at the instance of other heirs, and they had no alternative but to receive *diya*. Another special feature of the Muslim criminal law was that the death sentence was required to be executed by the heirs of the deceased (Jois, 1984).

Prisoners awaiting trial were detained in prisons in the Muslim period of India. The duties of the *Kotwal* were to check the number of the persons in the prison and ascertain their answers to the charges against them. Imprisonment as punishment was not expressly provided for under the Islamic criminal law, and thus there was generally no need of prisons as penal instruments. But due to the provision of *diya* in that law, many prisoners, after conviction, had to spend their days for their inability to pay compensation. Again the discretion left to the *Qazi* to impose *tazir*, that is in offences not categorized under *hadd, qisa* and *diya*, enabled him to award imprisonment if he so wished (Choudhuri, 1995).

From the above discussion, it is seen that during the Muslim rule in India the criminal justice system marked a significant change from that of the Hindu period. Special emphasis was given to the constitution and working of different courts (Bharti, 2002).

III. Modern India (A.D. 1757–1947)

On 31December 1600, Queen Elizabeth I of England granted a charter to the East India Company of London to trade into and from the East Indies, in the countries and parts of Asia and Africa for a period of fifteen years. The provisions of the Charter of 1600 were only in connection with the trade and were not intended for acquisition of dominion in India. Legislative authority was given to the company in order to enable it to regulate its own business and maintain discipline amongst its servants. With the passage of time the company continued securing more and more powers and privileges from the British crown. Being encouraged by the constant support of the British government, the company went on expanding its spheres not only in the business field but also in the political arena (Bharti, 2002).

The Battle of Plassey of 1757 was the first landmark in the history of the company's political success in India. However, the company's political power was established by the success in the Battle of Buxar of 1764. Thereafter, the company continued to expand its rule in India till 1857. The Revolt of 1857 proved fatal to the company's political career in India (Smith, 1998). The British crown assumed direct charge of the Indian affairs, as the Government of India Act, 1858 deprived the East India Company of the Indian government. The Proclamation of Queen Victoria of England on November 1, 1858 outlined the principles on which the Crown would govern India. The place of the President of the Board of Control was taken by a Secretary of State for India, who now became, in subordination to the cabinet, the fountainhead of authority as well as the director of policy in India (Jois, 1984). British rule in India continued till 1947 (Bharti, 2002).

In order to control the vast area and population of India, the British had revamped the existing criminal justice system of India. They modified the existing laws, passed new laws and introduced new principles. The criminal justice system, as it exists today, was mostly evolved during the British period (Bharti, 2002). The steps taken by the British to establish a well-defined and uniform criminal justice system in India are discussed below.

1. Organizing the Police

Lord Cornwallis was the first British administrator who tried to improve the police system. He appointed a Superintendent of Police for Calcutta in 1791 and thereafter extended his efforts to the *mofussil*. Cornwallis took police powers out of the hands of the *zamindars* of Bengal, Bihar and Orissa, and ordered, in 1793, the District Judge to open a police station for every 400 square miles and to place a regular police station officer over it. He was known as the *Daroga*. The *Kotwal* continued to be in charge of the police in the town (Choudhuri, 1995).

The period during 1801 to 1860 turned out to be a period of clumsy attempts in organizing the police system in the country. Each province made attempts to organize it in divergent ways. In

1816, Sir Thomas Munro, in such an attempt, took the Superintendent of Police in Madras out of the hands of the judge and placed him in the hands of the peripatetic Collector, who had the indigenous village police under his control (Jois, 1984). This policy was soon followed by other provinces (Bharti, 2002).

In 1843 Sir Charles Napier set himself the task of introducing a police system on the lines of the Royal Irish Constabulary in the newly conquered territory of Sind, now in Pakistan. As per his plan, while the police force was to continue under the authority of the Collector, yet in each district they were to be supervised by an officer whose sole duty was to control and direct them. Napier created a separate police organization directed by its own officers. Direction throughout the area of Sind was in the hands of the Inspector General of Police and in each district with the Superintendent of Police. The latter was accountable to the Inspector General of Police as well as the District Collector. In 1848, Sir George Clarke, the Governor of Bombay, appointed full-time European Superintendents of Police in many districts. In 1853, the police system in Bombay was remodelled on Napier's lines (Jois, 1984).

The revolt of 1857 drew the attention of the government of India to the urgency of police reorganization. Accordingly, a commission was appointed in 1860 to study exhaustively the police needs of the government. Its main recommendations were embodied in the Indian Police Act of 1861. The aims of the Act as enshrined in the Act itself were to re-organize the police and to make it a more efficient instrument for the prevention and detection of crime. Notably, this Act is still in force in India without any significant change (Bharti, 2002).

2. System of Courts and Codification of Laws

Although the British had acquired control and obtained rights of fiscal administration of Bengal, Bihar and Orissa in 1765, the company did not take responsibility for the administration of justice. As a result the criminal jurisdiction in these provinces was still left with the puppet *Nawab*. Thus a system of dual government was established, under which the company, whilst assuming complete control over the revenues, left in other hands the responsibility for maintaining law and order and administration of justice. The system proved disastrous (Jois, 1984).

The company introduced many reforms to bring about improvements in the court system. The Judicial Plan of 1772 prepared by Warren Hastings was the first major step in this regard. This followed a series of reforms. Consequently, the company assumed full responsibility for the administration of justice and a dual system of courts, namely, (i) the Company's Courts and (ii) the King's Courts came into existence in India. The King's Courts and the Company's Courts formed the dual system of courts, having their separate jurisdictions and applying different laws (Choudhuri, 1995). The Supreme Courts mostly applied English law, both civil and criminal, with certain exceptions relating to Hindus and Mohammedans. The Company's Courts in the *mofussil* area applied only the regulations of the government which were passed before 1834. English law was not applied by the Company's Courts. In cases for which there was no ascertainable law or custom, the judges were required to exercise their discretion according to justice, equity and good conscience. In criminal cases, Mohammedan law of crimes, as modified by the Regulation, was applied by the *mofussil* courts in Bengal and Madras provinces, but in Bombay a regular code superseded the Muslim law of crimes (Kulshreshtha, 1968).

The existence of the dual system of courts created many difficulties and conflicts. In order to achieve uniformity, certainty and efficiency, it was considered necessary to bridge the gap by legislative measures (Smith, 1998). The Draft Penal Code, which was drafted and submitted to the Governor-General in 1837, was revised and enacted into law in 1860 by the Indian legislature (Kulshreshtha, 1968). The Indian Penal Code, based on English principles, wholly superseded the

Mohammedan criminal law. A general Code of Criminal Procedure followed in 1861, and the process of superseding native by European law, so far as criminal justice is concerned, was completed by the enactment of the Evidence Act of 1872 (Jois, 1984). The British, by codification and by introducing the English principles of equity, justice and good conscience, made significant improvement in the preceding criminal laws (Bharti, 2002).

After codification of laws, the next step to reform the existing judicial system was to amalgamate the two sets of the courts, i.e. the Supreme Courts (the King's Courts) and *Sadar Adalats* (the Company's Courts). In 1858, the assumption of direct control of the government of India by the Crown made the task easier (Kulshreshtha, 1968). The British Parliament passed the Indian High Courts Act, 1861 which empowered the Crown to establish, by Letters Patent, High Courts of Judicature at Calcutta, Madras and Bombay abolishing the Supreme Courts and the Courts of *Sadar Diwani* and *Sadar Nizamat Adalat*. The jurisdiction and powers of the High Courts were to be fixed by the Letters Patent. Accordingly, the High Courts at Bombay, Madras and Calcutta were established in the year 1862. Subsequently, High Courts were established at other places in India. Each High Court was empowered to have supervision over all courts subject to its appellate jurisdiction. With this, the number of courts was decreased; the quality of work of the lower courts improved; efficiency of the judges improved; procedures were simplified; and the appellate procedure also became uniform. The establishment of High Courts was a significant step in the evolution of the criminal justice system in India (Bharti, 2002).

The Privy Council, a committee under the king of England to hear appeals from colonies, was the highest court of appeal from India (Jois, 1984). Later as per the provisions of the Government of India Act, 1935 the Federal Court of India was inaugurated at Delhi on 1 October 1937 (Kulshreshtha, 1968). The Federal Court functioned successfully and effectively during the transitional period in Indian history, when there was no written constitution. It built up great traditions of independence, impartiality and integrity, which all were inherited by its successor, the Supreme Court of India, established on 26 January 1950 under the constitution of India (Basu, 1994).

3. Jail Reforms

As the British continued to follow the criminal justice system of the Muslim period for a long time, the jails, as part of the whole system, were administered by the East India Company without any change. As the company was reluctant to spend money on jails, the condition of the jails was deplorable. In many jails, there was no separation between male and female prisoners by day or night. Up to 1860, the management of district jails had devolved upon the District Magistrate (Kulshreshtha, 1968). There was no manual of rules or regulations for the guidance of the jail staff. In the presidency of Bombay a simple Code of Rules was framed in 1860, and this was followed by 'Gaols Rules' framed in 1866. In Bengal, the Jail Code was compiled in 1864 which defined *inter alia* the duties, responsibilities and powers of the various officers in the jails (Choudhuri, 1995).

With a view to understanding the problems in the jails and to bring about reforms, various committees were appointed in the latter half of the nineteenth century. A few recommendations of these committees were carried into effect from time to time, but the reforms never reached a satisfactory level. Finally, the Prisoners Act of 1894 was enacted, followed by the Reformatory Schools Act of 1897. The Prisons Act of 1894 provided that convicted prisoners may be confined either in association or individually in cells. It fixed nine hours' labour a day for convicts sentenced to labour (Jois, 1984). The British appointed another committee in 1919 known as the Indian Jails Committee. As a result of the recommendations of this committee a number of changes were introduced in the rules governing the jail system of the country (Choudhuri, 1995). Significantly, many of the British-based prison laws still continue to govern Indian prison administration (Bharti, 2002).

IV. Present Criminal Justice System of India

The present criminal justice system of India is the product of a continuous effort on the part of rulers who controlled the affairs of the country from time to time. In every phase of Indian history the rulers contributed to the development of the criminal justice system. However, most of them treated the criminal justice system more as an instrument to subjugate the masses rather than as one to protect their rights. The British rulers who made well-thought-out efforts for the establishment of a sound and well defined criminal justice system in India were also not free from this weakness. They too looked at the criminal justice system more as an instrument to uphold colonial rule in India and less for the administration of fair criminal justice to the people (Bharti, 2002).

Various components of the present criminal justice system of India are briefly discussed below.

1. Police

The Revolt of 1857 led the British administrators to serious rethinking about reorganization of the police throughout India and to make it an effective and highly disciplined instrument of civil administration. In 1860 the government of India appointed the First Police Commission. On the recommendations of the Commission, the Police Act, 1861, was enacted, which imposed a uniform police system. The act established the police on a provincial basis with an Inspector General of Police as its head. Initially the Police Act of 1861 was not applicable to many parts of the country, and in such areas local Police Acts were in force, but subsequently, it was made applicable to most such areas by making amendments in the local police acts by the provincial/state governments or regulations of the central government. The Police Act of 1861, which is still in force with minor modifications, regulates the organization, recruitment and discipline of the police force in India (Bharti, 2002).

The constitution of India (1950) puts police and public order (including railway and village police) in the State List of the Seventh Schedule, giving the state legislatures the powers to legislate on these subjects. The constitution, however, assigns a definite role of supervision and coordination to the Union Government also in the matters pertaining to police (Basu, 1994). While police and public order are within the state field of legislative competence, preventive detention for reasons connected with the security of a state, the maintenance of public order and persons subjected to such detention are under concurrent jurisdiction of Parliament as well as state legislatures. Article 249 of the constitution gives powers to Parliament to intervene in state police administration if there is enough justification for doing so. The police forces in India are broadly divided into two, namely, (1) state police and (2) central police organizations (Bharti, 2002).

The police system of the pre-independence period developed by the British rulers still continues in India. The Police Act of 1861 still governs the basic structure of police in India. The new Code of Criminal Procedure of 1973, which deals with the powers of the police in great detail, has also not made any significant change. Though some efforts have been made to modernize the police and improve the administration and training, most of the old methods and procedures of policing still continue (Bharti, 2002).

2. Judiciary

At the top of the entire judicial system exists the Supreme Court of India. The Supreme Court acts as a federal court for determination of disputes between the constituent units of the federation. It is the highest interpreter of the constitution and thus plays the role of its guardian and saviour. For this purpose, the framers of the Indian constitution vested the power of judicial review with the Supreme Court so that any law or order enacted, promulgated or passed by the state authorities which contravenes the provisions of the constitution could be declared null and void. Under Article 32 of the constitution, it is to act as the protector of the fundamental rights of the people. The Supreme Court is the highest court of appeal in the country in civil as well as criminal matters (Bharti, 2002).

The jurisdiction of the existing High Courts, the law administered by them and the powers to make rules of the Court were allowed by the constitution to continue, as were immediately before then commencement of the constitution (Basu, 1994). The constitution contains provisions relating to High Courts under articles 214 to 231. It provides a High Court for each state or for a common High Court for two or more states. A High Court may have one or more benches at different places in its jurisdiction for keeping in view the convenience of the people. The High Courts enjoy original and appellate jurisdiction including powers of revision and review. The High Courts in the presidency towns of Calcutta, Bombay and Madras possessed an original jurisdiction, both civil and criminal, over cases arising within the presidency towns, whereas other High Courts did not enjoy such original jurisdiction (Basu, 1994). Though the original criminal jurisdiction of the Bombay and Madras High Courts has recently been entrusted to City Sessions Courts, the original civil jurisdiction of these High Courts is still retained in respect of actions of higher values. The City Sessions Court has also been set up in Calcutta, but the High Court of Calcutta still retains its original criminal jurisdiction over more serious cases (Nair & Jain, 2000).

Further, the constitution of India contains provisions regarding appointment of District Judges, recruitment of persons other than District Judges to the judicial service, control over subordinate courts, etc. in Part VI, Chapter VI— Subordinate Courts. Hence the courts of and below the District and Sessions Judges are called subordinate courts. District and Sessions Court is a principal civil court and also a criminal court to try serious offences as provided in Schedule I of the Cr.P.C., 1973 (Kelkar, 1996). Detailed provisions about criminal courts, their jurisdictions, etc. are found in Chapter II of the Code of Criminal Procedure, 1973. Section 6, Cr.P.C., provides that besides the High Courts and the courts constituted under any law, other than the Cr.P.C., there shall be, in every state, the following classes of criminal courts, namely: Courts of Session; Judicial Magistrates of the first class and, in any metropolitan area, Metropolitan Magistrates; Judicial Magistrate of the second class; and Executive Magistrates.

The above description of the judiciary as a component of the criminal justice system shows that a well-defined hierarchy of criminal courts exists in India to administer criminal justice. The very fact that the constitution itself contains elaborate provisions for the judiciary, including the subordinate courts, indicates the importance the framers of the constitution accorded to this important organ of criminal justice administration (Bharti, 2002).

3. *Correctional Services*

The correctional system of contemporary India mainly consists of prisons, probation and parole. The prisons, reformatories, Borstal institutions and other institutions of like nature are included in state lists under the constitution of India (Basu, 1994). The legal base for prisons is section 4 of the Prisons Act, which requires the state governments to provide accommodation for prisoners in their territories, in prisons which, as per section 3, means any jail or place used permanently or temporarily for the detention of prisoners. Further, under section 417 of the Code of Criminal Procedure, 1973, a state government may direct in what place a person liable to be imprisoned or committed to custody is to be confined (Choudhuri, 1995).

The government of India set up an All India Jail Manual Committee to prepare a Model Prison Manual for the use of various states in India. The committee finalized a Model Prison Manual in 1960. It *inter alia* recommended diversification of institutions; setting up of boards—(a) Central Bureau of Correctional Services, (b) Central and State Advisory Boards, and (c) Board of Visitors,

Review Board and Service Board in each jail; adequate training of staff; personnel discipline; educational programme for all prisoners; vocational training; and aftercare and rehabilitation (Choudhuri, 1995).

The administration of prisons being a state subject under the constitution of India, the recommendations of the All India Jail Committee are not of a mandatory nature and only provide guidelines to achieve some uniformity in all the states. However, the central laws, i.e. the Prisons Act of 1894 and the Prisoners Act of 1900, which still govern the management of prisons in the country, provide an overall uniformity in the administration of prisons. The prison manuals of the state governments are based on the central acts (Choudhuri, 1995). Prison establishments in different states/union territories comprise several tiers of prisons or jails. The most common and standard jail institutions in India are Central Jails, District Jails and Sub-Jails. The other types of jail establishments are Women's Jails, Children or Borstal Schools, Open Jails and Special Jails (Bharti, 2002).

Conclusion

The criminal justice system in India has evolved over a period of 3,000 years. Initially, the Law or *Dharma*, as propounded in the *Vedas* was considered supreme in Ancient India, for the king had no legislative power. But gradually, this situation changed and the king started making laws and regulations, keeping in view the customs and local usages. The punishments during Ancient India were cruel, barbarous and inhumane. As regards the procedure and quantum of the punishments, there were contradictions between various *Smritis* and in certain cases even among the provisions found in one *Smriti* itself. The system of awarding punishments on the basis of *varna* contravened the concept of equality of all human beings as propounded by the *Vedas*. The discriminatory system of inflicting punishments and contradictory provisions in different legal literature made the criminal justice system defective and confusing (Bharti, 2002).

During the Muslim rule in India, though, enlightened monarchs like Sher Shah Suri and Akbar showed great zeal to administer justice impartially, yet as a whole the administration of justice during the Muslim period in India suffered from defects. The concept of equality was applicable only to the Muslim population in India, and thus the bulk of the population, i.e. non-Muslims, was subjected to humiliating discrimination. The Hindus suffered in almost similar manner as the people of lower *varna* suffered at the hands of the people of higher *varna* among the Hindus. The major defect of Muslim criminal law was that most of the crimes were considered private affairs of the individuals. Many offences, including murder, could be compounded by the payment of *diya*, i.e. bloodmoney, and human life was considered rather cheap, assessible in terms of money. The criminal justice system developed by the Muslim rulers continued in India even after the British took control of India. It was in 1860 that the codification of laws changed the discriminatory provisions of Muslim criminal law (Bharti, 2002).

The British, after assuming power in India, found the then-prevailing criminal justice administration defective and decided to bring about drastic changes in it. Lord Cornwallis made detailed studies of the existing conditions of criminal justice administration. He introduced many reforms to revamp the whole system. Lord Hastings took a special interest in reorganizing the police force to deal with the criminals and maintain law and order in the country. Lord Bentinck created the post of District and Sessions Judge and abolished the practice of *sati*. In 1843, Sir Charles Napier introduced a police system on the lines of the Royal Irish Constabulary. He created the post of Inspector-General of Police to supervise the police in the whole province. Subsequently, the Indian Police Act of 1861 was enacted on the recommendations of a commission which studied the police needs of the government. They codified the existing laws and established the High Courts and Prisons Laws (Bharti, 2002).

Thus, the British introduced reforms wherever necessary. They adopted new principles by modifying the existing laws wherever required and made new laws where they felt it was a must. The institutions of police, magistracy, judiciary and jails developed during the British period still continue without significant changes in their structure and functioning. However, the British rulers also, while restructuring the criminal justice system, did not fully implement the concept of equality. The reforms introduced by them treated all Indians and non-British Europeans equally, but the British always enjoyed special privileges. It was only with the constitution of India coming into being that the right to equality before law was fully recognized and incorporated in the constitution as a fundamental right (Bharti, 2002).

The description of various components of the present criminal justice system of India shows that most of the major criminal laws such as the Indian Penal Code of 1860, the Police Act of 1861, and the Indian Evidence Act of 1872 are still in force with some peripheral amendments. Except for some significant changes such as separation of the judiciary from the executive and abolition of jury system, even the new Code of Criminal Procedure of 1973 is a replica of the old Cr.P.C. of 1898. The structure of the police and its working style has not changed much. However, establishment of police commissionerates in some of the states has certainly been a welcome development and has enhanced performance parameters.

With the constitution coming into force, the higher judiciary has taken a new role of interpreting the constitution and declaring laws keeping the spirit of the constitution in view. The constitutional provisions for appeal to the Supreme Court in certain criminal matters as of right is certainly an innovative reform introduced by the constitution in the judicial system of India (Bharti, 2002).

Considerable developments have been made in the correctional services in the post-independence period. The retributive theory of punishment has given way to reformative and rehabilitative theories. Separate prison establishments have been opened for women and young prisoners. Prison reforms have laid emphasis on improving the conditions in the jails.

To sum up, even though efforts have been made to effect radical transformation, we still find ourselves clogged in transition. Consequently, the indelible legacy of the British era remains. Thus, most of the criminal laws, procedures, institutions and principles evolved during the British period still govern the functioning of various components of the criminal justice system of India (Bharti, 2002).

Notes

1 Major parts of this chapter are derived from the previous work of the author: Bharti, D. (2002). *The constitution and criminal justice administration*. New Delhi: APH Publishing Corporation. Republished with permission.
2 A detailed chapter on Manusmriti and its role in criminal justice administration is in Chapter 9 of this book.

References

Basu, D. D. (1994). *Introduction to the constitution of India*. New Delhi: Prentice-Hall of India.
Bharti, D. (2002). *The constitution and criminal justice administration*. New Delhi: APH Publishing Corporation.
Chopra, P. N. (1913). *The gazetteer of India. Indian Union. Vol. 2. History and culture.* Vol.4 Administration and Welfare (1886). Publications Division, Ministry of Education and Social Welfare, Government of India.
Choudhuri, M. (1995). *Languishing for justice: Being a critical survey of the criminal justice system*. Nagpur: Datt Sons.
Jois, M. R. (1984). *Legal and constitutional history of India*. Bombay: N. M. Tripathi; Littleton, CO: Fred B. Rothman.
Kelkar, R.V. (1996). *Outlines of criminal procedure*. Lucknow: Eastern Book Co.
Kulshreshtha, V. D. (1968). *Landmarks in Indian legal history and constitutional history*. Lucknow: Eastern Book Co.
Nair. J., & Jain, U. C. (2000). *Judiciary in India*. Jaipur: Pointer Publishers.
Singh, D.R. (1994). Evolution of criminal justice. *Indian Journal of Public Administration, 40*, 385.
Smith, V.A. (1998). *The Oxford history of India*. Delhi: Oxford University Press.

5

MALDIVES

Towards the Reformation of the Criminal Justice System

Aishath Ali Naz and Aminath Shifaya Ibrahim

Introduction

An analysis of the crime statistics published in the Maldives Police Service website (Maldives Police Service, 2015) from 2010 to 2014, revealed the following patterns on reported offences. There was a percentage increase in the reported levels of assault, illicit drug use, theft, domestic violence and issues related to embezzlement between the years 2012 and 2013. There was a rise in reported offences such as vandalism, illicit drug use, theft, robbery, domestic violence and bounced cheques between the years of 2011 to 2012 (Maldives Police Service, 2015). Furthermore, reported levels of criminal offences were highest in the year 2012, while overall reported percentage of offences declined in the year 2014 in comparison to the previous 4 years. Fatal assaults and armed crime are on the rise in the Maldivian society. Specifically, the year 2012 and the first 4 months of 2015 (Maldives Police Service, 2012) witnessed a series of brutal murders, bringing the issue of homicide to the national forefront. Most of these homicides are increasingly being linked to criminal gangs. A majority of the offenders are Maldivian youth with past criminal history (Maldives Police Service, 2012). The murders are committed mostly on the streets or at public places, and deaths are caused by stabbing with sharp objects such as knives or machetes.

Research conducted in the Maldives (Maldives Police Service, 2012) and existing crime statistics (Maldives Police Service, 2012) indicate that criminal groups and gangs are operational in the capital city and other parts of the country. They are involved in drug smuggling within the country and with bordering countries (Maldives Police Service, 2012). They are also involved in theft, robbery and in criminal forgery. Millions of Maldivian rufiyaa have been recovered in operations carried out in cases of theft and robbery (Maldives Police Service, 2012).

Among other crimes, prostitution is on the rise. In the year 2012 alone, 27 locations were raided in connection to prostitution, with 98 people being detained, out of whom 63 were foreigners who were later extradited to their country of origin (Maldives Police Service, 2012). It has been reported (Human Rights Commission of the Maldives, 2014) that in the Maldives, children as young as 12 years of age are involved in commercial sex work. From an estimated 1,139 female sex workers in the country, 8% of female sex workers mapped in a study from 12 different islands were under the age of 18 years (Centre for Community Health and Disease Control, 2010–2011).

Over the past decades, the abuse of illicit drugs has been identified as the major challenge facing the Maldivian youth. In the Rapid Situation Assessment of Drug Abuse (UNESCAP and UNDP, 2003), it was reported that almost half of all drug users (47%) were below the age of 20 years (UNFPA, 2005), that the mean age of drug use initiation was 16.8 years, and that 97% of drug users were males (Sri Lanka Maldives Country Unit, 2014). The most commonly used drug is opioids, especially 'brown sugar', hashish oil and other cannabinoids (UNESCAP and UNDP, 2003). Furthermore, like in other societies, drug abuse is interlinked with criminal activity. Therefore, it is not surprising that drug related offences remain among the highest ranking of all reported offences over the last few years (Maldives Police Service, 2015). Also, there are reports on growth of terrorist links of youth with ISIS (Swami, 2015) and cybercrimes (Yoosuf, 2012).

In the present chapter an attempt is made to explore the crime situation in Maldives (as provided in the Introduction) and to discuss on various components of the criminal justice system of Maldives that deal with the crime situation in Maldives.

Criminal Justice System in the Maldives

1. Criminal Justice Processes

Professor Paul Robinson (Robinson, 2004a & b) opines that the "Maldivian criminal justice system systematically fails to do justice and regularly does injustice, that the reforms needed are wide ranging and without dramatic change the system and its public reputation are likely to deteriorate further". This study obligated the government to acknowledge the existing injustices and work speedily through its reform agenda. It has to be observed that while some of the issues have been rectified, others still remain in the process.

The new Penal Code of the Maldives overhauled and restructured criminal offences and their punishments. The legislation was passed on 13 April 2014, to be effective one year later. However, the Majlis passed an amendment on 12 April 2015 postponing the effective date by another three months (to 13 July 2015). However, the effective date may further be delayed. The Penal Code prescribes offences, requirements of offence liability, offence elements, penalties of offences, offence grades and implications, defences against offences, sentencing guidelines and punishment along with all the procedures relating to determining of penalties (Section 10, Penal Code of Maldives). The general purpose of the Code as stated in Section 11(b) is to establish a system of prohibitions and penalties to deal with conduct that unjustifiably and inexcusably causes or threatens harm to individual or public interests entitled to legal protection, including Islam, life, lineage, mind and property (Penal Code of Maldives). Interestingly, Maldives is the first Islamic country to have a comprehensive and fully codified penal code without leaving out any essential Islamic criminal law principles (Suood, 2014).

a. Criminal Law-Making Process

The Parliament of the Maldives (*People's Majlis*) is unicameral and invested with the power to enact, revise or amend the constitution and legislations. Since the inception of the 2008 constitution (Hussain, 2008), various important criminal law–related legislations have been passed (Penal Code (Law No.: 9/14), Drugs Bill (Law No.: 17/13), Prison and Parole Act (Law No.: 14/2013), Anti Torture Act (Law No.: 13/2013) and Anti Trafficking Law (Law No.: 13/13) Bills can only be submitted to the People's Majlis (Majlis) either by the government (through its Parliamentary Group Leader or an appointed member) or any other Opposition Member of Parliament. There are three readings in the passage of a Bill through Majlis. After third reading, if the Bill survives it will be sent to the president for assent. Once the president assents the bill it will become an Act of Parliament and will be published in the gazette. The president has the authority to send the bill back to Majlis for further consideration without assenting.

b. Sequence of Criminal Proceedings

This flow chart in Figure 5.1 represents the (current) sequence of criminal proceedings for an adult and a juvenile who is charged as an adult.

2. Policing in the Maldives

The first police force of the Maldives was established by law in 1933 under colonial rule. However, unlike other nations in the Commonwealth, the Maldives did not have a police legislation even though it gained its independence in 1965 (Commonwealth Human Rights Initiative, 2011). The police force was subsequently separated and re-established in 1972 as part of the National Security Service (NSS) paramilitary force under the Ministry of Defence and National Security. The police force continued to function as part of NSS till 2004 (Commonwealth Human Rights Initiative, 2011). By March 2004, there were plans to create a civil police service, and with this intention, a Change Management Committee was set up (Reform delayed 2006) (Commonwealth Human Rights Initiative, 2011). However, when massive anti-state protests broke out in Malé in August 2004, it triggered the administration to push forward plans to set up the civil police service.

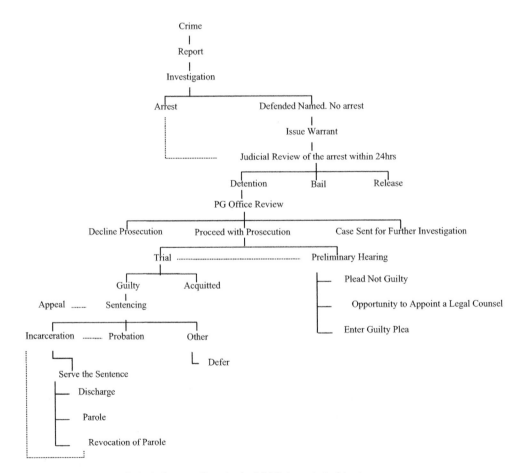

Figure 5.1   Sequence of criminal proceedings in the Maldivian criminal justice system.

In September 2004, the Maldives Police Service (MPS) was created as a civilian law-enforcing body under the Ministry of Home Affairs. Meanwhile the NSS was renamed the National Defence Force in April 2006 and remained under the Ministry of Defence. Hence, policing in the Maldives underwent significant changes. However, lack of necessary legislation and guiding police powers hindered the establishment of a recommendable police culture. In 2006, the Maldivian President Maumoon Abdul Gayoom, who was in power since 1978, initiated a constitutional reform process later refined into a Roadmap for the Democratic Reform Agenda. The reform process included the introduction of a multiparty system along with an independent judiciary and greater accountability through the People's Majlis or Parliament along with the formation of independent oversight bodies such as the Human Rights Commission and the Judicial Service Commission. In 2008, after the first multiparty democratic elections in the Maldives, President Maumoon Abdul Gayoom, who was in power since 1978, was defeated by Mohamed Nasheed of the Maldivian Democratic Party (MDP). In the period which followed, much was done for the purpose of strengthening the country's political, legislative and institutional reforms based on rule of law and commitment to human rights, thus facilitating democratic policing.

In 2008, the parliament passed the Maldives Police Act (Commonwealth Human Rights Initiative, 2011), and the constitution was ratified, thus providing a legal framework to initiate substantive police reform. The fundamental principle of the Maldives Police Service is to uphold the rule of law and to create an unbiased and organized police service which is free from extraneous influences. In doing so, they have to safeguard human rights, ensure democratic norms and provide legal protection due to all in the Maldives. The MPS became organized as a professional service and is expected to be free from political influences and accountable to the public. It is now established as a civil service but not as part of the Maldives Civil Service, as they are exempted from the provisions of the Employment Act.

Under the Maldives Police Service Act 2012 (Commonwealth Human Rights Initiative, 2012; Maldives Police Service Act, 2012), the MPS is now entitled to efficiently police the entire territory of Maldives. The MPS has the task to promote and preserve public order, prevent crimes and protect public property. As part of policing, they have to take measures to stop and prevent organized, serious and major crime and ensure the movement of land and sea by controlling and regulating the movement of the traffic of vehicles. They are to safeguard the tourist facilities, collect and compile information about the offenders and maintain the criminal records. They have to identify juvenile crimes, take the appropriate actions as specified in the law, prevent computer, internet and digital or cybercrime and take the required action in the law against such criminal activities and utilize modern methods of investigations including diverse forensic means. The MPS must also act as first responders in emergency situations.

2. Maldivian Judiciary

The judicial authority of the Republic of Maldives is vested in the courts (Article 7, Constitution of the Republic of Maldives, Hussain, 2008). On 7 August 2008, with the ratification of the new constitution of the Republic of Maldives, the Maldivian judiciary entered a new era of modernization, transformation and progress. According to Article 141 of the constitution, "the judicial power is vested in the Supreme Court, the High Court, and such Trial Courts as established by law". The judges are independent and subject only to the constitution and the law. When deciding matters on which the constitution or the law is silent, judges must consider Islamic Shari'ah. Furthermore, it is stated that in the performance of their judicial functions Judges must apply the constitution and the law impartially and without fear, favour or prejudice (Article 142, Constitution of the Republic of Maldives, Hussain, 2008). As under any democratic constitution, the 2008 constitution requires the courts to be independent and subject only to the constitution, which must be applied impartially and prudently.

The key legislation relating to the administration of judiciary in the Maldives is the Judicature Act 2010. This legislation was a bold effort which revolutionised, restructured and streamlined the administration of justice. The purpose of the Act is to determine the tiers of courts of the Judiciary, their jurisdiction and the principles governing their respective functions in accordance with the constitution. The courts' constitutional mandate is to protect the fundamental rights of all citizens, to resolve legal disputes in a fair and transparent manner and to ensure justice through an independent, honest and effective judicial system (Articles 141, 142 and 143, Constitution of the Republic of Maldives, Hussain, 2008). Despite the ratification of the 2008 constitution and the progressive contemporary legislations, the transformation of the judiciary into a truly democratic, impartial and neutral (removed from partisan politics) entity, still remains the most difficult challenge facing the country.

The Supreme Court is the highest authority for the administration of justice in the Maldives (Article 141(b), Constitution of the Republic of Maldives; Sections 10 & 11 Judicature Act, 2010), and it plays an essential role in the administration of the court system. The Supreme Court also has special powers to give orders relating to a matter or a case submitted to the court, to administer justice, to take necessary actions to prevent the misuse of the judicial system and to uphold the confidence in the judicial system. Further, on its own initiative or at the behest of a concerned party, the Supreme Court has the power to prevent the exploitation of the judicial system and to issue various orders in accordance with the law if anyone is found to have violated the law or any principles of the Supreme Court regulation (Section 22, Judicature Act 2010).

Until August 2008, the High Court was the highest authority in the administration of justice, and this institution was directly under the control of the president. With the adoption of the new constitution, the High Court has become the second-highest tiered court in the Maldives, below the Supreme Court in appellate jurisdiction. However, in comparison to the status of the High Court pre-2008 constitution, the new High Court has been provided with added powers by the Judicature Act (Section 36 Judicature Act 2010). The High Court exercises original and appellate jurisdiction in both civil and criminal cases. It hears cases in the first instance as well as cases on appeal from the lower courts and the Tribunals. According to Section 37 of the Judicature Act, the High Court has original jurisdiction to adjudicate matters on first instance, except matters accepted by the Supreme Court; firstly, in relation to a law or a part of a law which contradicts the constitution and secondly, in cases where a regulation created under a law is seen to either fully or partly contradict the constitution or a statute.

The lower courts are divided into two types: 1. Superior Courts (Courts sit in Malé); Magistrate Courts located in the islands (formerly Island Courts).

The superior courts established under the Judicature Act are Criminal Court: with the exception of juvenile delinquencies committed by children as defined in the constitution, the Criminal Court

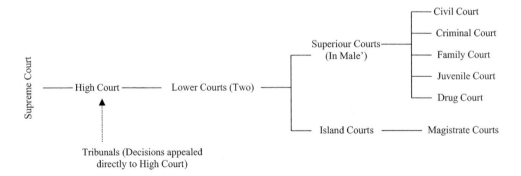

Figure 5.2 Court structure.

has the jurisdiction to adjudicate on all matters relating to criminal offences that have not been exempted by another law (Schedule 2, Judicature Act 2010). Civil Court: Civil Court has the jurisdiction to adjudicate all the civil cases with the exception of family matters (Schedule 1, Judicature Act 2010). Juvenile Court: Addition to the matters that are stipulated by another law as being within the jurisdiction of the Juvenile Court, juvenile delinquencies committed by children as defined by the constitution and matters submitted requesting the extension of the period of detention of those children who have been detained for various offenses (Schedule 1, Judicature Act 2010). Family Court: Family Court has the jurisdiction to adjudicate matters related to family affairs.

Other Superior Courts can be created by law. Such is the case of the Drugs Court, established by the 2011 Drugs Act (Knaul, 2012). The functions of the superior courts are stated in Section 57 and Schedules 1–4 of the Judicature Act. Judges of the superior courts are appointed by the Judicial Services Commission, which decides on the number of judges sitting in each court. Magistrate courts are situated in the atolls, with a Magistrate court in each inhabited island. According to Section 67 of the Judicature Act, there should be a Magistrate Court in each inhabited island of the Maldives except for those islands where four divisions of the Superior Courts are situated (Section 67, Judicature Act 2010). Section 64 of the Judicature Act requires a resident magistrate in all islands with a population of above 500. If the population of the island is 500 or fewer, a magistrate of the Judicial Area (Schedule 5, Judicature Act 2010) to which the island belongs to will be assigned the responsibilities of the magistrate court (Schedule 5, Judicature Act 2010). Magistrate courts have jurisdiction over both criminal and civil matters, but their jurisdiction is limited. Serious criminal offences or civil cases in which the amount or the subject matter in dispute exceeds a certain amount of Maldivian rufiyaa (local currency) are dealt with by the superior courts (Knaul, 2012).

3. Prison Administration in Maldives

On 19 September 2003, a young inmate was brutally murdered in the Maafushi prison, which held a prison population of about 1,100 inmates. Subsequent to this event there were prison riots, and many more were killed and injured. This incident became a precipitant of change, which initiated prison, police, human rights and political reform in the country. In the initial stages of prison reform, a number of consultations were held by the then-Department of Penitentiary and Rehabilitation Services (DPRS) with various national and international agencies. These consultations resulted in publications which identified the prisoner's profile and the gaps and recommendations for pathways to reforming the prison system in the country (Alder & Polk, 2004a, 2004b; Harding & Morgan, 2004; Macdonald, 2003; Robinson, 2004a, 2004b; UNDP, 2010; UNESCAP & UNDP, 2003).

Minister of Home Affairs

Commissioner of Prisons

Deputy Commissioner of Prisons

Inspector of Prisons

Directors of Prisons

Deputy Director of Prisons

Maldives Correctional Services Officers

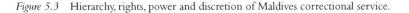

Figure 5.3   Hierarchy, rights, power and discretion of Maldives correctional service.

The Minister of Home Affairs is the lead of the hierarchy of the Maldives Correctional Services. The Commissioner of Prisons, who reports directly to the Minister of Home Affairs, is in charge of all the prisons under the Maldives Correctional Services. He is to oversee and ensure the safety and security of the prisons; to look after the welfare of all the prisoners; to ensure that the prisoners get the opportunity for rehabilitation such that they are integrated back into society as productive members on release from the prison. The Commissioner also has to look after the Maldives Correctional Service Officers and other staff and is responsible in monitoring their discipline.

According to this Act, each prison will have a Director of Prisons who will run the prison in consultation with the Commissioner of Prisons by looking after all the administrative functions of the prison. The Director of Prisons is in charge of looking after the prison security and managing the welfare issues of the prisoners and ensuring the safety of the prison. The Director of Prisons is to maintain a proper registry of each inmate within that particular prison. Information such as identification details, reason for imprisonment/detention, who ordered it, time of detention/ imprisonment, medical histories, security risk level, past criminal records, recommended rehabilitation programs, eligibility for parole and date of release need to be included in each inmate registry.

The Inspector of the Correctional Services is nominated by the Minister of Home Affairs. It is the responsibility of the Inspector to ensure that the structures of the prison are in adherence to the specified standards, that the prisoners receive basic service and that their basic rights are respected. The Inspector of the Correctional Services is to see that all the prisoners are treated as specified in the prison regulations with regard to the provision of food, medical services and other basic rights that are given to the prisoners in this act. The Inspector is to conduct regular visits to the prisons and is mandated to listen to the complaints of inmates independently and thereby bring these to the notice of the Minister. Furthermore, in the event of any prison deaths, such deaths will have to be investigated and a report will need to be prepared and presented to the Minister.

The Prison and Parole Act that is now implemented by the Maldives Correctional Services makes it mandatory on the prison officers to interact with inmates in peace and kindness and offer them protection and safety. They are to assist the inmates with their welfare, facilitate the process of inmate rehabilitation and provide medical support when required. They are not to accept bribes, fees and gifts from inmates or to torture or indulge in acts of cruelty. The organization also has an Emergency Support Group, Prison Academy, Parole Offices, Rehabilitation Command, Operational Command and a Cooperate Command. The disciplinary board of the Maldives Correctional Service will investigate and take necessary actions against violations made by prisoners and the Maldives Correctional Service Officers and other staff.

Maldives Correctional Services is in the process of implementing the newly passed Prison and Parole Bill (At No. 14/2013). Currently, the Maldives Correctional Services is beginning to demonstrate the effect of initiating reform. Maldives Correctional Services have conducted training programs for Prison Officers (reported on 4 June 2015), and an Institute for Correctional Studies was inaugurated on 6 June 2015. Furthermore, with the initiation of the new rehabilitation model within the prison, it was reported that 71 prisoners recently received certificates for various courses conducted within the prison. For example, inmates were distributed certificates such as Certificate 3 in Electricians Course; Pest and Disease Control Course; Wood Carving Course Level 1; Qari Course Level 1; Stocking Flowers Workshop and training on how to make small Dhoani. Furthermore, in the Asseyri Prison (Visham, 2015), which is considered a low-security prison, programs such as handicrafts and carpentry courses, information technology level I courses, counseling programs, religious awareness programs and programs on teaching how to recite the Holy Quran have been conducted for the inmates. Besides this, the inmates have held regular exhibitions for the public under the name of "Inmates Creativity Exhibition" (Visham, 2015). It is of worth to note that currently the Maldivian prison system is witnessing the fruits of a long process of prison reform that has been initiated after much research, study and careful strategic policy and legislature change.

Conclusion

In this chapter an overview of the crime situation in Maldives, police, judiciary and prisons service was discussed. It is found that in spite of Professor Robinson's report (2004a, 2004b) implementation of the reforms in the criminal justice system has not taken its fullest strides. Though the court management is good, there are still issues in police management and prison management. However, these issues are solvable with effective implementation of laws and procedures.

The ultimate goal of the Maldives Police Service (MPS) is to become a democratic police organization, wherein intelligence-led policing will be ingrained in the implementation of all its activities. The MPS has to develop its capacity to adapt to complex situations, use pre-emptive approaches to policing, be socially responsible and work in harmony with community partners and stakeholders and go into joint partnership with the community in creating awareness of the importance of adherence to rule of law. The MPS has to enhance the transparency in Maldives Police's functioning and increase the awareness within the Maldives Police Service about the priorities and standards laid down for them on how to carry out their duties. There has to be greater emphasis on behavioral and attitudinal reform in the training imparted to police officers.

The MPS needs to engage closely with the Police Integrity Commission while deciding on policing priorities. Efforts have to be made to improve the mechanisms for evaluation and performance monitoring and to regularly conduct needs-assessment surveys related to policing. It is unfortunate that the public remains distrustful of the MPS, who appear to remain suppressed under political influence (Maldives Police Service, 2012). A large majority of the public continues to perceive the MPS as hostile to them and politically biased and regards the MPS as an institution which is failing to provide them with adequate security and protection.

Apart from settling the issues of police management, the issues of prison management and reforms are the need of the hour. Earlier, a number of concerns were raised about the operation of Maafushi Prison (Harding & Morgan, 2004). Maafushi Prison was criticized for not providing a safe and secure environment for staff or prisoners and having a lack of treatment programs, work or education for prisoners. Therefore, to avoid further prison riots and disorder, reforming the prison became a necessity. Recommendations were made to develop the prison on an incentive-based regime by creating a more positive and productive environment. Additionally, bringing broader structural changes to the prison work, reducing the prison population by reducing the number of people incarcerated before trial and those with long periods of drug use and the need to explore the role of new community-based penalties and introducing new parole and home leave schemes (Harding & Morgan, 2004) were suggested. Further recommendations were made to decriminalize the offence of drug usage and propose mandatory rehabilitation, provided that the offender had no other criminal charges.

Recommendations were also made to establish an effective restorative justice programme, which could be ideal to combat juveniles, or youth offenders, in order to minimize them from being incarcerated for minor offences; review and pass the Penal Code, Criminal Procedure Code, Evidence Bill, Drugs Bill and the Prison and Parole Bill and amend the existing local orders and prison rules and procedures. Further recommendations include establishing rehabilitation programs in prisons along with opportunity for rehabilitation of drug offenders and creating opportunity for employment within the prison industry (UNDP, 2010). The need to strengthen the DPRS database and strengthen the collaboration and information sharing between the MPS, PGO, Criminal Court, Correctional Service, the Parole Board and the Clemency Board were suggested (UNDP, 2010) as necessary components of prison reform. Proper implementation will enhance the image of correctional services in Maldives.

References

Alder, C. M., & Polk, K. (2004a). *Strategic plan for the reform of the Juvenile Justice System, prepared at the request of the Attorney General of the Maldives for the United Nations Development Program.* Malé: UNDP.

Alder, C. M., & Polk, K. (2004b). *Gender issues in the Criminal Justice System of the Maldives, prepared at the request of the Attorney General for the Maldives and the Minister of Gender, Family Development and Social Security, for the United Nations Development Programme.* Malé: UNDP.

Centre for Community Health and Disease Control. (2010–2011). *National aids programme.* Malé: Ministry of Health and Family.

Commonwealth Human Rights Initiative. (2011). *Implementation of the Maldives Police Service strategic plan 2007–2011: An analysis.* Retrieved from www.humanrightsinitiative.org/publications/police/Report_Maldives_Police_Strategic_Plan.pdf: Commonwealth Human Rights Initiative.

Commonwealth Human Rights Initiative. (2012). *Bill on the Maldives Police Service.* Retrieved from www.nipsa.in/uploads/country_resources_file/1033_Maldives_Police_Bill_2012_-_English_translation_v2.pdf.

Harding, R., & Morgan, N. (2004). *Strengthening custodial services in the Maldives, prepared for the Attorney General and the Ministry of Home Affairs of the Maldives.* Malé: Attorney General and Ministry of Home Affairs of the Maldives.

Human Rights Commission of the Maldives. (2014). *UPR submission September 2014.* Retrieved from www.hrcm.org.mv/Publications/otherdocuments/UPR_submission_Sept_2014.pdf.

Hussain, D. (2008). *Constitution of the Republic of Maldives, 2008: Functional translation in English made by Dheena Hussain for Ministry of Legal Reform, Information and Arts, Maldives is the Publisher.*

Knaul, G. (2012). Report of the Special Rapporteur on the independence of judges and lawyers: Advance report on the global thematic study on human rights education and training of legal professionals, 20 July 2012, A/HRC/20/20, UN do A/68/285. Geneva: United Nations Human Rights Council. Retrieved from https://www.refworld.org/docid/501666b1a.html.

Macdonald, D. (2003). *Review and revision of the current legal framework for drug abuse prevention and intervention in the Maldives: Issues paper, prepared for the United Nations Development Programme and the Narcotics Control Board.* Malé: UNDP.

Maldives Police Service. (2012). *Annual report 2011–2012.* Retrieved from www.police.gov.mv/s/annual_report_2011_2012.pdf.

Maldives Police Service. (2015, June 28). *Case statistics.* Retrieved June 28, 2015, from Maldives Police Service http://police.gov.mv/#casestat.

Robinson, P. (2004a). *Report on the criminal justice system of the Republic of Maldives: Proposals for reform.* Malé: UNDP.

Robinson, P. (2004b). *Draft penal code, prepared for the Attorney General of the Maldives.* Malé: UNDP.

Sri Lanka Maldives Country Unit. (2014). *Youth in Maldives: Shaping a new future for young women and men through engagement and empowerment.* Washington, D.C.: The World Bank.

Suood, H. (2014). *The Maldivian legal system.* Malé: Maldives Law Institute.

Swami, P. (May 14, 2015). *From Kerala family to ex-gangster, IS pulls Maldivian men.* Retrieved from www.msn.com/en-in/news/national/from-kerala-family-to-ex-gangster-is-pulls-maldivian-men/ar-AAaXUSz.

UNDP. (2010). *Prison assessment and proposed rehabilitation and reintegration of offenders report.* Retrieved from www.mv.undp.org/content/dam/maldives/docs/Democratic520Governance/prisons%20report.pdf

UNESCAP and UNDP. (2003). *Rapid situation assessment of drug abuse in Maldives.* Malé: UNESCAP and UNDP.

UNFPA. (2005). *Maldives: Youth voices report.* Malé: UNFPA

Visham, A. (2015). *Works done for the reintegration of convicts to society: Asseyri Prison.* Retrieved from Corrections.gov.mv/dhi/?p=335.

Yoosuf, A. (December 24, 2012). *Cybercrime has increased by 200 percent in Maldives: Police Chief.* Retrieved from www.haveeru.com.mv/news/46422.

6

NEPAL

Institutions in the Criminal Justice System and the Need for Reforms[1]

Mandira Sharma

Introduction

Nepal's criminal justice system needs reform. From the police to the army to public prosecutors, the governmental institutions responsible for dispensing "justice" have been consistently accused of not being effective in protecting the rights of civilians. Flaws in the system have been identified by local and international organisations for many years, but very few legal or substantive changes have been made over the past decade. A long awaited comprehensive penal code has not yet been enacted; and when it is, the law will have much to address.

The system suffers from broad structural and legal flaws. Its functioning is also significantly undermined by the illegal behaviour of governmental actors. Criminal justice in Nepal is pursued through an adversarial process through which, ostensibly, justice will be served by both the state and criminal defendants vigorously promoting their respective interests. In reality, poor, marginalised citizens are largely at the mercy of the state and often do not benefit from the protections they are entitled to by law.

On the other side of the spectrum, crimes committed by public officials almost always go unpunished. Members of the army who perpetrated gross abuses on civilians during the conflict period have thus far escaped justice despite the public exposition of their crimes. The army remains very powerful, and other governmental actors and institutions are loath to hold its members accountable for their crimes. Similarly, police officers are able to routinely inflict torture on detainees without any fear of prosecution. The politicisation of these crimes and the corresponding cycle of impunity continue to gravely undermine the legitimacy of the justice system as a whole.

This chapter outlines the functioning of the criminal justice system on a broad level, identifies particularly significant problems, and proposes solutions to these problems. Some of these reforms require changes in the letter of the law or the passage of new laws, while others recommend increased budgetary allocations or the creation of new governmental institutions. All of them will be necessary to eliminate the excesses and limitations of the system and form a stable foundation for the rule of law in Nepal.

I. Institutions in the Criminal Justice System

1. Police

The police are under the general supervision and control of the Ministry of Home Affairs. The cabinet appoints the inspector general of police. The police are subdivided into several forces such as the Nepal Public Police Force, Guard Police Force, Riot Police Force, and Traffic Police Force. Criminal investigation is carried out by the Crime Investigation Department (CID) of the public police, which is headed by the assistant inspector general of police of the Nepal Public Police Force.

The Nepal Police employs its police officers across the five regions, 14 zones, and 75 districts of Nepal. Each Regional Police Office (RPO) is headed by a deputy inspector general, while the Zonal Police Offices are under the command of senior superintendents. District Police Offices (DPOs) are commanded by superintendents or deputy superintendents. DPOs have local units with a mandate to investigate criminal cases in their territory. They are the most common investigative bodies, but not all districts have separate CIDs. In contrast, RPOs are supervising and coordinating bodies that are not directly involved with investigations. They serve as the middlemen between district CIDs and the Central CID at Nepal Police Headquarters in serious cases.

The CID is divided into units according to the nature of crimes and in order to make the investigation system more efficient. They are: Crime Investigation Groups, National Level Dog Section, Narcotic Control Unit, Crime Investigation School, Crime Research Branch, Foreign Branch, Anti Terrorist Branch, and the Scientific Resources Coordination Branch. The Foreign Branch is divided into three subsections: Foreign Politics, Interpol, and Telex. The Anti Terrorist Branch is divided into internal and external terrorist sections. The Scientific Resources Coordination Branch deals with criminal behaviour, fingerprinting, photography, and forensic science. The Crime Research Branch includes the Central Women's Cell, Records Section, Research Section, Crime Investigation Information Section, and White Collar Crime Section. Some of these branches, like the Women's Cell, were set up only in recent years. Such cells now exist in major cities, including Kathmandu, Biratnagar, and Pokhara but do not operate in most districts of Nepal.

2. Government Attorneys

The Office of the Attorney General in Kathmandu is the central and ultimate authority in the prosecution of crimes. There are also Appellate Prosecutor's Offices, whose attorneys work in the Appellate Courts, and District Prosecutor's Offices, whose attorneys are confined to the district courts. There are 16 Appellate Prosecutor's Offices and 75 District Prosecutor's Offices to carry out the work of the Attorney General.

The prosecution of crimes is the Attorney General's constitutional responsibility. Article 135(2) of the interim constitution of Nepal 2007 states that the attorney general should represent the government in cases wherein the rights, interests, or concerns of the government are involved. The article further states that the Attorney General has the power to make the final decision as to whether to initiate proceedings in any case on behalf of Nepal's government in any court or other adjudicative forum. The Attorney General also acts as the chief legal advisor to the government and advises government officials in all matters regarding constitutional and legal affairs (State Cases Act, Section 17).

District Government Attorneys are responsible for the prosecution of standard criminal cases throughout Nepal. They have the discretion, under Section 17 of the State Cases Act, to decide whether to initiate proceedings in response to a charge sheet filed by police. They are also required to be present during interrogations conducted by police. Appellate Attorneys represent the state in cases in which individuals have challenged an initial conviction in the district court, challenge acquittals of criminal defendants in the district courts.

Government attorneys currently play no role in criminal investigations. The police conduct investigations and present their findings to government attorneys with a recommendation of whether to proceed. Since prosecutors have no chance to participate in the information gathering of an investigation, they are forced to rely solely on the facts presented to them by the police. Given the well-documented tendencies of the police to disregard the laws binding them, it would be advisable to renew the role of government attorneys in overseeing investigations. This would also give them a more accurate idea, untainted by forced confessions or misrepresented evidence, of the merits of each case. It is important for different government institutions to check and balance one another's power in a transparent and well-functioning justice system.

Government attorneys have the final say in the decision of whether to initiate trial proceedings in a given case. But rather than using this authority to filter out cases with little merit, prosecutors tend to be little more than a rubber stamp of approval. In a recent study, the Centre for Legal Research and Resource Development (CeLRRd) found that government attorneys prosecuted 96% of cases submitted to them over the course of a six-year period (CeLRRd, p. 153). The data suggests that the attorneys rarely evaluate the evidence presented to them and instead automatically begin prosecution as a knee-jerk reaction to receiving a charge sheet from the police.

This problem seems to stem from a combination of poorly drafted laws and ineffectual government actors. Under the State Cases Act, public prosecutors are empowered to decide whether to file a case, but there is no provision prescribing any procedures to govern this important duty (Sections 17 & 18, State Cases Act). Prosecutors may be acting irresponsibly in failing to filter the cases presented to them, but they are not currently acting illegally. The almost complete absence of any pretrial sorting of cases causes consistently low success rates for prosecutions. Conviction rates hovered around 60% during the years of the CeLRRd study, and it is unlikely that these numbers have improved in recent years (CeLRRd, p. 154).

Although discretion is a necessary component of a prosecutor's job, guidelines must be created to aid the process of filtering out unsupportable cases before trial. It is encouraging that the judiciary seems less willing to accept the police officers' version of events, while at the same time it is very disturbing that so many meritless cases even reach trial. It is also significant that victims of crimes are so often frustrated in their pursuit of justice.

3. The Judiciary

Part 10 of the interim constitution delineates the structure and responsibilities of the judiciary. Under the constitution, the Supreme Court is the highest court, and its interpretation of the law is final and binding on all government bodies. The Chief Justice of the Court is appointed by the prime minister on the recommendation of the Constitutional Council. The Chief Justice then appoints the remaining judges in accordance with the recommendations of the Judicial Council. Unlike in some other countries, appointments to the Supreme Court are not for life; judges must mandatorily retire at the age of 65 (Interim Constitution, Articles 102, 103, & 105).

Below the Supreme Court in the judicial hierarchy are the Appellate Courts and District Courts. Each district of Nepal has a District Court, which is empowered to hear both civil disputes and criminal cases. The District Courts are meant to be courts of first instance, and in most situations they are. However, a case that implicates a fundamental right prescribed by the constitution can proceed directly to the Supreme Court. Parties to settled disputes in the District Courts can challenge the verdicts in the Appellate Courts. Judges may only be appointed to these courts by the Chief Justice of the Supreme Court on the recommendation of the Judicial Council (Interim Constitution, Articles 107 & 109).

Administrative officers of several government institutions also exercise judicial authority. Under the Forest Act, for example, District Forest Officers are permitted to sentence offenders to up to one year imprisonment (Forest Act, 1993, Section 65). Chief District Officers are also empowered under other laws (such as the Arms & Ammunition Act and Public Offences Act) to impose significant criminal sentences. These cases proceed without the procedural protections afforded to criminal suspects in the regular courts. In some situations, the same administrative officer will direct the entire process, from investigation to sentencing.

4. Prisons

Prisons in Nepal, on the whole, are overcrowded, understaffed, and housed in decrepit buildings. Prisons in the Tarai and in urban areas are particularly burdened. A study by CVICT and PRI, during which representatives from the organisations visited several prisons, found a number of problems common to each facility. The main issues with Nepal's prisons seem to be insufficient housing for prisoners, ancient facilities, a lack of rehabilitative programs, the detention of juveniles and the mentally ill alongside competent adults, and the fact that prisoners themselves are often responsible for keeping order and inflicting punishments (CVICT & PRI, p. 1933). Additionally, female prisoners often languish in the worst conditions of any prisoners.

Prisons such as Ghorahi, Bhimphedi, and Biratnagar were found by the study to be significantly overpopulated for their capacity. Health risks, such as open sewage systems, filthy toilets, and the incarceration of sick prisoners within the general population, were common (CVICT & PRI, p. 1933). The government has not taken any significant steps to reform the prison system, and it is unlikely that the facilities at these prisons have improved in recent years. During the armed conflict, the situation was even worse due to the large numbers of political prisoners incarcerated.

Only minimal efforts have been made to educate or otherwise improve the position of prisoners. Some prisons contain a library and hold adult education classes, but these facilities are not widely used by the prisoners. Further, most prisons lack work programs designed to teach their uneducated prisoners skills (CVICT and PRI, p. 1933). Without mechanisms in place to teach and empower prisoners, repeat offenders will continue to repopulate the prisons and keep them overcrowded.

Various reports suggest that children are still held in prisons alongside adults. This practice is conducted in blatant disregard for the Children's Act, the provisions of which are discussed in preceding sections of this chapter. There are significant reasons why the law requires children to be incarcerated in separate facilities. Juveniles are vulnerable to physical and sexual abuse at the hands of older and stronger inmates, as are the mentally disabled. Additionally, there is a better chance that juveniles can be rehabilitated through education and a more nurturing approach. Programs specifically aimed to prepare child offenders for their reintegration into society are, however, nonexistent in Nepalese prisons.

It is also significant to note that "trusted prisoners" are commonly used by the staff of prisons to maintain order and mete out punishments. This system speaks to the almost complete absence of effective protocols to govern the administration of prisons. It is also indicative of a grave lack of funds; that prison guards must outsource their work to the prisoners themselves means that there are not enough prison guards. This is a problem common to under-funded penal systems in countries all over the world.

In 2004–2005, the government decided to begin a program whereby convicted criminals could serve sentences of up to three years doing community service instead of spending the time behind bars. Provisions relating to this "open prison" system were codified in an amendment to the Prison Act. The implementation of these provisions of the Acts and Regulations related to imposing community service in lieu of incarceration, however, remains a distant dream.

Thus, it is suggested that the prison system must be legally guaranteed a significantly larger percentage of the budget for improving the infrastructures of the prisons, provide education and other programs to prisoners, and to have sufficient and well-trained staff in prison. Having prison service separate from the home would be another ways of avoiding international problems of prisons too.

II. Discussion and Conclusion

1. Issues in Policing, Crime Investigation, and Pre-Trial Detention

Article 24 of the interim constitution highlights specific fundamental rights relating to criminal justice. In accordance with international standards of criminal law, each person suspected or accused of a crime must be proven guilty beyond a reasonable doubt. Article 24(5) reinforces this principle, providing that "no person accused of any offence shall be assumed to be an offender until proven guilty." This procedural safeguard evinces the philosophy that wrongful conviction and incarceration is to be avoided at all costs. Unfortunately, the Nepalese police often investigate crimes and arrest suspects with the presumption that their targeted suspect is inevitably guilty. The law surrounding investigation and detention is not without faults, but it contains many sound provisions. The deep-seated attitudes and practices of the police (as well as the government's unwillingness to impose liability on officers for their violations) constitute the most pressing problems with this sector of the justice system.

Prior to the passage of the State Cases Act of 1964, investigation of criminal cases was the province of the judiciary. Influenced by the Anglo-American system of criminal justice, the royal government decided to reform its judiciary and eliminate judges' investigative responsibilities. This was an important development (further codified in the revised State Cases Act of 1992), as the current framework requires the judiciary to act as an independent arbiter of cases rather than as a force in investigating and prosecuting them. The police are therefore vested with the entire authority to investigate crimes and make arrests, while the Attorney General on the national level and district government attorneys on the local level have the discretion to initiate prosecutions.

One potential problem with such a strict division of powers is that prosecutors are actually prevented from having a meaningful role in investigations. The State Cases Act of 1992 eliminated monitoring and investigative responsibilities previously required of prosecutors. The resultant system is one which allows for unfettered discretion for police in investigations and renders detainees vulnerable to abuses. A study of the penal system in 2000 recognised this flaw, and Advocacy Forum's recent data shows that the police often disregard the rights of criminal suspects (CVICT & PRI, 2000).

A criminal investigation is usually triggered by the filing of a First Information Report (FIR). Anyone with information about the commission of a crime may file a FIR (Section 3, State Cases Act). The police station that receives the report or is made aware of the commission of a crime in any other way then has a duty to fully investigate the claims (Section 7, State Cases Act). This duty, however, is often neglected, especially when a complaint is lodged against a government official. FIRs relating to the conflict period and accusing members of the army or police of misconduct (usually serious crimes like torture or murder) have been routinely disregarded. The State Cases Act of 1992 does allow complainants to approach higher authorities if their FIR is initially rejected; the unwillingness of police to investigate a particular complaint can ultimately be ruled upon by the Supreme Court (Section 3(5), State Cases Act). The Supreme Court has ordered the investigation of cases that were willfully ignored by police for many years. However, the passage of time can be a significant barrier to effective evidence gathering. Requiring complainants to engage in a lengthy appeals process just to force the start of an investigation that will likely not be conducted in good faith is not a satisfactory practice. But regardless of the legal procedures compelling police to initiate investigations, their unwillingness to look into certain cases is symptomatic of cronyism, a culture of impunity, and corruption as well as systemic flaws.

While gathering evidence, police are required by the State Cases Act to have probable cause before searching the person or property of a suspect (Section 10, State Cases Act). The law provides additional protections in that each search must have two citizen witnesses, and the competent police official must document all items seized during the search. These laws are consistent with the demands of international law as well as the protection of each person's privacy and human rights. However, it is unclear to what extent the prescribed search and seizure procedures are actually followed by police and how they are held responsible for not observing these procedures.

Violations of legal protections of human rights also happen because police investigators lack the expertise and resources needed to conduct adequate inquiries into alleged crimes. Officers are often charged with investigating crimes, although most of their experience is in keeping the peace.

The investigative process is also hindered by a lack of technologies needed to gather sufficient evidence for a criminal prosecution. Without proper training and equipment and an internal system of accountability, the police rely almost solely on confessions and the testimony of witnesses.

On paper, the law regarding pre-trial detention is, with some exceptions, equitable and protective of detainees' human rights. Initially, each suspect must be informed of the grounds for his or her arrest as soon as possible after being placed in detention (Section 24(1), Interim Constitution). Further, each detainee must be produced before the court within 24 hours of arrest. As an additional protection, a government attorney must be present while the police take a suspect's statement (Section 9(1), State Cases Act). The fact that police are empowered to arrest criminal suspects without warrants may be a cause for concern, but this is a common practice in many countries and does not constitute a serious procedural problem, assuming that these detainees are produced before the court within the mandated 24-hour period. Indeed, this provision is necessary to effectively prosecute sophisticated offenders who may destroy evidence or otherwise evade justice (CVICT & PRI, p. 57).

These laws, however, are of no consequence to the actual practices of police throughout Nepal. Altogether 95.5% of all detainees interviewed in a recent survey were not provided with a notice of arrest, while over 50% were not taken to court within the required timeframe (Coalition Against Torture, p. 83). It is also evident that a government attorney is not present during most interrogations and that the law mandating their presence does little to deter torture and other abuses. The almost unitary unwillingness to abide by these laws suggests a problem caused more by the composition and traditions of the police than by systematic flaws. The issue is that the police, rather than strictly adhering to their obligations and responsibilities under the law, continue to be permitted to ignore these duties with impunity.

The most serious implication of the noted breaches of the law regarding arrest and detention is that detainees are often subjected to torture, coercion, and other abuses. A survey conducted by Advocacy Forum over the past year in 19 districts of Nepal reveals that 19.5% of detainees were tortured over the past year (Coalition Against Torture, p. 82). While this figure is a marked improvement from the past (especially when compared to the widespread and unchecked violations that occurred during the conflict), it is unacceptable that almost one in every five detainees endures severe pain at the hands of the police. Torture is a grave problem in Nepal. Its practice results from a combination of the aforementioned ingrained traditions and a present lack of any substantive law criminalising torture. The issue is dealt with at length in a recent publication, "Criminalize Torture," and will be further considered in later sections of this report.

Unless the violations of the law governing pre-trial detention (production in court within 24 hours, provision of notice of arrest, presence of government attorney during interrogations) are punished by suspension, demotion, and/or imprisonment, adherence to these provisions continuously remain questionable. In addition, the legal framework such as law to criminalize torture also needs to be enacted as a matter of priority.

2. Issues in Trial Process, Defence, Legal Aid, and Adjudication

Once a charge sheet has been filed by the government attorney, a trial in the District Court can proceed. However, this is rarely a prompt process, because District Courts almost invariably have excessive caseloads. In most of the years in the past, about 50% of criminal cases filed are not adjudicated until the next year or beyond. This problem stems from a combination of insufficient physical capacity and a lack of procedural shortcuts such as plea bargains that would relieve overburdened courts.

After the charge sheet is filed, a bail hearing is held. The sitting judge decides whether to grant bail depending on the nature and severity of the charges and a number of subjective factors. For any offence which is punishable by more than a three-year sentence, bail will be refused provided that the evidence submitted with the charge sheet provides grounds to reasonably establish the detainee's involvement in the crime. For lesser charges, bail may be offered at the discretion of the sitting judge. Typically bail will be granted with a bond of land, cash, or other property. In rare cases where the charges are not severe, bail may be offered without a bond. The amount of the bond often prevents average detainees, who either do not own property of sufficient value or are unable to appraise the value of the property they do own, from being released on bail. Additionally, detainees facing certain criminal charges (such as drug or black marketing related) are not entitled to bail.

Lengthy delays before trial and the inaccessibility of bail are symptomatic of the overall presumption of guilt that drives the criminal justice system. It is possible for a Nepalese citizen to be arrested without a warrant and without information about the charges against him, tortured and detained for days without being allowed to see a judge, and imprisoned for months or years without being convicted and without access to bail. The substantive law governing the pretrial process needs many changes, and the significant legal protections that do exist are infrequently implemented in practice.

Once the bail hearing and any appeals to that process have concluded, the District Court hears the oral testimony of witnesses and confirms evidentiary exhibits. Unlike courts in many other countries, witnesses in Nepal are heard before, not during, the final hearing. These hearings are often greatly prolonged due to the prosecution's difficulty in producing witnesses. After this process, the final hearing, during which the prosecution and defence each make oral arguments before the court, occurs. Judges are the sole arbiters of guilt or innocence, and at the conclusion of the final hearing, they will also decide on a sentence if they have found the accused guilty.

There are very few formal regulations for sentencing. The judge is given almost unchecked discretion to decide the type of punishment and length of imprisonment. In theory, the judge considers the aggravating or mitigating circumstances and the background and culpability of the convicted person when determining the sentence. However, since there are no specific guidelines, there is a great inconsistency from one court to the next. As such, severe punishments are frequently imposed for relatively minor crimes.

Section 24 of the interim constitution affirms a number of important "Rights Regarding to Justice" within the Fundamental Rights chapter of that instrument. The rights enshrined include many of the detention-related protections already mentioned in the previous section. Additionally, Subsection 7 provides that "No person accused of any offence shall be compelled to be a witness against oneself" (Section 24(7), Interim Constitution). This is consistent with widely accepted international guidelines on criminal justice and is an essential safeguard of the rights of the accused. Unfortunately, coerced confessions remain commonly used in criminal proceedings throughout Nepal.

In one study, 67% of respondents (all of them were detainees who had charge sheets filed against them by police) reported that they had been compelled to give evidence against themselves (CeL-RRd, p. 195). While this figure is from several years ago, recent data reveals that torture and other cruel, inhuman, or degrading treatment are still frequently inflicted on detainees in efforts to "gather evidence" (Coalition Against Torture, p. 82). As government attorneys are rarely present during interrogations, there is little to prevent police from using physical and mental coercion to compel the confessions they seek.

Although forced self-incriminatory statements are ostensibly inadmissible in court proceedings under the Torture Compensation Act and Evidence Act, this prohibition begs the question: why, then, do the police continue to torture and humiliate detainees in efforts to coerce confessions? The only possible answer is that the "evidence" they get from this process is frequently used to establish suspects' guilt during trials. Thousands of interviews with detainees each year reveal that, at the initial remand stage, judges very rarely ask detainees whether their statements were freely given (AF Annual Report, 2008, p. 30). It is therefore likely that this insensitivity continues during trials and that coerced evidence is commonly admitted in court and used to convict people.

As has been demonstrated, the principle of "innocent until proven guilty" is operative on paper but not in practice. Similarly, the right to legal counsel is guaranteed by law, but many defendants are prevented from accessing an attorney. The constitution provides that indigent people shall have access to free legal aid (Section 24(10), Interim Constitution). This right is ostensibly provided for by the Legal Aid Act of 1997. However, an effective infrastructure to guarantee legal counsel to all defendants in accordance with the law is not currently in place. Altogether 91% of respondents in CeLRRd's 2002 study who could not afford counsel were not given representation under the Legal Aid Act (CeLRRd, p. 218).

The Legal Aid Act was passed 10 years before the interim constitution and does not fully protect the fundamental right to free counsel prescribed by the latter document. There are two significant aspects of the law which greatly restrict detainees' access to legal aid. Section 3(2) provides that either the Central or District Legal Aid Committee "shall be authorized to grant or deny legal aid to a particular person" (Section 3(2), Legal Aid Act, 1997). This broad discretion is utilized too often and is not consistent with the guarantees of the constitution. Committees have decided to refuse legal aid to detainees accused of crimes such as human trafficking, sale of narcotics, and espionage (CeLRRd, p. 55). A system whereby the "right" to legal aid can be so easily revoked is unacceptable, especially in light of the tenuous investigative practices that lead to the charges in the first place.

Another provision of the Legal Aid Act also functions to prevent many detainees from receiving the representation they are guaranteed by the constitution. Section 3(1) limits legal aid to those who have proven that their income falls below a certain threshold (Section 3(1), Legal Aid Act). This measure ends up preventing many defendants from getting a lawyer. In practice, detainees are often unable to compile documents necessary to prove their income while held in police offices or prisons. This is again indicative of the correlation between wealth and access to justice in the Nepalese system. The conundrum is that indigent defendants are often unable to get bail because of their limited assets and then prevented from providing proof of their poverty due to their continued detention. The system conspires to condemn the poor without giving them a fair chance to defend themselves.

Even those detainees who can get lawyers aren't allowed access to representation when they need it most: during interrogation. Detainees are almost always denied a visit from a lawyer up until a charge sheet is filed against them. This allows the police to have full dominion over detainees and use illegal methods to coerce the all-important confession. Nepalese citizens have a constitutional right against self-incrimination, but when detainees are unaware of this and lack the support of legal counsel, the right has little substantive effect.

Finally, the government simply hasn't set aside enough funds to pay lawyers for providing free legal aid. There is only one legal-aid lawyer appointed for each district court, and other attorneys are hired very infrequently. Attorneys from the Nepal Bar and NGOs such as Advocacy Forum attempt to fill the gap by providing free legal services, but these individuals should not have to shoulder the constitutional responsibilities of the government. In the CeLRRd survey, this situation resulted in over half of all detainees interviewed proceeding through the criminal justice system without ever having the opportunity to consult a lawyer (CeLRRd, p. 83).

Under the Civil Code of Nepal (now repealed), a trial in a court of first instance must be completed within one year of the time of filing of the answer to a complaint (Number 14, Preliminary Chapter, Civil Code). However, this guarantee is often unfulfilled, as many cases are not adjudicated within a year of their filing. This was a problem before the conflict, and it has persisted to the present day. In 2002, a comprehensive study of the criminal justice system found that Nepal's courts were dangerously overburdened, with the accused waiting for lengthy periods before trial (CeLRRd, p. 83). As the conflict intensified in the following years, caseloads for courts in urban areas increased, while caseloads for courts decreased in rural districts under the thrall of the CPNM (ICJ, 2008, p. 19). Since the Comprehensive Peace Agreement, dockets have remained overloaded. In the period between July 2007 and July 2008, 55.5% of cases filed were not resolved in the same year (Annual Report of the Attorney General, p. 55).

One reason for this is that civil cases take up a substantial part of the docket; as a result, criminal defendants are often forced to endure long waits before trial. Another is the high percentage of frivolous or unfounded cases that go to trial as a result of government attorneys' unwillingness to exercise their discretion in initiating prosecutions. Finally, there are simply not enough courts or judges to handle the needs of the Nepalese population. A poor physical infrastructure compounds the problem. The executive and legislative branches naturally require and receive the vast majority of government funds, but the judiciary is still woefully under-funded.

Judges' impartiality and willingness to acquit those who have not been proven guilty beyond a reasonable doubt are the only checks on the otherwise inexorable progress of suspects toward prison. However, it is unclear whether the judiciary is competently fulfilling this vastly important responsibility. In the most recent report of the Attorney General's Office, 82% of cases adjudicated before District Courts and Chief District Officers (CDOs) resulted in convictions, a statistic which suggests that the standard of guilt beyond a reasonable doubt is not always honoured in the courts (Annual Report of the Attorney General, p. 55). This is clearly due to the manipulation of suspects by the police and the inability of government attorneys to exercise any discretion. The investigative capacity of the police is low, and they are often unable to produce compelling evidence even in cases in which a suspect's guilty is likely. As so many unfounded prosecutions proceed to trial, judges are forced to sift through the quagmire and acquit many suspects.

Further, the fact that public officials are immune from prosecution in Nepal has been well publicized but remains a significant flaw in the criminal justice system today. Human rights organisations have been lobbying for the government to hold its own employees accountable for their crimes for many years now, but to no avail. The credibility of the government as a whole continues to be undermined by an almost complete absence of mechanisms for accountability and transparency. An independent investigative and prosecutorial unit must be established to deal with allegations of crimes committed by members of the government.

Note

1 Earlier published as a chapter as Sharma, M. (2009). Criminal justice system in Nepal. In B. Sapkota (Ed.), *The Nepali security sector: An almanac* (pp. 277–293). Hungary: Geneva Centre for the Democratic Control of Armed Forces, Geneva, Switzerland and European Studies Center, Faculty of Humanities, University Pecs, Hungary. Republished with permission from the publisher.

References

Forest Act. (1993). Government of Nepal. Retrieved from http://extwprlegs1.fao.org/docs/pdf/nep4527.pdf.
Interim Constitution of Nepal. (2007). Retrieved from www.wipo.int/edocs/lexdocs/laws/en/np/np006en.pdf.
Legal Aid Act. (1997). Government of Nepal. Retrieved from http://www.lawcommission.gov.np/en/wp-content/uploads/2018/10/legal-aid-act-2054-1997.pdf.
Advocacy Forum. (2008, June). *Annual report 2008*. Nepal: Advocacy Forum.
Centre for Legal Research and Resource Development. (2002). *Baseline survey on criminal justice system of Nepal*. Nepal: CeLRRd.
CVICT and PRI. (2000, March). *Penal reform in Nepal: Plan of action and report*. Nepal: CVICT and PRI.
Government Cases Act (1992). Government of Nepal. Retrieved from http://www.lawcommission.gov.np/en/wp-content/uploads/2018/10/government-cases-act-2049-1992.pdf.
ICJ. (2008, February). Nepal: Justice in transition.

7

PAKISTAN

Criminal Justice Processes and Issues of Crime, Policing, Judiciary, and Prisons

Amit Thakre

Introduction

Pakistan is administered by federal parliamentary or federal republic government. Pakistan is predominantly an Islamic nation. Sharia (Islamic laws) have historical significance in the justice delivery mechanism in Pakistan (Azeem, 2013), and despite deriving a legal system from English common law (Wasim, 2008), the influence of Sharia is clearly evident on the criminal justice system of Pakistan (Johnson & Vriens, 2013). The justice disposition in Pakistan's contemporary era is fundamentally based on the religious rationale. Henceforth, the principles of equality and fairness in justice delivery in Pakistan are in accordance with the decree of the Holy Quran (Rehman, 2007).

To make sure that a law conforms to the order of Islam, Federal Shariat Courts were established on 26 May 1980 under President's Orders (Barakatullah, 2010). The Shariat Court is chaired by the Council of Ulama (An Islamic advisory board). The constitution of Pakistan enunciates principles within which the Pakistan's criminal justice system should function, viz., equality before the law, prohibition of discrimination, deprivation of life and liberty only in accordance with procedure established by the law, proof beyond reasonable doubt, detention in accordance with prescribed guidelines, and protection against double jeopardy (Mirza, 2010).

In Pakistan, most of the core statuary laws were formulated during the British era (1860 to 1910) (Blue & Hoffman, 2008), such as, the Penal Code (1860), the Criminal Procedure Code (1898), Prisons Act (1894), Prisoners Act (1900), and the Reformatory Schools Act (1897). The stated legislations were formulated with a coercive approach during the early British era, which needs serious reforms to be well-justified in the contemporary era of reformation (Lau, 1973). As per the reformative requirements, the Pakistan government established its first Law Reform Commission in the year 1958 under Mr. Justice S. A. Rahman (Hussain, 2011), followed by 1967 Law Reform Commission under Justice Hamoodur Rehman. Later on there were more Law Reform Commissions constituted in the years1978, 1993, and 1997 (Law and Justice Commission), and on 14 January 2005, the Law Reform Bill was proposed. The recommendations of the Law Reform Bill 2005 are currently under consideration by the Pakistan government as guidelines to mend the loopholes in the existing CJS of Pakistan (Abbas, 2011).

The current chapter in part I discusses the criminal justice system of Pakistan including the criminal justice processes and functioning of the criminal justice system in Pakistan. Part II discusses the issues of crime situation, policing, judiciary, and prisons in Pakistan.

I. Criminal Justice System in Pakistan

1. *Criminal Law-Making Processes*

The criminal justice system of Pakistan fundamentally consists of legislature, judiciary, and executive bodies (Lippman, McConville, & Yerushalmi, 1988). The process of making a criminal law is undertaken by the legislature by defining prohibited acts and sanctioning penalties. The state constitution also entitles the legislation that bills can be modified and rejected on its discretion. The legislature apart from a criminal bill is also responsible for passing and amending procedural bills. This includes defining the duties of executive (search, seizure, arrest, custody, bail grant, etc.) and judiciary powers (trail, proceedings, and sentencing). Figure 7.1 is a flowchart depicting the process of law-making in Pakistan:

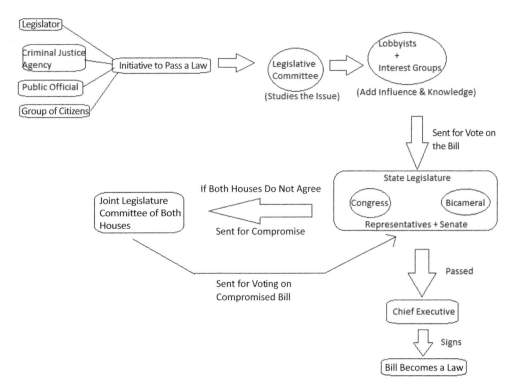

Figure 7.1   Criminal law-making processes in Pakistan.

(*Source*: Prepared by the author)

As demonstrated above, the initiation to pass a law in Pakistan can be done by a legislature, a criminal justice agency, a public official, or a group of citizens. This bill is studied by legislative committee, and assistance of lobbyists and interest groups is also taken, as they add influence and knowledge to the issue. Once finalized, the bill is forwarded to the state legislature, where Congress and bicameral bodies vote on it. If both houses do not agree, then it is forwarded to joint legislature committee of both houses, which study and try to reach a compromise. The compromised and modified bill is again reverted to the state legislature for approval. From here on, if both the houses of the state legislature pass the bill, it is finally sent to the chief executive. At this level, if the bill is vetoed, it could be dropped or sent back to the legislature again for further consideration. Finally, the chief executive signs on the bill to make it a law.

2. *Policing*

The duties, rules, and regulations for Pakistan's police are illustrated in The Police Act, 1861, which is a central law coming from the Police Act of the British India period (CHRI, 2010). The act still remains applicable in the province of Pakistan with certain modifications. However, in an effort to revamp the whole act, a centrally propagated order was brought into effect on 14 August 2002, but none of the new changes were ever implemented.

Following is the police structure and organization in Pakistan:

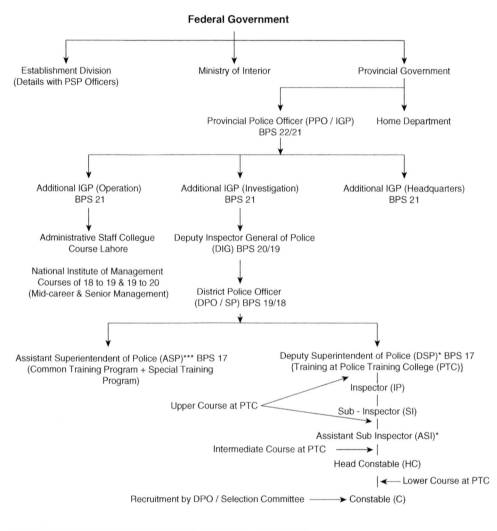

Figure 7.2 Representing police administration in Pakistan with special reference to recruitment and training. (*Source:* Fasihuddin, 2010)

At federal level, following are the institutions responsible for maintaining order in the society (Abbas, 2011):

- Federal Investigation Agency (FIA)
- Anti-Narcotics Force (ANF)
- Frontier Constabulary
- Frontier Corps $\left.\right\}$ These 4 are Field Organizations
- Pakistan Coast Guards $\quad$ (Under Federal Ministry of Interior)
- Pakistan Rangers
- National Highways and Motorways Police (NHMP)
- Pakistan Railways Police
- Islamabad Police, Islamabad Capital Territory

Pakistan police pursue their duties as per the Code of Criminal Procedure, 1898 (CrPC). Also, the procedures relating to evidence are stated in the (Raja, 2003). Policing in Pakistan is more of a provincial approach in which four main regions are identified across the country and respectively provided with provincial police departments. The four regions for policing based on provinces (along with number of police stations in them) are: Punjab (637), Sindh (440), Khyber Pakhtunkhwa (218), and Balochistan (84). Under the Police Act of 1861, the hierarchy of police in Pakistan is as follows (Suddle, 2003):

At the functional level, every district (headed by Senior Superintendent of Police) has sub-divisions (headed by Assistant/Deputy Superintendent of Police). Further based on area, crime rate, and population, it has two or more police stations (headed by Inspectors). The organizational setup of the Pakistan police is demonstrated in following flowchart:

To address the accountability issue, the Police Order 2002 introduced mechanisms at headquarters, departmental, and police station levels (Abbas, 2011). The recommendatory nature of Police Order 2002 places greater emphasis on the proactive role of policing, registering FIR within 48 hours, and conducting effective investigation. For this matter, establishment of the District Public Safety and Police Complaints Commission (DPSPCC) was proposed. However, change in governance and amendments in the Police Order have downplayed the promise of reform as stated in the report by International Crisis Group stating 'Amendments in Police Order have instead weakened civil accountability and internal discipline as well as heightened the political influence in crucial policing matters.'

3. Judiciary

It is the responsibility of the judiciary to ensure that the rule of law is observed and enforced in the state. The role of the judiciary extends to remedial measures as well through judgments prescribing rehabilitation, reformation, and reintegration of the wrongdoer. The judiciary is entitled to monitor and recommend processes pertaining to the legislature and the executive. All the above-mentioned roles of the judiciary have direct implications on how a state deals with its citizens, how citizens perceive the legitimacy of its state, and, finally, how effective the judiciary is in mitigating between the state and the citizen.

The reformation of the justice system of Pakistan witnessed the transition of society from the Hindu era (1500 B.C. until 1500 A.D.), the Mughal period (11 century A.D. to 19 century), and British rule to post-1947 (independence) changes (Hussain, 2011). The constitution illustrated provisions for a superior judiciary (Article 2 A of Pakistan Constitution), appointment and removal terms and conditions, and a degree of monetary control (which ruling came in the case of

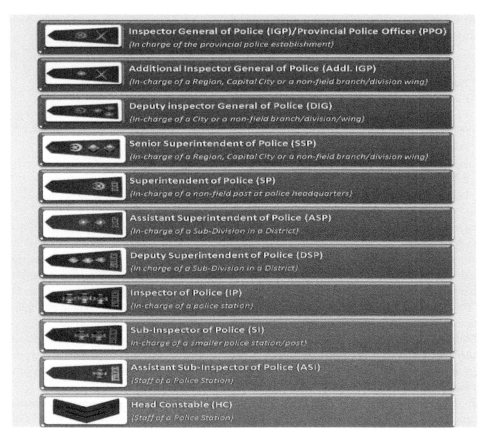

Figure 7.3   Hierarchy of police in Pakistan.
(*Source:* www.nipsa.in)

Government of Sind v Sharaf Faridi) (PLD, 1994 SC 105, Hussain, 2011). To balance the independence of the judiciary, special emphasis is placed on the need for an accountability mechanism, and hence was established the Supreme Judicial Council under article 209 of the constitution of Pakistan. Misconduct, abuse of power, and incapability issues are monitored by the two most senior judges of the Supreme and High Courts as members that are forwarded to the president for the final decision. The important functions of the Supreme Judicial Council are to ensure the adherence to the Code of Conduct by the judges, performance appraisal of the judiciary, and issuance of guidelines for the Supreme Court and High Court. The organizational and functional setup of the judiciary in Pakistan is as follows:

Apart from that, special courts and tribunals have been established in Pakistan to take up specific cases, such as courts for offences in banks, traffic courts, anti-corruption, anti-terrorism, anti-narcotics, drug courts, labour courts and insurance appellate tribunal, income tax appellate tribunal, and services tribunals (Barakatullah, 2010).

At grassroots level, the Jirga system in Pakistan is quite active (Taizi, 2007), similar to the Panchayati system in India. The Jirga system is chaired by the notable elders of the village, who mitigate and decide disputes in minor cases. The Article 4 to 9 of the Qanun-e-Shahadat ordered the proceeding before Jirga system (vested powers similar to civil courts) in alignment with magisterial proceedings.

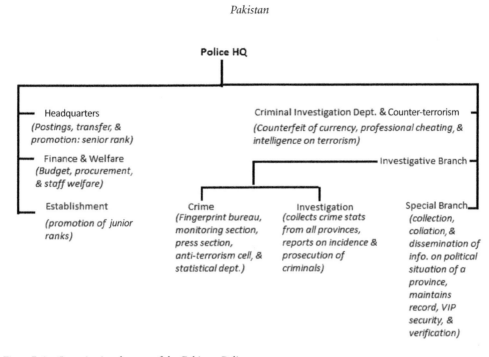

Figure 7.4 Organizational setup of the Pakistan Police.

(*Source:* Prepared by the author)

This includes cross-examination of the witnesses and administering oaths to the witness in accordance with their religion. Similarly, there are Qazi courts and Majlis-e-Shura, which were constructed solely for speedy justice in accordance with the Civil Procedure Code, 1913; but these courts were not established nationwide, and they remain functional only in the provinces of Balochistan and the North West Frontier of Pakistan. The appointment of the members of Qazi court and Majlis-e-Shura is made through the Public Service Commission.

4. Prison Administration

The prison system in Pakistan is inherited from the British regime, which was primarily designed for detainment and punitive measures against freedom fighters. In the 19 century, the purpose of confinement shifted from inflicting pain and agony to reformation and rehabilitation. The objectives of prison now became introspection and reintegration of offenders into society as law-abiding citizens.

Prison administration, duties of prison staff/officers, discharge of prisoners, work assigned, and treatment are done in accordance with the Prisons Act of 1894 of Pakistan. The Prisoner's Act of 1900 deals with sentencing, prisoner transfers, nature of punishment awarded, and matters related to presenting the court of law. The *Jail Manual of Pakistan* (a.k.a. the *Pakistan Prison Rules*, 1978) consists of 50 chapters and 1,250 rules covering management of prisons.

Currently, there are 99 prisons in Pakistan, including four women's jails (Khan, 2010). Apart from those, in every prison, women inmates are kept in a separate facility. In addition to detention center, there are two Borstal and juvenile institutions at Bahawalpur and Faisalabad.

The overall authorized capacity is 42,670 prisoners in all the provinces of Pakistan, but there are 78,328 prisoners, which means the overcrowding is 183.8% of authorized capacity.

ORGANISATION AND STRENGTH OF JUDICIAL HIERARCHY

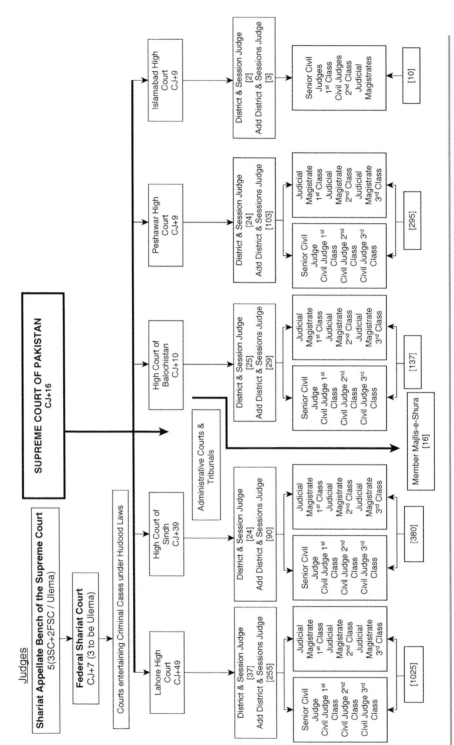

Figure 7.5 Organizational and functional setup of judiciary in Pakistan.

(*Source:* Hussain, 2011)

Sr. No.	Province-wise prison population and authorized capacity			
	Name of Province	No. of Prisons	Authorized Capacity	Prison Population
1.	Punjab	32	21,527	52,318
2.	Sindh	22	10,285	14,422
3.	Khyber Pukhtunkhwa	23	7,982	,7549
4.	Balochistan	11	2,173	2,946
5.	Azad Kashmir	06	530	663
6.	Gilgjt Balnstan	05	173	430
	Total	99	42,670	78,328

Figure 7.6 Province-wise prison population and authorized capacity.

(*Source:* National Academy for Prison Administration Report)

II. Discussion

1. *Crime Situation in Pakistan*

Crime data in Pakistan is collected and disseminated for public information by the National Police Bureau of Pakistan, which is based on First Information Reports registered at local police stations. The data at the national level is collected from four provinces and the capital, i.e., Islamabad. As per crime statistics in Pakistan, the assault rate[1] is 0.1, whereas the murder rate[2] is disturbingly high at 78.88%. Overall, the crime rate in Pakistan has increased to 76.84% in the last three years (2011–2104) (Ahmad & Ahmad, 2014). Apart from that, Pakistan is severely affected by the Golden Crescent illicit trafficking issue, which contributes to high opiate (0.8%) and cannabis (3.9%) consumption rates in Pakistan (Yaqub, 2013). Astonishingly, $4 billion per year is generated in Pakistan from drug trafficking's illicit market only (Archibald et al., 2013). The high concentration of substance abuse in Pakistan can also be attributed to increasing crime rates of various natures.

Aurangzeb (2012) in his study stated that the crime rate in Pakistan has increased multifold in the past few years, and it has negatively affected the sense of security among the citizens of Pakistan. Aurangzeb also discussed significant determinants of rising crime rates in, which are high unemployment rate, poor literacy level, and persistent issues with the justice system (lawlessness, double standards, and technologically handicapped institutions). The governance required to control the crime situation has not yet reached full potential in Pakistan. Such conditions are an outcome of political rather than research-oriented crime governance (Gillani, Rehman, & Gill, 2009). Further, governance in Pakistan is corroded by corruption, the criminal–politician nexus, and weak public administration mechanisms. Also, the reactive measures are inadequate to address the reported issues, leaving victims and their kin in stress and unsatisfied with the insufficient assistance coming from CJS machineries. This exposes the weak victim redress system in Pakistan.

The police culture in Pakistan is politicized, which extends to influence not only administration but policy formulations as well. This damages the victim support–oriented approach, and in response to this, recently the Chief Justice of Pakistan declared a new judicial policy that aims for effective victim assistance (Waheed, 2010). This step was taken in good spirit, but on implementation at national level, there's still a long way to go. Also, there's no specific empirical study on crime at the national level by any institution in Pakistan, which leaves a huge gap in knowledge for policy makers to formulate effective intervention and apprehension strategies. The only mass perception about Pakistan's justice system can be interpreted from a survey conducted by the Human Development Foundation, according to which 46.15% of the public holds a negative image of the justice system, whereas only 0.96% of respondents hold a good image of it (Waheed, 2010).

2. Issues in Police Administration

The Pakistan police have done little to establish gender parity in police recruitment. Historically, the first-ever women-only police station in Pakistan was founded by former Prime Minister Benazir Bhutto in 1994 in Rawalpindi (Jafar, 2005). Thereafter, the drive to further women's involvement in policing came to a halt when Bhutto's government came down in November 1996 (Waseem, 1996). Currently, efforts and initiatives are being taken by Pakistan's government to induct more women into policing.

Modernization of the police in Pakistan is currently a hot area under consideration. Experts in Pakistan hold a negative image of the police, calling them "poorly managed, ill-equipped, poorly trained, deeply politicized and chronically corrupt" (Abbas, 2012). The areas identified as being in need of upgradation are forensic labs, investigation facilities, and training. On a positive note, some of the constructive steps taken towards effective policing in Pakistan are as follows (CHRI, 2010):

- Gender crime cell (unit) is devoted to monitoring cases against women and assisting policy makers in implementing better inclusive strategies at the national level. Also, reinforcing gender sensitization and encouraging related research studies will be helpful in reducing crimes against women.
- To synergize all the efforts of police stations working across the provinces of Pakistan, the Police Record and Office Management Information System (PROMIS) is under development. This will link all the crime data of all the police stations in Pakistan so that they can take effective and coordinated steps.
- To create a database of fingerprints at the national level, the Automated Fingerprint Identification System (AFIS) was established.
- For better coordination among various police organizations through communication, a Nation-wide Integrated Trunk Radio System (NITRS) has been introduced.
- To emphasize evidence-based prosecution, the National Forensic Science Agency (NFSA) was approved on 31 March 2006 in Islamabad.
- With the rising menace of cybercrime, the National Response Center for Cyber Crime (NRCCC) was established to handle computer-generated/related crimes in an effective manner.

The low conviction rate in Pakistan (less than 10%) (International Crisis Group, 2005) is attributed to the poor conditions in which Pakistan's police are working. Abbas (2012) in his study mentioned the various dimensions of policing problems, such as delayed investigations due to widespread bribery, lack of proper training in evidence collection, unnecessary work burden (ex. superfluous VIP security), and political interference. In return of all this, there's also the issue of underpayment, lack of adequate housing facilities, and extremely slow promotions. The budgetary allocations are inadequate, whereby on an average Rs. 60,000 per police station per month is allocated, when in reality there's a minimum need of Rs. 150,000 per month (HRCP, 2013). This budgetary shortfall has direct implications on investigation processes, and more often than not, the major sufferers are the poor.

The Fraser Indian Police Commission of 1902–03 stressed the dire need to bring in police reforms, which were stated to produce incalculable benefits to the society. Later on, dozens of reports pertaining to police reforms in Pakistan were furnished before the government, and Fasihuddin (2010) identified some common factors indicated in all the reports, such as malpractices, outdated investigative methods, political interference, and lack of public support. Similarly, the report submitted by Abbas Khan (ex. IGP Punjab) gave some strong recommendations along the lines of the

Japanese Police Framework, which proposed replacing the old Police Act 1861 with the new one, establishing a Public Safety Commission and a strong National Police Agency. Fasihuddin (2010) in his study stressed democratization of the Pakistan police with respect to bridging a gap between officers (sensitive to policy matters) and middle-lower police personnel (engaged in eminent field issues). Also, the democratization of policing should be coupled with accountability and fair play to create a unified approach of the whole police department.

3. *Issues in Judiciary*

Historically, the governance of Pakistan went through numerous ups and downs. Since the first constitution of Pakistan (1956) passed, two institutions, the military and the judiciary, played vital roles in stabilizing governance and public order in Pakistan (Khalid, 2012). Under the autocratic rule of the governor general of Pakistan, many widescale social disorders shattered Pakistan, which was evened by the Superior Judiciary through courts' decisions and constitutional assemblies. There are some landmark judgements of the judiciary that helped: For e.g., Usif Patel's case (Shabbir, 2013), in which the consent of the governor general of Pakistan was made necessary for approval of every bill, and Asma Jilani's case (Iyer, 1973), in which imposition of martial law was made to support the government, not the public. In terms of positive impact on the society, the judiciary played an important role in shaping Pakistan's democracy as well by taking up the responsibility of being a guardian of human rights and mass liberties. The important functions of Pakistan bar councils are to appoint advocates to practice before the Supreme Court and to remove enrolled advocates on discretionary grounds, monitor and sanction punishments in cases of an advocate's misconduct, give guidelines for advocates practicing in courts of law, promote and support law reforms, set standards and procedures of legal education in the universities of Pakistan, provide affiliation of legal support and training institutions, manage the resources of Pakistan's Bar Council, and support associated matters as mentioned in Bar Council Act.

The Pakistan Bar Council is chaired by the Attorney General for Pakistan, ex-officio, and 20elected members voted on by the members of the Provincial Bar Councils of Balochistan (1), the North-West Frontier Province (2), the Punjab (11), and Sindh (6) (ref.). The 18th constitutional amendment has been a much-debated topic because it somehow limited the judiciary powers in areas of handing over a state's governance to the military. Unlike the 8th and 17th constitutional amendments, which favored a military regime, the 18th amendment shifted the ounce of discretionary powers in favor of political rulings, hence clearing issues pertaining to any forms of military takeover in the future (Rizvi, 2012). Hence, it can be concluded that contemporarily, the 18thconstitutional amendment gave more governing powers to the publicly elected bodies, prime minster, and judiciary in Pakistan.

In terms of further improvement needed in Pakistan's judiciary, Yasmeen and Ali (2011) stated in their study that there's a need to increase the number of judges (there are only 12 judges/million population in Pakistan), and the existing experience required for induction of civil judges should be increased from two years to five years. The pendency of cases in the Supreme Court is 20,147 (until 1 April, 2014), whereas in Lahore High Court, 180,000 cases are pending (Yasmeen & Ali, 2011). To work on it, the Supreme Court in 2014 gave direction to all judges in Pakistan to adopt a shorter format in deciding bail petitions and to avoid unnecessary augmentation of file work, which is the primary reason behind delayed justice (Hussain, 2011).

4. *Issues in Prisons*

Presently, there is only one national-level training institute for prison staff, which is the National Academy of Prison Administration (NAPA) in Pakistan. In prison, there's a shortage of manpower and budgetary allocations to meet bare-minimum standards in providing reformatory assistance to the prisoners (Abbas, 2011). The Human Rights Commission of Pakistan (2011) in its annual report made disturbing revelations about Pakistan's prisons, stating lack of modern security devices, poor medical treatment facilities, insufficient water treatment plants, and reforms needed in vocational and skill development programs running inside Pakistan's jails. On the administration level, prisoners are forced to board an overcrowded bus when going for hearings in courts. These are all consequences of cuts in budgetary allocations. Apart from that, children, adolescents, and hardened criminals are placed in common prisons, which fails the whole purpose of reformation, because in this way, prison becomes a nurturing ground for future criminals.

There is a gradual rise in the crime rate over the last few years (on an average 17.86% crime rise since 2007) (Gillani et al., 2009) in Pakistan but a low conviction rate (less than 10%) (Abbas, 2011) that leads to overcrowding of the prison population. As per the last recorded data, there are around 80,000 under-trial prisoners in Pakistan jails, and the number is ever increasing with the rising crime rate. The clearing up of cases is further delayed due to ineffective legal aid provisions in Pakistan. Similar to Bangladesh, the responsibility to provide legal aid to poor detainees falls on NGOs. This leaves the majority of poor inmates languishing in prisons waiting for their turn to be acknowledged by the Pakistan Bar Council's Free Legal Aid section, as per which only one case/year is taken up by the advocates free of charge. Moreover, the fee paid to advocates under the free legal aid scheme is Rs. 2000/month only. With this little incentive, the diligence required for the case is bound to dilute.

To reform the prison conditions, many crucial committees were formed during the last 50 years. These are:

Year	Committee	Chaired/Headed by
1950–1955	First Prison Reform Committee	Col. Salamat Ullah, Ex-IGP of UP
1956	East Pakistan Jail Reform Commission	S. Rehmat Ullah, CSP, Commissioner
1968–1970	West Pakistan Jail Reform Committee	Mr. Justice S. A. Mahmood
1972	Jail Reform Conference	Prison Reform Division, Govt. of Pakistan
1981–1983	Special Committee on Prison Administration	Mr. Muhammad Hayatullah Khan Sumbal, Home Secretary
1985	Prison Reform Committee	Mr. Mahmud Ali, Minister of State
1994	Jail Reform Committee	Maj. Gen. (Retd.) Nasirullah Khan Babar, Minister of Interior & Narcotics Control
1997	Jail Reform Committee	Mr. Justice M. Rafique Tarar, Pak Law Commission
1997	Pak Law Commission	Mr. Justice Sajjad Ali Shah, Chief Justice of Pakistan
2000	Task Force on Prison Reforms	Mr. Justice Abdul Qadir Sheikh
2005	National level meeting	Mr. Aftab Ahmed Khan Sherpao, former Minster for Interior

Figure 7.7 Important committees of prison reforms.

(*Source:* Prepared by the author)

A copy of the final report with the recommendations is forwarded to all the jails as per Provinces, National Reconstruction Bureau, Home Secretaries, and Prison Administration for implementation (Bhutta & Akbar, 2012). From judicial and legislative perspective, reforms should be brought in sentencing structure, as this will have direct implications on effectiveness of reformatory process of correctional institutions in Pakistan. The provision for seeking alternatives to imprisonment (sanctioning compensation, engaging in community service or rehabilitative treatments) for petty crimes/first-time offenders should be given based on the merits of the case. Also, the legal aid to NGOs assisting inmates (free legal aid) should be supplemented to curb undue detentions of under-trials.

One of the biggest lacunae lies in the lack of proper implementation of recommendations coming from special orders and meetings especially constituted to address prison issues. For example, it has been several years now since the Police Order (2002) gave recommendations in establishing a national-level coordination committee that is responsible for carrying out surprise inspections of prisons across the country, but so far, no such mechanism has been initiated. To maintain basic rights of prisoners, the Police Order (2002) also suggested constituting a public safety commission that will be accountable for adherence to international treaties and covenants in upholding human rights of the prisoners.

If the prisons are to become effective, it is important to give importance to the 'after-release' situation also. Pakistan prisons should revamp their own probation and parole systems. This requires adequate training facilities, technological upgrades, and good transport systems. Families and neighbors of prisoners should also be covered in the ambit of reformation and reintegration strategy, as the police, through healthy public relations, could motivate society in accomplishing successful reintegration of the released offender.

Khan (2010), in a detailed description of prisons in Pakistan, gave some operational suggestions that include provisions for expansion of correctional institutions along with recruiting additional manpower, carrying out frequent jail inspections by the judiciary and furnishing on-the-spot instructions, providing psychological counseling to all the inmates, encouraging work of excellence by prison staff via incentives/awards/proper recognition, and carrying out an in-depth study of prisons in Pakistan for effective reformation processes.

Conclusion

After 1947, the formation of Pakistan shaped a diverse culture with various ethnicities, socio-economic backgrounds, and languages. The complainants from diverse cultures are seeking justice from three different and simultaneously working legal systems in Pakistan, which are statute laws, Shariah laws, and tribal laws. The setup of a parallel legal system in Pakistan is as follows:

In Pakistan, the majority of the population residing in rural areas (62%) (World Bank Report, 2014) resorts to informal modes of legal systems in which the tribal laws are implemented through Jirga courts. In the case of formal laws, the statute laws are implemented through Civil Court and Lower/High/Supreme Court, and Islamic Shariah laws are implemented through Federal Shariah Court. Both forms of above-mentioned formal laws are enforced through state police departments.

The criminal justice system of Pakistan is contemporarily enduring the burden of undue delays in justice (Hussain, 2011). The delay in justice delivery mechanisms is further manifested into a large chunk of the prison population (nearly two-thirds) being under-trial prisoners. Pakistan's justice system needs to incorporate the recent amendment in legislation for granting bails easily and use it consistently. Otherwise, such displays of unusual delays in justice delivery mechanisms and subsequent languishing of under-trials creates negative public perception. Apart from that, the socio-economic health of Pakistan is also affected due to mass negative perception based on adverse effects on foreign relations and investment prospects.

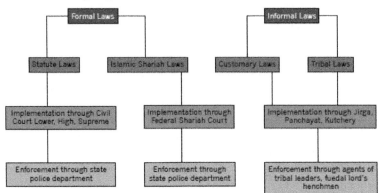

Figure 7.8 Parallel legal systems in Pakistan.
(*Source:* Tahira Khan, 2006)

Apart from fallacies of the criminal justice system of Pakistan, the public has also developed resentment towards the way the military is carrying out its justice system. Scores of people are detained on grounds of being held as suspects in terrorism, mostly from political backgrounds. The practice of manhandling by the Pakistan military is rampant in Balochistan, Khyber Pakhtunkhwa (KPK), and the Federally Administered Tribal Areas (FATA) (Nawaz, 2009). There has to be a mechanism to segregate habitual delinquent youths for rehabilitation purposes. For this, the Anti-Terrorism Act (ATA) 1997 should be amended to separately try cases of juveniles in juvenile courts.

Contemporarily, all the components of the criminal justice system in Pakistan are underperforming. Since all are interlinked and interdependent, maladjustment of one leads to malfunctioning of the rest. The lack of manpower and resources in the police, the judiciary, and prisons further weakens the effectiveness of crime governance in Pakistan. There's an emergent need for overhauling all systems so as to match up with rising and technologically advanced forms of crimes in recent times. The innovative, economical, and feasible strategies such as community policing should be practiced with a research-driven approach. For example, each of the four provinces should be researched to develop a comprehensive model depicting their various demographic features. Also, sincere efforts need to be put in by the law enforcement to improve public perception and amplify public involvement. After implementation, the strategies should be stringently monitored and followed up with feedback. This will provide sufficient room for further refinement. Also, such practices will create an important record of data that will be useful in future endeavors.

The grim picture of Pakistan's criminal justice system can be revived on two levels: first, to implement the recommendations of committees constituted for reforms and second, to synergize the efforts of all the stakeholders of the criminal justice system in Pakistan. On a positive note, some provinces of Pakistan have well-structured police and prison systems that support access to justice and potential for innovation.

There is a significant dearth of empirical literature in criminology and victimological areas in Pakistan. With the exceptional efforts of Fasihuddin, a high-level police officer in Pakistan, criminology is growing in Pakistan (Fasihuddin, & Pakistan Society of Criminology, 2008; Fasihuddin, 2013). With his founding of the Pakistan Society of Criminology (http://pscriminology.com) and *Pakistan Journal of Criminology* (www.pjcriminology.com), the literature on Pakistan's criminology is seeing great heights (Fasihuddin, 2013).

Notes

1 Number of recorded assaults by police per 1,000,000 population.
2 Number of record intentional homicide per 1,000,000 population.

References

Abbas, H. (2011). *Reforming Pakistan's Police and Law enforcement infrastructure.* Washington, DC: US Institute of Peace.

Abbas, H. (2012). *Stabilizing Pakistan through police reform.* Park Avenue, NY: Asia Society Report by the Independent Commission on Pakistan Police Reform.

Ahmad, A., Ali, S., & Ahmad, N. (2014). Crime and economic growth in developing countries: Evidence from Pakistan. *Journal of Basic and Applied Scientific Research, 4*(4), 31–41.

Archibald, C. P., Shaw, S.Y., Emmanuel, F., Otho, S., Reza, T., Altaf, A., & Blanchard, J. F. (2013). Geographical and temporal variation of injection drug users in Pakistan. *Sexually Transmitted Infections, 89*(Suppl2), ii18–ii28.

Aurangzeb. (2012). Determinants of crime in Pakistan. *Universal Journal of Management and Social Sciences, 2*(9).

Authoritarianism and Political Party Reform in Pakistan. (2005, September 28). *International crisis group Asia reports,* 102.

Azeem, H. M. (2013). *Criminal justice system in Pakistan.* Retrieved from http://hmazeem.blogspot.in/2013/02/criminaljusticesysteminpakistan.html.

Barakatullah. (2010). Judicial system of Pakistan. *Pakistan Journal of Criminology, 2*(3), 15–34.

Bhutta, M. H., & Akbar, M. S. (2012). Situation of prisons in India and Pakistan: Shared legacy, same challenges. *South Asian Studies, 27*(1), 171.

Blue, R., & Hoffman, R. (2008). *Pakistan Rule of Law Assessment—Final report.* Washington, DC: United States Agency for International Development.

Commonwealth Human Rights Initiative (CHRI). (2010). *Police organizations in Pakistan.* Retrieved from www.humanrightsinitiative.org/publications/police/police_organisations_in_pakistan.pdf.

Fasihuddin. (2010). Police and Policing in Pakistan. *Pakistan Journal of Criminology, 2*(3), 131–145.

Fasihuddin. (2013). Criminology and criminal justice system in Pakistan. In J. Liu, B. Hebenton, & S. Jou (Eds.), *Handbook of Asian criminology* (pp. 247–281). New York: Springer.

Fasihuddin, & Pakistan Society of Criminology. (2008). *Expanding criminology to Pakistan: A proposal for MSc criminology and an Institute of Criminology, research & criminal Justice in Pakistan.* Peshawar: Pakistan Society of Criminology.

Gillani, S.Y. M., Rehman, H. U., & Gill, A. R. (2009). Unemployment, poverty, inflation and crime nexus: Cointegration and causality analysis of Pakistan. *Pakistan Economic and Social Review,* 79–98.

Human Rights Commission of Pakistan (HRCP). (2013). *State of Human Rights.* Retrieved from www.hrcp-web.org/hrcpweb/report14/AR2013.pdf

Hussain, F. (2011). *The judicial system of Pakistan* (pp. 7–15). Pakistan: Supreme Court of Pakistan.

Iyer, T. K. K. (1973). Constitutional law in Pakistan: Kelsen in the courts. *The American Journal of Comparative Law,* 759–771.

Jafar, A. (2005). Women, Islam, and the state in Pakistan. *Gender Issues, 22*(1), 35–55.

Johnson, T., & Vriens, L. (2013). *Islam: governing under Sharia.* Washington, DC: Council on Foreign Relations.

Khalid, I. (2012). Role of judiciary in the evolvement of democracy in Pakistan. *Journal of Political Studies, 19*(2), 125.

Khan, M. M. (2010). The prison system in Pakistan. *Pakistan Journal of Criminology, 2*(3), 35–50.

Khan, T. S. (2006). *Beyond honour: A historical materialist explanation of honour related violence.* Oxford: Oxford University Press.

Lau, M. (1973). Sharia and national law in Pakistan. *Sharia Incorporated,* p. 373.

Lippman, M. R., McConville, S., & Yerushalmi, M. (1988). *Islamic criminal law and procedure: An introduction* (pp. 107–08). New York: Praeger.

Mirza, M. (2010). Role and responsibility of the public prosecution: a case study of Khyber Pakhtunkhwa Province. *Pakistan Journal of Criminology, 2*(3), 1–13.

Nawaz, S. (2009). *FATA—A most dangerous place: Meeting the challenge of militancy and terror in the federally administered tribal areas of Pakistan.* Washington, DC: Center for Strategic & International Studies.

Raja, S. A. (2003). Islamisation of Laws in Pakistan. *South Asian Journal, 1*(2), 94–109.

Rehman, J. (2007). The Sharia, Islamic family laws and international human rights law: Examining the theory and practice of Polygamy and Talaq. *International Journal of Law, Policy and the Family, 21*(1), 108–127.

Reichel, P. L. (2002). *Comparative criminal justice systems: A topical approach.* Upper Saddle River, NJ: Prentice Hall.

Rizvi, H. A. (2012, January 31). *Competition for power.* Retrieved from www.pakistantoday.com.pk/2012/01/31/comment/columns/competition-for-power/

Shabbir, S. S. (2013). *Judicial activism shaping the future of Pakistan.* SSRN 2209067. DOI: 10.2139/ssrn.2209067. Retrieved from https://papers.ssrn.com/sol3/papers.cfm?abstract_id=2209067.

Suddle, M. S. (2003). Reforming Pakistan Police: An overview. In UNAFEI (Ed.), Resource material series no. 60 (pp. 94–104). UNAFEI: Fuchu, Tokyo. Retrieved from https://www.unafei.or.jp/publications/pdf/RS_No60/No60_12VE_Suddle.pdf.

Taizi, S. (2007). *Jirga system in tribal life.* Retrieved from www.tribalanalysiscenter.com/PDFTAC/Jirga%20System%20in%20Tribal%20Life.pdf

Waheed, M. A. (2010). Victims of crime in Pakistan. *Resource materials series*, 81 (pp. 138–148). Japan: UNAFEI. Retrieved from www.unafei.or.jp/english/pdf/RS_No81/No81_00All.pdf.

Waseem, M. (1996). Ethnic conflict in Pakistan: The case of MQM. *The Pakistan Development Review*, 617–629.

Wasim, A. (2008). *Overview of criminal justice system in Pakistan.* Retrieved from https://mawasim.wordpress.com/2008/10/03/overviewofcriminaljusticesystem.

Yasmeen, S., & Ali, W. (2011). Role and functions of judicial system in Pakistan. *Science*, *30*(3).

Yaqub, F. (2013). Pakistan's drug problem. *The Lancet*, *381*(9884), 2153–2154.

8

SRI LANKA

Criminal Justice System and Rule of Law

Jeeva Niriella

Introduction

Ever since the beginning of human civilization, crime has been an unsolved problem. There is hardly a society which is not struggling with the problem of crime, and no one can escape the subject of crime in day-to-day life. Sri Lanka is not an exemption to this phenomenon. The media reveals many stories and information of crimes daily, and some of us might have encountered crimes more directly as victims. This may be one of the reasons that crime is one of the top concern subjects in Sri Lanka. Prevention of crimes, protection of the people from crimes and imposition of appropriate degree of punishment on the offenders are some of the major issues relating to the crime problem in Sri Lanka. The increase of crime rate including its brutality and rise of recidivism symbolize the dilemma faced by the main agencies (police, courts and correctional institutions) of the criminal justice system of the country today. These state institutions have the responsibility to apprehend, adjudicate, punish and correct the wrongdoers to achieve the safety of the people and a peaceful society. This could be possible by extending their functions to reduce the level of crime commissions, protect the rights of the parties in a criminal matter, ensuring the fair and speedy disposal of the criminal cases, improve the process of the rehabilitation of both offender and victim and reintegrating them into the society appropriately. However, there is a concern whether the main agencies of the criminal justice system of Sri Lanka adhere to the principles of rule of law in carrying out their tasks to achieve the afore-mentioned goals. This chapter intends to discuss the issues of criminal justice system by evaluating the provisions of the constitution and other relevant statutes relating to the functions of the said main agencies in Sri Lanka.

Criminal Justice System in Sri Lanka

Since criminal law is part of the criminal justice system, one may correctly claim that there is a strong relationship between an effective criminal justice system and the concept of rule of law. Therefore, the criminal justice system should constitute the unbiased mechanism to redress the grievances and bring action against perpetrators who committed crimes (or in other words who committed offences against the society) in order to uphold the notion of rule of law. Therefore, an effective criminal justice system is capable of investigating and adjudicating criminal offences efficiently, impartially and without improper interventions while ensuring the rights of the suspects and victims are being protected and also capable in reducing the crime rate, especially the recidivism rate.

In this context, the following discussion focuses on the rights guaranteed by the constitution of Sri Lanka (the supreme law of the country) and procedural laws relating to controlling the actions of the law enforcement agencies—the police—in order to protect the rights of the parties involved in a criminal matter, especially the suspect/accused.

1. Police and Law Enforcement[1]

In the event of a crime, the police are the agency that primarily plays the role in the criminal justice process whose function is first to arrest and detain the suspect, interrogate the relevant people during the investigative process, search the premises and then form the charges and finally lead the evidence in the trial. In this process, on one hand the police need freedom to enforce the law as they see fit, and on the other hand the rights of the citizens recognized by the constitution should not be violated when they use their power.

Police officers are the gatekeepers of the criminal justice process. They use their power of arrest to initiate the justice process. Generally speaking, a person will be said to be detained when a state official restrains the person's liberty including cases where the person reasonably perceives that he is not free to come and go as he pleases. Being free from arbitrary arrest is one of the fundamental rights guaranteed by the constitution of Sri Lanka.[2]

Chapter IV of the Code of Criminal Procedure Act No. 15 of 1979 governs the law relating to arrest and detention of the suspect and search the premises. According to section 23(1) of the Code of Criminal Procedure Act, making an arrest means that the police officer should not actually touch or confine the body of the suspect unless there is a submission to the custody by word or action by the police officer, and detain means keeping the person in police custody. However, today, arrest and detention do not necessarily mean confinement in a police station, but stopping a person in any place and interrogating him without any reasonable reasons or ground also may amount to an arrest and detention, which is arbitrary, and it leads to violation of the fundamental right guaranteed by section 13(1) of the constitution. For instance, *Sirisena v Perera* (1991) Sri Lanka Law Report (SLR) 97; *Wickramabandu v Herath* (1980) 2 SLR 348; *Piyasiri v Fernando* (1981) 1 SLR 173; *Namasivayagam v Gunawardae* (1989) 1 SLR 396; *Rajapakse v Kudahetti* (1992) 2 SLR 223 and more importantly *Somawathie v Weerasinghe* and *Lundstron v Herath*. In these cases it was further emphasized by the court that the protection of Article 13 (1) of the constitution is not confined only to a person who is arrested on suspicion of having committed or being concerned with an offence.

It is important to note here that the provisions of the Code of Criminal Procedure Act are not applicable in case of preventive detention. Preventive detention is where detaining a person is considered a threat to the state. When a state has declared any emergency situation under section 2 of the Public Security Ordinance No. 25 of 1947, section 5 of the same ordinance empowers the president to make regulations that are essential to ensure the public security. Section 5(2)(a) provides that the regulations made under section 5(2) may authorize the preventive detention of persons. Therefore, in such situations, any person can be detained for preventive purpose. Emergency Regulation No. 17 under Public Security Ordinance stipulates the legal permission for (preventive) detention of a person on the order of the Secretary of Defence with a view of preventing him from acting in any manner prejudicial to national security or to the maintenance of public order. Emergency Regulations No. 18 and 19 refer to the arrest of a person relating to offences prescribed in the Emergency Regulations. According to the Emergency Regulations 2005[3] preventive detention without trial on security grounds for up to one year is authorized. The regulation excludes judicial review[4] and declares all such detentions are lawful.[5] In addition to the Emergency Regulations, the Prevention of Terrorism Act No. 48 of 1979 also recognizes validity of the preventive detention of a person. According to the act, if a person who commits any of the offences mentioned in section 2 of the act or if the Minister of Defence in the country has reasons to believe or suspect that any person is connected with or concerned in any unlawful activity under this act, the minister may order such person to be detained.[6] However, a reasonable question arises as to whether this type of unlimited or unconstrained law can be enacted by the legislature, and this type of law violates the rights of the people which are recognized under rule of law.[7]

The right to be promptly informed of the reasons for arrest[8] is one of the rights guaranteed by the constitution. It protects individual privacy against certain types of arbitrary inferences of the law enforcement agencies. Nevertheless, it does not provide a general/unlimited constitutional right to privacy for people that obstructs the main objectives of the criminal justice. The Code of Criminal Procedure Act sets out its provision as to protect the above-said right. Section 23(1) stipulates that the person who is subjected to arrest should be informed of the reasons for such arresting. However, the permission given to the law enforcement officers by section 23(2) of the Code to use their force reasonably and appropriately when the accused/suspect forcibly resists the endeavor to arrest him or attempt to evade the arrest leads to violation of the guaranteed right. The phrase 'reasonably and necessary to affect the arrest' in the section is very much subjective to the circumstances. It legitimizes abuse of power.

The right to be brought promptly before a judge is another right guaranteed by the constitution of Sri Lanka.[9] The Criminal Procedure Code sets out some provisions with regard to producing the suspect without any delay. According to section 37 of the Criminal Procedure Code, a person who is arrested under suspicion for any offence should not be detained for more than 24 hours. However, according to section 115 in the Code, a Magistrate may extend the detention period for 15 days, considering the request made by the police officers, if there is a necessity of further investigation. This detention period was extended up to 48 hours in the case of cognizable offences with the amendment No. 2 to the Code in 2013.[10] The new provision has made a clear distinction between some cognizable offences and non-cognizable offences with regard to producing the suspect before the court. Since the new amendment is only applicable to the offences listed in the amendment, it also creates a difference between the cognizable offences listed in the new amendment and the offences which are not listed in the amendment.

Article 13 of the constitution[11] guarantees certain important fundamental rights for the accused: freedom from arbitrary arrest,[12] detention,[13] punishment and prohibition of retroactive penal legislation. Article 13(5) stipulates that every person shall be presumed innocent until he is proven guilty and, further, it provides that the burden of proving of the particular facts may, by law, be placed on an accused person. Article 11 states that no person shall be subjected to torture or to cruel, inhumane or degrading treatment or punishment. These articles could be interpreted as meaning that the law enforcement authorities cannot use any force, including physical or psychological, against the suspect/accused to get them to confess or give information relating to the particular crime. The rights intended to be preserved by the above-said articles are directly related to police functions of obtaining statements (interrogation) from the suspect/accused in a criminal matter.

Evidence Ordinance No. 14 of 1883 includes provisions relating to the admissibility of the statements made by the suspect or accused. It states that a confession[14] must be made voluntarily by the suspect if it is to be admissible as evidence in a criminal trial. In *Cooray* (1926) 28 NLR (New Law Reports) 74; *Kalubanda* (1912) 15 NLR 422; *Ukkubanda* (1923) 24 NLR 372; *Weerakkone v Ranhamy* (1926) 27 NLR 267; *Nambiar v Fernando* (1925) 27 NLR 404; and *Anandagoda* (1960) 62 NLR 24, the court emphasized that confessions means an admission made by the suspect or accused suggesting the inference of commission of the offence by him. Confession extracts from the suspect through coercion, trickery or promise[15] of leniency are inadmissible due to lack of the trustworthiness of such statements. In *Weerasamy* (1941) 43 NLR 152, the court held that the Crown should establish the relevancy of confession by leading evidence to show that it was made voluntarily. In *Amaris Appoo* 1 NLR 209; *Martin Singho* (1964) 66 NLR 391; *Kalimuttu* (1966) 69 NLR 349; and *Gunaseela Theoro* (1968) 73 NLR 154, the court emphasized that a confession extracted from the suspect under any influence or promise or by making any threat is inadmissible at the criminal trial. The rule of voluntariness (the exclusionary rule) applies to confession obtained at any time, whether the suspect is in police custody[16] or not.[17] However, a confession is admissible evidence against the accused if it comes under the sphere of Section 27[18] of the Evidence Ordinance or if the statement is made before a judicial officer, even if the suspect is in police custody.[19] *Piyadasa* (1967) 72 NLR 434 and *Sugathapala* (1967) 69 NLR 457 are classic examples.

The procedural law relating to obtaining statements from the suspect is governed by sections 110 and 111 of the Code of Criminal Procedure Act No.15 of 1979. According to section 111, a police officer should not offer or make any inducement, threat or promise to any person charged with an offence to induce such a person to make any statement with reference to the charge against the person. However, this provision does not prevent the suspect from making any statement of his/her own free will.[20]

According to section 110(1) and (2) of the Code of Criminal Procedure Act No. 15 of 1979, the police officer who is making an investigation may ask questions of any person regarding the crime. According to section 110(2) of the Code Criminal Procedure Act, any person supposed to be acquainted with the facts and circumstances of the case should answer the question other than questions which would have a tendency to expose them to criminal charges or to a penalty of forfeit. Therefore, the suspect is also bound to answer the question without remaining silent.[21] Some suspects are being ill-treated/tortured by the police officers during the police investigation in order to obtain confessions or information relating to the alleged offence. There are several instances where the suspects are being tortured in custodial interrogation. Some of them are as follows: the *Angulana* dual murder case, which is an unreported case where the two suspects were badly assaulted by the police officers to make them confess. *Samarasinghe Sudath Pushpakumara* is another case[22] where the suspect was arrested for the offence of robbery and forced to make a confession by admitting the commission of the offence of robbery with the notorious thief. In *Mulankandage Lasantha Jagath Kumara*,[23] the suspect was tortured while he was in the police custody and forced to make a confession. In the *Ranjith Sumangala*[24] case, the suspect was arrested and detained for several days, and police obtained a confession forcefully. The aforementioned cases are a few illustrations to prove that there is doubt in the applicability of the principles of rule of law in relation to custodial interrogation.

2. The Judicial Process

When the proceedings are instituted or in other words charges are made against the accused person after completing the police investigation, the court, which is the next agency of the criminal justice system, comes into play its role: conducting the trial to determine the culpability of the accused. In Sri Lanka, criminal offences are basically heard either summarily (by serving a charge sheet made by the police) in the Magistrate Court or by serving an indictment given by the Attorney-General, which is heard in the High Court. High Court trials can be carried out with a jury or with a trial at bar where three High Court judges are appointed by the Chief Justice to conduct the trial. In addition to these trials, there is a special circumstance where the Magistrate is allowed to conduct the preliminary inquiry with regard to the non-summary offences.

This particular part of the discussion mainly focuses on the rights guaranteed by the constitution to the accused during the period of the trial and how the Code of Criminal Procedure Act sets out legal provisions to protect the rights ensured by the constitution. Most of the procedural rights provided to an accused in the trial process are found in the Articles 11, 12 and 13(3), (4) and (5) of the constitution. Article 12 guarantees equal protection before the law without any discrimination based on race, religion, language, caste, sex, political opinion and place of birth etc. Therefore, any person who has violated the criminal law in the country should be tried according to the law of criminal procedure without any discrimination. In all criminal prosecutions, the accused shall enjoy the right to a fair trial by a competent court.[25] Article 13(3) covers a wide range of rights that the accused can enjoy in the criminal justice process, especially during the trial process. It ensures several rights such as right to be tried within a reasonable time without any undue delay, right to public trial, right against self-incrimination and right to be silent, right to understand the proceedings/right to information, right to participate in the trial and to be represented by an attorney at law/right to counsel, right to confront opposing witnesses, right to defend, right not to be convicted without a guilty mind, right to appeal, right not to be punished more than once for the same offence (right against double jeopardy) and right to be presumed innocent etc.

As far as the right to be tried within a reasonable time is concerned, in Sri Lanka, though there is no explicit constitutional provision which guarantees this right, section 163 of the Code of Criminal Procedure Act says: A preliminary inquiry should be concluded within a month. However, if there are any reasonable reasons, the Magistrate has the power to record and prolong the inquiry beyond the period of one month. One may state here that the purpose of this section is to minimize: (i) the time period the accused spends in pre-trial custody under restrictive bail conditions, (ii) mental stress, (iii) pre-trial anxiety of the accused and (iv) possible deterioration of evidence during the pre-trial period. However, there is no other provision to guarantee the above-said right other than section 163. Therefore, this is criticized by many accused and their counsels according to the axiom "Long delay and Never tried," which is very relevant to the criminal trials of Sri Lanka today.

With regard to the right to public trial, section 136 states that the proceedings in the Magistrate's Court maybe constituted of a public servant (police officer or any other public officer) or the victim of criminal offence, and in the High Court, the Attorney-General or State Counsel may institute the proceedings (section 191(i) of the Code of Criminal Procedure Act). These sections reveal that criminal trials should be held in the courts publicly.

The right to silence is also accepted by the provisions set out in the Criminal Procedure Act. According to 146 of this Code, the accused can remain silent without answering to the Magistrate.[26] However, it is important to note here that if the accused keeps remaining silent at the trial, it is unfavourable to him, as he appears guilty. Participation at the trial by him or with an attorney is respected in both summary and non-summary trials.[27]

Right to confront the witnesses is also recognized in the preliminary inquiry and in other trials. Section 148(2) states that the accused may pose questions to each witness produced against him. According to section 148(3), this right is guaranteed in the circumstances where the accused is not represented by an attorney. Section 199(5) says the accused is permitted to cross-examine all witnesses called for prosecution. This right is a necessary component of a fair trial.

Right to defence is another important legal right preserved by the constitution through the procedural laws in the country. According to sections 150 and 151 of the Code of Criminal Procedure Act, the accused is given the opportunity to defend him-/herself at the preliminary inquiry. The same right is well established in the High Court as a result of section 201(1) of this Code. Section 260 also declares that every person accused before any criminal court may by right be defended by an attorney.[28]

The Code of Criminal Procedure Act sets out some provisions to protect the right to understand the proceedings or right to information about the charges, evidence and statements made against the accused. According to section 146, a Magistrate conducting a preliminary inquiry should read to the accused the charge or charges in respect of which the inquiry is being held,[29] and he is entitled to obtain a (certified) copy of the evidence and statements given by the others to the police.[30] With regard to summary offences, section 182(1) states that when the accused is brought or appears before the court, the Magistrate should inform the charges made against the accused, and section 182(2) stipulates that the Magistrate should ask the accused to present reasons as to why he should not be convicted. According to section 195(b) and (c), the High Court Judge should serve a copy of the indictment and its annexes and inform the accused of the date of trial and also should be informed to select a jury if necessary at the beginning of the High Court trials.[31]

However, the (undue) delay of trial in many cases has made a serious doubt of the protection of the fair trial in Sri Lanka, which leads to less faith in the justice process in the country. The right not to be tried twice for the same criminal offence is also appreciated by the provisions in the Code of Criminal Procedure Act[32] and the Judicature Act (under the theory of double jeopardy). The objective of this particular provision is that if any person has been once tried by a competent court for a criminal offence and has been convicted/acquitted of such an offense, they should not be liable to be tried for the same criminal offence again.

At the post-trial stage of the criminal proceedings, perhaps the most important right for someone who has been found guilty of offense is the right to appeal against conviction. In Sri Lanka, a person convicted of a criminal offence can appeal against the conviction, the punishment imposed upon conviction or both.[33] An appeal is not a re-hearing of the trial, and only certain aspects of the trial decision may be appealed. Generally, this is limited to situations where the trial judge has made an error in application of the law, but findings of fact maybe addressed on appeal, though not for the purpose of re-trying the case. In particular, an accused has a right to appeal on the basis that the finding of guilt was unreasonable in the circumstances or cannot be supported by the evidence.

The established basic principle of the criminal law is that no person can be found guilty without proving *actus reus* and *mens rea*, which especially means that no person can be punished without proving the guilty mind of that person. The Penal Code and the special statutes which prescribe the criminal offences deal with the substantive law relating to this principle. The procedural laws relating to this particular principle can be found in the Evidence Ordinance and the Code of Criminal Procedure Act too.

The presumption of innocence lies at the heart of the criminal law and protects the fundamental liberty and human dignity of any person accused of a criminal offence. The fact that the state must prove the guilt of an accused beyond a reasonable doubt flows from the presumption of innocence in Article 13(5) of the constitution of Sri Lanka.[34]

Protection against cruel, inhumane or degrading treatment or punishment is well guaranteed in the constitution of Sri Lanka.[35] In Sri Lanka, the death penalty is a legally permissible mode of punishment.[36] According to the nature of the execution, one may say that the death penalty is a cruel and inhuman punishment. Then a question arises whether the imposition of capital punishment violates the provision of the constitution. In accordance with Article 16(1) of the constitution, all existing written laws and unwritten laws should be valid and operative, notwithstanding any inconsistency with the presiding provisions of the Chapter III (fundamental rights chapter) of the constitution, and imposing any form of punishment recognized by prevailing written law does not make any contravention of the provisions of Chapter III.[37] Therefore, imposing the death penalty is not unconstitutional or in violation of Article 11 of the constitution.

According to Article 13(6), no person should be held guilty of an offense on account of any act or illegal omission which did not, at the time of act or omission, constitute such an offense, an no penalty shall be imposed for any offense more severe than the penalty in force at the time such offense was committed. It further states nothing in this article has prejudiced the trial and punishment of any person for any act or illegal omission which at the time when it was committed was criminal according to the general principles of law recognized by the community of nations. Therefore, upon finding an accused guilty or a plea of guilty by the accused person, the court may impose a punishment on him/her. In Sri Lanka, the criminal law generally specifies the maximum sentences for the offences and a very few minimum sentences as mandatory, leaving a great deal of discretion in the hands of the trial judge in relation to the imposition of the sentence. Therefore, in Sri Lanka, the sentencing disparity is a frequent problem which is found in criminal cases where the proportionality between the punishment imposed and the offense committed cannot be found. Therefore, one may argue that sentencing disparities in similar cases may be considered as cruel punishment for some offenders.

3. Institutional Corrections—Prisons

Prison[38] is one of the important correctional institutions which is involved in the criminal justice process. The offenders who are sentenced by imprisonment are sent to this particular institution for rehabilitation. The most important task or the main objective of the prison institution is to rehabilitate the prisoner, thereby helping him/her to understand what was wrong with his/her behavior and helping him/her to become a productive citizen in the future after release from prison.

The prison system was established in Sri Lanka under the Prison Ordinance in 1877.[39] Every year, the direct admission of un-convicted prisoners is more than the number of convicted prisoners. In the year 2013, the percentage of the un-convicted prisoners was 77.4% and the convicted prisoners' percentage 22.6%.[40] Ratio of convicted to un-convicted prisoners in the year 2013 was 1:3. According to the information issued from the Department of Prisons, direct admissions of both convicted and remands prisoners have considerably increased during the last decade. Although the number of admissions of prisoners has increased, the capacity of the prison system has not extended in shape at the same rate. The prisons are overcrowded and lead to violation of certain rights of the inmates. Although prisoners do not have full constitutional rights like other free people, they are also protected by the constitution's prohibition of cruel and unusual punishment. This protection requires that prisoners be afforded a minimum standard of living. Prisoners also retain some other constitutional rights such as equal protection before the law of those who should be protected against unequal treatment on the basis of race, sex and religion etc.

The following prison regulations respect Article 11 of the constitution:

- Regulation 248, which says before the execution of the punishment, the medical report of the offender should be taken into consideration.
- Regulation 249 and 252(e), which say iron shackles and iron equipment cannot be used to punish any prisoner in the prison.

Article 4(d) of the constitution says that the fundamental rights which the constitution declared and recognized shall be respected and secured by all the organs of the government and should not be abridged, restricted or denied. Prison regulation 132, while respecting the above-said Article, states the main responsibility of the prison officers is to treat the prisoners humanely and kindly without any exception.

Under the directive principles of state policy and fundamental duties, the Parliament, the president and the Cabinet of Ministers should enact the laws in order to establish a just and free society. Therefore, all the Public Officers should take the necessary steps to provide an adequate standard of living for all the people in the country.[41] Prison regulation 13 says that the Superintendent of the prison should ensure the daily needs of the inmates are provided adequately. Regulation 15 says the superintendent should visit the prison hospital frequently, and according to regulation 22, he is responsible to provide medicine and other required needs to the sick prisoners according to the recommendations given by the prison doctor. Regulation 222 says all prisoners are entitled to nutritious meals, and according to regulation 50 they are entitled to clean drinking water and an adequate quantity of water for their daily basic needs. Segregation based on sex is one of the rights of the inmates in Sri Lanka. According to section 77 of the Prison Ordinance, male inmates should be kept separate from female inmates.

Although Sri Lanka has the above-said constitutional provisions and prison rules and regulations to protect the rights of the prisoners, many incidents have taken place in the prisons where the above-said rights were violated.[42]

Conclusion

The above discussion reveals the relationship between the concept of rule of law and the criminal justice system. It also discloses how Sri Lankan law, including the constitution and the other penal laws, especially laws of criminal procedure, provide the provisions to adopt the principles of the rule of law in the criminal justice system. However, violations of the rights of the suspects in the investigation process, rights of the accused in the trial and post-trial process and the rights of the inmates in correctional institutions (prisons) tell us the principles of rule of law are limited only to the statute books. It may not be the case with Sri Lanka, and this is the common phenomenon of many criminal justice systems in the world.

Notes

1 The appointment, promotion, transfers, disciplinary control and dismissals of police officers are not discussed in this chapter.
2 Article 13(1) of the Constitution stipulates that no one should be arrested except according to the procedure established by law, and the arrested person must be informed of the reasons for his arrest, and Article 13(2) of the Constitution states that every person held in custody, detained or otherwise deprived of personal liberty shall be brought before the judge of the nearest competent court according to procedure established by law and shall not be further held in custody, detained or deprived of personal liberty except upon and in terms of the order of such judge made in accordance with procedure established by law. Article 13(4) says that no person shall be punished with death or imprisonment except by order of a competent court, made in accordance with procedure established by law. The arrest, holding in custody, detention or other deprivation of personal liberty of a person, pending investigation or trial, shall not constitute punishment.
3 Emergency Regulation 19. See further, Regulation 1.
4 Emergency Regulation 19(10). See further, section 8 of Public security Ordinance: No emergency regulation and no order, rule or direction made or given there under shall be called in question in any court. *Visualingam* v *Liyange* (1984) 2SLR 123; *Adirisuriya* v *Navaratnam* (1985) 1 SLR 100.
5 Emergency Regulation No. 19(3).
6 Section 9(1).
7 See *Hidramani v Ratnawale* 75 NLR 67; *Gunasekera v Ratnavale* 76 MLR 316.
8 Article 13(1) of the Constitution stipulates that no one should be arrested except according to the procedure established by law, and the arrested person must be informed of the reasons for his arrest.
9 Article 13(2) of the Constitution says that every person held in custody, detained or otherwise deprived of personal liberty shall be brought before the judge of the nearest competent court according to procedure established by law and shall not be further held in custody, detained or deprived of personal liberty except upon and in terms of the order of such judge made in accordance with procedure established by law.
10 Section 2 of the Code of Criminal Procedure (Special Provisions) Act, No. 2 of 2013.
11 The Constitution of the Democratic Socialist Republic of Sri Lanka enacted in 1979.
12 Article 13(1) says that no person shall be arrested except according to procedure established by law. Any person arrested shall be informed of the reason for his arrest.
13 Article 13(2) says that every person held in custody, detained or otherwise deprived of personal liberty shall be brought before the judge of the nearest competent court according to procedure established by law and shall not be further held in custody, detained or deprived of personal liberty except upon and in terms of the order of such judge made in accordance with procedure established by law.
14 Section 17(2) of the Evidence Ordinance says that 'A confession is an admission made at any time by a person accused of an offence stating or suggesting the inference that he committed that offence.'
15 Section 24 of the Evidence Ordinance says that

> 'A confession made by an accused person is irrelevant in a criminal proceeding if the making of the confession appears to the court to have been caused by any inducement, threat, or promise having reference to the charge against the accused person, proceeding from a person in authority, or proceeding from another person in the presence of a person in authority and with his sanction, and which inducement

threat, or promise is sufficient in the opinion of the court to give the accused person grounds, which would appear to him reasonable, for supposing that by making it he would gain any advantage or avoid any evil of a temporal nature in reference to the proceedings against him.'

16 Section 26(1) of the Evidence Ordinance says that 'No confession made by any person whilst he is in the custody of a police officer, unless it be made in the immediate presence of a Magistrate should be proved as against such person.' In the following case law, it was emphasized that any confession is made by the suspect is not admissible evidence against him unless it is made in the presence of the Magistrate. E.g. *Tennakoon Mudiyanselage Appuhamy* (1958) 60 NLR 313.

17 Section 25(1) of the Evidence Ordinance says that 'No confession made to a police officer should be proved as against a person accused of any offence.' In following cases, the court decided that a confession made to a police officer is not admissible evidence against the accused: *Gnanaseeha Thero* (1968) 73 NLR 154; *Murugan Ramasamy* (1964) 66 NLR 265.

18 Section 27(1) of the Evidence Ordinance provides that when any fact is deposed to as discovered in consequence of information received from a person accused of any offence, in the custody of a police officer, so much of such information, whether it amounts to a confession or not, as relates distinctly to the fact thereby discovered may be proved.

19 Section 26(1) of the Evidence Ordinance.

20 Section 126 of the Code of Criminal Procedure Act says that

'any peace officer or person in authority should not make any inducement, threat or promise any person charge of with any offence to induce such person to make any statement having reference to the charge against such person but any peace officer or other person shall not prevent or discourage by any caution or otherwise any person from making any statement which he may be disposed to make of his own free will.'

Section 127 of the Code of Criminal Procedure says that a Magistrate should not record any confession statement unless, upon questioning the person making it, he has reason to believe that it was made voluntarily, and when he recodes any such statement, he should make a memorandum at the foot of such record.

21 Section 100(2) of the Code of Criminal Procedure Act No. 15 of 1979.

22 Asian Legal Resource Centre (AHRC)—UAC-012–2011.

23 Supreme Court Fundamental Right Appeal Case No. 471/2000.

24 AHRC Police Cases 1988–2011.

25 Article 13 (3) of the Constitution states that 'Any person charged with an offence shall be entitled to be heard, in person or by an attorney-at-law, at a fair trial by a competent court.'

26 Further see section 151(1)(2)(3).

27 Section 191 of the Code of Criminal Procedure Act, No.15 of 1979.

28 It is interesting to state here that the right to defend was recognized under Administration of Justice Law No. 44 of 1973, which governed the criminal procedure prior to the current Criminal Procedure Code No 15 of 1979. *Jayasinghe v Munasinghe* (1959) 92 NLR 527; *Premaratne v Gunaratne* (1964) 71 NLR 113; *Subramaniam v I.P. Kankesanturai* (1968) 71 NLR 204.

29 Further see section 150 of the Code of Criminal Procedure Act

30 Section 158 of the Code of Criminal Procedure Act.

31 Further see section 204 of the Code of Criminal Procedure Act.

32 Section 314 of the Code of Criminal Procedure Act; section 12 of the Judicature Act.

33 Section 320 (1) of the Code of Criminal Procedure Act; section 31 of the Judicature Act.

34 Further see sections 101–105 of the Evidence Ordinance.

35 Article 11 of the Constitution.

36 Section 52 of the Penal Code.

37 Further see Article 16(2).

38 Prison is the only correctional institution which is discussed for the purpose of this study.

39 Prison Ordinance No. 16 of 1877.

40 See Table 3.13 on page 24, Prison Statistics of Sri Lanka Published by the Statistics Division, Prison Headquarters Sri Lanka in 2008.

41 Article 27(1) of the Constitution.

42 *Superintendent v Amarasinghe* 2003 1SLR 270; *Amal Suddath Silva v Kodithuwakku* 1987 2SLR 119; *Saman v Leeladasa* 1989 1SLR 1; *Lama Hewage Laal, Rani Fernando and others v Police O.I.C of Seeduwa* 2005 1SLR 40; *Anthony Michael Emmanuel Fernando v Sri Lanka* (CCPR/C83/D/1189/2003); Case No.4705/2001 and 4706/2001- The case of the two Tamil prisoners assassinated in Kalchura prison on 6 January 2000.

PART II

Historical Perspectives of Crime and Justice

9

CRIMINAL JUSTICE TENETS IN *MANUSMRITI*

A Critical Appraisal of the Ancient Indian Hindu Code

K. Jaishankar and Debarati Halder

Introduction

The statute of Ancient India, which was basically Hindu ruled, was formed by the idea of '*Dharma*',[1] or principles of righteousness, as laid out in the different manuals clarifying the Vedic sacred texts, for example, '*Puranas*'[2] and '*Smritis*'.[3] The king had no autonomous authority but got his authority from 'Dharma', which he was required to maintain. The refinement between a common wrong and a criminal offense was clear. While common wrongs related primarily to debate emerging over wealth, the idea of sin was the standard against which wrongdoing was to be characterized (Basham, 1967; Jois, 1990).

The Maurya Dynasty, which had stretched out to significant parts of the central and eastern parts amid the fourth century BC, had a thorough punitive framework, which recommended mutilation and in addition capital punishment for even trivial offenses (Sharma, 1988). About the second century BC to the third century AD, Manu,[4] an important Hindu jurist, drew up the *Dharmasastra*[5] code, which was called *Manusmriti*.[6] The code recognized attack and other real wounds and property offenses, for example, burglary and theft (Pillai, 1983; Griffith, 1971; Thapar, 1990; Raghavan, 2002; Jaishankar & Halder, 2004).

Manusmriti managed the obligations of a ruler, the mixed castes, the principles of occupation in relation to caste, occupations in the midst of pain, reparations of sins, and the tenets administering particular types of resurrection. *Manusmriti* also managed the items of common sense of life and was generally a coursebook of human conduct. After Manu came *Dharmasastras* ascribed to Yajnavalkya, Vishnu, Narada, Brahaspati, Katyayana,[7] and others (Jayaswal, 1930). The later *Dharmasastras* were nearly pure legal textbooks. The *Manusmriti* was considered superior to the other *Dharmasastras* (McGrath, 2003; Jaishankar & Halder, 2004).

The Dharmasastras professed to be divine in birthplace and to have been passed on by ancient sages who can't be distinguished as authentic figures. Manu was found as early as the *Rig Veda*[8] (1200 BC), where he was depicted as Father Manu, the begetter of mankind. In the *Satapatha Brahmana*[9] (900 BC), Manu was portrayed as the father of humankind when he pursued the guidance of a fish and constructed a ship in which only he among other men endured the extraordinary surge. Thereafter he adored and performed penance, and a woman, Ida or Ila,[10] was created, and he began humanity with her. Manu was also the first king and the first to kindle the sacrificial fire. As the originator of social and moral order, he was the sage who uncovered the most legitimate of the *Dharmasastras* (Singh, 1998; Bhatia, 2001; McGrath, 2003; Jaishankar & Halder, 2004).

Manu's content, the *Manusmriti* or *Manava Dharmasastra*, is the earliest of the *Dharmasastras*. Its date is questionable, being somewhere close to 200 BC and 100 BC. It presumably achieved its present form around the second century BC. The geological skyline of *Manusmriti* was limited to the district north of Vindhyas (Mahajan, 1994). A fundamental Hindu text, the *Manusmriti* is vital for its exemplary depiction of such a significant number of social organizations that have come to be related to Indian culture (Olivelle, 2004). In the area of the content on raja dharma, the ruler's dharma, there are entries on Hindu law. It was these entries that were first noted by Western researchers, and thus the content wound up known as the Laws of Manu (McGrath, 2003). The *Manusmriti* is the definitive work on Hindu law. *Manusmriti* was basic law on which the Hindu law was modified by the British in India. The Sanskrit content was first converted into English in 1794, and interpretations into other European dialects quickly pursued (Doniger, 1991; Drapkin, 1989). Numerous scholars even have done Ph.D./D.Litt. on *Manusmriti* (Betai, 2003; Bahadur, 1998; Das, 1978, 1982; Jaishankar & Halder, 2004).

The Laws of Manu drew on jurisprudence, philosophy, and religion to make a remarkable, broad model of how life ought to be lived, out in the open and in private, by oppressed castes and in addition by priests and kings, by women and by men (Doniger, 1991). A few chapters deal with crime, justice, and punishment. The criminal justice system in ancient India was observed to be founded on the Varna[11] system, and the *Manusmriti* defined crime and punishment for every Varna[12] in a vertical hierarchy (Jaishankar & Halder, 2004).

The present chapter is a critical analysis of the criminal justice tenets found in the ancient Indian Hindu code, the *Manusmriti*. This chapter is divided into three parts. In the first part we discuss the tenets on administration of justice, in the second part crimes and punishment, and in the third part we provide a criticism of the code. Lastly, we discuss and conclude the chapter.

I. Administration of Justice

From the Vedic time period onward, the lasting state of mind of Indian culture has been justice and righteousness. Justice, in the Indian setting, is a human articulation of a more extensive widespread rule of nature, and if man was totally consistent with nature, his activities would be immediately just. Men in three noteworthy pretences encounter justice: in the feeling of a distributive equity, as moral justice, social justice, and legal justice. Every one of these types of justice is seen as a particularization of the general rule of the universe, seen as an aggregate living being. From the broadest to tightest origination, at that point, ancient Indian perspectives on justice are inseparably bound up with a feeling of economy (Wayman, 1970). Human institutions of justice—the state, law, and so forth—take an interest in this general economy; yet the conviction has stayed solid in India during that time that nature itself is a definitive and last referee of justice. At last, justice is cosmic justice (Underwood, 1978; Jaishankar & Halder, 2004).

The state played out its obligation of protection of society and the person through coercive implementation of the principles of justice, which are lessened for logic into the details of positive law. Through practical law enforcement, the state should really look to oppose the obliviousness of those men in the public arena who stay uninformed or unconvinced of the plain purposes for which they themselves, the state, and society exist (Bhattacharaya, 1990). In like manner, the customary Indian king has been attributed with *danda,* 'the sceptre', symbol of the power and authority of the state, which rules, unyieldingly by law and punishment (Menski, 1991). Manu demands in his exchange of the job of the king that in the event that he doesn't "inflict punishment on those worthy to be punished, the stronger would roast the weaker like fish on a spit".[13] "Having fully considered the time and the place (of the offence), the strength and knowledge (of the offender), let him justly inflict that punishment on men who act unjustly".[14] The activity of the coercive intensity of *danda* as to law enforcement is viewed as just in the most astounding sense, since particularistic legal codes are viewed as concrete and point-by-point encapsulations of the more theoretical and magnified principles of justice which are key to the universe (Underwood, 1978; Jaishankar & Halder, 2004).

The organization of lawful justice and infliction of punishment were performed based on the Varna[15] framework. *Manusmriti* says that it is just normal to consider Varna in the administration of justice. Manu shows that the king, as judge, ought to consider "the strength and knowledge" of the litigant. His strength and knowledge are evaluated based on the elements of his Varna. It was envisaged by Manu that Varna ranking will have two principal results; one to do with obligation and the other concerning the perpetrators and their victims. Crimes against persons were arbitrated with reference to the varna-status of the victim and the culprit. The punishment for a wrongdoing was progressively more extreme the higher the Varna of the victim and lower the Varna of the culprit (Das, 1982). One of the central obligations of the ruler was the upkeep and protection of the Varna framework through his power of *danda* (the sceptre). The king complied with this idea, since it is understood that Varna and the state are essential guides to the accomplishment of the last objective of life (Underwood, 1978; Lahiri, 1986). The legal distinctions of ancient India are solidly founded on an ideal of equity and justice expressed in terms of hierarchy rather than of equality (Jaishankar & Halder, 2004).

1. The Judges[16]

It is discovered that the jury framework existed in Manu's period, and Manu prescribed the king to give the power of judicial administration to *Brahmins* even in their absence. It is additionally astounding to note that the juries in the court of the *Brahmin* judge were likewise *Brahmins*. Manu has depicted such a court where there were three *Brahmins* versed in the Vedas and the scholarly judge delegated by the king as the court of four-faced Brahma. Manu has given the qualifications of the king, who can be the judicial administrator (Chakraborti, 1996). The person who is honest, who acts after due thought, who is astute, and who knows the individual estimation of prudence, delight, and wealth can be the judicial executive. A king who appropriately inflicts punishment thrives concerning those three means of happiness; however, on the off chance that he is not prudent and cheating, he will be decimated, even through the uncalled-for punishment which he orders. Manu felt that the judicial administration ought not to rest in the hands of a dimwitted ruler (Buhler, 1984). If the judicial administration were given to such a ruler, he would devastate the entire nation. Punishment can't be inflicted fairly by one who has no assistant, (nor) by a fool, (nor) by an avaricious man, (nor) by one whose mind is unchanged, (nor) by one dependent on exotic delights (Das, 1982). By this idea, we get to an understanding that Manu insisted on Brahmanical assistance in the administration of justice (Jaishankar & Halder, 2004). He additionally depicted the only administrator as a one who is unadulterated (and) loyal to his promise, who acts as per the institutions (of the hallowed law), who has great assistant(s) and is insightful in the infliction of punishment.[17]

2. The Dangers of Injustice[18]

Manu has connoted the significance of the juries, for they ought not to fall in the wheel of injustice (meaning that it will become a cyclical process of injustice if a person falls into the wheel of injustice), and in the event that they don't acknowledge a trial, they might be punished. Manu trusted that nobody ought to go to the court, yet in the event that there is an opportunity to go to the court, truth alone ought to be spoken. Perjury is a crime as per *Manusmriti*. In case justice was devastated by foul play, or truth by deception, and if the judges were insignificant onlookers, they will be considered offenders (Buhler, 1984). Manu trusted that "justice, being violated, destroys; justice, being preserved, preserves: therefore, justice must not be violated, lest violated justice destroy us".[19] Manu gave most extreme significance to justice and felt that the main companion who pursues men even after death is justice, and everything else is lost in the meantime when the body perishes. He has also divided the guilt of injustice to various people. One fourth of the blame of a treacherous choice falls on the guilty party, one quarter on the false witness, one quarter on every one of the judges, one quarter on the king. Nonetheless, if the guilty party who is deserving of punishment is punished, the king is free from blame, and the judges are spared from sin and the blame falls on the culprit alone. Manu recommends that the administration of justice, whether pure justice or injustice, be according to the order of the castes (Varna) (Buhler, 1984; Jaishankar & Halder, 2004).

3. Judicial Psychology[20]

Manusmriti has indicated that part of the judge's capacity is to test the core of the heart of the accused and the witness by studying their posture, mind, and changes in voice and eyes. Manu felt that the inner working of the psyche could be seen through the behaviour, the movements, the step, the motions, the discourse, and the adjustments in the eye and of the face (Buhler, 1984). Thus, it can be asserted that *Manusmriti* is the first legal code to take account of judicial psychology (Jaishankar & Halder, 2004).

4. General Principles of Law[21]

In the dispersion of stolen material, Manu does not demand segregation between Varnas. He has proposed that the king ought to re-establish the property stolen by hoodlums to men of all castes (Varnas). Manu is likewise mindful that kings of ravenous nature may develop. Therefore, he has demanded that a king who uses such (stolen property) for his own utilization is labelled a cheat. Since Manu's laws depended on Varna framework, every Varna has its own laws. So Manu proposes that the king, who knows the sacred law, must inquire into the laws of castes (Varna), of regions, of societies, and of families, and (along these lines) settle cases according to the particular law of each. Manu cautions that neither the king nor any worker of his will himself or herself should cause a lawsuit to be started or settle one that has been brought before them by some other man (Buhler, 1984). This idea is different from the current standard of law, where a judge can initiate a case (*suo-motu*). Manu gives an analogy that a ruler will find on which side the truth lies by derivations (from the actualities) like a hunter who follows the injured deer by the drops of blood. He additionally guides that the king, when occupied with legal procedures, must give careful consideration to truth, to the object of the dispute, and to himself, by the witnesses, to the place, to the time, and to the viewpoint (Jaishankar & Halder, 2004).

5. Witnesses[22]

Manu has depicted the qualification of people who can be witnesses. Householders, men with male issue, and indigenous people, (occupants of the nation, be they) *Kshatriyas, Vaisyas*, or *Sudras*, are skilled enough to give evidence (Buhler, 1984). Reliable men of all the four castes (Varnas) might be made witnesses in lawsuits, men who know their entire obligation and are free from rapaciousness; and others should be rejected. The people who must not be made witnesses are those who have an interest in the suit, family, companions, mates, and adversaries of the parties, men in the past sentenced for perjury, people enduring extreme sickness, and those polluted by mortal sin. The king likewise can't be made a witness. Manu upheld the utilization of judicial psychology when the king looks at the evidence of children and old and sick men, who are well suited to talk untruly. Similarly considered as conniving in like manner are men with disordered minds (Jaishankar & Halder, 2004).

While making the qualification of witnesses, Manu is distrustful about women and people of lower Varnas. Therefore, he insists that women should give evidence for women and for twice-born men for twice-born men (dwija) (*Brahmin, Kshatriya,* and *Vaisya*) of the same kind and men of the lowest castes for the lowest. We are likewise ready to discover a note on dying declarations. Manu has given special case for witnesses in situations where a crime happens inside a house, a forest, or a person who is about to die of homicide, and then whoever is close to the injured individual can be the witness. If a reasonable witness was not accessible at that point, witness can be given by a woman, by a child, by an old man, by a student, by a relative, by a slave, or by a hired worker (Jaishankar & Halder, 2004).

Manu advised the king that he should not look at the fitness of witnesses too strictly in all cases of violence, of theft and adultery, of defamation and assault. Manu offered significance to witnesses who can be included during the trial. At the point when a man initially not selected as a witness sees or hears anything and later analyzes it, he should announce it precisely as he saw or heard it. Manu disdains false witnesses and is vary about hostile witnesses and recommends that they may not be tolerated. However, he has also provided exception in the case that when the truth would cause death to a person, he suggests lying. For a situation at a later stage in the event that it is discovered that false evidence has been given in any suit, the judge should reverse the judgement, and whatever has been done must be considered as undone, and the case should be reinvestigated (Jaishankar & Halder, 2004).

II. Crime and Punishment

1. The Eighteen Causes of Legal Action[23]

Manusmriti divides crimes into eighteen types (Buhler, 1984; Chakraborti, 1996; Jaishankar & Halder, 2004). They are:

(1) non-payment of debts, (2) deposit and pledge, (3) sale without ownership, (4) concerns among partners, and (5) resumption of gifts (6) Non-payment of wages, (7) non-performance of agreements, (8) rescission of sale and purchase, (9) disputes between the owner (of cattle) and his servants, (10) disputes regarding boundaries, (11) assault and (12) defamation, (13) theft, (14) robbery and violence, (15) adultery (16) Duties of man and wife, (17) partition (of inheritance) (18) gambling and betting.

2. Verbal Assault[24]

In the definition of various crimes and punishment, *Manu* has entirely pursued the Varna framework. In instances of verbal attack, we can see the various types of punishment dependent on Varna. A *Kshatriya*, having slandered a *Brahmin*, will be fined 100 (panas[25]); a *Vaisya* 150 or 200; a *Sudra* will endure corporal punishment. A *Brahmin* will be fined fifty (panas) for defaming a *Kshatriya*; in (the case of) a *Vaisya*, the fine will be twenty-five (panas); in (the case of) a *Sudra* twelve. For offenses of *dwija* (twice-born men—*Brahmin, Kshatriya*, and *Vaisya*) against those of equivalent caste (Varna), the fine will be also twelve (panas); for talks which should not to be articulated, that (and each fine will be) twofold. A once-born man (a *Sudra*) who affronts a twice-born man with gross condemnation will have his tongue removed. If a *Sudra* makes reference to the names and castes (Varna) of the (twice-born men), an iron nail, ten fingers in length, will be pushed scorching into his mouth. If a

Sudra pompously teaches *Brahmins* their duty, the king will punish him by immersing hot oil in his mouth and into his ears (Buhler, 1984; Jaishankar & Halder, 2004).

A person who through arrogance puts forth false expressions with respect to the learning (of a caste-fellow), his nation, his caste (Varna), or the rituals by which his body was purified will be constrained to pay a fine of 200 (panas). A person who even as per the realities disdainfully calls another man one-eyed, faltering, or something like that will be fined no less than one *karshapana*.[26] He who maligns his father, his mother, his wife, his sibling, his child, or his teacher, and he who gives not the route to his preceptor, will be constrained to pay 100 (panas). For shared maltreatment by a *Brahmin* and a *Kshatriya* a fine should be forced by a perceiving (king); on the *Brahmin* the most reduced fine, however on the *Kshatriya* the middlemost. A *Vaisya* and a *Sudra* must be punished precisely in a similar way as indicated by their respective castes, yet the tongue of the *Sudra* will not be cut (Buhler, 1984; Jaishankar & Halder, 2004).

3. Physical Assault[27]

In instances of physical assault additionally, we can see the various types of punishment dependent on Varna. With whatever limb a man of a low caste hurts of a man of the three most noteworthy castes, even that limb will be cut off. A *Sudra* who raises his hand or a stick will have his hand cut off; he who in outrage kicks with his foot will have his foot cut off. A low-caste man who attempts to put himself on a similar seat with a man of a high caste will be marked on his hip and be expelled, or the king will make his buttock be cut (Buhler, 1984). In the event that out of haughtiness a *Sudra* spits on a superior, the king will make his lips be cut off; if he pees on him, the penis; in the event that he farts against him, the anus. If he lays hold of the hair of a superior, the king should unhesitatingly remove his hands; similarly, if he takes him by the feet, the facial hair, the neck, or the scrotum (Buhler, 1984; Jaishankar & Halder, 2004).

4. Harm to Property[28]

A man who harms the merchandise of another, be it deliberately or inadvertently, will offer fulfilment to the proprietor and pay to the king a fine equivalent to the harm. On account of harm done to leather or to utensils of cowhide, of wood, or of clay, the fine will be multiple times their value; similarly on account of harm to flowers, roots, and fruit (Buhler, 1984; Jaishankar & Halder, 2004).

5. Acts of Violence[29]

Manu has profoundly underscored the punishment of violent crimes. A king who wishes to accomplish Indra's[30] position of authority and win long-lasting and interminable fame ought to never for a minute neglect the man of violence. A violent man is to be viewed as the specific most exceedingly terrible sort of criminal, worse than one who is liable of verbal maltreatment or burglary or one who beats another with a stick. A king who endures the culprit of brutality rapidly goes to his own annihilation and causes scorn (Buhler, 1984). Neither for the well-being of friendship nor for monetary profit, however high, may the king set free men of savagery who are the reason for fear to every single living being (Jaishankar & Halder, 2004).

In the counteractive action of violent crimes, Manu has given the privilege of private defence. It is important to note that the Indian Penal Code (Sections 96–106) likewise gives the privilege of private defence. Twice-born men may wage war when they are ruined in the satisfaction of their obligations, to secure the twice-born castes (Varna) in (abhorrent) times, in their very own guard, and in order to protect women and *Brahmins* (Buhler, 1984). It might sound dismal that Manu was recommending the utilization of violence in special cases; in any case, it is acknowledgement of an essential human right. The law is unequivocal; it gives every individual an appropriate way to protect himself against outfitted assault, regardless of whether it costs the assailant his life. It declares that privilege of self-defence even when the assailant is one's guru or an educated *Brahmin*, two people whom one would typically be seen as sacrosanct. Later, shastras limit the privilege of self-defence to the case in which it is incomprehensible for the unfortunate victim to make his departure by fleeing and afterward confine the privilege to utilize violence in precisely the manner in which contemporary English law does, requiring the injured individual to avoid excessive injury to the assailant (Melling, 2002). Notably, Manu did not demonstrate any mercy for individuals of any Varna with respect to violent offences, though he was supportive of milder punishment for *Brahmins* (Jaishankar & Halder, 2004).

6. *Punishment*

Manu unequivocally trusted that the *danda*, a symbol of power and authority, was created by God, and just fear alone would make individuals not swerve from their obligations. Manu sturdily has pushed the theory of deterrence as the motivation behind punishment, and the infliction of punishment ought to be in accord with the principles of natural justice (Bose & Varma, 1982). The king, having completely thought about the time and the place of the offense and the quality and the knowledge of the wrongdoer, ought to fairly impose punishment on the guilty parties. The idea of the thought of the offense and wrongdoer with the end goal of punishment falls in accordance with the cutting-edge standards of justice advanced by Jeremy Bentham and Cesare Beccaria. Manu felt that nothing but punishment can control all the individuals in the earth and gave most extreme significance to punishment. In any case, he is cautious of punishment given without appropriate judgement and felt that it might annihilate the nation.[31]

Manu alerts the king that if he doesn't rebuff the guilty parties who are deserving of punishment, the more grounded would broil the weaker, similar to fish on a spit, and a circumstance will emerge in which might may overrule right. In a nation where punishment isn't appropriately dispensed, the ownership would not stay with anyone; the lower ones would usurp the place of the higher ones (Buhler, 1984). The entire world is maintained in control just by punishment, in light of the fact that there is nobody on the planet who will dependably act in an equitable way. Only the fear of punishment runs the world. Manu additionally expected that if there was no punishment, all castes (Varnas) would be tainted (by intermixture), all hindrances would be gotten through, and all men would see the (against one another) in consequence of mistakes with respect to punishment.[32]

Manu has distinguished ten places on the body in which punishment may be inflicted. The sexual organ, the tummy, the tongue, the two hands, the two feet, the eye, the nose, the two ears, moreover the (entire) body, and wealth (wealth is also considered as an extension of the body and it can be punished by confiscation of cattle or other property) are the ten places in a body fit for punishment (Buhler, 1984). From this view, we also realize that Manu upheld retributive justice. Manu is against unjust punishment and cautions that unjust punishment will decimate notoriety among men and popularity (after death) and will cause even the next world the loss of heaven. Manu gives phases of punishment to a blundering individual if he keeps on doing the wrongdoing; first by (delicate) rebuke, second by (unforgiving) upbraiding, thirdly by a fine, lastly by corporal reprimand. However, when the offender is not able to restrain such offence even by corporal punishment, then the four modes co-jointly should be applied.[33]

III. Criticism of Manu's Criminal Justice

Manusmriti has treated distinctive Varnas and gender as unequal for legal purposes. The Hindu law as classified by Manu depended on the principle of disparity. The punishment for a specific wrongdoing was not the same for all Varnas. Truth be told, the punishment changed relying upon the Varna of the victim and the Varna of the individual carrying out the wrongdoing. For a similar crime, the *Brahmin* was to be given a mild punishment, while the *Shudra* was to be given the harshest punishment of all. So also, if the victim of a wrongdoing was a *Shudra*, the punishment was mild, and the punishment was cruel if the victim was a *Brahmin*. For instance, if a *Brahmin* is granted capital punishment, it is adequate to shave his head; however, *Kshatriya, Vaishya,* and *Shudra* have to be killed. In the event that a *Kshatriya*, a *Vaishya*, or a *Shudra* more than once gives false evidence in the court, he is to be rebuffed and ousted from the kingdom, though the *Brahmin* isn't to be punished, he is to be just expelled (Buhler, 1984; Jaishankar & Halder, 2004).

If a man has sex with a consenting woman of his own Varna, he isn't to be punished. However, if a man of lower Varna has sex with a woman of higher Varna, with or without her consent, he has to be killed. If a *Brahmin* forces a *dwija* to work for him, he is to be rebuffed. Be that as it may, if a *Brahmin* forces a *Shudra* to work for him, he isn't to be punished, in light of the fact that *Shudras* have been created just to serve *Brahmins*. If a *Brahmin* manhandles a *Shudra*, he is to be fined mildly. However, if a *Shudra* mishandles a *Brahmin*, he has to be killed (Buhler, 1984). Then again, regardless of whether a *Brahmin* executes a *Shudra*, he is just to perform repentance by killing a cat, frog, owl, or crow and so on. Along these lines, a *Shudra* is to be slaughtered for mishandling a *Brahmin*, though a *Brahmin* is to be let off delicately regardless of whether he murders a *Shudra* (Nath, 2002; Jaishankar & Halder, 2004).

Manu obviously declares the matchless quality of Brahmanism by exempting *Brahmins* from any sort of punishment. On account of false evidence, every one of the three other Varna people ought to be fined and banished; however, a *Brahmin* should just be exiled. Manu has distinguished ten places on which punishment might be dispensed for three Varnas but exempts *Brahmins* to leave safe from the country. Manu proposes that it is better to tonsure the head of a *Brahmin* instead of giving him the death penalty; and yet men of different castes will endure capital punishment. Manu prompts the king not to kill a *Brahmin* even though he has carried out every single conceivable wrongdoing, and the king ought to expel him, grabbing his property and abandoning him safe. Manu even goes to the degree of affirming that "No greater crime is known on earth than slaying a *Brahmin*", and a king, in this way, must not imagine in his mind the thought of executing a *Brahmin*.[34]

Manu has broadly discriminated against women in the administration of justice. Unequal punishment was to be given for women who have perpetrated the same wrongdoing as men. Manu has endorsed capital punishment for women who are accused of infidelity. *Manusmriti* endorses that the spouse who contacts, meets, or even converses with a man who isn't her husband is to be fed to animals. Lesbians were savagely punished by having their fingers chopped off.[35]

Melling (2002) attempted to think about the distinctive punishments exacted on various classes for verbal maltreatment with the diverse ways fines are imposed for property crimes. He completed a correlation and underlined that an intriguing outcome has developed. In Chapter VIII 267 we read:

> A kshatriya who verbally abuses a Brahmin is fined 100 panas, a Vaisya 150 or 200, a Shudra suffers corporal punishment. If a Brahmin verbally abuses a Kshatriya, the fine is 50 panas, a Vaisya, half that, a Shudra, 12. . . . If a once-born grossly insults a twice-born, he shall have his tongue cut out.

Melling (2002) continues:

> It is tempting to read this text as privileging the higher castes at the expense of the lower. We might well guess that the same pattern would apply in all areas of the law; the higher the caste of the criminal, the lower the penalty, the higher the caste of the victim, the higher the penalty.

What, then, of this ruling, in Chapter VIII 336:

> In a case where a common man would be fined a single scratch-penny, the King will be fined 1000, that is the established rule. For theft, the penalty on a Shudra is 8 times the value of the object stolen, on a Vaisya, 16, on a Kshatriya 32 times, And on a Brahmin 64 times, or 100 times or even 132 times, since he knows the nature of the offence.

Melling (2002) further argues:

> True enough, the shastras give privilege and protection to the higher classes, in that they enforce respect to them and defend them against violence, but the shastras also enforce on the higher castes a higher level of responsibility in their dealings with others. We are certainly not dealing with a social ideal based on any notion of equality, but equally it is not based on privilege. When it comes to issues of property relations, the shastras remind us of the law code of the Incas of ancient Peru. The Inca punished crimes against property with great severity, and the higher the rank of the criminal, the more severe the penalty, but if a man could show he had been forced to steal to put food in his mouth, he was declared innocent, and the local Governor was put to death instead.

Be that as it may, it is troublesome for us to acknowledge Melling's (2002) contentions, as the examination he makes is definitely not a reasonable one. How might one compare a punishment of cutting the tongue or corporal punishment with that of a fine? Are both the same? Would we be able to compare the pain of these punishments? Melling (2002) likewise contends that Manu has demonstrated most extreme consideration of animal welfare and even of trees. Melling (2002) finds that the law fining savagery to animals and the law against the harming of trees demonstrate that the lawful scholars of ancient and medieval India were building up the law to declare human obligations to animals and to the earth. The facts may prove that Manu has demonstrated significance to animal welfare, yet one ought to be sufficiently reasonable to acknowledge the most stunning reality is that he has brought down a section of human beings (*Sudras*) to lower-level creatures. One may ponder that by what method can a man like Manu who demanded Dharma be very partial toward *Sudras* alone? The reason Manu has settled is that the justice depended on the *Varnashrma Dharma,* and he felt that discrimination against *Sudras* was right. Dharma implies nobility, and what sort of righteousness is the point at which one set of individuals be discriminated on the grounds of their community or group (Jaishankar & Halder, 2004)?

Unequal justice is observed to be the basis of *Manusmriti.* The contention between *varna-vyavastha* and the estimation of equality is more than self-evident. In fact, this arrangement of graded inequality is by all accounts the simple embodiment of the *varna-vyavastha.* It denies equal respect and equality before the law to all in the society. Regardless of whether it is the selection of names, the way of welcome, the method of engaging guests, the method of administering oath in the court, or the way toward taking out the funeral procession, at every last advance throughout everyday life, from birth to death, this arrangement of graded inequality is to be connected and observed (Nath, 2002; Jaishankar & Halder, 2004).

In the pre-independent India, it was the British who resurrected the *Manusmriti* and utilized it to outline the Hindu Civil Code. Prior to colonization, the *Manusmriti* was simply an obscure content, long overlooked and once in a while used to figure out what was acceptable social practice (Kishwar, 2003). The *Manusmriti* was extremely convenient in social control, in light of the fact that since the British were fewer in numbers, the *Manusmriti* was extremely convenient as a tool to social control of the Hindu population of the country and also the British utilized *Manusmriti* to rule in proxy. It was vital that their agents did not confront obstruction or insubordination, even in the social domain.

Attributable to its severe and exceptionally disruptive character, the *Manusmriti* helped in forestalling both individual and aggregate resistance from local authorities, who were normally upper caste and often *Brahmin*. That the *Manusmriti* represented an age-old and obsolete social code did not make a difference. It fit in extremely well with the British colonial project. It was likewise advantageous in giving ideological cover to abusive lawful advances the British needed to take in any case. For example, it didn't hurt that the *Manusmriti* upheld laws that legitimized gender discrimination or assaulted same-sex connections. Such mentalities were then similarly common in Europe, and it made it easier to disenfranchise women in matters of inheritance or introduce legal injunctions against same-gender sexual relations (just like the case in Britain amid the eighteenth century) (Jaishankar & Halder, 2004).

Notwithstanding, in post-independent India, under the leadership of Dr. B. R. Ambedkar, the Indian constitution was established, and he made efforts to see that no discrimination snuck into the constitution. The constitution of India (1950) was an exceptional accomplishment in the disposal of discrimination on the lines of caste in the administration of justice. The constitution of India has tried to make a more equivalent and just rule of law among people and groups than what existed under customary authorities, for example, *Manusmriti*. The Indian constitution endeavours to kill the mortification that individuals endured under the conventional social arrangement of caste and patriarchy, subsequently making new ground for acknowledgment of human dignity. The acknowledgment of both formal and substantive fairness that is going on under the rule of law in contemporary Indian society can encourage a more innovative thriving of a real existence of dharma or righteous conduct in self and society (Giri, 2002; Jaishankar & Halder, 2004).

In any case, regardless of the arrangements in the constitution for equality in justice, we can find Manu's reminiscences on the village justice system playing a major role in the dispensation of justice. Holden (2003), in her research on a few villages in India, found that the majority of the village justice system depends on caste and discovered that a considerable lot of the principles establishing the conventional *panchayat's*[36] choices have a clear source in the ancient Hindu tradition. Caste, which is presently a far different rendition of Manu's Varna, has occupied the central seat of village justice systems. However, one can't deny the roots of the caste system in the Varna system. All through mankind's history, oppressed castes have endured social discrimination of some sort. Any social framework that depends on unequal access will unavoidably prompt some type of social discrimination and disparity. Victims of older forms of discrimination will either continue to be victimized or simply become victims of new forms of discrimination. Caste and gender discrimination continue to cause grave harm, such that *Adivasis*[37] and *Dalits*[38] still face all manner of hardships, and all such social disparities should be battled with continued vigour (Jaishankar & Halder, 2004).

For Nietzsche, the human intelligence of Manu far outperformed that of the New Testament; for the British Raj, it was by all accounts the ideal apparatus with which to rule the Hindus. No comprehension of Hindu society is conceivable without it, given the wealth of its thoughts, its aphoristic significance, and its importance to widespread human problems. Manu remains next to the great epics, the *Mahābhārata* and the *Rāmāyana*. Numerous reporters see Manu as opposing and equivocal, and others see an unmistakable topical honesty (Penguin, 1991; Doniger, 1991). Indeed, even after a few centuries, it still generates controversy, with Manu's verses being referred to in support of the mistreatment of women and individuals from the oppressed castes (Olivelle, 2004). The criminal justice tenets of Manu are striking in their vision and application considering their times. However, the imbalance in rendering justice dependent on the Varna framework is a chink in the armour of Manu, the first lawgiver of India (Jaishankar & Halder, 2004).

To conclude, we feel it is worth mentioning what Jawaharlal Nehru (1951, p. 622) said about religion in the context of codes and law:

> Religions have helped greatly in the development of humanity. They have laid down values and standards and have pointed out principles for the guidance of human life. But

with all the good that they have done, they have also tried to imprison truth in set forms and dogmas, and encouraged ceremonials and practices which soon lose all their original meaning and become mere routine. While impressing upon man the awe and mystery of the unknown that surrounds him on all sides, they have discouraged him from trying to understand not only the unknown but what might come in the way of social effort instead of encouraging curiosity and thought, they have preached a philosophy of submission to nature . . . to the prevailing social order, and to everything that is. The belief in a supernatural agency which ordains everything has led to a certain irresponsibility on the social plane, and emotion and sentimentality have taken the place of reasoned thought and enquiry. Religion, though it has undoubtedly brought comfort to innumerable human beings and stabilised society by its values, has checked the tendency to change and progress inherent in human society.

Notes

1 Dharma means righteousness.
2 Puranas are ancient Indian Hindu mythological texts in which stories are given to highlight the importance of gods and goddesses.
3 Smritis are a set of texts which teach the eternal immutable dharma found in the Vedas. Many sages have written Smritis.
4 Manu is considered as the first lawgiver of India.
5 *Dharmashastra* is the 'science of dharma' and is a set of texts which teach the eternal immutable dharma, found in the Vedas. The *Dharmashastras* expanded and remodeled in verse form the *Dharmasutras*.
6 *Manusmriti* was the most important of *Dharmashastras* and is the most famous of the ancient texts. The *Manusmriti* prescribed rules for all of society, so that each person might live according to dharma. It is in the form of the dharma revealed by Brahma to Manu, the first man, and passed on through Bhrigu, one of the ten great sages.
7 Yajnavalkya, Vishnu, Narada, Brahaspati, Katyayana are ancient sages who are considered to be the authors of smritis or books of dharma.
8 *Rig Veda* is the oldest of the Vedas, and they are the ancient holy texts of Hindus.
9 *Satapatha Brahmana* is an ancient Hindu text.
10 She is considered as the first woman in the Hindu mythology and may be comparable to Eve of the Bible.
11 Without the knowledge of *Varnashrama Dharma* one may not be able to understand the nuances of *Manusmriti*. The Varna, popularly known as the caste system, is perhaps the most explosive topic in Hinduism. The word 'Varna' is derived from the root 'VR' meaning 'to screen, veil, covering, external appearance'. Varna also means colour. Varna was used to denote groups having different skin coloration. The Aryans were fair skinned and the Dravidians black skinned. Thus, white or fair complexion was considered as belonging to *Brahmins* (priestly), red to *Kshatriyas* (princely), yellow to *Vaisyas* (commercial), and black to *Sudras* (serving). But colour is only one of the many aspects of the term. Varna also denotes species, kind, character, and nature. Racial, tribal, and familial solidarity had also a part to play in the origin of the Varna system. The divisions may have been made based on religious beliefs, cult practices, and even eating habits. Above all, there is the theory that the *Varnas* derived their basis from the *Purushasukta* (*Rig Veda* 10.90) in dividing mankind into four socially separate interdependent categories, and this was incorporated in the Manu *Dharmasastra* (Singh, 1998; Bhatia, 2001).
12 Manu *Dharmasastra* expressed and fortified the Varna division. As indicated by Manu *Dharmasastra*, *Brahmins* were to be the profound and fleeting aides, teachers, and exponents of law; *Kshatriyas* were the warriors, princes, and rulers—in short, the nobility; *Vaishyas* took the tasks of agribusiness and merchantry; and *Shudras* included people who performed service to other Varnas—manual and agricultural labourers, craftsmen, bricklayers, and so forth. Except *Sudras*, all the other three varnas were called *dwija* or twice-born. The significance of twice-born is that after a birth, the three Varnas (*Brahmins*, *Kshatriyas*, and *Vaishyas*) are again born with the investiture with the sacred thread, the symbol of a child's admittance to membership in his Varna (Dongali, 1986). It is trusted that the Varna framework depended on the standard of division of labour and the reasonableness of the diverse groups for the distinctive classifications of occupations. Notwithstanding, the Varna system depended on disparity and every, Varna was arranged in a vertical chain of importance.
13 *Manusmriti*. Chapter VII. 20.
14 *Manusmriti*. Chapter VII. 16.

15 Even though Varna and caste are connected concepts, in some places in this chapter, the terms are used interchangeably.

16 *Manusmriti*. Chapter VIII. 8–11.

17 *Manusmriti*. Chapter VII. 20–31.

18 *Manusmriti*. Chapter VIII. 12–22.

19 Ibid.

20 *Manusmriti*. Chapter VIII. 23–6.

21 *Manusmriti*. Chapter VIII. 40–46.

22 *Manusmriti*. Chapter VIII. 61–123.

23 *Manusmriti*. Chapter VIII. 4–7.

24 *Manusmriti*. Chapter VIII. 267–78.

25 *Pana* is an ancient form of currency which may be considered the equivalent of the present-day rupee, the Indian currency.

26 *Karshapana* is an ancient form of currency, which may be considered equivalent to paise, the Indian currency.

27 *Manusmriti*. Chapter VIII. 279–87.

28 *Manusmriti*. Chapter VIII. 288–9.

29 *Manusmriti*. Chapter VIII. 344–51.

30 Indra is the Lord of Heaven in Hindu mythology.

31 *Manusmriti*. Chapter VII. 14–19.

32 *Manusmriti*. Chapter VII. 20–31.

33 *Manusmriti*. Chapter VIII. 124–130.

34 *Manusmriti*. Chapter VIII. 379–81.

35 *Manusmriti*. Chapter VIII. 356–372.

36 *Panchayat* means village justice system in which principles of natural justice prevail without any interference of the contemporary criminal justice system. However, it is ruled by the caste system.

37 Tribals of India.

38 A holistic term for all low-caste Hindus.

References

Bahadur, J. R. B. S. S. (1998). *Crime and punishment in Manusmriti and Economics*. Ph.D. thesis submitted to Dr. Hari Singh Gour University, Sagar.

Basham, A. L. (1967). *The wonder that was India*. London: Sidgwick & Jackson.

Betai, R. S. (2003). *Evolution of law of crimes in ancient India*. Delhi: Bharatiya Kala Prakashan. Based on the author's thesis, Ph.D. 1957.

Bhatia, H. S. (2001). *Vedic and Aryan India: Evolution of Political, legal and military systems*. Reprint. First Published in 1984/86. New Delhi: Deep and Deep Publications.

Bhattacharaya, C. A. (1990). *The concept of theft in classical Hindu law: An analysis and the idea of punishment*. Delhi: Munshiram Manoharlal Publishers.

Bose, S., & Varma, P. (1982). Philosophical significance of Ancient Indian Penology. *Journal of Indian Philosophy*, *10*(1), 61–100.

Buhler, G. (1984). *The Laws of Manu*. Delhi: Banarsidass. (Reprint from Oxford University's 1886 edition).

Chakraborti, H. (1996). *Criminal justice in Ancient India*. New Delhi: Vedams eBooks (P) Ltd.

Das, R. M. (1982). *Crime and punishment in ancient India: With a particular reference to the Manusmrti* (1st ed.), Bodh-Gaya: Kanchan Publications; Based on the author's thesis (D. Litt.—Magadh University, 1978).

Dongali, D. (1986). *Crime and punishment in ancient Hindu society*. Delhi: Ajanta Publications.

Doniger, W. (1991). *The laws of Manu*. London: Penguin Books Ltd.

Drapkin, I. (1989). *Crime and punishment in the Ancient World*, Lexington, MA: Lexington Books, xviii, 423 p., see "Ancient India and the Laws of Manu" at pp. 99–133.

Giri, A. K. (2002). Rule of Law and Indian society: Colonial encounters, post-colonial experiments and beyond. *Jura Gentium*, Centre for Philosophy of International Law and Global Politics. Retrieved from http://dex1.tsd.unifi.it/juragentium/en/index.htm?surveys/rol/giri.htm.

Griffith, P. (1971). *To guard my people: The history of the Indian Police*. Bombay: Allied Publishers.

Holden, L. S. (2003). Custom and law practices in central India: Some case studies. *South Asia Research, 23*(2), 115–134.

Jaishankar, K., & Halder, D. (2004). *Manusmriti*: A critique of the criminal justice tenets in the ancient Indian Hindu code. *ERCES Online Quarterly Review, 1*(3). (Now not available online).

Jayaswal, K. P. (1930). *Manu and Yajnavalkya—A comparison and a contrast; A treatise on the basic Hindu law.* Calcutta: Butterworth.

Jois, R. M. (1990). *Legal and constitutional history of India,* Vol. I & II. Bombay: N. M. Tripathy Ltd.

Kishwar, M. (2003). From *Manusmriti* to Madhusmriti: Flagellating a mythical enemy. *Manushi.* Retrieved from http://free.freespeech.org/manushi/117/*Manusmriti*.html.

Lahiri, T. (1986). *Crime and punishment in ancient India.* New Delhi: Radiant Publishers.

Mahajan, V. D. (1994). *India since 1526.* New Delhi: S. Chand and Company Ltd.

McGrath, J. I. (2003). *Dharmasastras.* Retrieved from http://philtar.ucsm.ac.uk/encyclopedia/hindu/ascetic/dharma.html.

Melling, D. J. (2002). A dream of justice, a vision of peace: Excerpts from a talk originally delivered to the Indian Classical Music Society at Gita Bhavan, Manchester. Cited and quoted in Jaishankar, K., & Halder, D. (2004). *Manusmriti:* A critique of the criminal justice tenets in the ancient Indian Hindu code. *ERCES Online Quarterly Review, 1*(3). (Now not available online).

Menski, W. F. (1991). *Crime and punishment in Hindu Law and under Modern Indian Law.* Bruxelles: De Boeck (series; Transactions of the Jean Bodin Society for Comparative Institutional History; vol. 58).

Nath, R. (2002). *Why I am not a Hindu.* Retrieved from www.infidels.org/library/modern/ramendra_nath/hindu.html.

Nehru, J. (1951). *Discovery of India.* London: Meredian.

Olivelle, P. (2004). *The law code of Manu.* Oxford: Oxford University Press

Pillai, A. (1983). *Criminal law.* Bombay: N. M. Tripathi.

Raghavan, R. K. (2002). *World Factbook of criminal justice systems: India.* Washington, DC: U.S. Department of Justice, Bureau of Justice Statistics. Retrieved from www.ojp.usdoj.gov/bjs/pub/ascii/wfbcjind.txt.

Sharma, S. D. (1988). *Administration of justice in Ancient India.* New Delhi: Sundeep Prakashan.

Singh, U. B. (1998). *Administrative system in India: Vedic Age to 1947.* New Delhi: APH Publications.

Thapar, R. (1990). *A history of India, Volume I.* London: Penguin.

Underwood, F. B. (1978). Aspects of justice in Ancient India. *Journal of Chinese Philosophy, 5,* 271–285.

Wayman, A. (1970). Varnaa's rama-dharma: Ends and obligations of man. In J. W. Elder (Ed.), *Lectures in Indian civilization.* Dubuque, Iowa: Kendall/Hunt Publishing Company.

10

WITCHCRAFT ACCUSATION, VICTIMIZATION AND DEMONOLOGY IN NEPAL

Binita Pandey

Introduction

The belief that witches exist and that through an alliance with the supernatural powers of darkness they can inflict injury and destruction upon body and property is as old as humankind (Putty, 1973). Prehistoric art depicts magical rites to ensure successful hunting. Western beliefs about witchcraft as sorcery grew out of the mythologies and folklore of ancient peoples, especially the Greeks and Romans (Witchcraft History, Ancient times, n.d.). Roman law made distinction between good magic and harmful magic, and harmful magic was punishable by law. When Christianity began to spread, the distinctions vanished. Witchcraft came to be linked with worship of the devil (A Short History of Witchcraft, n.d.).

The Englishman of the 16th and 17th centuries blamed "mysterious" harmful occurrences upon the evil powers which inhabited the realm of the supernatural co-existent with the beneficent powers. The belief in witchcraft and the harm which its adherents can inflict upon man and beast was very strong in medieval England. The popular or folk belief was that the devil entered into a formal pact with a wizard or a witch, and through their combined powers they inflicted suffering and death upon man and beast. The person in league with Satan or evil spirits was usually a woman, and she was known as "a compounder of philters and poisons, a caster of spells, a wicked woman, and a hideous hag". The belief in witchcraft, however, was limited neither to the medieval period in England's history nor to the imaginations of the "folk". Some of the most learned men in the country believed in it no less fervently than the folk. The witch mania grew like a weed, strengthened by ignorance, fear, and imagination until it reached its zenith in the 1650s and then gradually subsided until the repeal of the witchcraft laws in 1736 (Putty, 1973, p. 1).

Besides Europe and North America, there were major persecutions in such places as "Ancient Rome, Inca Peru, Aztec Mexico, Russia, China, India, and some Bantu empires of Africa" (Schnoebelen, 2009, p. 6). Thus, the belief in witchcraft in the influence of demonology is found in every part of the world, at some point of time despite all differences of culture languages and mentalities.

In Nepal witchcraft is the traditional superstitious practice existing in society, having a very long history, and is variously perceived. Different ethnic groups use different terms to describe a 'witch'. The common ones being *bokshi* (a woman having and practicing black magic), *kichkanya* (an evil spirit of a woman who possesses black magic and sucks blood out of people) and *chaudi* (a woman having and practicing black magic, more harmful and powerful than *bokshi*) (Global Health Problem [GHP], 2012). The *bokshi* (witches) and for that matter *dayan* (soul of dead witches) are believed to cause sickness in humans. When possessed by a ghost, witch or any other spirit or cursed by the god, they manifest in diseases in humans such as sleep disorder, loss of appetite, feeling of loneliness and sadness, headache, fever, aches and pains in different parts of the body, weakness, vomiting, hysterical and epileptic symptoms and acute stomach pain, all believed to be caused by the influence of a witch. Even the domestic animals such as cows and buffalos are rendered sick if they are possessed by the spirits (Randall, Simkhada, Teijlingen, & Wasti, 2011). Further, *bokshis* are believed to harm or cause illness through the evil eye (Gartoulla, 1998). It is also believed they are able to induce certain gods (e.g. *Devis*) or other supernatural powers (*Masaans, Bhutas*) to harm a victim or to send dangerous animals like snakes or tigers to kill him or her (Häußermann, 2006). Consequently on the belief of witchcraft, an old lady in the neighborhood is often made the scapegoat (Giri & Shankar, 2006).

It is very difficult to gain information on witchcraft, as it is not done in the open. Only a few cases appear in media when it becomes an issue of public concern. According to the Women's Rehabilitation Centre (WOREC), an astonishing 75 cases of gender based violence against women induced by allegation of witchcraft were lodged in 2012 alone, while yet another report of the Informal Sector Service Center (INSEC, 2012) reveals that a total of 54 cases of witchcraft allegations were reported (Poudel, 2013). Generally, it is found in the incidences of witchcraft accusation and subsequent violence that the victims mostly are widows, single and elderly women with no proper support and belong to illiterate, poor, *Dalit* and marginalized communities, often in some cases with a long family feud over properties or lands (Thapa, 2012).

It is a matter of national shame that people in Nepalese society are being accused of being witches even in the 21st century (Sancharika Samuha Nepal, n.d.). The tortures inflicted on accused witches are very degrading and inhumane. In the absence of proper legal protection, many widows and women in rural Nepal are often accused of practicing witchcraft, beaten, paraded naked and forced to eat excreta by illiterate and superstitious villagers (Joshi, 2009). Accordingly, there are numerous cases in Nepalese media that focus on women being branded and killed as witches in the Terai region. These common practices of traditional healers (Jhankri) claiming the women to be witches and punishing them have led to very painful incidences enhancing the violence against women in the Nepalese society (Joshi, 2008). So it is pertinent to bring the issue of witch accusation to light to make people aware about the severity of cases of witch accusation and also to provide information for the concerned institutions for taking reformative action. This chapter tries to assess the crime of witchcraft accusation and victimization in Nepal, including the relationships between victims and offenders and the interactions between victims and the criminal justice system, i.e. police personnel.

I. Laws Against Witchcraft Accusation in Nepal

At the international level, the pervasive problem of witch accusation in Nepal can be found in the report of the Universal Periodic Review, UN Human Rights Committee, CEDAW committee, Committee Against Torture, Committee on the Rights of the Child and the Special Rapporteur on Extrajudicial, Summary Executions and Special Rapporteur on Violence Against Women. These mechanisms have reflected the scenario of witch accusation in Nepal. For instance, the Special Rapporteur on Violence Against Women identified witchcraft beliefs as a cultural practice that is violent towards women. Likewise the Special Rapporteur on Extrajudicial, Summary or Arbitrary executions, Philip Alston (2009), stated that in Nepal, elderly women and widows in rural areas are often singled out and abused in exorcism ceremonies. The CEDAW committee in 2011 and the Human Right Committee in 2014 on the conclusion observation report had shown concern about the problem of prevalence of harmful traditional practices such as witch accusation and recommended undertaking drafting of laws against harmful traditional practices and ensuring full implementation of the law without delay as well as monitoring of its effective implementation.

Nepal didn't have specific laws to tackle the problem of witch accusation until 2015. The special act, Witchcraft Accusation (Crime and Punishment) Act, was enacted in 2015. Its major characteristics include (i) defining the acts as crime, (2) providing special measures to the victims of witch accusation, (3) determining crime and punishment and (4) miscellaneous measures.

The major aim of this act was to provide specific guidelines and replace the existing scattered laws on witch accusation, but in practice it is found, unless the issue is highlighted, that still the other acts are referred to in cases of witch accusation. Meanwhile, the Domestic Violence (Offence and Punishment) Act 2066 (2009) is still relevant, and it has even been examined by this act. The significant acts that are prohibited as the crime of witch allegation are: (i) accusing someone of being a witch, (ii) libel, slander, defamation of a person or offensive behavior to the family of accused witch, (iii) social ostracization and exile from community/society, (iv) witch accusation through the use of *Dhami, Jhankri, Tuna Muna, Tantra Mantra, Jharphuk* and related means, (v) beating, piercing, branding or torturing by using chemicals or poisonous or organic substances or by any other means or conducting cruel, inhumane and degrading behavior and (vi) causing grievous hurt.

It even provides punishment to the person who attempts these crimes, the inciter or conspirator to the enlisted crime, as equal to half of the punishment to the main perpetrator. It even increases the amount of punishment of the recidivist as per their repetition of the crime, and in cases of public officials, the punishment is increased. It further prohibits the act of damaging one's property in the name of witch accusation. So the new law attempted to protect the life, security and property of the accused person. Yet it seems there is still the problem of implementation.

In addition to this specific act, the newly enacted State Criminal Code 2074 (2017), in its Section 168(1)(2), has prohibited witch accusation as an inhumane and degrading act. It has also prescribed punishment of five years' imprisonment with and a 50,000 rupee fine. In addition, as per Section 169, the judges can even order provision of reasonable compensation to the victim. (But this Act was implemented from 17 August 2018 only.)

There were various laws in the country before the enactment of these acts. Unfortunately, those obsolete laws are still now used. They are:

1) *The Civil Code (Muluki Ain)* 2020 (1963):[1]

   a) *The Chapter on Homicide:* It is a more comprehensive chapter on deciding cases of homicide. Accordingly, in cases of witch killings, the court is found to decide the case in accordance with the Chapter on Homicide. This chapter provides the punishment for the main perpetrators, inciters and conspirators and the accessories to the crime and attempt to murder. It even provides for the doctrine of causation which can be found in the witch killings.

   b) *Chapter on Battery:* It defines the offence of hurt/battery and states if a person causes bloodshed (*Ragatpachhe*), wound, injury or grievous hurt (*Angabhanga*) or causes any pain or harm to the body of another person, the person shall be deemed to have committed the offence of hurt/battery. Based on some circumstances the ordinary hurt may be considered as a grievous hurt. Accordingly, in Number 14 it provides punishment to the perpetrators.

   In addition to *The Civil Code (Muluki Ain)* 2020, there have been references of the other acts in dealing with the cases of witch accusations and gender-based violence. They are:

2) *Libel and Slander Act* 2016 (1959): Section 8 of the of this act punishes if any person, with intent to defame any woman, says anything in a manner that she can hear or see it or express any kind of work or gesture or shows any article or undermines her privacy, and it shall be liable to a fine of 100 rupees to 500 rupees and may also liable to the punishment of imprisonment for a term not exceeding six months.

3) *Some Public (Crime and Punishment) Act* 2027 (1970): In Section 2 of the Act, it prohibits insulting women in public places by committing molestation and threatening or scolding or teasing or

committing any undue act or expressing any undue things to anyone through telephone, letter or any other means or medium with intention to intimidate, terrorize or cause trouble or to insult or defame or harass to him/her.

4) *Domestic Violence (Offence and Punishment) Act* 2066 (2009): The act has been enacted to prevent and control violence that occurs within the family and for matters connected therewith and for providing protection to the victims of such violence. Section 3 of the act deems one to have committed an offence of domestic violence if a person with whom he/she has a family relationship commits or aids or abets or incites the commission of any form of physical, mental, sexual or economic harm. Section 13(1) provides to a person who commits an act of domestic violence a fine of 3,000 rupees up to 25,000 rupees or six months of imprisonment or both. The act permits the court to grant an interim protection order to the victim. The act further provides camera proceedings and hearings, compensation to the victim and provision of a service center.

Nevertheless, despite these laws, the problem is the same, as the registered cases at Nepal Police, Women and Children Directorate, show that within seven years, from 2067/2068BS to 2073/2074BS,[2] there were altogether 236 cases of witch accusation reported. The number of cases on 2067/2068BS was 39, while in 2073/2074BS it was 24 (Women and Children Service Directorate Nepal Police, n.d.).

II. Findings of a Study

1. Method

The most popular —were selected as information sources for this study. These are the popular newspaper dailies that have the highest circulation and largest networks of reporters spread over Nepal. These daily newspapers are studied considering the resource availability and time available for the study. This was judged to be a time- and cost-effective means for developing some understanding on witch accusation in Nepal within the author's resource limits. The news about witchcraft accusation was studied through a purposive sampling method. The news stories were randomly collected through daily observation of nine different daily national newspapers of Nepal for the year 2012. In every incidence, the publication date, place (district), age and sex of victim, perpetrator's relationship with victim, allegation and violence against victim, its consequences upon them and their approach to police for complaint were studied through a tabulation method. Corrections were made for any duplication of the same news. A Master Table of information was developed and coding was done. Data were analyzed using both qualitative and quantitative methods. Quantitative data obtained from different sources were analyzed using simple statistical tools and methods such as percentages and numbers.

2. Findings

a. The Number of Victims, their Age and Sex

The researcher found that in Nepal, incidents of witchcraft accusation were reported throughout the year in 30 different districts, while in 10 districts the incidences were repeated. There are altogether 57 victims in 47 incidents. There are 11 male and 46 female victims who are of various ages (i.e. child, adult or elderly). The findings are given in Table 10.1 and Table 10.2.

Thus, it is seen that there is pervasiveness of witchcraft accusation in Nepalese society. Be it the urban areas or rural areas, there is a problem of witchcraft accusation. While there is media reporting of the crime in the district, similar incidences are found to be repeated. Table 10.2 shows in Nepal witchcraft accusation has spared neither men nor women. However, the number of women victims

Table 10.1 The Number of Victims on the Basis of Age Group

Age Group	Number
Below 18 years	2
19 years–59 years	25
60 years and above	10
Unknown	20
Total	57

Table 10.2 The number of victims according to gender

Sex	Number
Female	46
Male	51
Total	57

is found to be comparatively higher. Further, all groups of people, whether child, adult or elderly, are found to be accused as witches. According to the data, adults and elderly are likely to be accused as witches more. So from the data, it can be found that the women are more vulnerable in comparison to men, while elderly and adults are more vulnerable in comparison to children in cases of witchcraft accusation.

b. Accusation and Violence Against the Victims

There is strong belief in witchcraft in the society. When any calamity or misfortune occurs, the people in villages do not ask how and what; rather, they are found to ask the question why. For instance, when anyone in a village dies or suffers from an unknown disease, people suspect such events occurred due to the influence of suspected witches in the society. The news shows the people believe that witches can enter someone's body and force the individual to suffer symptoms of a certain disease or kill people or animals, cause disasters in villages, etc.

It was found in two cases that the accused person had to suffer by ordeal to prove their innocence by licking the feet of the village heads and touching the fire that was lit. In addition, in other incidents, it is found that the society inflicted violence against victims in various ways as shown in Figure 10.1.

These violences can be categorized as:

(a) *Physical violence:* In the process of witchcraft accusation the accused witches were beaten black and blue; attacked with sharp weapons (sickle, *khukuri* and axe), branded, eyes were hurt and the like. It was found that three people were beaten to death and one was burnt to death.

(b) *Social violence:* It was found during the accusation, in the village the accused witches' heads were shaved off on four sides, soot painted on their faces, they were forcefully fed human excreta, while some of them were banished from the society.

(c) *Verbal abuse:* Meanwhile, some of the accused witches were defamed by the villagers accusing them as witches and charging them with the crime of bewitching others.

(d) *Economic abuse:* In addition, it was found the villagers do not only physically cause violence to the accused witch but economically exploit them too. In one case it was found that after the accusation, the accusers even looted the accused's property.

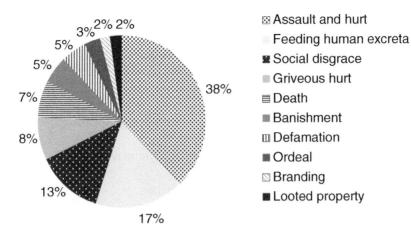

Figure 10.1 Violence against the accused witch.

Perpetrators

The perpetrators in witchcraft accusation consists of family members, local villagers or neighbours, witch doctors (*Jhankris* and *matas*), local group and even the educated member of society such as teachers, politicians and in one case police too. It is shown in Figure 10.2.

This data shows the victims are mainly attacked by the local people and villagers. Following that, they are treated badly by neighbors and family members. This shows the victims are in reality suffering from the violence from near and dear ones. If an individual does not feel safe at home, in their neighborhood and village, there arises doubt regarding the security of life, liberty and property of an individual, which is provided by the law, constitution and other human rights instruments in the country. Similarly, the involvement of witch doctors and even the local women and youth groups during witchcraft accusation illustrates that even the local service provider group uses their superior power to inflict violence upon the weaker section of the society. This makes the victim even more vulnerable. This situation shows that in society, there are always powerful groups suppressing the weaker ones in the name of tradition or culture.

In addition, in the incidence of witchcraft accusation, it was found that the numbers of perpetrators were difficult to ascertain, as they vary from a single person to a group of people consisting of more than 100. It is thus harder to determine who are the main perpetrators, conspirators and accessories of crime. Besides, there are still large numbers of other people who passively observe it. In criminal law, criminal liability arises even through omission of duty. In *Muluki Ain* 2020, Chapter of Homicide number 19 states when someone pleads for help to the persons present nearby and such persons who are between the ages of 17 and 65 years don't go to the rescue or go for help, they can be punished. On the contrary, it was found that if the family members of a victim tried to save them, they are assaulted, injured, defamed and in two cases even killed.

c. Impact on Victims

The violence resulting from witch accusation can have serious physical, emotional, financial and social consequences upon the victim, including:

(a) *Physical effects:* In the immediate effect of witch accusation, most of the accused witches were found to suffer from physical injuries. They have eyes damaged, hands broken, injuries in the

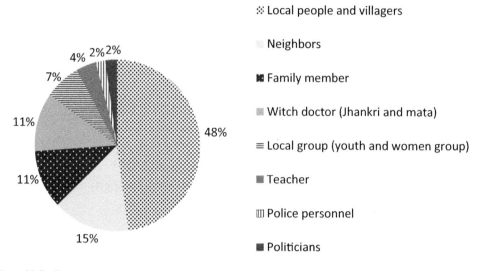

Local people and villagers

Neighbors

Family member

Witch doctor (Jhankri and mata)

Local group (youth and women group)

Teacher

Police personnel

Politicians

Figure 10.2   Perpetrators.

forehead, burning injuries, pain in backbones, etc. Consequently, many of them were taken to hospital for treatment, and some people even died of major injuries.

(b) *Social effects:* It was found that many accused witches are isolated in the society, while in some cases it was found after the accusation, the accused witches had to abandon their home and village.

(c) *Psychological effects:* It was found that after the witchcraft accusation, the victims are suffering mentally too. The victims are found to have diminished personality, anxiety, low self-esteem, depression, sleep and mental health disorders, post-traumatic stress, social isolation, marginaliza-tion, and in one case the victim was even found to attempt suicide.

(d) *Sexual effects:* In the process of witch accusation, it was found that even the private or reproduc-tive organs of the women were attacked. The accused witches were even paraded naked in the village. This shows in addition to the physical violence that the accused witches were sexually exploited and, after the violence, suffer from sexual injuries.

(e) *Education effects:* In the cases of two children being accused as witches, it was found that they had problems of poor attendance and low grades at school, transferring or leaving school. This shows that when children are accused as witches, it has negative effects on the education of the children.

(f) *Economic effects:* It was found that the witch accusation makes poor people even more vulner-able. It is observed that the accused witches are isolated in villages and do not participate in income-generating activities. In cases of banishment, the accused witches had to sacrifice their own property.

The government is also found not compensating the victims in such cases. Thus, poor people become even more economically marginalized due to witchcraft accusation.

In addition to this, family members of the accused witches are adversely affected by witchcraft accu-sation. In the course of study, it was found that even the family members have also gone through mental trauma and sometimes even been displaced or banished along with victims. Likewise, it was found that when the family members tried to save the victim, they were assaulted, injured, defamed and in two cases even killed.

d. Victims' Interaction with the Criminal Justice System

The act of witchcraft accusation in considered a crime through the legislation in Nepal. According to the reports from the news, after the violence, 32 victims are found to have reported at nearby police stations, and 4 complaints were filed in CDO offices. In 2 cases the police denied the filing of the complaint, and 1 person then approached the court for the complaint (when complaints are not registered by police, then people have recourse to the court to get the complaint registered). In 18 cases the status of the registering of the complaint is not known. Figure 10.3 shows the status of complaints and the receiving institution.

This data thus suggests that violence in the name of witchcraft is accusation is reported to the government by the victims in a quest for justice. It is thus the duty of the government to do proper investigation and punish the perpetrators.

e. Settlement of Dispute by Police Personnel

After the incident of the witchcraft accusation, most of the victims have approached the police for justice and protection. However, despite the clear provision in law, the victims are found to file the case in different categories like defamation, hurt, some public offense act, homicide, violence against women etc. Consequently, during the process of investigation, the police are found to act indifferently. It was found the police had released the perpetrator in 1 case with an admonishment, while in other cases, the police were forced by pressure from local people to release perpetrators. Eventually, in many cases, perpetrators managed to flee. The complaints were settled through mediation by police in four cases, and in two cases, local communities pressed police for further investigation. Nevertheless, in 20 cases, investigation and prosecution by police went on. This is shown in Figure 10.4.

The study shows most of the cases are in the process of investigation. It was further found during the investigation that the police are able to arrest few perpetrators, while others fled. Moreover, it was found that when the police tried to prosecute the perpetrators, the society created pressure to release the perpetrators. Thus, it is seen that there is unwillingness of people in society to name perpetrators, and additionally, it shows there are lots of people who think the supposed witches are evil towards the society, and the person who inflicts the violence toward them are saviors of the society. Meanwhile, the refusal by police personnel to file a case against the accuser shows they are also influenced by the society to save the perpetrators, and they are hurried to solve the dispute and close the case. In addition, it was further found in most of the cases that the police have tried to do mediation at the local level. Generally, mediation cannot be performed to settle the dispute of crimes which are listed

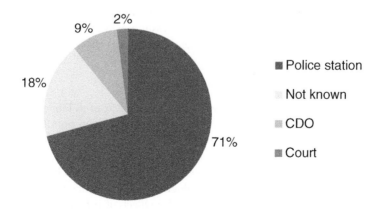

Figure 10.3 Complaint-receiving institution.

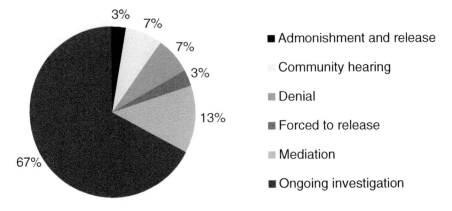

3% 7%

7%

3%

13%

67%

■ Admonishment and release

Community hearing

■ Denial

■ Forced to release

Mediation

■ Ongoing investigation

Figure 10.4 Investigation by police.

by the law. Unfortunately, the crime of violence against accused witches is not in that category. In some cases, the police misuse their power by using mediation; hence mediation processes should be regularized.

Similarly, in some cases, the dispute was decided through the local community using their customs and traditions, and this intervenes in the police work. This illustrates that still in Nepal, there is a prevalence of traditional methods of dispute resolution at local levels. However, the Nepalese laws do not recognize the legality of such community decisions. The law must decide what sort of cases can be adjudicated by such community action and what will be their legal status.

f. Availability of Remedy to Victim

In Nepal, there is only one exclusive provision in law about witchcraft accusation in society. The laws do not define victims' rights particularly. Accordingly, the reports of the news also showed that the victims were not able to get remedy or compensation after the incidence either from perpetrators or from the government. It was found that the victims who were hurt and admitted to hospital were not able to claim reimbursement for treatment expenses from perpetrators, and they are not guaranteed nonrepetition of such incidences in the future. Likewise, those who were ostracized from their villages couldn't return home. Only in a few cases, the victims got compensation from perpetrators or were rehabilitated in society, and in only one case did government give monetary compensation to the victim's family. This illustrates that in Nepal, the law is not supporting the victims of witchcraft accusation in terms of getting remedy through proper mechanisms. Nevertheless, the newly enacted act has some provision for protecting rights of victims, as it provides methods to get compensation from the perpetrators and even from the government. However, its effectiveness is yet to be assessed.

Conclusion

The result of the current study must be interpreted in the context of its limitations, which may be addressed by future research on witchcraft accusation and victimization from different perspectives such as the perspective of human rights, women's and children's rights, comparative study on the practice of witchcraft in different societies and alike. Importantly, the study was carried out with the data from 2011–2012, as the practice of witch accusation is still the same. The study showed that in Nepal, there is still the reminiscence of a demonological theory of crime in society in the form of witchcraft accusation. Though the law has prohibited such acts, it is found that in either urban or rural areas, the age-old practice of persecuting people in the name of witchcraft still persists under the influence of the demonological theory. Consequently, the people and society are found to inflict injuries upon the individuals on the belief that the suspected witch in the society is a devil. The study further illustrated this phenomenon of accusation, and subsequent violence has especially targeted the poorer and weaker sections of society, leaving them more vulnerable. In some cases, the perpetrators are only the close relatives of the victims and in some cases, the perpetrators hold high positions in the society and this situation puts the victims in difficulty in getting access to justice.

In addition, the high status of some perpetrators has even adversely affected the investigation and prosecution process by state mechanisms. Thus, the state needs to intervene in this practice immediately through the criminal justice system. The author recommends the government and NGOs/INGOs that work for human rights create awareness among the public on scientific evidence in cases of witchcraft and make the public aware of the perils of believing the demonology theory of crime. To sum up, the incidence of witchcraft accusation shows that there is a failure of the state's mechanism to control crime in society: the police are not able to investigate and prosecute the cases, while the courts are found to be less efficient in deciding in the case of witchcraft accusation, and the Nepalese society is still guided by the age-old, obsolete basis of the demonological theory of crime.

Notes

1 This law is soon to be replaced by a newly drafted civil code, criminal code and sentencing act in Nepal.
  1) State Criminal Code 2074 (2017)
  2) State Civil Code 2074 (2017)
  3) Sentencing Act 2074 (2017)
  These acts were implemented from 17 August 2018, replacing the whole content of the Civil Code 1963.
2 The data are kept according to the financial year at Nepal. The financial year starts with the third month of year in Nepal (approx. 15 June).

References

Alston, P. (2009). Promotion and protection of all human rights, civil, Political, economic, social and cultural rights, Including the right to development, A/HRC/11/2, United Nations Human Rights Council.

Gartoulla, R.P. (1998). *Therapy patterns of conventional medicine with other alternative medicines: A study in medical anthropology in Nepal.* Kathmandu: Research Center for Integrated Development (RECID) Nepal.

Giri, B. R., & Shankar, P. R. (2006). Faith healing in Western Nepal. *Nepal Journal of Neuroscience, 3*(1). Retrieved from www.neuroscience.org.np/132m.pdf.

Häußermann, C. (2006). Shamanism and biomedical approaches in Nepal—Dualism or synthesis? *Music Therapy Today* (Online 1st October), 7(3). Retrieved from www.wfmt.info/Musictherapyworld/modules/mmmagazine/showarticle.php?articletoshow=178.

Informal Sector Service Center. (2012). *A study on violence due to witchcraft allegation and sexual violence* (2nd ed.). Kathmandu: Author.

Joshi, S. K. (2008). Violence against women in Nepal—An overview. *The Free Library.* Retrieved fromwww.thefreelibrary.com/Violence Against Women in Nepal—An Overviewa01073875052.

Joshi, S. K. (2009). Violence against Women (VAW) in Nepal: Role of health care workers. *Kathmandu University Medical Journal, 7*(2).

Poudel, T. (2013). *Women violence in Nepal.* Retrieved from http://jcycnepal.wordpress.com/news-articles/articles.

Putty, E. R. (1973). *The formative impact of witchcraft on renaissance drama.* Bachelor thesis, Texas: Texas University. Retrieved from http://repositories.tdl.org/ttu-ir/bitstream/handle/2346/22390/31295001678951.pdf?sequence=1.

Randall, J., Simkhada, P., Teijlingen, E.V., & Wasti, S. P. (2011). In what way do Nepalese cultural factors affect adherence to anti-retroviral treatment in Nepal? *Health Science Journal, 5*(1).

Sancharika Samuha Nepal. (n.d.). *Those who are weak are witches Victimized women seek justice.* Retrieved from www.carenepal.org/bulliten/__sancharika%20leaflet%20english.pdf.

Schnoebelen, J. (2009). Witchcraft allegations, refugee protection and human rights: A review of evidence. *New Issues in Refugee Research*, Research Paper No. 169. Geneva: United Nations High Commissioner for Refugees, Policy Development and Evaluation Service.

Thapa, S. (2012). Witch hunt: Medieval practice in Modern Nepal. *World Pulse*. Retrieved from http://world pulse.com/node/62221.

Witchcraft History Ancient Times. (n.d.). Retrieved from swcta.net/moore/files/2011/01/Witchcraft-History. ppt.

Women and Children Service Directorate. (n.d.). Retrieved from https://cid.nepalpolice.gov.np/index.php/cid-wings/women-children-service-directorate.

11

CRIME AND JUSTICE IN ANCIENT SOUTH INDIA (SANGAM AGE)

Gleanings from Tamil Literature

P. Madhava Soma Sundaram, K. Jaishankar
and E. Enanalap Periyar

Introduction

Crime and issues related to crime have always been matters of interest to human beings in general, and Indians are no exception. Social, political and biological inequalities across continents and nations prompted deviations from the acknowledged norms of the general public. History is loaded with incidences where individuals abused the acknowledged norms or tenets recommended by the society. Each society had its own strategy and foundation to manage norm violations. These techniques for managing norm violations were dependent upon the scientific knowledge and the technical know-how of the society.

In ancient India, law as an idea depended on morals, devotion, social need and respectability. It was a law for the leading of day-by-day life and a set of generally accepted rules to oversee significant standards of socialization. Criminal law was considered as an organ of vigilance to shield the citizens from foul play. The king was the final authority for awarding of punishment, and he had the prerogative of pardoning (Kosambi, 1964). Ancient India had its own compilation of laws such as *Manusmriti, Naradasamhita, Dandaviveka, Kantaka* and *Arthasasthra*.[1]

Notably, the legal distinctions of ancient north India are firmly based on an ideal of equity and justice expressed in terms of vertical hierarchy (based on caste or Varna[2] of individuals) rather than of equality (Jaishankar & Halder, 2004; Ragozin, 1961). However, in ancient south India (in the Sangam[3] Age), criminal justice was in a developed form, and justice was equal for all, irrespective of caste or Varna. There were mentions of equal justice in *Thirukkural*,[4] a classic work of Tamil literature (*Kural (541 Chengonmai Adhikaram*, Just Governance chapter 55)), which conceptualizes that "*Government has to examine the crimes, which may be committed, to show no favor to anyone, and to inflict such punishment as may be wisely resolved on*" (Enanalapperiyar & Jaishankar, 2004a). This sense of equity and equality prompts a reading of Tamil culture, literature and justice administration, and this chapter makes an effort at that.

The main objective of this chapter is to peep in to the contributions of traditional Tamil society to the fields of criminology, criminal jurisprudence and criminal justice. This chapter is divided into two parts. The first part deals with the history, literature and justice administration of the Sangam Age. The second part deals with the portrayal of crime and justice in the Sangam Tamil literature.

I. History, Literature and Justice Administration During the Sangam Age

In India, till the second century B.C., the upland segments of the landmass with the Kaveri delta were possessed by individuals who are called megalith manufacturers. They are known not from their actual settlements, which are uncommon, but rather from their graves called megaliths. These were encompassed by enormous bits of stone which contained skeletons of the buried individuals as well as earthenware and iron items. Tridents, which later came to be related with Shiva, have likewise been found in the megaliths. Contrasted with the quantity of agrarian devices that were buried, those for battling and hunting are bigger in number. This demonstrates that megalithic individuals did not practice an advanced sort of farming. The megaliths are found in every single upland region of the peninsula, yet their focus is by all accounts in eastern Andhra and in Tamil Nadu of south India (Bharathi Tamil Sangham, 1968; Chattopadhyaya, 2009; Subramanian, 1976).

Their beginnings can be traced to around 1000 B.C., yet as a rule, the megalithic stage endured from about the fifth to the first century B.C. The Cholas, Pandyas and Keralaputras (Cheras) referenced in the Ashoka engravings were likely in the late megalithic period of material culture. By the third century B.C., the megalithic individuals had moved from the uplands into fertile river basins and reclaimed mucky deltaic territories. Under the improvement of contact with the components of material culture conveyed from the north to the extraordinary end of the peninsula by businessmen, conquerors and Jaina, Buddhists and some Brahmana missionaries, they came to have social classes. They came to practice wet paddy cultivation and established various villages and towns (Bharathi Tamil Sangham, 1968; Chattopadhyaya, 2009; Subramanian, 1976).

Social and monetary contacts between the north and the Deep South known as *Tamilakam or Tamizhakam* turned out to be critical from the fourth century B.C. The course toward the south called the *Dakshinapatha* was esteemed by the northerners in light of the fact that the south provided gold, pearls and different valuable stones. Prospering exchange with the Roman Empire added to the development of the three states individually under the Cholas, Cheras and Pandyas. These southern kingdoms would not have been created without the spread of iron innovation, which advanced timberland clearing and plough cultivation (Bharathi Tamil Sangham, 1968; Chattopadhyaya, 2009; Subramanian, 1976).

1. The Sangam Period

The Sangam Age in South India is a milestone in her history. The word *sangam* is the Tamil type of the Sanskrit word *Sangha*, which implies a gathering of people or an association. The Tamil Sangam was an academy of writers and poets who prospered in three distinct periods and in different places under the support of the Pandya kings. It is trusted that the first Sangam was gone to by divine beings and legendary sages, and its seat was *Then Madurai* (South Madurai). All the works of the first Sangam have perished (Bharathi Tamil Sangham, 1968; Chattopadhyaya, 2009; Subramanian, 1976).

The seat of the second Sangam was *Kapatpuram*, another capital of the Pandyas. It was attended by many poets and delivered a vast mass of writing, yet just *Tolkappiyam* (the early Tamil sentence structure) has endured. The seat of the third Sangam was the present Madurai. It has additionally created tremendous literature, yet just a small amount of it has endured. It is this portion which comprises the surviving collection of Sangam writing. The Age of the Sangam is the age in which the Sangam writing had a place. The Sangam writing establishes a mine of data on states of life around the start of the Christian era (Bharathi Tamil Sangham, 1968; Chattopadhyaya, 2009; Subramanian, 1976).

2. Sangam Literature

As per K. A. Nilakanta Sastri, the Sangam writing, which joins optimism with authenticity and great beauty with indigenous industry and quality, is properly viewed as comprising the Augustan time of Tamil literature. It manages mainstream matter identifying with public and social action like government, war philanthropy, exchange, adore, farming and so on. Among the literary works of the Sangam Age, *Tolkappiyar, Tiruvalluvar, Illango Adigal, Sittalai Sattanar, Nakkirar, Kapilar, Paranar, Auvaiyar, Mangudi Marudanar* and a couple of others are remarkable. Sangam literature comprises the earliest Tamil works (for example, the *Tolkappiyam*), the ten ballads (*Pattupattu*), the eight compilations (*Ettu-togai*) and the eighteen minor works (*Padinenkilkanakku*) and the three legends. The main benefit of the Sangam works is their outright commitment to guidelines and adherence to scholarly traditions (Bharathi Tamil Sangham, 1968; Chattopadhyaya, 2009; Subramanian, 1976).

The earliest content that the Tamils utilized was the *Brahmi* script. It was just from the late ancient and early medieval period that they began developing another rakish content, called the *Grantha* content, from which the modern Tamil is inferred. A portion of the substance of the Sangam literature is substantiated by the works of some Greek and Roman classical writers of the first and second centuries A.D., driving us to settle the time of Sangam Age, generally between the third century B.C. to the third century A.D. The Sangam literature was finally compiled in its present shape in around A.D. 300–600 (Bharathi Tamil Sangham, 1968; Chattopadhyaya, 2009; Subramanian, 1976).

3. Justice Administration During the Sangam Age

The Sangam literature gives insights about the administration amid the Sangam Age. Monarchy was the arrangement of government amid this period. The king was called *Vendan, Ko* and *Irai*. The local chieftains were known as *Velirs*. The law of succession was practiced, and the eldest child delighted in the privilege to succeed his father. Amid the Sangam time frame, the powers of the king were boundless. He was considered as the delegate of God. The term *Irai* (God) connotes this hypothesis. He was the protector of the law and justice. In his court, the ruler met the general population, heard their complaints and rendered justice. As per the Sangam verses, the kings of the Sangam Age like *Karikalan. Manu Needhi Cholan* and *Porkai Pandyan* were known for their fairness in delivering justice (Bharathi Tamil Sangham, 1968; Chattopadhyaya, 2009; Subramanian, 1976, 1992).

It is apparent that there was then a court of justice known as *Manram, avai, Avaik-Kalam*, in main urban areas, where both civil and criminal cases were examined, tried and decided. The judges were to a great extent guided by what is known as *Dharmanul* (Subramanian, 1992).

The pregnant perception of the Kural, to be specific, that it is not the spectre or danda that triumphs but an exemplary administration that runs on the basis of *Dharmaic* rule, is confirmed by the *Puram*, where the recognition of the *Dharmaic* rule is said to be fundamental to and beholden on a ruler. In more than one place in the *Silappadikaram* it is said that if justice was not legitimately rendered, the king would not endure, and he would perish. Truth be told, this is referenced as the main characteristic for the Pandyan kings (Subramanian, 1992). With such a high feeling of justice, at that point, the ancient Tamil chieftains investigated every possibility for dispensing appropriate equity to the offender and the victim. There was special department of justice consisting of highly learned people. The ruler was obviously the highest court of appeal (Subramanian, 1992).

II. Crime and Justice in Tamil Literature

1. Crime Prevention

One of the Tamil classics, *Silappadikaram* (the narrative of the anklet), discusses life and times of Kovalan and Kannagi and the justice system that prevailed in the Sangam Age. This classic brings to light the various nuances of the criminal jurisprudence. The king in a feeble minute requests the beheading of Kovalan without enquiring. The town watch who goes to the place finds from the disposition of Kovalan that he doesn't look like a man to manage stolen merchandise. Is this not the proof of forensic psychology that existed among ancient Tamils? The fact that Kannagi and Kovalan moved from *Kaveripoompatinam* to *Madurai* stage by stage at night to avoid the heat of the day reveals the evolved society devoid of thieves and robbers (Madras Police Department, 1959).

According to *Silappadikaram*, there are eight qualities for a thief, which are (Madras Police Department, 1959):

- Mandiram (This enables the thief to recite a few verses so as to become invisible, probably referring to the camouflaging techniques followed by armies around the world)
- *Deivam* (Thinking of their deity allows them to escape from any situation—probably a method of increasing concentration to escape from a difficult situation)
- *Marunthu* (With medicines, a thief will stupefy other persons—may be something akin to our modern-day biscuit bandits in the trains)
- *Nimitham* (Without proper auspicious signs, a criminal will not venture to commit a crime—may be a form of surveillance of the target's vulnerability)
- *Thandhiram* (It refers to the modus operandi of the offender)
- *Idam* (It refers to the place of offence—what we call today spatial or environmental criminology—and it is the fourth dimension of crime)
- *Kalam* (It refers to the geographical climate of the place—in the geographic school of crime, it was proposed that property crimes occur in hot climates and personal crimes occur in cold climates)
- *Karuvi* (It refers to the tool utilized to commit the crime)

The diverse ideas conceived in the classic *Silappadikaram* apply to the present-day setting too. In modern-day criminology, we talk about exploring a crime by breaking down the modus operandi, and we talk about prevention of crime through redesigning the environment and utilization of modern types of gear like PCs to perpetrate violations (online or cybercrimes). The seminal ideas of all of this are found in classic Tamil writings (Madras Police Department, 1959).

From *Silappadikaram*, crime prevention through surveillance is one of the thrust areas of criminology in the present. Involvement of the community in crime prevention activities is what present-day policing aims at. Thoughts like this are found in *Silappadikaram*. The frameworks of town watch were present in days of yore, as is obvious from a few verses in *Silappadikaram*. It additionally recommends that the king went out in disguise to check the watches and learn the complaints of the general public (Madras Police Department, 1959).

2. Forensic Science

Silappadikaram (the story of the anklet) provided a stronghold of forensic knowledge of ancient Tamils. The king, in a weak moment, orders the beheading of Kovalan without enquiring whether he is the person who has stolen the queen's anklet. Kannagi, the wife of Kovalan, breaks her anklet in order to prove to the king that the anklet in the possession of Kovalan was different from the queen's anklet, and the Pandya king realized that his goldsmith had misled him and that he was bereft of all reason when he ordered the killing of Kovalan (husband of Kannagi). He became broken-hearted and died on the spot. The final scene where Kannagi breaks her anklet in order to prove to the king that the anklet in the possession of Kovalan was different from the queen's anklets highlights the forensic knowledge and how proof is presented in a court of law in order to get justice (Madras Police Department, 1959).

The next classic to which we may turn our attention is *Sekilar's Periyapuranam*. This is the story about how Sundarar was prevented from entering a marriage by Lord Shiva so as to dedicate himself to the service of the god. Setting aside the supernatural element, the story gives us the picture of how justice was meted out in ancient days. The case was tried by a court at Thiruvennainallur, where Lord Shiva in disguise produced a palm leaf as proof. The court looked into the document and said that though it categorically supported the contention of the complainant, and it had to be legally admitted in evidence by proving its authorship before reliance could be placed on its contents. Sundarar's father's handwriting was available in certain documents in the possession of the court itself. This accepted handwriting was compared with his suspected one by the court, who found it to be the same. Lord Shiva in disguise won the case, and Sundarar bowed to the decision. The point to be borne in mind is the forensic clarity in document comparison and the speed with which justice was administered in those days. Even an impending marriage did not get precedence over court business, unlike today, where postponement of cases is the order of the day (Madras Police Department, 1959).

3. Policing

In *Patthupattu (Madurai Kanchi* 631–653), a Tamil classic of the second century A.D., there is a description of a dark, rainy night and thieves dressed in black, armed with the implements of house breaking, lurking in darkness. Unmindful of the rain, the patrolmen, renowned for their mastery of the ways of the thieves, with high energy and relentless vigil pursued their vigilance. In *Pandikovai,* a work of the seventh century A.D., robust youths keep vigil over Madurai, the Pandyan capital. Similarly, *Manimekalai* (7:68–9) refers to the men who patrol the highways and by lanes, alerting the citizens with their rattles (Madras Police Department, 1959).

In *Purannanuru* (37), there is a poetic fancy which brings to our knowledge the crocodiles hurrying up in the moats to catch the bright reflected images of the lanterns carried by the city night patrols, which appear to them as some kind of prey. All these references in the ancient Tamil literature point to an established and efficient policing system with able-bodied men (Madras Police Department, 1959).

Employing spies seems to have been common and part of royal administration in the ancient times. It is the duty of a king to keep in touch with various issues of the kingdom. The spy was an important means of keeping a finger on the pulse of public opinion (Enanalapperiyar & Jaishankar, 2004c). Thiruvallur's *Thirukkural* describes the qualities of an efficient spy. He should not be easily identifiable by appearance and should be an expert at disguise. When under disguise and otherwise, it should be possible for him to merge easily with the surroundings and ward off suspicion, and he should be unnerved by any scrutinizing stares. He should be able to protect secrets under all circumstances and never give himself away (Enanalapperiyar & Jaishankar, 2004c).

Ancient kings, it appears from *Thirukkural,* feared revenge and assassins. Against such possibilities, they had a network of spies. While comparing the spying system with the present, we need to understand the structure of the ancient kingdom envisaged in *Thirukkural* (Enanalapperiyar & Jaishankar, 2004c). The ancient kingdom is like a city or a district, as there were many such small kingdoms. Therefore, the spies of Thiruvallur's period are analogous only to the present-day police officers who collect intelligence and not to the spies who collect external intelligence from foreign countries. It is worth noting that when a police officer in Tamil Nadu took charge of the intelligence wing, he ordered his subordinates to read thoroughly the ten couplets of *Thirukkural* describing espionage. The qualities of the efficient spy developed by Thiruvalluvar still holds good for the present intelligence officers (Enanalapperiyar & Jaishankar, 2004c).

4. Administration of Justice

It is also interesting to note how old Tamil kings carried out justice administration. It is apparent that they relied on the dharma (rule of law) and had an administrative setup, particularly in the court of justice. Between the able bureaucracy and active local assemblies, which in various ways fostered a live sense of citizenship, there was a high standard of administrative efficiency and purity, perhaps the highest ever attained by the state (Madras Inspector General of Police, 1959).

The way that the rulers were accessible to the general population for the administration of justice and the review of their complaints is shown by the narrative of *Manu Needhi Cholan*, who had a bell of justice (*Araichimani*) that was kept at the passageway to the royal residence to be rung by aggrieved individuals to call the consideration of the king (Subramanian, 1992). Instantly in the wake of hearing the bell, the ruler would go to the court, call the gathering and enquire about the protest. The king is said to have heard objections, notwithstanding when he was in camp. Likely if the case was of an entangled sort, he asked skillful officers close by to attempt it or guided the issue to be settled by intervention by the scholarly men of the area within the presence of a government official. The king's court, besides being one of original jurisdiction, appears also to have had appellate jurisdiction (Subramanian, 1992).

Here let us see an example of a *Thirukkural* relating to administration of justice. Thiruvalluvar emphasized the rule of law, good governance by law, equality before the law and equal protection of the law. If there is a delay in identifying and redressing the people's grievances in time and failure in rendering justice to them according to the law, the reputation of the government will go down the drain and the government will have its natural end. Kural (541 Chengonmai Adhikaram 55) conceptualizes that "Government has to examine the crimes, which may be committed, to show no favour to anyone, and to inflict such punishment as may be wisely resolved on". This concept is reflected in A.V. Dicey's rule of law, which states that "a country should be governed by the Law of the land and not according the whims and fancies of any individual, group or government, however powerful they may be" (Enanalapperiyar & Jaishankar, 2004a).

5. Penology and Corrections

Thirukkural highlights the importance of punishment free of cruelty. Though in ancient times there were barbaric punishments, it is amazing that Thiruvalluvar has highlighted this issue. He has emphasized that a king should inflict punishments mildly and without cruelty. His thought on the removal of cruelty in punishment is echoed in the writings of modern-day penologists (Enanalapperiyar & Jaishankar, 2004b).

It is pertinent to highlight what Jeremy Bentham has said about the cruelty of punishment.

> Every particle of real punishment that is produced more than what is necessary for the production of the requisite quantity of apparent punishment, is just so much misery run to waste. Hence, the real punishment ought to be as small and the apparent punishment as great as possible. If hanging a man in *effigy*, would produce the same salutary impression of terror upon the minds of the people, it would be folly or cruelty ever to hang a man *in person*.
>
> *(Enanalapperiyar & Jaishankar, 2004b)*

Capital punishment for theft is not anything characteristic of India. Even in advanced countries of the West, this was in existence before the new jurisprudence came into force. In *Silappadikaram*, the Pandya king told Kannagi that the decapitation of a thief was the duty of the king, and it would never be considered an unrighteous act. However, when the king realized that his goldsmith had misled him and that he was bereft of all reason when he ordered the killing of Kovalan, he became brokenhearted and died on the spot. This gives an indication of the ideal of justice, which the kings of old held up before them, and the sacrifice they were prepared to make when they unwittingly made a mistake (Enanalapperiyar & Jaishankar, 2004b).

In *Thirukkural*, Thiruvalluvar emphasizes that a good king has the essential responsibility of protecting his people from dangerous anti-social elements by imposing even the death penalty. Hardcore offenders are like weeds to a farmer's crops: if he allows the weeds to grow along with his plants, the weeds will overcome the crops, strangling them, leaving the farmer with little or no crop yields (Kural 550 Chengonmai Adhikaram 55). From this *kural* we understand that Thiruvalluvar is a supporter of retributive and preventive theory of punishment. Even though this *kural* supports these theories, it is implicit that he emphasized that capital punishment should be provided only to hardened criminals. This falls in line with the modern thinking of the Supreme Court: to award the death penalty only in the "*rarest of rare cases*" (Justice V. R. Krishna Iyer's Judgement in *Bachan Singh vs State of Punjab*) (Enanalapperiyar & Jaishankar, 2004a, 2004b, & 2004d).

Is capital punishment just? Does it deter people from committing crimes? These are the usual questions at the heart of the increasingly heated debate about capital punishment. Of course, capital punishment is necessary, but the principle of 'rarest of rare cases' will be the right approach in this regard. The death penalty may seem inhumane, but what about the heinous acts of the criminal involved? Even though Thiruvalluvar's views are in line with the modern principles of penology such as reformation, rehabilitation and resocialization (in other *kurals*), he makes apparent that the "*lex talionis*" (eye for an eye and tooth for a tooth) principle is fitting for hardcore criminals (Enanalapperiyar & Jaishankar, 2004b).

6. *Victimology and Victim Justice*

A king named Manu Needhi Cholan killed his own son under the wheels of a chariot to provide victim justice to a cow whose calf was killed by the prince under the wheels of his chariot. *Silappadikaram* explains that Pandya king Nedunchezhyan, died on the spot when he understood that he was the cause of death of Kovalan, when Kannagi (wife of Kovalan), a victim, proved that. This shows that the king, who was considered to be the embodiment of justice in those days, was concerned about the victims and their rights. During the Sangam period, the king provided victim compensation, and also it was quite common for the early civilizations to extract payments for the victims from the offenders, which process is now known as restitution (Jaishankar, Madhava Soma Sundaram & Halder, 2008).

Conclusion

The literature of a country is a reflection of its people and their culture. With the availability of literature spanning more than 2,000 years, Tamil lends itself as an ideal language to put this hypothesis to the test. Going through the Tamil literature, one is amazed at the depth and breadth of the knowledge the scholars of the past possessed. The feeling that one has just scratched the surface of what has been done already becomes inevitable. No aspect of life has been left untouched or unadorned.

The knowledge the ancient Tamil scholars rendered to the field of criminology and criminal justice is immense. Tamil literature has not left any chink of vision and mission for the criminal justice system. It has highlighted issues of criminal justice such as the draconian laws, just adjudication, duties of police, intelligence and penology and correctional administration. It is remarkable that the quintessence of some of the modern ideas of planning, management and organization of criminal justice system are found elegantly and succinctly enshrined in some of the scholarly works of Tamil literature.

Notes

1 For a treatise on Indian legal codes, see Betai (2003); for Manusmriti see Das (1982) and Chapter 9 of this book by Jaishankar and Halder; and for Arthashastra see Shamasastry (1923).

2 For a discussion on the role of caste or Varna in criminal justice, see Chapter 9 of this book by Jaishankar and Halder.
3 The Sangam Age in south India is a landmark in her history. The Sangam Age is from 300 B.C. to 200 A.D. A detailed note on the Sangam Age is provided in part I of this chapter.
4 The *Thirukkural*, a book of justice and code of ethics, is the most popular, most widely esteemed Tamil classic of all time. The word *Thiru* denotes sanctity, and *kural* means the short verses (couplets). Thiruvalluvar, a poet and philosopher of India, wrote it 2,000 years ago in the first century B.C. The *Thirukkural* consists of 133 chapters on different aspects of life, and each chapter consists of ten couplets. It is global in perspective and has universal applicability.

References

Betai, R. S. (2003). *Evolution of law of crimes in Ancient India*. Delhi: Bharatiya Kala Prakashan. Based on the author's thesis, Ph.D., 1957.

Bharathi Tamil Sangham. (1968). *The Sangham age: Being essays on early Tamil literature together with English renderings of selected poems of the Sangham age*. Madras, India: Bharathi Tamil Sangham.

Chattopadhyaya, B. (2009). *A social history of early India*. New Delhi: Pearson Education India.

Das, R. M. (1982). *Crime and punishment in ancient India: With a particular reference to the Manusmrti* (1st ed.), Bodh-Gaya: Kanchan Publications; Based on the author's thesis, D. Litt.—Magadh University, 1978.

Enanalapperiyar, E., & Jaishankar, K. (2004a). Administration of Justice. In Tirukkural's Criminal justice Outlook. *Crime & Justice Perspective, 1*(3), 2. March 2004. Tirunelveli, India: Department of Criminology and Criminal Justice, Manonmaniam Sundaranar University.

Enanalapperiyar, E., & Jaishankar, K. (2004b). Punishment & justice. In Tirukkural's Criminal Justice Outlook. *Crime & Justice Perspective, 1*(4), 2. April 2004. Tirunelveli, India: Department of Criminology and Criminal Justice, Manonmaniam Sundaranar University.

Enanalapperiyar, E., & Jaishankar, K. (2004c). Spies & intelligence. In Tirukkural's Criminal Justice Outlook. *Crime & Justice Perspective, 1*(5), 2. July 2004. Tirunelveli, India: Department of Criminology and Criminal Justice, Manonmaniam Sundaranar University.

Enanalapperiyar, E., & Jaishankar, K. (2004d). Cruelty & punishment. In Tirukkural's Criminal Justice Outlook. *Crime & Justice Perspective, 1*(3), 2. September 2004. Tirunelveli, India: Department of Criminology and Criminal Justice, Manonmaniam Sundaranar University.

Jaishankar, K., & Halder, D. (2004). *Manusmriti*: A critique of the criminal justice tenets in the ancient Indian Hindu code. *ERCES Online Quarterly Review, 1*(3). (Now not available online).

Jaishankar, K., Madhava Soma Sundaram, P., & Halder, D. (2008). Malimath Committee and Crime Victims: Resurrecting the forgotten voices of the Indian Criminal Justice System. In: Natti Ronel., K. Jaishankar and Bensimon, M. (Eds.), *Trends and Issues in Victimology* (pp.112–127). Newcastle upon Tyne, UK: Cambridge Scholars Publishing.

Kosambi, D. D. (1964). *The culture and civilisation of ancient India in historical outline*. Poona: English Publisher.

Madras Police Department. (1959). *The history of the Madras Police: Centenary 1859–1959*. Published Under the Authority of the Inspector General of Police. Madras, India: B.N.K. Press.

Ragozin, Z. A. (1961). *Vedic India (as embodied principally in the Rig-veda)*. Delhi: Munshi Ram Manohar Lal Oriental Booksellers & Publishers.

Shamasastry, R. (1923). *Kautilya's Arthasastra*. Mysore: Wesleyan Mission Press.

Subramanian, N. (1976). *History of Tamilnad: To A.D. 1565*. Madras, India: Koodal Publishers.

Subramanian, R. (1992). Administration of justice in Tamil Literature. Retrieved from www.yabaluri.org/Web%20(1978%20-%202008)/administrationofjusticeintamilliteraturejan92.htm.

12

GOONDAS OF CALCUTTA
Crimes and Policing in the Colonial India

Sugata Nandi

Introduction

The word 'goonda' is the epithet for the ubiquitous South Asian urban criminal. The term, a slang of obscure origin, came into common parlance in Calcutta around 1900. In February 1923 the Calcutta Police were empowered with the Goondas Act [hereafter GA], with which the goondas became a criminal category demarcated by the law (Bengal Government, 1939). The GA was a local law applicable to Calcutta and its surrounding industrial rim, and its express purpose was to protect the city from violent property criminals lurking in the streets. The act proved so effective in Calcutta that police forces of several other cities, like Bombay, Kanpur and Delhi, were empowered with GAs modelled closely on the one in force in Calcutta. This chapter is a brief history of the goondas of colonial Calcutta and their policing from 1920 to 1947. It argues that the goondas, rather than constituting a self-evident criminal category, were repositories of perceived threats of the colonial police and the Indian respectable classes, and also that they represented different threats at different points in time.

This chapter is divided into four sections. First, it traces the genesis of goondas leading to the ratification of the GA. Second, it looks at those who were criminalized by the act, taking up a few typical cases. Third, it studies the various uses of the GA in the period under study. Last, it probes the way goondas have been linked to the worlds of communal violence and institutional politics, which from the 1920s down to this day are taken to be a problem plaguing several South Asian polities.

1. How Did the Goondas Come to Be?

The word 'goonda' connoted an outsider miscreant to the Calcutta Police and Bengalis of respectable classes or the *bhadralok* from around 1900. For example, in a report on a riot in north Calcutta in 1907, Bengalis of the respectable classes accused 'up-countrymen', i.e. men hailing from the neighbouring provinces of United Provinces and Bihar, of being goondas who looted their belongings taking advantage of the anarchy in the riot affected area (Government of Bengal, 1907). At this point of time, however, the goondas had not become a cause for concern either for them or for the police. This prevailing attitude changed from 1914. In that year Marwari traders of Barabazar, a north Calcutta neighbourhood, which was the business-cum-residential quarter for the said Hindu and Jain merchants from the modern-day Indian state of Rajasthan, sought police help to put down a spate of street property crimes they attributed to the goondas (Government of Bengal, 1920). The police heightened security in that area with special patrols and claimed to have stamped out goonda crimes. The goondas reappeared in 1919, this time as a far more serious threat. The Marwaris appealed to the highest civil bureaucrat of the Bengal government, the Chief Secretary, for special measures against the goondas of their neighbourhood and its surrounding areas (Hardgrove, 2004; Timberg, 1978). The government unlike in the past attached a high degree of importance to their complaint, because Marwari traders of Calcutta had emerged as important allies of the colonial government in India (Hardgrove, 2004; Timberg, 1978). They had supplied the Indian Army fighting for Britain on off-shore war theatres with jute gunny sacks and soldiers uniforms, and in exchange they amassed vast fortunes which enabled them to turn into industrialists in the 1920s. It was also the time when they were looking for ways to assert their presence in the Gandhi-led movements, which would bring them political importance and high social status. They followed the practice of hiring a large retinue of servants and private guards from United Provinces and Bihar, among whom some robbed their employers, taking advantage of their practice of send large amounts of cash through their servants' hands for business transactions (Bengal Government, 1921).

Responding to their complaint of goondamenace in Barabazar, Reginald Clarke, Commissioner of Police, Calcutta, therefore, attributed the origins of the problem to the Marwaris' practice of inducting 'up-country' guards and servants into Barabazar (Bengal Government, 1921). He said that Marwaris trusted these men with large sums of money, and they in turn found it easy to prey upon their employers. Hence there were a large number of cases of breach of trust, which Marwaris called goondacrimes. The Commissioner ended his observation saying that those Marwaris described as goondas were ninety per cent 'up-countrymen'. Nonetheless, keeping in mind the newfound importance of the Marwaris in the eyes of the government, he called for a new law which would enable the police to deport these miscreants from the city (Bengal Government, 1920). The law was ratified as the GA by the Bengal Legislative Council in February 1923. Contemplated as a local law applicable to Barabazar, the scope of the GA was extended to cover the Presidency Area, i.e., the area under the jurisdiction of the Calcutta Police and industrial rim surrounding the city.

While 'goonda problem' specifically meant a spate in violent property crimes in Barabazar, the scope of the act was extended to a much larger area, as elite and middle-class Bengal politicians saw in it a possible legal weapon with which the poor could be kept outside the realm of nationalist politics (Bengal Government, 1923). The Bill was tabled less than a year after the first mass movement of India, the Gandhi-led Non Co-operation movement (with which he had joined forces with the anti-imperial pan-Islamist Khilafat in 1920), had ended, which signalled the beginning of the mass phase of politics. Challenged by the newfound political importance of the poor, Bengal politicians turned the GA into a weapon which empowered the police to instill fear of their authority among the poor to keep them docile. To attain this end they called for its application on the riff-raff who donned the garb of political activists alongside those from respectable classes like students and idealist youths at times of the movements only to be exempted from punishment as common criminals (Bengal Government, 1923, Vol XI). During debate on the Goondas Bill they cited instances of how goondas from Barabazar had infiltrated ranks of Non-Co-operation and Khilafat agitators in 1921 and '22 in Calcutta. They imagined a typical goonda to arrive at Howrah, Calcutta's adjacent industrial township, by train, where he would live in the company of his country cousins in the slums of the mill districts and commit petty crimes. Later, as he would take to foraying into Calcutta and becoming a criminal without the fear of law, he would settle in the city and prey upon its defenceless law-abiding denizens (Bengal Government, 1923, Vol XI, p. 395). In their eyes such criminals or the goondas were different from the other common offenders because they used the fear of violent reprisals to silence their victims from reporting their crimes. For this reason the *bhadralok*-dominated Bengal legislature called for deportation without trial as the only suitable punishment for the goondas, as they were convinced that the said criminals would necessarily intimidate and prevail on witnesses to be acquitted by courts of law (Bengal Government, 1923, Vol XI, p. 461).

With the provision of trial by a court of law excluded from it, the GA became an extension of the already existing arbitrary powers of the Calcutta Police. What further enhanced the power of the police was the deliberate exclusion of a definition of the term 'goonda' in the Act; it merely said that its target was an 'extraordinary badmash', an uncommon criminal or a 'goonda or other rough' or 'a member of a gang of goondas' (Bengal Government, 1939, p. 97). Going by its provisions the Commissioner of Police, Calcutta or a District Magistrate from the industrial rim which came within the jurisdiction of the law had the power to send a confidential report on any person they suspected to be a goonda to the Bengal governor (Bengal Government, 1939, pp. 99–100). Having found the report convincing the governor instructed the commissioner to act against the accused using the GA. Immediately afterwards the police arrested him with a non-bailable warrant and submitted the report on him to two judges, usually from Sessions Courts, who advised the police on whether he was to be deported or not. The judges typically gave their opinion on any case on solely the merit of the confidential report given by the Commissioner of Calcutta Police or a District Magistrate. The accused was given to represent himself either in person or through a Prisoner's Petition. Rarely the judges examined witnesses, and they did so in complete secrecy without informing the accused, who on his part could call in witnesses only with their approval. After examining a case the judges typically informed the police whether they thought that the man in question was a goonda and should be deported and suggested a duration for which he was to remain outside the Presidency Area (Bengal Government, 1939, pp. 102–103). In case one of the judges opted against deportation, the police followed the opinion of the other. They guided the deportee away from the city to one of its two railways stations, where he was made to board a train to travel to the destination mentioned in his 'Order of Externment' (Bengal Government, 1939). On reaching the place he was to report to the local police station and had to seek their approval in case he was to leave that place even for a brief while. Violation of the order of deportation, i.e. in case the deportee returned to the Presidency Area or Calcutta proper any time before the end of his period specified in his order, he was to be punished with one year's rigorous imprisonment without trial (Bengal Government, 1939).

2. Who Were Deported and Why?

With the scope of the act defined in the legislature at the time of its ratification, the police marked out certain occupational categories as targets of the GA before it was brought into operation. Those who were goondas in the eyes of the police were mainly fruitsellers, small shoe-shop owners, shop-clerks, carters, porters, day-labourers, paan (chewing beetle leaf) vendors and private guards (Bengal Government, 1922). According to the police the majority of them were migrants, hailing from far-off places like the North West Frontier Province and the Punjab and also neighbouring provinces like Bihar and United Provinces (Bengal Government, 1922). They claimed that they found it difficult to prosecute these people, as they necessarily had legal occupations, which they used as a veneer to conceal their illegal activities, and in addition they used intimidation to silence their victims, which made it almost impossible for the police to gather evidence against them. The overwhelming majority of them lived and perpetrated crimes in Barabazar, its surrounding neighbourhoods and bazaars of north Calcutta. This meant that the police targeted those who eked out a living from the crowded streets and bazaars of Calcutta and who, as was not unlikely, often fell back on crimes to supplement their meager incomes (Bengal Government, 1922). It is these people who formed the mass of Calcutta, which from after 1919 fought pitched battles with the police during agitations whenever the latter tried to disperse them. To punish them with the GA implied the assertion of police power over recalcitrant elements from among them.

A classic example of this was Babu Khan, a gangster who virtually controlled a large area adjoining the Calcutta dock (Government of Bengal, 1923). He migrated to Calcutta from Bihar to work as a private guard in his early twenties, took to crime while acting as a hitman for his merchant employer and later became the target of police and the excise department for many years. He was accused in a number of cases involving smuggling in contraband articles and drugs, extortion, robbery, grievous assault and murder. Crime paid him handsomely, and he was a very rich man at the time of his arrest. He owned a number of houses in the dock area and commanded a following from among its inhabitants who went to the extent of claiming ownership of contraband articles smuggled by Babu to protect him from the law. The police failed to prove him guilty in a court of law, as he either silenced the complainants with threats or bribed witnesses to turn to his favour. When arrested under the GA Babu successfully stalled his deportation from the city, as he was being tried in another case. The police could force him out of the city three years later in 1926 when they found him instigating crowds to violence during a Hindu–Muslim communal riot in Calcutta. His ouster from the city marked the ultimate triumph of the police in subduing a man who had for decades evaded arrest and foiled police authority over a neighbourhood.

Another such case was Burra Mahabir a bully, extortionist, fraudster and robber who preyed on unsuspecting pedestrians on the Chitpore Road, one of the main arterial roads of north Calcutta (Government of Bengal, 1925). The police arrested him on several occasions but failed to prove him guilty as he intimidated his victims into submission and forced them withdraw cases against him. He extorted money from the shopkeepers of Chitpore Road and fatally assaulted them when they sought police help. He cheated people with fake offers of jewellery; in such cases also his victims were silenced with fear of reprisals. His ouster from Calcutta signified a police victory over the Chitpore Road, a main thoroughfare where he openly flouted police authority repeatedly with his crimes.

While men like Babu and Mahabir were notorious gangsters and they actually challenged the police with their influence over pockets of the city, the law-keepers used the act against any poor person who even seemingly challenged their authority during turbulent times. For example, Abdul Gaffoor, who was known as a pickpocket to the police, was deported from the city in 1931 during the time of the Civil Disobedience movement (Government of Bengal, 1931). He attained the status of a goonda in the eyes of the police when he hit a police sergeant in a scuffle while the movement was at its peak. Referring to this one of the judges observed that he was certainly a goonda as he was from the 'lower class and was ready for lawless violence'.

The police tried to establish that those deported under the GA exhibited common characteristics which made them appear as an easily distinguishable variant of criminals. In confidential reports of all the deportees the police tended to suggest that they belonged to families which migrated to Calcutta, took to crime from an early age and emerged as juvenile delinquents by adolescence. By late adolescence or early youth they became recidivists or repeat offenders when punishment did not restrain them. This culminated in their becoming fearsome criminals with a proclivity to use violence. For example, Jit Singh appears in his biography first as a boy from a family which migrated to Calcutta from the Punjab who started going astray in the company of known bad characters of his slum after the death of his mother while he was a teenager. Later, following his father's death during his late teens, he emerged as a juvenile delinquent in the eyes of the police. When he was in his early youth the police arrested him several times for theft and drug peddling. Later on he became a gangster and committed crimes of violence (Government of Bengal, 1931). During the time of his arrest under the GA the police observed that two of his elder brothers who remained in their ancestral home in Amritsar in the Punjab were leading law-abiding existences as workers in a printing press.

The case of Sheikh Nawab, who belonged to a family of poor migrants in Calcutta, appears similar from the confidential report on him (Government of Bengal, 1925). His case revealed how the police looked at slums as criminalizing agents. Nawab's family lived in a slum in Bagmari, which was located next to a swamp on the north-eastern fringes of the city. His father had a carpet shop in a bazaar near the slum which he ran with the help of his elder son, Nawab's brother. In the slum Nawab picked up the company of 'dangerous characters' and turned into a bully and an extortionist and belaboured constables when they tried to arrest him red-handed. Due to his utter dearth of fear of lone beat constables, a posse of policemen had to overpower him before his arrest. When his report was placed before the advising judges, they noticed that his father and brother were lawfully eking out a living as shopkeepers.

3. What Did the Goondas Act Accomplish?

The majority of the cases of GA deportees ranging from the gangster Babu Khan down to slum extortionist Sheikh Nawab come from the period 1923 to 1931, which shows that the GA was essentially a measure of the '20s, and a relatively small number of deportees suggests that the act was used to mete out exemplary punishment to a few to deter many from taking to violent crime. It remained in effect from 1923 till after the end of colonial rule in Calcutta and was modified into the Anti-Rowdy Act by Bidhan Chandra Ray, noted Gandhian Congressman and the illustrious Chief Minister of West Bengal, in 1952 (Dhareshwar & Srivatsan, 1996). In the twenty-five years of its existence during colonial rule, the GA was a law of extraordinary importance for the police up to 1929. By 1932 it lost its unusual importance. Thereafter from the mid 1930s till 1940 it commanded very little significance. In 1941 it was once again put into use with renewed vigour, and finally the act was zealously used by the police to enforce order in a riot-torn city during 1946.

The phase of the vigorous anti-goonda campaign of the Calcutta Police was synonymous with the career of Charles Tegart as its commissioner, regarded by many as an iconic colonial policeman, who led the Calcutta Police as its commissioner from 1923–29. Under his stewardship a Goondas Division was opened in the Calcutta Police which gathered information on individuals who would be deported by the GA (Curry, n.d.). Between 1923 and 1929 the police deported 213 individuals, and during this time apocryphal stories about Tegart's prowess spread through the city (Bengal Secretariat, 1924; Ghosal, 1974). One such story claimed that he roamed the streets of Calcutta in disguise in the night to hunt down goondas singlehandedly. For his part, Tegart hailed the GA as the much-needed measure with which the city would be safe for the law-abiding respectable classes and their property (Bengal Secretariat, 1924). He used crime statistics compiled annually by the police to claim that the act was bringing about a drastic improvement when it came to curbing ordinary crimes. For example, between 1922 and 1929 annual aggregates for cases of robbery, considered to be the worst form of goonda crimes, decreased from 122 to 15 (Bengal Secretariat, 1930). Two other ordinary offences, burglary and theft, also attributed to the goondas from 1922, showed a marked decline over these years. At the end of 1925 the Bengal governor expressed great satisfaction at the effects of the GA and said that the decline in the figures for robbery, burglary and theft showed that these were undoubtedly the work of the goondas (Bengal Secretariat, 1926). The fall in these offences continued in 1926, the year in which there was a large-scale riot in the city in which an incalculable amount of property was either destroyed or stolen (Bengal Secretariat, 1927). By 1929 the goondas lost their special importance in the eyes of the police, as the law-keepers shifted their attention to other everyday concerns of policing like the enforcement of traffic rules and the maintenance of public order (Bengal Secretariat, 1930).

In the 1930s the goondas almost disappeared from the list of serious threats to law and order perceived by the police, the politicians and the press. The police discovered a new threat in 1930 with the beginning of the Civil Disobedience movement, namely Bengali youths from the middle class (Bengal Secretariat, 1931). The Bengal government was alarmed to notice a resurgence of terrorism which aimed at the assassination of key European and Indian administrators and high officials. The terrorists were Bengali students and youths, both male and female. With them posing a threat the goondas receded into the background in the eyes of the police. This was reflected in the annual aggregates of GA deportees, which was 150 for the '30s (Bengal Secretariat, 1931–40).

The fear of terrorism and a large-scale anti-imperial mass movement overwhelmed the police to such an extent in the '30s that it concentrated its efforts at prevention of smuggling of arms and ammunitions through the Calcutta Port even as late as 1937, when these threats had actually waned (Bengal Secretariat, 1938). Immediately before the outbreak of the Second World War the police administration of the city remained unaltered through the years of the Second World War. In 1940 the Commissioner of Police lamented that intelligence gathering in Calcutta was outmoded and inefficient, and hence he stepped up efforts at hauling it up (Bengal Secretariat, 1941). As a consequence, the GA was used vigorously in 1941, and after a decade of dwindling numbers of deportations, the number of GA deportees shot up to fifty-six, the highest recorded figure for the colonial period (Bengal Secretariat, 1942). It did not signify, however, that the police attached a high importance to the goondas in a manner similar to that in the early '20s. It was part of an administrative strategy to drive out known offenders from the city to prevent possible trouble in times of war and not a response to a re-emergence of the goondas as a serious threat. Later, even the tumultuous anti-imperial movements of 1945 and '46 did not lead to re-appearance of goondas. Rather the youth and a section of the unionized factory workers looked intimidating to the colonial authorities. It all changed in August 1946 when the first Partition riot broke out in Calcutta.

4. How Were Goondas Linked to Riots and Politics?

An important part of the history of the goondas of Calcutta was the way they were linked to communal riots. In modern-day South Asia, they are often cited as sole originators and perpetrators of riots and similar outbreaks of violence. The first recorded instance of such detailed and meticulous causation for riot comes from Calcutta 1926. In that year the city suffered three spells of rioting over the issue of using streets as sites of religious assertion (Government of India, 1926). As a consequence of that Calcutta witnessed an unprecedented goondas panic, which finally led to the promulgation of emergency twice in the city, once immediately after the first two spells of rioting.

In 1926 the riot broke out on Good Friday in April as a Hindu Arya Samaj procession was passing by a mosque in north Calcutta where poor Muslims had congregated for their weekly prayer (Government of India, 1926). The Hindu processionists played music, which they claimed to be a part of their religious ritual. The Muslims objected to the playing of music, which led to a violent altercation between the two parties, which in turn culminated in a riot. At the time when the riot broke out the goondas appeared to be a waning threat, especially because the Calcutta Police had claimed that the goonda menace had been suppressed at the end of 1925 by stringent application of the GA. Within weeks after the outbreak of the riot the goondas emerged in police reports and in newspaper reportage as killers prowling the streets of the city who preyed upon unsuspecting victims, stabbed them and left them bleeding to death in the narrow alleyways as well as the main streets. They managed to slip away even before the police could appear on the scenes of crime. They matched the might of the military patrols with their guerrilla-esque strikes on lone victims braving the troops (Government of Bengal, 1926).

Soon it appeared that the goondas threatened everyone while the riot raged. For fear of riots, the postal service was temporarily stopped, the New Market, the then-elite shopping arcade of Calcutta, closed indefinitely, the Calcutta University closed sine die, violence spilled into bhadralok enclaves earlier known as safe havens, Muslims of the city feared attacks by faceless Hindu communalist assassins and the Hindus called for organizing defence parties to protect themselves from Muslim communal killers. Even policemen, including European officials, feared violent death at the hands of such killers while trying to disperse rioting crowds off the streets. For all the diverse sections of Calcutta residents the embodiment of the fear was the goonda. This resulted from mid-April in a public outcry calling for a suppression of the goondas with a heavy hand. For example, veteran Indian nationalist Bipin Chandra Pal urged the Calcutta Police to use the Lewis gun, a firearm used in the First World War.

The Calcutta Police, which was failing to desist crowds from rioting, found in the situation an opportunity to augment its arbitrary punitive powers to instill fear in the hearts of rioters. The result was an emergency law, the Presidency Area (Emergency) Security Act of 1926, which empowered the police to deport anyone on sheer suspicion of having a role in the riot (Government of Bengal, 1926). The act did away with the necessity of drawing up a confidential criminal biography and that of seeking the opinion of judges before actually deporting a person. The Bengal Governor used the act to declare emergency for a three month period from May to August and later from the beginning of October to the end of December (Bengal Government, 1927). By the end of the year the police had deported 404 persons by the emergency act (Bengal Government, 1927). During the second period of emergency they deported many known bad characters and others on suspicion that they were goondas with criminal intent to start a fresh spell of riots. The Bengal governor hailed this measure as a well-thought successful pre-emptory step which ensured that there was no recurrence of riots in the last three months of the year (Government of Bengal, 1926). With this he gave conclusive official approval to the conviction that the riot was the work of the goondas alone.

In 1946 the riot lasted for five days, August 16–20, but its consequences were devastating. It left at least 4,000 dead, 16,000 were left mortally wounded and 10,000 homeless according to one estimate (Government of India, 1946). It turned Calcutta into a cluster of Hindu and Muslim ghettoes, which became no-go areas for people of the other community (Government of Bengal, 1946). Stray murders, stabbings, acid throwing and bomb hurling kept the fear of a fresh spell of riots alive till December 1946. In March 1947 riots broke out again following the rumoured killing of a Hindu woman and her child (Chatterjee, 1991). Localized rioting occurred almost regularly till Independence on August 15, 1947 (Mansergh, n.d.).

Husain Shahid Suharwardy, the Muslim League Prime Minister (equivalent of modern day Chief Minister of a provincial government) of Bengal was widely believed to have let loose armies of goondas to attain Pakistan. He stood accused as the originator of riots of this one-year period. He faced a No Confidence in the Bengal Assembly after the riot of August 1946, where legislators of the Congress Party accused him of orchestrating a riot with the help of goondas (Bengal Government, 1946). Though Suharwardy and the Muslim League easily defeated the motion as they commanded a majority in the house, the conviction that he had used the goondas to bring about the riot grew stronger in Calcutta, a city dominated by the Hindus. Up to June 1947 every case of rioting was attributed to the goondas sponsored by the League and Suhrawardy (Bengal Government, 1947). After June 3, when India's last Viceroy Mountbatten officially declared the date of Partition of India along with Independence, a Hindu-dominated Congress ministry for the future Indian state of West Bengal assumed office. This emboldened the Hindus and the number of attacks on Muslims increased manifolds suddenly. Muslim League politicians led by Suhrawardy, who have been accused of patronizing criminals as communal killers, in turn accused Congressmen of victimizing the Muslims of the city with the help of Hindu goondas (Bose, 1974). Outbreaks of localized riots paralyzed life in the city completely in the weeks preceding Independence day on August 15 that Gandhi intervened by undertaking a fast in Calcutta to bring 'hot goonda-ism' to a stop.

The goondas of 1946–47 were markedly different from those of the previous years. They emerged as saviours of their co-religionists and slayers of the enemy community and found widespread though short-lived recognition as community leaders with important political connections (Das, 1994). As the police were largely ineffectual in quelling riots and a colonial government on its way out did not stamp out 'disorder' as before, the goondas of this period won the support of well-heeled respectable classes as well as the poor, who looked up to them as protectors. One such man was Gopal Chandra Mukherjee, then a Hindu youth in his early thirties who scraped out a living as a meat-shop owner and a wrestling trainer to police constables in Calcutta (Das & Ray, 1996). He lived in a mixed locality in central Calcutta which witnessed intense rioting. He saved the lives of many of his co-religionists and raised a private army of Hindu youths called Bharatio Jatio Bahini, named after

Subhas Chandra Bose's Indian National Army. Gopal, who was unknown before the riot, virtually controlled a large part of central Calcutta during 1946–47 (Das, 1991). He enjoyed the patronage of several important Hindu politicians of the Congress, who protected him from the clutches of the law. After Independence Gopal lost control of a part of his gang, but remained influential in pockets centering around his neighbourhood and was known for his proximity to Bidhan Chandra Ray, the Chief Minister of West Bengal (Das, 1991; Das & Ray, 1996). His connections with Ray come across as a typical example of the politician–criminal nexus, in which the goonda appears to be an extraordinary criminal due to political patronage which protects him from the police and the courts.

Conclusion

The goondas emerged as a serious urban criminal category in Calcutta at a time when poor migrants from provinces other than Bengal, who had flocked to north Calcutta in search of a living, turned into a mass which played a decisive role in nationalist politics. During the same time a community of Indian merchants was looking for opportunities to assert their newfound high social status even in police protection against street criminals. The goondas, whom a European-led police force, the Bengali Hindu *bhadralok*-dominated provincial legislature and the wealthy Marwari traders identified as a grave threat to law and order in Calcutta, were people who lived off the streets, took to crime to supplement their meagre incomes and challenged police power over a pocket in the city either in ordinary times or had done so during the time of anti-imperial political agitations. The typical goonda was imagined as a migrant who had gone astray from adolescence and had chosen crime over a life of hard and less remunerative honest labour. He became a violent offender with no fear of the law as an adult.

The GA was the legal weapon which gave exemplary punishment to a few such offenders by deporting them from Calcutta without trial. The greatest number of them were deported between 1923–29, when the colonial government and Bengal politicians were anxious to turn the restive poor migrants docile. In the 1930s as educated Bengali youths took to terrorism the fear of the goonda waned. The goondas did not re-appear as a serious threat to the colonial Calcutta Police in the 1940s, as the originators of turbulence in the eyes of the law were students and unionized factory labourers. In 1946–47 they suddenly came to the forefront with the outbreak of riots since August 16, 1946. Earlier, during a communal riot in 1926, the colonial Bengal government and Indians of respectable classes of the city had singled out the goonda first as the source of communal violence leading to a spate of murders and then as the sole originators and perpetrators of the riot. Similarly in 1946 the sheer number of deaths brought the goondas back as communal killers, who unlike in the past enjoyed visible patronage of Indian politicians, both Hindu and Muslim. From within the matrix of political patronage emerged the goonda of Independent India, a violent gangster, not necessarily of migrant origin, who enjoyed support of high politicians offering him immunity from the law.

References

Bengal Government. (1920). Home department, Police branch, Confidential (1920). File No. 241/(1–8). WBSA.
    Bengal Government. (1921). *Annual report of Police Administration for the town of Calcutta and its suburbs [hereafter ARPATCS] for the year 1920.* Calcutta; Bengal Government Press, 1921, 7.
Bengal Government. (1922). Political department, Police branch (1922). The Goondas Bill. File No. P. 2-A-9(3) of 1921. WBSA.
Bengal Government. (1923a). *Bengal Legislative Council Proceedings [hereafter BLCP] (1923)* (vol. X, p. 427). Calcutta: Bengal Government Press.
Bengal Government. (1923b). *Annual reports of Police Administration for Calcutta for the years 1923–29.* Calcutta: Bengal Government Press.
Bengal Government. (1926). *Official record of the Proceedings of the Bengal Legislative Assembly (hereafter BLAP)* (Vol. LXXI, pp. 92–3). Calcutta: Bengal Government Press, 1946.

Bengal Government. (1927). *ARPATCS for the year 1926*. Calcutta: Bengal Government Press, Resolution 1.

Bengal Government. (1939). Bengal Act I of 1923 (The Goondas Act, 1923), The Bengal Code, Volume IV, Bengal Acts 1920–1930 (5th ed., pp. 97–101). Calcutta: Bengal Government Press.

Bengal Legislative Assembly Proceedings. (1947). Calcutta: Bengal Government Press, Vol. LXXII, No. 3, 153 and BLCP, Vol. XI, 408–9, 417, 422.

Bengal Secretariat.(1924). *ARPATCS for the year 1923* (p. 10). Calcutta: Bengal Secretariat Book Depot, 10.

Bengal Secretariat. (1926). *ARPATCS for the year 1925*. Calcutta: Bengal Secretariat Book Depot, Resolution 1.

Bengal Secretariat. (1927). *ARPATCS for the year 1926*. Calcutta: Bengal Secretariat Book Depot, Resolution 1.

Bengal Secretariat.(1930a). *ARPATCS for the year 1929* (pp. 7, 10). Calcutta: Bengal Secretariat Book Depot.

Bengal Secretariat. (1930b). *ARPATCS for the year 1929*. Calcutta: Bengal Secretariat Book Depot, Resolution 1–2.

Bengal Secretariat.(1931). *ARPATCS for the year 1930* (p. 2). Calcutta: Bengal Government Press.

Bengal Secretariat.(1938). *ARPATCS for the year 1937*(p. 9). Calcutta: Bengal Secretariat Press.

Bengal Secretariat. (1941). *ARPATCS for the year 1940* (p. 10). Calcutta: Bengal Government Press.

Bengal Secretariat. (1942). *ARPATCS for the year 1941* (p. 10). Calcutta: Bengal Government Press.

Bengal Secretariat Compiled from ARPATCS for the years 1930–39 (1931–40). Calcutta: Bengal Secretariat Press.

Bose, N.K. (1974 Reprint). *My days with Gandhi* (p. 255). Hyderabad: Orient Longman.

Chatterjee, P. K. (1991). *Struggle and strife in Urban Bengal 1935–47: A study of Calcutta based urban politics in Bengal* (p. 190). Calcutta: Dasgupta and Co.

Curry, J. C. (n.d.). *Tegart of the Indian Police* (pp. 10–11, 14–15). Kent: The Courier Company Limited.

Das, S. (1991). *Communal riots in Bengal, 1905–1947*. Delhi: Oxford University Press.

Das, S. (1994). The "Goondas": Towards a reconstruction of the Calcutta underworld through police-records. *Economic and Political Weekly, 29*(44), 2877–2879, 2881–2883.

Das, S., & Ray, J. K.(1996). *The goondas: Towards a reconstruction of the Calcutta Underworld*. Calcutta: Firma KLM.

Dhareshwar, V., & Srivatsan, R. (1996). Rowdy sheeters: An essay on subalternity and politics. In S. Amin & D. Chakrabarty (Eds.), *Subaltern studies IX: Writings on South Asian society and history* (pp. 201–231). Delhi: Oxford University Press.

Ghosal, P. (1974). *Poolish Kahini* (Vol. II, pp. 59–61). Calcutta: Mandala Book House.

Government of Bengal. (1907). Papers regarding the Calcutta Riots. File No. 149/07 K.W. West Bengal State Archives, Kolkata, India. [hereafter WBSA]. Home department, Political branch, Confidential.

Government in Bengal. (1920). Control of goondas in Calcutta. Political department, Police branch, Confidential File no. 241/(1–8). WBSA.

Government of Bengal. (1923). Case against Babu Khan under the Goondas Act. File no. 295, Serial nos. 1–6. WBSA, Police Department, Confidential.

Government of Bengal. (1925). Action against Mahabir Singh alias Burra Mahabir under the Goondas Act. File no. 296, Serial Nos. 1–4. WBSA, Political Department, Police Branch, Confidential.

Government of Bengal. (1926). Declaration of a state of Emergency (for the second time) under the Presidency Area (Emergency) Security Act 1926. File no. 246, Serial nos. 25–26, WBSA, Political department, Police branch. Communal Rioting in Calcutta, Second Phase 22nd April to 9th May 1926. File no. 229, serial nos. 1–20. WBSA, Political department, Police branch, Confidential.

Government of Bengal. (1931). Action against the Goonda Abdul Gaffoor under the Goondas Act. File no. 274, Serial nos. 1–4. WBSA, Police Department, Confidential.

Government of Bengal. (1946). Report of the Commissioner of Police on the Disturbances and Action taken by the Calcutta Police between the 16th and 20th August inclusive. No file number. WBSA. Home department, Political branch, Confidential.

Government of India. (1926). Report of J. E. Armstrong, Commissioner of Police on Calcutta Riots. File no. II/XXV/1926. National Archives of India, New Delhi, India [hereafter NAI], Home department, Political branch.

Government of India. (1946). Secret Report on the Political Situation in Bengal for the Second half of August. File no. 18/8/46 Poll. NAI, Home department, Political branch.

Hardgrove, A. (2004). *Community and public culture: The Marwaris in Calcutta*. New Delhi: Oxford University Press.

Mansergh, N. (n.d.). Pandit Nehru to Mountbatten, 21 July 1947. *Transfer of Power, XII*, 283–285.

Timberg, T. A. (1978). *Marwaris: From traders to industrialists*. New Delhi: Vikas.

13

OPIUM PRODUCTION IN INDIA, PAKISTAN AND AFGHANISTAN

Historical Milieu and Counter-Measures

James Windle

Introduction

Opium is the coagulated juice of the opium poppy (*papaver somniferum*). It has been consumed, in prepared form, for centuries in many regions of the world for religious, cultural, medicinal and/or recreational purposes. More recently, opium is used to manufacture drugs—such as codeine, heroin and morphine—for sale in both licit and illicit markets. South Asia is home to three of the world's largest sources of illicit opium: Afghanistan, India and Pakistan. Heroin is illicitly manufactured in all three countries. This chapter provides an introduction to the size and scope of opium production in three South Asian nations, provides historical context to demonstrate how each country became a major source of opium before describing the current market conditions and scrutinizes current counter-measures employed in Afghanistan, India and Pakistan. The discussion and conclusion will draw from the existing theoretical literature on crime prevention, namely the situational crime prevention and routine activity approach, and on experiences from other countries to frame discussion on what could work and what most likely won't work in suppressing and preventing the supply of opium.

1. Opium in India

While there is evidence of opium trading in India as early as the mid-sixteenth century (Watt, 1908; McCoy, 2003) trade expanded significantly from 1773 when the British East India Trading Company—who had already secured authority over much of northern India—declared a monopoly over supply and export. Colonial India quickly became the world's largest source of opium: some was sold licitly to markets permitting opium imports; some was sold illicitly to markets where opium imports were prohibited, most notably China. In terms of revenue and exports, the Indian opium trade peaked around 1880, after which it gradually declined until 1897, when it unevenly increased before sharply dropping after 1911 (Windle, 2012).

According to Windle (2012), the declining significance of opium to colonial India resulted from three cultural, economic and political factors:

1) India gradually lost market share to rising Chinese production from the 1860s onwards;
2) The opium trade had lost much significance to Indian farmers and the colonial Indian government. Innovations in the transport infrastructure had linked rural communities to national

markets. This allowed farmers to produce and sell bulkier or more perishable goods. In many areas crops produced in opium's place were more profitable and their markets more stable. Furthermore, alternative crops had become more profitable to the government as export items;

3)   In Britain there had been a gradual shift in the perception of opium as a relatively harmless drug to be tolerated towards one of opium as a threat to health. This took place at a time when America began lobbying for a global prohibition on opium (see Windle, 2014a).

By 1947, when India got independence, the development of the international drug control regime had obliged states to limit opium exports to medicinal/scientific purposes. India, therefore, rejuvenated the flagging opium trade by producing opium for the pharmaceutical industry (Dev, 1957; Haq, 2000). The administrative and legal control mechanisms developed during the colonial period (see Windle, 2012) continued to be administered as before (Asthana, 1954), with added innovations designed to prevent diversion.[1] Minimum qualifying yields (MQY) were introduced to eliminate corrupt and inefficient farmers, and farms could only be licensed if they touched or were near another licensed farm (Dev, 1957). Six states were de-licensed between 1948 and 1960 in order to concentrate licensed opium production in three touching, accessible and controllably states: Madhya Pradesh, Rajasthan and Uttar Pradesh (Deshaprabhu, 1966). The MQY became gradually more stringent, and farmers were offered cash incentives for surrendering excess opium to the monopoly (Kohli, 1966). These innovations improved the yield per hectare, suggesting that farmers became either more efficient or diverted less (Windle, 2012).

During the 1960s, India, supported by the UN, established a near monopoly on the international trade in licit opium for medical/scientific purposes (Haq, 2000). The 1970s were the 'golden years' of India's licit opium trade. By the early 1980s its position as the world's leading producer was unstable. Competition from Turkey, Australia, France and others forced India to cut its export price from US$60 to US$45 per kilo, and, consequently, to de-license 73,000 farmers (Windle, 2012). This led the Economist (1981, p 83) to quip that India was 'stranded with an illusory monopoly and an opium glut'.

As the number of licenses began to contract, concern was expressed that formerly licit opium was being diverted into the black market (Burger, 1995). In 1981, the UN—receptive to Indian concerns over rising diversion and loss of jobs—passed a resolution urging opium-importing countries to purchase Indian opium (Haq, 1998). Regardless of the resolution, India's share of the global licit market has fluctuated on a gradual declining gradient from between 40% and 60% in the 1980s to around 10% since 2003. The number of licensed farmers has concurrently gradually declined (Windle, 2012; see Kramer, Jensema, Jelmsa, & Blickman, 2014).

In 2012, India passed the National Policy on Narcotic Drugs and Psychotropic Substances, which opened the opium trade by opening up the monopoly to private companies. The intention was to develop the flagging industry by allowing private companies to hold up to a 49% stake in a company where the state is the major shareholder. While it was hoped that private influence would improve efficiency, opening the industry to the private sector quickly resulted in de-licensing. This has, in turn, led some farmers to illicitly produce opium (Kramer et al., 2014).

Administrative and technological control measures have improved since the 1950s. They, however, continue to be founded upon the basic structure established in 1799: unlicensed opium farming is prohibited and subject to stringent punishment. Farmers are licensed to cultivate and produce an amount dictated by and sold only to the state at a fixed price. At the end of each season, farmers transport their opium to state opium agents for weighing and examination for adulterants. The opium agents transport the produce under armed guard to opium-refining factories (Newman, 1989; Richards, 1981; Windle, 2012).

At present, the Central Bureau of Narcotics (CBN) oversees Divisional Opium Officers who, supported by village Lambadars, inspect and monitor licensed farmers. To prevent corruption, two independent witnesses and the license holder accompany the officials. To ensure authenticity, the Opium Officer returns at a later stage to take a random sample (Rahman, 2012; Smith & Kethineni, 2007). The CBN annually calculates, for each of the three licensed states, the quantity of opium to be produced, the set price paid to farmers and the MQY (CBN, 2014; Mansfield, 2001). A major innovation has been the issuing of 'smart card' licenses that contain the licensee's personal information, the area they are permitted to cultivate, the results of previous monitoring and the amount of opium previously surrendered to the CBN. The use of satellite imagery was introduced in 2003 to support ground monitoring (US State Department, 2010); however, the Lambardar continues to be the primary means of monitoring (Paoli, Greenfield, & Reuter, 2009). Failure to meet the MQY implies that the remainder was sold illegally and, as such, the farmer loses the right to secure future licenses (CBN, 2014; Haq, 2000; Rahman, 2012).

Precise national-level estimates of diversion rates are largely conspicuous by their absence (Mansfield, 2001). Several academic and government researchers have, however, produced estimates ranging from 10% in the mid-1980s to 6–7% (INCB, 1993), 25% (Laurent, Dusinberre, & Hoots, 1996) and upwards of 50% (Haq, 2000) in the 1990s. Estimates in the first decade of the 21st century have ranged 10%—deemed too conservative by foreign diplomats stationed in India (Paoli et al., 2009)— and 30% (Mansfield, 2001). Romesh Bhattacharji, a former Narcotics Commissioner of India, has suggested that diversion tends to fluctuate: Increasing when harvest is limited by bad weather or disease, but when the crop was good the diversion would be about 20%.

In 1994, Karan Sharma—a former Mandsaur Deputy Narcotics Commissioner—established a model farm to test how high the MQY should be set. The test farm yielded 62kg of opium from 1hectare. Sharma suggested that careful and experienced farmers should be able to produce as much as 100kg per hectare: the MQY was, at the time, set at 40kg per hectare (cited in Haq, 2000). In 2001, after interviewing opium farmers and administrators, Mansfield (2001) suggested average yields of 60–65kgs could be obtained from one hectare, while 80–100kg is possible. Assuming that little over the MQY is surrendered to the state, the yield estimates provided by Sharma and Mansfield suggests diversion rates of between 35% and 60% (Windle, 2011a). A separate indicator of the extent of diversion from licit channels is that since the mid-1980s, significant numbers of heroin-manufacturing laboratories have been detected within licensed opium-producing areas (Mansfield, 2001; Paoli et al., 2009). India additionally remains a major manufacturer of illicit heroin (from diverted opium), which supplies India's 2.1 to 2.8 million consumers (Paoli et al., 2009).

2. Opium in Pakistan

In 1947, colonial India was partitioned and Pakistan became an independent sovereign state. While India inherited all opium-producing regions, Pakistan inherited the colonial administrative and legal structure to control opium production. In 1955, an opium factory was built in Lahore. In 1956 farmers were licensed to produce opium in Peshawar, Mardan and Abbottabad in the North West Frontier Province (NWFP)[2] (Asad & Harris, 2003; Khan, 1982). The state used former employees of the Indian opium monopoly who had chosen to reside in Pakistan to administer the new Pakistan Opium Agency (Haq, 2000).

While all opium was supposed to be surrendered to the state, to be sold by the monopoly to registered opium addicts (Hasnain, 1982), inefficient monitoring of licensed opium sales resulted in many merchants bypassing the state and buying opium illicitly produced in NWFP and Federally Administered Tribal Areas (FATA) (Khan, 1982; Murphy, 1983). Controls on opium sales were further relaxed in 1971 (Haq, 2000) to a point whereby there was 'no organisation and no control' (Train, 1974, p. 3) of either production or consumption (Qayyum, 1993). Consequently, production was inflated by increasing demand (Haq, 2000).

It was, however, external factors which launched Pakistan as a major global opium producer. In the late1960s (Windle, 2014b) to early 1970s Europe and North America's primary source of illicit heroin gradually declined through the suppression of opium production in Turkey and heroin manufacturing in France (Murphy, 1983). At this time, demand was increasing throughout Europe and North America. As such, European traffickers may have looked to Pakistan as an alternative source, and in 1975 the first heroin laboratories appeared in NWFP and Baluchistan Province (INCB, 1975; Qureshi, 1982).[3] Then, in 1979, opium production and heroin manufacturing increased in neighbouring Afghanistan as a consequence of the Soviet invasion. This was coupled with the closing of Iran's borders—due to the Islamic Revolution and later the Iran–Iraq War—blocking the primary trafficking corridor from South Asia to Europe. These events increased Pakistan's and later India's importance as a major transshipment point for South Asian heroin destined for Europe, North America and, by the late-1980s, Iran (see, Murphy, 1983; Haq, 1998).

Domestically, in 1979, the state monopoly was closed by the Enforcement of Hadd Ordinance, which prohibited the non-medical/scientific production, trade and consumption of intoxicating drugs. The ban on production was punitively enforced through forced eradication and the prosecution of farmers (Khan, 1982). The ban was supported by a one-year spike in production in 1979, which created a surplus which deflated the farm-gate price of opium. That is, the risk to farmers had increased at a time of declining reward (Murphy, 1983). Production dropped significantly (Khan, 1982) and the sudden removal of an important cash crop, without the support of alternative incomes, pushed many farmers deeper into poverty (Murphy, 1983; see, Qureshi, 1982).

Opium made a comeback around 1986, and relatively high production levels remained for the next decade, after which there was a sharp decrease: partly resulting from alternative development and eradication programmes (for an in-depth examination of the intervention see Windle, 2016b). Whilst projects differed in substance and effectiveness, overall they had rural development as a foundation, and for the purposes of this chapter, some generalisations can be made. Illicit opium-producing areas would receive assistance in constructing transport, agricultural and social welfare infrastructures. Agricultural extension workers were used to introduce high-yielding varieties of existing crops or establish new crops, such as tobacco or fruit trees, whilst instructing farmers in modern agricultural techniques. All this was often completed through continual discussion with tribal leaders (see Gillett, 2001; Murphy, 1983; Williams & Rudel, 1988).

Once the development project began to produce tangible results, the state implemented phased eradication programmes.[4] Each September, areas were targeted for suppression. State representatives would then meet with tribal leaders and opium farmers in the targeted areas and inform them of the enforcement schedule. Agricultural extension workers were on hand to provide advice on substitute crops and modern agricultural techniques (Boner, 1991; Qureshi, 1987; Zahid, 1987). Any opium poppies discovered following the initial warnings were eradicated. Eradication was primarily manual (Qureshi, 1987), although there was some aerial spraying with herbicides (Asad & Harris, 2003; Economist, 1986). Farmers re-cultivating after this initial eradication were prosecuted (Qureshi, 1987). In addition to interventions in Pakistan making opium a less attractive crop, parallel increases in Afghan opium output reduced the farm-gate price of Pakistani opium, further reducing the attractiveness of opium as a cash crop. Individually, the projects have been responsible for suppressing opium production and, to varying degrees, improving livelihoods throughout FATA, NWFP and Gilgit in the Northern Areas. The cumulative effect being that Pakistan was declared 'poppy free' by the UNODC in 2001 (UNODC, 2008; see Windle, 2016a).

3. Opium in Afghanistan

Afghanistan, like Pakistan, is a comparatively recent source of opium, entering the global market during the mid-1950s (INCB, 1973). While opium was first prohibited in 1969, the ban was under-resourced and seldom imposed (INCB, 1970), especially during the periods of violent conflict after 1978. The combined conflicts of the 1980s and 1990s devastated Afghanistan's agricultural resources and rural infrastructure, leaving opium as one of the few available cash crops in many areas (Ministry of Counter-Narcotics, 2009), a situation magnified by many Mujahedeen warlords who facilitated heroin production, manufacturing and distribution (Felbab-Brown, 2010). Production steeply increased throughout this period.

The 1992 overthrow of the Communist government launched a warlord era (Windle, 2011b) in which multiple warlords and criminal organisations fought for control of territory and the profits from illicit trades (Felbab-Brown, 2010; Goodson, 2002). Consequently, by 1994 Afghanistan had overtaken Burma as the world's largest source of illicit opium. Some stability was eventually established by the Taliban, who initially enforced a strict ban on opium. By 1996, however, they became aware of the resentment many farmers felt at losing opium revenue and repealed prohibition, before protecting and taxing the trade (Felbab-Brown, 2010; Rubin & Sherman, 2009). This de facto legalisation increased the number of provinces producing opium from ten to 23 (Goodhand, 2008).

Prohibition was re-enacted in 2000 with an opium ban which reduced the national area under cultivation by 91%. Sources have suggested that the intervention was 'inhumane and draconian', with local community leaders ordered to forcefully eradicate crops and punish farmers with public humiliation, imprisonment, flogging, execution (Farrell & Thorne, 2005) and destruction of property. Mansfield (2011), conversely, suggests that there was less violence and much more brokerage and implied coercion in many areas. There is, however, agreement that the economic impact of the ban forced many farmers and landowners to borrow money to repay debts incurred during the previous growing season. Others fled to Pakistan to avoid repaying debts or sold livestock and in some cases children (Mansfield, 2004).

Widespread popular resistance to the opium ban weakened the Taliban's authority just prior to the American led invasion: resulting in their removal from power (Felbab-Brown, 2010).[5] During the conflict, rural infrastructures were further damaged (Ministry of Counter Narcotics, 2006), and the state disintegrated into warring and rent-seeking factions. Production increased on a steep incline from then onwards (Windle, 2011b).

The opium trade is rewarding for many of the Afghan economic and political elite. Many warlords appointed to legitimate political/bureaucratic positions after 2001 had previously exerted authority over aspects of the opium and/or heroin trade (Baldauf & Bowers, 2005; Paoli et al., 2009). While former warlords avoided formal ties with overt criminal activity in order to enter legitimate state institutions, several of them exploited their position by protecting 'former' contacts (Shaw, 2006; see Byrd, 2010; Goodhand, 2008).

A less iniquitous obstruction to drug control is the awareness that a sharp decline in production would have severe economic and political repercussions. Afghanistan is one of the least developed countries in the world: around 39% of Afghans survive below the poverty line, and 33% are food insecure. In 2009, opium was produced by 12.9% of the rural population (UNODC, 2009), and a quarter of all economic activity was centred upon opium (Byrd, 2010) while in 2014, 13% of the country's GDP came from opium (UNODC, 2016). There is a concern that suppression would strengthen the insurgency and alienate rural populations (Felbab-Brown, 2010, 2015; Fair & Jones, 2009), an acceptable concern considering the outcome of the Taliban ban. Hence, while the opium trade represents a barrier to long-term economic growth and foreign investment (Fishstein & Mansfield, 2014; World Bank, 2005), support for a policy which could diminish the income of a third of the population, destabilise the economy and ignite anti-government feelings is understandably low.

Representative of state weakness is that since 2006, drug control has been centred upon the 'Good Performance Initiative' and 'Governor Led Eradication'. The schemes motivated provincial and district governors to ban and eradicate opium production by rewarding reductions in the area under cultivation with developmental funding. More often than not, governors must negotiate with local powerholders (i.e., warlords, strongmen or tribal leaders) to eradicate crops in their sphere of influence (Byrd, 2010; Mansfield, 2011; Mukhopadhyay, 2009). Governor- and local powerholder–administered suppression has tended to centre upon forced eradication and punishments rather than the development of alternative incomes and is often 'imposed where farmers have no alternatives' (Fishstein & Mansfield, 2014, p. 2). The lack of developmental aid has pushed many (ex-)opium farmers deeper into poverty and debt (Mansfield, 2011; Pain & Kantor, 2010). Furthermore, many local powerholders have facilitated insecurity for personal gain, and there are reports that opium bans have been administered to control prices. Others have siphoned resources into their own pockets or inequitably distributed them (Felbab-Brown, 2010, 2015; Pain & Kantor, 2010). While the challenges are numerous, the Afghan opium trade is not, however, a lost cause.

Discussion and Conclusion

This section will discuss how counter-measures in India, Pakistan and Afghanistan could be improved by drawing insights from two criminological perspectives: situational crime prevention and routine activity approach.

Counter-measures to prevent the diversion (theft) of opium from the state monopoly in India should be done by looking in to the example of Turkey—another major source of opium to the pharmaceutical industry—which has limited diversion to almost zero. Turkey did this by employing what criminologists call situational crime prevention techniques (see Clarke, 2008). That is, Turkey increased the effort and risk of diverting opium while removing excuses and reducing rewards by increasing the relative rewards of compliance (i.e. the state paid a fair price). A major element of this policy has been the 'poppy straw method' (Windle, 2016b). Although the poppy plant is cultivated in the same manner as in India (or Afghanistan and Pakistan), at harvest the farmer is prohibited from incising poppy pods to collect the opium gum. Instead, farmers cut and crush the poppies. The crushed poppies (the poppy straw) are then sold to the state, which extracts morphine from the straw using specialist and expensive technology (Mansfield, 2001). The next major element is that farmers are subjected to extensive surveillance throughout the process, especially during the harvest period. Surveillance is implemented by the military and local police, village elders and—as an entire community's crops could be eradicated for the excess production of one farmer—local communities (Windle, 2016b).

Although careful analysis of the 'local political, organisational and personal realities' (Laycock & Tilley, 1995, p. 575) of Indian opium poppy farming would be required, India could implement similar control mechanisms. The question then remains: why has Turkey enforced much more stringent controls than India? The answer appears to lie in the impact the trade has on foreign states. Diverted Turkish opium was a major source of heroin to American and Western European markets. Turkish controls were partly the result of decades of pressure from the USA and UN to control its farmers (see Windle, 2014b, 2016b). Historically, little Indian opium has been exported. This may have limited the external pressure which partly motivated Turkey. This said, while India remains a minor source for foreign markets, the rising illicit cultivation in Arunachal Pradesh and growing exportation to China (Datta, 2014; Kramer et al., 2014) and other states (Seghal, 2014) could result in external pressure being exerted on India to control its opium farmers. Furthermore, the engagement of the private sector in India's opium industry may result in more stringent regulation and a move towards the poppy straw method as stakeholders look to improve profits by reducing diversion.

The routine activity approach can offer some insight into what should be done.[6] Traditionally the routine activity approach has focused upon the act rather than the actor and ignored cultural, economic and social causes of crime. In fact, the development of the routine activity approach and the related rational choice theory represented a shift away from theories centred on social deprivation towards that of reducing opportunities to offend (Garland, 1994; Matthews, 2014). Proponents of these approaches, furthermore, often return to the argument that as not all poor people commit crime, poverty is an insufficient contributor to criminality (Wilson, 1985; see Farrell, 1998 for this argument applied to drug crop production). We can, however, reverse this argument to show how, for opium production, the routine activity approach dictates a need for structural change.

Routine activity theory emphasises how opportunities for offending are presented by the routine activities of everyday life (Cohen & Felson, 1979; Osgood, Wilson, O'Malley, Bachman, & Johnston, 1996). It predicts that for crime to take place, a motivated offender must converge in time and space with an attractive target, while there must be an absence of capable guardians or handlers. Routine activities thus provide the context within which decisions are made (Felson, 1986). The approach provides a useful way of understanding the prevention and suppression of opium poppy farming:

- Opium farmers are often *motivated* by survival.[7] As discussed above, they often make rational decisions that not growing opium outweighs the often quite slim chance of punishment by the state;
- Opium is an *attractive target*. Farming techniques are often passed down from generations, there is a ready market, and merchants will often buy opium at the farmgate, removing the expensive and in some cases risky trip to market;
- Major opium growing areas often lack *capable guardians*. The state may be limited by conflict or geographical isolation, or the local representatives may be corruptible and thus incapable of acting as guardians. The local community, one of the more important forms of guardianship, may support opium farming and thus act as a guardian against state intervention.

In short, drawing on the routine activity approach, the Afghan and Pakistani governments and foreign donors should consider that farmers make rational decisions based upon survival rather than profit. Policies should seek to alter the risk/price analysis by providing farmers with something to lose. That is, provide farming communities with alternative incomes, social goods (i.e. clean water, education, healthcare) and, often best of all, security. Indeed, recent evidence from Afghanistan demonstrates how farmers have stopped growing opium if other crops prove more profitable (Fishstein & Mansfield, 2014). This said, previous experiences of states which have suppressed opium suggest that successes often hinge on the state possessing the capacity to enforce prohibition and monitor opium farmers. Development alone is insufficient (Windle, 2016a).

For the state to provide guardians, it must either use local powerholders as a proxy or extend security forces into opium-growing areas. Repressive interventions which remove opium without first providing alternative incomes often weaken state authority in opium-growing areas, consequently limiting the capability of potential guardians or resulting in their ejection from the areas. Providing alternative incomes and social goods can boost the state's political capital, thus allowing the state to slowly extend its authority, establishing capable guardians whilst altering the risk/reward calculations by providing farmers with something to lose. Furthermore, the provision of social goods and alternative incomes may motivate the community to act as capable guardians in place of the state. In short, the primary objective of opium suppression interventions should be to build political capital and gain entry into isolated and hostile opium-producing areas.

Notes

1 'Diversion' is the technical term by which drug policy refers to theft.
2 As of 2010 renamed Khyber-Pakhtunkhwa.
3 This said, while it is commonly accepted that events in Turkey impacted Pakistan, Windle (2013) advises against assuming a simply causal link, as by the early1970s, Turkey was contributing little to the global market.
4 USAID crop substitution projects were the exception and usually demanded a more prompt cessation of production (Williams & Rudel, 1988; Qureshi, 1982).

5 A variety of cases have shown that any measure negatively and significantly impacting the welfare of opium farmers can harm rural–state relationships and have been contributing factors in the democratic (Windle, 2014a) or violent removal of existing regimes (Chouvy & Laniel, 2007; Paoli et al., 2009; Windle, 2013).

6 For a balanced critique of the routine activity approach, rational choice theory and situational crime prevention, see Roger Matthews (2014).

7 This should not be read as suggesting that opium farmers are a homogenous group. Different farmers have different levels of reliance upon opium, depending upon their land size, access to alternative markets and livelihoods, water and labour and whether they rent or own their land. That is, some farmers are in better positions to leave opium for other crops or livelihoods. Furthermore, not all farmers in high-opium-producing areas choose to grow opium. For many farmers, opium is perceived as a risky crop which may divert resources from less risky and more profitable crops (Mansfield & Pain, 2008).

References

Asad, A., & Harris, R. (2003). *The politics and economics of drug production on the Pakistan-Afghan Border.* London: Ashgate.

Asthana, S. (1954). The cultivation of the opium poppy in India. *Bulletin of Narcotics, 6*(1), 1–10.

Baldauf, S., & Bowers, F. (2005). Afghanistan riddled with drug ties. *Christian Science Monitor,* May 13, 2005.

Boner, A. (1991). Pursuing the elusive poppy. In *World development.* New York: UNDP.

Burger, A. (1995). Narcotic drugs: Security threat or interest to South Asian States? In M. Weinbaum & C. Kumar (Eds.), *South Asia approaches the millennium: Re-examining national security* (pp. 167–183). Oxford: Westview.

Byrd, W. (2010). Responding to the challenge of Afghanistan's opium economy: Developing lessons and policy implications. In P. Keefer & N. Loayza (Eds.), *Innocent bystanders: Developing countries and the war on drugs.* London: Palgrave MacMillan.

CBN (Central Bureau of Narcotics). (2014). *Licit cultivation.* Retrieved from http://cbn.nic.in/html/operation scbn.htm.

Chouvy, P., & Laniel, L. R. (2007). Agricultural drug economies: Cause or alternative to intra-state conflicts? *Crime, Law and Social Change, 48*(2), 133–150.

Clarke, R. R. (2008). Situational crime prevention. In R. Wortley & L. Mazerolle (Eds.), *Environmental criminology and crime analysis* (pp. 178–194). London: Willan Publishing.

Cohen, L. E., & Felson, M. (1979). Social change and crime rate trends: A routine activity approach. *American Sociological Review, 44*(4), 588–608.

Datta, S. (2014, July 3). Satellite data reveals Arunachal a Hotbed of opium farming. *Hindustan Times.*

Deshaprabhu, S. B. (1966). *The wealth of India: Raw materials.* New Delhi: Publications and Information Directorate, CSIR.

Dev, S. (1957). The all-India narcotics conference, 1956. *Bulletin of Narcotics, 9*(1), 1–3.

Economist. (1981, April 4). Les Fleurs Du Mal. *The Economist.*

Economist. (1986, December 20). Heroin brings more trouble. *The Economist.*

Fair, C., & Jones, S. (2009). *Securing Afghanistan.* United States Institute of Peace. Retrieved from www.usip.org/publications/securing-afghanistan-getting-track.

Farrell, G. (1998). A global empirical review of drug crop eradication and United Nations crop substitution and alternative development strategies. *Journal of Drug Issues, 28*(2), 395–436.

Farrell G., & Thorne, J. (2005). Where have all the flowers gone? Evaluation of the Taliban crackdown against opium poppy cultivation in Afghanistan'. *International Journal of Drug Policy, 16*(2), 2005, 81–91.

Felbab-Brown, V. (2010). *Shooting up: Counterinsurgency and the war on drugs.* Washington, DC: Brookings Institute.

Felbab-Brown, V. (2015). *No easy exit: Drugs and counternarcotics policies in Afghanistan.* Washington, DC: Brookings Institute.

Felson, M. (1986). Linking criminal choices, routine activities, informal control, and criminal outcomes. In D. Cornish & R. Clarke (Eds.), *The reasoning criminal.* New York: Springer.

Fishstein, P., & Mansfield, D. (2014). *Despair or hope: Opium Poppy cultivation in post-2104 Afghanistan.* Kabul: AREU.

Garland, D. (1994). The commonplace and the catastrophic: Interpretations of crime in late modernity. *Theoretical Criminology, 3*(3), 353–364.

Gillett, S. (2001). Tribesmen, politics, opium and development in Dir, Pakistan. *Asian Affairs, 32*(3), 268–278.

Goodhand, J. (2008). Corrupting or consolidating the peace? The drugs economy and post-conflict peacebuilding in Afghanistan. *International Peacekeeping, 15*(3), 405–423.

Goodson, L. (2002). Afghanistan's long road to reconstruction. *Journal of Democracy, 14*(1), 82–99.

Hasnain, R. (1982). Effectiveness of laws enforcing organisations interdiction of narcotic drugs. *International conference on demand and supply of opiates in Pakistan,* September 19–23, 1982. Islamabad: Pakistan Narcotics Control Board.

Haq, M. E. (1998). The politics of medicinal opium: Resurgence of Indian international drug trafficking in the 1980s. *South Asia, 21*(2), 121–143.

Haq, M. E. (2000). *Drugs in South Asia: From the opium trade to the present day.* New York: St. Martins.

INCB (International Narcotics Control Board). (1970). *Report for the International Narcotics Control Board for 1969.* E/INCB/9.

INCB (International Narcotics Control Board). (1973). *Report for the International Narcotics Control Board for 1972.* E/INCB/21.

INCB (International Narcotics Control Board). (1975). *Report for the International Narcotics Control Board for 1974.* E/INCB/19.

INCB (International Narcotics Control Board). (1993). *Report for the International Narcotics Control Board for 1992.* E/INCB/1993/1.

Khan, D. J. (1982). Trafficking routes of opiates for domestic and international markets. *International conference on demand and supply of opiates in Pakistan,* September 19–23, 1982. Islamabad: Pakistan Narcotics Control Board.

Kohli, D. N. (1966). The story of narcotics control in India (Opium). *Bulletin of Narcotics, 18*(1), 3–12.

Kramer, T., Jensema, E., Jelmsa, M., & Blickman, T. (2014). *Bouncing back: Relapse in the golden triangle.* Amsterdam: TNI.

Laurent, L., Dusinberre, D., & Hoots, C. (1996). *The geopolitics of drugs.* Boston: Northeastern University Press.

Laycock, G., & Tilley, N. (1995). Implementing crime prevention. In M. Tonry & D. Farrington (Eds.), *Building a safer society, crime and justice: A review of research.* Chicago: University of Chicago Press.

Mansfield, D. (2001). *An analyses of Licit poppy cultivation: India and Turkey.* London: Foreign and Commonwealth Office.

Mansfield, D. (2004). *What is driving opium poppy cultivation? Decision making amongst opium poppy cultivators in Afghanistan in the 2003/4 growing season. Paper for the UNODC/ONDCP second technical conference on drug control research.* Received from www.davidmansfield.org.

Mansfield, D. (2011). *Where have all the flowers gone?* Kabul: AREU.

Mansfield, D., & Pain, A. (2008). *Counter-narcotics in Afghanistan: The failure of success?.* Retrieved from AREU www.areu.org.af/index.php?option=com_docman&Itemid=&task=doc_download&gid=617.

Matthews, R. (2014). *Realist criminology.* London: Palgrave Macmillan.

McCoy, A. (2003). *The politics of heroin: CIA complicity in the global drug trade.* Chicago: Hill.

Ministry of Counter Narcotics. (2009). *National drug control strategy: An updated five-year strategy for tackling the illicit drug problem.* Retrieved from www.afghanconflictmonitor.org/AFGHANISTAN_NationalDrugControlStrategy_January2006.pdf.

Mukhopadhyay, D. (2009). Disguised warlordism and combatanthood in Balkh: The persistence of informal power in the formal Afghan state. *Conflict, Security & Development, 9*(4), 535–564.

Murphy, J. (1983). Implementation of international narcotics control: The struggle against opium cultivation in Pakistan. *Boston College of International and Comparative Law Review, 6*(1), 199–247.

Newman, R. K. (1989). India and the Anglo-Chinese Opium agreements, 1907–14. *Modern Asian Studies, 23*(3), 525–560.

Osgood, D. W., Wilson, J. K., O'Malley, P. M., Bachman, J. G., & Johnston, L. D. (1996). Routine activities and individual deviant behaviour. *American Sociological Review, 61*(4), 635–655.

Pain, A., & Kantor, P. (2010). *Understanding and addressing context in rural Afghanistan: How villages differ and why.* Retrieved from www.areu.org.af.

Paoli, L., Greenfield, V., & Reuter, P. (2009). *The world heroin market: Can supply be cut?* Oxford: Oxford University Press.

Qayyum, A. (1993). *The challenge of narcotics in Pakistan: Legal and administrative dimensions.* Islamabad: Pakistan Narcotics Control Board.

Qureshi, T. (1982). Programmes to reduce the abuse of drugs in Pakistan. *International conference on demand and supply of Opiates in Pakistan 19–23 September, 1982.* Islamabad: Pakistan Narcotics Control Board.

Qureshi, T. (1987). Poppy crop replacement: A means of agricultural transformation. *Regional seminar on the replacement of opium poppy cultivation,* December 14–19, 1987. Chiang Mai, Thailand.

Rahman, S. (2012, May 4). Opium smuggling hits new high. *India Today.*

Richards, J. F. (1981). The Indian empire and peasant production of opium in the nineteenth century. *Modern Asian Studies, 15*(1), 59–82.

Rubin, B., & Sherman, J. (2009). *Counter-narcotics to stabilize Afghanistan: The false promise of crop eradication.* New York: Centre for International Cooperation.

Seghal, M. (2014, July 9). UN report reveals Indian heroin is going global as supply reaches as far as Canada. *Mail Today.*

Shaw, M. (2006). Drug trafficking and the development of organised crime in post-Taliban Afghanistan. In D. Buddenberg & W. Byrd (Eds.), *Afghanistan's drug industry: Structure, functioning, dynamics and implications for counter-narcotics policy* (pp. 25–46). New York: World Bank.

Smith, B., & Kethineni, S. (2007). Cultivation and use of opium in rural India: Bottom-up insights into anti-drug efforts. *Asian Journal of Criminology, 2*(1), 19–33.

Train, C.S. (1974). *For the record.* In FC0 9/2130. British National Archives: Kew.

UNODC (United Nations Office of Drugs and Crime). (2008). *Illicit drug trends in Pakistan.* Islamabad: UNODC.

UNODC (United Nations Office of Drugs and Crime). (2009). *Afghanistan opium survey 2009.* Retrieved from www.unodc.org.

UNODC (United Nations Office of Drugs and Crime). (2016). *World drug report.* Vienna: UNODC.

Watt, G. (1908). *The commercial products of India.* London: Murray.

Williams, M., & Rudel, L. (1988). *U.S. economic assistance to Pakistan: A review of the period 1982–87.* Washington, DC: Devres.

Wilson, J.Q. (1985). *Thinking about crime.* London: Vintage Books.

Windle, J. (2011a). Poppies for medicine in Afghanistan: Historical lessons from India and Turkey. *Journal of Asian and African Studies, 46*(6), 663–677.

Windle, J. (2011b). Ominous parallels and optimistic differences: Opium in China and Afghanistan. *Law, Crime and History, 2*(1), 141–164.

Windle, J. (2012). Insights for contemporary drug policy: A historical account of opium control in India and Pakistan. *Asian Journal of Criminology, 7*(1), 55–74.

Windle, J. (2013). Harms caused by China's 1906–17 opium suppression intervention. *International Journal of Drug Policy, 24*(5), 498–505.

Windle, J. (2014a). How the East influenced drug prohibition. *The International History Review, 35*(5), 1185–1199.

Windle, J. (2014b). A very gradual suppression: A history of Turkish opium controls, 1933–1974. *European Journal of Criminology, 11*(2), 195–212.

Windle, J. (2016a). *Suppressing illicit opium production: Successful intervention in Asia and the Middle East.* London: I.B. Tauris.

Windle, J. (2016b). Preventing the diversion of Turkish opium. *Security Journal, 29*(2), 213–227.

World Bank, (2005). *Afghanistan—State building, sustaining growth, and reducing poverty.* New York: World Bank.

Zahid, S. (1987). Enforcement of the ban on poppy cultivation in Pakistan. *Regional seminar on the replacement of opium poppy cultivation*, December 14–19, 1987. Chiang Mai, Thailand.

14

HOMICIDE IN ANCIENT, MEDIEVAL, BRITISH, AND CONTEMPORARY INDIA[1]

K. Jaishankar and Debarati Halder

Introduction

("Hatya"), killing or homicide, is a socially unethical act well recognized by the Indian criminal justice system since ancient times. Similar to other criminal law jurisprudences, the modern Indian criminal law jurisprudence also categorizes homicide into two categories: (1) lawful or simple homicide and (2) unlawful homicide. However, it is interesting to note that even though the modern criminal law in India, including the Indian penal code, was originally made by the colonial rulers and although legal provisions regulating traditional crimes, including culpable homicide, murder, and so on, were made in the shadow of English criminal laws, the concepts of intentional and accidental homicide were present in ancient Indian scripts dating back to 200 BCE to 100 BCE (Jaishankar & Haldar, 2004).

In India, criminal justice administration has been influenced by culture, religion, and colonization, viz., the Hindu religion and culture, Muslim religion and culture, and British colonization. The recognition and categorization of homicide have developed based on the above. The penology of homicide has also undergone changes accordingly. The ancient Hindu culture introduced the theory of "sin," which played a major role in correctional administration in relation to simple homicide cases or homicides of lesser gravity. While the ancient scriptures also prescribed severe punishments for other categories of homicides, the Muslim invasion brought in different understandings regarding homicide and related punishments. The colonial rulers, on the other hand, introduced homicide laws which were partly influenced by English laws and colonial cultures of punishing the killers of members of the ruling community and partly influenced by existing Hindu and Muslim cultures and laws regarding homicide.

Interestingly, some categorization of homicide has existed since ancient times, and this includes killing in self-defense, killing under provocation, killing of women and unborn children, and so on. However, the penology for the same may have undergone sea changes due to different interpretations of criminal justice by the then rulers. Similarly, the methods by which homicide is committed have also undergone changes because of developments in science and sociology; for instance, the present-day pattern of homicide may include murder by way of acid burns, lethal drugs, machine guns, or lethal bombs. Also, India is one of those few countries where capital punishment still exists for "rarest of rare cases" (doctrine developed by the Supreme Court of India in *Bachan Singh v State of Punjab* 1980). Such cases may include murder committed in "extremely brutal, grotesque, diabolical, revolting or dastardly manner so as to arouse intense and extreme indignation of the community"

(Garg, 2013, para 16). Several activists are working toward eradication of capital punishment, as it may be perceived as "lawful murder" (Suresh et al.,2014) and some question the appropriateness of the "rarest of rare" doctrine (Venkatesan, 2012; Bhadra, 2014). This gives an interesting understanding of contemporary Indian criminal jurisprudence regarding treatment of homicide of the gravest nature.

In this chapter, we aim to analyze the concept of homicide in India in the historical and contemporary perspectives. The chapter will follow doctrinal methodology whereby it will develop its arguments based on the ancient scriptures, existing criminal codes, and relevant literatures on ancient, medieval, and colonial criminal justice systems, case laws, and news reports. The chapter is divided into four sections. The first section deals with ancient Hindu codes regarding homicide, the responses to homicide, and related punishments; the second section deals with the concept of homicide in the medieval period; the third section deals with a British colonial understanding of homicide in India; and the last section deals with the contemporary understanding of homicide in post-independence and contemporary India.

I. Homicide in Ancient India

The ancient Indus civilization gifted the world with several wonderful intellectual works; the finest of them are the ancient legal codes prepared by sages of different periods. The earliest of these codes are the "Dharma Shastra." Each of these codes, or *samhitas*, was prepared by different sages and the oldest, and most authoritative of these is the *Manusmriti* or Manu Samhita, prepared by Sage Manu. It dates back to approximately 1500 BCE. While *Manusmriti* (for a detailed study on *Manusmriti* and crimes see Jaishankar & Haldar, 2004) was the first to codify the crimes, punishments, *raja Dharma* (duties of the kings), general conduct of people, trade practices, and so on, further codes were developed by learned Brahmans of later ages who were ministers to emperors before and during the Greek invasion in India. One such code is Arthasashtra, prepared by Kautilya, Vishnugupta, or Chanakya (350–275 BCE), who was the minister in the court of Mauryan Emperor Chandragupta. Even though Arthasashtra is a verse on economics and political science, it also mentions crimes, punishments, and the criminal justice system (Shamasastry, 1923). The ancient Hindu understanding of the criminal justice system is heavily influenced by these two codes (Lahiri, 1986).

Manusmriti categorized homicide into three main groups: (1) legal, (2) illegal, and (3) unintentional homicide. The three types of homicides are discussed below.

1. Legal Homicide

Legal homicide could include punishment of death handed down by the kings. *Manusmriti* prescribes four types of "*danda*" or punishments, which are as follows: (1) *vak danda* or admonition, (2) *dhik danda* or censure, (3) *dhana danda* or pecuniary punishment, and (4) *badha danda* or physical punishment, which also includes the death penalty (Lahiri, 1986, p. 168). *Badha danda* could include punishments such as the severance of limbs, beating and whipping, putting heated oil in the ear, imprinting marks on the visible parts of the body of the offender, and so on. But these might not result in death unless a death sentence was also given along with such punishments (Lahiri, 1986: 170).

Manusmriti categorizes 21 types of offenses where capital punishment can be given, including intentional homicide caused by force, a woman killing her husband, children, or spiritual guru, a woman administering poison with the intent to kill, and so on (Lahiri, 1986, pp. 191–192). Notably, among all these crimes, killing of a Brahmin by a member of a lower caste, killing of a Brahmin woman by a Brahmin man, and causing death to an unborn child were held to be the worst kinds of offenses and carried a mandatory death sentence. In cases of death sentence, *Manusmriti* prescribed seven basic ways of execution: beheading, causing death by pushing a sharp-edged weapon called "*shula*" through the anus of the offender, causing death by drowning, cutting the limbs, pushing a red-hot iron rod into the mouth of the offender, burning to death, and devouring by hunting dogs (Lahiri, 1986, p. 170). However, these types of execution were not allowed to be carried out by ordinary civilians nor even by the members of the highest Varna, that is, the Brahmans. It may be noted that death punishments were waived for Brahmins for most offenses. In cases where Brahmins were found guilty of offenses that were punishable by death, they were given other types of sentence, including pecuniary fines or banishing (Jaishankar & Haldar, 2004).

2. Illegal Homicide

As can be seen from the above list of offenses punishable with death sentences, intentional and willful homicides were recognized as illegal and liable to be punished by the *Manusmriti* and the *samhitas* prepared by other sages like Katyan and Yagyabalka. Such homicides could include the following types: the intentional and willful killing of a Brahmin man or woman; intentionally and willfully causing death to any man or woman or child out of rage and anger by anyone belonging to any caste; intentionally and willfully causing grievous hurt which results in subsequent death; killing and subsequently burning the body; intentional and willful feticide by a mother; killing an unborn child by harming the mother either with a sharp weapon or by slow poisoning; intentional and willful killing of a husband or children by a woman; intentional and willful killing of an upper-Varna member by a member of a lower Varna, for example, the Shudra, and so on (Lahiri, 1986; Jaishankar & Haldar, 2004). *Manusmriti* does not prescribe any special punishment for any special kind of homicide, but it does mention the killing of Brahmins as the highest offense and terms the offender as "*mahapataka*," or "ultimate offender."

The essential elements that were mentioned by the *Manusmriti* for treating a homicide as an illegal homicide are (1) intention to kill, (2) willfulness, and (3) knowledge of the consequences of the harm. It may be noted that even though *Manusmriti* treated women as inferior to men belonging to any other Varna, even the Shudra, intentional and willful homicides by women offenders were recognized as offenses punishable with death; similarly, intentional homicide of women by men and others was also recognized as offenses punishable with death. It may further be noted that *Manusmriti* also condemns *atmahatya* or suicide, especially when it is caused by self-strangulation, use of a sharp weapon, or poisoning; when it is due to frustration in love either caused by the partner or by the society; or when it is due to anger or rage (Lahiri, 1986; Jaishankar & Haldar, 2004). In such cases, the punishment included dragging of the corpse (of the one who committed suicide) by means of the same rope, or other weapon that was used in the suicide, along a public road (Lahiri, 1986; Jaishankar & Haldar, 2004). *Manusmriti* also prohibited any other person to perform the formal cremation of such dead bodies. It may be assumed that these measures were adopted to show the society that *atmahatya* or suicide is no lesser offense.

3. Unintentional Homicide

Manusmriti as well as later Hindu codes also recognized unintentional homicide. In this category the following four types of homicides are included: death caused to an *atatayee* (attacker) in the course of self-defense; death caused by a child who is under 12 years of age and does not have the maturity to understand the consequences of the harm; death caused by sudden provocation and anger and when the offender was not aware of the consequences and did not intend to kill; and death caused by the offender when under the influence of liquor or directed by someone when the offender is under "*moha*" (hallucination or infatuation) and when the offender neither intended to kill the victim nor was aware of the consequences of the harm inflicted (Lahiri, 1986; Jaishankar & Haldar, 2004).

In the last two circumstances the *Manusmriti* prescribed a procedure of penance by way of treating the wrongdoing as "sin." In the case of the first type of homicide, the person who has caused the death must provide evidence of willful, sudden attack on himself or on his kith or kin or on the community that he was protecting or was associated with (Lahiri, 1986; Jaishankar & Haldar, 2004). However, in such cases, both *Manusmriti* and Arthasashtra prescribed punishment other than physical torture or death (Shamasastry, 1923). Such punishments were prescribed mainly to make the offender atone for misdeeds that were caused more by mistake than by intent. In the second type of homicide, however, both *Manusmriti* and Arthasashtra had exempted child offenders under 7 years of age but prescribed examination of the maturity of a child offender between 7 and 12 years of age (Shamasastry, 1923) (interestingly, these provisions are available in the Indian penal code introduced by the British in 1860). Notably, however, *Manusmriti* did not exempt a Shudra from killing a Brahmin even if such homicide was unintentional (Lahiri, 1986; Jaishankar & Haldar, 2004).

Also, by introducing Varna-based (caste-based) social structures, *Manusmriti* introduced the legalized concept of honor killing. This may be evident from cases where death sentences were given for willful and consensual intercaste sexual relationships. Even though there were instances of mixed marriages where a woman from a higher Varna could be married to a man from a lower Varna in some later *samhitas*, this was strictly forbidden between a man and a woman from the Shudra and Brahmin communities and vice versa. It may further be noted that such honor killing was not permitted by ordinary civilians, as it had to be sanctioned by the lawful authorities. It is an unfortunate fact that such traditions of honor killing, for intercaste marriages or intracaste marriages still exist in Indian society, even though this is no longer supported by the authorities (Vishwanath & Palakonda, 2011). In earlier times some monarchy forms of government authorized such killings, though it is not legally proscribed and supported by any authority today. But some village systems do still support honor killing.

II. Homicide in Medieval India

India started losing its "Hindu" character by the end of the 11thcentury CE when foreign invaders, especially the Turks, started capturing northwestern areas of India and rolled out their own criminal justice systems to rule the captured areas. "In 712 CE, Mohammad Bin al Q'asim overran Sind. The Arabs, the Turks, the Afghans and the Mughals invaded India in hordes" (Ghosh, 1987, p. 24), and India entered the medieval period, when Qutbuddin Aibak became the ruler of Delhi in 1206 with the establishment of the Sultanate of Delhi. This brought about a new era for the criminal justice system in India that was influenced by Islamic philosophy (Ahmad, 1941). Over the next few centuries, until 1858 when the British took over the ruling of India from the last Mughal emperor, Bahadur Shah Zafar, the criminal justice system underwent many reforms, some of which still exist today. Before delving into the subject of homicide in the medieval Indian criminal justice system, a brief introduction to the origin of Muslim laws is needed. Islamic law is mainly based on Quranic verses. The code of laws for people belonging to Islam is known as Sharia, which finds its sources from the Quran and also the examples set forth by the Prophet Mohammed as the code of conduct for every Muslim (Coulson, 2011).

The invasions by Turks and later by Afghans, being followers of Islamic laws, brought Islamic laws to India. But it needs to be stated that the early invaders, including Aibak, the first Muslim ruler in India, did not feel the need to completely replace the existing set of laws and administration, including civil and criminal legal administrations. Islamic laws were imported more to regulate the people following Islam in India than to forcefully change the existing systems for the invaded (Ahmad, 1941). Rather, when the Muslim invaders made India their home, they created a mixed set of civil and criminal judicial and administrative systems which gave enough space for both Hindu and Muslim laws to govern people following the respective religions.

The Islamic criminal justice system as introduced by the Turks, the Slave dynasty, and then the Mughals maintained a threefold typology of homicide similar to that used in ancient Hindu India, namely, legal homicide, illegal homicide, and unintentional homicide. The Sharia laws dealt with specific types of crime, which included crime against individuals, crime against property, crime against God, unethical conduct, and illicit sexual conduct. Accordingly, Sharia laws followed specific types of punishments which included *Qisas*, "blood fine," and the doctrine of "eye for an eye" (Ahmad, 1941) for illegal homicides, including murder and death for disputes over property; *Hudud* (restriction) for offenses against religion, including adultery and illicit sexual relationships (MirHosseini, 2011), robbery, and theft; and *Diyya* (financial compensation) for bodily harm. An in-depth study of the penology of medieval India shows that legal homicides or death sentences sanctioned by the king or the judge existed in India, but the legal procedure of dealing with such homicides was different from that of the ancient Hindu period.

Legal homicide or death punishments sanctioned by laws were given in cases of murder, treason, theft from the royal treasury, adultery by married men as well as women, and grave mistakes and enmity against the ruler by officials. In cases of murder, grave bodily injury leading to death, intentionally causing death out of rage, and so on, the victim's kin could enter a demand for *Qisas* (the right of the victim's kin to kill the murderer), which could be granted by the state. *Qisas* was applicable in certain cases of unintentional homicides as well. However, it is interesting to note that *Qisas* was not awarded for non-Muslim victims. In such cases, if the non-Muslim victim or his kin could prove that he was a proper taxpayer, the state was empowered to award *Diyya* to be extracted from the Muslim perpetrator. However, there was discrimination regarding the amount of *Diyya* to be paid to a non-Muslim compared to a Muslim victim (Friedmann, 2006, pp. 42–50). Painful execution procedures were prescribed for the capital offenses, mentioned above, other than homicides caused by interpersonal problems. These included stoning to death (especially in cases of adultery), systematically cutting off limbs until the offender is dead, throwing the offender from height, trampling of the body of the offender by trained elephants, and poisoning the offender (especially in cases of officials who had failed in their duties) (Ahmad, 1941).

It needs to be noted that the Islamic criminal law as practiced by Muslim rulers in India did not prescribe death sentences for some kinds of homicide in the first instance.

Systems of jail term, pecuniary fines, lashing, and so on were used to provide the offender an opportunity to learn from the mistakes. Death sentences were given as final punishments (Ahmad, 1941). In such cases, there was no distinction between Hindu and Muslim subjects. Notably, many kings, including the Mughals, had a preference for public execution. This was done specifically to set an example to other people about the consequences of wrongdoing.

As can be seen from the above paragraphs, illegal homicide in the criminal justice system in medieval India included intentional and willful causing of death by one to another. However, the Muslim rulers did not disturb the existing categorization of illegal homicide to a great extent, especially for non-Muslim subjects, except in the case of *Qisas*, as has been discussed earlier. But similar to the ancient Hindu system, causing death in the course of exercising the right to self-defense and causing death by children under the age of 12 were recognized by the Muslim laws in India (Ahmad, 1941) as unintentional homicide, falling outside the purview of illegal homicide. It may be interesting to note that in several of these situations, as well as in cases of robbery, theft, and death caused because of such instances, the governors or the *Qazis* (priests) were liable to pay the compensation to the victims (Ahmad, 1941).

III. Homicide in British Colonial India

The East India Company ruled certain parts of India between 1757 and 1858, and during that time they did not alter the existing Mohammedan laws (Jois, 1984) and allowed the laws on homicide to be practiced by the courts. In 1858, with the defeat of India's last Mughal emperor, Bahadur Shah Jafar, began the colonial rule of the British, which lasted until India's independence in 1947. Although different parts of India were colonized by other European invaders, including the Dutch and the French, during the last few decades of Mughal rule, the British colonial rulers successfully captured the whole of India and brought major reforms to the existing penal system as well as the civil procedure system in India. Notably, the British rulers maintained the existing laws of the "natives" for succession or for other civil matters including marriage, but they created a set of uniform codes in the form of the Indian penal code (1860) under the chairmanship of Lord Macaulay and the Indian Evidence Act under the chairmanship of Sir James Fitzjames Stephen, to regulate criminal justice administration. The court system was changed to the British system. Even though the procedures for investigation, evidence, prosecution, and appeal had been present since ancient times in India, the system was revamped with the introduction of the penal code and the evidence act following British courts where the supreme judicial authority was invested in the British monarch. This introduction of the new penal code shredded some of the categories of legal homicides and introduced others.

It needs to be mentioned here that on many occasions since ancient times invaders used women and children as pawns to forcefully bring villages and cities under their control. This included raping women and using children as slaves as well as the creation of local customary laws which suppressed basic rights of women in Hindu and subsequently Muslim societies. These included child marriages, female feticide, sacrificing of children in the name of religious practices, genital mutilation of children, and burning of brides in the pyres of their husbands. By the end of the 17th century onwards, the problems of dowry harassment and killing of young brides by physical torture also erupted in Indian society. The British colonial rulers introduced a positive penal reform by categorizing such sorts of homicides as illegal homicides. There were specific laws made to criminalize bride burning or the system of *Sati Daha*, the sacrifice of children, feticide, and infanticide. Causing death by grievous harm in the form of punishment was also condemned as illegal homicide. Similarly, rape and sexual assault on women and honor killing were condemned as heinous criminal activities. The penal code also prohibited caste/religious violence (including communal riots) by way of killing members belonging to other castes, class, religion, or creed. While these were coded under specific provisions, the Indian Penal Code (IPC) brought in the concept of "culpable homicide" and homicide amounting to murder through sections 299 and 300, respectively.

Culpable homicide according to section 299 of the IPC is the causing of death by acting with the intention of causing death or with the intention of causing such bodily injury as is likely to cause death, or with the knowledge to cause death by such an act. The explanations attached to the provision further clarify that (1) a person who causes bodily injury to another who is already suffering due to some disease or infirmity or disorder and the death is accelerated due to the physical condition of the victim shall be deemed to have caused his death; (2) where death is caused by bodily injury which could have been resisted by proper medication, the person who had caused such death would be deemed to have caused the death; (3) causing of the death of an unborn child in the mother's womb would not be considered as homicide, but when the death is caused to a living child of whom any body part is brought forth from the womb even though the child may not be fully born or breathing may amount to culpable homicide. Culpable homicide is categorized as one of the illegal homicides, but it was differentiated from murder on the ground of intention, willfulness, and knowledge of inevitable results. However, section 300, which defines murder, provides several exceptions that may be categorized as culpable homicide not amounting to murder and also as unintentional murder. These include homicide caused by sudden provocation or without knowledge of the grave consequences.

Unintentional homicide may also include homicide by way of private defense, homicide by children, and also homicide by way of prevention of crimes. It should be noted that some of these categorizations had remained since ancient times, and they were formally recognized by the British laws. Ironically, the very British who emphasized the "rule of law" also used those laws to kill inno-cent people who were against their "British Raj." There were many mass murders committed by the British during their rule, for example, the Jallianwala Bagh massacre. The British also fanned the hatred between Hindus and Muslims, and there were large communal riots that killed many innocent individuals. The partition of India and Pakistan caused millions of people to be uprooted from their homeland, and the riots during that time killed more than 5 million people.

IV. Homicide in Post-Independence and Contemporary India

Although the laws on homicide remained the same in post-independence India, patterns of homi-cide have changed significantly. The Indian lawmakers preferred to keep the Indian Penal Code introduced by the British, and the laws on homicide within this code have been and continue to be amply used; while there are special laws like the Dowry Prohibition Act, 1961, which also has provi-sions for the punishment of dowry death (also amended in the Indian Penal Code). This law alone has not prevented dowry deaths, and a significant number (15% according to the National Crime Records Bureau, 2013) of recorded cases of homicide in India are from dowry deaths (UNODC, 2014). Also, communal riots continued in post-independence India, more recently being added to or replaced by terrorist attacks, including the 26/11 Mumbai attacks, which killed more than 500 people. In spite of the partition of India and Pakistan, Kashmir is still a contentious area for both countries, and several hundred people have been killed there either by the armies or by terrorists. Armed violence or aggression by Maoists also killed many people in many parts of India (IAVA, 2011a). Post-independence India saw an increase in murders/homicides which was again dealt with the same British laws, which have continued to be used in contemporary India, although homicide has decreased considerably over the last 15 years. The numbers of homicides rose considerably in post-independence India, although there had been a marginal decline in recorded murders since the start of the 21st century. The National Crime Records Bureau (NCRB) shows that murder increased fourfold from 9,802 cases in 1953 to 37,399 cases in 2000 but has since declined by over 10% to 33,201 cases in 2013 (National Crime Records Bureau, 2013, p. 13; see also Marwah, 2014).

Except for a few armed attacks in Kashmir and Maoist-dominated areas (IAVA, 2011a), India does not have a gun culture, unlike North and South American countries, for example, where the gun culture forms the major reason for homicides. Although there is no gun culture in India, to some extent, the use of illegal guns to commit homicide is prevalent in both rural and urban areas. A study by Kohli and Aggarwal (2006) found the prevalence of firearm fatalities in New Delhi, with around 90 victims being killed by firearms. Interestingly, the number of homicides based on firearms reduced between 1999 (112,147) and 2008 (6,219) (IAVA, 2011b, p. 1).

Many reasons are used as motivation to commit murders in contemporary India, and many clas-sifications are offered to explain these reasons. Nagpaul (1985, pp. 149–153) has developed a typology, based on causal factors, of homicides occurring in post-independence and contemporary India. They are: (1) homicides arising from property disputes, (2) family violence, (3) family violence concerning dowry, (4) situational homicides, (5) village feuds and political conflicts, (6) senseless homicides, and (7) infanticides. Alternatively, Periyar's (2018) research, which studied the victim–offender relation-ship in cases of revenge murders, developed the following typology as a base for homicides that occur in rural India: (1) intercaste issues, (2) intracaste issues, (3) class-based issues, (4) marital-based issues, (5) communal-based issues, (6) land dispute issues, and (7) others. The National Crime Records Bureau (2013), in its publication "Crime in India," presented its statistics on murder based on 13 typologies/motives. They are: murder for gain, property dispute, personal vendetta or enmity, love affairs/sexual causes, dowry, lunacy, witchcraft, terrorism/extreme violence, political reasons, com-munalism, caste conflict, class conflict, and other motives (National Crime Records Bureau, 2013; Marwah, 2014).

In 2013, the most common motives behind murders were shown as "personal vendetta or enmity" and "property dispute," which accounted for 10.3% and 8.4% of total murder cases, respectively. The other significant causes were "love affairs/sexual causes" (7.1%), "gain" (5.0%), and "dowry" (4.1%) (National Crime Records Bureau, 2013, p. 55). The statistics of homicide victimization in contemporary India still show females as the major victims of murder and culpable homicide, predominantly for reasons such as dowry deaths, infanticide, and honor killing. Females and young people were the main victims of murder in 2013 according to the NCRB statistics. "The share of female victims was 27.1% of the total murder victims (9,180 out of 33,901) and the youth victims (18–30 years) was maximum at 44.0% (14,910 out of 33,901 victims)" (National Crime Records Bureau, 2013, p. 59). However, individual empirical studies based on medical autopsies show males as major victims of homicide in India (e.g. Mohanty et al.,2005; Gupta, Prajapati, & Kumar, 2007). The reason may be the higher exposure of males to risk-based situations outside their homes compared to females, and females are more victimized in their own homes.

In contemporary India, the dynamics of homicide have changed in both urban and rural areas. While domestic and familial ("interpersonal") attacks make up many of the homicides that occur in rural areas, it is primarily "strategic benefit" that underlies homicides in the cities. A study by Dikshit, Dogra, and Chandra (1986) revealed that homicides were committed for financial gain in urban Delhi. Thus, lack of social cohesion in the urban areas is a key factor in many homicides, while the greater level of social cohesion in rural areas continues to be the reason behind many homicides there, due to adultery, revenge, love affairs, and so on. A study by Mohanty, Mohanty, and Patnaik (2013), done in rural southern India, found previous enmity and familial disharmony as the main reasons for homicide. There is a strong victim–offender relationship in the rural-based homicides. Similar situations were found when the offender is a female and the victim is a male. Studies on female homicide offending by Rani (1983), Saxena (1994), and Kethineni (2001) found that most of the female offenders have killed either their husbands or closest family members, and the majority of them were from rural areas.

Also, due to globalization, large-scale migration of rural people to urban areas has taken place. This phenomenon has created culture conflict between the urbanized people and the new migrants, which has often resulted in rapes or murders. A classic example of this is the rape and murder of a 23-year-old physiotherapy student in a moving bus in 2012 in New Delhi (aka the Nirbhaya incident). A small number of American-style school shootings and cyber-based murders have been committed in contemporary India (Jaishankar & Halder, 2009). In addition, sensational and unique homicides occurred in the past decade in the urban regions. For example, the recent murder of an Infosys software company employee, Swathi (June 2016), in broad daylight in Nungambakkam railway station in Chennai by Ramkumar (the accused); the killing of Sheena Bhora by her mother Indrani Mukerjea (2015); the Laila Khan case (2012), where Laila, her mother, and her siblings were killed by her stepfather; the Sandhya Pandit case (2012), where she was killed by her own son Raghuveer Singh; the Arushi Talwar–Hemraj murder case (2008), where Arushi and her domestic help Hemraj were purportedly killed by her own parents; and the Nithari killings that occurred in 2006 in a neighborhood of New Delhi, where 20 victims were raped and murdered by a rich businessman, Surender Kohli, and his domestic help (FB Staff, 2015). Examples from the earlier decade, such as Naina Shani (1995), who was killed by her husband Sushil Sharma and burned in a *Tandoor* (clay oven), and Jessica Lal (1999), a model that was killed at a party by Manu Sharma, were sensational cases. Notably, most of the sensational cases that occurred in urban India involved the killing of women. This shows the conflict of patriarchy with the modern values of women, wherein modern women who resist the patriarchy ruling or try to create new value systems copying the West are killed to be silenced.

Even though the analysis might indicate a rise of homicides in contemporary India, the rates of homicide in contemporary India are comparatively lower than in many other countries (IAVA,

2011a; UNODC, 2014). They have also been falling for some time, as noted by UNODC (2014, p. 26): "India has seen its homicide rate decline by 23 percent over the last 15 years, while Pakistan and Nepal have both seen slight increases in their homicide rates." Although India's homicide rates are relatively low compared to those of other countries, its conviction rates for homicide are also very low. Nagpaul (1985, p. 152) cites reasons for this, such as the purchase of eyewitnesses by the offender or the offender's family, eyewitnesses may be one of the close relatives who may not be willing to be a witness, or offenders may create false evidence. Overall, the Indian criminal justice procedure is designed in such a way as to favor the accused rather than the victim.

Conclusion

In this chapter, an attempt has been made to analyze the responses to homicide in India from historical and contemporary perspectives. Homicide in India was always treated as the most heinous crime, although the level of punishment in ancient India for the same crime varied between various Varnas. In medieval India, the Muslim laws provided harsher forms of punishment based on Islamic laws. The British later made sweeping changes in the laws during their time of rule and provided punishment for homicides following the same principle of "*lex talionis*" (retributive justice, sometimes referred to as "an eye for an eye"), and these are still followed in contemporary India.

There are no clear-cut statistics regarding homicides during the ancient, medieval, and British India periods. In post-Independence and contemporary India, the National Crime Records Bureau, which was founded in 1986, is the only authentic source of homicide-related data. Many researchers on murders/homicide have utilized the NCRB data (Dreze & Khera, 2000; Marwah, 2014). Apart from the NCRB statistics, there are few empirical studies on homicides, but they were mostly done from a victim's perspective (Dikshit, Dogra, & Chandra, 1986; Mohanty, Mohanty, & Patnaik, 2013) with fewer studies on homicide offenders (Kethineni, 2001). There is a need for more empirical studies on homicide to find the patterns of homicide in India.

Note

1 Earlier published as a chapter as Jaishankar, K., & Halder, D. (2017). Homicide in India: Historical and contemporary perspectives. In F. Brookman, E. R. Maguire, & M. Maguire (Eds.), *The handbook on homicide*. Wiley-Blackwell Series of Handbooks in Criminology and Criminal Justice (pp. 486–498). Hoboken, New Jersey: Wiley-Blackwell. ISBN: 978–1–118–92447–1. Republished with permission from the publisher.

References

Ahmad, M. B. (1941). *The Administration of Justice in Medieval India: A study in Outline of the Judicial System under the Sultans and the Badshahs of Delhi Based Mainly upon Cases Decided by Medieval Courts in India between 1206–1750 AD*. Aligarh, India: Aligarh. Historical Research Institute for Aligarh University.

Bhadra, S. (2014). *Indian judiciary and the issue of capital punishment*. Retrieved from http://cafedissensus.com/2014/01/01/indianjudiciaryandtheissueofcapitalpunishment.

Coulson, N. J. (2011). *A history of Islamic law*. New Brunswick, NJ: Aldine Transaction.

Dikshit, P. C., Dogra, T. D., & Chandra, J. (1986). Comprehensive study of homicides in *South Delhi, 1969–79*. *Medicine, Science, and the Law, 26*(3), 230–234.

Dreze, J., & Khera, R. (2000). Crime, gender, and society in India: Insights from homicide data. *Population and Development Review, 26*(2), 335–352.

FP Staff. (2015, August 28). Five controversial murders that shocked India before Indrani Mukerjea's arrest. *Firstpost*. Retrieved from www.firstpost.com/india/beforeindranimukherjeasarrestfivecontroversialmurdersthatshockedindia2408592.html.

Friedmann, Y. (2006). *Tolerance and coercion in Islam: Interfaith relations in the Muslim tradition*. Cambridge: Cambridge University Press.

Garg, A. (2013). *Death sentence: Extent of judicial discretion and need of guidelines.* Retrieved from www.legalservices india.com/articles/deat.htm.

Ghosh, S. K. (1987). *Communal riots in India (meet the challenge unitedly).* New Delhi: Ashish.

Gupta, S., Prajapati, P., & Kumar, S. (2007). Victimology of homicide: A Surat (South Gujarat) based study. *Journal of Indian Academy of Forensic Medicine, 29*(3), 29–33.

IAVA (India Armed Violence Assessment) Brief. (2011a). India's states of armed violence: Assessing the human cost and political priorities. *Small arms survey issue brief no. 1,* September 2011. Retrieved from www.indiaava. org/fileadmin/docs/pubs/AVAIB1statesofarmedviolence.pdf.

IAVA (India Armed Violence Assessment) Brief. (2011b). Mapping murder: The geography of Indian firearm fatalities. *Small arms survey issue brief no. 2,* September 2011. Retrieved from www.unodc.org/documents/ southasia/webstories/IndiaAVA_IB2_2011_Mapping_Murder_1.

Jaishankar, K., & Haldar, D. (2004). *Manusmriti:* A critique of the criminal justice tenets in the ancient Indian Hindu code. Retrieved from www.erces.com/journal/articles/archives/v03/v03_05.htm.

Jaishankar, K., & Halder, D. (2009). Cyber bullying among school students in India. In K. Jaishankar (Ed.), *International perspectives on crime and justice* (pp. 579–598). Newcastle, London: Cambridge Scholars.

Jois, M. R. (1984). *Legal and constitutional history of India* (vol. 1). New Delhi: Universal Law.

Kethineni, S. (2001). Female homicide offenders in India. *International Journal of Comparative and Applied Criminal Justice, 25*(1), 1–24.

Kohli, A., & Aggarwal, N. K. (2006). Firearm fatalities in Delhi, India. *Legal Medicine, 8,* 264–268.

Lahiri, T. (1986). *Crime and punishment in Ancient India.* New Delhi: Radiant.

Marwah, S. (2014). Mapping murder: Homicide patterns and trends in India. *Journal of South Asian Studies, 2*(2), 145–163. Retrieved from http://escijournals.net/index.php/JSAS/article/view/571/364.

MirHosseini, Z. (2011). Criminalizing sexuality: Zina laws as violence against women in Muslim contexts. *SUR International Journal on Human Rights, 8*(15), 7–33.

Mohanty, M. K., Mohan Kumar, T. S., Mohanram, A., & Palimar, V. (2005). Victims of homicidal deaths—An analysis of variables. *Journal of Clinical Forensic Medicine, 12,* 302–304.

Mohanty, S., Mohanty, S. K., & Patnaik, K. K. (2013). Homicide in southern India—A five year retrospective study. *Forensic Medicine and Anatomy Research, 1*(2), 18–24.

Nagpaul, H. (1985). Patterns of homicide in North India: Some sociological hypotheses. *International Journal of Offender Therapy and Comparative Criminology, 29*(2), 147–158. doi: 10.1177/0306624X8502900207.

National Crime Records Bureau. (2013). *Crime in India—2013.* New Delhi: Government of India: National Crime Records Bureau. Retrieved from http://ncrb.nic.in/StatPublications/CII/CII2013/Home.asp.

Periyar, E. E. (2018). *Victim—Offender relationship: An ethnographic study of revenge murders in Tirunelveli District.* Unpublished PhD thesis submitted to the Manonmaniam Sundaranar University, Tirunelveli, Tamil Nadu, India.

Rani, B. M. (1983). Homicides by females. *Indian Journal of Criminology, 11*(1), 8–17.

Saxena, R. (1994). *Women and crime in India: A study in sociocultural dynamics.* New Delhi: InterIndia.

Shamasastry, R. (1923). *Kautilya's Arthashastra.* Mysore: Wesleyan Mission Press.

Suresh, V., Singh, P., Bhadro, S., et al. (2014). Say NO to death penalty. *Report of meeting of all India human rights organisations and activists,* March 8, 2014, Chennai. Retrieved from www.indiaresists.com/saynotodeathpenalty.

UNODC. (2014). *Global study on homicide 2013: Trends, contexts and data.* Vienna: United Nations Office of Drugs and Crime (UNODC). Retrieved from www.unodc.org/documents/dataandanalysis/statistics/ GSH2013/2014_GLOBAL_HOMICIDE_ BOOK_web.pdf.

Venkatesan, V. (2012). A case against the death penalty. *Frontline, 29*(17). Retrieved from www.frontline.in/static/ html/fl2917/stories/20120907291700400.htm.

Vishwanath, J., & Palakonda, S.C. (2011). Patriarchal ideology of honour and honour crimes in India. *International Journal of Criminal Justice Sciences, 6*(1–2), 386–395.

PART III

Politics of Crime and Justice

15

TERROR AND TRAFFICKING IN AFGHANISTAN, PAKISTAN AND INDIA

A Routine Activity Approach

Tony Murphy

Introduction

This chapter demonstrates the value of criminological theory in understanding key crime events in a number of South Asian countries. Although we can study issues of crime and justice in South Asia as we might do in any other region or country of the world, the processes and threats associated with terrorism and organised crime are especially prominent in this region. In particular, the illicit trades in drugs and people—trafficking—are noteworthy. Such activities evolve, and in doing so they present problems for domestic law and order and indeed wider security matters. Afghanistan, Pakistan and India are focal points within the chapter. They exhibit many of the problems associated with fostering a secure law and order environment, and they have been closely associated with trafficking and terrorist activities in recent years.

A number of possible theoretical lenses are available as a means through which to explore and ultimately understand those crime events. Traditional criminological theories continue to prove to be a valuable reference point, or a tool for understanding crime on some level, as well as a platform upon which more recent theories have been able to build, filling in explanatory gaps or responding to critique of those original theories. Theory often builds on theory after all. In this context, the chapter utilizes a re-working of traditional criminological theory—classicism—through the focus on routine activity theory (Cohen & Felson, 1979) and builds on this further by reconciling it with dimensions ordinarily associated with other theoretical models. In essence, the chapter demonstrates how it is possible to move beyond the conceptual constraints of a theory and apply it to contexts beyond those ordinarily associated with the theory. Thus here, routine activity theory is used to better understand terrorism and trafficking. In order to do this, the foundational principles of the routine activity framework are interrogated and then subsequently treated in a more expansive manner. At the outset, the nature of the threats in the case study countries is outlined.

1. Terrorism in South Asia

In Afghanistan, Pakistan, India and the disputed territories between India and Pakistan, terrorism can be viewed in a critical manner; defining acts as being 'terrorism' in nature is dependent upon one's political perspective. Furthermore, drawing a line between legitimate combatant behaviour and terrorist activities can be difficult. However, what is not contestable is the fact that there have been and continue to be acts of extreme violence borne out of political and religious differences, inflicted upon both civilians and foreign and domestic combatants—for example, civilians, international troops within ISAF and Afghani security forces have all been targets within Afghanistan. Terrorism in this region also extends to actions connected to the disputed ownership and governance of lands, specifically in the context of India and Pakistan since independence from Britain in 1947. Religious and cultural intolerances have seemingly been strong drivers for violence, and in the instance of Afghanistan in particular, and to a lesser extent Pakistan, we also see opposition to foreigners and other nation-men who are part of the *war on terror* since 9/11, sitting on the other side of a bloody ideological divide. As we can see in Figure 15.1, there has been a noticeable increase in events defined as being 'terrorism' in nature in recent years in the region.

That noted, we must seek to understand the conditions that have made such parts of the world conducive to the development of terrorist organisations, the conditions which have drawn in foreign terrorist organisations—for example Al-Qaeda—and insurgencies, and the drivers of recruitment in to those organisations at individual and group levels. What is it about parts of South Asia that has enabled insurgent and terrorist organisations to take a foothold? Can we attribute this to the failed or weak state narrative; are such places suffering from acute economic and political inequalities which have created antagonism and conflict; can we point to cultural characteristics of places such as Afghanistan and connecting regions; or perhaps we can cite the presence of extremist religious doctrines? Credibly, all of these dynamics have been of influence.

Martin (2014) attempts to distinguish between the different *causes* of terrorism, and in doing so, he cites processes at both individual and group levels. At the individual level he notes how it is possible to consider rational, psychological and cultural origins, whilst at a group level attention is brought to political activism as a genesis for action. Whittaker (2012) offers a similar type of analysis. Martin notes that regardless of the *precipitating cause* of a particular terrorist's behaviour, there are common motives, and these include the responses to perceived injustices, a strategic choice and moral influences (from the perspective of the terrorist or terrorist group). Intuitively, this mirrors what we have seen in Afghanistan in recent years. There, terrorist acts can be viewed as a part of a strategy to drive out and inflict defeat on enemy forces who occupy an alternative ideological position, and this

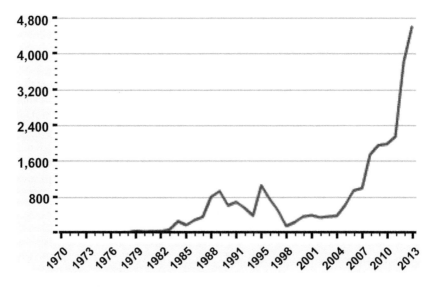

Figure 15.1 Terrorism incidents over time in South Asia.

(*Source*: Adapted from Global Terrorism Database, 2014)

occurs in the context of a conflict driven by a skewed understanding of injustice—on the part of the *jihadists*—and a sense of moral duty, again influenced by a warped interpretation of religion. Here, we see the impact of an ideological doctrine which requires self-sacrifice in defence of the religion whilst simultaneously reassuring a would-be terrorist that they are to be rewarded in the afterlife should they die fighting for the cause (see Laqueur, 1998).

Naturally, criminological theories that focus on structural dynamics within societies can also be brought into the account. In this context, we can see how within those regions experiencing economic problems and military crises, or where policies alienate or antagonise groups, there is a heightened vulnerability to insurgent forces and thus terrorist activities (Goldstone, 1986, within Martin, 2014, p. 47). Quite clearly we see this in events in Afghanistan—through the rise of the Taliban in the early 1990s and their relationship with Al-Qaeda. Notably also, international influences, *vis-à-vis* religious ideology, are also vital to consider. The terrorism in Afghanistan and Pakistan can be attributed in most part to religious differences and a worldview borne out of it, spread by an international jihadi agenda that has manifested itself in political action and, ultimately, violence.

Martin (2014) argues, in accordance with Whittaker (2012), that political violence is common in some social and political contexts—we can see this in Afghanistan; the country has a long tradition of conflict and a pervasive warrior culture. In modern times the conflict with Russia exemplifies this. That conflict, according to Martin (2014, p. 151), played a key role in spreading jihadist ideology throughout the Muslim world as the *Mujahideen* ("holy warriors") effectively pushed out a foreign superpower aggressor. Such cultural characteristics have seemingly been exacerbated through the role of extremist religious positions and insurgencies which serve to channel and inflame that trait. Further still, terrorists may view themselves as an 'elite vanguard', who are not content with discussion but who instead see action (and violent action) as a necessary process in achieving their political goals (Martin, 2014). Thus, what we have seen in some parts of Afghanistan is a warrior culture influenced by extreme versions of Islam, with a sense of moral or religious duty to defeat an enemy who is depicted as diametrically opposed to their belief system and where political violence is a strategic choice to achieve their stated goals.

Whittaker (2012) also develops an account of how cultural legacies of violence and modern cultural relationships with violence can play a role in determining such behaviours. The insurgencies which have brought foreign Al-Qaeda operatives in to the theatre of conflict in Afghanistan found a natural home. We can see the development and prominence of Al-Qaeda in Afghanistan as being in no small part a result of the Taliban seizing power from a weak central government in Kabul in the early 1990s. The Taliban shared an extremist interpretation of Islam and ruled through violence. It is no wonder then that a more global terrorist organisation with compatible world views felt welcome there and took Afghanistan as its base (Whittaker, 2006, within Whittaker, 2012).

Interestingly, Martin (2014) and Grabosky and Stohl (2010) have noted how the targets of terrorist actions become 'depersonalised', and they have symbolic labels attached to them owing to the ideological divide which develops. Thus, they become desirable targets. It is easy to recognise this within the conflict in Afghanistan and the accompanying propaganda materials, and indeed in related conflicts in Iraq and Syria—a brief YouTube search demonstrates this.

Logically, we can view much of this discussion in the context of strain theories, associated initially with Merton (1938) and subsequently developed by a range of other experts, including Passas (2000). In this narrative, crime, in this instance terrorism, can be viewed as being somehow a response to inequalities and lack of opportunities for some groups in regions of South Asia. It is a fairly intuitive step to view the traditional cultural and religious divisions of Afghanistan as manifesting themselves within inequitable relationships of power. This might stem from local or regional processes and also interactions at an international level—inequalities resultant from processes of globalisation or political and economic sanctions imposed by strong international communities: the United Nations; World Bank; International Monetary Fund and so on. One outcome of such processes is feelings of alienation and anger towards other groups, those perceived to be fostering injustice—other nations, other religious or cultural groups or power elites in a given country. Strain theories dictate that individuals and groups can respond to such strains or injustices (perceived or real) in a retaliatory or rebellious way. Extreme religious doctrine then gives such anger and alienation a focus, and it brings into view a common enemy. The use of violence and instilling fear in the *enemy* then becomes a rational or at least strategic route towards achieving stated goals, which are often political in nature— driving out Western influences and defeating the *infidels*.

2. Trafficking in South Asia

Recent estimates suggest that the majority of the world's illegal opiates are grown in Afghanistan; for the year 2009 this was thought to be approximately 90% of the global supply (UNODC, 2014). Furthermore, the impacts of the trade are telling; It is clear to see that the "boom in opium production in Afghanistan echoes loudly through the political and social fabric of the region" (UNODC, 2014).

How do we begin to understand the prominence of trafficking operations in South Asia? Well, the market is king. Individuals and groups operating in illegal markets, including the trade in people and drugs, are motivated by the financial rewards that are possible. Those actors are driven by the market—illicit markets meeting demands that are not catered for within licit economies. Peter Reuter famously considered the role of market principles in the regulation of illegal industries in the USA, and he explored the role of violence within this (Reuter, 1983). Violence and organised crime seemingly go hand in hand wherever illicit markets are there to be tapped. And such markets are vast. Experts such as Castles and Miller have described how the movements of people have become an industry in itself—the 'migration industry' (for example, see Castles & Miller, 2003). The 'migration industry' worldwide is now thought to have exceeded in size the international illicit drugs trade (Aas, 2013, p. 37). However, as one might expect, understanding the true scale of such activities is problematic owing to a lack of disclosure, unknown illegal operations and law enforcement difficulties.

Naturally, much of the activity within that *industry* reflects a desire on the part of those being transported to seek a better life in the given country of destination. This can be broadly labelled as 'people smuggling'. Often this involves movement to Europe or North America, and the journey can be treacherous and often fatal. Undoubtedly this type of movement of people is prolific in South Asia, typically with those countries being the point of origin for would-be migrants. Yet the focus in this chapter is around the forced trafficking of individuals. Here the process is against the will of the person, and usually the purpose of trafficking is for labour or more commonly to fuel the sex trade. The United Nations Office on Drugs and Crime (UNODC) published a report in 2012 and demonstrated that 79% of human trafficking is related to sexual exploitation, and the vast majority of the victims are women and girls (UNODC, 2012). Sometimes, those trafficked—to other countries or to other regions within the same country—are duped in to the process. They may agree to go with traffickers under false pretences, and the promise of work seems to be a common deception.

The United Nations defines human trafficking in relation to the following:

> The recruitment, transportation, transfer, harbouring or receipt of persons by means of the threat or use of force or other forms of coercion, of abduction, of fraud, of deception, of the abuse of power or of positions of vulnerability or of the giving or receiving of payments or benefits to achieve the consent of a person having control over another person, for the purpose of exploitation. Exploitation shall include, at a minimum, the exploitation of the prostitution of others or other forms of sexual exploitations, forced labour or services, slavery or practices similar to slavery, servitude or the removal of organs.
>
> *(UNODC, 2012, p. 16)*

Although significantly wordy, the definition captures the complex nature of trafficking. Unfortunately, South Asia is a significant player in this industry. UNODC data (UNODC, 2012) paints a picture of a worryingly high level of trafficking in South Asia, and India is a notable case study (see Kiley, 2005). Yet the problem is certainly not restricted to any one country, and the international dynamics of trafficking further complicate the matter. Most worrying, perhaps, is the heavy burden of victimisation which falls on the shoulders of children in this region. For example, Figure 15.2 demonstrates how poorly South Asia (as part of a wider region of South Asia, East Asia and the Pacific) ranks in relation to this, although not quite as poorly as Africa and the Middle East.

Aas (2013) has made the link between the development processes within 'poor' countries and the security environment in the West. That is, international inequalities and restricted development create an environment conducive to the development of organised crime activities. In a similar vein to terrorist activities, this creates challenges for the security of countries on the other side of the world and, indeed, law enforcement challenges within the origin countries. Whilst again, akin to accounts of structural conditions or *strains* influencing the terrorism landscape in regions of South Asia, we see similar processes at work here in the context of trafficking. In light of what Passas (2000) terms 'global anomie', we can recognise some processes of international inequalities *vis-à-vis* legitimate opportunities and pathways to success as shaping the desires of would-be organised crime groups. Countries such as Pakistan, India and Afghanistan are exposed to hegemonic cultural aspirations in a modern globalised, capitalist and consumerist world, but the stark reality of the extreme inequalities within those countries dictates that innovative means of acquisition are logical outcomes for many. The violent rejection of those ideas and the subsequent adoption of alternative ideas that challenge such hegemony is another possible outcome *vis-à-vis* terrorism.

Again, echoing what we see in relation to the development and harbouring of terrorism, weak states, that is where states are unable to maintain conventional processes of governance over their lands, are vulnerable to criminal networks (Aas, 2013). Such territories are attractive to criminals on the basis of the scope they offer them to operate unmolested and without disruption. Such

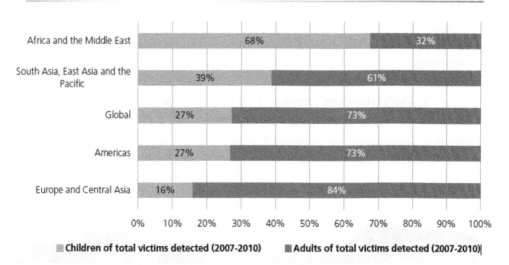

Share of child victims detected by region, 2007-2010

Figure 15.2 Victims of trafficking.

(*Source*: Adapted from UNODC, 2012, p. 10crop)

environments are further enhanced by the possibility of a 'state–crime nexus', where tangible informal networks or connections can exist between political and civil state actors and criminal drug enterprises (Aas, 2013). 'Selective law enforcement' is one outcome of this (Muller, 2012, with Aas, 2013). Muller explored this in the context of Mexico, but quite clearly we can identify comparable processes in parts of Asia, and Chin (2009) explores this in detail. Relatedly, an investigative report for Channel 4 News in Britain demonstrated some of these issues in relation to people trafficking. Law enforcement complicity and corruption were seemingly apparent in the operations of the child sex industry within Indian cities (Kiley, 2005). Similarly in Afghanistan, evidence of such corruption continues to be found (see Swarts, 2014).

The issues of competencies and resources are also important in developing an understanding of those illicit trades. This is clear to see in the major policy responses to the drug trade in the region. For example, the UNDOC's programme for Pakistan (2010–2014) has focused around promoting the rule of law, to 'enhance the legislative regimes, increase the knowledge and capacity of drug enforcement officials and improve interdiction capabilities' (UNODC, 2014). Similar programmes elsewhere also focus on the capabilities of law enforcement to disrupt and prosecute traffickers.

Trafficking, whether relating to drugs or people, can be broken down in to three discrete steps. Initially, this involves the production of drugs or recruitment, including the forceful taking of people. Production of opiates, for example, requires poor or ineffective governance structures in order that operations are not interfered with. Corruption or state complicity improves the situation further still. In order to recruit those who are to be trafficked, there is often a strong motivation to go—as a result of their economic situation—and those people are thus vulnerable to being duped by a trafficking gang. Or the poor law enforcement landscapes enable gangs to snatch people against their will and offer little in terms of investigatory follow-up, especially in rural areas (Kiley, 2005). This might be a result of acute shortages in resources or competencies but also complicity or 'selective law enforcement'.

The next stage involves the movement or trafficking itself, and again lax law enforcement structures and corruption allow drugs and people to be moved in an unsolicited manner. From Afghanistan, drugs are moved to neighbouring countries through porous borders, and much of this is then moved into Europe and Russia via Turkey and the Balkans (UNODC, 2010)—see Figure 15.3. People who are trafficked from within India may be moved internationally, but much of the movement is internal—to the major cities for the purpose of forced prostitution (UNODC, 2012). The final stage, consumption of the drugs or those trafficked, which is shaped by market forces, then takes place both domestically and further afield internationally. In the context of Afghanistan, the heroin consumption on the streets of Europe, Russia, Central Asia, Oceania and the USA helps to fuel the trade—see Figure 15.4.

3. Understanding Terror and Trafficking: A Revised Routine Activities Model

In its most basic form, routine activity theory (Cohen & Felson, 1979) requires that we understand the incidence of crime as determined by three immediate factors. Those elements include

- the existence of a motivated offender
- the existence of a suitable or vulnerable target
- the absence of capable guardianship (that is, the absence of a means to successfully prevent a crime or respond to a crime *in situ*)

(Cohen & Felson, 1979)

In light of what we have explored in this chapter, it is possible to understand the dynamics of trafficking and terrorism in parts of South Asia in a broader theoretical manner. Clearly, such activities

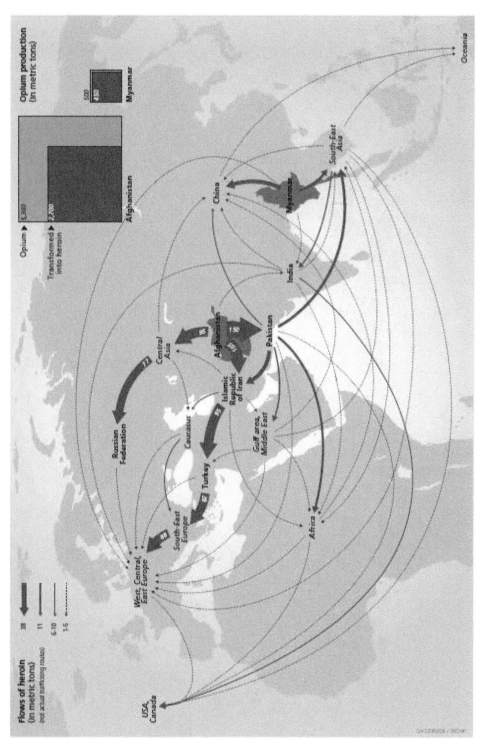

Figure 15.3 Global flows of Asian heroin.

(*Source:* Adapted from UNODC, 2010, p. 45)

Use of opiates including heroin, 2008-2009 (or latest year available)

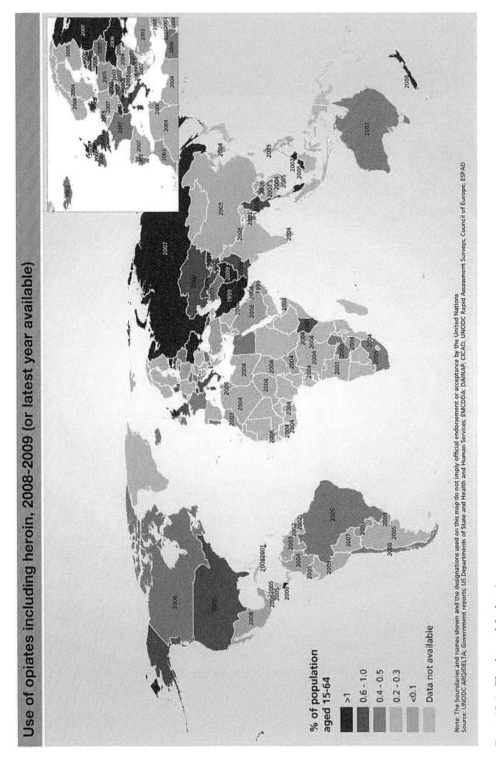

% of population aged 15-64
- >1
- 0.6 - 1.0
- 0.4 - 0.5
- 0.2 - 0.3
- <0.1
- Data not available

Note: The boundaries and names shown and the designations used on this map do not imply official endorsement or acceptance by the United Nations.
Source: UNODC ARQ/DELTA; Government reports; US Departments of State and Health and Human Services; EMCDDA; DAINAP; CICAD; UNODC Rapid Assessment Surveys; Council of Europe; ESPAD

Figure 15.4 The demand for heroin.

(*Source*: Adapted from UNODC, 2010, p. 21)

are widespread, and we can identify a number of drivers, connected to the social, cultural, political and economic conditions, and routine activity theory allows us to put such influences into a logical framework. Thus, by utilising the three nodes of analysis we can make sense of the activities, despite the necessity here to move the framework beyond its intended usage. And so, by utilising the model, we can identify the following:

- The motivations for individuals and groups to become involved in terrorism and trafficking are located in the social, cultural, political and economic conditions and events within the countries of the region. We see this in the role of the markets and accounts of *strain*, the vulnerability of such places to extreme ideologies and insurgencies and the conditions conducive to conducting illegal operations in an unchallenged manner.
- Suitable targets are prevalent as a result of those wider social, cultural, political and economic dimensions within the region. The conditions required for the existence of groups of vulnerable peoples at the mercy of the *people trade*—the most vulnerable being women, young girls and the economically deprived—are brought about by gross income inequalities, desperation and inequalities in power and security. Similarly, occupying foreign troops (for example ISAF) and opposing domestic factions represent vulnerable targets. They are vulnerable in the sense that they are visible, and they are not fully in control of the territories within which they operate. They are also highly suitable targets owing to their symbolic importance. The weak-state narrative and the cultural dynamics of Afghanistan accounts for the presence of those targets and their vulnerability. The ideological and political landscape is telling.
- An absence of capable guardianship is evident in many parts of South Asia resultant from law-and-order and governance vacuums. A failure in terms in resources or competencies, and even 'selective law enforcement', creates the opportunities for traffickers and terrorists to operate without harassment. Thus state corruption, acute inequalities and the conditions of war or quasi-war over many recent years have created challenges for governance and stability. Organised crime groups and terrorists thrive in structures of poor or ideologically driven forms of governance (Martin, 2014; Whittaker, 2012). The blurring of boundaries between official/state bodies and criminal enterprises is also noteworthy, and 'state complicity' in crimes further erodes the existence of capable or willing guardianship. Chin (2009), Aas (2013) and Grabosky and Stohl (2010) have explored such interfaces between state agencies and criminal enterprises. Chin, for example, demonstrates a convergence between state and criminal narcotics enterprises, pointing to corruption and ineffective governance regimes. Aas has noted how wider official or *legitimate* economies in Asia benefit from organised crime activities.

Thus here we see the outlines of a more expansive application of routine activity theory. It is also important to note that there are a number of parallels between organised crime and terrorism, despite caution being raised by some commentators. The relationships between them have been explored successfully by a number of authors (including Makarenko, 2004; Grabosky & Stohl, 2010), yet this remains a relatively under-reported account within criminology. In parts of South Asia the relationships between those two activities are particularly noteworthy. Makarenko (2004), for example, demonstrates a number of crime–terror 'interfaces' (please read for further details). The illicit trade in heroin for instance, presents an obvious case study of how organised crime and terrorist activities coincide in parts of Afghanistan. One might point to the use of funds from the heroin trade to resource terrorist activities. Grabosky and Stohl (2010) explored a number of connections between those activities, and they cite the phenomenon of 'narco-terrorism'. This relates to the involvement of terrorist organisations in the drugs trade as a means through which to fund their activities. Others have directly explored this in the context of Afghanistan. Singh (2011) offers a useful case study. He demonstrates that the situation in reality can be slightly more complex than the uni-dimensional relationship of illicit drugs supporting terrorism, but this has seemingly been the case in some instances.

Grabosky and Stohl's analysis briefly touched on routine activity theory as an explanatory framework. Within this they note how motivations for offending are multiple but may include factors such as greed, rebellion, indignation, the pursuit of security, power, revenge and excitement (Grabosky & Stohl, 2010). And so one question we might ask is how such motivations are *created*. The local, regional and international influences on places such as Afghanistan or Kashmir shape everyday experiences such that this becomes conducive for motivating terrorist behaviours amongst some members of the population. Similarly, the conditions created in those locales, plus other areas in South Asia, are conducive to the rise and influence of organised crime networks—particularly the illicit trades in drugs and people. Grabosky and Stohl (2010) also consider the role of group influences in motivating terrorists—the desire to be a part of a group or fraternity of some sort—and once this is coupled with a sense of outrage or hatred for another group, that desire to collectively act or respond is exacerbated. In the context of Afghanistan, Pakistan and India we see religion as an obvious driver, both in terms of extremism and sectarianism. The exploration of 'opportunities' and 'guardianship' by Grabosky and Stohl was less expansive, but this nevertheless demonstrates how we might develop our *handling* of the three nodes of analysis within routine activity theory. Similarly, Martin (2014) attempted to apply routine activity theory to terrorism, although this did not focus on South Asia, and it was done fleetingly. Yet there is then a precedent set for thinking about routine activity theory in the contexts of terrorism and organised crime, and this chapter has sought to further develop such analysis.

It is often helpful to visually present theoretical frameworks in order to consider the interplay between the various dynamics under consideration. Thus, in Figure 15.5a typical depiction of the routine activity framework is included. As is evident, this is focused around factors associated with the immediate environment which can encourage crime. Here, the 'hot spots' represent the coming together of those conditions conducive to crime. Note how the application of the framework tends to be in relation to everyday behaviours and scenarios:

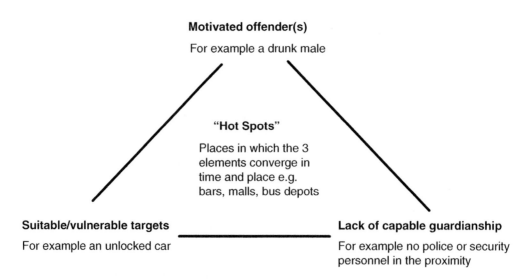

Figure 15.5 A typical depiction of routine activity theory.
(*Source*: Adapted from Tibbetts, 2011)

Motivated offender

Offenders can be driven by political, cultural, economic and social factors, and this can operate locally, nationally and internationally. This might include ideological opposition and religious intolerance (in the instance of terrorism); the opportunities afforded by illicit markets (e.g. *people trade* and drugs trade) and the monetary rewards from such markets; economic hardship and a failing of, or the inequity of, local and national economies and the conditions this creates, conducive to both organized crime activity and terrorism; and other factors associated with sociological, biological and psychological positivist thinking and some critical theories.

Locations and environments conducive to crime
e.g. activities associated with terrorism and organized crime

Suitable targets

The existence of vulnerable targets is resultant from the failed governance and economic structures in some parts of South Asia. Groups of poor young people (often girls) are at the mercy of the *people trade*. Equally, occupying foreign troops and opposing domestic factions (state security forces or not) are obvious targets, created by the political and social conditions (also spanning religious and cultural spheres) in places like Afghanistan. Such *targets* have been and continue to be at the mercy of terrorist activities. Despite some ability on their part to negate threats and fight back, they will continue to be vulnerable to such attacks and be important symbolic targets.

Absence of capable guardianship

Most notably, this can be understood within the law-and-order and governance vacuums apparent in many parts of South Asia. This extends to corruption, acute political inequalities and in the instances of Afghanistan and Kashmir, the state of war or quasi-war over many recent years which has created challenges for governance and stability. Even with the at times copious numbers of international troops on the ground in Afghanistan, creating an effective security environment has remained difficult and arguably impossible. Organised crime groups thrive in structures of poor governance, whilst terrorism is allowed to take a foothold in the absence of strong-willed, effective and moderate systems of governing. In Afghanistan, the post-war administration has thus far proved to be highly ineffective. We can further add to this with the blurring of boundaries between official/state bodies and criminal enterprises, and even 'state complicity', where the premise of capable or willing guardianship is further interrogated. Again in Afghanistan, there is a body of evidence pointing to state corruption and complicity.

Figure 15.6 A more expansive application of routine activity theory.

It is, however, possible to re-work the framework to reconcile it with wider influences, those beyond the immediate nature of the event, as demonstrated earlier in the chapter. We are able to employ a more dynamic and expansive level of analysis in relation to the framework. In short, we can move it beyond the rational-actor model and borrow from other theoretical models. Thus, beyond the immediacy of the environment, we can consider the social, cultural, economic and political conditions that influence a given space. We can also extend our thinking beyond the immediate vicinity of the environment into regional, national and international influences. More than this, we can also consider influences over time—traditions, cultural legacies, the spreading of ideologies, the conditions created by poor governance and processes of development and so on. This can be viewed in the context of *creating* motivation for crime, that is, drivers for criminal behaviours beyond impulse. It can also be seen within the creation of suitable targets where those targets have become vulnerable as a result of those wider regional, national and international events and processes. Finally, the absence of capable guardianship can be viewed as a consequence of those same types of processes. This is depicted in Figure 15.6, where the focus is around terrorism and organised crime in South Asia.

Conclusion and Implications

As a model for understanding law-and-order responses to organised crime and terrorism, a more expansive application of routine activity theory demands that we consider how policies and practices work with the three nodes of analysis at local, national and international levels. Thus, the policy questions emergent from this include:

1. How can we reduce the supply of motivated offenders? How can we change or interrupt illicit markets? How can we reduce or temper the ideological divisions and religious hatred operating locally between different sects and more widely in the context of jihadist ideologies? How can we reduce the stark inequalities in wealth and power which fuel reactions conducive to crime?
2. How can we reduce the numbers of vulnerable targets—those people susceptible to trafficking or terrorist activities? How can we ensure that families and children are not left in economically and socially vulnerable positions at the mercy of gangs in the trafficking trade who may kidnap or dupe? How can we ensure universal security and protection for all?
3. How can we create more robust processes of *guardianship*, locally, nationally and internationally? How do we foster stronger and fairer governance regimes, effective surveillance and motivated and competent law enforcement? What role can domestic and international legislation play? How can we disrupt organised crime operations abroad? How can we guard against the spread of ideology and insurgencies that have shaped places such as Afghanistan and the disputed territories in South Asia?

Such questions reflect the acute challenges facing those who are tasked with making a difference.

References

Aas. K, (2013). *Globalisation and crime* (2nded.). London: Sage.
Castles, M., & Miller, J. (2003). *The age of migration: International population movements in the modern world.* Basingstoke: Palgrave McMillan.
Chin, K. (2009). *The golden triangle: Inside Southeast Asia's drug trade.* Ithaca, NY: Cornell University Press.
Cohen, L., & Felson, M. (1979). Social change and crime rate trends: A routine activity approach. *American Sociological Review, 44*(4), 588–608.
Global Terrorism Database. (2014). *Incidents over time: South Asia.* Retrieved from www.start.umd.edu/gtd/search/Results.aspx?region=6.
Grabosky, P., & Stohl, M. (2010). *Crime and terrorism.* London: Sage.

Kiley, S. (Presenter) & von Planto, C. (Producer). (2005). *India: Land of missing children* (Television series episode). In Gregory, F. (Executive Producer), Unreported World. London: C4.

Laqueur, W. (1998). *The new terrorism: Fanaticism and the arms of mass destruction*. New York: Oxford University Press.

Makarenko, T. (2004). The crime-terror continuum: Tracing the interplay between transnational organised crime and terrorism. *Global Crime, 6*(1), 129–145.

Martin, G. (2014). *Essentials of terrorism: Concepts and controversies*. Thousand Oaks, CA: Sage.

Merton, R. K. (1938). Social structure and Anomie. *American Sociological Review, 3*, 672–682.

Passas, N. (2000). Global Anomie, dysnomie, and economic crime: Hidden consequences of neoliberalism and globalisation in Russia and around the world. *Social Justice, 27*(2), 16–43.

Reuter, P. (1983). *Disorganized crime: The economics of the visible hand*. Cambridge, MA: MIT Press.

Singh, A. (2011). Narco-terrorism: A case study of Afghanistan. *Scholar's Voice: A New Way of Thinking, 2*(1), 75–88.

Swarts, P. (2014, May 14). Afghanistan corruption still severe problem, U.S. watchdog says. *The Washington Times*. Retrieved from www.washingtontimes.com/news/2014/may/14/afghanistan-corruption-still-severe-problem-us-wat/?page=all#!

Tibbetts, S. (2011). *Criminological theory: The essentials*. Thousand Oaks, CA: Sage.

UNODC. (2010). *World drug report 2010* (United Nations Publication No. E.10.XI.13). New York

UNODC. (2012). *Global report on trafficking in persons 2012* (United Nations Publication No. E.13.IV.1). New York.

UNODC. (2014). *Central Asia*. Retrieved from www.unodc.org/unodc/en/drug-trafficking/central-asia.html.

Whittaker, D. (Eds.) (2012). *The terrorism reader* (4th ed.). Abingdon: Routledge.

16

WAR, CRIME, JUSTICE AND SOCIAL ORDER IN AFGHANISTAN[1]

John Braithwaite and Ali Wardak

Introduction

Thomas Hobbes lived through the terror and security dilemmas of the English Civil War. His conclusion was that life is nasty, brutish and short until a Leviathan (Hobbes, 1651) emerges who can be granted legitimacy to pacify a space by dominating all other armed factions inside it. The Leviathan could be a monarch or some other authority that takes central control of a state. Afghanistan has since 1978 suffered much worse violence from various warring factions (including those who formed states) than England endured during Hobbes's lifetime. After 2001, a Leviathan, President Hamid Karzai, backed by the NATO-led International Security Assistance Force (ISAF), increased security at first in the way predicted by Hobbes (Braithwaite & Wardak, 2013).

This chapter views Afghanistan less as a war and more as a contest of criminalized justice systems. The Taliban came to power because they were able to restore order to spaces terrorized by armed gangs and Mujahideen factions. After the Taliban's 'defeat' in 2001, their resurgence was invited by the failure of state justice and security institutions. The Taliban returned with a parallel court system that most Afghans viewed as more effective and fair than the state system. Polls suggest judges were perceived as among the most corrupt elements of a corrupt state. Police were widely perceived as thieves of ordinary people's property, not protectors of it. While the US diagnosis of anomie in Afghanistan up to 2009 was aptly Hobbesian, its remedy of supporting President Hamid Karzai as a Leviathan was hardly apt. The West failed to ask in 2001, 'What is working around here to provide people security?' One answer to that question was jirga/shura (for more about jirga/shura see Chapter 1 of this book). A more Jeffersonian rural republicanism that learnt from local traditions of dispute resolution defines a path not taken (Braithwaite & Wardak, 2013).

Part I of this chapter is limited to the Hobbesian part of our analysis and Part II to a Jeffersonian analysis, which gives priority to empowering and reforming traditional rural justice. In Part I, we first provide a Hobbesian analysis of the rise of Islamist and other forms of tyranny. Then we connect this to the criminalization of the state, the criminalization of the justice system and the criminalization of war, all of which in Part I are seen as Hobbesian maladies. Part II discusses possible Jeffersonian paths to escape those maladies.

Part I. The Hobbesian Analysis

1. *Pacification as a Modern Path to Islamist Tyranny*

In 1998, terrible Christian–Muslim violence broke out in two hotspots of religious political competition in Indonesia: Ambon and Poso (Braithwaite Cookson, Braithwaite, & Dunn, 2010). It subsequently spread more widely across the provinces of Maluku and Central Sulawesi at a cost of more
than 10,000 lives. At both hotspots, the conflict took two disastrous turns that escalated the conflict.
One was that, in response to rallies organized by radical Islamists in Jakarta, thousands of young men
joined Islamist militias such as Laskar Jihad and sailed to Ambon and Poso, armed to the teeth, sweeping into villages, burning them to the ground, killing Christians who had not managed to flee. The
second disaster was that elements of the security forces took sides. For example, large sections of the
local police in Ambon sided with the Christian community; large sections of the military sided with
the Muslim cause. Some professional military snipers sold their assassination services to both sides
(Braithwaite & Wardak, 2013).

A Hobbesian war of all against all prevailed in these two provinces for a time, allowing the most radical Islamic groups to establish terrorist training camps there, assisting Indonesia to become the country
with the highest frequency of terrorist bombings in the world until 2002, after which Iraq, Afghanistan
and Pakistan took over this mantle. At these terrorist training camps in Maluku and Central Sulawesi,
the Bali bombers, who took 200 lives, were trained. These camps are now closed. Christian–Muslim
violence still exists but has returned to the low levels that prevailed prior to 1998. There were three
main factors in this accomplishment. One was that religious leaders pleaded with the fighters to return
home peacefully. These included leaders in Saudi Arabia, who issued a Fatwa for the cessation of fighting, and local Muslim leaders in Javanese and Sulawesi villages from whence the young militiamen
had come, and from the villages they had gone to defend in Ambon and Poso. Second, Muslim leaders
joined with Christian leaders in inter-faith reconciliations that connected to bottom-up village-level
traditions of reconciliation that were pre-Christian, pre-Muslim. Third, the security sector stopped taking sides and started enforcing the peace against spoilers from all sides. In the course of the 2000s, an
imperfect but fairly firm peace consolidated in both provinces (Braithwaite & Wardak, 2013).

Bangladesh from 1998 saw a rather parallel story with the rise of a Salafist group, Jamaat-ul-
Mujahideen Bangladesh (JMB), which organized hundreds of terrorist bombings across Bangladesh,
peaking in 2004–05 (ICG, 2010; South Asian Terrorism, Portal, 2012). JMB saw a state of sectarian
violence, police failing to do their jobs, lawlessness, weak governance and a general condition of
citizens feeling unsafe within certain rural hotspots of disorder, particularly in Rajshahi Division.
It grasped this anomie as an opportunity to consolidate its movement. It enforced a rule of Shari'a
law, allowing people to feel safer, and then used these rural areas as bases from which terrorist training and operations could be mounted across Bangladesh. As with the Indonesian militias of the late
1990s and early 2000s, in Bangladesh, a multidimensional state and civil society response from the
mid-2000s has effectively eliminated JMB as a source of terrorism in recent years (Fink & El-Said,
2011, pp. 5–7), though it is a threat that could return. Indeed, Indonesia and Bangladesh—the largest
Muslim-majority nations—are today not terrorist hotspots in the way that so many other Muslim-
majority societies such as Afghanistan, Pakistan, Yemen and Somalia have become. Bangladesh security experts whom John Braithwaite interviewed said that the *modus operandi* of JMB was the same as
that of the Taliban: to build a base from rural areas with a rule-of-law vacuum that are being terrorized by gangs (Braithwaite & Wardak, 2013).

This observation led us to this chapter's focus on a Hobbesian analysis of the rise of the Taliban.
We conclude that the international community's response to the Taliban has also been Hobbesian:

to install Hamid Karzai as a Leviathan. In 2001, the international community was still obsessed with the Yugoslavia breakup scenario, for which there was no historical precedent or basis for fear in Afghanistan. Nevertheless, international support for a highly centralized Leviathan was justified by 'the assertion that the country would break apart without firm control at the top' (Barfield, 2010, p. 8). In Woodward's (2011) *Obama's Wars*, he quotes US President Barack Obama as saying in meetings with his national security team that his objective is not to build 'a Jeffersonian democracy' in Afghanistan (Braithwaite & Wardak, 2013).

The conclusion we develop in Part II of this chapter is that the tragedy that is Afghanistan is a product of decades of policies that have been altogether too Hobbesian and insufficiently Jeffersonian. We must remember that Jefferson's republican vision was of rural, decentralized, deliberative checks and balances on challenges of domination and violence. The alternative we develop is of the kind of rural village republicanism supported by a democratic state—the Panchayat vision that we also see in the political thought of Mahatma Gandhi (see also Braithwaite, Charlesworth, & Soares, 2012). Village justice, according to this analysis, is more important than state justice, though state justice is also interdependently important to securing a world freed from terror and violence (Braithwaite & Wardak, 2013).

2. War, Society and Criminalization of State in Afghanistan

Prior to a Communist coup in 1978, Afghanistan had many problems but remained generally peaceful for about five decades under King Mohammad Zahir Shah and President Mohammad Daoud Khan. During this period (especially between 1973 and 1978), Afghanistan was slowly beginning to consolidate state institutions. It was gradually becoming a freer society, especially for women. Compared with other developing nations at a similar level of development, there was promise in the education system. The tragedy of Afghanistan was partly born of the latter strength. Like many educationally free universities around the world in the late 1960s and early 1970s, Kabul University was vibrant with student radicalism (Barfield, 2010 p. 213). What distinguished the radicals of Kabul University from those at the Sorbonne or Berkeley was that its radical factions of the left came to be backed by the full might of the Soviet empire (or of Mao's China), and its Islamic radicals came to be backed by radical circles in Pakistan, Iran and other parts of the Muslim world. After the Soviet invasion, the latter were also backed by Pakistan's Inter-Services Intelligence Directorate (ISI), the US Central Intelligence Agency (CIA) and money, men and munitions from Saudi Arabia and some other Arab nations (Braithwaite & Wardak, 2013).

With this backing, the Communists and then the Islamists were able to take over the Afghan state. Between them, they managed to destroy the fragile promise of Afghanistan. In a succession of wars in which the Communists and the Mujahideen were the main protagonists, more than 1.2 million Afghans are estimated to have lost their lives. In the course of these wars, Afghanistan's economic, political, educational and cultural infrastructure was decimated. Successive classes of warlords captured corrupted institutions, while smaller gangs and militia groups were allowed to carve up the countryside. Eventually, the destroyed promise of the state education system meant that the only way many young Afghans could get an education was in *madrassas* (Islamic seminary schools). Many *madrassas* were funded by the likes of Osama bin Laden in the border areas between Afghanistan and Pakistan and in some Pakistani cities (Braithwaite & Wardak, 2013).

When the Soviet Union decided that sending guns and advisers was no longer enough to prop up its chaotic Communist client, it invaded Afghanistan, in December 1979. The Mujahideen were then able to draw in countervailing support from the United States, Western Europe, Pakistan, Saudi Arabia and Osama bin Laden. This was enough for them to defeat the Soviet Union and contribute greatly to the collapse of global communism. The last ruler of the former Communist regime of Afghanistan, Dr Mohammad Najibullah, renounced communism in the same way that Russia did, declaring instead support for Islam and democracy. The regime remained a Russian client and managed to hang on with Russian military aid. Though Gorbachev's and then Yeltsin's Russia was no longer its Cold War adversary, the United States did not seize the opportunity to work with Russia to support the transition from communism to democracy in Afghanistan. Instead, the United States wallowed in satisfaction at its expensive Cold War triumph there, refused to take responsibility for cleaning up the mess Cold War rivalry had created and jumped at the fiscal opportunity to sever the flow of funds to Afghanistan. The United States outsourced regional security for Afghanistan to Pakistan. The vacuum where great powers had once competed opened up a world in which Afghanistan could become a key site of a dangerous rivalry between regional powers—especially India and Pakistan. This cocktail of instability was further compounded by the state on its western border, Iran, arming Afghan Shi'ite militias inside Afghanistan (Braithwaite & Wardak, 2013).

Not only has the United States suffered terrorism as a result of its decision to abandon Afghanistan after the Soviet withdrawal (Wardak, 2002), Pakistan and India have also suffered ravages of terror as a result, while Russia now loses 14,000 young people a year to heroin sourced from Afghanistan—a number close to that of the young soldiers it lost throughout its Afghan war. Iran likewise bleeds from heroin trafficking out of Afghanistan, typically accounting for more than one-quarter of the world's opiate seizures (Paoli, Greenfield, & Reuter, 2009, p. 238). Between the Soviet withdrawal from Afghanistan and the early 2000s, it had already lost no fewer than 3,700 police killed in fights with drug traffickers (Ashouri & Rahmdel, 2003; Paoli et al., 2009, p. 238). At the end of the war with the Soviets, the Afghan state was much more salvageable than it was in 2001, when the West finally re-engaged with Afghanistan (Braithwaite & Wardak, 2013).

This is the Hobbesian lesson from Afghanistan. If the short-term interests of neighbouring states allow a war of all against all within a lawless state, all manner of sinister forces might incubate inside that space. This poses longer-term threats, even nuclear ones around the Pashtun belt that straddles Afghanistan and Pakistan, where the risk of Pakistan's nuclear weapons falling into the hands of terrorists is one of the greatest threats the world faces. This is no less than the lesson of Somalia, of Yemen and of other parts of Pakistan. While the Hobbesian diagnosis of disorder is perceptive, we seek to explain why the Hobbesian remedy of a Leviathan with a strong police and military made things worse in Afghanistan, just as it has in Pakistan (Braithwaite & Wardak, 2013).

While fighting among Mujahideen groups backed by different neighbours and regional powers delivered the most decisive blows in recent history to the Afghan state, it built on a longer history of state fragmentation as a result of civil war, clientelism of external powers, the geopolitical reality that Afghanistan was a buffer between competing empires (Russian, British) and competing alliance systems (Soviet, American) (Rubin, 2002), unstable succession from polygamous rulers (Saikal, 2004) and other causes. Some past military decimations were even more fragmenting than recent ones; for example, Genghis Khan destroyed many towns and most irrigation infrastructure in the thirteenth century, turning most of the surviving population back to nomadism (Rubin, 2002, p. 22). Propping up Hamid Karzai's government with the Northern Alliance warlords/leaders as a Leviathan without an effective separation of powers served to further erode state legitimacy. This led to a weak-state–strong-society pattern of Afghan development (Migdal, 1988). The renowned hospitality of Afghan civil society flourished by ordinary people learning to depend on their village and clan for security, justice and economic opportunities. They learnt not to depend on the state. Among the most critical of the supportive non-state civil society institutions were jirgas (for more, see Chapter 1 of this book).

The collapse of the Taliban at the hands of the US military campaign supported by the Northern Alliance warlords did not at first deliver a massive injection of Western support for state building. Once the initial rout of the Taliban was accomplished in 2001, the attention of Western powers was focused mostly on what was seen as the more difficult challenge of Iraq. The Bush administration had come to power with a platform averse to state building, so the priority in Afghanistan was killing or capturing remnants of al-Qaeda and the Taliban (Braithwaite & Wardak, 2013).

In the years after 2001, the realization began to dawn that former Northern Alliance warlords/ leaders and relatives and friends of President Karzai were pillaging the state. The authority of that state to monopolize the use of force did not extend much beyond Kabul, and even within Kabul, its legitimacy was plummeting. Progressively, Western support for state building poured in more voluminously. It poured into a bucket with holes controlled by a Leviathan who captured the leaks. It was a Leviathan unchecked by an effective separation of powers. The fatal mistakes were made early of putting criminals in charge, bedding down a culture of impunity and creating an electoral system that was winner-take-all and stunted the development of political parties. Worst of all, the constitution and the occupation concentrated power in the hands of one person: the president. That president then doled out positions with discretionary power to buy support from corrupt powerbrokers (Braithwaite & Wardak, 2013).

The Bonn agreement in 2001 did not usher in an effective 'constitutional moment' (Afsah, 2011, p. 157) because it enabled a personalized division of spoils rather than an institutionalized division of powers. Key ministries and other important positions in the first two crucial post-Taliban administrations were given to those anti-Taliban warlords who were involved in the destruction of Kabul, the killing of hundreds of its innocent residents, rapes and widespread looting (Afghanistan Justice Project, 2005; Grossman, 2006; Nordland, 2012). These ministries—especially Interior, Defence, Foreign Affairs and the National Directorate of Security—were then staffed by the warlords' factional followers and have become major networks of institutionalized abuse of power, corruption and nepotism (Grossman, 2009). More importantly, all these have had negative implications for the legitimacy of the post-Taliban Leviathan and its international backers, who promised to promote human rights and democracy in the new Afghanistan (Braithwaite & Wardak, 2013).

The Afghan state failed to secure inclusiveness, to deliver security and justice, to prevent corruption, address the issues of war crimes and crimes against humanity and to control the drug trade. Taliban fighters who had fled or surrendered in 2001 mostly sought to reconcile and submit to the Karzai government, right up to the level of Taliban military commander and minister of defence (Afghan, 2011, pp. 308–309; ICG, 2011, p. 6; Ruttig, 2011, p. 6). While Karzai himself wished to reciprocate reconciliation overtures from Taliban leaders in 2001 and 2002, his American overlords were at best indifferent to this as a priority. At worst, the United States was sympathetic to dominant Northern Alliance elements in the government who killed, imprisoned and persecuted Talibs with whom President Karzai or provincial leaders had reached reconciliation agreements (ICG, 2011, p. 11).

3. Criminalization of the Justice System After 2001

The Afghan government is a savage criminal enterprise that a few people run (Former member of parliament quoted in Nixon, 2011, p. 11). Prisons are full of people who have committed no crime but are too poor to bribe their way out of trouble, while serious criminals can pay enough to avoid ever serving their sentences. Just over half of Afghans fear for their safety in the local area (Asia Foundation, 2009), and many feel more secure and are more optimistic about justice prevailing in areas controlled by the Taliban (Mason, 2011, p. 1).

Mason's (2011) book *The Rule of Law in Afghanistan: Missing in Inaction* documents the ways the Afghan state has failed to compete with the Taliban in offering rule-of-law services. David Kilcullen, at the launch of the book in Canberra, described the Taliban as an 'armed rule of law movement'. His chapter (Kilcullen, 2011) describes the greater appeal of Taliban Shari'a courts in comparison with corrupt state courts for resolving disputes that matter locally, such as land conflicts, and for making the resolution of agreements stick, albeit brutally at times. These Shari'a courts consist of one *qazi* and two *ulema* and are part of the Taliban's administrative structure (Ruttig, 2010, p. 17). Kilcullen (2011) describes how the Taliban have an ombudsman (see also Peters, 2009, pp. 108–109) to whom citizens can complain about the shadow state services offered by the Taliban, including its courts. Peters (2009, pp. 108–109) found a sudden increase in wealth by a Taliban member can result in an investigation and in demotion or physical punishment if illicit bribes or kidnapping are the reason. A recent field study of the Taliban justice system—*Shadow Justice: How Taliban Run Their Judiciary*—further confirms these observations (Giustozzi, Franco, & Baczko, 2012). The 6 January 2012 ISAF State of the Taliban Report, based partly on interrogations of 4,000 arrested Taliban, leaked to *The New York Times* (2012), concludes that there is independence in the administration of this ombudsman function and in its enforcement of the Taliban Code of Conduct, the integrity of which ordinary Afghans have come to respect (at pp. 3–6).

Kilcullen (2011) contrasts the Taliban's justice services with the vicious and procedurally unfair Islamic justice meted out by al-Qaeda in Iraq, which the people of Iraq could not wait to turn on and evict. At the opposite extreme, Kilcullen (2011) finds the rather reintegrative justice and welfare services of Hezbollah in Lebanon, which support people in solving problems of injustice more holistically than the services provided by the Taliban. Finally, Kilcullen (2011) takes us on a journey across time and space to show from the writings of the ancient Greek Herodotus (1954) how military commanders with a small local base could expand that base during periods of Hobbesian anarchy by providing quality justice and security services to ever-widening circles of frightened citizens (Braithwaite & Wardak, 2013).

While it would be wrong to say there are no pockets of good policing practice, the consensus among commentators has been that the billions in American and European aid have built a tyrannical policing culture with weak community policing capabilities (Bayley & Perito, 2010; ICG, 2007, 2008; Murray, 2007; Wilder, 2007). Community policing has been the casualty of a policing culture corrupted and militarized by its leaders. In 2006, the Ministry of the Interior launched the Afghanistan National Auxiliary Police (ANAP) with international funding, which was intended to build community policing capability. Rather than realizing this intent, 'the program was used to regularize existing militias' (Lefèvre, 2010, p. 1). Another reason it did not work as a community policing initiative was that recruits overwhelmingly came from outside the areas they were assigned to police (Lefèvre, 2010, p. 6). ANAP was closed in 2008, only to see similar initiatives launched with the same weaknesses: the Afghan Public Protection Program and Local Defence Initiatives. These programmes may in reality discourage recruitment by the Afghanistan National Police, becoming their rivals rather than their auxiliaries. The training is less arduous than joining the police. ANAP recruits received the same pay and uniform as regular police after ten days' training (ICG, 2007, p. 13). The successors to ANAP have been led by the US military and have drawn their inspiration from the 'Sons of Iraq' arming of 100,000 local irregulars in the fight against al-Qaeda in Iraq starting in 2006. They also harnessed the tradition of the *arbaki*. The *arbaki* were unpaid militias formed by the tribal jirga, which have operated in specific cultural tribal settings for centuries. The auxiliary militias formed by the US military since 2006 differ from the *arbaki* in not being under the regulatory influence of the jirga and being paid, meaning that they are 'uncontrollable when payments stop' (Ruttig, 2010, p. 10). They are harnessed to the military objectives of one side in a war as opposed to having community policing objectives. Therefore, the auxiliaries neglected 'the jirga's inherent principle of mitigating conflicting interests and rather tend to deepen conflicts' (Ruttig, 2010, p. 10).

Another problem is that peaceful areas where militias have handed in their weapons to support democratic policing do not benefit from these aid programmes. Leaders from these peaceful areas complain that the American funding for auxiliaries goes to the most criminal gang leaders who have dragged their feet on handing in weapons. This is a direct contribution to the criminalization of the state: [T]he government ends up rewarding criminal jihadi commanders instead of peaceful members of the community. To some, this may form an incentive to take up arms in the hope of accessing government funding and employment (Lefèvre, 2010 p. 22).

Accessing government funding and employment illegitimately is closely connected to institutionalized corruption in the Afghan justice 'system' and in other state organs. One reason for the greater appeal of Taliban courts is that 'unlike the state courts, their decisions are not dependent on the ability to pay bribes' (Ledwidge, 2009, p. 7) Ladbury and CPAU (2009) found that: "The general perception was that the Taliban had indeed captured the justice market and were perceived to be reasonably efficient and fair—at least when compared to the formal system which was neither. There was no mention of unreasonable or unjust punishments" (p. 24).

Another problem is the patrimonial form of rule Hamid Karzai put in place. It is not that Karzai is personally one of the more corrupt individuals in Afghanistan. His style is genteel, and he seems to aspire to an Afghanistan that is an independent, democratic and prosperous society. It is not that he is a corrupt or brutal tyrant, more that he is a weak leader enjoying enormous control over a highly centralized presidential system. He uses that control in a patrimonial fashion to buy personal support from any powerbroker who threatens him or demands booty; his government is referred to by many Afghans as *hokomat-e-maslahati*—a government formed on the basis of a 'marriage of convenience' among rival individuals and groups each serving their personal and/or factional interests. President Karzai seems to allow a small circle of corrupt individuals at the political centre to build their wealth and power by expanding factional patronage systems. Ironically, this small circle also includes some smartly dressed, secular, Western-educated 'advisers' who advocate democracy and human rights but are deeply involved in patronage, nepotism and corruption (Braithwaite & Wardak, 2013).

Corruption has been particularly acute in the judiciary. There is perhaps no place in the world outside Afghanistan where it is nearly impossible to buy urban land without bribing a judge. Afghanistan is one of the few places in the world, if not the only place, where you can find a national survey that shows citizens are more likely to experience having to pay a bribe in their dealings with the judiciary than in their dealings with the police, the military and customs officials (the 2008, 2009 and 2011 Asia Foundation surveys, though with more mixed results in 2006 and 2010; see Asia Foundation, 2011, p. 102). Equally unusually, citizens are more likely to view the judicial branch as acting in 'their own interests' than members of the legislative or executive branches (Asia Foundation, 2010, p. 101, 2011, p. 112). On the positive side, these same surveys do show a little improvement across time in citizen attitudes to the judiciary. Even more positively, Afghanistan after 2009 became the only country in the world about which one could say hundreds of judges have been punished or dismissed for corruption (Braithwaite & Wardak, 2013).

4. The Criminalization of War

When UK Prime Minister Tony Blair justified the 2001 intervention in Afghanistan, he gave great prominence to the need to control the narcotics trade out of the country. A decade later, NATO had surrendered not only to 'bribery for peace' but also to a 'narcotics for peace' philosophy that was accepting of Afghanistan continuing to supply most of the world's heroin. NATO's philosophy became much worse than tolerating impunity for the corruption, drug deals and war crimes of the warlords it supported. Led by the Bush administration, 'torture for peace' became part of the philosophy of the 'war on terror'. The detention and torture of suspected insurgents at Guantanamo Bay and at the notorious Bagram prison, 'extraordinary rendition' of detainees and the repeated killing of civilians in night raids and in the CIA's drone attacks are well documented (*BBC,* 2009; Centre for Constitutional Rights, 2006; Human Rights Council, 2011; *The Guardian,* 2011; UNAMA, 2011). In Afghanistan, extrajudicial execution by NATO forces increasingly displaced arrest and trial (Braithwaite & Wardak, 2013).

The criminalization of NATO justified in the minds of the Taliban further criminalization of their *jihad*. The Taliban had never engaged in or approved suicide attacks on civilians until 2002; right up to the level of their foreign minister, and up to Mullah Omar, they strongly condemned the suicide attack on New York of 11 September 2001 (also see Strick van Linschoten & Kuehn, 2012). From 2002, the Taliban took a leaf out of al-Qaeda's book and, with technical support from them and from ISI-protected suicide bomb factories in Pakistan, the Taliban turned to terror. Armed gangs on all sides turned to funding their fighters partly through the heroin trade. This leads us to hypothesize that *the longer a war continues in stalemate, the more criminalized it becomes, especially if visible precedents of impunity abound early on.* This is hardly an original insight; it is a Hobbesian one. It is also Durkheimian, about anomic spaces where the rules of the game are no longer settled, where openings are created for all manner of sinister forces, not just those of the principal war makers and not only the brutishness of organized criminal groups. Hence, for example, personal revenge murders in Afghanistan are passed off as war killings or accommodations between armed factions (von Biljert, 2009).

We further hypothesize that the remedy is not so much in shifting the balance back from the war model to a criminal law-enforcement model for fighting terrorism and insurgency, though that is also needed. Rather, the more fundamental solution we advance is grounded in a restorative justice approach to defeating impunity. It can be built peacefully from the fabric of surviving traditional community justice institutions—jirga and shura—that are deeply grounded in Afghan culture and society (see Chapter 1 of this book).

Part II. Jeffersonian Alternative

Part I of this chapter (Braithwaite & Wardak, 2013) argued that insurgents sometimes grab power when they build legitimacy through restoring order to dangerous, anomic rural spaces. This is an alternative path to legitimacy to that provided by Hobbes's Leviathan. It is a path to power that exploits limitations of the Hobbesian solution. Part II of this chapter is about the Afghan path initially not taken—complementing Hobbes with Jefferson: state building combined with the strengthening of traditional rural ordering that delivers security.

1. State, Society and Social Order in Afghanistan

While state formal social control at the macro level has historically been weak and problematic (Shahrani, 1996), social order in Afghan society has mainly been maintained through the exercise of informal social control at micro and meso levels (Barfield & Nojumi, 2010; Glatzer, 1998; Wardak, 2002). One important consequence of this has been that when the Afghan state collapsed following the Soviet invasion, social order continued to exist in Afghan rural villages, where the overwhelming majority of Afghans live. Even today, there exists a higher level of social order in Afghan rural villages compared with large urban centres, where tens of thousands of Afghan and NATO-led International Security Assistance Force (ISAF) from nearly fifty countries concentrate. Ironically, the main sources of violence and disorder in Afghan rural villages are the very forces—the Taliban, the ISAF and the Afghan state—that try to impose order. But their imposed orders have proven fragile, artificial and unsustainable (Wardak & Braithwaite, 2013).

Afghan and international strategists over the past twelve years failed to restore lasting order and stability in Afghanistan because they did not understand the complex relationships between the Afghan state and society at various levels. They failed to understand that the state and various non-state institutions contribute to the formation and the maintenance of social order in Afghan society in different spheres of life and at different levels. Importantly, there has also been a lack of political will on the part of the Afghan state and the international community to fully explore the complexities of this kind of understanding and translate it into policy. Drawing on Wardak's (2006) work on the formation and maintenance of social order in Afghan society, we identify the main agencies of social control as the extended family, kinship groups, tribes, ethnic groups and the state (for more see Chapter 1 of this book).

2. *Finding a New Path to Non-Violence and Justice in Afghanistan*

A cease-fire in a war President Karzai, NATO and the Taliban cannot win (Braithwaite & Wardak, 2011) is the last best hope to lay a foundation for all sides to work to disempower themselves in favour of village jirgas/shuras and a plural, inclusive republican constitution. Most Western military commanders have held to the view that, even if they cannot defeat the Taliban militarily, killing Taliban fighters maintains military pressure, and this might help them cut a better peace deal. Braithwaite and Wardak (2011) argue that this approach is wrong, particularly where it counts most: for high-level Taliban. The military pressure that *high-level* Taliban members feel most is from the Pakistan ISI, who assure them that if they do not keep fighting the Americans, they will hand them over to the Americans to be sent to Guantanamo Bay or be killed. In the past, the ISI has quite often won credit from the United States by advising them of the whereabouts of senior Taliban commanders who were suing for peace. NATO military pressure on *mid-level* commanders has led to the replacement of older Taliban who long for peace and who fight for their valley and their people with young men who are more radical, more bloodthirsty and more disconnected from their valley and their people. This is because they have been indoctrinated in Pakistan-based religious schools and further radicalized by drone attacks and the repeated killings of civilians in Afghanistan and Pakistan (Wardak & Braithwaite, 2013).

Killing *low-level* Taliban members is also counterproductive because of Pashtun revenge culture: 'If you kill me, my brothers will kill you'. One way they do this is by joining the Afghan Army and Afghan National Police and killing their foreign trainers—known as 'green-on-blue' attacks. The evidence is that low-level operatives who are killed have their places taken by younger relatives. Moreover, night raids that kill members of the Taliban also kill innocent citizens in collateral damage; resentment over this also fuels the insurgency (Wardak & Braithwaite, 2013).

Criminologists should be capable of seeing killing in Afghanistan through a broader lens than just a war lens. They should be able to see it through the eyes of victims, for example. Oxfam survey (Waldman, 2008, p. 12) results show that ordinary Afghans certainly fear being killed by the Taliban, but fears of warlords, criminal gangs, international forces, drug traffickers (which, were they combined with 'criminals', would be perceived as the top security threat), Afghan police and armed men hired to do the bidding of Afghan government officials are all extremely high; and fears of the Afghan Army, family violence and inter-tribal violence are also quite high. What is needed is a paradigm shift that responds to this fear of violence and war-weariness as a political resource to motivate a multidimensional cease-fire combined with concrete steps towards disarmament and replacement of militarized policing with community policing and with regulation of violence by both jirgas and courts (Wardak & Braithwaite, 2013).

3. *Expanding Pacified Spaces and Democracy via Village/Town Moots*

Afghanistan is a case study of how hard it is to build a democracy from the top down via a state executive, even with unprecedented support for that state from all the world's major powers and initially with the overwhelming support of the relieved citizens of Afghanistan in 2001. Insecurity is a central reason democracy is not working in Afghanistan. The Asia Foundation (2010, p. 4) found that the percentage of Afghans afraid to vote in national elections is rising and, in mid-2010, was 60 per cent, 83 per cent in the south-west of the country. Most flourishing democracies started to build democratic institutions first in towns that were very small by contemporary standards—towns like Lubeck in Germany and Bruges in Flanders, which remain small today, and like Hamburg, Boston, York and Florence, which have become large cities. Most people prefer democracy to autocracy, yet they must learn to be democratic before they can enjoy its benefits. Throughout history, citizens have learnt to be democratic in sub-national institutions like guilds, town councils and village moots. Among the things these institutions delivered was space for citizens to settle disputes and allegations of crime without autocratic edicts from the courts of feudal masters. These feudal courts fused judicial and executive authority. It proved more possible to break away judicial authority than executive authority (particularly to wage war) from the courts of kings and feudal overlords (Wardak & Braithwaite, 2013).

Through this prism, it is hard to understand why the discipline of criminology has not been more theoretically assertive in debating the possibility that criminal adjudication has always been a key site where citizens learn to be democratic. The institution of the jirga/shura (see Chapter 1 of this book) shows that, in conditions of a Hobbesian war of all against all; it is in local crime control that citizens most crave a democratic voice. Yet the Afghan case also shows how forces of tyranny—local Taliban tyrants and local NATO and Afghan military commanders—can co-opt this craving for participatory, reconciliatory local regulation of crime. Even when they do, a little local space is still created with the possibility that citizens at the periphery can learn to be democratic. There is no simple, straight path from tyranny to democracy. Just sending in peacekeepers to hold a national election is not such a path. Top-down peacemaking and constitutional development are important but will only take root if the soil of democracy is cultivated locally and spreads out from 'islands of civility' (Kaldor, 1999).

Conclusion

Our conclusion is that criminologists need to be part of a debate about the path to democracy that starts at the periphery of a society rather than at the centre. This debate sees it as important to jump-start the journey to democracy in the judicial branch within rural and small-town spaces as much as in the executive branch in the capital. In mature democracies where citizens feel increasingly remote from and cynical about their government, criminology can lead a debate about whether the judicial branch rather than electoral politics provides the more fertile soil for democratic renewal. The argument is that most young citizens might enjoy better prospects of learning to be meaningfully democratic in participatory restorative justice conferences in schools and neighbourhoods than in Labour Party branch meetings. If movements of scholars like the Taliban continue to be more open to this insight than communities of liberal scholars, more poor nations may be co-opted to tyranny by Islamic and other armed rule-of-law movements (Wardak & Braithwaite, 2013).

The reality of Afghan society is that it has historically resisted the imposition of social order from above: the drastic failures of King Amanullah Khan's modernist, Western-inspired radical reforms in the 1920s and the Afghan Communists' Soviet-inspired 'socialism' in the 1980s are lessons not to be lost. Both tried to impose modernity on a very traditional Afghan society. Similarly, the imposition of different versions of theocracy by the Mujahideen and Taliban in the 1990s and early 2000s drastically failed. In order for Afghanistan to live in a lasting peace with itself, its neighbours and with the rest of the world, its local traditional institutions need to be bridged with modernity. It may not be too late for the United States and its Western allies to help build peace and promote justice in post-Taliban Afghanistan from below—through an Afghan form of rural republicanism—supported by a Hobbesian Leviathan from above. This Afghan *bottom-up and, at the same time, top-down* approach is more likely to deliver effective justice and provide lasting peace to all Afghans. Peacekeepers may be required to protect both the Afghan state and its society, including those involved in bottom-up reconciliatory work. Top-down imposition of a new social order supported by Western military power and night raids to search for and kill Taliban fighters are likely to prove counterproductive in the long run (Wardak & Braithwaite, 2013).

Note

1 This chapter is a revised version of two previous articles of the authors: 1. Braithwaite, J., & Wardak (2013). Crime and war in Afghanistan: Part I: The Hobbesian solution. *British Journal of Criminology, 53*(2), 179–196. doi: 10.1093/bjc/azs065; 2. Wardak, A., & Braithwaite, J. (2013). Crime and war in Afghanistan: Part II: A Jeffersonian alternative? *British Journal of Criminology, 53*(2), 197–214. doi: 10.1093/bjc/azs066. Republished with permission.

References

Afghan, S. (2011). Kandahar after the fall of the Taliban. In W. Mason (Ed.), *The rule of law in Afghanistan: Missing in inaction.* New York: Cambridge University Press.

Afghanistan Justice Project. (2005). Casting shadows: War crimes and crimes against humanity 1978–2001. Retrieved from www.afghanistanjusticeproject.org/index.htm.

Afsah, E. (2011). Is Constitutionalism possible without governance? International standards and the Afghan Legal System. In A. Nollkaemper, (Ed.), *International law in domestic courts.* Oxford: Oxford University Press.

Ashouri, M., & Rahmdel, M. (2003). Final Report—Iran, report submitted for the project Modelling the World Heroin Market: Assessing the Consequences of Change in Afghanistan Production, Tehran, Mimeo.

Asia Foundation. (2010). *Afghanistan in 2010: A survey of the Afghan people.* Kabul: The Asia Foundation.

Asia Foundation. (2011). *Afghanistan in 2011: A survey of the Afghan people.* Kabul: The Asia Foundation.

Barfield, T. (2010). *Afghanistan: A cultural and political history.* Princeton, NJ: Princeton University Press.

Barfield, T., & Nojumi, N. (2010). Bringing more effective governance to Afghanistan: 10 pathways to stability. *Journal of Middle East Policy, XVII*, 40–53.

Bayley, D. H., & Perito, R. M. (2010). *The police in war: Fighting insurgency, terrorism, and violent crime.* Boulder, CO: Lynne Rienner.

BBC. (2009). Ex-detainees allege Bagram Abuse. Retrieved from http://news.bbc.co.uk/1/hi/world/south_asia/8116046.stm.

Braithwaite, J., Charlesworth, H., & Soares, A. (2012). *Networked governance of freedom and Tyranny: Peace in Timor-Leste.* Canberra: ANU E Press.

Braithwaite, J., Cookson, M., Braithwaite, V., & Dunn, L. (2010). *Anomie and violence: Non-truth and reconciliation in Indonesian peacebuilding.* Canberra: ANU E Press.

Braithwaite, J., & Wardak, A. (2011). Is killing Taliban a good idea?, *Inside Story,* Retrieved from http://inside.org.au/is-killing-taliban-a-good-idea/.

Braithwaite, J., & Wardak, A. (2013). Crime and war in Afghanistan: Part I: The Hobbesian solution. *British Journal of Criminology, 53*(2), 179–196. doi: 10.1093/bjc/azs065.

Centre for Constitutional Rights. (2006). Report on torture and cruel, inhuman and degrading treatment of prisoners at Guantanamo Bay, Cuba. Retrieved from http://ccrjustice.org/files/Report_ReportOn Torture.pdf.

Fink, N. C., & El-Said, H. (2011). *Transforming terrorists: Examining international efforts to address violent extremism.* New York: International Peace Institute.

Giustozzi, A., Franco, C., & Baczko, A. (2012). *Shadow justice: How Taliban run their judiciary.* Kabul: Integrity Watch Afghanistan (IWA).

Glatzer, B. (1998). Is Afghanistan on the brink of ethnic and tribal disintegration?. In W. Maley, (Ed.), *Fundamentalism reborn? Afghanistan and the Taliban.* New York: St Martins.

Grossman, P. (2006). Truth, justice and stability in Afghanistan. In N. Roht-Arriaza & J. Mariezcurrena (Eds.), *Transitional justice in the twenty-first century, beyond truth versus justice* (pp. 255–77). Cambridge, NY: Cambridge University Press.

Grossman, P. (2009). *Transitional justice and DDR: The case of Afghanistan.* New York: International Center for Transitional Justice. Retrieved from http://ictj.org/sites/default/files/ICTJ-DDR-Afghanistan-CaseStudy-2009-English.pdf.

Guardian, The. (2011). Afghan civilians killed by RAF Drone. Retrieved from www.guardian.co.uk/uk/2011/jul/05/afghanistan-raf-drone-civilian-deaths.

Herodotus. (1954). *The histories.* Trans. A. de Selincourt. Harmondsworth: Penguin Books.

Hobbes, T. (1651). Leviathan. Retrieved from Project Gutenberg www.gutenberg.org/ebooks/3207.

Human Rights Council. (2011). Report of the United Nations High Commissioner for Human Rights on the Situation of Human Rights in Afghanistan and on the achievements of technical assistance in the field of human rights, UN General Assembly, A/HRC/16/67. Retrieved from http://daccess-dds-ny.un.org/doc/UNDOC/GEN/G11/103/31/PDF/G1110331.pdf?OpenElement.

International Crisis Group (ICG). (2007). *Reforming Afghanistan's police.* Kabul and Brussels: International Crisis Group.

International Crisis Group (ICG). (2008). *Policing in Afghanistan: Still searching for a strategy.* Kabul and Brussels: International Crisis Group.

International Crisis Group (ICG). (2010). *The threat from Jamaat-ul Mujahideen Bangladesh.* Dhaka and Brussels: International Crisis Group.

International Crisis Group (ICG). (2011). *The insurgency in Afghanistan's heartland.* Kabul and Brussels: International Crisis Group.

Kaldor, M. (1999). *New and old wars: Organized violence in a global era*. Cambridge: Polity Press.

Kilcullen, D. J. (2011). Deiokes and the Taliban: Local governance, bottom-up state formation and the rule of law in counter-insurgency. In W. Mason (Ed.), *The rule of law in Afghanistan: Missing in inaction*. New York: Cambridge University Press.

Ladbury, S., & Cooperation for Peace and Unity (Afghanistan) (CPAU).(2009). *Testing hypotheses on radicalisation in Afghanistan: Why do men join the Taliban and Hizb-i Islami?* Kabul: Department for International Development.

Ledwidge, L. (2009). Justice and counter insurgency in Afghanistan: A missing link. *RUSI Journal, 154*, 6–9.

Lefèvre, M. (2010). *Local defence in Afghanistan: A review of government-backed initiatives*. Kabul: Afghanistan Analysts Network.

Mason, W. (2011). Introduction. In W. Mason (Ed.), *The rule of law in Afghanistan: Missing in inaction*. New York: Cambridge University Press.

Migdal, J. S. (1988). *Strong societies and weak states: State—Society relations and state capabilities in the third world*. Princeton, NJ: Princeton University Press.

Murray, T. (2007). Police-building in Afghanistan: A case study of civil security reform. *International Peacekeeping, 14*, 108–26.

New York Times. (2012). State of the Taliban, 2012. Retrieved from https://archive.nytimes.com/www.nytimes.com/interactive/world/asia/23atwar-taliban-report-docviewer.html?emc=eta1.

Nixon, H. (2011). *Achieving durable peace: Afghan perspectives on a peace process*. Oslo: Peace Research Institute Oslo (PRIO).

Nordland, N. (2012, July 23). Top Afghans tied to '90s carnage, Researchers say. *New York Times*. Retrieved from www.nytimes.com/2012/07/23/world/asia/key-afghans-tiedto-mass-killings-in-90s-civil-war.html.

Paoli, L., Greenfield, V., & Reuter, P. (2009). *The world heroin market: Can supply be reduced?* New York: Oxford University Press.

Peters, G. (2009). *Seeds of terror: How heroin is bankrolling the Taliban and Al Qaeda*. New York: Thomas Dunne Books.

Rubin, B. R. (2002). *The fragmentation of Afghanistan: State formation and collapse in the international system* (2nd ed.). Karachi: Oxford University Press.

Ruttig, T. (2010). *How tribal are the Taleban?* Kabul: Afghanistan Analysts Network.

Ruttig, T. (2011). *The battle for Afghanistan: Negotiations with the Taliban: History and prospects for the future*. Washington, DC: New America Foundation.

Saikal, A. (2004). *Modern Afghanistan: A history of struggle and survival*. London: IB Taurus & Co.

Shahrani, N. (1996). State building and social fragmentation in Afghanistan: A historical view. In A. Banuazizi & M. Weiner (Eds.), *The state, religion and ethnic politics: Afghanistan, Iran, Pakistan*. New York: Syracuse University Press.

South Asian Terrorism Portal. (2012). Jama'atul Mujahideen Bangladesh (JMB). Retrieved from www.satp.org/satporgtp/countries/bangladesh/terroristoutfits/JMB.htm.

Strick van Linschoten, A., & Kuehn, F. (2012). *An enemy we created: The myth of the Taliban/Al-Qaeda Merger in Afghanistan, 1970–2010*. London: C. Hurst and Co.

UNAMA. (2011). Treatment of conflict related detainees in Afghan Custody, Report by UN Office of the High Commissioner for Human Rights. Retrieved from http://unama.unmissions.org/Portals/UNAMA/Documents/October10_%202011_UNAMA_Detention_ Full-Report_ENG.pdf.

von Biljert, M. (2009). Unruly commanders and violent power struggles: Taliban networks in Uruzgan. In A. Giustozzi, (Ed.), *Decoding the Taliban: Insights from the Afghan Field*. New York: Columbia University Press.

Waldman, M. (2008). *Community peacebuilding in Afghanistan: The case for a national strategy*. Oxford: Oxfam International.

Wardak, A. (2002). Jirga: Power and traditional conflict resolution in Afghanistan. In J. Strawson (Ed.), *Law after ground zero*. London: Cavendish.

Wardak, A. (2006). Structures of authority and local dispute settlement in Afghanistan. In H.-J. Albrecht (Ed.), *Conflicts and Conflict Resolution in Middle Eastern Societies: Between Tradition and Modernity* (pp. 347–370). Berlin: Duncker & Humblot.

Wardak, A., & Braithwaite, J. (2013). Crime and war in Afghanistan: Part II: A Jeffersonian alternative? *British Journal of Criminology, 53*(2), 197–214. doi: 10.1093/bjc/azs066.

Wilder, A. (2007). *Cops or robbers? The struggle to reform the Afghan national police*. Kabul: Afghanistan Research and Evaluation Unit.

Woodward, R. (2011). *Obama's wars*. New York: Simon & Shuster.

17

ORGANISED CRIME, GANGS AND THE COMPLEXITY OF GROUP OFFENDING IN BANGLADESH

Sally Atkinson-Sheppard

Introduction

Organised crime and gangs are widely discussed topics in criminological literature. There is a general consensus that mafias are a specific form of organised crime group that engage in a market for protection (Gambetta, 1993) and crime and violence (Paoli, 2002,2003,2004) and are distinguishable from organised crime groups in general because of the way they collude with corrupt politicians and members of the state (Hess, 1998). In contrast, organised crime groups are generally thought to 'attempt to regulate and control the production and distribution of a given commodity or service unlawfully' (Varese, 2010, p. 27) but have less of a focus on protection, and do not necessarily engage directly with corrupt politicians or the police.

Academic debate tends to argue that gangs are one of several things; one view sees them as marginalised young people who form groups as a sub cultural resistance to wider social exclusion and who are different to more organised forms of criminality. This thinking was developed by Thrasher (1927) and has continued to gain momentum, particularly in the Western world, ever since. The Eurogang programme, for example defines the gang as 'any durable, street-oriented youth group whose involvement in illegal activity is part of its group identity' (Van Gemert, 2005, p. 148). A definition they argue can and should be used as a basis for comparative gang studies around the world (ibid.). Another view is that street-based gangs operate as the lower echelons of organised crime networks (Levitt & Venkatesh, 2000) or that street-based gangs begin as peer groups and advance into more organised criminal groups (Hallsworth & Young, 2006; Densley, 2012). Despite this wide-ranging and virtually global debate, the nature of organised crime and gangs in Bangladesh remains largely unknown.

In 2010, Shafi conducted one of the only studies into crime and violence in Dhaka and argued that crime is pervasive, particularly in poor areas, but that crime reporting is low, thus the extent of criminality in Dhaka is largely unknown. Shafi (2010) discusses endemic organised crime led by '*mastaans*' who work in alliance with corrupt politicians and the police, something also argued by Zafarullah and Rahman (2002, p. 1021), who propose that 'mastaans operate under the 'shelter of godfathers, who are mainly ministers, members of parliament and business leaders'. Lewis (2012) discusses the role that mastaans play in connecting slum dwellers with politicians and securing votes during elections. However, he also argues that 'they may also play a more parasitic role, operating on the fringes of criminal extortion and other forms of violence' (p. 211).

Furthermore, The Coalition to Stop the Use of Child Soldiers (2007) suggests that:

> Children in urban slums are vulnerable to recruitment by criminal gangs commonly known as mastaans. High levels of unemployment, patronage from political parties, together with inadequate, inefficient and corrupt law enforcement agencies have all contributed to the growing culture of 'mastanocracy'. Their connections with political parties make it possible for them to engage in extortion and other crimes with impunity.
>
> *(p. 11)*

Despite the extant literature many questions remain unanswered, including: What is the nature of the mastaans? Are they mafia groups, organised criminals, gangs or something else? How do mastaans operate and exist? What role do young people play in these criminal groups? And what relationship do mastaans have with other criminal groups and gangs?

As a way to address some of the lacunas in knowledge, I conducted a three-year ethnographic study into gangs and organised crime in Dhaka, with a specific focus on the involvement of street children in Bangladeshi mafia groups, the mastaans. The context in which this study occurred—a corrupt and violent political situation (Moniruzzaman, 2009), a 'quintessential developing country' (Lewis, 2012), endemic poverty (UN-HABITAT, 2002), pervasive slums (*RISE*, 2013) and persistent child labour (Ruwanpura & Roncolato, 2006) mean that several of the most widely acceptable criminological theories and their underpinnings, namely that crime is expressive, was challenged by the data derived from this study.

This chapter considers the landscape of criminal groups in Dhaka. It begins by exploring the mastaans and how and in what instances street children are hired as the 'illicit labourers' of these groups (Atkinson-Sheppard, 2016). The chapter then moves on to explore a variety of other criminal groups, including organised crime groups which are distinct from the mastaans, 'rich or upper-class' gangs, 'student groups' and then, finally, extremist groups and the ways in which terrorism is conceptualised in Bangladesh. The chapter considers the nature of these groups and the associations they have with one another. The chapter concludes with a reflection on the complexity of criminal groups in Dhaka and the implications of this for global understandings of crime and violence.

Research Methods

There were three phases of data collection included in this study:

Phase 1: Participant Observation

I conducted a total of three years' worth of participant observation, most of which occurred while I worked for an international development organisation in Dhaka. This observation was essential to understanding the social, political, economic and cultural factors that provide the context to this study.

Phase 2: Interviews with Adult Practitioners

I carried out a total of 80 interviews (38 semi-structured and 42 unstructured) and two focus groups, the first with six participants and the second with five. The participants included police officers, senior prison officers, military security officers, paralegals, NGO workers, police and prison reform workers, journalists, diplomats and community members.

Phase 3: An Embedded Case Study of Street Children and the Organisation That Supports Them

There were 22 children involved in this embedded case study. There were 10 girls and 12 boys, and their ages ranged from 8 to 15. All were associated with an organisation that provides holistic support to children that live on the streets. I visited the children on a weekly basis for over a year and conducted participant observation and workshops which explored general themes of crime and violence and, finally, semi-structured group interviews with all 22 of the children.

Data analysis continued throughout the research; each phase helped to develop and refine the next phase, and each data set was triangulated against each other. The data was catalogued, coded and descriptive, and then analytical analysis occurred. The data was contemplated in light of theories of gangs and organised crime from around the world; gaps appeared, and thus I sought theories from development studies including: child labour, social protection and patronage. This all helped to frame the study from a perspective that was relevant to the context in which it occurred and led to a Bangladesh-specific theory of street children's involvement in organised crime, discussed throughout this chapter.

Exploring the Landscape of Gangs and Organised Crime in Dhaka

1. Mastaans, Gangs and 'Illicit Child Labourers'

The basis of this study was an exploration of the mastaans, their nature, the gangs that work for them and the street children that became embroiled in the lower echelons of these criminal groups. Mafias are often argued to be a distinct form of organised crime, specifically because of the relationships they form with the state and their ability to operate in a market for protection (Gambetta, 1993). This role that mafias play, in what Sergi (2015) terms *concurrent governance*, helps to explain the ways in which these groups collaborate with corrupt politicians and the police, which in turn facilitates the role they play in a market for protection, crime and violence.

In 2017, I argued—for the first time—that mastaans are Bangladeshi mafia groups. By drawing on theories of protection (Gambetta, 1993; Varese, 2010), violence (Paoli, 2002) and behavioural theories of mafias (Sergi & Lavorgna, 2016) I developed a 'social protection' theory of the mafia and proposed that 'mastaans work in alliance with corrupt members of the state, they provide access to services, resolve disputes, commit extortion and carry out a wide array of criminal activity, much of which relies on their monopolisation of violence to protect their illegal industries' (Atkinson-Sheppard, 2017a, p. 1).

There is a general consensus that organised crime groups, including mafias, need some level of organisation to operate effectively. There is an ongoing debate among criminological scholars about the nature of hierarchies, which demonstrate that mafias often evolve to suit the context in which they occur. For example, Calderoni (2014) argues that the concept of distinctly hierarchical structured mafias that regularly infiltrates the mainstream media is misleading; instead *Ndrangheta* bosses in Italy often play a role in the tactical delivery of criminal business, questioning the rigidity and structure of these mafia groups.

This study explored the nature of mastaans in Bangladesh. I argue that mastaans operate in a hierarchical structure similar in many ways to Hallsworth and Young (2006) echelons of group offending which includes three distinct levels: organised crime, street gangs and peer groups. However, I propose a modified pyramid; mastaans sit at the top of the criminal hierarchy in Dhaka, gangs are employed to manage business on the streets and at the lowest echelon, street children are hired as the 'illicit labourers' of these groups (Atkinson-Sheppard, 2016).

The crimes that mastaan groups are involved in are multi-faceted; they 'operate in a market for social protection, acting as patrons allowing poor people to access services and social mobility, protecting economic transactions and resolving disputes. The role of mastaans has also diversified into other forms of organised crime. They commit extortion and carry out a wide array of criminal activity' (Atkinson-Sheppard, 2017a, p. 17). Gangs and street children are hired to conduct a variety of crime on behalf of the mastaans, including political violence, extortion, 'land-grabbing', drug dealing and contract killings (Atkinson-Sheppard, 2016).

One criminological perspective, often derived from studies of gangs in the Western world, defines the gang as 'any durable, street-oriented youth group whose involvement in illegal activity is part of its group identity' (Van Gemert, 2005, p. 148), yet this definition does not sufficiently explain the gangs that work for the mastaans. Firstly, gangs that operate at the middle echelon of mastaan groups are not individual entities but part of a larger picture of organised crime. Thus an alternative definition of the gang as part of a spectrum is more useful (Levitt & Venkatesh, 2000; Hallsworth & Young, 2006; Densley, 2012). Secondly, mastaan groups exhibit traits similar to mafia groups from around the world, yet criminological literature has yet to develop a way to explain or conceptualise young people who operate on the fringes of mafia-related activity.

Furthermore, and taking a different stance, considering children as gang members misses important drivers for their involvement in crime; street children are highly vulnerable; they live in abject poverty and often have to work to earn a living to provide for themselves and their families. As the children involved in this study explained, involvement in mastaan groups is primarily seen as a means to acquire protection and to earn an income, essential for their survival on the streets (Atkinson-Sheppard, 2017b). For this reason, I proposed that children who are hired to work in organised crime groups, including mastaans, should be conceptualised as 'illicit child labourers' (for more details please see Atkinson-Sheppard, 2016, 2017a, 2017b) and the act considered a form of modern slavery.[1] In doing so, steps can be taken to raise awareness of the plight of these children and develop ways to better protect vulnerable children in Bangladesh and wider afield.

The main objective of the study was to consider the mastaans and the role they play in Bangladesh society. However, while data was gathered on a variety of issues related to the mastaans, additional themes emerged; these themes included *other* forms of organised crime in Dhaka and the ways in which mastaans interact with these groups, demonstrating a complex landscape of crime and violence. Discussions throughout this chapter consider these additional groups and reflect on the nature of group-related crime in Dhaka and the interplay between groups operating in the nation's capital city.

2. Organised Crime Groups and Gangs

2.1 Organised Begging

On arrival in Dhaka one of the first things I noticed was the presence of street children begging at car windows at busy intersections of the city. I also witnessed these children give the money they received to men who were standing, sheltering from the sun, in doorways or alleyways adjacent to the roads in which the children begged for money. Media reports suggest that this is a common occurrence in Dhaka; children are abducted and then beaten or starved. The worse the child's disfigurement, the more money they can earn by begging on the streets. A report in the British Newspaper *The Guardian* revealed that the leader of a begging group was arrested and confessed that:

> He and his accomplices abducted children, kept them for months in confined spaces or even in barrels and deprived them of food. Permanently disabled by their confinement and

virtual starvation, the children were then sent on to the streets of the city either accompanied with a woman posing as their mother or alone, according to police.

(Hammadi & Burke, 2011)

The CNN Freedom Project is working to end this 'modern-day slavery' and featured a story of a seven-year-old boy who was abducted and forced to beg on the streets. The boy tried to escape but was violently beaten. CNN reports:

> The boy was slashed many times, his healed wounds now forming a large cross in scar tissue across a section of his chest and from his throat to his pelvis. But he survived, and he and his family have been placed in a witness protection program. The boy is now the star witness in a case that has exposed a criminal gang that, according to investigators, has snatched children off the streets, maimed them and sent them out to beg for money.

(p. 1)

The Guardian article describes these gangs as operating in a 'racket' (Hammadi & Burke, 2011). However, very little information is known about the nature of these criminal groups or the relationships they may form with mastaans or other types of gangs.

I asked the participants about this phenomenon; they explained that 'organised begging' was a prevalent issue in Dhaka and that begging groups were well established and often managed by bosses living in different parts of the city, demonstrating a level of organisation, and the exploitation of vulnerable children. The participants described instances when children were maimed as a mechanism to acquire greater sympathy and thus extra money from passersby. For example, as one participant explained: 'Sometimes the begging gangs break their [street children] legs, it's a whole institution. They are very organized' (Hammadi & Burke, 2011).

As discussed earlier in this chapter, Varese (2010, p. 15) argues that 'organised crime groups attempt to regulate and control the production and distribution of a given commodity or service unlawfully'. Thus these begging groups demonstrate a form of organised crime; they are organised, and their objective is to monopolise the begging market via illegal means. The groups are managed by a boss and have different echelons, with street children operating at the bottom, street-based level. According to the participants there is no direct association between mastaans and 'begging gangs', but it is probable that protection money is paid by these gangs to acquire permission to work in areas controlled by mastaan groups. Nevertheless, the exploitation of vulnerable children potentially demonstrates a form of modern slavery and is comparable to discussions about the 'illicit child labourers' of mastaan groups.

2.2 Gangs Involved in Theft, Robbery and Drugs

The participants spoke about a variety of gangs involved in theft or robbery. For example, a journalist explained that 'there are some criminals that work in groups that throw a substance into people's eyes, burn their eyes and then rob them'.[2] In addition, a police officer discussed 'pickpocketing groups':

> One pickpocketing group operates all over Dhaka; in all areas. The leader is a very rich man who lives in a high story building in Uttara. He is the boss of the pickpockets. He has workers in every area, who all have sub-leaders, and they have people who do the pickpocketing. The money goes to the boss, the rich man. There were three groups in Dhaka but recently they joined together. The sub-leaders are all interlinked but the money still goes to the chief.[3]

This demonstrates a type of organised crime (Varese, 2010). The groups aim to regulate and control a particular type of commodity: pickpocketing, via illegitimate means. The participants also described many examples of gangs that sell drugs in different areas of the city. They explained that in some instances gangs sell drugs on a small scale but that there is often an organised element to these groups, which invariably has some type of association with a mastaan. A UN Security Advisor described the structure and activities of an organised crime group involved in drug selling: 'In many instances the drug dealers are well-placed socially, they have good linkages with mastaans. The boss has agents in areas, they are powerful in their areas and they move around a lot to stay undercover. They have sub leaders'.[4] This illustrates the hierarchical nature of these groups, their aspiration to monopolise areas of the city and the importance of developing relationships with the mastaans.

2.3 Fake Police Officer Groups

One participant, a police officer, described what he termed 'fake police officer groups'. These groups 'have handcuffs, fake IDs and work with CNG[5] drivers. When a CNG driver has a customer from outside of Dhaka the fake police officers stop the CNG, jump in with a gun and say "this is the police, you have fake currency". Obviously, the people will deny it but the fake police officers will demand the money anyway. We've seen a recent rise of this type of activity; there are more than 20 of these groups operating in Dhaka'.[6]

The participants also described several other forms of gangs or organised crime groups that threaten people over the phone and claim they have associations with mastaans. For example, a UN Security Advisor explained that 'People call you on your house phone and demand money, they say they have strong links with mastaans. People become scared and they don't know what to do, the people making the call say they know everything about you, your address, your car registration. This has happened to several UN people'.[7] The UN Security Advisor explained that he has little information to substantiate any relationship between these groups and mastaans, but this example does demonstrate tentative links of criminal groups with mastaan-related activity.

3. The 'Rich or Upper-Class' Gangs

Hallsworth and Young (2006, p. 4) argue that group-related offending occurs in three different but often interlinked echelons:

Peer groups are relatively small, unorganised and transient entities that coalesce in public spaces. Members are usually friends who share similar life trajectories and experiences and simply 'hang around' together. Delinquency and criminal activity are not integral to the identity or practice of this group, but they can occur in certain situational contexts.

The gang is a relatively durable, predominantly street-based group who see themselves and are seen by others as a discernible group and for whom crime and violence is intrinsic to the identity of group practice and solidarity. It is a mutation of the peer group.

The **organised crime group** is composed principally of men for whom involvement in criminal activity is intrinsic to their identity and practice. Crime is an occupation and business venture.

Previous discussions in this chapter have highlighted the difficulties in applying this definition to understandings of mastaans and the role that street children play in these criminal groups. However, discussions within the study did highlight a different type of 'gang' in Dhaka for which this definition is both useful and relevant.

The participants discussed the 'rich or upper-class gangs' who come from affluent areas of the city including Dhamondi, Gulshan, Baridhara and Uttara. The participants believed these groups to be 'relatively new to Bangladesh; they have been apparent for the last 8 to 10 years or so'.[8] The 'Gulshan boys', a name used frequently by the participants to describe 'rich' gangs who were sometimes but not necessarily from the Gulshan area of Dhaka, consist of young men from privileged families who, according to the interviewees, 'are not politically affiliated, because they don't need to be'.[9] Members of these 'rich or upper-class gangs' are usually aged 12 to 18, enrolled at English-language schools and live in apartments or houses, never on the streets or in slums.

Gangs of Gulshan boys have around six to eight members. The activities of these groups consist of 'hanging out together, driving fast cars, taking drugs and finding girlfriends'.[10] The types of drugs or alcohol that the Gulshan boys use include 'yaba, fencidile and beer'.[11] In addition, the Gulshan boys are also involved in graffiti, sometimes displayed on the walls in the more prosperous areas of the city in a bid to 'to give their message, their identity'.[12]

Discussions with the interviewees highlighted that the Gulshan boys are essentially friendship groups, often formed at school, that act as a way for predominantly young men to acquire solidarity and a sense of belonging. For example, the data suggests that most of the activities of these types of gangs involve groups 'meeting at tea stalls in the evening and chatting'.[13] Crime, for the Gulshan boys, is expressive rather than driven by a need to survive (as highlighted in previous discussions about illicit child labourers). For example, as one interviewee explained: 'Their main motivation for crime is interest and excitement'.[14]

Nevertheless, some interviewees believed the Gulshan boys to be involved in more serious offences, such as theft, robbery or drug dealing. In addition, sex outside of marriage—a taboo subject in Bangladesh—was highlighted to be a frequent activity of the groups, as the following explains: 'They have free sex, they say "I catch your girlfriend, you catch my girlfriend". It is a new culture in our society. There is also "lounge culture"; restaurants take money from young people and these restaurants have many private rooms where rich boys have parties. The "Gulshan boys" will go to these parties'.[15]

Drivers for involvement in the Gulshan boys are largely related to frustration, as one participant explained:

> The Gulshan boys have lots of pain from frustration, cultural gaps, some have lots of wealth but don't use it properly. Also, the political situation doesn't align with what they want, jobs are hard and this creates frustration. They want to mix with their girlfriends but can't; they want to be like the west but can't; they want to drive their cars fast but can't. This is linked to frustration in Bangladesh society, we have a lot of frustration: financial crisis, wealth discrimination, 95% of the country is the extreme poor. So when the young boys see their friends driving the big car with beautiful girlfriends they want this. Rich boys go to parties; poor ones go back home. The younger ones, the poorer ones want to go to the parties too. The frustration is there.[16]

Thus the nature of the Gulshan boys demonstrates 'peer group-related' (Hallsworth and Young, 2006, p. 4) behaviour, as well as, in some cases, gangs. Definitions of gang, derived from an Anglo-American context are useful in this instance.

The interviewees were asked whether there was a relationship between the mastaans and the Gulshan boys, and an interviewee said, 'The Gulshan boys are not mastaans and they are not linked to the mastaans. In Gulshan, the area is controlled by mastaans and they protect the shop keepers from other groups. The Gulshan boys don't commit this type of crime, otherwise the people [the maastans] will kill them'.[17] The interviewees were also asked whether the Gulshan boys could also be hired by older gang members or organised crime bosses. There was a general consensus that, as one participant explained, 'they cannot be hired because they are not interested in these jobs; they do not need the money'.[18] This is a sharp reminder of the inequality that exists in Bangladesh, which infiltrates life in the gang and demonstrates that gang membership—as understood from the perspective of the Gulshan boys—is an almost paradoxical privilege when compared to what drives street children's involvement in mastaan groups.

It is important to note that gathering data on these types of gangs was difficult. There is no direct translation of the term 'gang' in Bengali, and when asked, the participants assumed I was asking about the mastaan groups, discussed above. It was clear following the interviews that the notion of 'street gangs', rather than gangs that form the lower echelon of organised crime groups—be that mafias or otherwise—is a relatively new issue in Dhaka. It was also apparent that the presence of street gangs and their effect on overall society is limited and perceived by the participants to be of low concern, particularly when compared to the other types of criminal groups discussed in this chapter.

4. Student Groups

Bangladesh is a relatively new country after only gaining independence from Pakistan in 1971 (Lewis, 2012). The first leader was Sheikh Mujibur Rahman, known as 'the Father of the Nation', who, following his escape from captivity in Pakistan, formed the Awami League administration in 1972. Bangladesh is a democracy; however, the state is weak, and a fair and transparent democratic form of governance has, according to many commentators, eluded Bangladesh for years (Riaz, 2005).

There are two main political parties, the Awami League (AL) and the Bangladesh National Party (BNP) (Jahan, 2001), and Bangladesh has been headed by either Sheikh Hasina of the AL, the daughter of Sheikh Mujibur Rahman, or Khaleda Zia, widow of the BNP leader, Ziaur Rahman (ibid.). Political rhetoric is underpinned by feuds between the two parties and their respective leaders, which in many cases lead to violence that some argue is conducted by the student wings of both the AL and the BNP (Moniruzzaman, 2009).

According to the participants, political parties have student wings with different hierarchies. The AL has the *'Chatra league'* (student league), the *'jubo league'* (youth league) and the *'Chatra sabok league'*. In a similar way, the BNP has the *'chatra dol'* (student league), the *'jubo dohl'* (youth league) and the *chatra sabok dohl*. These groups are involved in recruiting new members for political parties and often become involved in political violence. As one participant explained, 'the student movement has always had an enormous amount of influence in Bangladesh'.[19]

The participants described how student groups are closely linked to the history of Bangladesh, as one journalist explained:

> To understand the student groups, you need to go back to the 1970s, following the 1971 war of independence in Bangladesh, when young people were politically affiliated, they had weapons and wanted to secure turfs for their respective political parties. Most major political movements here have roots in universities; hence students have played an influential role in developing Bangladesh. It was at universities, during the 1970s that ideologies were formed; to form the 'new Bangladesh'.[20]

The data suggested that student groups may also be involved in criminality aside from political violence. One participant explained that student groups were involved in collecting extortion money: 'student leaders are not really involved in lots of crime, just collecting the toll money'.[21] Therefore, the term 'student groups' describes politically affiliated groups of young people that can, in some instances, merge into criminality or work in close alliance with criminal groups, potentially including the mastaans. However, it is necessary to gather more data to explore the nature of these groups in greater depth.

5. Conceptualising Terrorism

This study focused specifically on organised crime, gangs and the involvement of street children in mastaan groups. Thus violent extremism and terrorism did not feature as a main component of the research. Nevertheless, the participants explained that Bangladesh is a unitary state and parliamentary democracy but that it has been exploited by extremist groups for decades. Participants described the following extremist groups in Bangladesh: 'Jamaat Islami which is a far-right Islamist political party who openly attempted to stop the independence of Bangladesh from Pakistan in 1971, believing it would have existed better as a united Islamic state'.[22] A security expert explained that 'Jamaat-ul-Mujahideen (JMB) allegedly aimed to replace the current state of Bangladesh with an Islamic state based on Sharia law. This group opposed the political system of Bangladesh and was officially banned by the government in February 2005. Six months later, it detonated 500 bombs at 300 locations in 63 of the country's 64 districts killing three and injuring over 100'.[23]

In a similar vein the 'Harkat-ul-Jihad-al Islami Bangladesh (HUJI-B) was established in 1992 and aimed to establish Islamic rule in Bangladesh. HUJI-B has reported links to international extremist groups including Al-Qa'ida and the Taliban and was proscribed by the government in 2005'.[24] It is important to note that in recent months and following the completion of this study there has been a spike in violent extremism in Bangladesh with Islamic State of Iraq and Levant (ISIL) and Al Qa'ida in the Indian Subcontinent (AQIS) both claiming attacks within the country, specifically related to the killings of atheist bloggers (*BBC News,* 2 May 2016) and the Holey Bakery attack of 2016 (*BBC News,* 6 May 2016).

The participants also discussed 'ultra-left or communist' groups and used the term 'insurgent groups'. These groups, driven by communist ideology, were argued to operate in the northwest, southwest and northeast of the country, particularly in the Chittagong Hill Tracts. The participants believed these groups to be involved in 'extortion, murder and exploitation of the people'.[25]

The term 'mastaan' has been favoured throughout this chapter to discuss mafia-type groups and as a way to ensure clarity for the reader. However, as a security expert explained, 'There is a big debate over what constitutes terrorism in Bangladesh. Many acts described as terrorism would not fall under international definitions and the term has wider usage; but the people are terrorised so Bangladeshis use the word terrorism'.[26] This was a prevalent theme throughout the research: the interviewees used the term 'terrorist' to describe mastaan groups yet also used the same term to describe violent extremists. This provokes some obvious issues related to understanding of both organised crime groups and terrorism. However, the participants did not appear confused by the dual nature of the term, suggesting that it is a well-integrated term in Bangladeshi society. This may signify something wider and potentially more significant: that perhaps the difference between organised crime and terrorism is not as easy to distinguish as often claimed.

Conclusion

The discussion held in this chapter about the Gulshan boys highlights several important issues for criminological understanding of the gang. Most literature related to gangs still arises from Anglo-American perspectives. This means that the definition of a gang as predominantly street-based groups fits. However, when this definition is applied in Bangladesh, as was done in this study, gaps and problems arise. Firstly, as demonstrated by the Gulshan boys, the Western definition of the gang is useful and in many ways correctly depicts the 'privileged few' in Dhaka; those groups of young men who come together, form friendship groups, take drugs and commit relatively low-level forms of criminality. Yet there are a plethora of other forms of potential 'gangs' in Dhaka that demonstrate different types of characteristics. It is for this reason that I propose a new way to conceptualise children who operate at the lowest echelon of the mastaans, as illicit child labourers. This categorisation moves away from understandings of gangs—and organised crime, which is couched in Western assumptions and into a realm more fitting of the location in which this study occurred: Bangladesh.

Conceptualising children's involvement in crime as illicit labour challenges extant criminological theory that argues that crime is expressive, highlighting the role that children's involvement in gangs and organised crime play in the informal economy. This has ramifications for global discussions of gangs and feeds into discourse related to 'Southern criminology', a new paradigm working to shift the focus of criminological literature from the 'global North' (Western Europe and North America) and into the 'global South' (Latin America, Africa, Asia and Oceania) (Carrington et al. 2016).

The implications of this for criminology and global understandings of crime and violence are as follows: Firstly, more studies into criminal groups, including mafias, organised crime groups and gangs, need to occur in places outside of the 'Western world'; a far better understanding of crime in the 'global South' must occur (ibid.). Secondly, we need new ways to conceptualise criminal groups and young people who operate on the fringes of organised crime groups, including mafias. By developing the conceptualisation of illicit child labourer, I hope to generate debate about ways to better reflect and protect children in Bangladesh and wider afield. Thirdly, to approach a study of crime in Bangladesh from an 'Anglo-American' lens is ethnocentric and likely to produce misleading results. While crime in Bangladesh has many similarities with crime in other places, there are some new things to learn: the complexity of criminal groups and the interlinkages between these groups amid a landscape of poverty, corruption and crime. It is the fluidity of criminal groups in Dhaka which is important; their ability to form and merge as the need takes them and something intrinsically linked to the context in which group-related offending occurs—amid abject poverty and crime driven by the need to survive.

Developing this type of understanding for other countries in Asia and the global South may help to explain the complexity of criminal groups across the region. The argument should thus be more focused on understanding groups in the context in which they occur; applying rigid definitions— which largely derive from Anglo-American origins—to a Bangladeshi context is ethnocentric and misleading. Rather, working from the 'ground up' and couching research methods in ethnography helps to begin discussions of crime and violence in a terrain largely missing from criminological discourse.

Notes

1 'Forced labour' constitutes a form of modern slavery according to the UK Modern Slavery Strategy 2015.
2 Semi-structured interview 4.
3 Semi-structured interview 10.
4 Semi-structured interview 12.
5 The term 'CNG' is widely used in Bangladesh to describe a small three-wheeled vehicle which runs on compressed natural gas and is used as a form of public transport.
6 Semi-structured interview 10.
7 Semi-structured interview 12.
8 Semi-structured interview 26.
9 Semi-structured interview 31.
10 Semi-structured interview 40.
11 Semi-structured interview 40.
12 Semi-structured interview 7.
13 Semi-structured interview 7.
14 Semi-structured interview 28.
15 Semi-structured interview 6.
16 Semi-structured interview 7.
17 Semi-structured interview 8.
18 Semi-structured interview 40.
19 Semi-structured interview 31.

20 Semi-structured interview 31.
21 Semi-structured interview 36.
22 Semi-structured interview 27.
23 Semi-structured interview 27.
24 Semi-structured interview 27.
25 Semi-structured interview 30.
26 Semi-structured interview 15.

References

Atkinson-Sheppard, S. (2016). The gangs of Bangladesh: Exploring organised crime, street gangs and "illicit child labourers" in Dhaka. *Criminology and Criminal Justice. 16*(2) 233–249.

Atkinson-Sheppard, S. (2017a). Mastaans and the market for social protection: Considering mafia groups in Dhaka, Bangladesh. *Asian Journal of Criminology.* Advance online publication. doi: 10.1007/s11417-017-9246-9.

Atkinson-Sheppard, S. (2017b) Street children and "Protective Agency": Exploring young people's involvement in organised crime in Dhaka, Bangladesh. *Childhood.* Advance online publication. doi: 10.1177/0907568217694418.

BBC News. (2016, May 2). Who is behind the Bangladesh killings?. Retrieved from www.bbc.com/news/world-asia-34517434.

BBC News. (2016, May 6). Bangladesh siege. Retrieved from www.bbc.com/news/world-asia-36692613.

Calderoni, F. (2014). Strategic positioning in mafia networks. In C. Morselli (Ed.), *Crime and networks* (pp. 163–181). New York: Routledge.

Carrington, K., Hogg, R., & Sozzo, M. (2016). Southern criminology. *British Journal of Criminology, 56*, 1–20.

CNN Freedom Project (2011, May 4). Child mutilated for refusing to beg. Retrieved from http://the cnnfreedomproject.blogs.cnn.com/2011/05/04/gang-profits-from-maimed-child-beggars/.

The Coalition to Stop the Use of Child Soldiers. (2007). *Child recruitment in South-Asian conflicts: Bangladesh.* London: Coalition to Stop the Use of Child Soldiers. Retrieved from www.eldis.org/document/A31519.

Densley, J.A. (2012). "It's a gang life but not as we know it": The evolution of gang business. *Crime and Delinquency,* 1–30.

Gambetta, D. (1993). *The Sicilian mafia.* London: Harvard University Press.

Hallsworth, S., & Young, T. (2006). *Urban collectives: Gangs and other groups.* A report prepared for the Metropolitan Police Service and Government Office for London. London: Metropolitan Police Service.

Hammadi, S., & Burke, J. (2011, January 9). Bangladesh arrest uncovers evidence of children forced into begging. *The Guardian.* Retrieved from www.guardian.co.uk/world/2011/jan/09/bangladesh-arrest-forced-begging?INTCMP=SRCH.

Hess, H. (1998). *Mafia and mafiosi: The structure of power.* Westmead: Saxon House.

Jahan, R. (2001). *Bangladesh: Promise and performance.* Dhaka: The University Press.

Levitt, S. D., & Venkatesh, S. A. (2000). An economic analysis of a drug selling Gang's finances. *Quarterly Journal of Economics, 115*, 755–789.

Lewis, D. (2012). *Bangladesh: Politics, Economy and Civil Society.* Cambridge: Cambridge University Press.

Moniruzzaman, M. (2009). Party politics and political violence in Bangladesh: Issues, manifestation and consequences. *South Asian Survey, 16*(1), 81–99.

Paoli, L. (2002). The paradoxes of organized crime. *Crime, Law & Social Change, 37*(1), 51–97.

Paoli, L. (2003). *Mafia brotherhoods: Organized crime, Italian style.* New York: Oxford University Press.

Paoli, L. (2004). Italian organised crime: Mafia associations and criminal enterprises. *Global Crime, 6*(1), 19–31.

Riaz, A. (2005). Bangladesh in 2004: The politics of vengeance and the erosion of democracy. *Asian Survey. 45*(1), 112–118.

RISE. (2013). A look into Dhaka, Bangladesh the most densely populated city in the world. Retrieved from http://risebd.com/2013/03/09/a-look-into-dhaka-bangladesh-the-most-densely-populated-city-in-the-world.

Ruwanpura, K. N., & Roncolato, L. (2006). Child rights: An enabling or disabling right? The nexus between child labour and poverty in Bangladesh. *Journal of Developing Societies. 22*, 359–372.

Sergi, A. (2015). Mafia and politics as concurrent governance actors. Revisiting political power and crime in Southern Italy. In P. C. van Duyne, A. Maljević, G. A. Antonopoulos, J. Harvey, & K. von Lampe (Eds.), *The relativity of wrongdoing: Corruption, organised crime, fraud and money laundering in perspective* (pp. 43–72). Oisterwijk: Wolf Legal Publishers.

Sergi, A., & Lavorgna, A. (2016). *Ndrangheta: The glocal dimensions of the most powerful Italian mafia.* Palgrave Pivot Series, London and New York: Palgrave Macmillan.

Shafi, S. A. (2010). *Urban crime and violence in Dhaka*. Dhaka: The University Press.

Thrasher, F.M. (1927). *The gang*. Chicago: University of Chicago Press.

UN-HABITAT. (2002). United Nations Human Settlements Programme (UN-HABITAT) Urban Indicators Database. Retrieved from www.Citypopulation.de/World.html.

Van Gemert, F. (2005). Youth groups and gangs in Amsterdam: A pretest of the Eurogang expert survey. In S. Decker & F. Weerman (Eds.), *European street gangs and troublesome youth groups*. Oxford: AltaMira Press.

Varese, F. (2010). What is organised crime? In F. Varese (Ed.), *Organised crime: Critical concepts in criminology* (pp. 27–55). London: Routledge.

Zafarullah, H., & Rahman, M. H. (2002). Human rights, civil society and non-government organisation: The nexus in Bangladesh. *Human Rights Quarterly, 24*(4), 1011–1034.

18

CRIMES OF WAR IN SRI LANKA[1]

International Crisis Group

Introduction

Both the Sri Lankan Security Forces and the Liberation Tigers of Tamil Eelam (LTTE) in Sri Lanka's civil war violated international humanitarian law throughout the 30-year conflict (*Crisis Group Asia Report*, 2007, 2008, 2009, 2010a, 2010b). However, the violations became particularly frequent and deadly in the months leading to the Sri Lankan government's declaration of victory over the LTTE in May 2009. There is an increasing body of evidence that the government security forces repeatedly violated the law by attacking civilians, hospitals and humanitarian operations and that the LTTE violated the law by killing, wounding or otherwise endangering civilians, including by shooting them and preventing them from leaving the conflict zone even when injured and dying.

Much of the international community turned a blind eye to the violations when they were happening. Some issued statements calling for restraint but took no action as the government continually denied any wrongdoing. Many countries had declared the LTTE as terrorists and welcomed their defeat. They encouraged the government's tough response while failing to press for political reforms to address Tamil grievances or for any improvement in human rights. The eventual destruction of the LTTE militarily came at the cost of immense civilian suffering and an acute challenge to the laws of war. It also undermined the credibility of the United Nations and further entrenched bitterness among Tamils in Sri Lanka and elsewhere, which may make a durable peace elusive. Now a number of other countries are considering "the Sri Lankan option"—unrestrained military action, refusal to negotiate, disregard for humanitarian issues—as a way to deal with insurgencies and other violent groups.

The International Crisis Group (2010c) report believes that tens of thousands of non-combatant Tamil men, women, children and the elderly were killed in the final five months of the war. In August 2009, Crisis Group began gathering evidence relating to the conduct of hostilities in the final months of the war. It includes eyewitness statements taken and deemed credible by Crisis Group as well as hundreds of photographs, video, satellite imagery, electronic communications and documents from a wide range of sources. The material is far from exhaustive; indeed, it covers only a small number of the violations that are likely to have taken place and touches on the alleged roles of only a handful of individuals. Though the report of the Crisis Group (2010c) is exhaustive, in this chapter, only a summary of the war crimes in Sri Lanka will be provided.

I. The War and Its Aftermath

1. The Defeat of the Tamil Tigers

By January 2009, the Sri Lankan government had effectively defeated the LTTE. The Tamil fighters were cornered in a small portion of the Northern Province known as the Vanni[2] and were surrounded by more numerous and better-armed Sri Lankan government forces[3](Shashikumar, 2009). Also in the area were over 300,000 civilians, most of whom had been repeatedly displaced from previously LTTE-held areas. The LTTE by this stage were running short of arms and supplies. Many of their cadres believed the situation was hopeless, and the Tamil civilian population was increasingly resentful of such policies as forced recruitment and the near-complete ban on leaving the Vanni (Human Rights Watch, 2008).

The LTTE's dire situation was a result of a series of critical errors made by their leader Vellupillai Prabhakaran. Their violations, including its August 2005 murder of the Sri Lankan foreign minister, Lakshman Kadirgamar, angered governments that supported and funded the 2002–2006 peace process. This lost them much of any remaining international legitimacy, and they were banned as a terrorist organisation by the European Union in May 2006. Prabhakaran had used the cease-fire in 2002 to purge the Tamil community of anyone seen as a threat. Hundreds of Tamil dissidents across the island were murdered. This left little space for Prabhakaran's ambitious and restless eastern deputy, Colonel Karuna, who split from the LTTE in 2004 along with 6,000 fighters and soon began cooperating with the government. With Karuna's support, Colombo was able to regain control over the Eastern Province by the middle of 2007.

In 2005, the LTTE leader ordered Tamils to boycott the presidential election, resulting in the victory for Mahinda Rajapaksa, a politician with a keen ability to tap in to growing Sinhala nationalism and resentment. The new administration stepped up arms purchases and began planning for a resumption of war with a commitment to destroy the Tigers. The cease-fire—which was always marred by violations, mostly by the LTTE—started breaking down in 2006 and was formally ended on 16 January 2008 by declaration of the government. This led to the departure of the Nordic observers with the Sri Lanka Monitoring Mission (SLMM).

By then the Sri Lankan security forces had begun pressing north in to the remaining LTTE-controlled areas. Prabhakaran had previously always out-manoeuvred government forces, but his desire for the LTTE to maintain the trappings of a state—with a population and standing army holding territory—limited his military options. The LTTE's widely expected return to guerrilla warfare never came. In addition to having many more personnel, the security forces were also better trained and armed than in earlier stages of the war. They had acquired an array of new weapons, from better artillery to more unmanned aerial vehicles (UAVs) that could monitor the conflict zone and act as forward observers to call in shelling (*The Island*, 4 January 2010). China and Pakistan stepped in to fulfil much of the weapons demand (*The Times of India*, 4 March 2009), and the Pakistani Air Force "extended technical assistance and training" (*Sri Lanka Air Force news*, 12 November 2009). The security forces had complete air superiority and adopted more aggressive tactics, sending commando units behind LTTE lines and pounding defensive positions with multi-barrel rocket launchers (MBRLs) and aerial attacks. The navy, with intelligence assistance from India and other countries, tracked and destroyed a series of LTTE arms shipments, successfully shutting down the LTTE's ability to re-arm.

Tougher military tactics were backed by a more aggressive political line, including censoring of military and civilian casualties and attacks on critics of the war. The government pressed for the LTTE to be banned internationally, adopted the rhetoric of the "war on terror" and stepped up security. Efforts at political reform were sidelined, with proposals to alleviate Tamil concerns endlessly delayed. There was a darker side to this: the number of disappearances soared, journalists were killed, beaten or silenced, politicians were threatened, non-governmental organisations (NGOs) attacked and international organisations such as the United Nations intimidated (*Crisis Group Asia Report*, 2007, 2008, 2009). A government inquiry into alleged abuses by the security forces and the LTTE collapsed and was denounced by a group of prominent international observers, who terminated their role in March 2008, finding "a lack of political will to support a search for the truth" (*Crisis Group Asia Report*, 2007, 2008, 2009). Any criticism of the government led to an accusation of being pro-LTTE from the country's firebrand, partisan media and outspoken officials. Even a meek comment from the UN's humanitarian coordinator prompted a Sri Lanka minister to describe him as "a terrorist" (*The Nation*, 19 August 2007). Rajapaksa cloaked himself in a mantle of Sinhala nationalism while his top general during the war, Army Commander Sarath Fonseka, warned minorities of their place in Sri Lankan society (Bell, 2008).

With the media effectively censored, critics of the war silenced, the international community both cowed and caught up in the "war on terror", and the Sinhalese population eager for victory, the government pressed ahead without restraint. The strategy from mid-2008 was to corral the LTTE and the Tamil population of the north in to an ever-smaller area from which independent observers, aid organisations and journalists would be excluded (Reporters Without Borders, 10 April 2009).

After the capture of LTTE headquarters in Kilinochchi in early January 2009, the security forces closed in on the LTTE, eventually trapping them and the civilian population in a few square kilometres of a narrow spit of land on the north-eastern shore. From January the character of the conflict changed distinctly. As the security forces dramatically reduced the size of the conflict zone, the government unilaterally declared a series of ever smaller so-called No Fire Zones (NFZs) and concentrated the civilian population in them (Mullaittivu, 22 and 31 January 2009). The government also claimed the civilian population was less than one-third its actual size and refused to allow in adequate food and medical supplies. At the same time, the LTTE continued to prevent civilians from leaving, including by shooting dead some of those who tried. While the government publicly condemned the LTTE's actions as "human shielding" and "hostage taking" and claimed the security forces were taking "maximum precautions to avoid civilian casualties" (MOD news, 17 February 2009), they in fact continued to advance without restraint. They forced the LTTE's front lines back into each successive NFZ, until the government announced Prabhakaran's death and declared the war over on 18 May.

Evidence gathered by the Crisis Group provides reasonable grounds to believe that during these months the security forces intentionally and repeatedly shelled civilians, hospitals and humanitarian operations. It also provides reason to believe that senior government and military officials were aware of the massive civilian casualties due to the security forces' attacks but failed to protect the civilian population as they were obliged to under the laws of war.

UN agencies, working closely with officials and aid workers located in the conflict zone, documented nearly 7,000 civilians killed from January to April 2009. Those who compiled these internal numbers deemed them reliable to the extent they reflected actual conflict deaths but maintain it was a work in progress and incomplete. The final three weeks of fighting alone likely saw thousands of non-combatants killed (UTHR, 10 June 2009). UN officials in New York have consistently distanced themselves from the internal figures, even though senior officials and diplomats in Colombo accepted them as credible (*CNN*, 29 May 2009; *SBS Dateline*, 28 February 2010; Sunday Observer, 14 February 2010; *Daily Mirror*, 13 February 2010). Crisis Group's evidence shows that many bodies were never taken to hospitals but instead were buried in shallow graves or collapsed bunkers. Based on the evidence collected, the Crisis Group believes the total number of civilian deaths in the final five months to be in the tens of thousands.

2. *The Aftermath*

Over 280,000 Tamil civilians crossed over to government-held areas in the last months of fighting and were unlawfully interned in emergency camps run by the security forces. The camps, located primarily in Vavuniya, were overcrowded and suffered from severe deficiencies of sanitation, medical care and food. Government intelligence agencies and Tamil paramilitaries repeatedly screened the internees for involvement with the LTTE, leading to reports of abuse. Embassies were for several months denied consular access to foreign citizens held in the camps, and the media were allowed in only for guided tours. The government restricted and tightly monitored access for the UN and humanitarian agencies and from July 2009 barred the International Committee of the Red Cross (ICRC) from the camps in Vavuniya. Restrictions on the ICRC remain in place as of May 2010. Although considerable international pressure led to the release of most of the internally displaced persons (IDPs) by the end of 2009, 80,000 civilians were there in camps. The government also has detained more than 10,000 individuals allegedly involved with the LTTE in separate camps with no outside access. These detentions are unlawful and pose particularly grave risks given the government's history of alleged enforced disappearances and torture.

Many Sri Lankans were ecstatic about the defeat of the Tigers. Most Tamils in the country and abroad were shocked and dismayed by the treatment of their compatriots in the North. While professing concern about the situation, key members of the international community did little. The Security Council refused to take up the war or the internments, with China, Russia and others saying it was a domestic matter. At the end of May 2009, the UN Human Rights Council (HRC) voted down a proposal for an investigation into alleged war crimes.[4]

International calls for post-war accountability returned after the August 2009 broadcast on British television of video showing what was said to be the execution of eight bound and blindfolded Tamil men by Sri Lankan soldiers in January 2009 (Miller, 25 August 2009). The Sri Lankan government immediately denied the charge, denounced the video as a fabrication by pro-LTTE propagandists and attacked Britain's Channel Four for broadcasting unfounded allegations (Channel 4, 26 August 2009, and 11 September 2009). Technical reports produced by government-hired experts claim to show a series of irregularities with the tape (*Defence News*, 3 September 2009). On 7 January 2010, the UN special rapporteur on extrajudicial executions, Philip Alston, announced that expert analyses commissioned by the UN had found the video to be authentic and called on the Sri Lankan government to allow "an independent" and "impartial investigation into war crimes and other grave violations of international humanitarian and human rights law allegedly committed in Sri Lanka" (UN, 7 January 2010; Blakely, 15, December, 2009).

Allegations that the LTTE leaders and the others were shot while surrendering with a white flag resurfaced in December 2009 when retired Army Commander and then presidential candidate Sarath Fonseka charged that the defence secretary and brother of the president, Gotabaya Rajapaksa, ordered their execution despite earlier promises of protection (The Sunday Leader, 13 December 2009). Gotabaya and other government officials have rejected the allegations (Asiantribune.com, 25 February 2010). President Rajapaksa went on to win another six-year term in January 2010, soon after which Fonseka was arrested to face courts martial for conducting political work while in uniform and for fraudulent arms dealing (*BBC News*, 8 February 2010).

An October 2009 report from the U.S. State Department offers a catalogue of reported violations of international humanitarian law (IHL), including government shelling of hospitals and areas with heavy concentrations of civilians and LTTE killing of civilians who attempted to flee areas under their control (U.S. Department of State, October 2009). The alleged incidents are consistent with thousands of civilian deaths. The U.S. report is careful to note that it does not "reach conclusions as to whether the alleged incidents . . . actually occurred" or constituted violations of international law (U.S. Department of State, October 2009). Unfortunately, few resources were devoted to the congressionally mandated report, and no reference was made to satellite imagery or human intelligence in the possession of different branches of the U.S. government. Even so, the report lists scores of "incidents and conduct which may constitute violations of IHL and/or crimes against humanity" based on eyewitness testimony and reports from credible organizations (U.S. Department of State, October 2009). The report presents a damning indictment of both sides and makes the case for a serious, well-financed and independent investigation all the more compelling (U.S. Department of State, October 2009).

II. Actions of the Sri Lankan Government

Crisis Group has eyewitness testimony or other evidence to support the allegations in this section. Times, locations and other circumstances are provided with as much specificity as possible but may be clarified as further evidence is discovered. The Sri Lankan government has denied any unlawful conduct in the last months of the war and rejected many of the allegations (*Defence News*, 18 May 2009). Yet the evidence Crisis Group has collected shows there are reasonable grounds to believe that the Sri Lankan security forces committed war crimes and that certain individuals should be investigated, including top government and military leaders.

1. Attacks on Humanitarian Operations

The main elements of this crime and a summary of relevant evidence are as follows:

* *The perpetrator directed an attack.* Witness statements show that the security forces repeatedly launched weapons at the food distribution centre and the UN site therein. The pause in fire after the intense shelling early in the morning of 24 January and multiple calls to the government and security forces to ask them to stop the fire demonstrates that they had control over the frequency and direction of their attacks. The LTTE positions within the NFZ were too close to the centre to fire, arcing artillery shells into it, and LTTE in general had little reason to fire on their own fighters or cause the UN and especially internationals to leave.
* *The object of the attack was personnel, installations, material, units or vehicles involved in a humanitarian assistance mission.* The humanitarian nature of the UN operation and food distribution centre was well established. The UN personnel and supplies carried into the area had been approved by the defence ministry and SFHQ-Vanni and inspected by the security forces. The food distribution was being coordinated by the government's representative. Shells struck within metres of UN personnel sheltering in bunkers, injuring at least two people associated with the UN and damaging at least one UN vehicle. Many civilians seeking food, shelter or assistance in the centre were killed, and materials were destroyed.
* *The perpetrator intended such personnel, installations, material, units or vehicles to be the object of the attack.* A number of government and military officials had detailed knowledge of the location of the food distribution centre and the UN personnel, vehicles and materials. The UN provided GPS data on their precise location, and witnesses saw UAVs flying over the food distribution centre. There was no warning to the UN, civilians or government representatives who had followed the security forces' instructions to go to the NFZ that the area would be shelled. After the shelling began, the government and security forces received further confirmation of the location of the centre and UN site and the fact that it was being shelled. As the shelling continued, the government was again advised of the location. Outgoing LTTE fire was sporadic and did not come from within the centre. The LTTE frontlines and vast majority of cadres were outside of the NFZ.

- *Such personnel, installations, material, units or vehicles were entitled to that protection given to civilians under the international law of armed conflict.* The UN personnel and material in the food distribution centre were involved in only humanitarian activities, as were the government representatives. At no time did they provide assistance to LTTE cadres or engage in any acts that may have been harmful to the security forces. UN personnel, vehicles and material had been searched and approved by the security forces before going into the Vanni. The government had declared the NFZ with the stated intention of protecting civilians and then directed the UN to relocate its personnel, vehicles and material there. The civilians in the area around the distribution centre were not taking part in the hostilities.
- *The perpetrator was aware of the factual circumstances that established that protection. The security forces and government approved the UN's location.* There were multiple communications confirming that the personnel and materials in the centre were not involved in the conduct of the hostilities.

2. Attacks on Hospitals

Dozens of attacks on hospitals and makeshift medical centres were reported in the final five months of the war. The government either denied these incidents entirely or claimed the facilities were being used by the LTTE for military purposes and therefore were legitimate targets. It also rejected reports of mounting civilian casualties and suffering, many of which were coming from medical personnel or witnesses who had been in hospitals. Four government doctors who managed the last medical centres until the end of the fighting were arrested upon leaving the war zone because of the information they had released. Hospitals remain protected under international humanitarian law, unless the facilities are "used to commit hostile acts, outside their humanitarian function". The mere presence of wounded combatants or LTTE doctors would have no effect on a hospital's protected status.

The main elements of the crime of intentional attacks on hospitals and a summary of relevant evidence are as follows:

- *The perpetrator directed an attack.* Witnesses observed fire from the Sri Lankan security forces that repeatedly struck these hospitals. The Sri Lankan Air Force admitted bombing the building that witnesses have identified as the Princess Margaret Hospital (PMH) annex, and they saw similar damage at the main PMH hospital building. The aerial video footage the security forces released with respect to the Puthukkudiyiruppu (PTK) hospital and PMH demonstrates their unobstructed access to detailed information about targets and their ability to strike with precision.
- *The object of the attack was one or more hospitals or places where the sick and wounded are collected, which were not military objectives.* ICRC statements and witness accounts confirm that the facilities were being used for medical purposes with hundreds of patients who were not taking any part in the hostilities. Witnesses did not observe any LTTE fire of any kind from within the facilities, nor did they see any heavy weapons fire in the hospitals' vicinity. Wounded cadres are not legitimate targets.
- *The perpetrator intended such hospitals or places where the sick and wounded are collected, which were not military objectives, to be the object of the attack.* Government and military officials had information—including aerial images, direct lines of sight and GPS coordinates and other information from the UN and others—confirming that these facilities were being used for medical purposes. Despite having that information, the Sri Lankan security forces attacked them repeatedly. Government officials stated publicly that the security forces would not accept responsibility for the safety of any civilians outside the NFZs—which would include at least PTK and PMH hospitals and for a time Putumattalan hospital.

3. *Attacks on Civilians*

The primary victims of these alleged attacks on humanitarian missions and hospitals were the Tamil civilians who went to these locations seeking food, shelter and medical care. But these were not isolated incidents. Crisis Group has collected evidence that provides reasonable grounds to believe the repeated shelling of civilians in the three NFZs, combined with the obstruction and undersupplying of food and medical care for civilians, was part of the government's overall military strategy in the Vanni. Much of the evidence discussed in the preceding subsections is relevant to the main elements of this crime. In summary:

- *The perpetrator directed an attack.* Witnesses have described dozens of occasions over five months in which the security forces fired heavy weapons that struck civilians or civilian objects in the NFZs. In many of these instances, it was physically impossible for the LTTE to direct heavy weapons fire at these targets given their proximity. The LTTE also had strong motivations not to target their own families and supporters and give them more reason to want to leave the NFZs.
- *The object of the attack was a civilian population as such or individual civilians not taking direct part in hostilities.* Witnesses have provided evidence that the people killed or wounded in these attacks had not taken up arms and were not engaged in acts that adversely affected the military operations of the security forces. Many of them were children, women, the wounded and the elderly who were undernourished, without proper shelter and had been on the run for months.
- *The perpetrator intended the civilian population as such or individual civilians not taking direct part in hostilities to be the object of the attack.* The government and military had directed the civilian population to go to the NFZs. They had knowledge from multiple sources about the civilian nature of the targets of their attacks, including aerial images, direct lines of sight and many communications from the UN, ICRC and others. These were not one-off shelling incidents. It was a pattern of behaviour over months in which the government and security forces were told repeatedly that they were shelling civilians and they chose to continue doing so and simply say they were not.

III. Actions of the LTTE

The evidence Crisis Group has collected also provides a strong basis for allegations of war crimes by the LTTE and its leadership. These alleged crimes are largely an extension of the rebels' long history of imposing controls on the Tamil civilian population in the areas they held, forcibly recruiting adults and children and brutally repressing dissent. As the security forces continued to advance into the Vanni and demand that the LTTE allow civilians to cross into government-controlled areas, the Tigers tightened their hold on the population. Even when their military defeat was clear at the beginning of 2009, they failed to take actions that could have protected civilians, such as agreeing to open a humanitarian corridor or attempting to negotiate surrender.

The security forces' continual shelling of and advance into the NFZs, along with growing frustration and disillusionment with the LTTE, convinced many civilians that the risks of being forced back into increasingly unsafe areas were greater than those of crossing the frontlines and submitting to a government with a history of violence against Tamils. In response, the LTTE gave orders to its cadres to turn civilians back from crossing and, if they refused, to fire upon them. They also prevented the departure of some who were severely wounded and seeking medical care and continued to forcibly recruit civilians to serve as fighters or labourers on the frontlines. Many of these individuals were killed in the fighting.

Eyewitness statements describe these events in detail, providing reasonable grounds to believe that LTTE cadres committed war crimes at the direction of their superiors. That evidence is summarised below, again using definitions in the Rome Statute of the ICC for illustration. The main elements of these crimes and a summary of relevant evidence are as follows:

- *The perpetrator killed one or more persons.* Eyewitness testimony establishes that LTTE cadres shot and killed numerous civilians who were attempting to flee the conflict zone. It also shows that LTTE commanders gave orders for cadres to do so.
- *The perpetrator inflicted severe physical or mental pain or suffering upon one or more persons.* There are many accounts showing that the LTTE shot and wounded civilians attempting to escape to government-held areas, forcibly recruited members of families into fighting, often leading to their deaths, and generally endangered the civilian population by not allowing anyone to leave an area that the LTTE knew was going to see significant civilian casualties. All of these actions were taken with the knowledge that they would inflict severe physical or mental pain or suffering on civilians.
- *Such person or persons were either* hors decombat *or were civilians, medical personnel, or religious personnel taking no active part in the hostilities.* The people fired on by the LTTE as they were attempting to escape, the family members of those forcibly recruited, and the population in the conflict zone in general were civilians. Indeed, the LTTE often retaliated against civilians precisely because they refused to fight for them or were otherwise acting against their interests.
- *The perpetrator was aware of the factual circumstances that established this status.* The LTTE had effective control over the population and knew that those killed or wounded in attempting to flee, and the vast majority of those put in danger by the LTTE's policies, were civilians.

Conclusion

The Sri Lankan security forces and the Liberation Tigers of Tamil Eelam (LTTE) repeatedly violated international humanitarian law during the last five months of their 30-year civil war. Although both sides committed atrocities throughout the many years of conflict, the scale and nature of violations particularly worsened from January 2009 to the government's declaration of victory in May 2009. Evidence gathered by the International Crisis Group suggests that these months saw tens of thousands of Tamil civilian men, women, children and the elderly killed, countless more wounded and hundreds of thousands deprived of adequate food and medical care, resulting in more deaths. There is evidence of war crimes committed by the LTTE and its leaders as well, but most of them were killed and will never face justice.

Evidence secured so far touches on just a handful of potential crimes. Many others were likely to have been committed during the period from January to May 2009. A long history of other atrocities by both sides has never been investigated, and the victims of Sri Lanka's conflict have been denied justice. This has eroded faith in the judicial system, the government and the security forces and has damaged Sri Lanka's democracy. All Sri Lankans, not just Tamils, have a right and responsibility to demand that justice be done.

The international community has a responsibility to uphold the rule of law, the reputation of international agencies and respect for international humanitarian law, most importantly the protection of civilians lives. Many countries facilitated or permitted the conditions under which these alleged crimes were committed. They did little to speak out against them and even less to prevent them. Even at this late stage, they have a responsibility to press for investigations and prosecutions as an integral part of their efforts to support the people of Sri Lanka in rebuilding their country.

To recover from this damage, there must be a concerted effort to investigate alleged war crimes by both sides and prosecute those responsible. Sri Lanka is not a member state of the International Criminal Court (ICC), and the UN Security Council is not likely to refer these crimes to the ICC in the short term. While some of the LTTE may go on trial in Sri Lanka, it is virtually impossible that any domestic investigation into the government or security forces would be impartial given the entrenched culture of impunity. A UN-mandated international inquiry should be the priority, and those countries that have jurisdiction over alleged crimes—including countries such as the US where dual nationals or residents may be suspected—should vigorously pursue investigations.

Notes

1 Revised version of selected parts of the Report of the International Crisis Group (2010). War crimes in Sri Lanka. *Crisis Group Asia Report No. 191*, May 17, 2010. Published with permission from the publisher.
2 The Vanni consists of all or part of five administrative districts designated by the government—Kilinochchi and Mullaitivu Districts in whole and Vavuniya, Mannar and Jaffna Districts in part.
3 It is difficult to know the true number of LTTE cadres and Sri Lankan soldiers who fought in the final months of the war. One knowledgeable witness estimated that there were ap-proximately 8,000 to 10,000 cadres in the LTTE's military wing in September 2008, including Land and Sea Tigers but not the secretive and relatively small Air Tigers and Black Tigers. In an interview published in April 2010, Defence Secretary Gotabaya Rajapaksa said that the combined strength of the army, navy and air force grew from 125,000 in 2005 to 450,000 in 2009, with the army at a strength of 300,000.
4 On 27 May 2009 the Human Rights Council (HRC) passed a resolution tabled by Sri Lanka with 29 in favour, 12 against and 6 abstentions. Those voting in favour were Angola, Azerbaijan, Bahrain, Bangladesh, Bolivia, Brazil, Burkina Faso, Cameroon, China, Cuba, Djibouti, Egypt, Ghana, India, Indonesia, Jordan, Madagascar, Malaysia, Nicaragua, Nigeria, Pakistan, Philippines, Qatar, Russian Federation, Saudi Arabia, Senegal, South Africa, Uruguay and Zambia. Those voting against: Bosnia and Herzegovina, Canada, Chile, France, Germany, Italy, Mexico, Netherlands, Slovakia, Slovenia, Switzerland and United Kingdom of Great Britain and Northern Ireland. Those abstaining were Argentina, Gabon, Japan, Mauritius, Republic of Korea and Ukraine. The resolution praised Sri Lanka and failed to call for any inquiry. The HRC rejected a tougher text proposed by European countries condemning the actions of both sides and calling for unrestricted access to detained civilians and a domestic inquiry into alleged war crimes.

References

Asiantribune.com. (2010, February 25). Some Western powers wanted a regime change in Sri Lanka. Asiantribune.com.

BBC News. (2010, February 8). Sri Lanka election loser Sarath Fonseka arrested. *BBC News*.

Bell, S. (2008, September 23). Inside Sri Lanka: A life given over to war. *National Post*.

Blakely, R. (2009, December, 15). Sri Lankan war crimes video is authentic: Times investigation finds. *The Times*. Retrieved from www.timesonline.co.uk/tol/news/world/asia/article6956569.ece#cid=OTC-RSS&attr=797093.

Channel4. (2009, August 26). Sri Lanka calls "war crimes" video a fake. Retrieved from www.channel4.com.

Channel4. (2009, September 11) Sri Lanka steps up death video rebuttal. Retrieved from www.channel4.com.

CNN. (2009, May 29). Paper: 20,000 killed in Sri Lanka conflict. *CNN*. Retrieved from www.cnn.com/2009/WORLD/asiapcf/05/29/srilanka.death.toll/index.html.

Crisis Group Asia Report. (2007, June 14). N°135, Sri Lanka's human rights crisis.

Crisis Group Asia Report. (2008, February 20). N°146, Sri Lanka's return to war: Limiting the damage.

Crisis Group Asia Report. (2009, June 30). N°172, Sri Lanka: Politicised courts, compromised rights.

Crisis Group Asia Report. (2010a, February 23). N°186, The Sri Lankan Tamil diaspora after the LTTE.

Crisis Group Asia Report. (2010b). Asia briefing no. 99, Sri Lanka: A bitter.

Daily Mirror. (2010, February 13). Govt. says Ex-UN spokesman Weiss spreading lies.

Defence News. (2009, May 18). All Tamil civilians have been rescued without shedding a drop of blood. Ministry of Defence News. Retrieved from www.defence.lk/new.asp?fname=20090518_02.

Defence News. (2009, September 3). Technical analyst exposes "C-4" gutter journalism. Retrieved from www.defence.lk/new.asp?fname=20090903_05.

Human Rights Watch. (2008, December 15). Trapped and mistreated: LTTE abuses against civilians in the Vanni. Human Rights Watch.

International Crisis Group. (2010c, May 17). War crimes in Sri Lanka. *Crisis Group Asia Report no. 191*.

The Island. (2010, January 4). Opposition's claim Mahinda bought only Ammo countered. *The Island*. Retrieved from www.army.lk/detailed.php?NewsId=1723.

Miller, J. (2009, August 25). Execution video: Is this evidence of "war crimes" in Sri Lanka? Retrieved from www.channel4.com.

MOD News.(2009, February 17). Civilian safety is the top priority—Defence secretary. *MOD News.*

The Nation. (2007, August, 19). Jeyaraj slams Ban Ki-moon. *The Nation on Sunday.* Retrieved from www.nation.lk/2007/08/19/news6.htm.

Reporters Without Borders. (2009, April 10). Call for journalists to be let into area where "a major humanitarian crisis" is unfolding with no media presence. Press Release, Reporters Without Borders.

SBS Dateline. (2010, February 28). War stories. *SBS Dateline.* Retrieved from www.sbs.com.au/dateline/story/transcript/id/600331/n/War-Stories.

Shashikumar, V. K. (2009, July–September). Lessons from the war in Sri Lanka. *Indian Defence Review, 24*(3).

Sri Lanka Air Force News. (2009, November 12). Pakistan Air Force chief arrives in Sri Lanka. Retrieved from www.airforce.lk/news.php?news=135#.

The Sunday Leader. (2009, December 13). Gota ordered them to be shot'—General Sarath Fonseka. *The Sunday Leader.*

Sunday Observer. (2010, February 14). Civilian deaths: Gordon Weiss' comment a false utterance—Mahinda Samarasinghe. *Sunday Observer.*

The Times of India. (2009, March 4). Sri Lanka still sourcing arms from Pak, China. Retrieved from http://timesofindia.indiatimes.com/India/Sri-Lanka-still-sourcing-arms-from-Pak-China/articleshow/4220337.cms.

U.S. Department of State. (2009, October). *Report to congress on incidents during the recent conflict in Sri Lanka.* Washington, DC: U.S. Department of State.

United Nations. (2010, January 7). Deeming Sri Lanka execution video authentic. UN expert calls for war crimes probe. Retrieved from www.un.org/apps/news/story.asp?NewsID=33423.

UTHR. (2009, June 10). A marred victory and a defeat pregnant with foreboding. *UTHR, special report no. 32.* Retrieved from www.uthr.org.

19

MADARIS AND SUICIDE TERRORISM IN PAKISTAN

Is There an Association?[1]

Fashiuddin and Imran Ahmad Sajid

Introduction

Soldiers fight to protect a cause and sometimes also get killed in the process. However, the suicide terrorists fight by killing themselves to kill others in order to protect the cause. It is a tactic of warfare with such rigour that the world never experienced before. While a suicide attack is not a phenomenon unknown to history, nonetheless, since 9/11 there was a significant shift and new dimensions to the phenomenon. The trend in suicide attacks in Pakistan is alleged with the Madaris (plural of Madrassah, meaning Muslim education institutions, Islamic seminaries). The Madaris are constantly labeled as factories of terrorists and suicide bombers (Stern, 2000). The February 15, 2010, story of one of the leading newspapers of Pakistan—*The News*—while quoting Dr. Fauzia Saeed, a social scientist from Pakistan with a PhD from the University of Minnesota, reported that "Every suicide bomber is coming from Madrassah" (Khalid, 2010). Reporting the same seminar, *The News* severely criticized the role of Madaris in Islamabad. This is not limited only to Pakistan's self-defining "progressive" circles but has become a common norm for the leftists around the world to accuse the Madaris of promoting terrorism and producing suicide bombers, though little evidence supports their claims (Stern, 2000, 2001).

In Pakistan, the Madrassah structure was used against the Russian invasion of Afghanistan in the last quarter of the previous century. However, during the Afghan Jihad, no suicide tactic was used against the Russians. Nonetheless, the suicide attacks are used against the US and allied forces in Afghanistan as well as in Pakistan—against the security forces and also against the civilians. Now that the Madaris were used against Russia and the students of the Madaris were made into holy warriors, it is quite logical to assume that the same *Mujahideens* (holy warriors) who battled against Russia are also fighting against the US. In this process, they are using every means to compel US to withdraw its forces from a land they consider their own. Suicide attack is one of these means utilized by the supposed *Mujahideens* who were produced by the Madaris (See Box 1 for the logical relationship).

Box 19.1 Madaris–Suicide Logical Relationships

Madaris	→	produced	→	Mujahideen
Mujahideen	→	fought	→	Russia

1. Madaris fought Russia

Mujahideen (Madaris)	→	fought	→	Russia
Russia	→	replaced by	→	US

2. Mujahideen (Madaris) fight US

Mujahideen (Madaris)	→	Fight	→	US
Suicide terrorist	→	Target	→	US

3. Madaris produce suicide terrorists

At first glance, the conclusion seems valid. However, a little more depth of analysis and reasoning raises numerous questions regarding the claim. Why were Madaris not opting for suicide attacks against Russia but are using them against US and NATO forces? Besides this, a more fundamental question one would ask is whether the Madaris are really involved in producing suicide bombers. Is there any actual link between suicide terrorists and Madaris? Does the research support the common perception? These are a few questions which this chapter will discuss.

I. History of Madaris

Acquiring knowledge has got a significant position in Islam. The Muslims are encouraged to acquire knowledge, and for this purpose there are no geographical boundaries. One of the *Hadith* (sayings of the Holy Prophet Muhammad (SAW)) states that "seeking of knowledge is the duty of every Muslim (man and woman)." In the initial years of Islam, the teachings of the Koran and *Hadith* were being imparted through the mosques. However, as Islam started to expand gradually throughout the East and the West of Arabia, it became necessary to cater for the needs of the non-Arab Muslims for religious knowledge and understanding. Thus, a cadre of Muslim experts was created who would develop sophisticated writings and textbooks on *Fiqa* (Islamic jurisprudence), *Sunna* (Prophet's traditions), *Hadith* (Prophet's sayings), and *Tafseer* (the interpretation of the Koran). It began the tradition of Madrassah, the center for higher learning, the initial purpose of which was to preserve religious conformity through uniform teachings of Islam for all (Anzar, 2003).

The first proper Madrassah was established by the Saljuk minister Nizam-ul-Mulk Tusi in Baghdad in the year 1067 (Anzar, 2003). Tusi introduced two types of education in this Madrassah: scholastic theology to produce spiritual leaders and earthly knowledge to produce government servants. Similar kinds of Madaris were later established by Tusi all over the empire, which, in addition to imparting Islamic knowledge, also imparted education in varying fields such as science, philosophy and public administration and governance. Haqqani credits Nizam-ul-Mulk as being the father of the Islamic public education system (Haqqani, 2002). Further, Tusi himself is the author of a renowned book (among early Muslims) on public administration called *Siyasat Nama* (the way to govern).

For much of the later centuries, the Madrassah system remained unchanged. It produced numerous renowned scholars in both religious and secular fields, e.g., Ibn Rushd, the mathematicians al-Zarqali and al- Bitruji and the physicians Ibn Zuhr, Al-Ghazali, Ibn Sina and Ibn Khaldun, to name a few. However, with the gradual decline of the Muslim world at the hands of the Crusaders, Mongols and later by European colonization, Muslim scholarship also went into decay, resulting in closing of the door to *Ijtihad* (independent reasoning) (Anzar, 2003). However, the Indian sub-continent was one of the many regions where the Muslim Madaris went through a radical shift.

1. Indian Sub-Continent and Madaris

One editorial paper by Jamiatul Uloom-ul-Islamia, Banuri Town, Karachi, finds that before the arrival of the East India Company on the Indian Sub-continent, Madrassah education was the only formal means of educating the Muslim masses. Delhi, Agrah, Lahore, Multan, Jonpure, Lakhnaw, Kherabad, Patna, Ajmer, Deccan, Madras, Bengal and Gujarat were the famous cities for their institutions of advanced education. The paper also finds that "before the arrival of the British to Bengal, there were about eighty thousand (80,000) Madaris in Bengal, which averages at 400 population per Madrassah" (Bainat, 2010). Similarly, in the times of Muhammad Shah Tughlaq, there were 1,000 Madaris in the city of Delhi (Nadvi, 1989). The source of income for these Madaris was the properties allotted to them by the Nawabs (local rich and royal chief). However, with the arrival of the British and their commitment to introduce an alternative system of education in India, the old system of Madaris gradually started disintegrating. Particularly, the 1857 war of independence brought a very hard time on Madaris in the Indian sub-continent, as Madaris were alleged for producing *Mujahideens* (holy fighters) for this war (Nadvi, 1989).

The education system that is prevalent in Indian and Pakistani Madaris today was devised by Mullah Nizam-ud-Din Sihalvi (d. 1747), Lakhnaw, India. The curriculum he devised included 21 different subjects. Medicine, physics, history, geology and mathematics were compulsory subjects. However, these very important subjects are taught nowhere in Madaris in India or Pakistan today. Further, the curriculum consisted of 72 renowned and authentic books on these subjects (Usmani, 1989, 2005).

After the war of independence in 1857, Maulana Qasim Nanotvi established Madrassah Deoband at a small village in Soharanpur district in 1867. It was the first formal Madrassah establishment after 1857. It was different though. The Madaris before the British arrival were funded by the Nawabs (Nadvi, 1989). However, Dar-ul-Uloom Deoband was funded through public charities and dona-tions. The other difference, though no reference is available for this, was that this new Madrassah imparted only religious knowledge to the students. Secular education was left to the British edu-cation system. This was the beginning of the present environment which prevails throughout the majority of the Madaris in India and Pakistan. This radical shift in Madaris education in the Indian sub-continent reduced the influence the *Ulema* (religious scholars) had on the society. Further, the role of Madaris was significantly reduced. Their graduates were excluded from government employ-ment, and there was very little substitute for this (Nadvi, 1989).

The reason for this "pauperization" of Madaris needs to be researched in details. In brief, on the one hand, the British missionary policy of Christianization of the masses through missionary schools and colleges created fear amongst the Muslim *Ulema* about the future of the faith. On the other hand, preservation of the religion as a duty compelled them to take steps and revert to the very basics of the religion. The picture seems to be similar to as when the Mongols started conquering the Muslim states. At that time, the same thing happened. The Madaris reverted to the very basics of the religion, and the doors of *Ijitihad* were closed down. Mufti Taqi Usmani also concludes that the secularization of educational policies of the British in India and the bias towards religious education created a stir in the Muslim scholars. They feel apprehension over the future of religious teachings. This was the reason why the education system was divided into two realms—religious and secular—by Muslims of the sub-continent (Usmani, 1989, 2005).

This brief historical picture concludes that whenever Muslim society is under invasion from another force, it reverts to the very basics. Particularly after the 1857 war of independence, the Madaris reverted to the very basic subjects of the curriculum—*Serf-o-Nahw* (Arabic grammar), *Fiqh, Tafseer, Hadith* etc.—because of the perceived threat to the faith. It is pertinent to note that neither a single book out of 72 books mentions any teaching on suicide jihad/suicide terrorism, nor do the subjects promote radicalism. Similarly, never in the history of the Madaris in the Indian subcontinent were they ever used as safe haven for terrorists.

2. Pakistan and Madaris—a Deep-Rooted Relation

The Madaris system in Pakistan is not much different from the pre-independence system. Even after the creation of Pakistan in 1947, the role of Madaris remained restricted, and the doors for government employment were still closed to their graduates (Rehman, 2009). The objectives of the religious institutions remained the same as they were under British rule in India: preparing *imams* (leaders) for mosques, teachers for schools, orators for weekly sermons and religious leaders to carry out rituals and social responsibilities such as *nikah* (marriage contracts), divorce, inheritance and funerals (Rehman, 2009).

However, Akhtar Ali Shah (2011), a senior police officer of Pakistan, sees Madaris as an deeply intertwined part of the social fabric of Pakistani society. After an historical analysis of the role of Madaris in the politics of Pakistan, he concludes that Madaris have been providing livelihood, education and essence of identity to those millions who happened to be the *sons of lesser gods* (Shah, 2011). Prakhar Sharma (2009, p. 38) holds the similar view. According to him, the people of Afghanistan (and Pakistan) consider Madrassah and religious scholars to be integral parts of their history and identity, but the West generally views them as a breeding ground for extremists (Sharma, 2009).

3. Statistics on Madaris in Pakistan

There were a total of 12,448 *Deeni Madaris* in Pakistan in 2008, of which 363 (3%) are in the public sector, whereas 12,085 (97%) are in the private sector. The total enrolment in the *Deeni Madaris* is 1.603 million, of which 0.454 million (3%) are in the public sector, whereas 1.558 million (97%) are in the private sector. The total male enrolment in *Deeni Madaris* is 0.999 million (62%), whereas the female enrolment is 0.604 (38%). The total teachers in *Deeni Madaris* are 55,680, out of which 1,694 (3%) are in the public sector and 53,986 (97%) are in the private sector. There are 42,997 (77%) male teachers and 12,683 (23%) female teachers.

When Pakistan came into being in 1947, the presence of Madaris was very limited as compared to today. However, as the time moved on to 1971, the Madaris rose up to 897, a 72% increase in 24 years. During the next 17 years there was also a significant increase in Madaris, i.e., 68% increase. Astonishingly, there was 76% increase in Madaris between 1988 and 2005. Figure 19.1 shows a normal increase in number of Madaris between 1947 and 1988. However, the curve suddenly moves upward during 1988 and 2005. Why this sudden rise in Madaris? It is always attributed to the Afghan War against the Soviet Union during the 1980s and the successive Taliban rise to the power in Afghanistan during 1996–2001.

Out of the total 12,448 Madaris, only 321 (3%) are in the public sector, while 97% are in the private sector. The private Madaris are imparting education to a total of 1,558,554 students, out of which 971,343 (62%) are boys while only 587,211 (38%) are girls, which is not significantly different than the educational enrollment in public-sector schools and colleges (about 44% girls in all schools). The teacher–student ratio is 1:28 on average. The number of registered Madaris is only 6,803 (55%) (Shah, 2011). It is pertinent to mention here that the Madaris also give admission to foreign students.

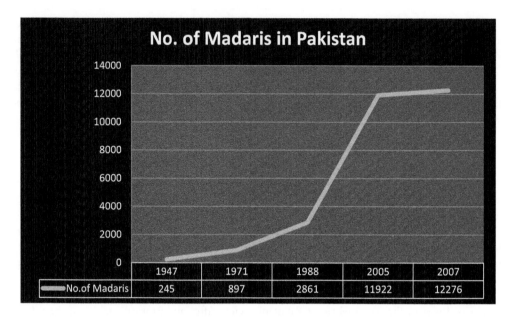

Figure 19.1 shows the line chart titled "No. of Madaris in Pakistan" with the following data:

	1947	1971	1988	2005	2007
No.of Madaris	245	897	2861	11922	12276

Figure 19.1 Details of Madaris in Pakistan (1947–2007).

(*Source*: Government of Pakistan, 2009; Shah, 2011; Usmani, 1989, 2005)

According to one report of the Ministry of Interior, there were 2,606 foreign students in Madaris of Pakistan in the year 2005 (Shah, 2011).

The province-wise breakdown of Madaris also presents an interesting picture. A significant number of Madaris are located in the Punjab (44%) followed by Khyber Pakhtunkhwa (KPK) 21% and Sindh 15%. There is a very small number of Madaris in Balochistan. FATA, with a population of 3,341,070, contains 498 Madaris, which makes it 1 Madrassah for every 6,709 people, compared to 14,956 in Punjab, 16,327 in Sindh, 1,1420 in Balochistan and 7,976 in KPK (Government of Pakistan, 2009). It is easy to infer that there are more Madaris per population in FATA and KPK than the other provinces of Pakistan.

It is to be noted that FATA and KPK are the regions which are severely hit by suicide terrorism. Further, these two are the Pakhtun-dominant regions as well. It may seem fit to jump to the conclusion that the more the Madaris the more the suicide attacks in the region. However, it is very naïve and seems to be an over-simplification. This point will be discussed later.

II. Suicide Terrorism, Religious Motivation and Madaris in Pakistan

1. Is There Any Association Between Madaris and Suicide Terrorism?

With every suicide bombing in Pakistan, fingers are pointed towards the possibility of a relationship between the bomber and an Islamic school, a Madrassah (Georgy, 2011). Usually a young boy of 13 to 18 is suspected to have done the deadly blast, who, in the educated guess and considered opinion of the investigation staff, is said to have had some links with the tribal groups, as the sketch being prepared by the officer in light of the statements of eyewitnesses is reportedly indicative of his ethnicity and background. A more general depiction of the story is like this:

- A hand/foot/skull is found from the scene of the crime
- Footage from CCTV/mobile is attained

- A boy of 12–14 or 15–17 is seen and suspected
- White clothes, new shoes, beads in hands, white cap/turban/hanki on head
- Small beard, medium height
- Afghani, Tribal, or Pushtoon by appearance
- Sketch prepared from eyewitnesses and footages/videos
- Probably a student of Islamic Madrassah

This is the most common practice of our media and investigation staff in Pakistan—to fix the responsibility on some unidentified suicide bomber who is reported to be a religiously motivated tribal or Afghani of a tender age and, in most probability, one who has been radicalized in some Islamic school of an unidentified place or with some unknown Islamic school master(s). This is generally believed and released to the media even before any forensic science applications, laboratory tests or tracing of a police criminal record or national identity card database (Khalid, 2010). This practice saves the police from many hurdles and the fatigue of a cumbersome investigation, as police of the cities have no authority and jurisdiction in Pakistan's tribal territories. Moreover, the propaganda against Madaris is trumpeted vehemently to those who want a ready scapegoat in the long war on terror. Madaris or some radical militant Islamic fundamental groups are the first to be blamed for carrying out suicide terrorism. However, is there any relationship between suicide terrorism and the Madaris? Is it the Madrassah structure and system which promotes suicide terrorism? Is a common norm in Madaris to carry-out suicide terrorism? Do the data support the same claim?

2. Is There an Association Between Madaris and Suicide Terrorism?

As we discussed earlier, the more the Madaris the more will be suicide attacks in the region is too simplistic to conclude. It is visibly found that KPK and FATA share more available Madaris per population than the other parts of the country (498 Madaris, which makes it 1 Madrassah for every 6,709 people, and in FATA, 7,976 for KPK) (Government of Pakistan, 2009). Similarly, Figure 19.2

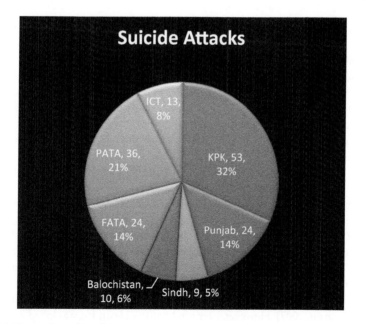

Figure 19.2   Suicide attacks in the Administrative Units of Pakistan.

(*Source:* Irfan and Usmani, 2011)

shows that KPK and FATA are the two regions which are severely hit by suicide attacks. KPK, with a total of 53 suicide attacks between 2002 and 2009, shares 31% of all attacks, followed by 24 attacks in the Punjab and 9 attacks in Sindh. However, FATA and PATA[2] also experienced 24 and 356, attacks respectively. Ethnically, both FATA and PATA are predominantly Pakhtun regions. Further, these are the regions where the military has started to move in the post-9/11 scenario. Never before 9/11 had KPK, FATA or PATA ever experienced any suicide terrorism. Post-9/11, they did, however, experience them more severely than anywhere else in the world. The question still remains: why post-9/11? The answer is in Robert Pape's (2005) findings, which we will discuss later.

The point of focus here is that first, we said that there were 1.6 million students enrolled in *Deeni Madaris* in Pakistan in the year 2008. Secondly, there was a total of 303 suicide attacks in Pakistan since 2002 (Mir, 2011). Astonishingly, 12,448 Madaris with 1.6 million enrolled students are producing only 303 suicide bombers in a decade! The facts denounce the claim of suicide bombers coming from Madaris or that religious motivation is seen in all suicide bombers. Holmes (2005), while analyzing statements issued by Al-Qaeda, has emphasized that Osama bin Laden's rationale for 9/11 has usually been secular rather than religious, focused towards "punishing Western injustices, not impieties" (Holmes, 2005).

Holme's (2005) conclusion also stands valid when we analyze the statements of one of the suicide bombers arrested before detonating himself in Lahore. He said that he became a suicide bomber when he saw the military operations in Lal Masjid (Red Mosque) and Bajur, meaning his motivation was not to bring Islam or *Shariah* (Islamic law) to the country but to take revenge against the (presumed) injustices of the military (Safi, 2009a). In the same interview, the suicide bomber revealed that none of his batch-mates at the training center at Miran Shah were from the *Deeni Madaris*; all were from the secular schools (Safi, 2009a). The KPK police also revealed the same findings through investigation (Khan, 2009).

Similarly, the religious scholars, at least in Pakistan, denounce suicide attacks. The supreme religious leader of Pakistan, Mufti Munib-ur-Rehman, who is also the Chairman Royat-e-Hilal Committee, issued that:

> Fighting in the way of Allah, for the uplift of religion, for the superiority of right things, giving your life, and when the time comes participating in Jihad, showing courage, vigilantism, and gallantry are not only valid in Islam but in the time of need it is also termed the Superior Prayers (Afzal Ibadat) and have superior degrees for the life hereafter. But vigilantism and gallantry is that when you come to the battlefield and fight, sometimes you also got killed but you do not start the battle with killing yourself first. In suicide attack, the attacker begins by killing himself and his own person, any valid argument for this has not come into my knowledge and to the extent I know the religion, I never came across any such justification from Quran and Hadith.
>
> *[translated from Urdu] (Safi, 2009b)*

While Mufti Munib is from the Barelvi school of thought (which is considered religiously liberal), the Deobandi school (a relatively religiously conservative school of thought) also denounces suicide attacks. One of the most influential Deobandi clerics of Pakistan, Maulana Hasan Jan, while signing a *fatwa* (decree) against suicide bombing in Pakistan, described the perpetrators as "cruel and ignorant people" and said that these people have "no knowledge and education." He said that suicide bombing was *haraam* (forbidden) and against the *Shariah* and added that the situation in Afghanistan and Iraq was different from Pakistan. He concluded: "We are completely against suicide activities in our country" (Hassnain, 2007). However, later on, Maulana Hasan Jan was killed in a terrorist attack on September 17, 2007, in Peshawar.

Analyzing the data over the past 30years, Pape (2005) asserted that religion is neither an essential nor a sufficient factor in the generation of suicide attacks and that the taproot of suicide terrorism is nationalism not religion. Christine Fair (2009) discusses the connection between Madaris and militancy at greater length in her book, *The Madrassah Challenge*. While remaining impartial, she argues that evidence counters the most sweeping contemporary claims that Madaris are extensively involved in the production of militants in Pakistan and elsewhere. In her study of 141 militant families in Pakistan, she finds out that only 19 were reportedly recruited from Madaris. Less than a quarter of the militants (33 of 141) ever attended a Madrassah. Of those 33, 27 attended a Madrassah for four or fewer years, and most also attended public schools. Eighty-two out of 141 were well educated by Pakistani standards (at least 10th grade) (Fair, 2009). These findings indicate that the militants in general are not uneducated, nor they are exclusively from Madaris. While Christine Fair (2009) tried to find an association between Madaris and militancy, she failed to consider the presence of military or foreign occupation as the essential condition for suicide terrorism.

Moreover, Naushad Ali Khan, a police officer in Khyber Pakhtunkhwa Police department, and Superintendent of Police (Research) find that none of the "living bombers" (those who couldn't blow themselves up and got arrested) had exclusively religious education. Only 10% had only secular education, and 90% had both religious and secular education. Further, the majority were from tribal origins (70%), a predominantly Pakhtun territory (Khan, 2009).

Finally, Pape's (2005, p. 96) conclusion stands significantly valid that "religions do play a role in suicide terrorism, but mainly in the context of national resistance."

3. *Why Suicide Attacks? Foreign Occupation Not Islamic Fundamentalism*

Since independence of Pakistan in 1947, not a single suicide terrorist attack was ever recorded. The first known suicide attack in Pakistan was carried out on November11, 1995, on the Egyptian Embassy in Islamabad. A suicide bomber rammed a pickup truck packed with explosives into the gate of the Egyptian Embassy in Islamabad, killing 15 people and wounding 59 others. There were no other suicide attacks during 1995 and 2002 (*New York Times*, 1995). The bloom of suicide attacks in Pakistan grew after the US invasion in Afghanistan.

The director of the Chicago Project on Security and Terrorism (CPOST) and the author of the book *Dying to Win: The Strategic Logic of Suicide Terrorism* and *Cutting the Fuse: The Explosion of Global Suicide Terrorism and How to Stop It*, Robert Pape (2005) presented his thesis that religion is not the basic motivation of suicide terrorism and that Islamic fundamentalism is not the cause of suicide terrorism.

He finds out that during the period 1980 to 2003, there were 343 completed suicide terrorist attacks. About 88% of these attacks had ideological affiliations. The world leader (in terrorist attacks) during this period is *not* an Islamic group but was the Tamil Tigers of Sri Lanka—a Marxist group, a secular group, a Hindu group. The Liberation Tigers of Tamil Eelam (LTTE) in Sri Lanka did more suicide attacks (78 suicide attacks) than Hamas or Islamic Jihad in Israel. The other leading group for suicide attacks is the PKK of Turkey, which is purely a secular Marxist, anti-religious suicide terrorist group, which carried out 14 suicide attacks in Turkey. Over 50% of these suicide attacks were not associated with Islamic fundamentalism (Pape, 2005) (see Table 19.1).

Pape (2005) questions the myth of suicide terrorists coming out of Islamic fundamentalism on the basis of data and argues that what most people think is that suicide terrorism is driven by religion, particularly Islamic fundamentalism. However, the data negates it. The facts don't fit in it. What is common in 95% of the worldwide suicide terrorist attacks is not religion but a specific strategic objective to compel democratic forces to withdraw combat forces from the territory the terrorists consider to be their homeland. From Lebanon to the West Bank to Chechnya and Iraq

Table 19.1 Suicide Terrorism Attacks Worldwide (1980–2002)

Total Suicide Attacks	343
Ideological Affiliations	298
Tamil Tigers in Sri Lanka	78
PKK in Turkey	14
Al-Aqsa Brigade	25
Popular Front for the Liberation of Palestine (PFLP) on West Bank	6
Syrian Social Nationalist Party (SSNP)	8
Baa'th Party in Lebanon	8

(*Source:* Robert Pape, 2005)

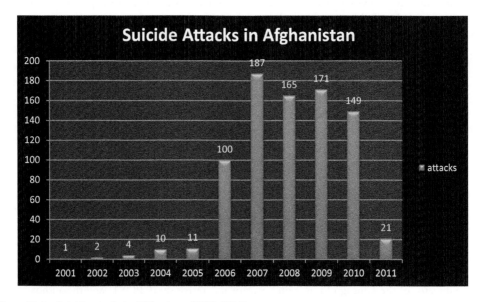

Figure 19.3 Suicide attacks in Afghanistan (2002–2011).

(*Source*: Chicago Project on Security and Terrorism (CPOST) Database)

and Afghanistan today, every suicide terrorist campaign has been waged by terrorist groups for this strategic objective. While it doesn't account for every suicide attack, it does, however, account for over 95% of the attacks of all the suicide terrorism we have experienced since 1980.

The point to focus on is that foreign occupation triggers the secular and religious suicide terrorism, much like smoking triggers lung cancer. In Afghanistan before 2001, there were zero suicide attacks in the history of this country. For the first few years, there were some tiny numbers of suicide attacks, but in 2006 suddenly there was a spike, and it stayed high (Figure 19.3). Why? Looking at the targets of the suicide attacks, the majority were the US and Allied troops (73.7%). Over 90% of the suicide attackers were Afghan nationals. A few percent were from the border regions, and only 5% were from the regions out of the conflict. But why sudden spike in 2006?

The plausible reason seems to be this: In the first few years, there were only a few thousand US troops in Afghanistan, and they were stationed specifically in Kabul, not spread around the country, basically giving security to Karzai. Then in 2006the UN gave the mandate to the US to spread around Afghanistan. First, the forces went north, where the Northern Alliance were allies with the US, so there was no such problem, and then they moved to the west with allies. Then in 2006 the forces moved to the South and East (Pakhtun territories), and that's when the suicide attacks explode suddenly. We can find some identical pattern and similar phenomenon in Pakistan in this respect.

According to Figure 19.3, before the US occupation of Afghanistan, suicide attacks were very rare in Pakistan (only one case before US occupation). However, as the US attacked Afghanistan, suicide terrorism started to grew gradually. However, the point is, it didn't grow suddenly after the US invasion. For the first few (five) years, till 2006, the suicide attacks remained relatively fewer in number in Pakistan as well as in Afghanistan. However, the count mushroomed in 2006–07. In 2006, as mentioned earlier, the US forces moved to the east and south of Afghanistan to occupy the Pakhtun territories, and at the same time the international community put pressure on Musharraf (the then-president of Pakistan) to withdraw its 100,000 troops from the Indian border to the Western Pakhtun area. The aim was to indirectly militarize the other half of the Pakhtun area in Pakistan (as the Pakhtun lives on both sides of the Pak–Afghan border). This excessive militarization, which had never happened in the past like this, triggered the suicide terrorism, both in Afghanistan and in Pakistan, from 2006 onward.

We find out earlier in Figure 19.4 that KPK, FATA and PATA experienced significantly more suicide terrorist attacks than any other part of Pakistan. In Pape's (2005) paradigm, it is obvious to conclude that this was a response to the military operations in these areas (predominantly Pakhtun areas).

The major target of these attacks were security forces (57%) (CPOST database). The trend continues, and the curve didn't go down significantly (Figures 19.3 and 19.4) in both of the countries—Pakistan and Afghanistan. Robert Pape (2005) claims that this suicide terrorism is not a global jihad but a local opposition to the US and NATO military presence in Afghan territory. The suicide attackers are not just Afghan nationals but Pakhtuns from the south and the east in Afghanistan and west in Pakistan (see Table 19.2 for details of suicide attacks in Pakistan).

Questions are raised about the confidence in the data Robert Pape (2005) collected through CPOST. However, the data of SATP and Pakistan Body Count (PBC) does not significantly vary from that of CPOST. In Figure 19.4, the data from CPOST, PBC and SATP are shown side by side.

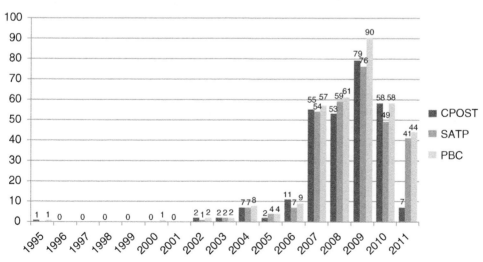

Figure 19.4 Trend in suicide attacks in Pakistan since 1995.

(*Sources*: [1] Chicago Project on Security and Terrorism (CPOST) Database. [2] South Asian Terrorism Portal (SATP). [3]. Pakistan Body Count (PBC))

Table 19.2 History of Suicide Attacks in Pakistan (1995–2011)

Suicide Attacks in Pakistan

Year	Attacks			Killed			Wounded			Lethality		
	CPOST*	PCB**	SATP***	CPOST	PCB	SATP	CPOST	PCB	SATP	CPOST	PCB	SATP
1995	1	1	-	17	15	-	60	60	-	17	15	-
1996	-		-	-		-	-		-	-		-
1997	-		-	-		-	-		-	-		-
1998	-		-	-		-	-		-	-		-
1999	-		-	-		-	-		-	-		-
2000	-	1	-	-	3	-	-	3	-	-	3	-
2001	-		-	-		-	-		-	-		-
2002	2	2	1	26	27	15	76	91	34	13	13.5	15
2003	2	2	2	66	65	69	102	115	103	33	32.5	35
2004	7	8	7	143	82	89	270	399	321	20	10.25	13
2005	2	4	4	24	83	84	80	230	219	12	20.75	21
2006	11	9	7	139	161	161	263	230	352	13	17.888889	23
2007	55	57	54	724	842	765	1315	2008	1677	13	14.77193	14
2008	53	61	59	769	940	893	1729	2426	1846	15	15.409836	15
2009	79	90	76	1038	1090	949	2847	3462	2356	13	12.111111	12
2010	58	58	49	1160	1153	1167	2775	2954	2199	20	19.87931	24
2011	41	44	41	628	625	628	1183	1386	1183	15	14.204545	15
TOTAL	**311**	**337**	**300**	**4734**	**5086**	**4820**	**10700**	**13364**	**10290**	**15**	**15.09199**	**16**

(Sources: [1] Chicago Project on Security and Terrorism (CPOST) Database. [2]. Pakistan Body Count (PBC) [3] South Asian Terrorism Portal (SATP)*)*

★Chicago Project on Security and Terrorism/★★Pakistan Body Count/★★★South Asian Terrorism Portal

The bars in the figure do not show any significant variation between the two. It is inferred on the basis of these two independent data sources that the basic motivating factor behind suicide terrorism is not religion, though religion is used in the national context to fight the unjust and oppressive militaries and their allies, not to bring *Shariah* or Islamic rule in the land.

Conclusion

Madaris hold a significant position in the Muslim societies, and Pakistan is no different. Their influence is deep rooted in Pakistani society, its history and politics. Madaris are a platform to mobilize the masses of Pakistan against or for any cause or force. Though conservative in orientation, the Madaris hold independent thinking, and their independence is dear to them. Indeed, reforms are a need of the hour in the Madaris of Pakistan. However, blaming the Madaris for producing suicide terrorists is only a myth created by the Western and Pakistani print and electronic media, the purpose behind which is not still clear. The media need to reconsider their policies of bias, and the reporting should be on the basis of research.

Notes

1 Revised version of the article: Fasihuddin & Sajid, I. A. (2011). Are suicide bombers coming from Madaris (Islamic Seminaries)? *Pakistan Journal of Criminology*, 3(4), 79–106. Published with permission.
2 PATA (Provincially Administered Tribal Area) includes Malakand Agency, Swat, Shanglah, Upper-Dir, Lower-Dir, Chitral and Buner districts of KPK. It is administratively connected with KPK.

References

Anzar, U. (2003). *Islamic education: A brief history of Madrassas with comments on curricula and current pedagogical practices*. Retrieved from www.uvm.edu/~envprog/madrassah/madrassah-history.pdf.

Bainat. (2010, June). History of religious Madaris. *Monthly* Bainat [Urdu], *73*(6). Retrieved from www.banuri.edu.pk/ur/node/1105.

Fair, C. C. (2009). *The Madrassah challenge, militancy and religious education in Pakistan*. Lahore: Vanguard Books.

Georgy, M. (2011, February 11). *Brainwashing drives young Pakistan suicide bombers.* Pakistan: MARDAN. Retrieved from www.reuters.com/article/2011/02/11/us-pakistan-bombers-youth-feature-idUSTRE71A35I20110211.

Government of Pakistan. (2009). *Pakistan education statistics 2007–08*. Islamabad, Pakistan: Academy of Educational Planning and Management, National Educational Management Information System. Ministry of Education.

Haqqani, H. (2002, November). Islam's Medieval outposts. *Foreign Policy Magazine*.

Hassnain, Z. (2007, May 7). Clerics worried by lack of respect for fatwas on suicide. *Daily Times*. Retrieved from www.dailytimes.com.pk/default.asp?page=2007%5C05%5C07%5Cstory_7-5-2007_pg7_11.

Holmes, S. (2005). Al-Qaeda, September 11, 2001. In D. Gambetta (Eds.), *Making sense of suicide missions*. New York: Oxford University Press.

Irfan, M., & Usmani, Z. (2011). Suicide terrorism and its new targets—Pakistan. In U. Niaz (Eds.), *Wars, insurgencies, and terrorist attacks, a psychosocial perspective from the Muslim world* (pp. 78–94). Karachi: Oxford University Press.

Khalid, R. (2010, February 15). Every suicide bomber is coming from Madrassa. *The News*. Retrieved from www.thenews.com.pk/TodaysPrintDetail.aspx?ID=224355&Cat=2&dt=2/15/2010.

Khan, A. N. (2009, April). Suicide bombing in the NWFP: The need for research and information collection on human bombers. *Pakistan Journal of Criminology*, *1*(1), 1.

Mir, A. (2011, September 13). Ten years after 9/11: Suicide attacks declining in Pakistan. *The News*. Retrieved from www.thenews.com.pk/TodaysPrintDetail.aspx?ID=67436&Cat=6.

Nadvi, A. H. (1989). *Hindustan ki Qadeem Darsgahen* [Urdu]. [Old Schools of India]. Lahore: National Book Foundation.

New York Times. (1995, November, 20). Bombing at Egypt's embassy in Pakistan kills 15. *New York Times*. Retrieved from www.nytimes.com/1995/11/20/world/bombing-at-egypt-s-embassy-in-pakistan-kills-15.html.

Pape, R. (2005). *Dying to win: The strategic logic of suicide terrorism* (1st ed.). New York: Random House.

Rehman, K. (2009). Madrassah in Pakistan: Role and emerging trend. In A. Pandya & E. Laipson (Eds.), *Islam and politics, renewal and resistance in the Muslim World*. Islamabad: Institute of Policy Studies.

Safi, S. (2009a). *Geo News, Exclusive Jirga—Interview with a Suicide bomber—2nd July 2009 (Part 1 of 3)*. Retrieved from www.youtube.com/watch?v=nq88egK755k.

Safi, S. (2009b). *Geo News, Exclusive Jirga—Interview with a Suicide Bomber—2nd July 2009 (Part 3 of 3)* Retrieved from www.youtube.com/watch?v=OeOExvUZHKw&feature=relmfu.

Shah, A. S. (2011, January). Role Madrassahs in the politics of Pakistan. *Pakistan Journal of Criminology*, *3*(1).

Sharma, P. (2009). Role of religion in Afghan politics: Evolution and key trends. In A. Pandya & E. Laipson (Eds.), *Islam and politics, renewal and resistance in the Muslim World*. Islamabad: Institute of Policy Studies.

Stern, J. (2000). Pakistan's Jihad culture. *Foreign Affairs*, *79*(6).

Stern, J. (2001, January–February). Meeting with the Muj. *Bulletin of the Atomic Scientist*, *57*(1).

Usmani, T. M. (1989, 2005). *Our education system [Hamara Nizam-e-Taleem Kya Hua] Urdu*. Karachi: Maktaba Darul Uloom.

20

POST-CONFLICT CRIME AND VIOLENCE IN NEPAL

Trends, Dynamics and Drivers

D.B. Subedi

Introduction

Nepal's lengthy transition from war to peace has not been very peaceful. Although direct violence induced by the Maoist armed conflict has ended since the signing of the Comprehensive Peace Agreement (CPA) in 2006, the post-peace agreement period has seen a dramatic upsurge in crime and violence.[1] As this chapter shows, a comparison of data between 2012 and 2015 reveals a steady growth in crime and violence. Proliferation of small arms and light weapons (SALW) threatens public security, while organized crime and mobilization of young people in contentious politics has grown, especially in urban areas across the country (Ghimire & Upreti, 2010).

The current scenario of crime and violence begs some critical questions: Why has Nepal experienced an upsurge in post-conflict crime and violence when the country is on a path to peace? What factors and drivers explain the on-set of post-conflict crime violence in Nepal? Engaging with these questions, this chapter aims to study post-conflict crime and violence in Nepal. It analyzes post-conflict crime and violence using a three-dimensional analytical framework in which the three dimensions are economic and structural dimension, institutional dimension and political and social dimension.

This chapter is based on multiple fieldworks in Nepal between 2008 and 2014. The fieldwork included interviews with Maoist ex-combatants, leaders of major political parties, civil society leaders, government officials and security personnel, youth groups, peace-building professionals and the private-sector leaders in Kathmandu, Morang, Sunsari, Parsa, Chitawan, Banke, Dang and Dhangadi districts. Upon requests from participants, anonymity is maintained when reporting or quoting verbatim from interviewees.

I. Trend of Crime and Violence in Post-Conflict Nepal

The context of crime and violence has changed since 2006. In the pre-CPA period, the Maoists People's Liberation Army (PLA)[2] and the state security forces were involved in committing politically motivated violence and human rights abuses, while in the post-conflict period armed groups, ex-combatants, youth gangs, criminal groups and politically affiliated groups are major actors of crime and violence (Interdisciplinary Analysts, Nepal Madhesh Foundation, Small Arms Survey, & Saferworld, 2011).

Homicide rates and rates of crime and violence have increased, mostly in big cities like Kathmandu, Birgunj, Biratnagar and Nepalgunj as well as semi-urban areas and urbanizing hubs across the country. A comparison of three years' crime data, as shown in Table 20.1, suggests that crime and violence from across the country have increased by nearly 26 percent between 2012/13 and 2014/15.

As Table 20.1 shows, an increase in homicide rate by nearly 16 percent between 2012 and 2015 depicts the overall trend of unlawful killing, which is higher than an average homicide rate in conflict time. Between 1996 and 2006, the total number of deaths from the armed conflict was around 15,000, with average deaths 1,500 per year, while average homicide rate in between 2012 and 2015 is roughly 4,200. While no study is available to provide a detailed account of homicide and its causes, my fieldwork suggests that youth gang violence, circulation of small arms and light weapons and criminal violence kidnapping are major causes of the growing homicide trend after 2006.

Social crime and crime related to women and children have nearly doubled, while the suicide rate has increased significantly. Crime related to travel and transport has decreased between 2012 and 2015, whereas theft and burglary and organized and economic crime have also increased. As Table 20.1 reveals, the sharp rise in social crime and crime related to women and children is a key feature of crime and violence, although the notion of social crime is very vague and includes a wide array of issues, from examples from crime related to the dowry system to sexual and gender based violence (SGBV). As SGBV is legally punishable, it is a form of social crime in Nepal. Although there are wide discrepancies in SGBV data in Nepal, studies show that between 12 percent and 50 percent of women in Nepal suffer some form of sexual violence (Deuba & Rana, 2005; Puri, Forst, Tamang, Lamichhnae, & Shah, 2012). SGBV violence during the Maoists' armed conflict was rampant, although very few cases have reported because of lack of victim protection mechanisms in rural areas. SGBV including domestic violence often goes unreported because either it is considered to be a 'family affair' or victims have acute financial dependency on the perpetrator, who can effectively circumvent any legal recourse.

Respondents from Kathmandu, Biratnagar, Birgunj, Nepalgunj, Dhangadi and Nuwakot mentioned that the recent trend of crime has a mix of economic, political and social motivations. The following figure shows respondents' views about the most pressing issues or type of crime and violence post-conflict.

According to the Ministry of Home Affairs, 34,314 people hold licensed firearms in Nepal, most of them in the Kathmandu Valley and the Terai districts. Civil-society organizations estimate that there are about 55,000 small arms in circulation. According to estimation, around 440,000 private

Table 20.1 Comparison of Crime and Violence Data Between 2012 and 2015

Types of criminal violence	Total cases in 2012/2013	Total cases in 2013/2014	Total cases in 2014/2015
Homicide	4,059	4,117	4,686
Suicide	3,977	3,974	4,504
Theft and burglary	1,069	1,042	1,128
Organized and economic crime	2,893	3,019	3,001
Social crime	6,276	7,109	10,133
Crime related to women and children	1,123	1,468	2,019
Crime related to travel and transportation	1,831	1,678	1,641
Miscellaneous	349	225	273
Total	**21,577**	**22,632**	**27,385**

(*Source:* Compiled by the author based on fieldwork in Kathmandu, 2014)

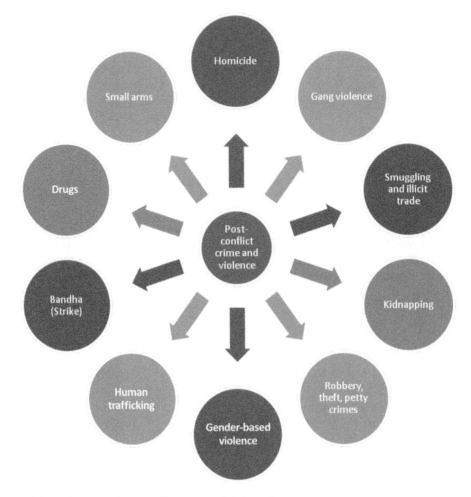

Figure 20.1 Major types of post–conflict crime and violence issues.

firearms are in Nepal, of which only about 55,000 are believed to be legally registered, meaning that around 330,000 are unregistered weapons (Karp, 2013). However, interviews with police officials and civil society members revealed that the actual circulation of SALW could be much higher because homemade guns and weapons are cheap[3] and easily accessible just on the other side of the border. The open border between Nepal and India also facilitates a free flow of people across the border every day, and this has historically become a route for smuggling of goods, trafficking of children, women and girls, cross-border crime, money laundering and fake (Indian) currency and circulation of small arms, which increased after 2006 mainly because of political instability and growing criminality in Terai.

II. Approaches to Analyzing Post-Conflict Crime and Violence

Although post-conflict crime and violence have become common phenomena in countries emerging from war, the literature on this critical problem is still growing. Much of the scholarly work on this issue draws from works of sociologists and economists, who focus on structural inequalities and economic deprivation as drivers of crime and violence. From a sociological point of view, prevailing structural inequalities including urban poverty, unemployment, income inequalities between rich and poor, the perception of relative deprivation of certain individuals and groups and the conditions of social exclusion and marginalization of the urban poor are considered to be the major factors to drive gang-led crime and violence in the post-conflict period (see Cramer, 2010; Lee, 1996; Moser & Holland, 1997; Tranchant, 2013).

The 'economic approach' to crime and punishment propounded by Becker (1968) and then contributed by other scholars like Jack Hirshleifer (2001) argues that lack of opportunity to enter the labor market is a driver of crime and violence. There is a very widespread view that youth unemployment is a key cause and driver of insurgency or civil war (Urdal, 2004). However, a key criticism of this approach is that there are no grounds empirically for the commonly made claims that there is a strong, automatic causal connection from unemployment, underemployment, or low productivity employment to violence and war (Cramer, 2010). A general weakness of the economic approach is its limitation to recognize other factors, for example social factors, which, when combined with economic factors, can drive crime and violence. For example, ex-combatants who feel socially disintegrated (ex-combatants are away from the society for a long time and even when they are brought in they are not integrated within the society as many do not like them) and economically uprooted tend to engage in criminal behavior and violence (Collier, 1994), although caution should be taken in generalizing ex-combatants as actors of crime and violence.

Some scholars have taken an institutional approach to comprehend post-conflict crime and violence. This approach assumes that prolonged armed conflict makes state security and justice and democratic institutions either dysfunctional or weak and incompetent to contain crime and violence (Bryden & Hanggi, 2005). Weak security institutions, therefore, undermine the state's capacity to maintain legitimate control over violence, and it creates a unique war-to-peace condition that is conducive to proliferation of small arms and light weapons (SALW), flourishing of warlords, criminal rackets and petty crimes (Ebo, 2005; Hanggi, 2005; Suhrke, 2012). This approach advocates strengthening state institutions, often under the rubric of liberal peace-building paradigms, through peace-building initiatives like security sector reform (SSR) and disarmament, demobilization and reintegration (DDR) programs. Institutional reform, in this case, may also gear towards breaking patterns of the war economy and support post-conflict politics to be more legitimate, accountable and responsible for public well-being, safety and security. Finally, the social cultural approach to security and violence posits that war and armed conflict disintegrate society and create conditions that legitimize violence in everyday life (Suhrke, 2012, p. 2). Armed conflict creates a "culture of violence", which produces a socially permissive environment for continuity of the use of violence, even though the violent conflict has officially ended (Steenkamp, 2005). Understanding post-conflict crime and violence therefore necessitates uncovering the effects of the legacy of armed conflict in the everyday lives of people. Hence, the networks and dense relationships between perpetrators, what is often called social capital, cannot be ignored, as network and social capital are powerful facilitating factors for post-conflict crime and violence (Belloni, 2009; Gilbert, 2009; Micolta, 2009).

Drawing on the literature and also based on data collected from fieldwork, I argue that the nature of crime and violence in post-conflict Nepal is so complex that it requires a framework that takes a maximalist understanding of crime and violence. Therefore, this chapter analyzes post-conflict crime and violence in Nepal by taking into account three analytical dimensions: socio-economic dimensions, institutional dimensions and political and social dimensions, as shown in Figure 20.2. This analytical framework is applied to analyze and understand causes and drivers of post-conflict crime and violence in the following sections.

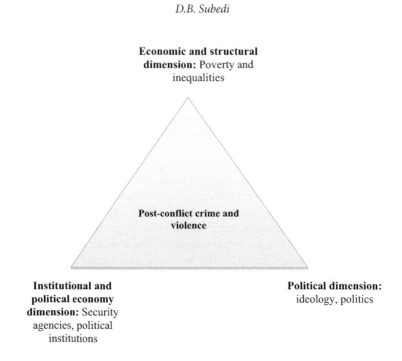

Figure 20.2 Analytical framework.

(*Source*: Designed by author based on literature review and fieldwork)

III. Economic and Structural Dimension

1. Unemployment and Criminal Violence

There are discrepancies of data on employment, unemployment and under-employment in Nepal. The working-age population, aged between 15 to 59 years, has increased from 54 percent in 2001 to about 57 percent in 2011 (CBS, 2012). The change in the population numbers is giving the demographic dividend, the unemployment rate among 15- to 24-year-old people has remained high at 3.6 percent (CBS, 2011). A recent report by the International Labor Organization (ILO), however, states that the unemployment rate for the year 2013/14 is 2.1 percent, while the average unemployment rate between 2005/06 and 2012/13 was 1.8 percent (ILO, 2014).

Unemployment of youth, especially between 15 and 25 years of age, is a major factor for economic crimes, particularly in urban areas. The youth unemployment rate in urban areas in the year 2013/14 was 13 percent, which is significantly higher than the average 7.6 percent urban unemployment rate between 2005/06 and 2012/13 (ILO, 2014). By contrast, youth unemployment in rural areas was 2.1 percent in the year 2013/14. The rural–urban difference in unemployment rate explains why crime and violence are more concentrated in urban and peri-urban areas than rural areas.

Unemployed youth, especially those from urban areas like Kathmandu, Biratngar and Birgunj, Nepalgunj have become the targets of criminal recruitment by organized criminal groups and loose youth gangs who have economic motivations for crime. Unemployment and poverty have become push factors for many young people who have joined armed groups and gangs, especially in the Terai Region and eastern hills. My conversation with a police officer in Kathmandu in May 2014 revealed that most youth involved in criminal activities come from urban slums where disenfranchised, marginalized and unemployed youth dwell. However, a great deal of caution should be taken in generalizing the correlation between poverty and crime, because Kathmandu Valley has a better national poverty indicator, but it has higher rates of crime and violence.[4]

Lack of education and marketable vocational skill are factors that contribute to unemployment and under-employment. Nepal's vocational system is limited, while the education system is not tied to preparing young people to enter the job market. As a result, the system produces half-educated but highly ambitious youth who are vulnerable to recruitment by armed groups and organized criminal gangs. Ten years of insurgency in the past pushed many young people out of school. The consequence was that a generation of youth was deprived of the education, skill and knowledge necessary to access the job market. These youth who lack education and skills and are unemployed were targeted by the Maoists in the past, and they are now targets of criminal groups and armed groups. Economic vulnerability of young people resulting from unemployment therefore continues to be a driver of recruitment in political radicalization, crime and violence.

2. Rural–Urban Migration and Rapid Urbanization

My fieldwork found that a strong links between urbanization and economic crime in cities is spurred by growing rural-to-urban migration. The Maoist insurgency was principally concentrated in rural areas, and as a result, the urban areas enjoyed relative calm and stability during the conflict period. Yet the armed conflict produced more than 200,000 conflict-induced internal displaced persons (IDPs) who migrated involuntarily from rural to urban areas such as the Kathmandu Valley, Biratnagar, Pokhara, and Nepalgunj and Dhangadi. Thus, the recent spate of urbanization in Nepal was driven by the Maoist insurgency as well as its impact on the societal and economic systems in the rural areas.

While youth[5] gangs and criminal gangs have rapidly proliferated in urban areas including the Kathmandu Valley after 2006 (Saferworld, 2012), conflict-induced rural–urban migration resulted in formation of unplanned urban slums. Over time, precarious life in urban slums coupled with the economic and political disenfranchisement of young people became drivers of economic crime.

IV. Institutional Dynamics

1. Policing and Post-Conflict Crime and Violence

The Nepal police is the principal institution to deal with crime and violence, although two other key institutions, the National Investigation Department (NID) and the Armed Police Force (APF), also work in collaboration with the civilian police to curb crime and violence. The total number of civilian police as of April 2015 is 67,417;[6] about 240 police for per 100,000 population.

Need for a professional paramilitary police force capable of dealing with the Maoist insurgency was felt in the first few years of the insurgency. The government's tussle with the Royal Palace to mobilize the army to contain the insurgency further intensified its need to establish a paramilitary force which would be fully under the control of a civilian government. As a result the APF was established on 24 October 2001. Currently it is a force of more than 30,000 security persons. The AFP's mandate is basically concentrated on patrolling border and custom areas and on crisis management and arms control. The National Investigation Department is a national intelligence body which provides information to the Ministry of Home Affairs, the Nepal Police (NP) and the APF to control crime, terrorism and violence. The Ministry of Home (MoH) is the highest legislative body which governs and regulates the function of all three security agencies.

The role of civilian police is significant in controlling crime and violence in the country's civilian security architecture. Although the security sector did not collapse during the armed conflict, as is the case in many war-torn countries elsewhere, the NP suffered heavy losses, result-ing in weak institutional capacity to curb crime and violence in the immediate aftermath of the armed conflict.

The Maoist insurgency, which started by attacking a police post in the Rolpa district, heavily tar-geted the civilian police in the first few years of the insurgency. This was because the Maoists assessed that the NP was never prepared to fight a guerrilla war and partly because the Maoists would not want to antagonize the military until they consolidated their own military strength. Consequently the NP suffered heavy losses: for instance, a total of 768 police posts were destroyed/damaged by the Maoists,[7] most of the police posts from rural areas in the hills were merged to district police offices to avert further damages while thousands of policed were brutally killed, and several hundred police personnel quit the job under actual and perceived security threats by the Maoists. Suffering moral defeat and losses of infrastructure and human resources, the police force was then mostly confined within district headquarters and urban areas.

As soon as the peace agreement was signed, the Terai region experienced violent identity politics spurred by the sense of social and economic injustices and exclusion experienced by the Madehsi people in Terai. It was immediately followed by proliferation of armed groups and criminal gangs in the Terai region. This was another setback to the police, as police posts from the border areas in Terai were increasingly displaced by the attacks of armed groups and criminal gangs. This resulted in a massive security vacuum in Terai, providing "safe haven" for violence and criminality, especially in Morang, Sunsari, Saptari, Siraha, Dhanusa, Rautaht, Bara, Parsa, Banke and Bardia.

Weak institutional capacity of security providers had impacts on the prevalence of post-conflict crime and violence in Terai: kidnapping and killing particularly targeting people from the *Pahadi* community peaked mostly between 2008 and 2010, when the police posts were displaced from villages. On the other hand, effects of rapid political change and somewhat chaotic transition had significant impact on the ability of policing in the post-conflict period, which provided favorable conditions to the rise of various criminal groups and youth gangs in Kathmandu Valley. More than two dozen youth gangs with criminal activities were reported active in Kathmandu in 2012 (Subedi, 2014b). In 2013, I explored how more than 100 gangs, both formal and informal, with political and criminal orientations, could be operating in the Kathmandu Valley between 2009 and 2011. Outside of Kathmandu, youth gangs were reported to be active in every major urban areas such as Biratnagar, Chitwan, Birgunj, Nepalgunj and Dhangadi, where they engaged in economic crimes by extorting businessmen, smuggling goods (often across the border between Nepal and India) and influencing and manipulating public construction tenders.

The Special Security Plan (SSP), introduced by the government in July 2009, was a major response to the growing need to address criminality and security in the Terai region. Although the plan was criticized for not making its details public in a way that would provide impunity to the police force and could potentially authorize security officials to use excessive force and commit human rights abuses, the police officers I spoke with in Morang and Banke districts believed that the SSP has become successful in curbing criminal activities in Terai. However, despite the criticism, there is opti-mism within the civilian police institution that the police personnel today enjoy high moral strength in comparison to the time between 2007 and 2011. I also found that criminality and violence is markedly reduced in Terai districts, particularly after 2011.

Security providers in Nepal, including police, have taken an "interventionist approach" with emphasis on "overt and covert operations" rather than fostering police–community interactions and collaboration and cooperation. The SSP is an example of the interventionist approach. Nonetheless, recognizing community participation in security delivery, the NP developed the idea of "community policing" in early 1990s. Although this idea was almost dysfunctional for a long time, it was recently revived, resulting in the formation of the Community Service Center (CSC), a civilian–police cooperation and collaboration. In Kathmandu as well as Morang, Parsa, Banke and Dhangadi districts, the CSC has become a platform for engaging communities in addressing petty crimes and violence in collaboration with local police. In Banke district, the CSC was found to have worked to address drug-addiction issues. The CSC was engaged with school students to raise awareness because a respondent said "school and college students mostly between 14–20 years are the major targets of local drug dealers".[8] The respondent also mentioned that drug dealers have increasingly targeted young people from semi-urban and rural areas because the economic capacities of households in villages are improving due to remittances from foreign labor migration and because the presence of security forces is limited in rural areas. Thus policing in remote areas is one of the major causes of drug-related economic crime at present.

2. Political Intervention in Policing

A common perception across the fieldwork districts suggests that political interference in everyday policing is one of contributors to growing insecurity, crime and violence. A police officer interviewed in Inaruwa, Sunsari, in November 2011 stated, "Political protection of criminals and armed group members" is a rampant problem in Terai". In the Terai region, a major problem is an overlap between identity politics and criminality. As most of the criminal groups that operated in Terai between 2009 and 2011 had overlapping political and criminal motivation, addressing criminality should rest in the hands of political actors more than the in those of security actors, hence the police. That only a dozen out of more than 100 armed groups operating in Terai had political orientation (see Subedi, 2011) means that addressing insecurity needs to shift from a "blanket approach" to a systematic "double-pronged" security strategy: tackling criminality and political armed groups separately. In the last few years, political protection and impunity of violent gang leaders has surfaced as a major security issue. At the time of the fieldwork, more than 10 most-wanted youth gang leaders were reportedly protected by major political parties in Kathmandu. Although almost all major political parties have allegations of having criminal gangs, the cases of Parshuram Basnet and Dinesh Adhikari are notable for public security concerns. When the gang members of Parshuram Basnet, a gang leader with official ties to the Nepal Communist Party of United Marxist and Leninist, attacked journalist Khilanath Dhakalin in 2011, the incident not only revealed the nexus between politics and young gang culture, but it also promoted a massive civil society movement against criminality and impunity (Adhikari, Gautam, Pudasaini, & Sharma, 2014). Similarly, when police encountered Dinesh Adhikari (nicknamed Chari), with affiliations to the CPNUML in Dhading district, in August 2014, the face of political protection of gang leaders (often known as *don*) and the deeply problematic culture of impunity surfaced blatantly. A respondent in Kathmandu said: "That several major political parties, the Nepali Congress, Nepal Communist Party, Madhesi Democratic Forum (BijayaGachhadar group) have provided protection and impunity to Dons who are still in the most wanted list of the Nepal Police is no longer a secret issue".

Both political and economic motivations shape the nexus between politics and criminality. The culture of using youth gangs in manipulating voters during elections started after 1990 and flourished particularly after 2006. While youth gangs insulate power for political leaders at local level, the gang leaders also are "money-making machines", as they act as proxy actors in collecting forced donations (Subedi, 2014c). In recent times, youth gang leaders are found to have been involved in grabbing public construction contracts, using muscle power as well as political protection. A Maoist commander who is implicated in misappropriation of allowances of ex-combatants now owns a construction company in Kathmandu. A mutual ex-change of money and power with political protection has given rise to a "criminal economy", which is thriving at the cost of political instability.

V. Political and Social Dimension

1. Politics and Ideology

Youth wings of political parties and ex-combatants are two key actors of post-conflict violence in Nepal. Engaged in both political and economic violence, these key actors' motivation to violence is driven by a combination of political ideology and contentious politics. The history of youth engagement in politics can be traced back to the 1950s, when the Nepali Congress party and the left-wing parties formed their student wings in a bid to mobilize young people in revolutionary movements, which uprooted the Rana Oligarchy in 1951. However, the number of political parties has grown significantly over the last 20 years of Nepal's democratic transition, as shown in Table 20.2:

A notable consequence of proliferation of political parties is that a competitive political space for mobilizing youth in politics has emerged. As shown in Table 20.3, even political parties and identity groups that emerged after 2008 Constituent Assembly (CA) election had already formed their youth wings.

Table 20.2 Number of Political Parties Registered With the Election Commission (EC) Since 1991

Year of Election	Number of Parties Registered With the EC	Number of Parties That Contested in the Election
1991	44	20
1994	65	24
2008	119	55
2013	140	122

(*Source:* Subedi, 2014b)

Table 20.3 Youth Wings of Political Parties

S.N.	Political Party/Ethnic and Identity Group	Youth Wing/Organization
1	Unified Communist Party of Nepal (Maoist) (UCPNM)	Young Communist League (YCL)
2	Communist Party of Nepal Unified Marxist and Leninist (CPNMUML)	Youba Sangh and Youth Force
3	Nepal Congress (NC)	Tarun Dal
4	Communist Party of Nepal—Maoists (CPN-M)	National Volunteer Bureau (NVB)
5	Madhesi Janadikar Forum—Democratic (MJF-D)	Democratic Youth Forum
6	Nepal Sadhbhawan Party	Madheshi Commando
7	Madhesi Janadhikar Forum (MJF)	Nepal Youth Forum and Madhesi Youth Force
8	Nepal Sadhbhavana Party (Mahato)	Madhesh Rakshya Bahini (Madhesh Security Brigade)
9	Communist Party of Nepal Maoist (CPN-M) Matrika Yadav Group	Youth People's Security Force
10	Revolutionary Communist Party Nepal led by Mani Thapa	The National Red-Guard Army
11	Rastriya Prajatantra Party (RPP)	National Democratic Youth Organization
12	Terai Madhesh Loktantrik Party	Terai Madhesh Sewa Surakshya Sangh
13	Rastriya Prajatantra Party Nepal (RPP-N) (Kamal Thapa)	Youth Front
14	Federal Limbuwan State Council (FLSC)	Federal Limbuwan State Council Limbuwan Volunteers (LVs)

S.N.	Political Party/Ethnic and Identity Group	Youth Wing/Organization
15	Federal Democratic National Party (FDNP) led by Laxman Tharur	Tharuhat Autonomous State Council Federal Volunteers
16	Tharuhat Swyatta Parishad	Tharu Sena
17	Khas Chettri Samaj	Chettri Samaj Youth Front
18	Bahun Samaj	Bahun Samaj Youth Front

(*Source:* Author's fieldwork, 2013 and 2014)

A number of youth wings of political parties, particularly the Young Communist Leagues (YCL), Youth Force (YF) and Limbuwan Volunteers (LVs), are involved in disruptive actions such as strikes, inter-group clashes, intimidation and forced donation requests to businesspeople, manipulating government tendering process and attacking ideologically differing individuals or groups (Crozier, Gunduz & Subedi, 2010).

YCL is the youth wing of the CPNM, which operated as a para-military group. Although the UCPNM publicly reiterated repeatedly in January 2008 that the party had given strict instructions to the YCL to refrain from using violence, various sources have shown YCL cadres were involved in extortion, abductions, intimidation, threats and murder (Carter Centre, 2011).

Although the CPNM declares that it has dissolved YCL in 2011, the legacy of violence among YCL cadres has not withered away. YCL-led violence was worse particularly when the Maoists came to the government in 2008, partly because YCL enjoyed the advantages of state power and also partly because of the political violence of Maoists (ICG, 2010).

Youth Force (YF), which is the youth wing of the CPNUML, has become a major contestant and rival of YCL; as a consequence, clashes and inter-group fights between them have occurred frequently, often leading to violence at the local, regional and national levels. Clashes between YCL and YF during the election of the constitution assembly in 2013 were major sources of election violence. For example, nine persons were injured when a clash between YF and YCL broke out in Bagheswori VDC 7, Chokde village in Nuwakot districts, in February 2010. Similarly, YCL and YF cadres clashed violently at Dhurkotrajasthal of constituency number 3 of Gulmi district on 10 November 2013, resulting in severe injuries of several cadres on both sides.[9]

Among the youth wings of newly formed identity groups, the Limbuwan Volunteers (LV), the youth wing of the Sanghiya Limbuwan Rajya Parishad, an ethnic outfit active in the eastern hills, is notable because of its violent activities, especially in Jhapa, Ilam, Panchthar and Taplejung districts.

Political ideology and political extremism are central to violence produced by youth wings of political parties and identity groups. The political youth groups form bonded "social capital"[10] within their in-group members, so their membership inclusion/exclusion, which is deeply embedded in their political schooling and ideology, produces conditions for inter-group rivalry, often leading to violent clashes. I also found that some members of youth wings tend to go beyond ideological control and reportedly become involved in criminal violence, while some youth leaders I interviewed in Kathmandu expressed frustration towards their dependency in terms of political activism and mobilization. This phenomenon can have two potential consequences. First, political apathy could rise among some youth leaders who are not happy with the way they are being treated by their mother political parties. Second, given that political youth groups often enjoy political protection and impunity in exchange for muscle power they offer to their political mobilizers, this dangerous political barter system between patrons (party leaders) and clients (political youth wings) is a major ideological threat to tackling the post-conflict crime and violence.

2. Ex-Combatants, Crime and Violence

There is a general agreement that a post-conflict society that receives ex-combatants who are unemployed and lack marketable skills is more likely to experience ex-combatant-led insecurity and violence (Colletta, Kostner, & Wiederhofer, 1996). Collier (1994) argues that ex-combatant-led insecurity has both micro (at the community level) and macro (national level and beyond) implications. While the studies on the relationship between failed or incomplete reintegration programmes and ex-combatant-led violence are well established, caution should be taken in generalizing all ex-combatants as actors of post-conflict violence, because depending on personal and social circumstances, some ex-combatants integrate better than others and eventually engage in peaceful livelihoods (Subedi, 2014b).

In Nepal, United Nations Mission in Nepal (UNMIN) verified 19,602 Maoist ex-combatants, while 4,008 members of the Maoist army were verified minors and late recruits (VMLRs)[11] who were deemed ineligible to remain in cantonments (Subedi, 2014a). The VMLRs were rehabilitated in late 2010, with a rehabilitation package delivered through the United Nations Inter-Agency Rehabilitation Programme (UNIRP), whereas the verified ex-combatants languished in cantonments for more than six years due to a lack of political consensus over a reintegration modality. On 1 November 2011, the government reached an agreement on a reintegration and rehabilitation proposal for ex-combatants, with three different policy options. According to the first option, out of the 19,602 combatants, a maximum of 6,500 ex-combatants would be eligible to be integrated into the Nepal Army (NA) on an individual basis if they met the standard recruitment norms of the NA. The second option was to provide an accompanied and facilitated rehabilitation package worth a minimum of Nepali rupees (NRs) 600,000 to a maximum of NRs 900,000, including a provision for educational support and vocational training opportunities.[12] The third option offered an alternative pathway to voluntary retirement from the PLA by providing ex-combatants with a lump-sum cash package categorized into four levels: those falling in the lowest rank received NRs 500,000, while the three remaining higher categories received NRs 600,000, NRs 700,000 and NRs 800,000, in ascending order respectively (Interview with a government official, Kathmandu, January 2013). A total of 15,602 ex-combatants opted for voluntary retirement, 6 preferred rehabilitation packages, and only 1,444 registered their interest in army integration.[13] Thus, a substantial number of ex-combatants returned to communities without any accompanying reintegration support. A large number of these ex-combatants have resettled elsewhere other than their villages of origin. Many of them have spent the cash in household-related consumption, and as a result, a substantial number of ex-combatants are still unemployed, facing economic hardships and livelihood insecurity (Subedi, 2014d).

My fieldwork found that ex-combatants in Nepal constitute a heterogeneous social category which has responded to violence and Maoist politics differently. Based on their personal, social and economic circumstances, ex-combatants can be classified into three categories: the socially and economically engaged group, the informal interest group and the politically active ex-combatants.

A small group of ex-combatants have engaged, both socially and economically. Economically, the ex-combatants who could be identified in this group have started some form of farm- and non–farm-based micro-enterprises such as poultry and vegetable farming, cow rearing, grocery shops, vegetable shops, stationery shops, mobile phone repairing centers, beauty parlors and internet cyber cafés. Except for a few exceptions, the majority of ex-combatants in this category have a profound sense of social, moral and economic obligations towards their families. It is this sense of morality and obligation that has motivated them to accept the peaceful livelihood options. The ex-combatants from this category seem politically less active; many of them do not have strong connections with their wartime mobilizers, although they are in regular contact with fellow ex-combatants. They possess a degree of war fatigue, partly because of their high expectations of the war and partly due to their current impoverished situation.

A considerable number of ex-combatants have a tendency to reorganize themselves into small formal and informal groups based on their shared interests, reciprocal relationships and a common purpose that brings them together, forming informal interest groups. An ex-combatant referred to this as a friendship group and acknowledged that such groups exist throughout the country.[14] By contrast, some ex-combatants have formed formal interest groups. For instance, the VMLRs who were released from the cantonments in 2010 with a modest rehabilitation package have now formed a National Struggle Committee to promote collective bargaining with the government and the UCPNM. A demand for equality of benefits as per their colleagues, the verified ex-combatants, is the binding factor. Finally, I found some ex-combatants are politically more active than others. Ex-combatants' access to former rebel leaders and high-ranking PLA commanders has provided some of them with the privileges of power and position in the Maoist party and its sister organizations. One interviewee mentioned that several ex-combatants who had returned to their villages had been provided by the UCPNM with particular positions in the party as well as in YCL.[15] The existence of a strong culture of patronage politics within the Maoist hierarchy requires ex-combatants to access the high-level leadership if they aspire to hold an important position within the Maoist organization.

Although some form of commonality as well as differences exists between the three groups, I found that while social and economically engaged ex-combatants have gradually refrained from violent attitudes and behavior, ex-combatants who would belong to informal interest groups and be politically active are found to have engaged in political violence and even in criminal activities, as shown in Table 20.4.

Table 20.4 Nature and Types of Ex-Combatants-Led Crime and Violence

S.N.	When	Low-Level Crimes and Violence in Which Ex-Combatants Were Involved
1	7 August 2013	The Kathmandu police arrested two ex-combatants, Surya Timsina and Tika Ram Magar, with the charge of planting bombs in the house of Naba Raj Bhusal in Kathmandu.
2	July 2013	Two Maoist ex-combatants held with six live bullets, donation slips and a toy gun in Kathmandu.
3	May 2013	The Unemployed Association of Nepal blocked the highway and disrupted public movements.
4	April 2013	Police arrested three people, including former Maoist ex-combatant Yam Bahadur Thapa of Gorkha, with a semi-automatic rifle, revolver, bullets, swords, *khukuris* (Nepali traditional knife) and knives.
5	February 2013	Police raided the rented room of Lenin Bista, a VMLR, in Madhyapur Thimi, Bhaktapur, and arrested him with equipment used for operating an illegal voice over internet protocol (VOIP) call centre, an illegal business in Nepal.
6	8 January 2013	Police arrested Maoist ex-combatant Nir Kumar Karki from Solukhumbu in connection with the murder of Fudorji Sherpa.
7	November 2012	VMLRs called for indefinite strikes in the eastern part of the country, affecting normal daily life.
8	16 October 2012	Ex-Maoist combatant Badri Pandey of Jevanpur Dhading arrested in Kathmandu with a pistol and two bullets.
9	September 2012	In Surkhet, police arrested two ex-combatants, Ramesh Thapa and Prem Bahadur Karki, on charges of stealing a motorbike.
10	April 2011	Ex-combatants from Yangshila cantonment terrorized and caused violence in the village near the camp.
11	April 2011	Ex-combatants from Yangshila mercilessly beat up villagers in Kerabari village.
12	January 2011	Police arrested five people who identified themselves as ex-combatants and have formed a criminal racket in the eastern part of the country.

(*Source:* Subedi, 2014a)

Increasing evidence of ex-combatants' involvement in post-conflict violence is a major concern for post-conflict crime prevention and public security. However, this is equally a political issue that also must be seen from the perspectives of re-mobilization of ex-combatants by their wartime mobilizers and other actors of crime and violence. Therefore, this issue would warrant a separate discussion, taking account of how the legacy of war penetrates into political mobilization and political activism in post-conflict Nepal.

Conclusion

Post-conflict crime and violence in Nepal is a complex phenomenon, conditioned and characterized by the emergence of new non-state actors of crime and violence and the political environment of war-to-peace transition. Ex-combatants, armed groups and youth gangs have emerged as "new actors" of crime and violence. Political youth groups and criminal gangs become immune to legal action as they were given political protection and in a way crime and politics have joined hands for sharing mutual benefits. Armed conflict has left a mark in such way that present-day violence can be seen as the residue of atrocities, direct violence and impunity that flourished during the Maoist conflict between 1996 and 2006. The country is still embroiled in social and identity conflicts inherited as an outcome of social, political and economic exclusion that the people from marginalized groups have suffered for ages. As is clearly seen in this chapter, crime and violence in the Terai region is driven by a complex mix of criminality and identity politics, with significant implications to policing and delivery of public security.

What aspects or drivers of crime and violence could be dealt with to maintain law and order and contain crime and violence? The answer to this is not straightforward because closely interlinked economic, institutional and political/social factors drive post-conflict crime and violence, posing challenges to security actors in terms of preventing and controlling crime and violence. War-induced urban growth and rural–urban migration has formed crowded cities with minimum economic opportunities for youth and urban poor. This is further complicated by lack of employment opportunity. The weak institutional capacity of the, police mainly due to effects of armed conflict and violence in the Terai, means that institutional strengthening cannot be overlooked. Politics, however, features prominently along the way, as political intervention in policing is partly a driver of growing crime and violence. This suggests that transformation towards an accountable political culture is as crucial as institutional strengthening of the police. Ideological underpinnings of political activism and mobilization are another set of factors that have produced multiple effects, from political protection of youth gangs to engaging youth in violent politics and aspirations to remobilization of ex-combatants. A complex mix of these different dimensions and drivers of crime and violence means that addressing crime and violence should be as much a securities endeavor as a political reform process.

Notes

1 Nepal was engulfed in an armed conflict between the Communist Party of Maoist Nepal (CPNM) and the government between 1996 and 2006. After signing the Comprehensive Peace Agreement (CPA) in November 2006, the Maoists are now in mainstream politics with their presence as the third-largest party in the Constitution Assembly, while a break- away faction of the Maoists led by Mohan Vaidhya boycotted the CA election. (For more on Maoist parties and Nepal's peace process see (ICG, 2009, 2011; Mishra, 2012; Subedi, 2014a.)

2 The military wing of the Maoists in the war.

3 On average, a homemade pistol can be bought at between 8,000 and 10,000 Nepali rupees (roughly 80 to 100 USD), while a sophisticated homemade gun (*KatuwaBanduk*) costs roughly NRS 20,000.

4 The districts with the lowest proportion of poor as a share of the respective district's population are Kaski (4%), Illam (7.3%), Lalitpur (7.6%), Kathmandu (7.6%) and Chitwan (8.9%). However, Kaski and Chitawan have higher rates of youth gang–led crime and violence.

5 It is worth noting here that young persons aged between 18 and 40 years of age are officially considered youth.

6 http://nepalpolice.gov.np/organization-structure.html

7 Author interview, February 2013.

8 Interview with a female respondent in Negpalgunj, January 2014.

9 Author interview, Kathmandu 2014.

10 For more about the idea of "bonded social" capital, see Putnam (1995).

11 Minors (child soldiers) born after May 25, 1988, or who joined the Maoist army after the cease-fire agreement on May 25, 2006, are considered disqualified ex-combatants. Later, the United Nations Inter-Agency Rehabilitation Programme (UNIRP) termed them Verified Minors and Late Recruits (VMLRs).

12 One US dollar is roughly equivalent to Nepali rupees 85.

13 Out of the 19,602 ex-combatants, 2,456 were missing, while 94 deaths were reported absent at the time of update and re-verification that took place in November–December 2011.

14 Interview with an ex-combatant, Chitwan, 2013.

15 Interview with an ex-combatant, Kohalpur, Banke district, 2013.

References

Adhikari, A., Gautam, B., Pudasaini, S., & Sharma, B. (2014). *Impunity and political accountability in Nepal*. Kathmandu: The Asia Foundation

Becker, G. S. (1968). Crime and punishment: An economic approach. *Journal of Political Economy, 76*(2), 169–217.

Belloni, R. (2009). Shades of orange and green: Civil society and peace process in Northern Ireland In M. Cox (Ed.), *Social capital and peace-building: Creating and resolving conflict with trust and social networks* (pp. 5–21). London and New York: Routledge.

Bryden, A., & Hanggi, H. (Eds.) (2005). *Security governance in post-conflict peacebuilding*. New Brunswick and London: Transaction Publishers.

Carter Centre. (2011). *Political party youth wings in Nepal*. Atlanta/Kathmandu: The Carter Centre. Retrieved from www.cartercenter.org/resources/pdfs/news/peace_publications/democracy/nepal-political-party-youth-wings-022811-en.pdf.

CBS. (2011). *The third Nepal living standard survey 2010/11*. Statistical Report Volume II. Kathmandu the Central Bureau of Statistics (CBS).

CBS. (2012). *National population and housing census 2011: National report* (Vol. 1). Kathmandu: Government of Nepal, National Planning Commission Secretariat, Central Bureau of Statistics (CBS).

Colletta, N. J., Kostner, M., & Wiederhofer, I. (1996). *Case studies in war-to-peace transition: The demobilization and reintegration of ex-combatants in Ethiopia, Namibia, and Uganda*. Washington, DC: World Bank.

Collier, P. (1994). Demobilization and insecurity: A study in the economics of the transition from war to peace. *Journal of International Development 6*(3), 343–351. doi: 10.1002/jid.3380060308.

Cramer, C. (2010). *Unemployment and participation in violence*. World Development Report 2011, Background Paper: School of Oriental and African Studies, London. https://openknowledge.worldbank.org/bitstream/handle/10986/9247/WDR2011_0022.pdf?sequence=1.

Crozier, R., Gunduz, C. & Subedi, D.B. (2010). *Private sector and public security: Perceptions and responses*. Kathmandu: National Business Initiative (NBI) and International Alert.

Deuba, A. R., & Rana, P. S. (2005). *A study on linkage between domestic violence and pregnancy*. Kathmandu: SAMANTA- Institute for Social & Gender Equity.

Ebo, A. (2005). Combating small arms proliferation and misuse after conflict. In A. Bryden & H. Hanggi (Eds.), *Security governance in post-conflict peacebuilding* (pp. 137–158). Geneva: Geneva Centre for the Democratic Control of Armed Forces (DCAF).

Ghimire, S., & Upreti, B. R. (2010). The post-conflict trojan horse: Upsurge of urban crimes as a challenge to state building. In *The remake of a state: Post-conflict challenges and state building in Nepal* (pp. 211–240). Kathmandu: NCCR North-South and Kathmandu University.

Gilbert, L. (2009). Analysing the dark side of social capital: Organised crime in Russia. In M. Cox (Ed.), *Social capital and peace-building: Creating and resolving conflict with trust and social networks* (pp. 57–74). London and New York: Routledge.

Hanggi, H. (2005). Approaching peacebuilding from a security governance perspective. In A. Bryden & H. Hanggi (Eds.), *Security governance in post-conflict peacebuilding* (pp. 3–19). New Brunswick and London: Transaction Publication.

Hirshleifer, J. (2001). *The dark side of the force: Economic foundations of conflict theory.* Cambridge: Cambridge University Press.

ICG. (2009). *Nepal's faltering peace process (Asia report no. 163).* Brussels and Kathamdu International Crisis Group (ICG).

ICG. (2010). *Nepal's political rites of passage (Asia report no. 194).* Kathmandu and Brussels: International Crisis Group (ICG).

ICG. (2011). *Nepal's fitful peace process.* Kathmandu/Brussel: International Crisis Group.

ILO. (2014). *Nepal labour market update.* Kathmandu: International Labour Organisation. Retrieved from www.ilo.org/wcmsp5/groups/public/—asia/—ro-bangkok/—ilo-kathmandu/documents/publication/wcms_322446.pdf.

Interdisciplinary Analysts, Nepal Madhesh Foundation, Small Arms Survey, & Saferworld. (2011). *Armed violence in the Terai.* Kathmandu www.smallarmssurvey.org/fileadmin/docs/E-Co-Publications/SAS-Saferworld-2011-armed-violence-in-the-Terai.pdf.

Karp, A. (2013). *Legacies of war in the company of peace: Firearms in Nepal. Nepal armed violence assessment issue brief no. 2.* Geneva: Small Arms Survey.

Lee, S. (1996). Poverty and violence. *Social Theory and Practice, 22,* 67–82.

Micolta, P. H. (2009). Illicit interest groups, social capital and conflict: A study of the FARC. In M. Cox (Ed.), *Social capital and peace-building: Creating and resolving conflict with trust and social networks* (pp. 75–91). London and New York: Routledge.

Mishra, B. P. (2012). *Revisiting the Nepalese peace process.* Kathmandu: Human Development and Peace Campaign (HUDEP) Nepal.

Moser, C., & Holland, J. (1997). *Urban poverty and violence in Jamaica.* Washington, DC: World Bank Publications.

Puri, M., Forst, M., Tamang, J., Lamichhnae, P., & Shah, I. (2012). The prevalence and determinants of sexual violence against young married women by husbands in rural Nepal. *BMC Research Notes, 5*(291), 1–13.

Putnam, R. D. (1995). Turning in, turning out: The strange disappearance of social capital in America. *PS: Political Science & Politics, 28*(4), 664–683.

Saferworld. (2012). *Perceptions of public security and crime in the Kathmandu valley.* Kathmandu: SaferWorld.

Steenkamp, C. (2005). The legacy of war: Conceptualizing a "Culture of Violence" to explain violence after peace accords. *The Round Table: The Commonwealth Journal of International Affairs, 94*(379), 253–267. doi: 10.1080/00358530500082775.

Subedi, D. B. (2011, January 23). Tackling insecurity in Terai. *Newspaper Opinion, My Republica.*

Subedi, D. B. (2014a). Dealing with ex-combatants in a negotiated peace process: Impacts of transitional politics on the DDR programme in Nepal. *Journal of Asian and African Studies, 49*(6), 672–689. doi: 10.1177/0021909613507537.

Subedi, D. B. (2014b). Ex-Combatants, security and post-conflict violence: Unpacking the experience from Nepal. *Millennial Asia: An International Journal of Asian Studies, 5*(1), 41–65. doi: 10.1177/0976399613518857.

Subedi, D. B. (2014c). *Forced donations, political funding and public security in Nepal: The private sector's perspectives and responses.* Kathmandu: National Business Initiative.

Subedi, D. B. (2014d). *Post-conflict recovery and peacebuilding in Nepal: Exploration of economic and social reintegration of Maoist ex-combatants* (Doctoral), University of New England.

Suhrke, A. (2012). The peace in between. In A. Suhrke & M. Berdal (Eds.), *The peace in between: Post-war violence and peacebuilding* (pp. 1–24). London and New York: Routledge.

Tranchant, J.-P. (2013). Addressing and mitigating violence: Unemployment, service provision and violence reduction policies in Urban Maharashtra. *Evidence report no. 17.* Institute of Development Studies. Retrieved from http://opendocs.ids.ac.uk/opendocs/bitstream/handle/123456789/2871/ER17%20Final%20Online%20v2.pdf?sequence.

Urdal, H. (2004). *The devil in the demographics: The effect of youth bulges on domestic armed conflict, 1950–2000: Conflict prevention & reconstruction. Paper no. 14.* Washington, DC: World Bank. Retrieved from www.eldis.org/vfile/upload/1/document/0708/DOC14714.pdf.

21

RELIGIOUS TERRORISM IN BANGLADESH

Patterns, Trends and Causes

Subrata Banarjee, Md. Shakhawat Hossain
and Mohammed Jahirul Islam

Introduction

Following the constitution and history of the liberation war, Bangladesh has been viewed as a moderate, democratic, secular state that has made tremendous changes in education, culture and economics and in human development. The political history reminds us that a large number of people sacrificed their lives for the freedom of the country. After the cruel incident of 1975 in which the father of the nation was killed brutally, the country faced some military and quasi-military rule. Finally, after the success of the democratic movement, democracy arrived in 1990. After that, Bangladesh managed to conduct four free and fair general elections in 1991, 1996, 2001 and 2008. Since then, Bangladesh has come in the line of economic and sustainable development (Zaman, 2012).

In the past, Bangladesh has faced a lot of multiple problems including chronic poverty, lack of education and health problems, natural disasters and a huge population, but terrorism was absent during that time. With the rise of global linkage, political patronage and revolution in the political sector, terrorism has evolved (Bajpai, 2002). Bangladesh has not experienced any terrorism since the birth of the country in 1971, but after some days, a group of leftist extremist parties committed some terrorist activities. At the same time, the terrorist and extremist groups have created a linkage with some militant groups in South, Southeast and West Asia (Roy, 2007).

Religious militancy and terrorism are inter-linked to one another. After the period of 1999, Bangladesh has experienced several terrorism attacks. Religious militancy groups, in August 2005, conducted a series of bomb attacks across the country. Surprisingly, the government of that period didn't take any proper steps to reduce such terrorist activities. It is reported by various news sources that the former political leaders might be patronizing the extremists' groups (Zaman, 2012).

Howell (2003) has identified four factors which analyze the reasons for growing terrorism: (i) increasing population; (ii) growing disparities in wealth and benefits; (iii) the expansion of religious terrorism; and (iv) advanced technology and access to it. On the other hand, Wilkinson (2005) has listed a wider range of causes: (i) states themselves; (ii) ethnic conflicts; (iii) groups believing in extreme-left ideology; (iv) groups espousing extreme-right ideology; and (v) religious fanaticism.

Roy (2007) points out that the Bengal Muslim search for a collective identity was clearly caught between the two opposite pulls of an extra-territorial Islamic ideology and of a local geographical Bengali culture. For the above causes, the religious terrorism increased. Riaz (2008) specified several reasons why the Islamist militant organizations have thrived. First, domestic politics have created an environment for their proliferation. Second, Bangladeshi state institutions are weak in certain geographical areas. Third, a new popular culture glorifies militancy, and fourth, they have received support from beyond the borders of Bangladesh. The origin and development of Islam and its proliferation divides on four dimensions: (a) immigration, (b) sword, (c) patronage, (d) social liberation (Barkat, 2006). This chapter deals with patterns, trends and causes of religious terrorism in Bangladesh.

This chapter uses secondary sources for collecting data. Due to security concerns in accessing the terrorist group and unavailability of official data, secondary sources have been mainly used for analysis. A content analysis of the secondary sources such as newspaper reports, internet publications, books, magazines, journal articles and intelligence documents has been done. The terrorist incidents from 1999 to 2001 in Bangladesh were taken into consideration and analyzed.

I. History of Religious Terrorism in Bangladesh

In 1971, Bangladesh finally achieved independence from Pakistan after a bloody, nine-month-long liberation war. An independent and secular Bangladesh became the only country in the sub-continent with one dominant language (called Bangla) and with very few ethnic and religious minorities. Present Bangladesh, as a state and a nation, inherits traditions and historical precedences of the Indian sub-continent. Most importantly, Bangladesh has a unique way of life that has evolved through time immemorial and has been based on a balanced mix of tradition, religion and culture (Chatterjee, 2010). Consequently, Bangladesh has long enjoyed a reputation as a secular Muslim country that is culturally more Bengali than Muslim.

Another terrorist organization also emerged soon after the birth of Bangladesh in the form of an insurgency movement. The political wing of the separatist insurgent group, Parbatya Chattagram Jana Shanghati Shamity (PCJSS), demanded autonomy, its own legislature on behalf of the people of Chittagong Hill Tracts (CHT), comprised primarily of three hill districts named Khagrachari, Rangamati and Bandarban. The government of Bangladesh rejected these demands, and as a consequence, the frustrated PCJSS leaders formed their party's armed wing, Shanti Bahini, and took up arms to struggle. With the exception of occasional cease-fires between the government and the insurgents, the insurgency continued for about 23 years. In 1997, a peace accord was signed between the PCJSS and the government of Bangladesh whereby the PCJSS agreed to surrender its weapons.

In 1998, Shantu Larma, the leader of the PCJSS, became the chairman of the CHT Regional Council, a post equivalent to a state minister, which he holds to date. Today, CHT is regularly finding its place in the print and electronic media due to the ongoing conflict between PCJSS and the United People's Democratic Front (UPDF), two opposing pro–and anti–peace-treaty rivals, respectively. Lack of political vision, criminals sheltered by political godfathers and corruption in law enforcement agencies gave birth to organized crime that jeopardized the country's overall law and order situation (Datta, 2003). Since 1991–92, a huge arrival of Rohingya refugees from Myanmar entered into the south-eastern part of the country and then spread across the country, as well as transnational insurgent groups moving to and fro from both neighbouring countries through unprotected inaccessible border areas, have all contributed to undermining the country's security situation (Sans, 2002). Even in the recent past, a huge cache of arms and explosives was confiscated at CHT.

The first major bomb blast in Bangladesh by religious fanatics took place on 7 March 1999, in a public cultural program at Jessore, a south-west district of Bangladesh. It killed 8 and injured about 100 and, most importantly, made a strong public statement on behalf of those fanatics (Rahman, 2005). Since then, there has been a major shift upwards in the tempo and style of terrorism. Between March 1999 and January 2005, militant Islamists killed at least 156 people in Bangladesh and injured more than 1,000 (Ali, 2006). Bombs were detonated mostly at secular cultural gatherings, courthouses and Sufi shrines. Notable ones among them were the bomb attacks at Chayanat program during celebration of the Bangla New Year on 14 April 2001 at Dhaka University, a bomb attack at the Ahmadiyya mosque, bomb-blasting Cinema Hall and a hand-grenade attack against the Bangladeshi-born British High Commissioner to Bangladesh (Roul, 2011).

A hand-grenade attack on 21 August 2004 on a political procession led by the country's opposition leader in the National Parliament (presently Prime Minister) was probably the worst of all. The bomb attack that shocked the country most was the blast of 17 August 2005, when 459 bombs exploded in 63 of the 64 districts in the country between 11:00 and11:30 a.m. This is the first time Jama'atul Mujahedeen Bangladesh (JMB), a nationally banned organization, claimed credit for the bomb blasts. In the leaflets, written in both Bangla and Arabic, found with the bomb devices, JMB claimed that it is time to implement Islamic law in Bangladesh. More militant actions immediately followed the simultaneous bomb blasts, and it created a reign of terror in the minds of the common people. Eventually, six militant leaders, including the JMB leader Sheikh Abdur Rahman, were arrested, put through judicial trial, and found guilty. On 30 March 2007 all of them were executed.

The JMB was reportedly in a shambles due to arrest of its present chief, Saidur Rahman, military wing chief, Shiblu, and acting chief Anwar Alam, Elias Nazmul, over a one-and-a-half-month period beginning on 12 July 2010. Our nearest country, India, has a long history of insurgency problems, especially in the states which are in close proximity to Bangladesh. India's Home Minister, Palaniappan Chidambaram, brought into focus the internal security of India at the conference of Chief Ministers on 17 August 2009 by saying that while militancy was on the decline in Jammu and Kashmir, the situation in the north-eastern states continues to remain volatile (*Zee News*, 2010). Assam, Manipur, Tripura, Nagaland, Mizoram, Meghalaya and Arunachal Pradesh, the seven states of northeastern India popularly known as Seven Sisters, have experienced a large number of armed and violent rebellions for a long time.

Additionally, Bangladesh is situated in the famous Crescent region and close to the Golden Triangle, both located in Myanmar. This makes it a transit point for the smuggling of heroin and illegal arms from Myanmar. From Bangladesh, communication to India, Pakistan and Afghanistan is quite easy. In the past, some students, mainly from religious education institutes (commonly known as Madrasa), of Bangladesh migrated to Pakistan and later moved to Afghanistan to join the Afghani Jihad in the proxy war against the then-Soviet invasion. Some also joined the same war by moving directly from Bangladesh. Many of them came back and apparently provided the backbone of JMB and other religious militant organizations in Bangladesh (Roy, 2010).

II. Patterns of Religious Terrorism in Bangladesh (1999–2011)

Figure 21.1 represents a range of terrorist activities in 1999. Most of the terrorist groups came from the Islam-based organization Jamaat-ul-Mujahideen Bangladesh. The most common terrorist

Table 21.1 Religious Terrorist Groups in Bangladesh

Year	JMB	HuJiB	JMJB	HuT	Chatroshibir	Extremist	Communist Party	Ethnic Group	Terrorist Group	Total
1999	0	2	0	2	1	4	0	0	1	10
2000	1	1	0	0	2	2	1	0	0	7
2001	7	3	8	2	1	3	0	2	4	30
2003	8	4	4	3	2	5	9	2	2	39
2004	5	3	2	3	2	1	3	2	2	23
2005	9	2	4	2	4	1	2	3	1	28
2006	2	0	1	1	1	1	0	0	2	8
2007	4	0	0	0	0	0	0	0	0	4
2008	0	0	0	1	0	0	3	0	2	6
2011	3	1	3	5	2	3	5	2	5	29
Total	39	16	22	19	15	20	22	11	19	184

(*Source:* The Daily Prothom Alo, The Daily Ittefaq, The Daily Jugantor, The Daily Star *1999–2011*)

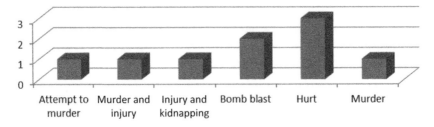

Figure 21.1 Types of terrorist attacks in 1999.

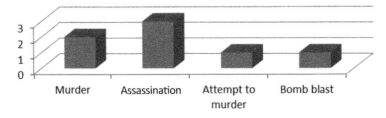

Figure 21.2 Types of terrorist attacks in 2000.

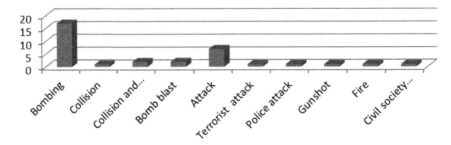

Figure 21.3 Types of terrorist attacks in 2001.

activity was bomb blast. After 1999, the number of bomb blastings increased at a larger rate. Attempt to murder, murder, injury, bomb blast and hurt were the common forms of terrorist activities of that period of time.

The maximum terrorist incident was assassination. At the same time, murder and attempt to murder had also been committed by the terrorist group Jamaat-ul-Mujahideen Bangladesh. In general, bomb blast and bombing (manually thrown bombs) were the major forms of terrorist incidents during the whole period.

During 2001 the rate of bombing activities increased over the previous year. Several terrorist groups of the border-based area also combined to commit crime. The use of firearms started in that period of time, and Bangladesh faced threats and violence. Bombing, collision, bomb blast, attack, terrorist attack, police attack, gunshot and gun firing were the most forms of terrorist incident in Bangladesh during 2001.

Figure 21.4 shows that bomb attack, murder, grievous hurt, slaughtering, collision, stabbing, attack and threat were the major forms of terrorist attack during 2003.

In 2004, several terrorist attacks occurred in Bangladesh. The grenade attack on the procession of Awami League (AL) was a great success for the Jamaat-ul-Mujahideen Bangladesh (JMB), a terrorist

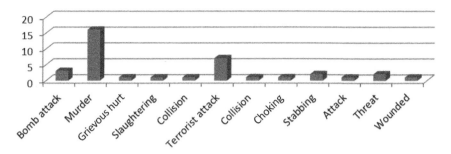

Figure 21.4 Types of terrorist attacks in 2003.

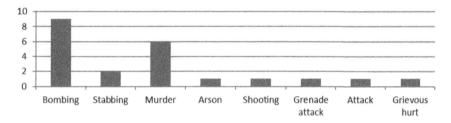

Figure 21.5 Types of terrorist attacks in 2004.

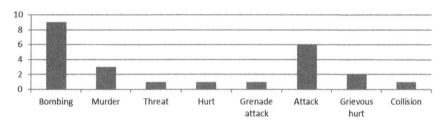

Figure 21.6 Types of terrorist attacks in 2005.

organization. JMB also colloborated with several unknown foreign organizations for establishing Islamic Rule in Bangladesh. This group's members are well trained in making grenades and attacking people with grenades. They have attacked several police stations with firearms and weapons. They have also motivated several innocent people to join their group and generally people are afraid of them.

During 2005, money laundering, human trafficking and attacks on the general public also increased. By their terror activities, the terrorist group JMB showed their power. The bombing on 17 August 2005 in the whole of Bangladesh caused a great harm to the security system of Bangladesh. The terrorist group attacked 63 districts at a fixed time. This kind of collective bombing killed a large number of people. Notably, the government also protected the terrorist group as the terrorist group's ideology was similar to the party in power.

The number of terrorist activities decreased tremendously during 2006 compared to previous years. The government took several counter-terrorism steps and the number of terrorist incidents decreased. However, the methods of terrorist attacks changed and a cinema theater was attacked where many people were killed.

During 2007, the nature and pattern changed frequently, in which activities gathered more profit for the terrorist group that committed these types of crime. Political power and political conflict existed in that period. The leader of the terrorist group tried to understand the motive of the general

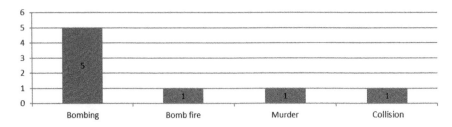

Figure 21.7 Types of terrorist attacks in 2006.

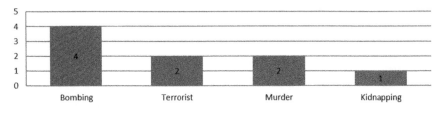

Figure 21.8 Types of terrorist attacks in 2007.

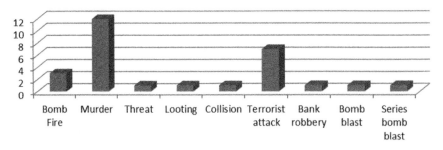

Figure 21.9 Types of terrorist attacks in 2011.

public. Finance from several countries created a strong position for the terrorist group. JMB tried to motivate the people by publishing and writing religious-based documents. The Rapid Action Battalion (RAB) responds effectively to counter religious-based terrorism in Bangladesh. RAB arrested the leader of the terrorists and found out the origin and financial activities. After seeing them, the government stopped the bank account of the terrorist leader so that the party's members didn't get any more support from the party.

In 2011, hazardous activities occurred, perpetrated by the members of the terrorist group. However, the incidence of bombing decreased. Invention of new techniques for committing illegal activities increased. With online communications the Bangladesh terror groups were able to create new pathways of terror attacks. Domestic and international strategies were applied to combat terrorism-related activities from Bangladesh. Looting and series bomb blasts were the new forms of terrorist incidents in Bangladesh. The government used modern weapons and tactics to fight against terrorist groups.

III. Trends of Terrorist Attacks in Bangladesh (1999–2011)

From the above discussion, we can see that most of the terrorist activities occurred during the period between 2001 and 2005. The network of the terrorist organization was linked outside the country. A favourable socio-political environment of violence, criminalization of politics, sympathy

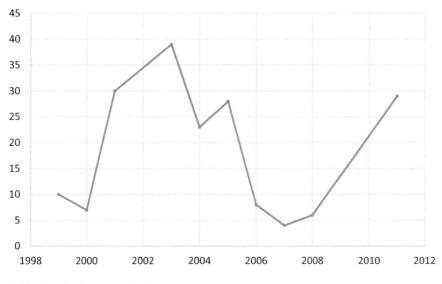

Figure 21.10   Trends of terrorist attacks.

(*Source*: The Daily Prothom Alo, The Daily Ittefaq, The Daily Jugantor, The Daily Star, *1999–2011*)

to Islamist militants, glorifying Islamists militants in the popular culture were the main factors that were responsible for the increase in the religious-based terrorism in the country (Riaz, 2008). But when the secularist government came to power in the country, they tried to take steps against the extremist groups with a strong hand.

IV. Causes of Terrorist Activities in Bangladesh

The causes of Terrorist activities in Bangladesh are: 1. Jihad, 2. establish Islamic rule, 3. to create fear, 4. to establish an Islamic State and 5. financing religious terrorism.

1. Jihad

The major religious-based organizations think that with jihad, they will establish a religious-based country. So they sacrifice their lives by suicide bombing, bomb blast and bomb explosion. The leader of the organization motivates the ordinary members of the party to become jihad. Jihad is the major cause of religious terrorism in Bangladesh. The persons who commit jihad think they are closer to God by becoming involved in such activities.

2. Establish Islamic Rule

The majority of the people of Bangladesh are Muslims. So the terrorist group wants to create Islamic rule in the country, but they do it in an illegal way.

3. To Create Fear

The major terrorist group tries to inform everyone about their presence in the country. They commit illegal activities in the society. Creating fear is one of the valuable activities or primary steps of doing terrorist activities.

Table 21.2 Terror Financing

Name of Organization	Financed By
JMB	England, Saudi Arabia, Pakistan, Libya, Kuwait
Extremists	Money laundering
Chatro Shibir	Money Laundering, Charitable fund. Pakistan, Saudi Arab, Muslims NGO
JMJB	Funds collected from Zakat
Communist Party	Ransom, extortion, contract killing
HUJIB	Afghanistan, Arabs, Pakistan
Terrorist Group	Communist Party of India, China, extortion, ransom
Ethnic Group	Extortion
Hizb-ut Tahir	UK, Pakistan militant group

(*Source:* SATP, 2011)

4. To Establish an Islamic State

Islam can't bear any illegal activities, but the terrorist group tries to establish an Islamic state in an illegal way. The people of Bangladesh are peace loving; however, terrorist groups do not want peace and they kill innocent people to achieve their goal of establishing an Islamic state.

5. Financing of Religious Terrorism

Due to the rise of terrorism globally, terrorist organizations find it easier now to transfer funds between them. Day by day, it is easier to close together by using modern communication systems and creating ties among the global militant groups (Azad, 2009). The leaders of the militant group shared their beliefs and attitudes with some of the Muslim countries including Iraq, Kuwait, Iran and Saudi Arabia. Some of the Bangladeshi citizens, those who are living in the UK and USA, also donated money for militant activities. Otherwise, the militant parties' members received funds from different sources like sadka, jakat and membership fees.

Conclusion

Since independence, Bangladesh has faced some internal and external security challenges. Leftist movement in the north and south-western part of the country and ethnicity-based insurgency movements in the south-eastern part of the country have marked the security dynamics from the beginning of its existence. Involvement of neighboring states in supporting the insurgency movement, spread-out effects of their own problems and the close proximity of Bangladesh to known drug and illegal arms routes through Myanmar all have negatively affected the country's security situation.

The terrorist group members are well trained and use technological equipment for terrorist activities. On the other side, Bangladesh has an inadequately staffed and equipped police force and a moderate standing military to combat terrorism. The police force is inadequate in number, and they suffer from a credibility crisis among the general populace. The elite police force RAB may be utilized for special and focused operations. Rapid modernization of the relatively large force may not be possible immediately.

Bangladesh needs to take counter-terrorism measures nationally, regionally and internationally. When facing a common problem like terrorism, countries should put aside their differences and work together. There are bi-lateral and multi-lateral issues among the countries in the South Asia region. Sharing of intelligence and expertise to counterterrorism may prove to be vital in the future. Participation of the general populace in the fight against terrorism is the most important parameter for a sustained effort leading to success.

Bangladesh should also adopt a counter-terrorism strategy that utilizes all elements of national power simultaneously—judicially and systematically—to fight terrorism. In this comprehensive national strategy, use of military and security forces will continue to provide a deterrent and disruptive effect. Initially, Bangladesh will need to prepare its military and security forces to disrupt, in the process degrade and finally uproot the existing terrorism and terrorist organizations from the country.

Preparing the military and security forces would mean reorganizing them and making them capable of countering terrorism. In the event of scarcity of manpower at district level, a small group from the military may be assigned in the capacity as RAB or other police force to each district to form the nucleus of the special operation force. The use of helicopter gunships, aerial operations and real-time monitoring of an area of operation by satellite round the clock may need to be added to existing operational capabilities by the military. There must be improvements in surveillance in terms of technology and human intelligence, investigation and interrogation capability of the military and security forces. These efforts may need to be supplemented by advanced interception, forensic analysis and capability to counter cybercrime.

Police and paramilitary forces may be utilized to protect key infrastructures. Critical government sectors such as transportation, public health and telecommunication may be directed to build an indigenous security mechanism. Every key sector should be self-sufficient in providing first-degree security to its own infrastructures. The military and police forces can provide training and preparation for their staffs for indigenous security needs. However, a public sense of protection should be promoted throughout the country to reduce the burden on police and paramilitary forces. Protection of land and maritime borders is vitally important for the physical protection of the country. Border Guards Bangladesh and Bangladesh Coast Guard must be adequately staffed and equipped to ensure protection of the country from illegal weapon trafficking, smuggling and drug dealing.

References

Ali, S. (2006). *Faces of terrorism in Bangladesh.* Dhaka: The University Press Limited.

Azad, A. K. (2009). Funding terrorism: Can it be stopped? In I. Ahmed (Ed.), *Terrorism in the 21st century: Perspectives from Bangladesh.* Dhaka: The University Press Limited.

Bajpai, K. P. (2002). *Roots of terrorism.* New Delhi: Penguin Books.

Barkat, A. (2006). Economics of fundamentalism and the growth of political Islam in Bangladesh. *Social Science Review, The Dhaka University Studies, 23*(2).

Chatterjee, P. (2010). *A story of ambivalent modernization in Bangladesh and West Bengal. The rise and fall of Bengali Elitism in South Asia.* New York: Peter Lang Publishing Inc.

Datta, S. (2003). Bangladesh's political evolution: Growing Uncertainties. *Journal of the Institute of the Defense Studies and Analyses, 27*(2), 233–249.

Howell, W. G. (2003). *Power without Persuasion: The politics of direct presidential action.* Princeton, NJ: Princeton University Press.

Rahman, Z. (2005). Terrorism, the case of Bangladesh. *Paper presented at first bi-annual international symposium of the Center for Asian Terrorism Research (CATR),* Denpensar, Bali, Indonesia, October 19–21, 2005.

Riaz, A. (2008). *Islamist Militancy in Bangladesh, a complex web.* New York: Routledge.

Roul, A. (2011, January 28). Terror and politics. Lashkar-e-Taiba, HuJI and assassinations in Bangladesh. *Asia Security Initiative.*

Roy, A. (2007). *Islam in history and politics, perspective from South Asia.* New Delhi, Oxford University Press.

Roy, B. (2010). A brief anatomy of Bangla terrorism South Asia Analysis Group. Retrieved from www.southasiaanalysis.org/%5Cpapers27%5Cpaper2623.html.

Sans, M. F. (2002, March). *10 years for the Rohingya refugees in Bangladesh: Past, present and future.* Holland: Medecins Sans Frontieres.

South Asia Terrorism Portal. (2011). Terror financing. Retrieved from www.satp.org.

Wilkinson, P. (2005). *Root causes of terrorism: Myths, reality and ways forward.* New York: Routledge.

Zaman, R. U. (2012). Bangladesh-between terrorism identity and illiberal democracy: The Unfolding of a tragic Saga. *Perception, XVII*(3), 151–177.

Zee News. (2010). Terrorism, nexalism, insurgency continue to threaten India.

PART IV

Crime and Justice Policies

22

HUMAN TRAFFICKING IN SOUTH ASIA

Regional Cooperation and Responses

Zahid Shahab Ahmed

Introduction

Poverty has a direct link with some social evils, especially human trafficking. It has been reported in the *Human Security Report* (HSC, 2005) that the victims of trafficking mostly belong to countries suffering from weak or corrupt governments, economic downfall, social upheaval, organised crime and violent/civil conflicts. The same report goes on, claiming that "poverty appears to be the single most significant driver of human trafficking" (HSC, 2005, p. 88). Most commonly, the victims of trafficking are women and children. Therefore, inter-governmental agencies, such as the United Nations, have been stressing the need to strengthen laws against human trafficking in South Asia for the protection of women and children.

The SAARC (South Asian Association for Regional Cooperation) region and its people have been exposed to heinous crimes, particularly trafficking in women and children for prostitution. It appears that there are cross-border linkages between the groups trafficking women and children into sex industries in South Asia and beyond. Although there is no exact estimate of the number of people trafficked from South Asia, according to an estimate, 150,000 people are trafficked from the region annually, mostly women and children. Most of those trafficked are transported to the Middle East and Southeast Asia, among other regions (UNODC, 2008, p. 8). The victims are mostly lured by promises of good jobs, or good marriages for example with a rich Arab, or recruitment in the film industry. Nonetheless, there is a demand for cheap labour in different parts of the world, and rackets of human traffickers, by exploiting people in poor countries, meet the needs of that demand. According to some estimates, internationally, human traffickers make roughly US$32 billion (Thakuria, 2007).

It is important to find out how traffickers operate locally and regionally in South Asia. From a 2007 operation in Sri Lanka, in which 20 children were protected from being trafficked to Singapore, it has been found that there are groups operating in the region with strong extra-regional linkages (HT, 2007). There are groups also operating within the region for intra-regional human trafficking. According to an estimate, 25,000 women and children from Bangladesh and 15,000 from Nepal are trafficked to India annually (Thakuria, 2007). There are no estimates available to tell how many usually stay in India in transit to some other destination, in either the Gulf countries or Southeast Asia.

Table 22.1 shows where the victims of human trafficking from South Asia end up being exploited, tortured and abused.

Table 22.1 Destinations for the Victims of Trafficking From South Asia

Country	Destinations
Afghanistan	Pakistan, Iran, India, Slovenia, Greece
Bangladesh	India, Pakistan, Middle East
India	Middle East
Nepal	India, Middle East, Southeast Asia (Malaysia, Hong Kong and South Korea)
Pakistan	Middle East, Iran
Sri Lanka	Middle East, the Maldives

(*Source:* DOS, 2011, pp. 32–33)

The figures of human trafficking, either intra-regionally or inter-regionally, show the gravity of this problem in South Asia. Considering the nature of the crime, the South Asian countries have no other option but to cooperate with each other in eliminating human trafficking in all its forms.

Regional Cooperation Against Human Trafficking

To date human trafficking, is perhaps the only issue that was taken on its agenda by the South Asian Association for Regional Cooperation (SAARC)[1] due to a strong advocacy campaign led by civil society groups and NGOs in South Asia. This could be because, at the beginning of SAARC, the idea was to keep the contentious or sensitive issues aside and let the process move on with a strong foundation of consensus in softer areas of cooperation—human security. Another reason for the lack of the participation of NGOs was and largely has been the over-bureaucratic system of SAARC, which predominantly allows the governments to propose, permit and implement projects in different areas.

SAARC could not avoid engaging in cooperation in sensitive issues, because terrorism was taken up by SAARC as an important agenda in 1987, even though terrorism often has been an issue triggering tensions between India and Pakistan—the two biggest SAARC members. After deliberations at various levels, the SAARC Regional Convention on Suppression of Terrorism was signed at the Third SAARC Summit held in Kathmandu in 1987. This created a scope for cooperation at SAARC against transnational crimes, and some hope in the civil society and NGO circles that they can push for their agenda via SAARC.

By virtue of their nature, collective actions against human trafficking demand cooperation of agencies dealing with state security, such as armed forces, law enforcement agencies, intelligence agencies and so on. This issue therefore has implications for bilateral relations too, especially in the case of India and Pakistan, having a history of four wars and intelligence agencies launching missions against the other country. Considering the political situation of the region, it was a big move that there was an agreement against terrorism.

There were strong efforts from the civil society to guide the SAARC process of issues, such as human trafficking. In the early 1990s, NGOs from India, Pakistan and Bangladesh lobbied for a declaration on the issue of human trafficking to be passed through the SAARC. More specifically in 1996, NGOs from India, Pakistan, Sri Lanka and Nepal created a coalition against trafficking in women and children. In this regard, the *Unnayan Bikalper Nitinirdharoni Gobeshona* (UBINIG)[2] of Bangladesh organised a regional workshop of NGOs working in this area to define the course of action for lobbying at SAARC. But processes at SAARC were sluggish to respond to the advocacy led by NGOs (Akhter, 1999). Consequently, the coalition of NGOs speeded up lobbying because they wanted this issue to be on the SAARC agenda for the scheduled Ninth Summit to be held in the Maldives in 1997.

Prior to the summit in the Maldives, women's groups (NGOs) also produced a common position paper for the SAARC countries. Lobbying was greatly successful because members of NGOs from Bangladesh, India and Nepal met the heads of state in their respective countries and informed them of the severity of the problem of human trafficking in the region (Akhter, 1999). The effectiveness of the lobbying was manifested in the declaration of the Ninth SAARC Summit, which for the first time acknowledged trafficking in women and children as a serious social problem (SAARC, 2008a, p. 114). In addition, at the summit a decision was made to do a feasibility study of cooperation on eliminating human trafficking via SAARC.

Because the SAARC process was still slow to finalise and sign the convention against human trafficking, NGOs moved ahead with more advocacy campaigns and lobbying. In this regard, notable is the example of the SAARC People's Forum (Colombo, 1998). At the forum, the main issue was to stop SAARC from limiting the scope of the prospective convention to only trafficking in women and children for prostitution, because a whole range of other issues, mainly labour, causes human trafficking. They were basically the *RESISTENCE* Network members from South Asia, the premier South Asian anti-trafficking network, who lobbied for a comprehensive convention to deal with human trafficking in the region, but these efforts proved to be unfruitful because at the Tenth SAARC Summit (Colombo, 1998), heads of state stressed the finalisation of the draft text of the Regional Convention on Combating Trafficking in Women and Children for Prostitution. Also, the leaders approved the convention to be signed at the Eleventh SAARC Summit (SAARC, 2008a, p. 141). Nonetheless, NGOs kept on lobbying the convention to be named at a SAARC Convention on Preventing and Combating Trafficking in Women and Children.

At the time when there were hopes of getting the convention drafted and ratified by the SAARC member states, the geopolitical environment of the region changed. The issue was then pushed to the back burner, because terrorism occupied the centre stage after the 9/11 incident and the 2001 terrorist attack on the Indian Parliament. It was during this time that the Eleventh SAARC Summit was postponed until 2002—a delay of three years. However, as soon as the SAARC process recovered to its routine affairs in 2002, the SAARC Convention on Preventing and Combating Trafficking in Women and Children for Prostitution was signed at the Eleventh SAARC Summit (Kathmandu, 2002) in accordance with the commitment of the heads of state at the Tenth SAARC Summit (SAARC, 2008a, p. 154). However, the convention entered into force only after it was ratified by all the member states in November 2005 (MADADGAAR, 2007).

The late ratification of or even hesitation in committing to multilateral agreements is not an exclusive phenomenon at SAARC. The responses of SAARC members towards the United Nations Convention against Transnational Organised Crime, implemented in 2003, also show mixed levels of commitments at the global level. Afghanistan, Bangladesh, India, Pakistan and Sri Lanka, are the SAARC members to have ratified the UN convention. Nepal has only signed, it and Bhutan and the Maldives have not even signed the convention. Further going into details, only India has ratified the following agreements: Protocol to Prevent, Suppress and Punish Trafficking in Persons, Especially Women and Children, supplementing the United Nations Convention against Transnational Organised Crime (implemented in 2003); and the Protocol against the Smuggling of Migrants by Land, Sea and Air, supplementing the United Nations Convention against Transnational Organised Crime (implemented in 2004). But New Delhi ratified these two UN agreements in 2011. Since December 2000, Sri Lanka is only a signatory to both protocols (UNODC, 2011). This in a way show that SAARC members feel the complexity of any multilateral cooperation against transnational crimes, either regional or global; therefore, hesitate to even commit to certain agreements forcing them to make reforms and actions at domestic levels. Nonetheless, the ratification of UN conventions would be complementary to the work of SAARC in this area.

It is important to underscore that through this action, the SAARC became the first regional body to have produced a treaty against trafficking—three years ahead of the European convention on this issue.[3] The convention is really a step in the right direction because it demonstrates the member states' commitment to the overall welfare of women and children by protecting them against heinous crimes, such as trafficking. Through the agreement, the members are asked to put curbs on employment agencies facilitating trafficking. There is focus on both prevention and protection with even a clause urging the member states to promote awareness of the problem of trafficking in women and children through media programmes (SAARC, 2002, pp. 2–3).

The convention has come under criticism due to its limited scope and incomprehensive definition of "trafficking", which according to Article 1 of the convention "means the moving, selling or buying of women and children for prostitution within and outside a country for monetary or other considerations with or without the consent of the person subjected to trafficking" (SAARC, 2002, p. 1). On the other hand, the civil society groups and NGOs have been demanding the definition to be changed to the following: "all acts involved in the recruitment, transportation, forced movement and/or settling and buying of women and children within and/or across borders by fraudulent means, deception, coercion, direct and/or indirect threats, abuse or authority for the purpose of placing a woman and/or child against her/his will with or without her/his consent in exploitation and abusive situations, such as, forced prostitution, marriage, bonded slavery and slavery like practices, begging, organ trade, drug smuggling, use in armed conflict, etc." (Raghuvanshi, 2002, p. 3). The later definition is adapted from the UN Protocol to Prevent, Suppress and Punish Trafficking in Persons, Especially Women and Children, supplementing the United Nations Convention against Transnational Organised Crime.[4]

Since the development and approval of the contention, civil society groups and NGOs have been unhappy with this tokenistic move of SAARC. If, on the one hand, some NGOs limited their response to suggested policy recommendation and workshops, others like the South Asian March against Child Trafficking (India) have been proactively campaigning against SAARC. An example of that is the demonstration organised by the organisation, involving hundreds of former child victims of trafficking, bonded and child labour, to question the relevance of the SAARC convention/actions against human trafficking. The group stated that the SAARC promises on this issue have been "inadequate and undelivered" (SAMACT, 2007). At this event, Kailash Satyarthi,[5] the leader of the march, said, "If SAARC cannot tackle the most heinous organised crime of human trafficking with adequate political will and honesty, what else can we expect for the rituals of annual SAARC summits . . . children from Bangladesh are bought and sold like animals" (SAMACT, 2007).

The agreement of cooperation against trafficking in women and children has been around for over eight years, and still not much has been done to take actions against networks responsible for human trafficking in South Asia and beyond. In addition, SAARC is yet to create an institution to implement the collective mission stated in the convention against trafficking. Nonetheless, the Task Force was created in response to the directions provided by the heads of state in the declaration of the Eleventh SAARC Summit (Kathmandu, 2002) to monitor the evaluation of cooperation in this area (SAARC, 2008a, pp. 154–155). The Task Force met in 2007, 2008, 2009 and 2010. There have been agreements on sharing of relevant information by the governments and NGOs, but nothing has happened yet. Moreover, during a special session of the Task Force held in 2010, it was decided to establish two regional toll-free help lines dedicated to help the victims of trafficking in the region. It is an interesting action-oriented development but was not launched until September 2011 (SAARC, 2011).

Considering some NGOs in the SAARC region have expertise in the area of preventing human trafficking and rehabilitation of the victims of this crime, SAARC has engaged them in implementing its agenda. SAARC also realises that it was due to the lobbying of certain NGOs that led the organisation to take up this issue on its agenda. Therefore, the task force responsible to implement the convention has been a forum of interaction among government officials and the members of relevant NGOs from all the member states. For example, for the meeting in July 2007 held in New Delhi, Pakistan was represented by a member of the Federal Investigation Authority and the head of the Lawyers for Human Rights and Legal Aid (LHRLA). The involvement of the civil society groups could be the reason that the meeting concluded on a clear action plan. It was decided that information on best practices would be shared by both government agencies and NGOs to combat trafficking with the SAARC Secretariat by November 2007 and afterwards annually (MADADGAAR, 2007). This has not happened yet and is due to no follow-up being conducted by the SAARC Secretariat, which has a limited staff. Therefore, SAARC needed to hand over the task to proactive NGOs working in this area, and such an institute could be funded under the Social Window of the SAARC Development Fund (SDF) (Lama, 2008, p. 15).

At the 2007 meeting of the task force, another decision was made that the government of India would prepare a Standard of Operating Procedure (SOP) to implement various provisions of the convention and would share it with the SAARC Secretariat by September 2007. New Delhi has not developed an SOP as of September 2011 (MADADGAAR, 2007). Without an SOP, the convention will remain unimplemented because there are no additional details available, for example, related to the repatriation of victims. Those details are crucial for both government bodies and NGOs because that will allow them to approach relevant authorities across the region.

SAARC Against Transnational Crimes

Even though not exclusively against human trafficking, SAARC has been engaged in cooperation or dialogues at various levels to expand the scope of its cooperation against a variety of transnational crimes, such as terrorism, drug smuggling, piracy, and human trafficking. It is, therefore, worth having a look into those processes to find out where the cooperation is heading.

Cooperation against human trafficking in general and trafficking in women and children specifically is yet to show any signs of significant regional measures in this area. This could be because this issue is still considered a social/gender issue at the SAARC Secretariat; therefore, it falls under the realm of the Social Affairs Division and not the one dealing with security aspects. Nonetheless, human trafficking is an important aspect of SAARC meetings on security matters, especially conferences of police chiefs and ministerial meetings, as will be discussed later. However, due to the issue of trafficking still being labelled as a social issue, the task force has not been included in meetings of police chiefs and other security-/law enforcement-related dialogues.

The cooperation in criminal matters has moved on, not only through bodies responsible for data collection and dissemination on terrorism and drug smuggling, namely the SAARC Terrorism Offenses Monitoring Desk (STOMD), and the SAARC Drug Offenses Monitoring Desk (SDOMD), but also with the help of an Expert Group on Networking among Police Authorities. This group has been responsible for monitoring the progress of both STOMD and SDOMD and cooperation in other related matters. From 1996 until 2010, SAARC has organised eight meetings on cooperation among police of the member states. In 2008, at the Seventh Conference of SAARC on Cooperation in Police Matters held in Islamabad, a range of critical issues was discussed, such as terrorism, human trafficking, organised crime, drug trafficking, money laundering, police training, police reforms and SAARCPOL. This is just the beginning, because police institutions are only responsible to domestically tackle crimes, and therefore at later stages the cooperation amongst border security forces will be crucial to restrict the movement of criminals within the SAARC region.

All the above -mentioned SAARC mechanisms have collaborated to address inter-related matters such as the production and smuggling of drugs with a view that these illegal crimes are also sources of funding for terrorist groups in South Asia (Rosand, Fink,& Ipe, 2009, p. 8). This depicts that SAARC bodies are networking amongst themselves to launch comprehensive measures against collective issues faced by the SAARC countries. The issue of arms smuggling has appeared in high-level meetings, but only with reference to the availability of weapons to terrorists. However, cooperation against drug trafficking has been present in the SAARC agenda for more than two decades.

SAARC has constantly been progressing to expand its agenda on cooperation in criminal matters. In April 2008, the first biannual conference of SAARC Police Chiefs was organised in Islamabad, at which a range of issues was discussed, including SAARCPOL, STOMD and SDOMD. In this regard, at the Fifteenth SAARC Summit held in Colombo in 2008, the SAARC Convention on Mutual Legal Assistance in Criminal Matters was signed (SAARC, 2008b, p. 210). If cooperation among the law enforcement agencies succeeds to progress, then it is likely that the much serious issue of terrorism will also be address, because STOMD has a potential to become an early-warning mechanism with the SAARC region (Rosand, Fink, & Ipe, 2009, p. 8).

The proposal on SAARCPOL—a replica of EUROPOL or INTERPOL—has initiated the government of Nepal, and the idea is to create a regional organisation on the lines of INTERPOL in Europe. If the SAARCPOL project manages to obtain approval at the SAARC summit level, then surely it will boost the process of identity formation in South Asia, which will be in addition to comprehensive cooperation among the security agencies of the SAARC member states. However, in the present climate of virtually no trust between India and Pakistan, it seems unlikely that the SAARCPOL proposal will see reality, at least in the near future.

The ideas of SAARCPOL and a Security Organisation for South Asia (SOSA), the latter presented by Naik (2004), have been considered too early for the SAARC because these involve a comprehensive cooperation of security agencies. In this regard, the issue of cooperation among intelligence agencies is likely to become a bone of contention, especially when such organisations have designed and launched terrorist activities in neighbouring countries, such is the case of India and Pakistan (Naik, 2004, p. 9). There is an example of INTERPOL-like bodies at sub-regional levels being productive in Africa with practical cooperation among law-enforcing agencies through a 24/7 communications network (Naik, 2004, p. 9). Therefore, there are higher hopes with SAARCPOL that it could boost cooperation in security matters with the SAARC region. There has been no agreement reached in the Ninth SAARC Police Conference on Cooperation in Police Matters to establish SAARCPOL. It is important to mention that the proposal of SAARCPOL is under discussion among the police chiefs for the past five meetings, but with no further moves (Radhakrishnan, 2011). Constant deliberations on the same proposal show the level of difficulty of cooperation in this area, especially when setting up of an institution demand changes in domestic legal frameworks.

In recent years, the cooperation against transnational crimes has captured the centre stage at the SAARC, and this is evident through high-level meetings. Since 2006, meetings of the SAARC interior/home ministers are taking place, as these are the persons with highest authority on domestic security issues. Therefore there is a greater likelihood of some serious practical measures against crimes bothering South Asia. Until 2010, there have been three meetings of the SAARC interior/ home ministers. At the third meeting held in Islamabad in 2010, the SAARC ministers adopted the Islamabad SAARC Ministerial Statement on Cooperation against Terrorism. In the statement, ministers emphasised the need for greater cooperation and the linkages between various crimes, such as terrorism, illegal trafficking in drugs and psychotropic substances, illegal trafficking of persons and arms, and threats to maritime security (SAARC, 2010, p. 1). Prior to this in 2009, the ministers had also demanded for the urgent ratification of the SAARC Convention on Mutual Legal Assistance in Criminal Matters (signed at the Fifteenth SAARC Summit, Colombo in 2008) through the SAARC Ministerial Declaration on Cooperation in Combating Terrorism (2009).

In the security sector, the cooperation has mostly been restricted to consensus building—more words and fewer actions. Reaching an agreement on controversial issues, such as terrorism, has definitely been time-consuming at the SAARC. Consequently, the actions have been delayed too. Cooperation in the security areas has to reach up to the level of practical measures, beyond merely sharing of information. However, through cooperation in criminal matters, such as terrorism, drug smuggling and human trafficking, the SAARC has a practical opening of transition towards developing a security orientation of its own, which could be welcomed by its member states.

Even though the meetings of police chiefs, interior ministers and so on look promising for a comprehensive SAARC convention on cooperation in criminal matters, there is still a loophole with reference to the exclusion of the task force dealing with the issue of human trafficking from these processes. Human trafficking is also a security and a legal matter; therefore, it needs to be integrated into ongoing SAARC dialogues on other security aspects.

SAARC is expanding the scope of deliberations on transnational crimes by suggesting more issues at the dialogue tables. This could be because the officials at SAARC want at least the process of consensus building in this area to move on, irrespective of collective actions against transnational crimes. Nonetheless, consensus on important issues like human trafficking has to be based on a rational approach. In 2010, the International Organization for Migration (IOM) reviewed SAARC Convention on Human Trafficking and put forward the following recommendations: there is a need to expand the scope of the document and legal definitions in the Convention; there should be an independent monitoring process for evaluating the process of the Convention; increased cooperation among SAARC countries should emerge from harmonization of domestic trafficking definitions, laws and punishments (IOM, 2010). If SAARC countries are serious in addressing the problem of human trafficking, then they should really act upon the recommendations from IOM as a basic requirement.

Conclusion

It is a significant development at SAARC that an agenda promoted by civil society groups and NGOs, though only partly, was adopted by SAARC. However, still NGOs want the SAARC convention dealing with human trafficking to be comprehensive in scope by covering all aspects of human trafficking and not just prostitution. This is because the majority of women and children in South Asia are trafficked for cheap labour, both within and outside the region. It is also a good development that representatives of NGOs are included in the Task Force, but their role has to be expanded to take care of the major portion of the implementation of the convention. Nonetheless, the incomprehensive SAARC processes have delayed the complete execution of the convention, because it is still labelled as a merely social issue. Thus, it is excluded from cooperation under SAARC in the areas of security and law enforcement. To complement its regional agenda, SAARC via India, which has ratified the UN legal frameworks dealing with human trafficking, could encourage other member states to commit to global conventions.

Notes

1 SAARC was established in 1985 and currently has the following eight members: Afghanistan, Bangladesh, Bhutan, India, the Maldives, Nepal, Pakistan and Sri Lanka.
2 Unnayan Bikalper Nitinirdharoni Gobeshona (UBINIG) stands for Policy Research for Development Alternatives. UBINIG has branches across Bangladesh, but its first office was opened in Dhaka in 1984.
3 The Council of Europe produced convention on Action against Trafficking in Human Beings in 2005.
4 According to the UN protocol, the following is the definition of human trafficking: "'Trafficking in persons' shall mean the recruitment, transportation, transfer, harbouring or receipt of persons, by means of the threat or use of force or other forms of coercion, of abduction, of fraud, of deception, of the abuse of power or of a position of vulnerability or of the giving or receiving of payments or benefits to achieve the consent of a person having control over another person, for the purpose of exploitation. Exploitation shall include, at a minimum, the exploitation of the prostitution of others or other forms of sexual exploitation, forced labour or services, slavery or practices similar to slavery, servitude or the removal of organs" (UNODC, 2004, p. 42).
5 Kailash Satyarthi is a renowned child rights campaigner from India who shared the 2014 Nobel Peace Prize with Malala Yousafzai of Pakistan.

References

Akhter, F. (1999). *The resistance against trafficking.* UBINIG. Retrieved from http://membres.multimania.fr/ubinig/saarc2.htm.

DOS. (2011). *Trafficking in persons report.* Washington, DC: Department of State (DOS), United States of America.

HSC. (2005). *Human security report (HSC).* New York: Human Security Centre, LIU Institute for Global Issues, The University of British Columbia, Canada.

HT. (2007). *Trafficking of Sri Lankan children to Singapore.* Human Trafficking (HT). Retrieved from www.humantrafficking.org/updates/775.

IOM. (2010, 23 April). *IOM conducts review of South Asian Association for Regional Cooperation (SAARC) Convention on Human Trafficking.* Retrieved from www.iom.int/cms/en/sites/iom/home/news-and-views/press-briefing-notes/pbn-2010/pbn-listing/iom-conducts-review-of-south-asian-assoc.html.

Lama, M. P. (2008). *Monitoring of SAARC policies and programmes.* Kathmandu: South Asia Centre for Policy Studies.

MADADGAAR. (2007). *First meeting of the regional task force to implement SAARC conventions relating to trafficking in women and children and promotion of child welfare,* held on July 26, 2007, New Delhi, India, attended by Mr. Zia Ahmed Awan, President LHRLA, MADADGAAR. Retrieved from www.madadgaar.org/Press%20Releases/SAARC-Meeting.html.

Naik, N.A. (2004). A security organization for South Asia: Mechanism for conflict resolution in South Asia. In R. Thakur & O. Wiggen (Eds.), *South Asia in the world: Problem solving perspectives on security, sustainable development and good governance* (pp. 269–278). Tokyo: United Nations University Press.

Radhakrishnan, R. K. (2011). Top SAARC police officers discuss drug trafficking and terrorism. *Hindu.* Retrieved from www.thehindu.com/news/international/article1603126.ece.

Raghuvanshi, A. (2002). South Asian Regional NGO consultation meeting on SAARC conventions on children. *Save the Children.* Retrieved from www.crin.org/docs/resources/publications/869SAARCReport.pdf.

Rosand, E., Fink, N. C., & Ipe, J. (2009). *Countering terrorism in South Asia: Strengthening multilateral engagement.* New York: International Peace Institute.

SAARC. (2002). *SAARC convention on prevention and combating trafficking in women and children for prostitution.* South Asian Association for Regional Cooperation (SAARC). Retrieved from www.saarc-sec.org/userfiles/conv-traffiking.pdf.

SAMACT. (2007). *Demonstrators question the relevance of SAARC protocols outside the SAARC summit venue in New Delhi.* South Asian March Against Child Trafficking (SAMACT). Retrieved from www.globalmarch.org/news/030407.php.

SAARC. (2008a). *Declarations of SAARC summits: 1985–2008.* Kathmandu: South Asian Association for Regional Cooperation (SAARC).

SAARC. (2008b). Fifteenth SAARC Summit, Colombo, August 2–3, 2008. In *Declarations of SAARC summits, 1985–2008* (pp. 199–211). Kathmandu: South Asian Association for Regional Cooperation (SAARC) Secretariat.

SAARC. (2010). *Adopted Islamabad SAARC Ministerial statement on cooperation against terrorism.* Kathmandu: South Asian Association for Regional Cooperation (SAARC).

SAARC. (2011). *Gender related issues.* South Asian Association for Regional Cooperation (SAARC). Retrieved from www.saarc-sec.org/areaofcooperation/detail.php?activity_id=10.

Thakuria, N. (2007). Combating human trafficking in South Asia. *Burma Digest.* Retrieved from http://burmadigest.info/2007/10/27/combating-human-trafficking-in-south-asia.

UNODC. (2004). *United Nations Convention against transnational organised crime and the protocols thereto.* Vienna: United Nations Office on Drugs and Crime (UNODC).

UNODC. (2008). *Human trafficking: An overview.* Vienna: United Nations Office on Drugs and Crime (UNODC).

UNODC. (2011). *Signatories to the United Nations convention against transnational crime and its protocols.* Vienna: United Nations Office on Drugs and Crime (UNODC). Retrieved from www.unodc.org/unodc/index.html.

23

RELIGIOUS, SOCIETAL REFLECTION AND RIGHTS OF TRANSGENDER IN INDIA

Asha P. Soman

Introduction

Transgender people are devoid of fundamental human rights and legislations in many countries. Especially penal laws are reluctant to accept them and give them full rights as normal human beings. Laws have been particularly influenced by the religious injunctions in sexual relationships (Qadri, 2005, p. 444.) This is true in the case of India. Being a country of diversities which is reflected in religion also, the plight of the transgender people is getting worse in the country (*Consilium.europa*, 2012). The converse is going on the legalisation of prostitution in India, and if this talk comes into reality and a law is passed in this respect; then the already vulnerable transgender people will find their life more suffocating. Legalising some social evil will not change the life of the people affected by it in the affirmative; social stigma will still follow them, and prostitution is one such area, especially when the transgender is the issue.

This is not the sole situation in India; globally the stance towards transgender is similar. There is the need for international attention towards the protection of rights of transgender and in India the issue of the lesbian, gay, bisexual and transgender (LGBT) community, especially the gay community, has attracted much discussion because of the significant verdicts of the Supreme Court of India on section 377[1] of the Indian Penal Code in *Suresh Kumar Koushal and Anr. vs. NAZ Foundation and Ors.* (2013)[2] and *Navtej Singh Johar & Ors. versus Union of India thr. Secretary Ministry of Law and Justice* (2018).[3]

The Delhi High Court in the year 2009 decided in the affirmative about the decriminalisation of homosexuality from the purview of Section 377 of the Indian Penal Code, 1860, and this decision gave courage to the LGBT community to come out of the defenceless existence they were having. But the 2013 Supreme Court verdict has turned the picture upside down and took it with the question whether public morality or constitutional morality should be advocated. Notably, in 2018 the Supreme Court decriminalised homosexuality and struck down Section 377 IPC. This has created hopes for the transgender community in the country.

More than one million *Hijras* live in India, and among this very large prevalence, most of them have undergone '*nirvan*'—sex change by ancient surgical means. This indicates that the intense transgender condition is far more prevalent than traditional Western psychiatrists and psychologists have ever been willing to admit. Chances of contracting HIV/AIDS are very high among them. These large numbers also speak of the countless tragedies occurring in the current climate of oppression, degradation and violence against transgender women, not only in India but in many other traditional societies all around the world (Ai.eecs.umich, 2012). This chapter explores the religious, societal reflection and rights of transgender in India.

I. Religious and Societal Reflection of Transgender

India has more than 4,000 years of recorded history of *Hijara* or *Hijra*. Ancient myths bestow them with special powers to bring luck and fertility (*Newstatesman*, 2012). Traditionally *Hijaras* have become the part of the Indian society, and they are culturally (Devi, 2012) accepted also. In Hinduism, '*Hijaras*' or 'eunuch' is mentioned in various scriptures and the epics like *Ramayana* and *Mahabharata* and also in the *Kama Sutra*. The word *Hijara* denotes physiological males who have feminine gender identity. This term is considered derogatory in Urdu. The British in India tried to eradicate *Hijaras*, and they considered them as signs of breach of 'public decency', and they were labelled as *Criminal Tribes* under the Criminal Tribes Act of 1871. After independence they were de-notified in 1952.

The *Hijara* population consists of people that were assigned male at birth but have strongly feminine gender expression and identity (Niresh, 2012). Deprived of their traditional roles as caretakers of harems, their main occupations are *badhai*—the offering of blessings in return for money or begging or sex work. Seen to be outside the pale of 'normal' society, they cannot really seek employment anywhere, nor do many of them have the necessary education or documentation that marks them as citizens with entitlements and rights.

As far as *Hijaras* are considered, society treats them as outcasts, and they are always treated as sex objects (Ai.eecs.umich, 2012). Why can the 'normal' people not see them as normal? Why are they always tortured and laughed at? Societal recognition is something of great importance, especially in a country like India. No one has the frame of mind to go to them and help them to have a 'decent' life. The apt word here is 'dignified' life, and that is what is lacking in their 'life'.

The world over, transgender people suffer from neglect and trauma. Earlier and now, recognising transgender is considered as something against morality and public decency and now legality also, after the apex court verdict on gay rights which is associated with transgender rights also. In India, transgender are called by different names like '*Number 9*', '*Hijra*', etc. It is unfortunate that the society is least bothered about the psychological situation of their fellow human beings to call them as a number. Members of these communities are those who have been left out by their families or who run away from their homes because of the humiliation they faced there, and some of them may undergo the ceremony called '*nirvana*' to become female in a complete sense. *Nirvana* (castration) or sex-change surgery among the *Hijara* community means cutting off the penis, testicles and scrotum. This is done either by a medical practitioner or a member of the *Hijara* family. These communities earn their daily bread by begging, performing religious ceremonies during birth of 'male' babies, weddings, etc. and most painfully through sexual work.

Considering official matters, most of the columns in governmental forms have female and male columns, but what about transgender—where should they mark? Will it be proper to call them '*third sex*' in order to include their identity in state identity-proof documents and also on the passports?

In India, in buses there are ladies' seats, in trains there are ladies' compartments, in railway stations there are ladies' waiting rooms and in hospitals there are male wards and female wards; then what about transgender people? Right to health is a fundamental right under Article 21 of the Indian constitution, and the same is not available to them. Do they do not have the right to get their share of rights? For instance, if they suffer from a disease and go to a hospital and if they are put in the ladies' ward, ladies will object, and in the men's ward they will exploit them, and unfortunately, they do not have the money to get separate rooms. Does the society have the right to segregate them? Can the state be justified here? The answer to these questions is a big 'NO'.

As far as constitutionally guaranteed rights of the *Hijaras* in India are considered, many of the rights guaranteed under Article 21 including right to life, personal liberty, health, privacy, education, etc. are at a crossroads. Along with it comes the violation of all the other fundamental rights, which is a serious stroke over the Indian democracy—that so many fundamental rights of a section of society is being violated solely because of their sexual orientation is something unjustifiable. The Indian constitution is framed in line with the Universal Declaration of Human Rights, 1948; hence, violation of these rights of *Hijaras* amounts to violation of the internationally recognised fundamental human rights also.

Unfortunately, the government is doing nothing in the proper manner to help them in order to come out from the stinking shell of the flesh trade and the discriminative attitude of the society. Transgender face social isolation, stigma, rejection, verbal abuse, harassment and threats of violence in every society and every walk of life. The world over, when something happens in the affirmative about recognising the rights of sexual minorities like gays, lesbians, transgender, it is mostly welcomed with violence. In this respect, many Indians might remember about the movie *Fire*—lesbian story.

Globally, life standards are improving, but still some stereotypes exist about certain matters, and one such matter is sexual education and sexual orientation. Even the educated mass too in many parts of the world considers it uncomfortable to talk about sex, and this is even more true in India; this ignorance is resulting in the spread of HIV/AIDS and consideration of the rights and living situations of the sexual minorities. As far as the *Hijara* community is considered, people are reluctant to speak about them, and when they see them, they became a part of the joke which they want to share with family and pals. Why is the society forgetting they are also human beings with the same flesh and blood?

II. Rights of Transgender in India

1. Penal Laws and Supreme Court Judgements

Right to freedom from discrimination and persecution on grounds of sexual orientation is not overtly listed as the grounds of discrimination in the UN Human Rights Conventions. However, both the UN Human Rights Committee and the Committee on Economic, Social and Cultural Rights have stated that the prohibition of discrimination in the ICCPR and the ICESCR includes sexual orientation. The UN Committee on the Rights of the Child has also emphasised that the prohibition of discrimination encompasses sexual orientation. Moreover, the European Court of Human Rights has declared that discrimination on grounds of sexual orientation is a breach of the European Convention for the Protection of Human Rights and Fundamental Freedoms (ILO, 2012).

The world over, the LGBT community faces various kinds of encroachments on their rights. Violations they face include killing, imprisonment, torture and abuses aimed specifically at sexual minorities, such as practices aimed at forcibly changing their sexual orientation; these are in violation of Article 3 of the UDHR—right to life, liberty and security of person.

Section 10 of the IPC, defines 'man' and 'woman'—the word 'man' denotes a male human being of any age; the word 'woman' denotes a female human being of any age. Section 8 of the IPC defines the term 'gender'—the pronoun 'he' and its derivatives are used of any person, whether male or female. Here the question arises of what is the status of *Hijara* under section 8 who has not performed 'nirwana', and what is the status of *Hijara* under section 10 for one who has done the sex-change surgery and become a female? Will they be treated as male or female under section 8, and will they be treated as 'woman' under section 10 after having the sex-change surgery and becoming female? Apart from these confusions, as the IPC often uses the word 'person' and rarely uses 'man' or 'woman', to a greater extents, *Hijras* are covered by the statute, but this is not the case with other statutes of the country.

If they are treated as women, then the state is duty bound to ensure them the protection given to women under the constitution and other legislation. If this is the matter, then are the *Hijara* community in India, especially who has done the sex-change surgery, entitled to get constitutional protection? What is happening is the clear violation of the constitutional mandates. Justice Verma Committee was constituted to recommend amendments to the criminal law so as to provide quicker trial and enhanced punishment for criminals accused of committing sexual assault against women. So if *Hijaras* get the status of woman or if they already have this status, then they should also get the benefit of Justice Verma Committee findings and other legislations and welfare schemes also.

Protection of rights and protection against discrimination to a great extent lies with the law enforcement agencies—the police. Regrettably, protectors are becoming predators as far as the *Hijara* community is considered. They are tortured and harassed by the police, and this makes their situation more vulnerable. They face sexual and other types of physical and mental abuse at the hands of the police, so having this fear, they never go to the police station to lodge a grievance.

"When anti-social elements treat you badly, you approach the police. But whom should you approach when police personnel themselves exploit you sexually?" Sita, a member of the transgender community, asks, highlighting the pattern of institutionalised exploitation of the transgender community. She adds, police earlier used to harass them for gay sex, but after the Delhi High Court decriminalised section 377 of the IPC, they harass the community on the pretext of being prostitutes (*The Hindu*, 2012). Notably, after the 2013 verdict of the Supreme Court of upholding the validity of section 377, it was expected that these communities were going to be tortured more, and they are back to the situation of extreme vulnerability. However, the Supreme Court of India decriminalised homosexuality in 2018, and this has created hope for this community.

2. *Rights of Transgender*

Discrimination against transgender people is a rights issue worldwide, but the existence of a well-recognised and defined transgender group in India makes the problem particularly conspicuous (Niresh, 2012). According to L. Nageshwar Rao, senior advocate, transgenders are deprived of their fundamental rights available to the other two sexes—males and females—and are not considered as the third sex.

> The transgenders are deprived of social and cultural participation, are shunned by family and society, have only restricted access to education, health services and public spaces and have restricted rights as citizens such as right to marry, right to contest elections, right to vote, employment and livelihood opportunities and various human rights such as voting, obtaining passport, driving license, ration card, identity card etc.
>
> *(Ibnlive, 2012)*

The most serious trauma faced by the transgender people is the neglect of the family. Still India is suffocating over superstitions, and rural India gives little respect to a transgender and their family. So the families, because of the fear of societal ostracism, show their unacceptance to the transgender, and it will finally result in their leaving home. One can very well understand societal attitude towards transgender by watching Indian movies; many of the movies depict them as comic characters.

It is not that India is blind towards the rights of the transgender. The central government has allowed the inclusion of 'other' gender in passports and voters' identity cards. This has given legal recognition to the gender identity of transgender people in India. The 2011 Census includes them, and the government (Delhi) has introduced pension schemes for them.

The Criminal Laws (Amendment) Act, 2013, has amended the IPC, Criminal Procedure code, 1973 and the Indian Evidence Act, 1872, with respect to provisions relating to sexual offences. New provisions are gender neutral, giving the scope of protection to the *Hijara* community also, but how far they will be effective is the real question, as these provisions will also have to pass through the hands of the police personnel, who are much abusing their power.

Though the Protection of Women from Domestic Violence Act, 2005, has gone a long way in advancing women's rights and protecting women from domestic violence, it has not benefited the transgender women and transsexual women, who face appalling physical and sexual violence at the hands of their family members on account of their gender identity (*Lawyerscollective*, 2012).

HIV prevalence is between 17.5 and41 percent in the *Hijara* population, which is more than fifty times higher than the general Indian adult population (Niresh, 2012). Though transgender people and sometimes other people do sex-change surgery, there are no guidelines in India that regulate such surgeries, such as which hospitals can do it, who can do it and other necessary requirements.

As far as police atrocities against *Hijaras* are considered, they are attacked by the police sexually, mentally and physically. Justice Altamas Kabir, former Supreme Court Judge, has also emphasised the need for a legal remedy to the problems of the transgender community (*Indlaw*, 2012).

The pressing need to address transgender rights exists in almost every realm of Indian society (Niresh, 2012). The Indian constitution is considered the emporium of rights. If a close analysis is done on all the constitutionally guaranteed rights, especially the fundamental rights, it is of no doubt that every constitutional expert in the country will point towards the refutation of a plethora of ensured rights of transgender community. *Hijaras* in India follow their own culture, and they also face ostracism from their families. Every *Hijara* has their own story, but the substance of every real-life story will be of neglect and indictment which they faced and are facing from their family, society and the government.

The Right to Information Act, 2005, in India is treated as one of the strongest 'weapons' in the hands of the general public against the abuse of the authorities. Section 3 of the Act confers the right to information to all citizens, and section 6(1) uses the term 'person' also. Though the act does not define the term 'person', as it gives rights to 'all citizens', *Hijara* community also comes under the purview of the act. Unfortunately they are not aware of it and are not taking the use of the legislation for their betterment and also for knowing their rights. Though the term 'person' in most of the laws mention natural-born persons, it least addresses the *Hijara* community.

The Indian Succession Act of 1925 uses terms like 'person', 'male', 'female', 'child'; but it does not mention the property distribution to a *Hijara*. Under section 20 of the Hindu Succession Act, 1956 even a child in the womb has the right over property, but whether the *Hijara* community has any property right in India is another matter of concern.

What can be presumed as far the legislation in India is considered is that the *Hijara* community can be included in the term 'person' used by the statute unless it is otherwise defined by the statute. In all such circumstances the meaning of the term 'person' can be treated as 'natural-born person'— including those who have done the sex-change surgery. Even if taken in this vein, how far they will get the benefit of these legislations is again a matter of question, and an additional question arising here is how many have claimed their rights under these legislations so far.

Another aspect is whether the *Hijara* community has the right to vote in the absence of an identity card showing their gender. Society is made up of manmade laws—legislature makes the laws and amends the laws; then what is the hurdle in including the transgender community into the arena of rights, which are their due, being human beings and citizens of this country?

Bullying and sexual abuse from classmates prompt many *Hijara* to drop out of school, resulting in high illiteracy rates and exacerbating unemployment. But even *Hijaras* who are educated face great difficulty in finding a job. For example, Mitra, a *Hijara*, finished college with a three-year degree in hotel management but still faced great obstacles to getting a job. According to Chandini, a transgender, "there are 2,000 sexual minorities in Bangalore and most of the transgenders are graduates and well educated, but due to lack of opportunity are forced into begging and are victim of sexual harassment" (*Times of India*, 2012).

3. Notable Proactive Steps to Protect Transgender

But not all rays of hope are closed for the *Hijara* community in India. The State of Tamil Nadu is taking progressive measures for the transgender community in the country—the High Court of Tamil Nadu has ordered the government to ensure wide publicity through electronic and print media that transgenders are entitled to get registered in electoral rolls, and the education department has created a third category for admission in educational institutions. The government has also provided for small loans and training for transgender self-help groups, and the government is also giving subsidies to all those transgenders who wish to undergo surgical treatment to change their sex (*Indlaw*, 2012). Regarding the protection and welfare of transgender, other states in India can go for the Tamil Nadu model.

The National AIDS Control Programme—III of India acknowledged safety and privacy concerns of *Hijaras* by establishing HIV surveillance sites specifically for *Hijaras* in 2005. In 2008, the State of Tamil Nadu formed the first transgender welfare board in the Asia-Pacific region. The board addresses issues like education access and social security for transgender people. The welfare board made big strides in transgender health in Tamil Nadu by instituting free gender-reassignment surgery in select government hospitals. The right for transgender people to check 'other' as their gender on voter identity cards allows many transgender Indians to vote for the first time (Niresh, 2012).

Former Delhi High Court Chief Justice A.P. Shah recommended the government recognise the transgender community on the basis of their sexual orientation and start welfare schemes for them as a matter of right. He also recommended that every state government, like Tamil Nadu, form a transgender welfare board and transgender commission to protect the human rights of the marginalised community (*The Hindu*, 2012). A.K. Sikri, Judge, Supreme Court, when he served as the Chief Justice of Punjab and Haryana High Court, opined:

> It is important for the judiciary to come out with bold pronouncements in support of this community. In the case of the disabled, courts have always taken a firm stand in their favour, which has made a lot of difference to their lives. I hope it is going to be the same for this community in future.
>
> *(The Hindu, 2012)*

Notably, this has happened when the Supreme Court of India decriminalised homosexuality that raised hopes for the transgender community.

Organisations like *Sangaam*, *Salaam*, *Sahodhari*, *Santi Seva* and *Parcham* are working for the emancipation of transgender communities in India (*AJWS*, 2012). The Indian Passport Office and recent census have included them with the title 'third gender' and 'other', respectively. The governments of Tamil Nadu, Karnataka and Delhi have been taking affirmative steps for the development and welfare of transgender people, and in this respect, the State of Tamil Nadu, including the judiciary there, has given a model for the whole nation.

Conclusion

Globally, life standards are improving, but still some stereotypes exist about certain matters, and one such matter is sexual education. Compared to other sexual minorities, *Hijaras* face more and virulent forms of social ostracism. Here, the emphasis is on the whole arena of their problems which they face because of their sexual minority status. What is emphasised here is their dignity as human beings, their life as human beings and their pathetic situation as human beings. They are also human beings of blood and flesh. No one has the right to question their identity. No one has the right to tell them to be someone else whom they cannot be—the so-called normal human being. Most importantly, no one has the right to ostracise them from the mainstream of society. Unfortunately, they are subjected torture in all its form, and this needs to end.

Following are some suggestions which will help to bring the *Hijara* community to the mainstream of society:

- There is the need for international attention towards the protection of the rights of transgender people, especially *Hijara* and also the LGBTs. There is the need to amend the international documents so as to include sexual minorities' rights also, and in this respect the United Nations can play a significant role.

- Statistics are needed to start any welfare approach. They might not be accurate, but they will give a rough idea of the number of *Hijaras*. At the international level, the initiative can be taken by the United Nations and other such organisations. In India, there is the need for an all-India survey on them including all their life aspects. This will help to frame or modify laws in favour of *Hijaras* and the LGBT community.

- Government should take initiatives to protect the interest of the *Hijara* community and also should ensure that they are not discriminated against and abused, especially by the police authorities.

- There is the need to take affirmative action from all the three wings of the government—legislative, executive and judiciary—in protecting *Hijara* rights. States should ensure them civil and political, social, economic and cultural rights, especially right to vote, property rights, employment opportunities, etc.

- The police force in India needs to be informed about protecting the rights of transgender people. Many *Hijaras* are victims of police torture and abuse. In fact, police officers can help these people to get in touch with any NGOs which are working for their welfare, and in this way they can help this community to come out from the undignified life they are having.

- If any police officer is found to abuse the power and torture the *Hijara* community or any vulnerable section, then they should face departmental enquiry and criminal prosecution, and there needs to be an amendment in the concerned laws in this respect, as this will help to reduce police atrocities towards the *Hijara* communities.

- There is the need to make LGBTs aware about themselves and to inculcate in them self-respect—it is the duty of society, government, organisations like the National and State Human Rights Commissions (NHRC and SHRCs) and NGOs to help them to recognise themselves as part of the society and human community.

- Prostitution is something closely associated with the *Hijara* community; it is the failure of the state mechanism that a section of the society has to depend on prostitution and begging for its survival. They are forced to do prostitution because there is no possibility of getting any other employment. This situation needs to be changed. With the help of NGOs, central and state governments could give them vocational training so that they can earn their daily bread without going for prostitution, and this will give them more acceptance from the society.

- Education is the only way which can make any change in the life of the *Hijra* community in India. But the problem is a perception that they do not wish to give up begging and other things they are doing that pay them well also. This attitude needs to be changed among the community, and for this, the main part is of the society itself. Those who make fun of them in daylight go to them at night to satisfy their sexual urges and call them prostitutes the next morning; this shows the double face of the society. It is the duty of every member of the society to give them a helping hand to come out from the vulnerable life. Educational facilities should be given to transgender people, and necessary steps should be taken against discrimination against them at educational institutions. We must include in the school curriculum of all syllabuses in India the rights of transgender people and make the small children aware of sexual minorities and teach them to respect them also as individuals with dignity and as citizens of the country.

- Similar steps should be taken to give them jobs in the government and private enterprises. Employment opportunity is another stepping stone for *Hijras*, as it will give them financial security, and this can be achieved by giving them reservations in employment and also allowing financial support to start small-scale industries. Here, the government can play a leading role, but it needs to be ensured that proper implementation of the schemes will take place.
- NGOs should take serious initiatives with respect to the pathetic situation of *Hijaras* and also with respect to the denial of their rights and recognition as human beings by the society and the government. They can visualise this through street plays and awareness programmes and also by making movies.

Notes

1 Section 377 of the IPC: Unnatural Offence: *Whoever voluntarily has carnal intercourse against the order of nature with any man, woman or animal, shall be punished with imprisonment for life, or with imprisonment of either description for term which may extend to ten years, and shall also be liable to fine. Explanation—Penetration is sufficient to constitute the carnal intercourse necessary to the offence described in this section.*
2 In this 2013 verdict, the Supreme Court of India criminalized homosexuality and turned down the verdict of the 2009 verdict of the Delhi high court that ruled that section 377 of the Indian Penal Code (IPC), which criminalized sex between adult homosexual men, was unconstitutional.
3 In this 2018 verdict, the Supreme Court of India decriminalized homosexuality and struck down section 377 of the Indian Penal Code.

References

Ai.eecs.umich. (2012). *Human rights violations against the transgender community—A study of kothi and hijra sex workers in Bangalore, India—September 2003*. Retrieved from www.ai.eecs.umich.edu/people/conway/TS/PUCL/PUCL%20Report.html.

AJWS. (2012). Human rights day 2010: Transgender rights in India. Retrieved from www.ajws.org/who_we_are/news/archives/features/human_rights_day_2010.html.

Consilium.europa. (2012). Retrieved from www.consilium.europa.eu/uedocs/cms_data/librairie/PDF/EN_LGBT.pdf.

Devi. (2012). *Transgenderism in India*. Retrieved from www.genderevolve.blogspot.in/2005/09/transgenderism-in-indian-culture.html.

The Hindu. (2012). Transgender community demands civil, not special rights. Retrieved from www.thehindu.com/news/cities/Delhi/article3414880.ece.

Ibnlive. (2012). Supreme Court seeks state govts' stands on transgenders' rights. Retrieved from www.ibnlive.in.com/news/supreme-court-seeks-state-govts-stands-on-transgenders-rights/296986-3.html.

ILO. (2012). Retrieved from www.ilo.org/wcmsp5/groups/public/—ed_protect/—protrav/—ilo_aids/documents/legaldocument/wcms_128059.pdf.

Indlaw. (2012). Judiciary supports equal rights to transgenders. Retrieved from www.indlaw.com/guest/DisplayNews.aspx?C9088C63-1AF7-4EBA-8831-895AC4BAE53B.

Lawyerscollective. (2012). Retrieved from www.lawyerscollective.org/blog/comments-criminal-law-amendment-bill-2012.html.

Newstatesman. (2012). India's transgendered. Retrieved from www.newstatesman.com/world-affairs/2008/05/hijras-indian-changing-rights.

Niresh, V. (2012). *Trailblazing initiatives in India for transgendered population*. Retrieved from www.akiliinitiative.org/trailblazing-initiatives-in-india-for-transgendered-populations.

Qadri. (2005). *Ahmad Siddique's criminology problems & perspectives*. Lucknow: Eastern Book Company.

Suresh Kumar Koushal and Anr.Vs. NAZ Foundation and Or. (2013). MANU/SC.1278.

Times of India. (2012). Transgenders seek their rights. Retrieved from www.articles.timesofindia.indiatimes.com/2010-06-23/bangalore/28282702_1_transgenders-sexual-minorities-ration-card.

24

TRANSITIONAL JUSTICE PROCESSES IN BANGLADESH

Ummey Qulsum Nipun

Introduction

The word 'justice' is very closely related with the term 'victim'. In the process of transitional justice (TJ)[1], much importance is given to the maintenance of victims' rights in comparison to other traditional methods of providing justice. According to the 1985 UN Declaration of Basic Principles of Justice for Victims of Crime and Abuse of Power, Article 1 en 2:

> 'Victims' means persons who, individually or collectively, have suffered harm, including physical or mental injury, emotional suffering, economic loss or substantial impairment of their fundamental rights, through acts or omissions that are in violation of criminal laws operative within Member States, including those laws proscribing criminal abuse of power. . . . The term 'victim' also includes, where appropriate, the immediate family or dependents of the direct victim and persons who have suffered harm in intervening to assist victims in distress or to prevent victimization.

Criminal justice procedures mainly work to protect the society by preventing law violations and punishing and rehabilitating offenders. Victims' rights are something to ponder when the situation of providing justice to a mass community arises. Justice can be served both in a distributive and in a corrective manner (Winthrop, 1978). A distributive justice process deals with socio-economic equity and equal distribution of wealth. Corrective justice emphasizes reciprocity and retaliation as means for establishing justice in society. And theoretically transitional justice (TJ) comprises the full range of processes and mechanisms associated with a society's attempts to come to terms with a legacy of large-scale past abuses in order to ensure accountability, serve justice and achieve reconciliation. These may include both judicial and non-judicial mechanisms—with differing levels of international involvement (and none at all)—individual prosecutions, reparations, truthseeking, institutional reform, vetting and dismissals or a combination thereof (UN Doc. S/2004/616, para. 8).

Experiences of the application of TJ measures around the world promoted this research to consider the case of Bangladesh. For example, in the Cambodia tribunal of Khmer Rouge (ECCC), there was involvement of United Nations (UN) to maintain the international standard of prosecution. This hybrid court worked with a target of rehabilitating victims as well as trial of the offenders. ECCC achieved huge amount of financial support from UN to conduct the whole process. A historical example of success in TJ has been set up by Germany. Reparation and reconciliation were the main tools in achieving this success. Another example of application of TJ mechanisms presented by Lambourne (2009) is the Gacaca court, which performed in its traditional way and successfully established victims' rights in Rwanda. This was not only a fast prosecution but also a financially impressive attempt of the government, and also there was no role played by an international court or the UN.

Theoretically all the aforementioned mechanisms of TJ work to serve justice to the victims by repairing the condition of the victims, through seeking the truth behind the event besides the prosecution of the offenders. Following this theme, in 2009 the International Crime Tribunal (ICT) was established in Bangladesh to prosecute the war criminals of 1971 genocide. This long due prosecution could not be done in these four decades because of the unwillingness of the government and also due to power sharing with the political party of the war criminals. Victims of the 1971 war want to get justice and expected the highest punishment of the war criminals. But after the trial declaration, followers of accused persons created unrestful conditions (regular recessions, strikes, burning vehicles and people) to protect their leaders from the sentence. There was no effective international supervision to take care of the increasing viciousness in Bangladesh regarding this trial and the consequences of the decisions. Although this is a trial of war crimes against humanity, a sentence to death and abolition of the right to appeal is against standard law of human rights.

Cambodia, Germany and Rwanda—all these countries have proven records of applying reparation and reconciliation successfully followed by the trial of the perpetrators. Although all these cases have faced international criticism, the end results have been found to be peaceful and democratic (Lambourne, 2009). But in the case of Bangladesh, application of the TJ mechanism turned into a dilemma because it caused victimization of the present generation. Bangladesh could not reach the opportunity of delivering a peaceful transitional justice but rather faced a worse result. However, there are some positive sides of this application. This attempt of applying TJ in Bangladesh also raised interest and awareness among the people of this generation about their history and also made them think about the reasons behind existing state-led violent conditions. Their active online movement in Facebook and blogs and their regular physical appearance in the place named Shahbagh made the government execute the trial decisions without delay. All these helped us to choose Bangladesh as a case study for further investigation from theoretical perspectives. That is why this chapter will consider the trial of war criminals in Bangladesh to analyze whether justice has been properly defined in Bangladesh. The relevance of applied methods to this attempt will also be discussed.

This chapter will discuss the mechanisms of transitional justice processes and, briefly, the fields of its application. Of focus in this chapter will be the TJ processes of reparation to reconcile the condition of the victims. It will not consider the application of acknowledgement or apology as a part of TJ processes; this is seen in the case of a mass violation of human rights or the event of atrocity, when it is not always possible to make the perpetrator confess the fault through a trial process. Usually these processes require an extended period of time and/or other ways of exerting influence. Additionally, successful international applications of the aforementioned processes will be discussed.

The main goal of this chapter is to explore whether transitional justice could be an option in reestablishing human rights and ensuring the practice of transitional justice in Bangladesh. To reach this goal, the following research questions have been proposed: What is the role of transitional justice processes in prosecuting war criminals of Bangladesh? What are the consequences of applying transitional justice mechanisms in Bangladesh in comparison with other countries in which similar situations have occurred? Why did it take 40 years to start a trial process against the main perpetrators in the Bangladesh case? This chapter will try to answer the research questions.

I. Transitional Justice Mechanism in Bangladesh

Transitional justice procedures are proposed for Bangladesh to solve the issue of war criminals who violated human rights in 1971. The 1971 war took place between Pakistan and Bangladesh because then ruling Pakistan government did not grant the Bangladeshis the freedom of speech in their mother tongue Bangla and did not allow for fair participation in activities that help in the nation's growth. Several events occurred within the time period of 1952–1971, which lastly turned into this war. Finally on 16 December, Bangladesh won the right from Pakistan. *International Mother Language Day* (21 February) is the global acknowledgment of the 1971 incident. Pial (2010) found that in 1972 the war criminals received a 'general amnesty/mercy' as declared by the founder of the nation Sheikh Mujibur Rahman. Later, former President Ziaur Rahman ordered destruction of all documents containing evidence of that declaration. An online daily newspaper (Tehelka.com (n.d.)) disclosed that the political party of the war criminals named Jamaat-e-Islami (JI) was once declared banned just after the liberation war. But later in 1975 they reappeared in politics, grew active, took part in elections and even got access to be in a ruling position together with other parties.

Since their reappearance in state politics, JI was never considered inferior by the other national parties and or treated as anti-liberation. All these helped them to grow more active in state politics. They even got a mandate in elections, got access into the national parliament with the help of other state parties and took part in decision-making for the country. State ruling party Bangladesh Awami League (2009–2013) initiated the trial process, as it has been stated in their election manifesto in 2008. In the year 2012/13, they started executing the prosecution of the seven criminals who helped Pakistanis during the war. Through this, the government achieved very strong emotional support of the citizens.

In 2009, Bangladesh's government decided to apply the first and foremost option of *prosecution* to provide justice to the victims (e.g. freedom fighters, direct victims and their immediate families) of the atrocity of 1971. Initially the trial procedure got the full attention and emotional support of the country's people. According to the legal procedure of applying the TJ mechanism, a trial can take place by maintaining the international prosecution procedure either in domestic court or by forming an international crime tribunal (ICT). Cammegh (n.d.) found that an ad-hoc ICT was formed to prosecute this elongated trial. Common people were given power to suggest to the prosecutor government to give the death sentence to offenders. The human rights–based non-government organization Amnesty International (2013) termed this public determination a symptom of a culture of violence because death sentencing without any space of appeal is another violation of human rights law.

Amnesty International opposed the decision of the tribunal, as the state has defied the right of appeal. Nonetheless, an ultimate decision of death sentence and jail to the criminals was declared by the International Crimes Tribunal (Bangladesh) (ICTB) and execution of the decisions has already started. The *Express Tribune* with the *International New York Times* (2013) published the result as declared by the tribunal, which declared the death sentence for five and life imprisonment for two (one of the accused had already been hanged). Government also banned the political party (named Jamat-E-Islami) of those criminals. But these decisions of government have not been accepted by the followers of the accused people, and they started to protest against the decision through regular recessions, strikes and burning vehicles and people. They want to protect their leaders from the death sentence. Now the country is going through severe violent conditions. Although this is a trial of war crimes, the sentence of death and abolition of the right to appeal is against the standard law of human rights.

Faiz (2013) stated that Amnesty International performed its initial responsibility by discussing with the prosecutor government the *Basic Principles and Guidelines on the Right to a Remedy and Reparation for Victims of Gross Violation of International Human Rights Law and Serious Violation of International Humanitarian Law*. Desai (2013) reported how the ICT has been highly criticized due to its procedural flaws in prosecution. The ICT also had to face the interference made by the state and consider the demands of citizens. International political leaders considered a suggestion that countries like Bangladesh should maintain the standard procedures of prosecution designed by International

Criminal Court, or they can hand over the responsibility to the ICC, as Rwanda, Cambodia and some other countries did.

II. Effects of Applied TJ Mechanism in Bangladesh

To decide if the application of the TJ mechanism in Bangladesh to prosecute the war criminals was worthy or not, we need to consider the effects of this decision. The positive side of this attempt is that a new generation became vocal in pushing the government for immediate execution of the trial decision. As the state already has waited 40 years to start the process for different reasons, the country's people expected that they would not keep the nation waiting for another long term to complete the prosecution. People from all backgrounds, professions, religions and beliefs gathered in Shahbagh (very close to the city center of the capital city, Dhaka) with a demand of the capital punishment of the accused war criminals. This domestic response was introduced as Gonojagoron Moncho, which attracted international attention along with huge media coverage (dailies, Facebook, blogs, Twitter, news channels).[2] This response was like a historic movement, as around 100,000 people participated in the procession and also stayed in Shahbagh roundabout (later named as Projonmo Chottor) for the whole month of February 2013.

International suggestions, as mentioned in the previous point, have been influenced by the negative aftermath of the trial decision. Declaration of the trial results made the supporters of the war criminals create violent conditions in the whole country. Every day they have been killing people, using children in making bombs and throwing cocktails into public transports and in other public zones. Innocent country people, women and children have been getting killed and burnt in this unrest condition. The official Facebook page of Save the Children in Bangladesh (2014) has summarized how children are suffering from this situation. In 2013, more than 20 children died in this continued political turmoil, and 36 children got severely wounded. But the prosecutor government was not active enough in reducing such sufferings of people caused by the trial decisions. Magnier (2013) reported the situation in the *Los Angeles Times* as riots in Bangladesh. All these made the prosecution process unsuccessful from the general people's perspective considering the degradation of the situation. After observing the aftermath of trials, even people who supported the trial decisions earlier changed their mind.

Discussion

The flipping sides of the whole transitional justice process as performed in the case of Bangladesh reached such a point that the government needed to decide how it could be further managed. Considering the effects of the application, this study found that the prosecutor government reached a dilemma of accepting one of the following options:

(A) Continuing the prosecution to serve justice to the genocide victims
(B) Halting the prosecution to save the general people from being victimized in political turmoil

Although the trial decision reignited the sense of patriotism among the young generations, it is also true that the decision of hanging the war criminals could not bring any good to the society, instead creating turmoil in the usual life of citizens. Kant gave us a reminder about the action and reactionary behavior of nature, which follows the laws of natural necessity, laws of physics and laws of cause and effect (Sandel, 2009). Newton's third law of physic says that for every action, there is an equal and opposite reaction. Before proceeding towards accomplishment of any law or action, we need to assume that there will be some reactionary events. Here the action of prosecution was performed to serve justice to a group that caused sufferings to the other part of the society as a reaction of that act.

War victims deserved	prosecution	of war criminals that	victimized	general people
	(action)		*(reaction)*	

Although the victims of war in Bangladesh deserved the trial of the perpetrators, the effect of this decision also requires consideration. Research question number one asked about the role of transitional justice processes in prosecuting war criminals of Bangladesh, and we found that this attempt of Bangladesh's government brought all its citizens closer to making a common decision. Awareness of the younger generation of the history of the country also increased due to this attempt. All these discussions about the theoretical procedure of TJ application helped us to think about the gaps in activities and decisions taken by the government. During the planning of the prosecution, the Bangladesh government considered only the emotional side of the country's people but not the characteristics of the offenders. Decisions made by the state enhanced the rights of victims, but on the other hand, it reduced the liberty of other communities. Eventually frustration, complexity and intolerance resulted, which affected the positive outcome of serving justice.

Moreover, there was no direct involvement of the victims of the genocide in the trial mechanism. Participation of the victims was totally denied, even though it was supposed to take place through different avenues like victim impact statements (VIS).[3] Nonetheless, the Bangladesh government did not take any attempt at improving the life of the victims. They used to receive a very meager government subsidy through which they are living a very inhuman life. There is no provision for health treatment, accommodations, livelihoods and other fundamental rights in the regular life of freedom fighters and their families. No procession has ever been made to demand the establishment of fundamental rights of the freedom fighters and improved services for them. The Ministry of Liberation War Affairs (n.d.) in Bangladesh has a special grant for them, but it is barely active in serving the honorable community of freedom fighters. Moreover, it has been reported that the existing government project has no direct impact on the lives of the victims because of continued corruption, low budget and lack of proper monitoring.

To reply question number two, which asked about the impacts of this attempt and a comparison of international examples with the Bangladesh case, we need to scrutinize the whole situation again. As the prosecution decision caused further victimization of the general people and the government has been unable to handle this situation, the country's people lost their faith in the government and its procedure for managing the country. Capital punishment of the war criminals was the sole demand of the people, and victims also expected the same, but the TJ mechanism turned out to be ineffective in the case of Bangladesh because of the violent situation created by the criminals' supporters. The major goal of applying TJ mechanisms is to provide justice to the survivors and to the victims. Lambourne (2009) discussed *The Model of Formal Legal Justice* that has been applied in Cambodia, Rwanda, East Timor and Sierra Leone for peace building and transitional justice provision. Under this model, an ad-hoc international crime tribunal was established. With the help of citizens and states, restorative justice mechanisms have been performed to restore peace in the community and also to repair the situation through victim–offender reconciliation, circle sentencing and community conferencing. There was no option of punishment in this process but instead application of the restorative justice theories and transitional justice mechanisms like truth commissions etc. In performing the model of *formal legal justice*, the state authority was also aware of the acceptability of the restorative justice process to the community. They maintained the proper level of accountability and thus ensured the respect and dependency of the citizens to the state and the law, its structure and affectability.

Through this model, Lambourne quantified the elements of transitional justice: accountability or legal justice, truth or knowledge and acknowledgement, socio-economic justice and political justice.

But unfortunately, victims of Bangladesh's liberation war (freedom fighters, direct victims and their immediate families) never received any significant assurance of the trial or reparation to reconcile the condition of human rights violations in the last 40 years. That is why reparation always has been promoted and prosecution is discouraged.

Question three asked about the reasons behind such a delay in starting the trial process against the main perpetrators of the Bangladesh case. At this point, we will consider the issues that lengthened the trial decision to find the answer to this research question. Desai (2013) appreciated the reconciliation process that has been initially undertaken by Sheikh Mujibur Rahman after 1971. But after this long gap, in 2009 his daughter decided to prosecute the forgiven ones. That historic declaration of general mercy in 1973 could be continued as a part of reparation, as the political party of those criminals reappeared in Bangladesh politics, took part in national elections and got access in Parliament. That is why no one ever considered making any attempt to prosecute them in the last 40 years. If we consider the Khmer Rouge case in line with the Bangladesh one, we can find some similar reasons behind such a delay in starting the prosecution. As reported by MacKinnon (2009) in the online daily *The Guardian*, the Cambodian government also had to wait almost 30 years to proceed with the trial because of the fugitive perpetrators and denial of the others about their crime.

All these facts indicated the political unwillingness of the Bangladesh government to prosecute a politically stable party. After 40 years, an attempt has been made to change this one, which also resulted in political unrest inside the country. International observers, leaders and rights activists are hoping strongly that it should be a matter of reconciliation instead of a revengeful trial (Cammegh, n.d.). The forms of reparation could further create a peaceful environment for Bangladesh, which has already lasted for 40 years as an aftermath of general amnesty. Expansion of that attempt could be continued by applying the full and effective processes of reparation instead of this sudden decision of prosecution. Ferstman, Goetz and Stephens (2009) enlisted the processes of reparation as restitution, compensation, rehabilitation, satisfaction and guarantees of non-repetition. Arthur (2009) presented Argentina as a glorious example of establishing justice through 'Transition to Democracy'. Elizabeth Lira named the Chile government as the best example for providing health assistance and paying pension to the victims (De Greiff, 2006).

Conclusion

When a retributive procedure takes place, it also ignites the desire for revenge (Darley, 2009). Revenge has been defined as an individual behavior that establishes justice by personal effort regardless of the sense of right and wrong. Activities of the supporters of the war criminals can be considered at this point, as their actions are being driven by the sense of vengeance. That is the reason for promoting TJ mechanisms given by the global leaders to establish a unique way of ensuring the offender–victim participation in the justice process. VIS, reformation of criminal justice procedures and restorative justice have been found to be popular and effective tools of providing justice to society.

This chapter talked about the procedures for conducting different transitional justice mechanisms to serve justice to the victims of a past wrongdoing. To exemplify the whole concept, the case of prosecuting war criminals in Bangladesh has been presented. The Bangladesh government tried to perform the TJ mechanism but ignored the possible effect of such an attempt. There was no participation of the victims in this process. Only the tool of *prosecution* has been considered by the Bangladesh government as the means of providing justice to the victims of genocide 1971. But it could take the full form of social justice if the retribution against the war criminals could be followed by reparations for the victims. Eventually the applied mechanism also made a specific group ferocious enough to cause the victimization of the citizens of the country. The trial decision also spurred further violation of human rights as the government defied the scope of appeal. So the TJ mechanism could not be found successful in the case of Bangladesh like in other countries. Another point is that the victims of this past event have not ever been compensated to reestablish their rights as part of a transitional justice provision.

Justice comprises not only the prosecution of the wrongdoers but also the reconciliation of the situation of the victims. When the goal is to provide justice to the victims of a past event, those striving for it should also consider the condition and strengths of the opponents, specifically if the prosecution takes a long time to happen. In the case of Bangladesh, 40 years have passed before the start of the trial process. In this long time, perpetrators grew old, and their political party gathered sustainability through participation in the politics of the country. These situations hindered the government's ability to run the prosecution smoothly, as it did not consider applying the other forms of TJ mechanisms.

From a theoretical point of view, it can be said that the recent victimization of the country's people made by supporters of the war criminals in Bangladesh could be reduced if *amnesty* from the TJ mechanisms was applied. Cowen (2006) also gave us a reminder that retribution is less effective in peace building where *reparation* can maintain the democracy by offering forgiveness to the oppressors to some extent. If we consider the libertarian or Nozickian standards, restitution is not a feasible option for the victims of genocide. But partial restitution can be offered to the identified victims who lost property due to their temporary refugee condition in India during the war. As an extension of applying transitional justice mechanisms, restitution can play its role in reconciling the victims of mass atrocities. The Bangladesh government will take the full responsibility of calculating the amount of financial compensation and will manage the full fund to serve the victims and their families as appropriate. Provision of life-long health treatment, education facilities and establishment of livelihood opportunities for the direct victims, their immediate family members and freedom fighters will be confirmed by the state as part of the reparations. As this chapter argued in favor of reparations along with the prosecution of the war criminals, there is also a suggestion about rehabilitation of the victims who lost their lands, houses and livelihoods regardless of gender, race, religion and ethnicity in 1971. At this point, the Bangladesh government may also consider the request made by Akhtar (2012) that stranded Pakistanis in Bangladesh need to be rehabilitated from their stateless condition.

Considering the thoughts of Haidt (2001), it can be said that justice can only be achieved in the case of war criminals of Bangladesh when punishment of the past wrongdoers will not cause further violation of human rights and will also be followed by the reconciliation of the situation of the victims. The Bangladesh government can honor the abovementioned recommendations by following the theories of transitional justice mechanisms. Considering all these, a modified and sophisticated version of retribution can be evaluated to reduce the possibility of victimization and thus to serve justice to the war victim community of Bangladesh.

Notes

1 TJ processes were originated to work for people through different sectors of social sciences for the greater welfare of a nation with the help of other sectors, e.g. law, political science, psychology, economics etc. These processes have been constructed with an aim to prosecute the people accused of the violation of laws and rights and to reconcile the conditions of the violated and the violator groups. Since the completion of World Wars I and II and the other cold wars, international leaders decided to rebuild the peace all around the world. TJ is an attempt towards carrying out that decision, as it works at reconciling past wrongdoing. This is kind of a balance between the decisions of restorative and retributive justice procedures. Lambourne (2009) explains that the retributive method deals with the punishment of the offender and the restorative process welcomes reconciliation of the victim through rehabilitation of both of them. Being influenced by these two processes, TJ performs in a neutral way where there is scope for the offenders to apologize and to take part in disclosing the truth behind the offence. TJ also covers the reparation of the situation of the victims even sometimes with the help of offenders.
2 All information and pictures of Shahbagh Projonmo Chottor can be found in this link: http://jamiajournal. com/2013/02/18/shahbagh-projonmo-cries-of-a-resurgent-bangladesh/

3 Hoffman (1982) considered the victim impact statement the accused's constitutional right and defines it as a statement given by the victims about the changes of their lives that happened due to all kinds of physical, economic and social losses suffered by them and their families. It doesn't include any suggestions regarding the punishment.

References

Akhtar, N. H. (2012, December 19). Bring the stranded Pakistanis home. *The Express Tribune*. Retrieved from http://tribune.com.pk/story/481701/bring-the-stranded-pakistanis-home.

Amnesty International. (2013, September 17). Bangladesh: Death sentence without right of judicial appeal defies human rights law [Press release]. Retrieved from www.amnesty.org/en/for-media/press-releases/bangladesh-death-sentence-without- right-judicial-appeal-defies-human-rights.

Arthur, P. (2009). How "Transitions" reshaped human rights: A conceptual history of transitional justice. *Human Rights Quarterly, 31*(2), 321–367.

Cammegh, J. (n.d.). *The Bangladesh war crimes tribunal: Reconciliation or revenge?*. Retrieved from www.crimesofwar.org/commentary/the-bangladesh-war-crimes-tribunal-reconciliation-or-revenge-2.

Cowen, T. (2006). How far back should we go?: Why restitution should be small. In: J. Elster (Ed.), *Retribution and reparation in the transition to democracy* (pp. 17–32). Cambridge: Cambridge University Press.

Darley, J. M. (2009). Morality in the law. The psychological foundations of the desire to punish. *Annual Review of Law and Social Science, 5*,1–23. doi: 10.1146/annurev.lawsocsci.4.110707.172335.

De Greiff, P. (Ed.). (2006). *The handbook of reparations*. Oxford: Oxford University Press.

Desai, R. D. (2013, December 2). A justice denied as Bangladesh prosecutes war crimes [Weblog post]. Retrieved from www.huffingtonpost.com/ronak-d-desai/a-justice-denied-as-bangladesh_b_4363124.html.

The Express Tribune with The International New York Times. (2013, December 10). 1971 war crimes: Bangladesh court stays JI leader's execution. Retrieved from http://tribune.com.pk/story/643714/1971-war-crimes-bangladesh-set-to-hang-ji-leader.

Faiz, A. (2013, October 1). Bangladesh must overturn all death sentences. *Amnesty International* [Press Release]. Retrieved from www.amnesty.org/en/news/bangladesh-mp-war-crimes-death-penalty-2013-10-01.

Ferstman, C., Goetz, M., & Stephens, A. (Eds.) (2009). *Reparations for victims of genocide, war crimes and crimes against humanity: Systems in place and systems in the making*. Leiden, The Netherlands: Brill.

Haidt, J. (2001). The emotional dog and its rational tail: A social intuitionist approach to moral judgment. *Psychological Review, 108*(4), 814.

Hoffman, M. (1982). Victim impact statement. *Western State University Law Review, 10*, 221.

Lambourne, W. (2009). Transitional justice and peacebuilding after mass violence. *International Journal of Transitional Justice, 3*(1), 28–48.

MacKinnon, Ian. (2009, February 17). Khmer Rouge leader in dock as Cambodia genocide trial starts. *The Guardian*. Retrieved from www.theguardian.com/world/2009/feb/17/war-crimes-tribunal-cambodia.

Magnier, M. (2013, September 17). In Bangladesh, death penalty for Islamist leader sparks riots. *Los Angeles Times*. Retrieved from http://articles.latimes.com/2013/sep/17/world/la-fg-wn-bangladesh-death-sentence-20130917.

Ministry of Liberation War Affairs. (n.d.). Retrieved from http://mof.gov.bd/en/budget/10_11/mtbf/en/MBF_63_LiberationFY10_C.pdf?phpMyAdmin=GqNisTr562C5oxdV%2CEruqlWwoM5.

Sandel, M. J. (2009). *Justice: What's the right thing to do?*. New York: Farrar, Straus and Giroux.

Save the Children in Bangladesh. (2014, January 21). Media summary [Facebook status update]. Retrieved from www.facebook.com/savethechildreninbangladesh.

Tehelka.com. (n.d.). Bangladesh HC cancels registration of Jamaat-E-Islami. Retrieved from www.tehelka.com/bangladesh-hc-cancels-registration-of-jamaat-e-islami.

Winthrop, D. (1978). Aristotle and theories of justice. *The American Political Science Review*, 1201–1216.

25

'NIRBHAYA INCIDENT' AND JUVENILE JUSTICE POLICIES IN INDIA

A Situational Analysis

R. Rochin Chandra

Introduction

On a cold winter night of 16 December 2012, a 23-year-old paramedic student, Jyoti Singh (now known as Nirbhaya) and her male companion, Arwinder Pratap Pandey, were returning home after watching a movie in Saket, South Delhi. The two boarded an off-duty charted bus for Dwarka from Munirka. There were only six other persons in the bus including the driver (Sharma, 2016). Media sources reveal that one of the six lured the couple into a vehicle, saying that the bus would go in the same direction towards their destination (Biswas & Malik, 2013). Soon, the male companion noticed that the bus deviated from its normal route and the doors of the bus had been tightly shut. When he objected, the six men on the bus taunted the couple, asking what they were doing alone so late at night (Biswas & Malik, 2013). At this point, a scuffle broke out between Pandey and the group of men. He was battered, gagged and knocked with an iron rod. The men, then, dragged Jyoti to the rear end of the bus and took turns to rape her (Sharma, 2016). When she tried to fight back (started shrieking), the driver and the other men inserted an iron rod into her, and it was pulled out with so much force that the act brought out her intestines (Mosbergen, 2012). The police sources later described the iron rod as being a rusted, L-shaped tool used to operate a jack to change flat tyres on buses and trucks (Perappadan, 2016). After the beating and raping, the two were dumped half clothed and bleeding on the roadside. At around 11 p.m. a passerby rushed the couple to Safdarjung hospital, where they were given immediate treatment (Sharma, 2016). Jyoti died from her injuries 13 days later while undergoing an emergency treatment in Singapore.

All the accused were arrested and charged with sexual assault and murder. The driver and the primary accused, Ram Singh, reportedly committed suicide in Tihar Jail on 10 March 2013. The other four adult perpetrators—bus cleaner Akshay, gym assistant Vinay, fruit vendor Pawan and Ram Singh's brother Mukesh—were awarded the death penalty by fast-track courts (Walia, 2014). The sixth offender, Mohammad Afroz alias Raju, who was a few months short of 18 at the time, was tried separately from the other five men in a juvenile court. On 31 August, he was sent to a reformatory home for delinquent juveniles for three years—the maximum allowed by juvenile court under the Juvenile Justice Act, 2000.

The differential treatment of the juvenile in this case prompted a nationwide outcry for lowering the minimum age for a criminal trial from 18 to 16 so that the juvenile accused, who was believed to be the most brutal in the assault, would be tried in an adult court like the other five accused (Singh,

2014). These sentiments were also echoed by several distinguished scholars, who argued that the limitation of a maximum three years for a custodial sentence is so short that it is neither justifiable on grounds of deterrence nor adequate for any reform program (Pande, 2013).

In the meantime, Subramaniam Swamy, an opposition politician and lawyer, filed a petition in the Supreme Court which called for a minor offender's "emotional, intellectual and mental maturity" to be assessed when deciding whether to try them as a juvenile (Banerji & Mohanty, 2013). The move was widely appreciated by the general public, as they believed that giving milder punishment to the juvenile (youngest convict in the case) would encourage other people in similar situations to commit heinous crimes—after all, they know that they will be let off by the Indian courts due to their age (MBA Rendezvous, n.d.; Banerji & Mohanty, 2013).

In an effort to allay these concerns, Menaka Gandhi, Minister of Women and Child Development, drafted the Juvenile Justice (Care & Protection of Children) Bill, 2014, to amend the JJ Act, 2000. Significantly, the proposed bill sought to revise the age of juvenile criminality from 18 to 16 years and provided a transfer model, known as 'judicial waiver system'—which allowed the Magistrate to try the juveniles in adult courts for committing certain crimes. The amendments to Juvenile Justice Act, 2000, were passed by Lok Sabha (after heavy opposition) in May, 2015 and subsequently forwarded to Rajya Sabha for debate. The bill gained strong impetus in the parliament following the release of the juvenile from the correctional facility after three years of detention. This event aroused the public sentiments related to the 16/12 incident and led to nationwide protests demanding rigorous punishment and amendments in the juvenile law. Ultimately, the bill was passed by the Rajya Sabha in the winter session of the parliament and received the assent from the president, Pranab Mukherjee, on 31 December 2015, amid heated debated and protests.

Keeping in view the above situation, this chapter will try to understand the recent developments in juvenile justice policies in India. More precisely, an effort will be made to investigate the nuances in the Juvenile Justice (Care and Protection of Children) Act, 2015, with respect to juvenile delinquents. In the above statement, I used the term 'nuances' to mean the new judicial concepts and amendments brought into the laws governing juvenile delinquency in India.

I. Juvenile Justice Legislations in India: Definition of Heinous

According to Merriam Webster's dictionary, the term 'heinous' owes its etymological roots from the Middle French word 'haine', which denotes acts hatefully or shockingly evil. The whole essence of the above definition is well established in modern times, as this word is generally used by people to reflect a sense of horror evoked by intense hatred. While this interpretation affords a basic idea of what qualifies to be 'heinous', it is quiet surprising to note that there exists no statutory definition that accounts for what exactly heinous means (Virani, 2015). Thus, in the absence of a clear legal definition, the scope of 'heinous' is reduced to mere punishments—the term 'heinous' is most often quantified and equated with its punishment instead of being spelled out as to what actually constitutes being heinous (Virani, 2015).

Given the horrific 16/12 Nirbhaya rape case, this term gained significant attention in eyes of the policy makers. Still, it is worth noting that before the adoption of the new juvenile legal framework (i.e., JJ Act 2015), the term 'heinous' was not expressly defined in our laws governing juvenile delinquency, and rightly so. When the Juvenile Justice Act, 2000, was drafted, the then existing socioeconomic conditions did not appear so frightful as they exist now. Henceforth, the law makers did not anticipate that they will have to grapple with shocking social realities in the future.

Further, the ultimate idea behind creating the JJ Act was to render care and protection to the children. But while making the law, the legislatures failed to incorporate the qualifying remarks of the UN Convention, which provides for creating exceptions, when juveniles are convicted for committing crimes of a heinous nature.

In an effort to fill this grey area, the new juvenile legislation defines heinous offences as those "for which the minimum punishment under Indian Penal Code (IPC) or any other law for time being in force is imprisonment for seven years or more" (Nair, 2015). It also specifies a list of offences that would be treated as heinous offending. This list extends to encompass offences like rape, murder, acid attacks, kidnapping and other terror-related activities. Thus, any juvenile who is between the ages 16 and 18 and is accused of committing heinous crime shall now face legal consequences in adult court. From the above explanation, it is, therefore, clear that heinous crimes are typically characterized by extreme brutality. The seriousness of such crimes is relatively higher in degree than conventional execution of crimes.

II. New Legal Proviso of 'Jurisdiction Waiver' Incorporated in JJ Act, 2015

The tragic 2012 Delhi gang rape case triggered a substantive debate over the inadequacy of the youth justice law (JJ Act, 2000—now repealed) in the country to effectively intervene with adolescents who are a legitimate threat to public safety. In response to these concerns, the Minister of Women and Child Development, Menaka Gandhi, introduced the Juvenile Justice (Care & Protection of Children) Bill in the Parliament on August 12, 2014 (Shankar & Deshpande, 2015). She said that 50% of juvenile crimes were committed by teens who know that they get away with it. She also added that changing the law, which will allow them to be tried for murder and rape as adults, will scare them. The bill was passed by the Lok Sabha after incorporating certain amendments in May 2015. One of the highlights of the proposed bill which remained the bone of contention until the last minute before, ultimately, finding the approval of the upper house on 22 December, 2015, was the introduction of a new legal proviso called 'judicial waiver system' (JWS). The judicial waiver model accommodates the concepts of the Hague Convention on Protection of Children and Cooperation in Respect of Inter-Country Adoption, 1993 (Sridhar, 2016).

This model is based on the premise that when a child is charged with a heinous crime, he/she will be examined by the concerned JJ Board (consisting of a magistrate and two social workers) in order for them to determine if the child possesses the requisite degree of "mental, physical and emotional capacity" to commit such crimes, besides having the ability to appreciate the consequences of his/her wrong doings (Malhotra & Sugden, 2015). In this connection, the board may even seek the advice of child psychologists and other experts. Upon completion of a preliminary assessment, if the JJ Board is reasonably satisfied that child has committed a heinous offence and believe there is a need for a trial of said child as an adult, then the Board shall waive its jurisdiction and transfer the child to the competent Children's Court (regular/session court), having jurisdiction to try such offence (Ministry of Law Report, 2015). After receiving the report of preliminary assessment, the Children's Court shall decide whether to try the said child as an adult or to chalk out a suitable plan for his rehabilitation (Malhotra & Sugden, 2015). If found guilty, the child who was tried as an adult must then be sent to a place of safety (most preferably Borstal schools) until turning 21, when he would be transferred to jail (Malhotra & Sugden, 2015). In other words, judicial waiver permits juveniles between 16 and 18 years to be tried as adults for committing heinous crimes.

While the JWS is enforceable from January 15, 2016, it is essential to note that this 'get-tough policy' was intensely opposed by several influential figures, including those from Congress, Samajwadi Party, JD (U), TMC and other advocacy groups. Citing the regressive effects of the model, they said, "laws cannot be dictated purely by public sentiments. This concept [judicial waiver] can jeopardize the life of millions of children in age group 16–18 who come from illiterate families and extremely poor homes" (Singh, 2016; Madhukalya, 2015). Further, they argued that this law had potential for misuse by framing false cases against vulnerable children, especially when they involve cases of elopement and consensual sex (Singh, 2016). This argument is fairly consistent with the prevailing sentiments of family honour and pride in our society. For example, an angry father of a runaway girl is bound to restore his societal honor by filing a false FIR against the erring teenager, alleging that his daughter was unwillingly taken away and subsequently raped (Hegde, 2015). Considering this possibility, it seems reasonable to say that treating an innocent youth equivalent to that of an adult in a regular criminal justice system will only be a recipe for more crime and criminals in the long run. It will have devastating ill effects of criminalization, penalization and stigmatization on such minors.

III. Understanding Juvenile Delinquent Behavior: Nature vs Nurture

1. Why Psycho-Social Maturity of Juveniles Is under Debate

The Nirbhaya rape case stood as one of the most horrific in the rape culture in India, and rightly so, for two reasons: (a) the soaring degree of mental maturity displayed by the juvenile and (b) the methodical manner in which he committed the crime. Here, the cumulative understanding of the above factors gives an impression that 'true juvenility is not in the age but in the level of mental maturity of the offender and the offence he committed'.

Ironically, this formulation was dismissed by a wider section of psychologists and child advocates, who used scientific evidence to show that the brain does not attain full maturity during adolescence, and as a result of this relative 'developmental immaturity' teens are likely to make poor decisions, engage in risky behavior or act in a seemingly reckless manner. In other words, the differences in neurological, psychosocial and emotional development greatly distinguish youths from adults. Hence, these factors, according to adolescent development studies, should be essentially taken into consideration when deciding the culpability and punishment for crimes committed by youths.

2. Research Findings on Structural and Neurological Development of the Adolescent Brain

Adolescence is generally recognized as the 'period of transition' between childhood and adulthood, whereby an individual experiences significant growth and change. A growing number of studies on adolescent development suggest that the behavior of adolescents is most likely to be affected during the teenage years (NJJN Factsheet, 2012). It is especially true because this is the time when adolescents normally undergo profound and dramatic developments in different areas of the brain (NJJN Factsheet, 2012). Such development with regard to physical parts of the brain is known as 'structural' changes. As with structural maturity, the functional changes that occur in different parts of the brain are equally critical. They 'rewire' the way in which adolescents process information and make decisions, thus revealing the differences in the ways adults and adolescents use their brains (Kintigh, 2012).

A growing number of studies on structural growth of the brain suggest that there is a rapid development in the 'shape and size' of the brain between the ages 12 and 20 (Kintigh, 2012). By using the term 'shape and size', I intend to mean the frontal lobe, especially the pre-frontal cortex, which is one of the last parts of the brain to fully mature. The frontal lobe can be considered as the 'central executive' part of the brain, which controls higher-order functions such as planning, judgment, decision making, expression of emotions and impulse control (Reddy, 2016, p. 25). This region may not fully develop until the mid 20s, thereby leaving children to use the primitive brain functioning prior to its complete maturation (Kintigh, 2012, p. ii). Moreover, it is important to note that the maturation of the pre-frontal cortex is vital in terms of development of self-control; deficits in the pre-frontal cortex may lead to violence and behavioral problems (Reddy, 2016, p. 25).

Similarly, it is widely believed that teenagers are driven to engage in criminal activities due to their ever-increasing impulsivity and mood swings during the adolescent period. According to research, such behavioral responses in adolescents are often stimulated due to an under-developed limbic system, or emotional brain, which helps to manage and process emotions (NJJN Factsheet,

2012). Before adolescence, the limbic system uses fight-and-flight response instead of using higher-order cognition. However, during puberty, the limbic system that regulates reward sensitivity is relatively heightened (Kintigh, 2012, p. ii). In other words, adolescents normally derive extreme pleasure in sensation seeking. For example, adolescents may seek excitement by means of engaging in increasingly risky behavior (NJJN Factsheet, 2012). Sometimes, such drives might cause a youth to drift towards subculture values, and the rewards (pleasure) gained through these experiments, in turn, are heavily valued by teenagers. Hence, due to partial development of the limbic system, the adolescents often experience mood swings and impulsive behavior, thereby increasing their temptations to get involved in reckless activities (NJJN Factsheet, 2012, p. 1).

When discussing the probable cause of the teenage tendency toward law-violating behavior, the impact of dopamine cannot be overlooked. While dopamine is a chemical produced by the brain, it mainly helps to relate actions with the sensation of pleasure. The shift in levels of dopamine production during adolescence typically increase the threshold needed for stimulation that lead to feelings of pleasure (NJJN Factsheet, 2012, p. 2). As a result, youth may seek pleasure by experimenting with risky behavior in a fashion similar to that of the immature emotional brain.

Nevertheless, it is essential to note that the adolescents, due to their immature development, often fail to reason rationally before choosing to get involved in risky behavior. This is to say that the teenagers do not place an emphasis on logically assessing/evaluating the risks involved in real-time situations as opposed to their adult counterparts. Instead, they are more reward sensitive and may overweigh the fun or pleasure (i.e. reward of risky behavior) that they feel when they engage in criminal behavior. Such risk-taking tendencies, in my view, go to show that teenager are less likely to consider the long-term consequences of their actions, which might potentially affect their future and subsequently reduce their fear of punishment (Hodgdon, 2008). Hence, it seems reasonable to say that there is a developmental gap that inhibits teenagers from making mature decisions, thereby distinguishing them from adults.

3. Youth Offending: Peer Influence vs Psycho-Social Maturity

Psycho-social development emphasizes the ability of the youth to make mature decisions and judgements in real life scenarios. According to the author, this capacity in adolescent is hindered by a relevant psycho-social factor, i.e. 'influence of peers', which will be discussed in this section.

A steadily growing body of adolescent behavior research indicates that teenagers tend to behave differently in circumstances of high emotional context and low emotional context due to dramatic changes in the emotional and decision-making regions of the brain (NJJN Factsheet, 2012, p. 2). One of the most suitable examples in this connection is the differential impact of peer groups and parents on the decision making of the youth. Given a stimulating situation, a teen surrounded by friends has an increased potential to make a more emotionally based decision (NJJN Factsheet, 2012, p. 2). Conversely, when a teen is placed in a dull or quiet environment, accompanied by his immediate elders or parents, it is likely that he will make a more intellectual and consequence-based decision (NJJN Factsheet, 2012, p. 2). The above example is conclusive proof of the fact that the decision-making of youth is heavily influenced by the relative environments in which they are placed.

In general, adolescents spend more time with their peers than with parents (Kintigh, 2012, p. 4). Hence, it is quite natural that youths are easily influenced by and pay more attention to their peers than adults when they are with friends. This is particularly true because during adolescence, the youth are under constant pressure to achieve status among their peer group (Kintigh, 2012, p. 4). In other words, to avoid real and imagined rejection from peers, or to elevate their status in the peer group, the youth may succumb to peer pressure by initiating risky behavior in a group situation, thus making a more emotional than reasoned decision (Hodgdon, 2008). This may even explain why youths seek autonomy from parents.

While the earlier paragraph described the susceptibility of adolescents to change their behavior and alter their decision in response to peer pressure, the psycho-social factors like unformed self-identity and experimentation with questionable behavior support the claim that youth are in a way different from adults. According to the research on adolescent development, youth often face difficulties in forming their self-identity—one's self-concept, values, beliefs, attitudes etc. (Hodgdon, 2008). To resolve this conflict (i.e. to figure out who they are), they may resort to experimenting with different activities, including risky behavior and even engaging in criminal activities. In criminological theories, this phenomenon is well established under Matza's theory of drift, in which youths vacillate in and out of delinquency due to weak social control.

4. Understanding Psycho-Social Maturity of the Juvenile from the 16/12 Nirbhaya Rape Case

If testimony of the male companion (who accompanied the victim in the bus) and the confession made by the juvenile (convicted in the Nirbhaya rape case) is anything to go by, then it is wise to recall the facts and circumstances of that horrific incident in detail. According to the juvenile's confession, it was he who lured and convinced the two to board the bus in the first place. In fact, he also confessed that before Nirbhaya boarded the bus, he tried to convince another girl who was alone, and that failed after she hailed an auto. The second of those confessions confirmed his involvement in initiating the lewd comments (until before all six joined) and in egging the idea of sexually assaulting and brutalizing the girl by inserting the iron rod (and even hands) in her abdominal cavity (to the point of pulling her intestines) before throwing her (naked) and the male friend out of the moving bus. From the above gory details, it appears that the juvenile involved in the horrific gangrape of Nirbhaya was driven to initiate the brutal assault out of peer pressure, and his decision to insert the iron rod was very impulsive and emotional. Further, his act is fairly consistent with the youth's tendency for risk and sensation seeking behavior as discussed earlier. Yet these brain-development explanations were dismissed by the protesters and media industry (as it would send a wrong message to the society), who claimed that the said juvenile had the requisite degree of mental maturity to know what he was doing was wrong/criminal and was old enough to brutally assault the victim to the point of killing her.

IV. State Action After the Nirbhaya Incident: Verma Committee

On 23 December 2012, a three-member committee headed by Justice J. S. Verma Committee, the former Chief Justice of Supreme Court, was constituted to recommend amendments to the criminal law so as to provide for quicker trial and enhanced punishment to the persons committing sexual offences of extreme nature against women as an aftermath of the terrible Nirbhaya incident (PRS, n.d.). The other members on the Committee were Justice Leila Seth, former judge of the High Court, and Gopal Subramanium, former Solicitor General of India. The said committee took up the task very effectively and after extensive hearings and thorough scientific analysis submitted its report on 23 January 2013 (PRS, n.d.). It suggested several changes in the laws related to crime against women and enhanced the punishment for those convicted of sexual assault. The Verma Committee specifically considered the issue relating to reduction of the age of a juvenile from 18 years to 16 years. The Committee dealt with the matter in paragraphs 44 to 55 of the Report. In paragraph 44 the Committee said, "We have heard experts on the question of reduction of the age of a juvenile from 18 to 16 for the purpose of being tried for offences under various laws of the country" (p. 253).

The Committee doubted the possibility of the convict to emerge as a reformed person if he is sent to life imprisonment at the age of 16. The Committee (para 45) pertinently observed that

> Our jails do not have reformatory and rehabilitation policies. We do not engage with inmates as human beings. We do not bring about transformation . . . Children, who have been deprived of parental guidance and education, have very little chances of mainstreaming and rehabilitations, with the provisions of the Juvenile Justice Act being reduced to words on paper.
>
> *(p. 254)*

The Committee further regretted that

> We are of the view that the 3 year period (for which delinquent children are kept in the custody of special home) is cause for correction with respect to the damage done to the personality of the child. We are completely dissatisfied with the operation of children's' institutions. The sheer lack of counselors and therapy has divided the younger society into 'I' and 'them' (para 47, p. 254). It is time that the state invested in reformation for juvenile offenders and destitute juveniles. There are numerous jurisdictions like the United Kingdom, Thailand, and South Africa where children are corrected and rehabilitated; restorative justice is done and abuse is prevented. We think this is possible in India but it requires a determination of a higher order.
>
> *(para 49, p. 255)*

The Committee also took account of certain scientific factors relating to adolescent brain development. It noted that "adolescence is a period of significant changes in the brain structure and function and there is consensus among developmental neuroscientists on the nature of this change" (para 53, p. 257). Findings from Laurence Steinberg's adolescentrisk-taking model were extensively cited in the report. The committee made a specific mention of various relevant changes during early adolescence to late adolescence and early adulthood. For example, how the decrease in grey matter in prefrontal regions of the brain has a strong bearing on basic cognitive abilities and reasoning skills, how changes in activity involving the neurotransmitter dopamine have important implications for sensation seeking, how the increase in white matter in the prefrontal cortex due to myelination is important for higher-order cognitive functions and how increase in the strength of connections between the prefrontal cortex and the limbic system is especially important for emotion regulation etc. (p. 258).

Ultimately after a thorough evaluation of the issue, the Committee held that "We are of the view that the material before is sufficient for us to reach the conclusion that the age of 'juveniles' ought not to be reduced to 16 years" (para 54, p. 259).

V. UNCRC and Obligations on the Signatory Nations

India is a signatory of the United Nations Convention on the Rights of the Child of 1989, the United Nation Standard Minimum Rules for Administration of Juvenile Justice 1985, i.e. the 'Beijing Rules', and the United Nation Rules for the Protection of Juveniles Deprived of their Liberty 1990. India signed and ratified the convention on 11 December 1992. In early 2000, the UNCRC questioned India about the discriminatory nature of the definition of the term 'juvenile' under the Juvenile Justice Act, 1986, and recommended that it be amended to ensure that boys under 18 years are covered by the definition of juvenile, as girls already are (Raha, Manoharan & Ramakrishnan, 2015).

Henceforth, the 2000 Act was brought in to adhere to the standards set by convention. The nuanced act maintains this aim and seeks to improve implementation and procedural delays experienced by 2000 Act. The UNCRC states that signatory countries should treat every child under the age of 18 years in the same manner and not try them as adults.

While the 2000 Act was in sync with this requirement, the new act is not. Still, many other countries that have also ratified the convention try juveniles as adults in the cases of certain crimes. These countries include the UK, France, Germany etc. The United States is the only country that hasn't ratified the Convention on Children's Rights—it treats juveniles as adults in the cases of certain crimes (Mehta, 2015).

VI. Reflection of NCRB Statistics on Juvenile Crimes Before JJ Act, 2015

According to PRS Legislative (2015), the government cited National Crime Records Bureau (NCRB) data to show that there has been a surge in crimes committed by juveniles, especially in the 16- to 18-years age group. However, the Standing Committee on Human Resource Development examining the Bill stated that NCRB Data was misleading as it was based on FIR's and not actual convictions (Shankar & Deshpande, 2015).

NCRB data further indicates that the percentage of juvenile crimes, when seen in proportion to total crimes, has increased from 1% in 2003 to 1.2% in 2013. During the same period, 16- to 18-year-olds accused of crimes as a percentage of all juveniles accused of crimes increased from 54% to 66% (Mehta, 2015).

VII. Age of Criminal Responsibility in India: Present Status

The criminal jurisprudence in India is governed and regulated by two major legislations—the Indian Penal Code, 1860 (IPC), and the Code of Criminal Procedure Code, 1973 (CrPC) (Bhatia, 2016). The IPC is a substantive law which provides definition of crimes and prescribes the scope and extent of punishments, whereas CrPC lays down the procedure that is to be mandatorily followed while pursuing a criminal case. The IPC has set the age of criminal responsibility at 12 years. As per the provisions of Sections 82 & 83 of the IPC, an offence committed by a child below 7 years cannot be held to be criminally liable, while the criminality of those between 7 and 12 has to be judged by the level of their mental maturity.

It is believed that children cannot be treated as adults under the criminal justice system of the country and hence we require development of special laws to deal with youthful offenders. India fulfilled this obligation by enacting the Juvenile Justice (Care and Protection for Children) Act, 2000 (Bhatia, 2016). The fundamental aim of this act was to facilitate care, protection, treatment, development and rehabilitation of children (under 18 years) who come in contact with the justice system as the result of committing an offence. It is based on the premise that juveniles lack the physical and mental maturity to appreciate/take responsibility for their crime; and because their character is not fully developed, they still have the possibility of rehabilitation.

Notably, this act was amended in the year 2005 and most recently in 2015. Under the current law (JJ Act, 2015), a juvenile is defined as a person who has not attained the age of 18, while the age of criminal responsibility is reduced from 18 to 16 years. That means that juveniles between the ages of 16 to 18 years will now be tried as adults for committing heinous crimes like rape and murder.

Conclusion

This chapter describes the 16/12 Nirbhaya incident, explains the major policy shifts in juvenile justice over the past 20 years and traces the recent trends in processing juvenile offenders. In this context, some of the broader topics that were discussed are (a) the reduction of age for criminal trial from 18 to 16, (b) the introduction of the judicial waiver system and (c) the psycho-social maturity of juveniles to commit heinous crimes.

Given these developments in the juvenile justice framework, there is an imperative need to test the utility of the new law in terms of its operationalization, effectiveness and feasibility. For example, after lowering the age of criminality under the JJ Act, it is unclear whether the offenders between 16 and 18 years would be sentenced under the Borstal School Act, 1920, or the Juvenile Justice Act, 2015. Similarly, measuring the physical, emotional and intellectual maturity of a minor offender is yet another issue that calls for a thorough examination in light of increasing cases of false accusation against children who are involved in elopement and consensual sex. In this connection, the fallibility of such measurements and the lack of a 'reverse waiver option' for the juvenile courts to reconsider its waiver order are equally pressing concerns. Further, there is no concrete data or evidence (neither of India nor of any foreign country) to prove that lodging the juvenile offenders in adult jails resulted in lowering of overall criminal offending of juveniles—although one can find several reports on the devastating ill effects of such treatment (Singh, 2014). Hence, this aspect ought to be considered from the developmental and victimization perspectives of juvenile offenders. Ultimately, with changing times, there is a need to examine the changing philosophies of the juvenile justice system. How has one isolated incident of barbarity against women shifted India's juvenile justice ideology from reformation to punishment? Is the current juvenile justice law good enough to deal with bad juveniles, or it is even worse? It is these types of questions that should be researched in the times to come.

Acknowledgement

The author wishes to acknowledge his sincerest thanks to Professor K. Jaishankar for reviewing and editing this chapter. The author is also thankful to Professor(s) Arvind Tiwari, P. Madhava Soma Sundaram, Debarati Halder and Dr. Syed Umarhathab for their valuable input and constructive criticism, which enabled to improve the quality of this chapter.

References

Banerji, A., & Mohanty, S. (2013). *Indian teen sentenced to three years in Delhi gang rape case.* Retrieved from http://in.reuters.com/article/uk-india-rape-idUKBRE97U06S20130831.

Bhatia, S. (2016). *The minimum age of criminal responsibility in India: Is it to be blamed for the increasing youth crime?* Retrieved from https://rostrumlegal.com/ the-minimum-age-of-criminal-responsibility-in-india-is-it-to-be-bla med-for-the-increasing-youth-crime-by-stuti-bhatia.

Biswas, T., & Malik, S. (2013). *Juvenile raped 'Amanat' twice, once while she was unconscious: Police sources.* Retrieved from www.ndtv.com/india-news/juvenile-raped-amanat-twice-once-while-she-was-unconscious-police-sources-509360.

Hegde, S. (2015). *Rage of self-righteous republic.* Retrieved from www.thehindu.com/opinion/lead/lead-article-by-sanjay-hegde-on-justice-juvenile-bill-rage-of-the-selfrighteous-republic/article8022373.ece.

Hodgdon, H. (2008). *The future of children: Adolescent development & juvenile justice.* Retrieved from www.futureof children.org/futureofchildren/publications/highlight s/18_02_Highlights_01.pdf.

Kintigh, B. (2012). *Adolescent development: Juveniles are different than adults.* Retrieved from www.miccd.org/wp-content/uploads/2013/09/Youth-Dev-Issue-Brief.pdf.

Madhukalya, A. (2015). *As juvenile in Nirbhaya Case is released, the debate rages over bill.* Retrieved from www.dnaindia.com/india/report-as-juvenile-in-nirbhaya-case-is-released-debate-rages-over-bill-2157976.

Malhotra, A., & Sugden, J. (2015). *What India's Juvenile Justice Bill says about trying children as adults.* Retrieved from http://blogs.wsj.com/indiarealtime/2015/12/22/wWhat%20 India%E2%80%99s%20Juvenile%20 Justice%20Bill%20Says%20About%20Trying%20Children%20as%20Adultsthat-indias-juvenile-justice-bill-says-about-trying-children-as-adults/?mod=wsj_streaming_delhi-rape-the-aftermath.

Mehta, K. (2015). *Homes or hellhole.* Retrieved from http:// www.millenniumpostin/ homes-or-hellholes-117194?NID=210629.

Mosbergen, D. (2012). *Delhi bus gang rape victim has intestines removed as shocking details of assault emerge*. Retrieved from www.huffington post.com/2012/ 12/20/delhi-bus-gang-rape-victim-intestines-shocking-details _n _ 2340721.html.

Nair, S. (2015). *The many heinous crimes that make a juvenile an adult*. Retrieved from http://indianexpress.com/article/explained/the-many-heinous-crimes-that-make-a-juvenile-an-adult.

Pande, B. B. (2013). *Justice cannot follow a tough act*. Retrieved from www.thehindu.com/todays-paper/tp-opinion/justice-cannot-follow-a-tough-act/art icle5162042.ece.

Perappadan, B. S. (2016). *Rape survivor airlift was govt., not medical, decision*. Retrieved from www.thehindu.com/news/national/rape-survivor-airlift-was-govt-not-medical-decision/article4246109.ece.

Raha, S., Manoharan, A., & Ramakrishnan, S. (2015). *New juvenile justice law cleared by the Lok Sabha violates basic tenets of the Child Rights Convention*. Retrieved from http://blog.mylaw.net/new-juvenile-justice-law-cleared-by-the-lok-sabha-violates-basic-tenets-of-the-child-rights-convention.

Reddy, K. J. (2016). Frontal lobe dysfunctioning in violent and criminal behavior. In K. Jaishankar., & N. Ronel. (Eds.), *Conference proceedings of the third conference of the South Asian Society of Criminology and Victimology (SASCV)*.(p. 25). Tirunelveli, India: South Asian Society of Criminology & Victimology & Department of Criminology and Criminal Justice, Manonmaniam Sundaranar University.

Shankar, A., & Deshpande, T. (2015). Legislative brief—The juvenile justice (Care & Protection of Children) Bill, 2014. *PRS Legislative Research*. pp. 1–3. Retrieved from www.prsindia.org/uploads/media/Juvenile%20Justice/Legislative%20Brief%20Juvenile%20Justice%20Bill.pdf.

Sharma, M. (2016). *16/12 Nirbhaya rape case: An incidence which shaken up whole Delhi full story*. Retrieved from www.indiantribune.com/dont-miss/1612-nirbhaya-rape-case-an-incidence-which-shaken-up-whole-delhi-full-story-5936.html.

Singh, R. (2014). *Are reforms really needed in the juvenile justice (Care and Protection of Children) Amendment Act, 2000*. Retrieved from www.legal servicesindia.com /article/print.php?art_id=1689.

Singh, H. (2016). *New Juvenile Justice Act: A setback for child rights*. Retrieved from www.huffingtonpost.in/harpal-singh/new-juvenile-justice-act-_b_8893144.html.

Sridhar, B. (2016). *The New JJ Act: "Facilitating Criminalization of Juveniles"*. Retrieved from www.newindianexpress.com/columns/The-New-JJ-Act-Facilitating-Criminalisation-of-Juveniles/2016/01/07/arti cle3214869.ece.

NJJN Factsheet. (2012). Retrieved from www.njjn.org/our-work/adolescent-brain-research-inform-policy-guide-for-juvenile-justice.

Virani, P. (2015). *Crime and commensurate punishment*. Retrieved from www.thehindu.com/opinion/op-ed/the-juvenile-justice-bill-and-rights-of-children/article7448576.ece.

Walia, S. (2014). *Two years since the Delhi gang rape, here's what's changed—And what hasn't*. Retrieved from https://qz.com/312738/two-years-since-the-delhi-gang-rape-heres-whats-changed-and-what-hasnt.

26

CRIME AMONG YOUNG OFFENDERS IN BHUTAN

Trends, Factors and Determinants[1]

Lham Dorji, Sonam Gyeltshen and Thomas Minten

Introduction

Young people in Bhutan (below age 24 years) constituted about 50% of the total population in 2014. The younger generation are better educated than their older folks (youth literacy rate was 86.1% compared to general literacy rate of 63%). The recent socioeconomic growth and development in the country has made life relatively easier for its citizens, especially for young people. They get free education and other life opportunities. The government, NGOs and society are committed to nurturing and harnessing their potential, but some of them seem to be getting trapped in a wide array of problems. What are those issues that are affecting some individuals and groups of our young populace? The crime, substance abuse and mental disorders related to the young population, among others, are a few inter-related issues that are emerging as policy concerns (Dorji et al., 2015).

Many of us believe that there is an upsurge in crime, substance abuse and mental health issues among young people in the country. These are the issues that need to be immediately addressed. Some foreign newspapers have started characterising Bhutan as no longer a Shangri-La (*The Guardian*, 2003). Crimes among young people that are [almost] comparable to the urban crimes in the developed countries are becoming notable. We often hear about murder, gang fight, rape, robbery, vandalism and drug offences in which young people are involved (Dorji et al., 2015).

Young people engaging in antisocial and criminal activities is not only morally wrong but can cause social disorder, affect collective good of the society and disrupt the country's progress towards the GNH (Gross National Happiness) goals; more so, because young people are supposed to devote their time and energy in building their own futures. Substance abuse among the younger generation is emerging as another worrisome social issue. The illicit drug abuse problem in the country may be lesser than in other countries, but it is still growing. The arrests associated with drug abuse remains one of the highest cases. Mental disorders among young people are noticeable, and it is only likely that more such cases will be observed. We are witnessing an increasing number of young people committing suicide. The government is already concerned about this growing trend (Dorji et al., 2015).

Bhutan's population is young, and this presents us the opportunity to exploit their potential and gain from the young demographic structure. This will require the entire society to safeguard them from new social and economic vagaries. To do so, we need to understand the nature, extent, trends and all possible causes of their problems. The present chapter is an effort towards that. However, since the research reported here focuses on the datasets limited to certain agencies and information collected from a group of population (young convicts), the findings should be considered only as suggestive of general trends rather than implying to the entire young populace in the country. More issue-specific and action researches are desirable and indispensable to come up with practical recommendations (Dorji et al., 2015).

The chapter consists of two parts. The first part is a descriptive analysis of crime data (of young Bhutanese people), sourced from the Royal Bhutan Police (RBP). The second part is a complementary discussion on the outcome of a qualitative research study with 44 young convicts (for in-depth interviews see Dorji et al., 2015). The overall aim of this chapter is to obtain better understanding of the "nature, extent, and trend of crime" that affects young Bhutanese people (Dorji et al., 2015).

I. Reported Crime Among Young People in Bhutan: An Analysis

The criminological studies in Bhutan are very limited. Other than regular crime records maintained by the Royal Bhutan Police (RBP) and crime statistics produced by the National Statistics Bureau (NSB), only a few studies on crimes and their causes had been conducted using police data (Dorji & Kinga, 2005). In absence of crime victimisation surveys, determining an explicit prevalence and extent of crime in Bhutan has been very limited.

Crime data such as that of police and court records are useful but not sufficient to generalise the crime situation because they do not capture the unreported crimes, which is popularly referred to as the "dark figure of crime" (Gibbsons, 1979). Nevertheless, criminologists could use such data to map the geography of crime and, to the extent possible, identify the socio-demographic characteristics of offenders. The official crime data are important to understand crime and to draw public attention and support towards crime prevention. Crime statistics are important because looking at them is not simply about numbers but about crime victims and the protection of the public well-being (Winsor, 2014).

The RBP's crime records of the past two and a half decades show that the overall reported or registered crime in Bhutan had been steadily increasing. Lham Dorji (2005, p. 80) noted: "not only is there variation in the frequency of crime across districts; there has been a steady increase in crime over time and across age categories". Dorji's study (2005) used only the RBP data, which, though suggestive, is restricted to those who had already offended and covered only those cases reported to the police. It may otherwise also be possible that the reported crime had increased due to improved policing and reporting over the years (Dorji et al., 2015).

It is too early to conclude whether the actual crime rate has increased in recent years because the present analysis uses only the RBP data. However, the total number of recorded crimes has increased by over 100% from 1986 to 2013. This excludes motor vehicle offences. In 2013, the RBP recorded 2,925 crimes against 1,243 crimes in 1986. The reported crimes have remained relatively stable until 2008 (with an average of 1,672 crimes per year). A sudden rise in the reported crime was noted beginning 2009. It reached a record high of around 3,500 cases in 2010, after which it started to drop (Dorji et al., 2015).

Among three broad categories of crime: (1) the crime against property was the most common one until 2013. The other broad categories are (2) the crime against human body and (3) others. The crime against property remained almost stable until 2003. From 2005 to 2008, the crime against property and human body started to decline. Interestingly, during the same period, there was a slight increase in other related crime. The crime against property peaked in 2011, and the crime against human body reached its highest point in 2010 (Dorji et al., 2015).

In many countries, young people are disproportionally represented in the statistics on crime and violence, both as victims and as perpetrators. Studies in other countries found that violent crimes are usually committed at a younger age. Adolescence (10–19 years) is considered as a stage of "breaking

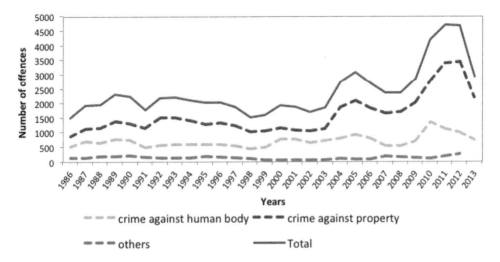

Figure 26.1 Crime among young people.

the rules". The same trend seems to apply to Bhutan as well. Over the years, crime among young people (12–24 years of age) has emerged as a new social issue and one of policy concern. In 2013 alone, the crime among young people constituted over 40% of the total recorded crimes. In response, the policy makers, researchers, development partners and legislators have started debating on both the causes and potential solutions to this social issue. The National Youth Policy specifically stresses achieving Gross National Happiness (GNH) by young people by ensuring a secular society, free from violence, crime, exploitation and intimidation, amongst many other initiatives (Department of Youth and Sports, 2010).

Understanding delinquency among young people has become very crucial in Bhutan. This analysis, therefore, is aimed at exploring the many facets of the crime among young people in the country. It looks into the nature of offences, socio-economic and demographic characteristics of young offenders, crime trends and the possible determinants of crime. The analysis of the recorded crime among young people for the period July 2012 to July 2014 in the country is presented in Figure 26.1. It includes crime trends, its distribution across age and gender and Dzongkhags (regions). It also presents categories of offences, possible determinants of crime and incidence of the repeat offences (Dorji et al., 2015).

Data for the analysis was sourced from the RBP's Youth Delinquent Monitoring System (YDMS). The YDMS is a database of crime history of young people (age below 25). It contains the bio-data of young offenders and other information such as time and place where crime took place and where it was recorded. The YDMS is purposed to monitor crime among young people in the country. It further contains self-reported reasons (by offenders) for criminal deviance. The YDMS dataset contained the crime records for the period from January 1, 2012, to August 4, 2014. However, for the present explorative analysis, the crime records from July 2012 to July 2014 could be used due to data inconsistencies and several missing observations [for some variables]. The dataset contained 2,321 cases across 19 different categories of crime (Dorji et al., 2015).

1. Seasonality of Crime

Studies elsewhere have found that some of the crimes (that young people carry out) take place during certain seasons and after certain hours. It must be for this reason, for example that, in 2015

Monggar Dzongkhag passed the curfew rule that prohibited a young person from being in the town after 8 p.m. The rationale for this was that many young people were found to be loitering in town, often leading to crime.

To look into the seasonality of crime, monthly cases from July 2012 until July 2014 were taken into account. Five months were observed with high crime occurrence: November 2012 (116 offences), March 2013 (110 offences), September 2013 (122 offences), December 2013 (171 offences) and February 2014 (127 offences). These observations indicate that crime among young people was a year-round phenomenon with little seasonal variation (Dorji et al., 2015).

2. Age of Offenders

The relationship between age and criminal offences has been observed since the beginning of criminology. Age is one of the strongest factors associated with criminal behaviour (Ulmer & Steffensmeier, 2015). It is observed that the registered crime increased by age until the age of 19. Not all adolescents showed the same propensity to commit crime, though on the whole, it increased during the entire adolescence. Data shows that after a small drop at the age of 20 and 21, crime again increased from age 22 to 24. The observations conform to the theory that the crime tends to peak in adolescence or early adulthood and then decline with the increase in age (Quetelet, 1984).

3. Gender

Gender representation among young offenders in Bhutan follows the international trend, as indicated by the presence of more male than female offenders. Only about 5% of the registered offenders were the females; the rest were the males (95%). This suggests that crime among young people in Bhutan is predominantly the male phenomenon. The males and females tend to commit different crimes, though sometimes patterns of offending tend to be similar (Schwartz & Steffensmeier, 2008). There is not much gender distinction when it comes to minor property and substance abuse offences. However, more males had committed serious crimes like homicide and offences related to firearms and weapons than the females. Data suggest that more males were involved in all categories of crimes except prostitution and related offences (Dorji et al., 2015).

4. Offence Categories

Different crimes were classified as per the Penal Code of Bhutan (2004) into five major categories and 5 subcategories. Among five major categories, the offences committed by young people fall under three main categories: the "offences against a person" (N = 697, 32%), the "offences against property" (N = 642, 29%) and the "miscellaneous offences" (N = 665, 30%). The offences under the other two categories, the "commercial crime, fraud, corruption and related offences" (N = 19, 1%) and the "offences against state and public order" (N = 163, 7%) were relatively lesser (Dorji et al., 2015).

On disaggregating the crime sub-categories, the "offences related to controlled and other harmful substance" (N = 635, 29%) came out to be the most common offence. The next in order were the "assault, battery and related offences" (N = 619, 28%) and then the "larceny, robbery, armed robbery and related offences" (N = 428, 20%). About 10% of the offences corresponded to the "burglary, trespassing, and related offences" and 5% to the "offences against the public welfare". Though a little less than 1% of the total crime was reported under homicide (also including attempts at homicide), it is to be noted that there were 22 such cases (Dorji et al., 2015).

There was not much variation in the nature of offences between the two age groups: adolescents (10–19 years) and young adults (20–24 years). The most common offences between these two age groups were the controlled substances, assault, battery and related offences and the larceny, robbery and related offences. However, subtle differences between the two groups were noted in some cases. For examples, slightly more adolescent offenders had committed the larceny, robbery, armed robbery and related offences and the burglary, trespassing and related offences. Contrarily, about 29.4% of young adult offenders had committed the assault, battery related crime compared to 26.6% of the same offence committed by adolescent offenders. Further, about 29.9% of young adult offenders had committed the offences related to controlled and other harmful substances compared to 27.7% adolescent offenders. Other crimes that occurred relatively more often among young adults than among adolescents were the sexual offences, money laundering and smuggling and the offences related to firearms and weapons (Dorji et al., 2015).

5. Reasons for Criminal Deviance Among Young People

Though data disallowed comprehensive causal analyses, an effort was made, to the extent possible, to determine reasons for criminal deviance among young people. This is because understanding the determinants of crime is crucial to helping develop crime control mechanism and designing the rehabilitation schemes (Dorji et al., 2015).

Using reasons for committing crime reported by offenders (2,166 cases) at the time of arrests and registration, simple analysis was done to understand why they had committed crime. More than half (56.8%, 1,210 offences) of the offences were reported to have been committed under peer pressure and in companionship. Another 12% (257) of young offenders reported poor socio-economic conditions necessitated them to commit crime. About 7% of young offenders reported that unemployment was the main reason for their criminal deviance. The self-reported reasons (given here) are not the top reasons as found out by the qualitative study (next part). Such incongruity in results is assumed to be due to the fact that at the time of arrests, the offenders would not have provided the reasons in detail as much as they had done when they were interviewed later using in-depth interview techniques. However, the next part presents the analysis of in-depth face-to-face interviews conducted among the sampled young convicts. The qualitative study was conducted to find out why they actually had committed the various crimes. Moreover, offenders could have simply reported that friends influenced them to commit crime to feign that their friends were the main culprits, particularly with the motives to turn away the blame or escape being incarcerated (Dorji et al., 2015).

More than half of the offences recorded to have been associated with deviant peers (1,210 offences) were the assault, battery and related offences and the offences related to controlled and other harmful substances. Another 20% of the burglary, trespassing and related offences and the larceny, robbery, armed robbery and related offences were driven by peer pressure. Out of 257 cases or offences recorded to have been committed due to the offenders' poor socio-economic conditions, 70% were related to the burglary, trespassing and related offences and the larceny, robbery, armed robbery, and related offences (Dorji et al., 2015).

6. Recidivism

The RBP records (July 2012–July 2014) show that among young offenders, those who repeated offences constituted a small proportion of the total offenders. Of 2,412 reported cases, a large majority (1,882 cases or 90%) were first-time offenders. About 9% of them had committed crimes twice, while less than 3% had offended for more than three times. Five young offenders had committed crime 5 times, and one person each committed 7, 10 and 11 offences during the two-year reference period (Dorji et al., 2015).

7. Distribution of Different Crimes Across Dzongkhags (Regions)

Of 2,412 cases of crime among young people across the country recorded with the RBP, 85 cases had no mention of places where the crime occurred. Thimphu Dzongkhag recorded the highest number of cases (821 cases), constituting about 35% of the total recorded crimes among young people in the entire country. The Dzongkha-wise occurrence of crime was determined based on the police station where the crimes were registered. Chhukha, Paro, Wangduephodrang and Sarpang Dzongkhags recorded 441 (19%), 198 (9%), 156 (7%) and 140 (6%) cases, respectively. Lhuentse and Gasa were two Dzongkhags with the fewest recorded crimes among young people. These two Dzongkhags registered five and nine cases within the two-year timeframe (Dorji et al., 2015).

In all Dzongkhags, young people constituted at least one-fourth of the total Dzongkhag population. Thimphu Dzongkhag had about 15% of the total young population in the country (in 2013). The other Dzongkhags with a higher concentration of young population were Chhukha, Samtse and Trashigang. Gasa Dzongkhag recorded the lowest population of young people (4%). The crime among young people was recorded to be the highest in Thimphu Dzongkhag, closely followed by Paro and Chhukha Dzongkhags (Dorji et al., 2015).

In 19 Dzongkhags, the assault, battery and related offences were reported as one of the top three crimes. The offences related to controlled and other harmful substances were listed as one of the top three crimes in 15 Dzongkhags and the larceny, robbery, armed robbery and related offences in 12 Dzongkhags. The burglary, trespassing and related offences came out as one of the top three crimes in seven Dzongkhags, while the sexual offences came out as one of the top three in three Dzongkhags. Just one Dzongkhag registered the offences related to public order and tranquility as one of the topmost crimes (Dorji et al., 2015).

With regard to the nature of crime in different Dzongkhags, the sexual offence was reported to be common in Dagana, Gasa and Zhemgang Dzongkhags, with Gasa and Zhemgang Dzongkhags recording two cases each within the reference period of two years. Dagana Dzongkhag reported seven sexual offence cases. This constituted almost half of all the crimes among young people reported in the Dzongkhag. The burglary, trespassing and related offences were common in Bumthang, Dagana, Paro, Punakha, Trashiyangtse, Trashigang and Trongsa Dzongkhags. More cases of the assault, battery and related offences, the offences related to controlled and other harmful substances and the larceny, robbery, armed robbery and related offences were reported to be common in Thimphu and Chhukha Dzongkhags (mainly Thimphu and Pheuntsholing Thromdes).

II. Young Offenders in Police Custody: A Qualitative Analysis

The central research problem that the authors wanted to address using the qualitative research approach was to explore the possible determinants of criminality among young Bhutanese prisoners. For this study, some young convicts (44 persons), hereon referred to as the participants, were selected from Chamgang Central Jail and the Royal Bhutan Police (RBP)-managed Youth Development and Rehabilitation Centre (YDRC), Tsimasham. The factors that we commonly account for deviant behaviour among young people are poverty, family dysfunction, substance abuse, peer pressure, unemployment, and low self-esteem. This chapter only presents interviews with the participants but not detailed analysis. For more see Dorji et al., 2015). This analysis mainly tried to seek answers to the question: What were the most probable reasons or factors for young convicts resorting to deviant behaviour and criminal activities (Dorji et al., 2015)?

Analysis and Discussion of the Participants' Interviews

The participants' explicit accounts of their crimes—above all their motives—for offending suggest the need to not only lend listening ears to their concerns but also to reassess how we manage their real plights. Notwithstanding the fact that most participants attributed their criminal deviances to substance abuse problems, this seems to be just symptomatic of many other underlying causes. The substance abuse, alcoholism and criminal deviancy seem to fuel each other in a vicious and destructive manner. Being intoxicated in certain cases has triggered violence and other criminal activities, while in other cases, young people have committed crimes to obtain funds for acquiring illicit substances and alcohol (Dorji et al., 2015).

Among many factors, the participants adduced family disruption and personality or mental health disorders to explain their criminal deviances. The narratives eloquently described multiple and interactive causes of these two notable issues: parental negligence, alcoholism problem in the family, parental divorce, poor parenting, loss of parents through death, family discord, negative family and social experiences, chronic poverty, unemployment, serious hardships, education deprivation, poor livelihood, discrimination, destitution, social stigma, hopelessness and helplessness, loss of self-esteem, anger, frustration and so on (Dorji et al., 2015).

Addressing these multiple and interactive factors of juvenile and youth crime may necessitate coordinated and integrated approaches. At present, many government and non-governmental agencies support vulnerable youths, but either their programmes duplicate or there is little systemic coordination among the youth-serving agencies. In this regard, synergised efforts among them and promoting local responsibility are necessary given that crime prevention, dispensation of justice to young offenders and their rehabilitation are complex processes (Dorji et al., 2015).

The primary institution of socialisation that is responsible for instilling in children and young people a sense of responsibility, humane conduct and development of wholesome personality and good citizenship is a family. The qualitative data indicated the presence of some relationships between family disruption and alcoholism, substance abuse and crime. This finding, though not proven statistically significant, may bear some significant implications for the prevention and treatment of substance abuse problems and other crimes among young people (Dorji et al., 2015).

This analysis identified family disruption bearing significant implications for children's adjustment and as one of the main risk factors for problematic behaviour among young people. Family disruption is loosely characterised by spousal conflict, divorce, broken homes, family alcoholism, negligent parents, parental deviance, poor family bonding, low level of parental involvement, child maltreatment, poor family management practices and so on. Economic hardships and lack of access to resources and opportunity also seem to have adverse impacts on the functioning of families, with negative outcomes for their children like truancy and dropping out of school, unstructured socialising with deviant peers, alcoholism, drugabuse, gang formation, and other antisocial behaviour (Dorji et al., 2015).

As most of the participants had pointed out, family disruption was one of the causes of their anger, frustration and other negative emotions, which encouraged their indulgence in substance abuse, alcohol consumption and delinquency. As might be expected, no government and society can guarantee a stable family for every child, but it is important that preventing crime among young individuals must include efforts to counteract the negative effects of family disruption.

In this connection, special attention must be given to young people who have lost their families and are seeking shelter with their friends or relatives. Of course, we do not see many street children, but this doesn't imply that there are no children with plights similar to that of street children in other developing countries. Special programmes are needed to take care of problems related to young people coming from dysfunctional families. The UN Convention on the Rights of the Child provides a framework for supporting such young people and ensuring their rights: survival rights, protective rights, development rights and participation rights. If the family adjustment initiatives, rescue of troubled young people and crime prevention measures are undertaken jointly by the agencies with fundamental stake in crime prevention like police, court, youth-serving NGOs, educational institutions, recreational groups, local governments and others, we might somewhat succeed in our efforts towards prevention and control of crime among young people (Dorji et al., 2015).

Parents must be made aware of their roles and responsibilities towards their children and of the importance of giving them constant moral guidance and support. In many cases, family breakdown, chronic poverty and alcoholism problems where young people are in trouble may render some parents impotent to take responsibility for their children. In other cases, though families may be reasonably rich, uninvolved parenting practices may deprive their children of proper moral, social and developmental guidance. The participants who came from somewhat well-to-do families described that they had suffered from poor and limited emotional connection with their parents and often took liberties to do whatever they liked (Dorji et al., 2015).

One thing which the consultative workshop participants (17 June 2015) felt important was parents' involvement with schools in tackling behavioural problems of their children. Schools seem to use every means to correct the wrongdoing students, but often some parents challenge school discipline decisions instead of getting involved to resolve the problem together. Creating awareness among such parents of their social liability to support, guide, supervise and monitor their children's activities may be useful for crime prevention and control (Dorji et al., 2015).

Some participants suggested the need to organise parental awareness programmes on the importance of proper parenting and equip neglectful parents with family management skills. One popular training approach is based on social learning principles, and it includes "training parents how to provide positive reinforcement for desirable behaviour, to use non-punitive and consistent discipline practices, and the family crisis management techniques" (Farrington & Welsh, 2003, p. 139). Incorporating positive parenting awareness programmes, behaviour management education, family management training and the programmes that bond parents and children within a larger preventive or intervention framework may contribute towards crime prevention and control.

Both the police records (part I) and this qualitative analysis (part II) showed that most offenders came from poor families. This suggests that poverty and deprivation have typically complex implications for crime by way of impacting individuals' behavioural, cognitive and attitudinal development. This analysis concludes that poverty and deprivation either directly drove young offenders into criminal acts as means to survive and get out of economic stress or impacted them indirectly by generating other drivers of crime like family instability, abusive conditions at home, forced premature autonomy, poor upbringing, low self-esteem, low educational attainment, frustration, anger, drug abuse, alcoholism and hardships. The educational attainments of most participants were rather low. They had to apparently drop their studies, mainly for the reasons that their families could not afford nominal school expenses (Dorji et al., 2015).

Most study participants admitted that they possessed some dispositional and environmental strains (prior to their criminal deeds), leading to various emotional and psychological disturbances. They recounted being angry, depressed, frustrated, hopeless, sensation seeking and resentful of their families, communities and society, which spurred them to externalise behaviour in the form of drug abuse, alcoholism and delinquency. The imprisonment period represents a timely opportunity to provide them mental healthcare services. Such services are necessary in the context of the presence of some mental health stigma among the Bhutanese people. It is said that Bhutanese people with mental problems generally face both internal and social barriers to availing themselves of mental healthcare services. The incarceration period may be exploited to treat young convicts with mental disorders and to prepare them for successful family and community re-integration. It was apparent that while the prison inmates appreciated the mental healthcare services available within the prison, many of them called for the improvement of mental healthcare services (Dorji et al., 2015).

In effect, all of them will one day or other have to return to their families, communities and society. The participants intend to exit from the prison, reformed in every respect. However, there were some sense of fear and disquietude (among them) that they might be compelled to return to the same risky environment and the same old routines, habits and behaviour that predisposed them to commit the previous crimes. The life's trajectories for them seemed less predictable. Currently, no satisfactory programme exists to facilitate the prisoners' reentry into their families and communities with some measure of self-worth. No traditional social agency exists to facilitate the prison–community transition, and thus, creating new agencies committed to help prison leavers readjust with their families and communities holds great promise of preventing or reducing recidivism.

Against this backdrop, the comprehensive re-entry support programmes are crucial for the prison leavers. Their wishes and aspirations must be given full consideration, exceptionally in providing them access to the services that can refine and enhance their livelihood. For example, a young ex-convict who had acquired some vocational skill and aptitude in the prison may wish to attend the formal vocational course. In such cases, he may be given an admission to the vocational institute not on the basis of his educational qualification but by judging his skills, aptitude and competence. Such consideration is justifiable because, firstly, the number of such cases may be small and manageable, and secondly, the cost to society of denying them such opportunities may become substantial in case they fall back and resort to antisocial behaviour.

Most participants professed that their crimes occurred under the influence of drugs and alcohol. Abuse of gangza (*cannabis sativa*) and chang (traditional liquor) seems to be common in schools and other learning institutions and among those who are jobless and idle. It was apparent that marijuana serves as a gateway or rite of passage to abuse of other dangerous drugs and a warning signs of criminal behaviour. It is unfortunate that gangza is grown in abundance in the wild, making it easily accessible to schoolchildren and young people. The commercial narcotic drugs are also easy to obtain in towns, smuggled in from the border areas (Dorji et al., 2015).

Some schools and volunteers periodically organise campaigns to root out cannabis plants. Though such programmes are beneficial, they are irregular, and sustainability remains an issue. Having a long-term plan and well-coordinated programmes to eradicate wild *cannabis sativa* plants from places near towns, schools and those places easily accessible to young people deserves high consideration. During the stakeholders' workshop (17 June 2015), many participants suggested setting up local-level committees representing different agencies and partners: local government leaders, health staff, schools, forest staff, community members and representatives from NGOs to control widespread growth of cannabis plants. The workshop participants agreed on the need to incorporate a cannabis eradication programme into the local development plan with a regular budget. The programmes, according to them, must involve local communities, schools, volunteers, monks, local government staff and so on (Dorji et al., 2015).

Another aspect of drug control is the easy availability and accessibility of commercial narcotic drugs. The stakeholder workshop's participants suggested the need to intensify vigilance on illegal cross-border drug smuggling and tough actions on drug lords and their traffickers. The RBP and Bhutan Narcotic Control Authority (BNCA) are doing their best, but there seems to be the need to toughen the effort to curb drug smuggling. Some of the workshop participants suggested using detection or sniffer dogs at critical checkpoints and for drug raids. They were of the view that having drug dogs placed at the major checkpoints can act as a strong deterrent to drug smugglers. Of course, using sniffer dogs may create an intimidating atmosphere for general motorists, but in the best interest of young people and others, the country has a significant obligation to provide the law enforcement agencies the tools to combat drug trafficking. Moreover, a canine sniff does not require opening the luggage and thus is less intrusive than the normal search (Dorji et al., 2015).

The way the study participants described how they had committed crime showed that most of the offences were committed in groups. Criminal activities among young people in peer groups were higher for theft, robbery, substance abuse, assault etc. and lower for murder and grievous crimes. We know and must appreciate that the RBP have been able to amicably crack down on gang formation in recent years, but not much can be done to intervene when young people are seen around in a group appearing so normal, though they may be up for some nuisance. Providing guidance and counselling services in schools may be one good measure to counter the negative effects of peer pressure.

Television programmes and movies seem to popularise violence and sexual urges among young people. For example, a few participants did mention their inclination to imitate heroes in the movies who usually emerge as victorious through the physical elimination of enemies. As described by one of the participants (convicts), porn movies seem to be easily accessible to children through illegal sale and online download. He said he was so habituated to watching porn movies from as early as the age of 12 that actually motivated him to rape a neighbour's girl child (Dorji et al., 2015).

Contemporary generations of Bhutanese youth have started to create a new public space for themselves in cyberspace through the internet and social media. New technologies allow young people to modify their identities and to create new and multiple virtual identities. In such cases, it is crucial for parents to exert strong parental control and monitoring of what their children are watching on television and doing on their phones or cyberspace social networks. In the larger context, creating a wide range of recreational facilities and services of interest to young people and making them easily accessible to them might divert their attention away from pernicious television programmes and violent and salacious movies and internet sites. School dropouts need to be engaged in learning and productive activities, but there seem to be a challenge in making youth development programmes attractive to them.

Arrests and sentencing are likely to deter offending behaviour because it makes young offenders understand the undesirable consequences on themselves and their families. The participants of this study have expressed repentances over their own criminal deeds and were inclined to reform and expressed their wishes for being released on parole or probation. In addition, most of them despised the severity, bias, and inconsistency of legal sanctions that left a few of them vengeful and inclined to reoffending. Most participants insisted on the need for fair and consistent punishment regardless of individual background and circumstances. There was some sense of injustice among them with regard to penal sentences imposed on them.

A dominant view among the participants was that they should not have been sentenced for longer durations that made them squander their prime years in the prisons rather than preparing them for productive citizenships. They justified this saying they had infringed the criminal laws on account of being immature, ignorant and unable to differentiate between criminal and socially acceptable acts and simply being mischievous. Many of them asserted that they gradually started to realise what is good or bad for themselves, their families and the society only after being held up in the prisons.

Going by their viewpoints, putting young people behind bars for the offences of a trivial nature may not deal with the kind of factors responsible for their crimes. It then becomes, according to them, the mere act of removing them from the crime situation but not showing them that they could become morally responsible and good citizens. Their views reflected a preference for restorative justice (Zehr, 1990; Zehr & Umbrelt, 1982) over punitive justice and affirmed the value of rehabilitation.

As the study participants maintained, while serious offenders deserve severe punishment, perpetrators of less serious crimes and first-time offenders should be treated humanely, decriminalised, and diverted from the prisons to the rehabilitation or correctional centres and observation homes if they are able to demonstrate promises for reform, social and moral righteousness, and good conduct. If the country opts to emphasise restorative justice for young offenders, it may entail establishing more rehabilitation centres across the country. Currently, the only rehabilitation centre for young offenders is managed by the RBP, which do not fully decriminalise young offender recruits. Experiences in other countries show that rehabilitation activities are normally carried out by the government agencies, NGOs and local communities.

Some participants had highlighted their experiences of being nervous, scared and dumbstruck during their court hearings. This suggest the need to assess the current trend in directing young perpetrators to conventional courts. A few of them complained of police antagonising them and foisting cases on them. Introducing special court procedures that recognise the immaturity of juvenile offenders and ensure fair and uninhibited hearings may enhance dispensation of fair, consistent and uniform justice. Legal services aid for young offenders may have positive implications on juvenile court procedures.

Special legal status of minor offenders was the recent advent, and this came about with the inception of the Penal Code of Bhutan (2002). The Penal Code legitimised a special status for children and youthful lawbreakers. In order to exercise such rights and legitimacy vouchsafed to them, it is high time that specialised and youth-friendly benches are set up across the courts at different levels. Undoubtedly, upsurges in crime among young people will only increase the pressure to reorganise and consider the need for youth courts. Further, providing training on psychology of children and youth justice and related procedures for judges and police has become imperative (Dorji et al., 2015).

Our effort to create an egalitarian society, where everyone is treated equally before the law, is often perplexed by certain legislations. The most talked-about law that the study participants were not contented with is the rape law. The participants felt there is the need to amend this law so that it does not discriminate between male and female. When rape takes place and is reported to the law enforcers, no matter who is culpable to offence or even when sexual acts are consensual, it is always the males who gets convicted.

In the opinion of participants, rather than formulating such law on the basis of ideas brought in from other countries, there should be adequate contextualising of it to our own country's long-established beliefs, customs and practices. The matter of the fact is that our society preferred early marriages (such as chung-nyen, jomo ngengi marriage tradition of Merak-Sakteng and grendheme marriage tradition of lower Kheng) not long ago. Though these traditions may no longer be relevant and sensible in today's changing contexts, our older generation had preferred early marriages (to reproduce as early as possible) to meet the manpower need for the farms. These customs and traditions are in decline but not completely wiped out, and they may be influencing (to a certain extent) how young people view sexuality (Dorji et al., 2015).

Some young rape convicts had knowledge about the rape law, but they had not taken it seriously and did not expect severe penal retribution. It would have been rational to first educate society about the rape law and legal liability for breaching it. As the society got educated about it, the enforcement could have been made stringent incrementally. For example, the statutory age limit for sex could have been set low in the beginning (instead of 18 years) and increased gradually when people got more informed and begin to understand that sexual acts with underage females are morally reprehensible and legally punishable. This would have prevented many young people from being incarcerated.

Conclusion

Young people represent a large segment of the society with an enormous potential to contribute towards the nation's success in the future. At the same time, while transitioning to adulthood, many of them stumble across so many challenges and become susceptible to various social afflictions brought about by changing social, cultural and economic contexts. Youth delinquency is on the rise, and it will only get higher unless the most appropriate counter-measures are taken. We are witnessing the crimes among young people such as murder, gang fights, robbery, vandalism and drug offences. Such rise in criminality among young people may affect the collective good of the society and disrupt the country's progress towards creating a happy and prosperous society (Dorji et al., 2015).

This chapter presented the results of the secondary data as well as the qualitative analysis with limited participants and only has a limited generalisability. To derive a comprehensive idea of crime scenarios in the country, such a study should be complemented by studies based on crime survey or crime victimisation survey data. This do not imply that such analysis is not useful. In fact, it did present many aspects of crime scenarios like nature of crime, occurrence, trend, possible causes and socio-demographic characteristics of offenders. The broader implications of findings of this analysis suggest the need for conscious and systematic efforts to address the underlying causes of juvenile and youth crime. Identifying the diversity of their needs and developing policies and programmes that can accommodate this diversity have become more crucial. This analysis illustrates that individual, family-specific and systemic issues interact to induce crime among young people. That is, multiple factors cluster together and act upon each other to generate delinquency.

Preventing and mitigating crime among young people require accurate identification of the risk factors that increase the probability of delinquent behaviour and the protective factors that prevent anti-social behaviour among young people. Though the current analysis identifies those risk factors in a limited way, it was based on the experiences of a sub-sample of young offenders. The result of this qualitative analysis cannot be generalised but may inform future research. There is then the need to conduct many action researches to understand the causes and correlates of delinquency. In fact, no adequate programme can be formulated without sound knowledge and facts about young people at risk of deviant behaviour, their problems and social influences on them. Relying only on the RBP crime records or some other administrative data to inform policy and programme designs can often be ambiguous due to underreporting of the crimes. Therefore, it is of paramount importance to undertake nationally representative crime and victimisation surveys for understanding crime among young people and designing effective interventions (Dorji et al., 2015).

We believe that empowering our young people is an essential element for improving community vitality. It is the responsibility of the government and the community to encourage our young people across the nation to make healthy choices by addressing their problems. The local leaders and parents have a huge responsibility to provide counselling services to young people who are at risk of turning unproductive and antisocial. Young people have a lot of potential. The only thing is we do not have well-integrated and comprehensive policy frameworks to make the best use of young people and their potential and make them contribute to the development of our country.

Finally, the challenge for the government is to identify the issues faced by young people (especially their causes) and to create policies that are well targeted and appropriate. While the interventionist and punitive approaches are necessary to prevent crime among the younger generation, it is important to develop policies and programmes which identify root causes and address the diverse challenges of young people and support them to reach their maximum potential through an integrated approach and in a sustainable manner (Dorji et al., 2015).

Note

1 This chapter is a revised version of the selective portions of the previously published work: Dorji, L., Gyeltshen, S. Jamtsho, C., Minten, T., Dorjee, T., Namgay, P., & Wangchuk, T. (2015). *Crime and mental health issues among young Bhutanese people.* Thimphu, Bhutan: National Statistics Bureau. Published with Permission.

References

Bhutan, R. G. (2004). *The Penal Code of Bhutan.* Thimphu.
Department of Youth and Sports, M. o. E. (2010). National Youth Policy 2010. Thimphu.
Dorji, L. (2005). *Youth in Bhutan: Education, employment, development.* Thimphu: The Centre for Bhutan Studies.
Dorji, L., Gyeltshen, S. Jamtsho, C., Minten, T., Dorjee, T., Namgay, P., & Wangchuk, T. (2015). *Crime and mental health issues among young Bhutanese People.* Thimphu, Bhutan: National Statistics Bureau.
Dorji, L., & Kinga, S. (2005). Juvenile delinquency as emerging youth problem in Bhutan. In L. Dorji (Ed.), *Youth in Bhutan: Education, employment, development.* Thimphu: The Centre for Bhutan Studies.
Farrington, D. P., & Welsh, B. C. (2003). Family-based prevention of offending: A meta-analysis. *Australian and New Zealand Journal of Criminology, 36,* 127–151.

Gibbsons, D. C. (1979). *The criminological enterprise: Theories and perspectives.* Englewood Cliffs, NJ: Prentice-Hall, Inc.

The Guardian. (2003). Bhutan: Fast forward into trouble. Retrieved from www.thegurdian.com/thegurdian/2003/june/14/weeeknd7.weekend2.

Quetelet, A. (1984). *Adolphe Quetelet's Research on propensity of crime at different ages.* Cincinnati, OH: Anderson Publishing Co.

Schwartz, J & Streffensmeier, D. (2008). *The nature of female offending patterns and explanations.* Burlington, MA: Jones and Barlett Publishers.

Ulmer, J. T., & Steffensmeier, D. (2015). *The age and crime relationship social variations, social explanations.* New York: SAGE Publications.

Winsor, T. (2014, November 18). Her Majesty's Inspectorate of Constabulary (HMIC), UK. Retrieved from www.justiceinspectorates.gov.uk/hmic/news/news-feed/victims-let-down-by-poor-crime-recording.

Zehr, H. (1990). *Changing lenses: A focus for crime and justice.* Scottsdale, PA: Herald Press.

Zehr, H., & Umbrelt, M. (1982). Victim offender reconciliation: An incarceration substitute? *Federal Probation, 46*(4), 63–68.

PART V

Victims and Victimization

27

WOMEN VICTIMS OF WAR AND CRIME IN AFGHANISTAN

Kirthi Jayakumar

Introduction

Sexual violence or gender-based violence refers to violence that is directed against a person on the basis of their gender (Council of Europe, 2011). Given that violence is antagonistic to the freedom of a person, it is a violation of the rights to life, liberty, security, dignity and equality between the genders. In that sense, gender-based violence amounts to a reinforcement of the inequalities that thrive between men and women. The repertoire of acts of violence falling under each category varies greatly and includes everything from domestic violence, sexual harassment, rape, molestation and sexual violence to female genital mutilation, forced marriages, honour crimes and trafficking (Council of Europe, 2011). The world at large witnesses tremendous violence against women—a phenomenon that cuts across borders, cultures, religions and ethnic structures in society.

Generally speaking, violence against women and girls comprises a range of different forms of violence including physical, psychological, sexual, verbal and economic violence. It can be carried out by anyone, within or without a familial or work setup, but the necessary element is that the targets of such forms of violence are women. In most jurisdictions across the world, some forms of violence against women are penalized (Lauritsen & Schaum, 2004).

The Convention on the Elimination of All Forms of Discrimination against Women in 1979 was the first official international piece of legislation that firmly decried all forms of violence against women. The Convention on the Elimination of All Forms of Discrimination against Women (CEDAW) is a human rights treaty for women's rights. It is commonly described as an international bill of rights for women. The convention was adopted by the United Nations General Assembly in 1971 and came into force in 1981. The convention is monitored by the CEDAW Committee, which is based in New York. CEDAW is one of the most highly ratified international human rights conventions, having the support of 186 state parties, and is constantly updated on the basis of general recommendations made by the committee. There are thirty articles in this convention that deal with several aspects of the lives of women in society. The substance of the Convention is based on three interrelated core principles: equality, non-discrimination and state obligation. The convention most importantly defines "discrimination against women", which means "any distinction, exclusion or restriction made on the basis of sex which has the effect or purpose of impairing or nullifying the recognition, enjoyment or exercise by women, irrespective of their marital status, on a basis of equality of men and women, of human rights and fundamental freedoms in the political, economic, social, cultural, civil or any other field". It also proceeds to condemn discrimination against women in all forms, through social and legal means.

In 1993, a Declaration on the Prohibition of All Forms of Discrimination Against Women denounced violence against women on all accounts and notes that violence against women impairs the enjoyment of women's human rights and is tantamount to being an impediment to the access of basic human freedoms (UNDPI, 1996). The declaration specifically defines violence against women and indicates that "violence against women constitutes a violation of the rights and fundamental freedoms of women and impairs or nullifies their enjoyment of those rights and freedoms" (UNDPI, 1996). The Beijing Declaration and Platform for Action adopted by the Fourth World Conference of 1995 defined violence against women in the Platform for Action as "any act of gender-based violence that results in, or is likely to result in, physical, sexual or psychological harm or suffering to women, including threats of such acts, coercion or arbitrary deprivation of liberty, whether occurring in public or private life".

Evaluating the kind of violence that occurs, the most commonly found occurring is domestic violence, which comprises physical, sexual and psychological violence that occurs within the familial setup and can be directed against any of the women in the family and can be carried out by relatives, not necessarily those related by blood. The second involves exploitative violence that generally includes trafficking, prostitution and forced marriage. The third category involves institutionally sanctioned violence where there is violence prevailing due to war, inadequacy of policies and legislation in times of peace or during unrest.

In 2011, the Thomson Reuters Foundation completed a survey that declared that Afghanistan was the "worst place in the world to be born a woman" (*Thomson Reuters*, 2011). The report explained that Afghanistan is "the most dangerous country for women overall and worst in three of the six risk categories: health, non-sexual violence and lack of access to economic resources." A survey of 213 experts in gender and issues concerning gender by the same foundation revealed that Afghanistan has high rates of maternal mortality coupled with heavily limited access to doctors and a state of almost a total lack of economic rights for women. It also explained that a UNICEF research project indicated that Afghan women have a 1-in-11 chance of dying in childbirth.

What makes women vulnerable? What makes them the perfect targets for violence in Afghanistan? The reason for women being made victims in a conflict-ridden background can be culled from a study of the political, cultural and social factors, coupled with the convenient backdrop that a history of conflict provides for gender-based violence. A mélange of criminology and victimology can explain the perpetrators' raison d'être for targeting women and reasons why women are easy victims. This chapter seeks to evaluate the situation in Afghanistan, tracing the trajectory from the inception of the Taliban rule until the present day. The situation as it prevails in Afghanistan will then be evaluated against criminological/victimological perspectives, to understand exactly why women are easy targets in a conflict-ridden society.

I. Violence Against Women in Afghanistan

Afghanistan redefines the very substance of conflict and its impact on gender violence. The impact of a state of war for decades together has ensured that gender violence remains not just protracted but also a deeply ingrained social mindset. As a country, Afghanistan historically never oppressed women or opposed the implemented enforcement of women's rights. Over time, these mindsets changed. In the nineteenth century, Afghanistan remained under the control of tribal groups and warlords. These institutions, driven by authority, controlled women. There was a breather for a while after 1973, when the People's Democratic Party of Afghanistan took over and attempted to once again reform marriage laws, women's rights in general and even took up cudgels in favour of women's education (Armstrong, 2003). In 1992, the Peshawar Accord was signed, in establishment of the Islamic State of

Afghanistan, by all the major Afghan anti-Soviet resistance parties, with the exception of Gulbuddin Hekmatyar's Hezb-e-Islami. The Peshawar Accord restored peace through an interim government (Saikal, 2006). However, War in Afghanistan was not far away, for it came back with a bang. This time around, Hekmatyar actively campaigned in antagonism towards women, having had a history of throwing acid into the faces of women and shooting them at University in 1970. Although there were bans on alcohol and the enforcement of veil use, (Maley, 1999) women remained integrated in the workforce, and the liberal provisions of the 1964 constitution were largely upheld. In 1996, Hekmatyar Gulbuddin became the prime minister of the integrated Islamic State of Afghanistan, and restrictions were increasingly imposed. Women who appeared on television or any form of media were fired at under Hekmatyar's orders. In the four years that followed, a massive civil war ensued, in which women were kidnapped and raped.

It was at this time that the Taliban were welcomed by the people. They were a group that comprised poor villagers educated in Wahhabi schools in Pakistan (Keddie, 2007). The Taliban regime was the death knell for progressive lifestyles of women in the country. With the advent of the Taliban, women were denied some of their most basic human rights and fundamental freedoms. The right to life, work, education, healthcare, freedoms of expression, movement and religion were no longer permitted women. When women asserted their rights under the Taliban regime, they were subjected to public lapidation, beatings and imprisonment. Women were not allowed to leave their households unless they had a burqa and had a male member of their family to accompany them. These policies rendered many women immobile and confined to their houses, because they were either too poor to afford a burqa or had no male relatives left after war. The women who remained at home had to paint their windows so no one could look in from outside (Rostami-Povey, 2007). The few women who once held respectable positions prior to the five years under Taliban rule were forced to beg to survive or to stay confined in their houses.

Women teachers who functioned before the Taliban regime could no longer teach at schools. This led to the redundancy of many schools and the imposition of a severe strain on the education system. Women in medicine were allowed to continue, because women could only be treated by female physicians. Despite that, a steady decline in access to medical care and healthcare ensued, because it was frowned upon for a woman to go to a hospital. The few that tried were beaten. Braving all of that, if a woman made it to the hospital, there was no guarantee that a doctor would see her (Skaine, 2008). A parallel market of human-trafficking, prostitution and slavery thrived (McGirk & Shomali Plain, 2002).

Though the Karzai government has to some extent changed this, the situation remains grim. Women are still under the domination of men, and a majority of women apart from those in Kabul are not allowed to be seen in public without a burqa. Education still eludes women, and healthcare access is frugal. The law is antagonistic to women's access to education and other social rights. Women are not allowed to go out except for legitimate purposes—but what legitimate is is still an obscure element, ushering in subjectivity. In 2008, Global Rights Nationwide indicated that 17% of the women were sexually abused by their husbands (Global Rights Nationwide, 2008). The National Penal Code equates rape with adultery.[1] Civil and family disputes are considered private and are not reported to the formal courts. However, the traditional dispute-resolution mechanisms or the Jirgas decide such cases. Women are punished, killed and given in exchange of crime (called bad) as a restorative justice mechanism (Afghan Women's Network, 2009).

II. A Criminological Dissection of Violence Against Women in Afghanistan

The general tendency is to identify Afghanistan as a black hole so far as women's rights go. By citing the lack of law, the presence of conflict, the general state of radicalism that misinterprets religion and law in a manner that affects women's rights adversely, most crimes are perceived as a by-product of a state of lawlessness. So far as violence against women goes, the issue is far more nuanced than just conjecture on lawlessness and conflict prevalence can explain. Some of the factors that could be potential causes for violence against women in Afghanistan have been elaborated below.

1. Patriarchy

Patriarchy literally means rule of the father in a male-dominated family. It is a social and ideological construct which considers men (who are the patriarchs) as superior to women. Sylvia Walby in "Theorising Patriarchy" calls it "a system of social structures and practices in which men dominate, oppress and exploit women" (Ray, 2013). Patriarchy is based on a system of power relations which are hierarchical and unequal where men control women's production, reproduction and sexuality (Ray, 2013). It imposes masculinity and femininity character stereotypes in society which strengthen the iniquitous power relations between men and women (Ray, 2013). Patriarchy is not a constant, and gender relations, which are dynamic and complex, have changed over the periods of history (Ray, 2013). The nature of control and subjugation of women varies from one society to the other, as it differs due to the differences in class, caste, religion, region, ethnicity and socio-cultural practices (Ray, 2013). The "processes that confer privileges to one group and not another group are often invisible to those upon whom that privilege is conferred" (Kimmel, 2004). The patriarchy rhetoric has significant political dimensions (Kimmel, 2004). The concept of "public patriarchy" refers to the institutional arrangements of a society, the predominance of males in all power positions within the economy and polity, both locally and nationally, as well as the "gendering" of those institutions themselves (by which the criteria for promotion, for example, appear to be gender neutral but actually reproduce the gender order) (Kimmel, 2004). Another manifestation of patriarchy is within the confines of the household—called and identified as "domestic patriarchy". Domestic patriarchy includes within its fold the elements and dimensions of male–female relationships, the dynamics of familial life and the mode of upbringing for the children of such families. Public patriarchy is the wider social setup that includes all actors beyond the family—which means the remainder of society, including the military and the police.

In essence, patriarchy is a form of structural violence (Barash & Webel, 2013). Structural violence refers to the kind of undercurrent of violence that is built into the structure of a society, a culture or an economic or political institution. In that it is an undercurrent, structural violence is indirect in its impact and arguably more insidious in comparison with actual physical violence (Barash & Webel, 2013). When a society forcibly imposes restraints on the development of its people or undermines the well-being and happiness of its people on any account—whether age, religion, gender, ethnicity, sexual preference or any other attribute—it amounts to a manifestation of structural violence (Barash & Webel, 2013).

Another factor that manifests because patriarchy is a form of structural violence is that patriarchy and hierarchy have a strong link (Taylor & Beinstein, 1994). Patriarchy elevates men, thereby devaluing women, and encourages a climate of domination that may be backed by force. The domination and subjugation hinges on gender in that the men dominate over and subjugate the women in society. This hierarchy remains a value that is passed onto succeeding generations, and because of the dominant nature, they become "male values", which enculturation carries forth while devaluing the female values of subjugation (Taylor & Miller, 1994).

Given that structural violence is invariably built into a social setup, it is often perceived as an "acceptable practice" or something that is "traditional" or "the norm". Therefore, the fact that it is violence is never really noticed or considered. In sharp contrast, direct violence is overt, visible and actually tangible. But in most instances, structural violence is the enabler for overt and direct violence. For example, the harassment of newlywed brides to beget sons is a clear case of structural violence, because it is a practice built into Afghan society to demand a price for the groom from the bride's family. But the manifestation of that violence can be direct, such as abusive behaviour, bride burning and domestic violence.

Afghanistan is a patriarchal society where all the major institutions are controlled by men (Nasimi, 2014). Although, since 2001, there have been many endeavours to elevate women and improvements have been observed, the foundations of discrimination against women have not been uprooted (Nasimi, 2014).

So far as Afghanistan goes, as Ahmed Rashid (2010) explains, many of the young men who fought for the Taliban were really orphaned young men who were aged between fourteen and twenty-four and were inculcated with "values" that grew out of a rather skewed interpretation of Islam by some mullahs who preferred radicalism to literacy. Consequently, they grew up in surroundings that showed and taught them precious little about women, making them perceive women as nothing more than unnecessary, unwelcome distractions that had the potential to tempt a man and lure him off the path he was chosen for. To this end, there was a belief that women were unnecessary in every sphere of life, whether domestic or otherwise. The Taliban also encouraged sexual abstinence (Rashid, 2010) and contended that men and women should not be in contact with one another, since women would weaken a warrior (Rashid, 2010). The radical manifestation of these ideas took the shape of active violence against women. Aside from segregation of women from men and the deprivation of property rights, violence became a common occurrence.

2. Cultural Interpretations of Religion

Technically speaking, nothing in Islamic law is skewed against women inherently. The verses of the Koran that are quoted as encouraging polygamy were actually the directives in the aftermath of a war, where widows and orphaned children outnumbered men, for a man to make good the lives of the women who were abandoned without means to live. The birth of Islam came at a time when the world was filled with barbaric practices, the time predating Islam now being known as Jahiliyya (Freeman-Grenville, 1981), an era of "ignorance of divine guidance". Legend has it that in the period that predated the birth of Islam, fathers were forced to bury their firstborns alive after they turned five if the firstborn was a girl. Among these manifestations of skewed perceptions of women, Islam had arrived as the divine guidance that would obliterate these practices.

In Afghanistan,

> references to Islam can be made by anyone, at any time, for any purpose. No matter the issue, a person may cite an appropriately vague hadith, said to represent the thousands of (often contradictory) opinions and life events of the prophet Muhammad or a recollection of what a mullah has once said. Such determinations—and they are not usually exclaimed with absolute certainty—of what is Islamic or not, are liberally distributed by Afghans, both young and old, and by those who hold university degrees and by those who use only their thumbprints to sign documents. The constant references to religion lead many Afghans to believe that any new rule imposed on them is mandatory to be a good Muslim.
>
> *(Nordberg, 2014)*

The general state of oppression that prevails in Afghanistan stems from a traditional cache of Pashtun practices. In most such traditional practices, the male elders in a family have an absolute say in the marriage of the young women in their families. They demand high bride prices for the girls in their families, thereby selling the girls off. Another manifestation of these traditional values is the practice of honour killings, where a woman found guilty of "sexual misconduct", or even refusal to marry, can be killed in order to preserve the family's honour. This has invariably encouraged the seclusion and segregation of women, right from their blue-canvas chaddars to actual physical isolation and confinement (Nasimi, 2014).

Although most often, the grounds cited to control women are invariably contended as having been founded in religion, it really is a cultural (mis)interpretation of religious tenets. For example, *namus*, or honour of a family—is considered a significant cultural value. Women are perceived as the flag bearers of a family's honour, for their chastity and good conduct is considered a representation of the decency and honour of a family vis-à-vis its social standing. Therefore, a violation of this code by failing to protect *namus* amounts to enough reason to kill the girl. However, no interpretation of the Koran has ever suggested encouragement for killing in the name of honour.

Afghanistan's population is structured into tribal communities that may or may not, with the majority falling in line with the former, practice Islam. The intermingling of tribal cultural practices and traditions with a religious outlook has tended for the two to be irretrievably mixed, to the point that they blur into one for those practicing the two. Consequently, women have been brutally beaten, tortured, burned, prostituted, raped and abused in the name of religion. On many occasions, religious, tribal and some political leaders in Afghanistan have been strong endorsers of harmful cultural practices by relying on their own interpretations of Islam which do not always fall in line with generally accepted norms under Sharia law and international law.

Part of this is also a proclivity towards cultural atavism despite external imposition of progress. Atavism essentially refers to the return to an ancient or ancestral type and when it comes to the perception of women, the society behaves in an atavistic way as the cultural practices are always in retrograde. Though Afghanistan has been a party to the UN Convention on the Elimination of All Forms of Discrimination Against Women, the constant state of disarray, the prevalence of frugal legislation concerning women and their status and the lack of access to justice have proven to be a suitable backdrop to create a state of cultural atavism (Rosenbush, 2014).

3. Masculinities of Violence

It is important to understand that masculinity is a social practice and not an identity (Connell & Messerschmidt, 2005). By perceiving it as an identity, there are attributes that are expected to be fulfilled in order to continue keeping that identity. Manliness must be validated by other men, in its reality as actual or potential violence, and certified by recognition of membership of the group of "real men" (Bourdieu, 1998). This leads to the creation of an expectation that must be adhered to. Especially during conflict in an armed militia, there is a rite of passage of sorts where those in combat are expected to assert their masculinities in a manner that would suitably weaken and break the enemy. The assertion of their masculinities invariably takes the form of violence, for that becomes the most symbolic representation and rendition of domination. The construction of masculinity is attributed to how much of a "warrior" a man is and how much "fight" he has in him. In many ways, this masculinity is "constructed through war" (Goldstein, 2001). Masculine, here, does not mean only domination by men but women and men after the assumption of masculinity, this masculinity being a social process and not an identity (Sivakumaran, 2007). Since it is a social process, it is fully possible for a woman to also be a perpetrator of violence against other women. In Sahar Gul's case (*BBC News Asia*, 2013), a child bride was tortured, beaten, brutally wounded and harassed by her husband's family, in which her mother-in-law and sister-in-law were major perpetrators too. In the words of UN Women Chief Phumzile Mlambo-Ngcuka, "Husbands are not the sole perpetrators of violence against women in the home: mothers-in-law, sisters- and brothers-in law, as well as other male family members have also been identified as abusers by studies conducted on violence against women in the country" (Deutsche Welle, 2014). The efforts of the US and its allies' troops to "control fanaticism in Afghanistan have resulted in Afghan men being further emasculated and depicted as unable to exercise control over their state and people" (Gilani, 2008).

4. Lack of Identity for Women Under Law

Skewed as the culture is, it is no surprise that the legislative structure, so far as women are concerned, is a reflection of the same. Sharia law contends that the legal standing of women vis-à-vis the law is confined to a minimal extent. Under the ambit of Sharia law governing procedure, the testimony of a woman is equal to half of what a man's testimony is worth. Women don't have property rights. Under family law, the custody of children is given to the father or the grandfather.

So divorce—even in cases of extreme abuse—is less likely to be sought, because a woman must be prepared to lose her children. These discriminatory practices against women are pervasive, occurring across ethnic groups in both rural and urban areas.

Many Afghans, including some religious leaders, reinforce harmful customs by invoking their interpretation of Islam. In most cases, however, these practices are inconsistent with Sharia as well as Afghan and international law. As long as patriarchy is perceived as the dominant culture and public value in Afghan society, violence and the tendency to commit violent acts will remain an integral part of culture and valued relationships. The lack of identity for women creates an institution of social learning that tends to convey a belief that women are not important or that women do not matter. The value attached to a boy or a man is significantly higher, so much so that a girl or woman dressed as a boy or man is given as much respect as a male is generally offered—notwithstanding the fact that the disguise may be an open secret (Nordberg, 2014).

The social learning theory indicates that deviant behaviour is acquired through the assimilation of knowledge through the observation of others, their behavioural patterns, their value systems and actions (Ellis, 1989). The learning is invariably influenced by the people that an individual remains in the company of, associating with them on a regular basis directly or indirectly. Patterns of domestic violence within the household, the regular discounting of women as unimportant, the perception of women as chattel and even the belief that women are the scions of honour for a family's reputation are passed on by imbibitions to the males in a household. This learning is then reinforced and emphasised with time.

Conclusion

A grand part of the prevailing culture of violence in Afghanistan stems from a skewed cultural backdrop that is augmented by external factors. The presence of a continuous state of conflict since the mid-nineties up until now, the general state of lawlessness and the radicalization and cultural interpretation of religion have augmented a structural form of violence: patriarchy. A nuanced approach to the state of affairs in Afghanistan will need not only a legal bent of mind but a heavy inclination towards anthropological and cultural understanding. For the duration that Afghanistan has been under the control of US troops and its allies' forces, the concept of "women's rights" have become a buzzword of sorts. There are plenty of initiatives at the grassroots, inter-governmental and international levels but only a few of them owned and crafted by the people of Afghanistan themselves. In the process, there are many cases of imposed solutions that have little or no understanding of the cultural fabric of Afghan society backing them. Consequently, these imposed solutions fail, and the nation remains in the throes of a state where violence against women remains at a record high.

The key to making inroads into the Afghani milieu vis-à-vis women's rights is to start from the bottom. To know what the religious interpretations are, to be able to understand and qualify what the consequential impacts of their policies have been against a political landscape of tribal warlords and to comprehend the rationale that underlies the mindsets of those skewed against women are all necessary prerequisites to ensure that solutions to address violence against women remain comprehensive when crafted. To make those solutions feasible and practicable, it is important to involve the local people—the imposition of a solution is as good as there being no solution. The local population should own the idea, they should believe they have a stake to hold in the process, and they should see the benefits they can derive from implementing a solution as something they want to have for themselves, for the future.

Note

1 Adultery is sexual intercourse between a married woman and another married man. It is called Zinna in Islamic law, and upon testimony of four authentic witnesses (men), the adulterer and adulteress are subject to lashes and stoning based on Sharia law and the judgement of the Qaazi (religious judge).

References

Afghan Women's Network. (2009). Gender based violence in Afghanistan. Retrieved from www.aidsdatahub.org/sites/default/files/documents/Gender_based_Violence_in_Afghanistan.pdf.

Armstrong, S. (2003). *Veiled threat: The hidden power of the women of Afghanistan.* Berkeley, CA: Seal Press.

Barash, D. P., & Webel, C. P. (2013). *Peace and conflict studies.* New York: Sage.

BBC News Asia. (July 15, 2013). *Sahar Gul: The fears of a tortured Afghan Child Bride.* Retrieved from www.bbc.com/news/world-asia-23311414.

Bourdieu, P. (1998). *Masculine domination.* Stanford: Stanford University Press.

Connell, R. W., & Messerschmidt, J. W. (2005). Hegemonic masculinity: Rethinking the Concept. *Gender & Society, 19*(6), 829–859.

Council of Europe. (2011). *Ad Hoc Committee on preventing and combating violence against women and domestic violence* (CAHVIO). Strasbourg, France.

Deutsche, W. (2014). UN Women chief "seriously concerned" Afghan women's gains may be reversed. Retrieved from www.dw.de/un-women-chief-seriously-concerned-afghan-womens-gains-may-be-reversed/a-18100806.

Elaheh, Rostami-Povey. (2007). *Afghan women: Identity and invasion.* London: Zed Books.

Ellis, L. (1989). *Theories of rape: Inquiries into the causes of sexual aggression.* New York: Hemisphere Publishing Corp.

Freeman-Grenville, G. S. P. (1981). *Islam: An illustrated history and Qutb, Sayyid milestones.* IA: Mother Mosque Foundation.

Gilani, S. (2008). Politics and societies, reconstituting manhood: Examining post-conflict remasculinisation and its effects on women and women's rights in Afghanistan. *In-Spire: Journal of Law, 3*(2).

Goldstein, J. (2001). *War and gender.* Cambridge: Cambridge University Press

Keddie, N. R. (2007). *Women in the Middle East.* Princeton, NJ: Princeton University Press.

Kimmel, M. (2004). Global masculinities: Restoration and resistance. Retrieved from http://pendientedemigracion.ucm.es/info/rqtr/biblioteca/masculinidad/Global%20Masculinities.pdf.

Lauritsen, J. L., & Schaum, R. J. (2004). The social ecology of violence against women. *Criminology, 42*, 323–357.

Maley, W. (1999). Reviewed by Carl L. Brown, fundamentalism reborn? Afghanistan and the Taliban. *Foreign Affairs.* Retrieved from www.foreignaffairs.com/articles/54956/l-carl-brown/fundamentalism-reborn-afghanistan-and-the-taliban.

McGirk, T., & Plain, S. (2002). Lifting the veil on Taliban sex slavery. *Time Magazine.* Retrieved from http://content.time.com/time/magazine/article/0,9171,201892,00.html.

Nasimi, S. (2014). The devastating truth of women's rights in Afghanistan. *Open Democracy.* Retrieved from www.opendemocracy.net/opensecurity/shabnam-nasimi/devastating-truth-of-women%E2%80%99s-rights-in-afghanistan.

Nordberg, J. (2014). *The underground girls of Kabul.* Danvers, MA: Crown Publishing.

Rashid, A. (2010). *Militant Islam, oil and fundamentalism in Central Asia.* New Haven: Yale University Press.

Ray, S. (2013). *Understanding patriarchy.* Foundation Course, Delhi University. Retrieved from http://dramser.edublogs.org/files/2013/11/hrge_06-1uq0zmd.pdf.

Rosenbush, E. (2014). Editor's note. *Harpers.* Retrieved from http://harpers.org/blog/2014/12/introducing-the-january-2015-issue.

Saikal, A. (2006). *Modern Afghanistan: A history of struggle and survival.* London: I.B. Tauris & Co Ltd.

Sivakumaran, S. (2007). Sexual violence against men in armed conflict. *European Journal of International Law, 18,* 253–276.

Skaine, R. (2008). *Women of Afghanistan in the post-Taliban era: How lives have changed and where they stand today.* Jefferson, NC: McFarland.

Taylor, A., & Beinstein M. J. (1994). Introduction: The necessity of seeing gender in conflict. In A. Taylor & J. B. Miller (Eds.), *Conflict and gender.* New York: Hampton Press.

Thomson Reuters. (2011). The World's most dangerous countries for women. Retrieved from www.trust.org/spotlight/the-worlds-most-dangerous-countries-for-women-2011.

UNDPI (United Nations Department of Public Information). 1996. *Women and violence.* Retrieved from www.un.org/rights/dpi1772e.htm.

28

HUMAN TRAFFICKING IN NEPAL
A Victimological Perspective

Sandhya Basini Sitoula

Introduction

Human trafficking is one of the most severe forms of violence against human beings. It can be regarded as the worst form of human rights violation. The notion of human trafficking has been defined and discussed from various aspects. Some of the literatures define it as the illegal transfer of a human being from one place to another for the purpose of trafficking, more specifically commercial exploitation. Human trafficking is also taken as transfer and harboring of the person for labour exploitation. However, human trafficking has been defined in various ways by laws as per context. Some countries have considered trafficking as immoral offence and some have focused on trafficking linked with sexual exploitation. Some modern laws have linked trafficking also with illegal transfer of human organs.

> Trafficking in Persons shall mean the recruitment, transportation, transfer, harboring or receipt of persons, by means of the threat or use of force or other forms of coercion, of abduction, of fraud, of deception, of the abuse of power or of a position of vulnerability, or of the giving or receiving of payments or benefits to achieve the consent of a person having control over another person, for the purpose of exploitation. Exploitation shall include, at a minimum, the exploitation of the prostitution of others or other forms of sexual exploitation, forced labor or services, slavery or practices similar to slavery, servitude or the removal of organs. The 'consent' of the victim of trafficking shall be irrelevant where any of the means set forth above have been used. 'Consent' is irrelevant in case of children even if this does not involve any of the means set forth above.[1]

Trafficking of persons has flourished due to the patriarchal social structure, gender disparity, geographical inaccessibility, illiteracy and ignorance and exploitative socio-economic and cultural relation in the society.[2] People are trafficked for various reasons including purposes like commercial sex, domestic servitude, organ removal, debt bondage, labor and other forms of exploitation. Though trafficking is not a new problem, the appalling new dimension it has reached in recent years means it is now a crime of epidemic proportions. It is a global concern, and no region or country is immune.

Human trafficking has been in practice for a long time in Nepal. Girls and women have particularly been the targets of unscrupulous traffickers nationwide and was basically trafficked for the purpose of sexual exploitation. Needless to say, the dimensions of trafficking purposes, vulnerable groups, destinations, approaches and modus operandi have been changing constantly with the changes in socio-economic and political contexts. Nowadays, trafficking is occurring not only for sexual purpose but also in the name of labor migration. Lots of internal and within-country trafficking takes place, which was not the case long before.

In order to address trafficking, Nepal has enacted various laws. Nepal has a national framework for protection of victims of trafficking, most particularly in the form of Human Trafficking and Transportation Control Act, 2007, and its Regulation 2008. Likewise, various laws are also related to the issue of trafficking, which include Children Act, Foreign Employment Act, Labor Act and Muluki Ain.

Victims are the essential part of the trafficking crime. 'Victims' are those persons who, individually or collectively, suffer and sustain harm, which includes physical and psychological harm, economic loss, and substantial impairment of fundamental rights either through commission or omission of the activities which are considered illegal in the criminal laws. Generally direct harm is sustained by the victim of human trafficking; however, families and relatives are also victimized indirectly. In the offense of human trafficking, 'victim' means a person who is sold, transported or put into prostitution.[3] The concerns of the victims are always neglected in the traditional justice system. The sole focus is given to the rights of the accused, whereas the rights of the victim are shadowed. Trafficking laws are also not the exception. Lots of rights of trafficking victims are curtailed while they are trafficked, like right to freedom, right to reproductive health, right to privacy, right to dignity, right to choose profession, right to education, right to movement, right to choose and so on. Victims of trafficking own various rights that include the right to compensation, right to privacy, right to participate in the criminal proceedings, right to reintegrate and rehabilitate, right to be non-penalized, right to protection and the physical security and right to access information, advice and assistance.

Nepalese trafficking laws have also provided various rights to the victims of the trafficking. However, the sufficiency and the implementation status of those rights of the victims are to be considered. Though Nepal has enacted Human Trafficking and Transportation (Control) Act (HTTA), 2007, and its Regulation 2008, it seems that the provisions of the laws are not adequate from the perspectives of victims' justice. The victims of the trafficking usually belong to the most marginalized and backward communities; most of them are illiterate and poor. If the legal provisions and the court procedure are not friendly for the victim, there remains the risk of victims of trafficking being further victimized. The complex legal provisions and procedures may create obstacles for the victims including complaining the case to the competent authority. The social stigmatization associated with trafficking due to lack of awareness in society necessarily associates all the trafficking with sexual exploitation. The key issues and challenges faced by the survivors of trafficking are social rejection and lack of ownership of citizenship, which does not allow these survivors to successfully reintegrate into the society. Lack of economic opportunity is one of the major factors driving people to migrate and giving traffickers the opportunity to lure potential victims. Unless equipped with alternative livelihood options with a substantial and sustainable income level, there is a high risk for survivors to be re-trafficked.

The United Nations Declaration of Basic Principles of Justice for Victims of Crime and Abuse of Power[4] defined the term 'victim' as any person who, individually or collectively, has suffered harm, including physical or mental injury, emotional suffering, economic loss or substantial impairment of fundamental rights, through acts or omissions that are in violation of criminal laws operating within the member states, including those laws proscribing criminal abuse of power. It further advocates the right of the victim to be treated with compassion and respect for their dignity.[5] The responsibility of the state and the judiciary has also been highlighted in the declaration in the form of facilitating victims through formal and informal mechanisms.[6]

However, the three basic principles of this declaration can be highlighted as follows:

- Access to justice and fair treatment for the victim[7]
- Fair restitution to the victim and their families or dependents by the offender[8]
- Compensation to victims and their family given by the State[9]

In recent times, the term 'survivor' has been interchangeably used with 'victim'.

The present chapter advocates that human trafficking victims in Nepal should be provided with a package of services like legal counseling, psychological counseling, medical treatment, rehabilitation services etc. and dealt with use extra precautions.

I. Situation of Human Trafficking in Nepal

Human trafficking in Nepal is a serious concern. Nepal is mainly a source country for men, women and children subjected to forced labor and sex trafficking. The Trafficking in Persons Report (TIP) compiled by the US State Department rates Nepal as Tier 2, the explanation of which is,

> the government does not fully comply with the minimum standards for the elimination of trafficking; however, it is making significant efforts to do so. In the present situation human trafficking is not confined to Indian brothels with purpose of sexual exploitation. Human trafficking from Nepal has been extended to Gulf countries for sexual as well as labor exploitation. Similarly, not only women and children are trafficked but also adult male are being trafficked. People of any gender, caste, creed and geographical location are indiscriminately being affected by human trafficking. Causes of human trafficking in Nepal occur in many areas of the sex sector, in entertainment sector, hospitality, brick kiln, garment industries, in agriculture, in domestic working, street begging, and transplantation of organs.[10]

The scope of human trafficking in Nepal is difficult to ascertain due to the lack of reliable statistical information, the open and highly congested border with India and the clandestine nature of the crime. Past experiences of trafficking of women and girls for the purpose of forced prostitution or sexual exploitation, specifically to India, have gradually been expanding to internal, cross-border and international trafficking of girls, women, men and boys. While trafficking for sex and prostitution still exists in Nepal, a significant paradigm shift in the trends of human trafficking has taken place. Currently, the major forms of trafficking in Nepal occur in many areas such as in labour migration, organ transplantation and the adult entertainment industry.

NGOs like Child Workers in Nepal (CWIN) cite a growing internal child sex tourism problem, with an estimated 5,000 to 7,000 girls trafficked from rural areas to Kathmandu for commercial sexual exploitation. In addition, the Nepalese Youth Foundation estimated that there are over 20,000 child indentured domestic workers in Nepal. Bonded labor also remains a significant problem in Nepal, affecting entire families forced into labor as land tillers or cattle herders. Men and women also migrate willingly from Nepal to Malaysia, Israel, South Korea, the United States, Saudi Arabia, the United Arab Emirates (U.A.E.), Qatar and other Gulf states to work as domestic servants, construction workers or other low-skilled laborers, but some subsequently face conditions of forced labor such as withholding of passports, restrictions on movement, non-payment of wages, threats, deprivation of food and sleep and physical or sexual abuse. A number of these workers are subjected to debt bondage, produced in part by fraud and high recruitment fees charged by unscrupulous agents in Nepal. A lot of internal trafficking also takes place these days. People are lured for good employment opportunities with attractive pay and brought to different cities and tourist hubs from different remote areas and are forced to work in entertainment sectors, which many times are operated in very exploitative and degrading conditions.

The National Report 2011 of the National Human Rights Commission (NHRC) revealed that about 11,500 persons were trafficked or attempted to be traffic in the fiscal year (FY) 2011/12. The Global Slavery Index 2013 estimated that at least 250,000 to 270,000 Nepalese were enslaved—of which at least 6,250 to 6,750 persons were trafficked. In FY 2012/13, 144 cases of trafficking were registered with the Nepal Police. The modus operandi of traffickers in most of the cases is luring with false promises. According to the records of the Office of the Attorney General (OAG), women trafficking survivors in FY 2011/2012 were altogether 125, and in FY 2012/13, it was 203 woman trafficking survivors who initiated cases in different courts of Nepal. This clearly shows the high disparity of actual crime committed and cases prosecuted and initiated in courts.

II. Laws and Policies Regarding Counter-Trafficking in Nepal

1. Constitutional Guarantees

The interim constitution of Nepal, 2007, has guaranteed the rights of women as fundamental rights.[11] It has guaranteed the rights of women including forbidding physical or mental violence against women.[12] Further, the constitution has also provides right against exploitation as a fundamental right.[13] It has been explicitly mentioned that traffic in human beings, slavery and serfdom or forced labor in any form shall be regarded as exploitation and thus punishable.[14]

Article 29 explicitly guarantees the right against exploitation. It says that no practice of any kind that exploits women may be justified as culture or tradition.[15] The article explicitly bans selling of human beings and placing anyone in the condition of 'bonded labor' and 'slavery or servitude'[16]. Similarly, the act of engaging anyone in forced labor is prohibited too.[17]

2. General Legal Framework Under the Muluki Ain (Law of Land) 1964

Muluki Ain under the chapter of Human Traffic has defined 'traffic in human being' as a crime punishable with terms of imprisonment. It has provided that no person shall entice and take any human being out of the territory of Nepal with the intention of selling him/her or take him/her outside of the territory of Nepal and sell him/her. In case any person has taken somebody for sale in foreign countries and is arrested before he can do so, he/she shall be punished by imprisonment for a term of ten years. In case the sale has been completed, he/she shall be punished by imprisonment for a term of twenty years. In case the purchaser is traced within the territory of Nepal, he/she shall be sentenced to the same punishment as the seller.[18] It does not talk much about internal trafficking and labour exploitation as a form of human trafficking

Clause 2 of the same chapter prohibits the separation of a minor person or anyone having a mental disorder without consent of his/her legal guardian. It has also restricted the act of enticing such person or persons for separation from their legal guardians. Such an act is punishable by an imprisonment up to three years and fine of 500 rupees or both.

3. Human Trafficking and Transportation (Control) Act, 2007

Human Trafficking and Transportation (Control) Act, 2007, is the specific law to control the acts of human trafficking and transportation and to protect and rehabilitate the victims of such an act by enacting law. The act is applicable to any person inside or outside of Nepal accused of being involved in trafficking a Nepalese citizen. It has defined that the act of trafficking encompasses multiple forms of trafficking and exploitation, including the sale or purchase of persons, enforced prostitution, illicit removal of human organs and engaging in prostitution of internal and/or cross-border trafficking, transportation of anyone with undue influence, fraud and coercion.[19] The definition of human trafficking and transportation offences is at par with the requirements of the UN Protocol to Prevent, Suppress and Punish Trafficking in Persons, 2000. The act also establishes extraterritorial jurisdiction in case of the offences that are committed outside Nepal.[20] The act establishes proportional penalties and a more stringent penalty structure for several aggravating factors and allows judicial discretion in sentencing. Prescribed penalties for trafficking offences range from ten to twenty years' imprisonment along with a fine. If someone is involved in selling or purchasing a person, they will be liable for twenty years' imprisonment and a 200,000-rupee fine. This is the maximum punishment prescribed in this act. The maximum penalty for internal trafficking is twelve years of imprisonment and a fine of 100,000 rupees. If some is found guilty of extracting human organs in an illegal manner, they will be liable for ten years of imprisonment and a 200,000- to 500,000-rupee fine.

4. *Human Trafficking and Transportation (Control) Regulation, 2008*

This regulation was enacted as per section 29 of the Human Trafficking and Transportation (Control) Act for the purpose of implementation of the objective of the act. It contains the broad framework that provides various measures for functioning of rehabilitating centers and establishment of National Coordination Committee against Human Trafficking (NCCHT), District Coordination Committee against Human Trafficking (DCCHT). Provisions made by this regulation can be discussed as follows.

a. *Establishment of National Coordination Committee Against Human Trafficking (NCCHT)*[21]

The regulation has provided for the formation of the National Coordination Committee against Human Trafficking, which is comprised of member from the Women, Children and Social Welfare (MoWCSW), Ministry of Labour and Employment (MoLE), Ministry of Home Affairs (MoHA), Ministry of Foreign Affairs (MoFA), Attorney General Office, Nepal Police, institutions or persons working in the field of human trafficking and transportation (nominated by MoWCSW) and victims/survivors of trafficking (nominated by (MoWCSW). The secretariat of the committee will be under MoWCSW. The national committee is assigned with the following functions, power and duties.[22]

- To prepare and submit necessary policies and programs against human trafficking and transportation to MoWCSW.
- Implement and monitor the approved policy or program.
- Rescue victims/survivors from foreign lands. While rescuing, the committee can assist and coordinate the organizations working in this field.
- Monitor and direct the rehabilitation centre to work as per the guidance given by the Nepal government.
- Monitor and coordinate the district committee.
- Record the implementation of international and regional laws or conventions that Nepal is party to and develop minimum standards to provide seed money for the victims/survivors who have taken training.
- Prepare and implement rehabilitation centre guidelines.

b. *Establishment of District Coordination Committee Against Human Trafficking (DCCHT)*[23]

The government of Nepal can establish the District Coordination Committee Against Human Trafficking as per section 23 of the act, which is comprised of the Chief District Officer, District

Government Attorney Office, District Police Officer, institutions or persons working for human trafficking and transportation in the district (nominated by CDO), representatives from the Nepal Journalist Federation and Women Development Officer. Rule 7 of this regulation has prescribed the power, functions and duties of the district committee are as follows.

- To recommend that concerned agencies prepare identity documents of the rescued victims/ survivors in case their identity is unclear.
- To establish and operate the human trafficking and transportation control committee at the local level.
- Monitor the district-level rehabilitation centre as per the guidance of the National Committee.
- Implement programs as per the guidelines prepared by the National Committee.
- Rescue vulnerable persons from human trafficking and transportation within the district.
- Coordinate with all organizations working for human trafficking and transportation.
- Keep records of all the activities relating to human trafficking and transportation and submit a report to the National Committee every three months.

c. Establishment and Functioning of Rehabilitation Centre[24]

The District Committee can establish a rehabilitation centre to provide physical and mental assistance to rehabilitate and re-integrate victims/survivors into society. The committee additionally grants responsibility to manage the centre to nongovernmental organizations. Such responsibility is given considering the financial and technical capacity of the organizations. The organizations are then responsible or established to rehabilitate and reintegrate victims/survivors and must apply following minimum standards.

- Minimum physical and infrastructural standard to rehabilitate victims/survivors
- Capacity to provide psychological counseling and health service
- Capacity to arrange and provide necessary medical assistance
- Capacity to arrange and provide legal assistance
- Capacity to provide educational facilities

The centre established with all these facilities needs to be monitored by the District Committee by every six months.

d. Reintegration and Family Reconciliation[25]

The regulation has provided that the rescued victims/survivors need to be reintegrated in society and with their family members. The rescued victims/survivors should be kept in the rehabilitation centre at least for six months from the date of rescue. However, if the victims/survivors are children, alternative measures to settle them in a child protection centre need to be applied.

While reintegrating victims/survivors with family, the centre must apply measures like finding the family, counseling the family members and coordinating the overall process.

5. Complimentary Laws

A. *Children Act, 2048:* This act prohibits the selling and buying of children and dedicating them to a god or goddess.[26] It also prohibits using children as beggars.[27] This act has also prohibited engaging and using children in an immoral profession.[28]

B. *Foreign Employment Act, 2064:* Prohibits migrating children to a foreign country as employees.[29] It has further provided that only a license holder agent can migrate the employee to the foreign country.[30]

C. *Muluki Ain, 2020, Chapter on Abduction and Taking Hostage:* Muluki Ain in the Chapter on Abduction and Taking Hostage has defined the terms 'abduction' and 'taking hostage'. It has provided that if abduction or hostage taking is done for selling, to make slaves, to make someone join labour or for making them join prostitution, the offender shall be given seven to fifteen years' imprisonment and a fine up to 200,000 rupees.[31]

D. *Child Labor (Prevent and Regulate) Act, 2056:* The Child Labor Act has prevented employing children under the age of 14 years. It also mentions that children should not be made to do any task as a labor by fear or by any means.[32]

E. *Birth, Death and Other Vital Events (Registration) Act, 2033 (1976):* The purpose of this act is to establish and to consolidate the system of registering incidents like birth, death, marriage, divorce and migration etc. Under the section 2(a) of the act, incidents like birth, marriage, divorce and migration are defined as vital personal events requiring registration. Section 2(b) defines migration as change of residence of a person from one VDC or municipality to another VDC or municipality within Nepal for a period of more than six months. As per this act, such migration shall have to be registered. The movement of people from Nepal to other countries is also defined as migration. The period of time is taken as an essential element of migration under this act, as no movement from one place to another for a period of less than six months is considered migration.

F. *The State Cases Act, 2049:* This act has listed the crime of human trafficking in its schedule and provided that investigation and prosecution be conducted by the government. Likewise, District Court Regulation, 2052, has provided that the hearing of trafficking cases shall be conducted in closed hearings.

6. *Other Government Strategies*

The government of Nepal has taken several strategies for prevention of offences of trafficking in persons. They include:

- Formulation of laws and ensuring law enforcement measures;
- Prioritizing the issues of addressing trafficking in periodic plans;
- Allocating budget to assist in the rescue and rehabilitation of victims of trafficking;
- Developing community-based institutional mechanisms (i.e. village child protection committees or VCPC) and supporting community-based structures (i.e. para-legal committees or PLC, women's groups and children's clubs);
- Expanding educational opportunities to girl children by providing scholarships;
- Vocational training and income generation opportunities to adolescent girls and their families;
- Awareness raising among the targeted groups; and
- Introducing and expanding social protection plans targeting the most vulnerable groups and families.

III. Nepalese Legislation on Trafficking: Analysis From Victimology Perspectives

In order to impart justice in a real sense for human trafficking survivors, the trafficking policies and laws should be composed in such a manner that they focus not just on the prosecution of perpetrators but also on respecting, protecting and restoring the rights of trafficked persons. The trafficking process itself is very lengthy and exploitative in nature. It curtails several fundamental rights and freedoms of its victims. So in order to dispatch real justice, laws and policies should be in place to address the overall harm done to victims and to prevent further and re-victimization through the criminal justice system and court proceedings.

It has been suggested through various experiences that the state must implement victim-sensitive policies and laws in order to successfully prosecute traffickers. Trafficking survivors are often reluctant to report, come before a court to give statements or cooperate with police because they fear retribution from perpetrators. Also, in most situations, the perpetrator is someone close to them or a neighbor/friend/relative, which further puts pressure on the survivors, who are often afraid to come out from their situation.

In this scenario, addressing these issues is a big challenge. It involves a broad range of interrelated measures, including measures to protect their physical and psychological safety and privacy, provision of adequate and timely information, victim-sensitive advice, language translation services and legal representation free of charge, victim-sensitive mechanisms, exemption from deportation, temporary residence status and emergency shelter so that they can participate in the investigation and prosecution of the case. Protective measures such as witness protection programs should be in place, as witnesses are one of the prominent pieces of evidence of the crime so that the perpetrators do not intimidate victims of trafficking, particularly where a professional criminal network or syndicate is involved in a very organized manner.

The special rights and needs for the protection and support for trafficking victims and witnesses are as follows.

1. Trafficked Persons Shall Not Be Penalized

Trafficked persons should be treated differently than other law violators. They are not supposed to be treated as criminals despite the fact that they might be engaged in certain criminal activities such as prostitution in some countries. They should be given exemption if found as illegal immigrants and should not be prosecuted or deported for their status as illegal migrants.

Neither can they be subjected to prosecution for using false documents, leaving the country illegally or having worked in the sex industry. It is a very insensitive approach to prosecute trafficking victims. It not only obstructs victims from receiving justice and enjoying their ensured basic human rights but can also weaken a state's ability to prosecute perpetrators.

If victims are not taken in a sensitive manner and are prosecuted for their unwilling/forced crime, they might be afraid and reluctant to come out from their situation and initiate any complaint or report trafficking incidents to the police. They may deny cooperating with authorities and actually act as witness of the crime. This will ultimately have adverse effects in prosecution and will decrease the chance of prosecuting the real perpetrators. It will hence encourage the perpetrator to carry out their business and drive the sex industry underground into the hands of organized crime.

In the Nepalese context, our laws don't have any specific provisions which explicitly explain that trafficked person shall not be detained, charged or prosecuted for the illegality of their entry into or residence in countries of transit and destination or for their involvement in unlawful activities to the extent that such involvement is a direct consequence of their situation as trafficked persons.

However, HTTA has provided that if a person knows or there is reasonable ground to believe that he/she is being bought, sold or engaged in prostitution or taken for the same and he/she does not get help to get rid of prostitution from those acts or somebody creates obstacles or stops or takes into control or use force, in such case, if he or she believes that it is impossible to get rid from such control and on such faith the perpetrator happens to be killed or injured in the course of release, such person shall not be liable for any punishment, notwithstanding anything in the prevailing law.[33] Nepalese law is not on a par with the various international instruments, which provide immunity to the trafficked person for committing various illegal activities, which has resulted as the consequence of trafficking. In cases of cross-country trafficking, many times, the issues of fake passports or visas or illegal status become the big questionable issues. They shall not be liable for the activities such as producing a fraudulent travel or identity document or procuring, providing or possessing such document.

2. *Physical and Psychological Security of Victims*

Victims can play a very prominent role in the prosecution process if they feel secure and protected. So providing security to the victims is one of the important aspects in securing and promoting justice for them. There are different provisions enlisted in different international instruments regarding providing physical and psychological security to victims. However, Nepal doesn't have any specific law in this regards. If we analyze Nepalese trafficking legislation from this perspective, there is a provision enshrined in HTTA that provides physical protection of the victim and witness. But it largely lacks provision for psychological protection and security, which in most cases are seen to be prerequisite. Victim protection measures need to be strengthened so that the victims and their families in trafficking cases feel safe to testify against traffickers.

Under Article 26 of HTTA, it mentions that if a person provides reasonable grounds and asks the nearest police office for security against any type of retaliation for reporting to the police or providing a statement in court or remaining as a witness, that police office should provide security during traveling in the course of attending the case proceeding in the court. However, it seems that the protection is provided once they request for it. Secondly, it is provided for a limited time and basically when the victim is travelling to attend the case proceedings. It doesn't have talk about extending the protection up to the desired time as per victim needs. The protection has been made conditional; however, it should be made unconditional.

3. *Right to Privacy of Victims Shall Be Ensured*

Maintaining and ensuring privacy is the essential need of trafficking victims. It is one of the crucial aspects of the victim justice system. Various international instruments have made provisions for the protection of the privacy of the trafficked person. Conceptually, it is very unethical to disclose the identity of the victim if they approach you for help and protection. Disclosing the identity of a victim might hamper a victim's access to justice. It will also have negative consequences in the overall process of victim rehabilitation and re-integration to the community and society at large. It will put victims' self-esteem in danger, and they will be bound to face social stigma regarding their past life and horrors.

In the Nepalese context, right to privacy is not simply a legal right but also the fundamental right guaranteed by the interim constitution of Nepal 2007. Nepalese laws are favorable for the protection of the identity of the victims. HTTA has the provision enshrined in it for the protection of the identity of the victims. It explicitly mentions that privacy of the victims should be ensured and guaranteed. For seeking it, court regulations have provision of the in-camera hearing and procedures in place. However, the problems lie in the implementation of the laws. The main jurisprudence behind non-disclosure of the identity of the victim and in-camera court proceedings are not understood by many judicial officers. It has been encountered in many cases that the identity of the victim is changed, but the address and the identity of the close relatives like her father and other relatives' names are not.[34] Similarly, in the in-camera/closed hearing, even though the practice of closing the door of the courtroom is done, due to lack of proper infrastructure, people were found peeping inside from the windows and ventilation doors.

4. Victims' Participation in Court Proceedings

Victims are the backbone of the criminal proceedings. They are the prime witnesses of the crime and very give reliable evidence in the process. It will be very cost-/time-effective if victims are taken into consideration throughout the investigation process. If they are not accommodated in the process, there is the high risk of missing important evidence and clues that can be very insightful in the case. So victims should be communicated with properly and should participate in the overall process of criminal proceedings. In the absence of the victim's participation, the investigators shall be confined to the statements of the suspects. The participation of the victims in the proceedings is not only important for the successful prosecution of the case, but it is also the right of the victim to get adequate information about his/her own case. They are the foremost beneficiary of the case proceedings, so it's always their enshrined right to know what is happening in the case by which they have been victimized.

The criminal justice system of Nepal, however, seriously fails to observe the 'crime from the perspective of victimology'. The victim has no more role than that of the 'prosecutor's witness'. Nepal only has the practice of a criminal justice system that basically deals with the rights of torture victims. It lacks the victim justice system approach regarding the rights of crime victims. They even don't have access to the prosecutors, as the police have no practice of presenting the victim before the prosecutors.

5. Right to Information, Timely Advice and Assistance

In order to encourage victims to come forward and fight for their guaranteed legal rights, they should have access to information, advice and assistance. These are the very basic rights that should be provided to them in each step of the proceedings. Various international instruments have provided the right to information, advice and assistance to the victim. According to Nepalese HTTA, it has a provision that says the victim can even keep a separate law practitioner to represent his/her case even though it is the state party case and a public prosecutor is the responsible person to initiate the case. Likewise, the provision of a translator and interpreter is also important from the perspective of victim justice. Many times victims belong to the indigenous community and cannot understand the language used in court proceedings, so in those situations, it is very crucial to have a translator so victims can actually know about the process in detail. Most trafficking victims are not aware of their rights, and even if they know their rights, they are afraid of testifying against traffickers, who might threaten and harass them and their family. Trafficked persons should be well informed about their legal rights, options and services so that they can make informed decisions about their future.

6. Right to Compensation

Right to compensation is a huge relief on the victim's part if it is executed as per his/her need. It is one of the crucial aspects in the criminal justice system that seen through the victimology perspective. The traditional justice system simply talks about the punishment of the offender and completely neglects the compensation part for the victims. In the modern jurisprudence of justice, simply punishing the perpetrator is not sufficient. It should also have provisions regarding compensation, rehabilitation and restitution for victims.

In Nepal, HTTA has mentioned the provision of compensation to the victim. It has provided that the compensation to the victim shall not be less than half of the fine levied as punishment to the offender. However, it is not clear in the act whether the compensation is to be provided only by the principal offender or from other offenders who assist or abet in the offense. This has created problems in the implementation of the laws. It is also found that in some cases where the principal offender is not found, the court has refused to provide compensation to the victim from other offenders.[35] The right of the victim to get compensation has been totally dependent on the arrest of the principal offender. So there should be a clear provision in the act stating that the compensation shall be made not only from the principal offender but can be drawn from other co-accused too.

Right to compensation is one of the basic doctrines in a victimology perspective of the criminal system. However, the existing provision in Nepalese laws seems to be that the victim's right to compensation is highly dependent upon the economic capacity of the perpetrator. In case the perpetrator has nothing as his belongings or is not capable enough to pay for compensation, the victim's right to compensation is jeopardized. Similarly, if due to investigation flaws the perpetrator is not convicted, the victim will get nothing as compensation. Hence, it is necessary to make the state responsible for the compensation if the principal is not able to pay compensation to the victim or is not convicted as per the law. Also, there is not any provision for interim relief, as court proceedings are often very lengthy and might take several years to reach a final decision, and until the final decision comes out, victims are not entitled to compensation. The law should be amended to provide victim compensation beyond the amount the perpetrator is fined.

7. Victims' Right to Rehabilitation and Reintegration

The most significant provision of this act is that it provides measures for rescue, rehabilitation and reintegration of victims of trafficking. Section 12 of the act has provided that the government holds the responsibility to rescue any of its citizens from foreign lands. Section 13 has provided for the establishment of rehabilitation centres for physical and mental treatment, social rehabilitation and family reconciliation of the victims. While analyzing the Nepalese legal provision for the rehabilitation and reintegration of the victims of trafficking, though there are a few important provisions for the rehabilitation and reintegration of the victims, there have been problems in the proper implementation of the provisions because of the financial and other resources. It seems that the government has shifted its responsibility to other organizations for rehabilitation and reintegration. For example, the rescue and reintegration component in the NPAT (National Plan of Action against Trafficking)[36] suggests that the government perceives rescue and reintegration as a task limited to NGOs and the community.[37]

NGOs actively working in rescue and rehabilitation have their own problems and challenges, and in many instances it is impossible for them to launch rescue missions with a lack of government support. The government should initiate the rescue mission on its own and invite NGOs to participate in it, not the vice versa, which is the current trend being followed. The government should invest in long-term income-generating programs for survivors in order to make them self-sufficient and self-reliant, which is itself a very important tool for the reintegration process. The legal provisions for rehabilitation should include assisting in repatriation and providing safe housing and legal medical and psychological support to the victims.

Conclusion

If we compare current legislation and government initiatives to the previous one in regard to human trafficking laws, it seems much more progressive and victim-oriented, even though it seriously lacks proper implementation and execution. It can be seen that the current laws don't envision either a compensation fund or interim relief for victims while during the court process. It also doesn't talk about the possibility to file a civil suit for compensation and other damages in these cases. There is no uniformity in compensation being provided across the country. Victims hardly benefit from the proceedings except in the mental satisfaction of punishment to the offenders, and sometimes the perpetrator are acquitted on very technical grounds or due to investigation flaws. The provision for fines from the perpetrator mentioned in the act is very little, and only half of the amount is received by the victim upon the successful end of the case, which often is very time consuming, and the rest of the amount goes to the government exchequer.

Apparently, because of the lack of protection and proper counseling of the victims, many of them turn as hostile witnesses in the court. We also have very regressive provisions in our law that penalize the victim/witness if they happen to change their statement in the court from the former statement they provided in police. This is totally against the victimology perspective, and it doesn't look around for the cause of changing the statement, which most of the time is due to the threat and undue influence imposed upon the victims. In a number of trafficking incidents that take place across the border, the trafficked person does not possess legal travel documents, including identification papers. In such a situation lies the danger of double victimization of the victim.

Martin Luther King rightly said that "Injustice anywhere is a threat to justice everywhere". So if victims are protected and made secure, they can help in prosecuting the perpetrator and make the investigation process easier, which otherwise will need lots of countries' resources.

The denial of victim access to justice might lead to the creation of many more victims/survivors and it would encourage the perpetrators to commit more crime. Victims are the backbone of any investigation. To eventually get victory and establish access of justice for the victim, they should be protected.

Reintegration is an important part in the victim justice system. However, there are various challenges to reintegrating the victims of trafficking. Due to social stigma, the family of the victim rarely accepts the victim. So it is very necessary to make survivors self-sufficient and self-reliant to lead their lives in whatever way they want.

Notes

1 Article 3 of United Nations (UN) Protocol to Prevent, Suppress and Punish Trafficking in Persons, Especially Women and Children 2000, supplementing the UN Convention against Transnational Organized Crime.
2 Gauri Pradhan, "An Overview on Different Definitions of Human Trafficking and its Conceptual Framework." *Presented in the seminar organized by National Human Rights Commission*, July 2004.
3 Human Trafficking and transportation (Control) Act 2007, Section 2(C).
4 General Assembly Resolution 40/34 of 29 November 1985.
5 See UN Declaration of Basic Principles of Justice for Victims of Crime and Abuse of Power 1985 Article 4.
6 Formal mechanism refers to the assistance to the victims through compensation, restitution and informal mechanisms as resolution of disputes, including mediation, arbitration and other practices. For detail see Article 6–13 of UN Declaration of Basic Principles of Justice for Victims of Crime and Abuse of Power 1985.
7 Article 4–7, Ibid.
8 See Article 8–11, Ibid.
9 See Article 12 & 13 Ibid.
10 *Human Trafficking Assessment Tool* (2011). (p. 15). USA: American Bar Association Rule of Law Initiative.
11 Interim Constitution (2007), Article 20.
12 Sub article (1) of Article 20 provides, "No discrimination shall be made only on the ground of someone being woman". Sub-article (2) says, "Every woman shall have the right to reproductive health and right concerning reproduction". Sub-article (3) provides, "No one shall be subjected to physical, mental or any other forms of violence, and any such act shall be liable to punishment in accordance with law".
13 Interim constitution (2007), Article 29.
14 Ibid, Article 29(2).
15 Article 29(2) of the interim constitution has provided that no one can be subjected to exploitation in the guise of custom, tradition and usages.
16 Article 29(3) of the interim constitution has provided that selling of human beings, subjection to slavery and forced labour are prohibited.
17 Article 29(4) has provided that no one shall be subjected to forced labour.
18 Muluki Ain (1964), Chapter of Human Trafficking, Clause 1.

19 Human Trafficking and Transportation (Control) Act(2007), Section 4.
20 Ibid, Section 1.
21 Human Trafficking and Transportation (Control) Regulation (2008), Rule 3.
22 Ibid, Rule 4.
23 Ibid, Rule 6.
24 Ibid, Rule 11.
25 Ibid, Rule 16.
26 Sec. 14 of The Children Act(2048), Section 14.
27 Ibid, Section 13.
28 Ibid, Section 14.
29 Foreign Employment Act (2064), Section 7.
30 Ibid, Section 10.
31 Muluki Ain(2020), Chapter on Abduction and Taking Hostage, Section 3.
32 Child Labor (Prevent and Regulate) Act (2056), Section 4.
33 Human Trafficking and Transportation (Control) Act, Section 16.
34 In many cases decided by the Kathmandu District Court, it was seen that the identity of the close relatives like father or husband and the address of the victim was not changed. There is no use in changing the name of the victim in this condition.
35 In the case of *Government of Nepal vs. Ram Bhadur Tamang and Kanchi Tamang*, Case of 2065, (Decision Date 2066 Bhadra 9), Kathmandu District Court refused to provide the compensation to the victim, citing as the reason that the accused was not the principal offender. The detail explanation of this case will be done in the next chapter of case analysis.
36 The Ministry of Women, Children and Social Welfare/HMG developed this policy with the cooperation of the International Labor Organization International Program on the Elimination of Child Labor. The government of Nepal approved this policy in July 1999.
37 For example, the NPAT action plan states, "Institute a referral system for victims of sexual exploitation for NGOs for care and counseling".

29

POLITICAL CRIME VICTIMIZATION IN BANGLADESH

Md. Shakhawat Hossain

Introduction

Political crime is a major concerning and alarming issue in the present situation of Bangladesh, and it hampers the sustainability of the country. Day by day, political crimes are increasing at an alarming rate, and it has attracted regional and international attention for its seriousness and has created an anxiety for international peace. A large number of people are always fearful about the impact of political crimes and their effect on the people of Bangladesh. Misconduct towards public and the political leaders also has increased at a higher rate. It has become a centre of discourse in contemporary Bangladesh.

Victimization or violent demonstration has occurred due to the demand for release of the accused in the war crimes trial committed by the Jamaat-e-Islami and Islamic Chhattra Shibir that increases political crime (*ASK*, 2013). The cost of political crime victimization is higher than any other crime victimization. It also hampers the economic condition of the country and decreases the values and norms of the society. Common people, the victims of political crime, suffer a lot. The grenade attack of 2004 left many people injured and killed. The increasing rate of terrorism and militancy encompasses the field for committing political crime across the state and victimizes innocent people.

The effects of political crime impact negatively globally and nationally. Nationally, when political instability arises, it hampers the security, education and communication systems as well as the economic system of the country. The people who are being victimized by political crime face crimes such as theft, robbery, dacoits, hurt, grievous hurt, political murder, loss of huge amounts of money, corruption, illegal lobbing, trafficking, drug dealing and drug business etc. Nowadays, torture, cross-fire, extrajudicial killing, enforced disappearances have also occurred very seriously than before in Bangladesh. In 2012, 70 extrajudicial killings, 53 cross-fires, 24 enforced disappearances and 132 public lynchings have occurred (Odhikar Report, 2013). Economic crisis, political culture, socialization problems, low ethics and morality, to show power and political clashes are some of the main reasons for political crime victimization in Bangladesh.

The people of Bangladesh learned to grow and survive from the political aggression and suppression of the Pakistani ruling party, both military and civil. The Pakistani state violated the principle of equality of opportunity, and the people felt exploited due to political clashes and the low-morality problems of the ruling party authorities. After independence, Bangladesh has faced terrorism committed by Sarboharas and Nakshals to increase the political violence and victimization rate. Now they have established themselves as a local criminal organization rather than a terrorist organization

(Syed, 2011). At the same time, political violence was also created because of Bengali nationalism. The problems arose deeply when Mujib set up Rakkhi Bahini to protest the rebel people of the country. Moreover, the establishment of Jatiya Rakkhi Bahini with autonomous power was the main indicator of political violence and terrorism (Riaz, 2008). On December 28, 1974, when the Mujib government declared a state of emergency and suspended all civil and political rights, several political parties protested against the decision of the government.

On the other hand, Bangladesh is situated in the in famous Crescent and close to the Golden Triangle, both located in Myanmar. This makes it a transit point for the smuggling of heroin and illegal arms from Myanmar. From Bangladesh, one can easily reach Pakistan and Afghanistan. In the past, some students, mainly from religious education institutes of Bangladesh, migrated to Pakistan and later moved to Afghanistan to join the Afghani jihad in the proxy war against the then-Soviet invasion. Some also joined the same war by moving directly from Bangladesh. Many of them came back and apparently provided the backbone of JMB and other religious militant organizations in Bangladesh (Roy, 2010). At the beginning of the judgments of war criminals, the Islamic Chattro Shibir attacked Hindu villages, and more than 50 temples and 1,550 homes were destroyed (*The Dhaka Tribune*, 2013).

Political crime and terrorism are interlinked to one another because most of the terrorist attacks would happen due to power-related conflicts or to show power in an illegal way. The vast majority of the reported crimes show that the weak political system and absence of good governance are the keys to the rise of terrorism as well as political crimes in Bangladesh. In many cases, the politicians patronize the terrorist groups for their political interests. The regime between 1991 and 1996, the BNP, provided these groups with liberal facilities, including training camps, bank accounts, facilitation for arms purchases and freedom of operation from Bangladeshi soil. As a result, these terrorist groups, on the run in India's Northeast under persistent pressure from Army operations, found a much-needed breathing space to regroup and relaunch their offenses against India (Gill, 2004).

During the period of the Awami League (1996–2001), the Harkat militants had attacked Shamsur Rahman, the renowned poet of Bangladesh. Six persons were killed and over 100 injured when two bombs planted by suspected religious extremists exploded at a cultural function in Jessore district. Seven persons of the Ahamadiya group were killed and some 40 injured when a bomb planted by Islamic terrorists exploded during Friday prayers at the Kadiani Mosque in Khulna. Organized crimes, political crime and violence, especially by the government-party cadres like Jainal Hazari of Feni district and others under government patronage, were strongly criticized by the opponents and the media.

During the BNP-Jamat regime (2001–2006), the top BNP leaders including the prime minister publicly denied the existence of terrorist activities in Bangladesh. For example, JMJB chief Siddiqul Islam Bangla Bhai had escaped from police dragnets and subsequently waged a reign of terror with backing from ruling-party lawmakers. Police arrested Bangla Bhai several times, but he was released with the supervision of political leaders. In sum, there are many examples where police released the militants without investigating the charges brought against them. An investigation by *The Daily Star* found that most of the JMB and JMJB leaders were in the past members of the Islami Chhattra Shibir (ICS), the student front of ruling coalition partner Jamaat-e-Islami Bangladesh (JIB). Unfortunately, the previous BNP government did not take any concrete actions against these terrorist organizations. In other words, to some extent, terrorists received political support from their allies. As a result, they managed to secure international funding to organize the groups.

Media reports showed that the sources of funding for continuing violence in politics come from both local and international sources. In the parliament, most of the MPs are businessmen, while others have law backgrounds, and notably some MPs are the donors for violent activities in politics. Some of the countries such as Iran, Iraq, Saudi Arabia and other charitable organizations have also given sponsorship. It is found that HUJI-B and JMB also raise funds from the madarasa's students and some local and international NGOs. Crimes such as smuggling, customs fraud, tax evasion and illegal money laundering also enhance the activities of political violence (Rahman & Kashem, 2012).

Day by day, the threat of political crime endangers the livelihood of the citizens of the country. According to the report of Ain-O-Salish-Kendro, in 2013, there were 848 incidents, 22,407injured and 507 died, and in 2014, there were 664 incidentsand8,373 injured and 147 died (ASK report, 2013, 2014). But the recent victimization has surpassed all of the previous records. From 5 January to 23 February due to election conflict and war criminal tribunal, 119 people died, out of which 4 were from AL, 27 from BNP, 13 from Jam-mat, 1 CNG driver, 3 truck drivers, 30 passengers and the rest unknown persons (Bangladeshpolitico.blogspot.com).

In the contemporary era, the trend and intensity of political crime have attracted the attention of criminologists, sociologists, researchers, law enforcement agencies, policy makers and human rights activists. Given the situation, there is a need to explore the nature of political crimes in Bangladesh. This chapter is a move in that direction. This analysis will be helpful to find out the victimization status of innocent people that indicates the fear of the culture and cruelty, human rights violation and distrust of general people in law and order. It would be very helpful for the policy makers and the government to take relevant steps so that such incidences will not further occur.

I. History of Political Crime in Bangladesh

Political crime is one of the burning and concerning issues not only for Bangladesh but also for the whole world. In the present world, most of the developed and under-developed countries face the problem of political crime. Due to political crime, the number of victims has increased day by day. Moreover, crime victimization is an important cause of political participation, and reports indicate that crime victims' participation in politics is more than compared to non-victims (Bateson, 2012). Political crime in Bangladesh has become an integral part of politics because the politicians want the power of the state at any costs. The numbers of political crimes are increasing at an alarming rate, and it has hampered the livelihood of innocent people.

Political crime may be defined as law violation by politicians for their vested interests and violation of law by people attempting to express their opinion on the political structure of the state (Ahuja, 1996). On the other hand, political crime can be defined as acts carried out by individuals or groups with a goal of accomplishing political power for a specific party at any cost (Datta, 2005). Political victims are the people who have suffered physically, psychologically and economically both personally and collectively violation of national and internationally recognized law (Bouris, 2007) by politicians.

Political crime as a system of behavior consists of a number of characteristics. Political offenders usually don't engage in criminal activities as a full-time career; persons who commit political crimes don't conceive of themselves as criminals and don't identify with crime or criminal behavior; they violate the law only when such behaviors seem to be the most appropriate means for achieving certain ends which are not personal but are deemed desirable for the larger society. The action usually taken by the offenders is public rather than private, and political offenders carryout their illegal activities in pursuit of an ideal (Clinard & Quinney, 1967).

Political crimes are used as a tool for political gains since 1971 when Bangladesh got independence from Pakistan. In Latin America, there are two mechanisms by which political crime victimization hampers democracy. Firstly, for the reason of political crime and that it negatively impacts the victimization rate is that citizens disengage with politics. It is merely observable that high levels of violent crime are hypothesized to lead to lower levels of participation in the democratic process (Buvinic, Morrison, & Shifter, 2002). Secondly, crime victimization caused due to authoritarianism is either in the form of dictatorship or repressive policing measures (Diamond, 1997).

Beginning in 2015, before and after the election period, Bangladesh has faced violent incidents. In the last 66 days of hartal (a closure of shops and offices as a protest or a mark of sorrow) and blockade,

384 incidents occurred, as a consequence of which 1,853 people were injured and 77 people died (Ain-O-Salish Kendro,2015). However, the report of Odhikar declared that from January to March 2015, due to political crime, around120 people were killed and 3,230 were injured (Odhikar, 2015). On the other hand, the report of Ain-O-Salish Kendro (*ASK*, 2015) found that 88 people died by the attack of law enforcement agencies (Odhikar, 2015). Between February and March 2013, after the judgments of war criminals, the Islamic Chatroshibir killed three Awami League supporters and a dozen security forces (Human Rights Watch, 2013). From 28 February to 21 March 2013, 82 persons were killed by Jamaat Shibir activists (Ain-O-Salish Kendro, 2013). Moreover, 22 people died and 59 people were injured as the result of terrorist-related crimes in the year 2015 in Bangladesh (SATP, 2015).

Political crime comes out at a higher rate when the political parties want to regulate the culture of street power.The practice of hartal started after the independence of Bangladesh and during the 1972–75 regime. For 22 days hartal has occurred, and since then it has been increasing (Rahman, 2014). Political crime is not new to Bangladesh, but the events after 6 January 2015 witnessed 90 days of blockade and hartal and it gave a new dimension in the political culture of Bangladesh. In previous times political demonstrations included hartal and blockade.In those demonstration sometimes they destroyed cars using sticks or hockey sticks but of late the demonstrations have become violent with the usage of petrol bombing and firing at cars, buses and trucks. Nowadays, hartals have become common instruments for political parties to press for their demands where the parties generally commit violent activities (Uddin, 2014).

In the present scenario, political crime is a major discourse in Bangladesh, due to which the citizens of the country have faced several dangerous issues, especially on blockade, hartal, firing and petrol bombing (a new dimension in the political culture of Bangladesh). The result of the crime of that period is much more dangerous and destructive. It impacted several other sectors including education, communication, health and development as well as the economic sector.Violent demonstrations have occurred due to the demand of release of the accused in the war crimes trial committed by the Jamaat-e-Islami and Islamic Chhattra Shibir that increased political crime (*ASK*, 2013).

There has been a gradual growth of political crime in Bangladesh due to political instability as a major threat to domestic and international security. Some of the reasons are liable to increase the political crime in Bangladesh. In that case, money and power playa nexus role to increase the relationship between the criminals and the politicians (Priyangika, 2000). Bangladesh has continued to suffer from a territorial demarcation with regard to geographical realities, environmental management, expanding population, poverty, scarcity of land and other physical resources.These reasons along with the political instability are the reasonable logic for increasing political crime (Peiris, 1998).Again, the excessive interference of politicians in decision-making of the departmental functions weakens the morale of the governmental administration as well as the criminal justice system (Paranjape, 2009).

II. Statistics of Political Crime in Bangladesh

Prothom Alo outlined a special emphasis on political crime and victimization after the independence of Bangladesh.Traditionally and historically, writers and journalists have tried their best to show the impact and victimization of internal conflict among the parties, party-to-party conflict, politician and law enforcement agency clashes, the situation after the election period and also the condition of the marginalized people of Bangladesh.

1. Political Violence in Bangladesh During Two Different Governments (1991–2015)

Due to the political violence in the past 22 years, 2,519 people lost their lives.And at the same time, about 1.5 million people were injured.According to media reports (*Prothom Alo*) from 1991 to1998, 285 people lost their lives during the period. In1991, 18 people; in 1992, 45 people; in 1993, 20 people; in 1994, 24 people; in 1995, 29 people; in 1996, 49 people; in 1997, 69 people; and 31 people died in 1998. Further analysis of the data showed that in the past 22years, which means the electoral years, the most people have lost their lives. In 1991, 18 people; 49 in 1996, 500 in 2001, 120 in 2006 (not selected), and in 2013, 304 people lost their lives in the last 10 months. In the years of 2007 and 2008, the lowest number of people reported dead was 11 people.

Awami League (AL) Regime: From 2009 to 2013, 564 people were killed. The political clash and feud of the Awami League and its associated organizations reported 130 people dead. During 60 hours of hartal from 7 to 9 October of Jammat-BNP, 15 people were killed in political clashes. Earlier, in the nine-month clash from January to September of 2013, 289 people were killed in political clashes.

BNP Regime: From 2001 to 2006, 872 people died due to political violence or political interest. And in 1991 to 1996,174 people were killed in political conflict. In the terrorist attack, 200 Awami leaders died and the 21st grenade attack killed 24 leaders of the AL. In the political conflict among the AL-BNP, 75 died; in the BNP-BNP clash, 75 died; in the Jammat-BNP clash, 10 leaders died; and in the AL-AL internal conflict, 14 people died (Hasan, 2013).

Another report of *Prothom Alo* (6 January to 5 March) estimated that in two months of hartal and blockade, 115 people died, out of which 90 percent were innocent and were civilians. Around 62 died by petrol bombing, and 36 died due to crossfire. The rest of the 17 died due to clashes or gun firing. The dead people were day laborers, workers students, foreigners, children, women and police personnel (Hasan, 2015).

As per Ain-O-Salish Kendro (ASK) report, the number of people killed in political violence in the last 15 years is: In 1999, 233; 2000, 208; 2001, 500; 310 in 2002, 203 in 2003, 52 in 2004, 34 in 2005, 120 in 2006, seven in 2007, and four in 2008, 42 in 2009; 76 in 2010, 58 in 2011, 84 in 2012 and 304 in 2013.

Report of 2014 indicated that, in 2013 AL-BNP there were 148 incidents and 2330 people were injured and 31 died. AL-Jammat Shibir, 14 incidents has occurred and for that 130 people were injured and 9 died. The conflict among the AL-shibir, AL-JP, BNP-JP, AL-Jammat Shibir, AL-Jasad, AL-BNP-Jammat Shibir, BNP-Jammat, BNP-Shibir, BNP-Jammat Shibir, AL-Hefajote Islam, AL-BNP-Jammat Shibir, AL-BNP-Shibir, AL-BNP-Hefajote Islam, Hefajote Islam-Ahole Sunnah, AL-AL, BNP-BNP, JP-JP and AL-CPB Bashod, AL-Police, BNP-Police, Shibir-Police, Jammat-Police Hefajote Islam-Police; there were 848 incidents and from them 22407 people were injured and 507died (*ASK*, 2014).

In 2014, there were 664 incidents and the violence included; violence against the party to party, internal to external parties, and political parties to police. In these incidents 8,373 people were injured and 147 people were killed (*ASK*, 2015). In 2015, 556 incidents occured and 3,051 people were injured and 122 died due to blockade and hartal (*ASK*, 2015).

In the last 22 years, 2,519 people were killed in political violence and 0.5 million people were injured across the country (Hasan, 2015). Another report published in *Prothom Alo*, mentioned that in six years (2009–2014) 908 people were killed (Shorifuzzaman, 2013).

III. Individual Cases of Victimization

1. Ahmed Rajib Haider

A blogger and activist of the Shahbagh movement was found being stabbed on February 15, 2013, after the organizers decided to discontinue the 24-hour blockade. Police found the body, bearing several stab wounds, near his house. He also posted many blogs on the Liberation War and Jamaat activities. About eight hours before being murdered, Rajib posted a status on Facebook calling upon the people to boycott Jamaat's media houses, coaching centers, cultural organizations and commercial institutions (*The Daily Star*, February 16, 2013).

2. Avijit Roy

Unidentified assailants killed writer and blogger Avijit Roy and badly wounded his wife Rafida Ahmed Banna at Dhaka University campus after the couple came out of the Ekushey Boi Mela. His writing drew the ire of religious fanatics and Baki Billah, a blogger. A Twitter account named @AnsarBangla7 posted a bloodied photo of Avijit and Banna, saying, "May be its Avijit Roy's bloody wife Husband's Head. #Beheaded He was a top Target for the last 3/4 years." Avijit is well known for his books, *Biswaser Virus* (*Virus of Faith*) and *Sunyo theke Mahabiswa* (*From Vacuum to the Universe*) (*The Daily Star*, February 27, 2015).

3. Oyasiqur Rahman Babu

Barely a month after the brutal murder of Avijit Roy, another blogger and online activist was hacked to death in broad daylight. Oyasiqur Rahman Babu (aged 27) was attacked by three cleaver-wielding youths in the capital's Tejgaon Industrial area around 9:00 a.m. Two of the attackers were aged about 19 and said they took part in the killing without even knowing Oyasiqur or reading any of his write-ups. They just acted as per instruction of a person called Masum, who recently graduated from a madrasa (*The Daily Star*, March 31, 2015).

4. Ananto Bijoy Das

Blogger Ananta Bijoy Das had been in a state of dread since the brutal murder of Bangladesh-born US writer and blogger Avijit Roy on February 26. Frustrated with the lack of progress in the Avijit murder case, the 32-year-old had posted a status on Facebook on March 15. Ananta, known for advocating science and secularism, was viciously hacked to death by a group of masked men in Sylhet City in a continuation of attacks on free thinkers. An organizer of local Gonojagoron Mancha, which champions the call for maximum punishment for war criminals, he was on his way to work when the attack happened around 8:45 a.m. He used to blog for Mukto-Mona, or Free Mind, the site Avijit Roy had launched. In many of his blogs and Facebook posts, he wrote against religious fundamentalism (*The Daily Star*, May 13, 2015).

5. Niloy Neel

In a chilling attack on free speech, unidentified assailants hacked to death a secular blogger inside his house in the capital in broad daylight. Niladri Chattopadhyay, alias Niloy (aged 28), who also was a Gonojagoron Mancha activist, is the fourth blogger to have been killed in 2015 by suspected Islamist militants. Four men armed with cleavers entered his Goran house in Khilgaon posing as potential tenants and then killed him in his bedroom in the night. He was hacked over a dozen times in the neck, face, shoulder, chest and hands. Ansar-Al-Islam (AQIS, Bangladesh Branch) took the responsibility of this murder. The time of the murder was carefully picked, as most men were at mosques attending Jumma prayers (*The Daily Star*, August 8, 2015).

Discussion and Conclusion

Political crime means the type of crime which is committed for fulfilling political purposes such as establishing political power on behalf of a political leader or their supporters, especially for gaining state power. The culture of politics in Bangladesh has created the field to commit illegal activities by the political leaders. In the contemporary phenomenon, the criminalization of politics and the politicization of criminals have been liable for increasing the rate of political crime. East Pakistan has shown the seeds of political turmoil and of violence and now it has grown in a great way in contemporary Bangladesh. Since independence from Pakistan, each and every regime in Bangladesh has the practice of indulging in political crimes. The party in power always attacks the other party, and when the other party comes to power, it attacks them back.

The police in Bangladesh don't perform their proper duty to the citizens; they are regulated by the ruling parties' authority and not by the law. The government doesn't take sufficient steps to reduce the political crime and provide necessary facilities for the victims. The civil society personnel do not join with each other and they are highly divided and not helpful.

Political crime is a serious and crucial issue in Bangladesh. Most of the citizens of the state are fearful of becoming victims of political crime. The nature and seriousness of the political crime have attracted the attention of every level of people. The death of many innocent people hasn't led to any offenders being arrested yet. The chapter outlined the political clashes, civil disobedience, terrorism, hate crime and political assassination, illegal surveillance, torture and deadly force as the major forms of political crimes in Bangladesh. As for the causes of crime, some of the indicators like political conflict among the parties, monetary gain, internal conflict, lack of good governance, unemployment, anarchy and terrorism are responsible for political crimes. The severity and gravity of the political crimes focus on issues like hurt, grievous hurt, theft, dacoits, land disputes and others.

The social consequences of political crime may be diverse. It has created fear of crime, ideological and social conflict, terrorism, prevention of free speech and parallel illegal governance. Political crime is the result of the lack of good governance and lack of enforcement of the relevant law agency and the lack of consciousness of the majority of the people of the country (Islam & Hamid, 2007). To eradicate political crimes in Bangladesh, the government, civil society and people with conscience can also play an effective role by increasing awareness about the political system and structure. People with conscience should be involved in politics who will not perpetuate political crimes; though this suggestion is farsighted, future citizens can be protected from political crimes only by this.

References

Ahuja, R. (1996). *Sociological criminology*. New Delhi: New Age International Publishers.

ASK (Ain O Salish Kendro). (2013). Human rights situation in Bangladesh, Dhaka Reporters Unity, Dhaka.

ASK (Ain O Salish Kendro). (2014). Human rights situation in Bangladesh.

ASK (Ain O Salish Kendro).(2015). Human rights situation in Bangladesh.

Bateson, R. (2012). Crime victimization and political participation. *American Political Science Review, 103*(2), 231–47.

Bouris, E. (2007). *Complex political victims*. Bloomfield: Kumarian Press.

Buvinic, M., Morrison, A., & Shifter, M. (2002). La violencia en America Latina y el Caribe. *Seguridad Ciudadana: Espejismo o realidad?* 60–107.

Clinard, M. B., & Quinney, R. (1967). *Criminal behaviour systems: A typology*. New York: Rinehart, Holt and Winston.

Datta, S. (2005). Political violence in Bangladesh: Trend and causes. *Strategic Analysis, 29*(3), 427–447.

Diamond, L. (1997). Introduction: In search of consolidation. In *Consolidating the Third Wave democracies: Themes and perspective*. Baltimore, MD: The Johns Hopkins University Press.

Gill, K. P. S. (2004). *Freedom from fear: Bangladesh-A Lengthening shadow of terror*. New Delhi: SATP.

Hasan, S. (2013). The politics of dead, rally of rescuers. *Prothom Alo*, Dhaka, November 5.

Hasan, S. (2015, March 6). The unprecedented movement: Hostage of civil people. *Prothom Alo,* Dhaka, p. 1.

Islam, M. J., & Hamid, S. S. (2007). *Alleviating corruption in Bangladesh: An agenda for good governance*. Empowerment through Law of the Common People, Human Rights and Corruption.

Odhikar. (2012, February 1). Human rights monitoring report 1 to 31 January. Dhaka, Bangladesh.

Odhikar. (2013). Human rights monitoring report of 2012. Dhaka, Bangladesh.

Odhikar. (2015, April) Human rights monitoring report, March 1 to 31, p. 25.

Paranjape, N.V. (2009). Criminology and penology (13thed.). Allahabad: Central Law Publications

Peiris, G. H. (1998). Political conflicts in Bangladesh. *Ethnic Studies Report, XV1*(1).

Priyangika, N. (2000). *Bitter political feud between the government and opposition in Bangladesh*. Dhaka, Bangladesh: International Committee of the Fourth International.

Prothom Alo. (November, 5, 2015).

Rahman & Kashem. (2012). *Understanding religious militancy and terrorism in Bangladesh*. Dhaka: SSRC.

Rahman, K. M. (2014). Management and economy in Hartals: The case of Bangladesh. *Journal of Comparative International Management, 17*(1), 24–42.

Riaz, A. (2008). *Islamist militancy in Bangladesh, A Complex Web*. New York: Routledge.

Roy, B. (2010). A brief anatomy of Bangla Terrorism South Asia Analysis Group. March 4, 2008. Retrieved from www.southasiaanalysis.org/%5Cpapers27%5Cpaper2623.html.

Shorifuzzaman. (2014, December, 29). 908 killed in six years of political violence. *Prothom Alo*, Dhaka.

South Asia Terrorism Portal (SATP). (2015). Major incidents of terrorist violence in Bangladesh. Retrieved from www.satp.org.

Syed, F. A. (2011). Left movement in post-Independence Era. *The Daily Star*, Dhaka, p. 8.

Uddin, M. J. (Ed.) (2014). *BCS professors Prokashoni*. Dhaka: Professors Prakashon.

30

TRADITIONAL PRACTICES AND VICTIMIZATION OF WOMEN IN NEPAL

The Case of Chhaupadi

*Binita Pandey, Manisha Rajak, Pramila Pantha
and Roshi Bhandaree*

Introduction

Nepal is a mountainous country rich with natural habitats and places along with culture, tradition and religious affairs. Since ancient times, the people in Nepal have developed their own language, culture and heritage. Today Nepal stands with unique cultural phenomena and diversity in the international arena. However, among these cultural practices, there are some practices folded with blind beliefs and superstitions followed in society which violate the range of basic human rights of an individual. Even the international community has shown concern about the harmful traditional practices prevalent in Nepal. For instance, CEDAW committee has recognized in Nepal there are the problems of child marriage, the dowry system, son preference, polygamy, widows, accusation of witchcraft, Chhaupadi, Jhuma, Deuki and Dhaan- khanne tradition obstructing the obligation of Nepal to fulfill the human rights commitment in an international forum (Committee on Elimination of Discrimination of Women [CEDAW], 2011, p. 4).

The word *Chhaupadi* is derived from Achham's local *Rawte* language, wherein "*chhau*" refers to menstruation, "*padi*" to women. Thus, the word "Chhaupadi" indicates women during the time of menstruation. In Nepal the process of menstruation in women is not considered as a natural phenomenon and it is not treated as a matter of individual privacy. Rather, it is observed from social, cultural and religious points of view. It is believed this *Chhaupadi* tradition was started in the time of Lord *Indra*. It is said that *Indra*, the King of Heaven, was accused of killing a Brahmin and committing illicit acts with women. Nevertheless, *Indra* in remorse went on a quest to redeem his sin, and consequently, for these acts, all women were said to be punished through menstruation (Volunteer Summer Nepal, n.d.). Later, this belief has influenced the social and cultural behavior of people.

Accordingly, it is believed that people observe this time of menstruation in women from the viewpoint of "purity" and "impurity". It is believed in the period of menstruation, a woman/girl is considered bodily impure. Consequently, during the time of menstruation, a woman is only allowed to sleep, sit or stay in her home during her period. It is believed if a menstruating woman, particularly an unmarried one, touches a man, he will fall ill. If anyone touches her, he or she needs to be purified by taking a bath and drinking cow's urine or they will become sick. Similarly, if she touches a tree it will not bear fruit and will soon dry, and if she touches a pregnant woman, the child will be miscarried or be born with malformations. The women have to stay away from temples and other holy places. It is also believed that if these women are given milk, the cow will stop producing milk (Ghimire, 2005).

Thus, in the *Chhaupadi* tradition, the girls and women are forced to stay in a shed for thirteen days during their first and second menstrual cycle, seven days in their third cycle and four days of every other menstrual cycle. The practice of *Chhaupadi* is also followed by women during childbirth and for up to eleven days after the delivery (Directive Regarding *Chhaupadi* Elimination, 2008). Even their babies are sent to live in these sheds with their mothers. During their menstrual cycles, women and girls are forced to stay outside their house at another place called *Chhaupadi Goth* (esp. in cowsheds or small huts). But this doesn't mean they are excused from other works. In fact, they are compelled to engage in hard labor such as working in the fields, fetching firewood, washing clothes and so on. In the Nepalese language, *Goth* means an animal shed. It is a simple shelter made out of stone, grass or sticks. These are sometimes built almost a mile away from the village. Hardly six feet wide and four feet high, they can barely accommodate two people. Although elite families build proper sheds, the poorer ones use extremely dilapidated and unhygienic outhouses made from mud, stone and wood with no windows. As a result, the shed generally has a dreadful living condition, and during winter, the temperature drops zero (Raut & Tandon, 2011).

This tradition has thus resulted on various adverse effects upon the women. It is found that the women suffer from poor mental health, the possibility of unnatural death due to attack by wild animals, rape, reproductive tract infection and pneumonia, malnutrition, fall of uterus because of heavy work, hindrance in education because of artificially created untouchability, humiliation, pneumonia, dysentery and hypothermia in children (Gautam, 2011).

The present chapter gives a detailed discussion of the evil practice of *Chhaupadi* in Nepal and its repercussions with findings of a content analysis.

I. *Chhaupadi* System in Nepal

Menstruation is a regular cycle that occurs in girls and women from menarche to menopause. It is purely a biological factor. However, it is not only related to women's body and health in Nepal. It is not clearly known when the practice of treating menstruation as impure started. Across Nepal, among the Hindu castes, it is rampantly found that there are practices of ostracizing girls when they have their first menstruation. Such girls are kept in a separate room and away from the view of male members of the family. But this is limited to only the first time, whereas in the *Chhaupadi* system of western Nepal, the women have to undergo this type of discriminatory treatment every time they have menstruation and throughout their life until menopause. Also, during child delivery also, women have to give birth to a child in the *Chhaupadi Goth* in the absence of others.

This tradition is rampant in the mid-western and far-western regions of the country. In the far west it is practiced mainly in Achham, Bajura, Bajang, Doti, Baitadi, Dadheldhura, Darchula, Kanchanpur and Kailali, and in the mid-west it is prevalent in Kalikot, Jumla, Humla, Mugu, Dailekh, Jajarkot and Surkhet Districts (Amgain, 2011). In these regions there is a widespread belief that the god and goddess will be enraged if the practice is violated. They believe the violation of the practice may lead to shorter life, death of livestock or destruction of crops. Similarly, there is blind belief that if a menstruating woman touches fruits, they will fall before they are ripe, and if she fetches water, the well will dry up (UNRCHC, 2011).

Every year, newspapers report stories of women raped, killed by wild animals, bitten by snakes or dead of cold during their stay in the *Goth*. But unfortunately only a few rape cases are reported because women fear the associated social stigma (AHRC, 2011). During a study conducted in Nepalese schools by Water aid in 2009, only 11 percent of the respondents declared not practicing any form of restriction or exclusion during menstruation. Recently, the *Chhaupadi* system has been blamed for the extraordinarily high rate of uterine pro-lapse in women, where, in one sample district, "over 60% of women are estimated to be living with the condition" (United Nations Populations Fund, 2009). According to Nepal's Monthly Monitoring and Annual Performance Review Worksheet 2009–2010, an average of 96 cases of menstruation disorders were reported each month by married and unmarried women in the district primary health center of Dolakha. In 2008, there were 281 deaths due to complications during delivery for 100,000 live births in Nepal. As per various experts, this figure is possibly underestimated. The neonatal mortality rate (during the twenty-eight days following the birth) reaches 32 for 1,000 live births, and a lot of newborns succumb to pneumonia or diarrhea after living their first days in a cowshed.

During *Chhaupadi* women face various forms of discrimination. They are prohibited to enter in their own house. They are forbidden to touch men, books and cows and not allowed to use the usual bed and cloths (NWC, 2008). They are restricted from going to the temples and are not allowed to touch cattle, green vegetables, plants or fruits. Access to basic things such as water taps and wells is also limited. Women practicing *Chhaupadi* can only bathe or wash clothes in a *Chaupadi dhara*—a separate well, stream or small rivulet near the village. They are not even permitted to participate in family- and community-level cultural as well as religious ceremonies or activities during their menstrual cycle (UNRCHC, 2011, p. 1).

Further, women are bounded by restriction in taking food. They are not permitted to take nutritious food and milk products. The women must survive on a diet of dry foods, salt and beaten rice (NWC, 2008). However, they must do other hard labor and manual work even when practicing *Chhaupadi*. This makes their condition much worse, and not having proper nutritious food and other kinds of discrimination deteriorates them more.

Consequently, this tradition has resulted in both mental and physical adversity for women. The women and infants are exposed to various infections and long-term ailments during their stay in the shed. There have been many cases of deaths and serious illnesses due to these practices. They are regularly suffering from infections like pneumonia, puerperal sepsis (post-partum infection), diarrhea and other chronic diseases, including mental disorders. This has led significantly to the low birth weight of children, high infant morbidity and mortality and high maternal mortality, resulting in a lower life expectancy for women. Even if a lady dies in the shed, the society doesn't allow the family to bring the dead body near their house (Khadka, 2014).

Studies by different scholars illustrate that to make this ill tradition prevalent in a society, many people and institutions play key roles (Khadka, 2014). At a household level, elders of the family and mothers-in-law are the main defenders, whereas at the community level, the main defenders are the local healers (*Dhamis, Fulpates, Jaisis*), old politicians, the caste system, the regional social system and local belief systems (Amgain, 2011). It can be found in the statement of the former minister from Doti district that

> The people in that part of the country are backward and blinded by superstition. We politicians have continuously tried to convince people to discard such superstitions, one reason may be that officials of the local bodies come from the same community and are not willing to cast off deep rooted traditions quickly.
>
> *(Ghimire, 2005)*

II. Laws Against *Chhaupadi* System in Nepal

The tradition of *Chhaupadi* degrades the condition of women. It restricts their liberty and hence denies their dignity to live freely. There are laws in Nepal which are determined to promote and protect the rights of women.

1. *The Constitution of Nepal 2072 (2015)*

This law promises protection of human rights. It has specifically provided the rights of women under Article 38, where it has prohibited any form of violence against women on the grounds of social or cultural tradition and practice. For instance, the constitution has provided that all citizens are equal before the law and no citizens shall be discriminated against on the basis of sex. Every person shall have the right to live with dignity. No physical, mental or other form of violence shall be inflicted on any woman, and such an act shall be punishable by law. Every woman shall have the right to reproductive health and other reproductive rights. Besides these, there is the right against untouchability and racial discrimination. It even prohibits torture and exploitation. Further, it provides rights like the right to live in a clean and healthy environment, right to have education and culture, right to social justice, right to religion, right to privacy, and it also protects the rights of children, stating that every child has the right not to be subjected to physical, mental or other forms of exploitation. Any such act of exploitation shall be punishable by law, and any child so treated shall be compensated as determined by law. In cases of violation of these rights, it provides the right to constitutional remedy in the manner set out in Article 133 or 144 of the constitution.

Before the enactment of this constitution, on the basis of "The Constitution of Kingdom of Nepal 2047," a case has been filed against the Government of Nepal in the Supreme Court. In the case of *DilBahadurBishwakarma and Other vs. Council of Ministers and Others* the Supreme Court of Nepal issued an order to His Majesty's government to perform following activities to eliminate *ChhaupadiPratha* from Nepal:

- The tradition of keeping menstruating and pregnant women in isolated *Chhaupadi Goth* shall be declared as ill tradition.
- The Ministry of Health shall send a group of doctors for conducting research tothe *Chhaupadi* practicing areas to find out the bad consequences of the practice of *Chhaupadi* for the health of women and publish the report.
- The Ministry of Local Development should implement programmes to create awareness in society against *Chhaupadi*.
- The Ministry of Women and Children should make protocols to prevent discrimination against women in the practice of *Chhaupadi*, and the Supreme Court should be informed about it.
- There is a need to do comprehensive research for enacting laws against the *Chhaupadi* tradition. In addition, the INGOs are also required to help in creating awareness among the people for eliminating the practice of *Chhaupadi* (*DilBahadurBishwakarma and Other vs. Council of Ministers and Others*, 2005, WPN 48.)

According to this judgement, the prime minister and cabinet secretariat have declared the practice of *Chhaupadi* as being of defective value. Likewise, the Ministry of Women, Children and Social Welfare prepared a directive, the *Chhaupadi* Tradition Elimination Guideline, 2064, to eliminate any kind of discrimination against women within the *Chhaupadi* custom. The major features of this guideline are:

1. Acknowledgement of Problem: It is an accepted fact that it is natural for girls to menstruate. However, in Nepal, the girls in mid-western and far western regions face discrimination and ill and degrading treatment. This tradition has been rooted in society due to illiteracy, blind belief and lack of awareness. Consequently it has resulted in devastating effects on personality development and security of women. Thus, in order to solve this problem in society, the government of Nepal has prepared a guideline to eliminate it.

2. It has further made long-term and short-term programmes to eliminate *Chhaupadi* in the society. The immediate programme includes:

    a) An awareness programme to be conducted to remove the old beliefs, values and customs related to the *Chhaupadi* tradition
    b) Providing health services and awareness about nutrition to the women and children affected by the *Chhaupadi* tradition
    c) Acknowledging the effort of people, family and community that tends to eliminate this tradition.

Likewise, the long-term programme includes:

    a) Implementing a programme for women to empower them from economic, social and political aspects
    b) Developing an equitable society which is based on human rights values through the development of a proper legal system

3. To implement such a programme, identification of the programme-implementing institution in the affected area, the target groups and the resource distribution needs to be done (Chhaupadi Tradition Elimination Guideline, 2007).

In addition to the constitution, court decision and specific protocol of *Chhaupadi,* there are various acts that provide protection of women's and children's rights in Nepal.

They are:

*   *State Criminal Code,* 2074 (2017): In its Section 168(3), it has prohibited *Chhaupadi* as an inhumane and degrading act and has prescribed punishment of three months' imprisonment or 3,000 Nepal rupees fine or both. In addition, judges can even order reasonable compensation to the victim. (Notably, this act was implemented only from 17 August 2018.)
*   *Civil Rights Act* 1955 (2012): Section 12 of Civil Rights Act 1955 has stated no one shall be deprived of his/her life or personal liberty.
*   *Children's Act* 1992 (2048): In its Section 4(3) it has provision of proper health care to pregnant mothers and mothers who have recently given birth to a child. Section 7 of the same act has mentioned that no child shall be subjected to torture or cruel treatment.

Nepalis bound by international human rights law, as it is a party to the United Nations (UN) Charter and seven of the nine core international human rights treaties currently in force. Article 279 of the constitution of Nepal, 2072 (2015) provides that the ratification of, accession to, acceptance of or approval of treaties or agreements that Nepal is to become party to shall be determined by law. Thus, Nepal's international obligations also form part of enforceable domestic law. It has further been stipulated by the Nepal Treaty Act which provides that provisions of Nepali laws that are inconsistent with the signed, accessed or ratified treaty, are void. In view of that, the problem of the *Chhaupadi* tradition can be tackled through a number of provisions under international human rights law. Firstly, the Charter of the United Nations (1945) has come out to reaffirm faith in human rights, in the dignity and worth of the human person and in the equal rights of men and women and to promote social progress and better standards of life. Likewise, the Universal Declaration of Human Rights addressed that all human beings are born free and equal in dignity and rights. It assures equal rights, freedom and non-discrimination to everyone. It also assures the right to liberty of persons, protection of persons from torture or cruel, inhumane or degrading treatment or punishment and specifies that all are entitled to equal protection against any discrimination. In article 25 it states the right to a standard of living adequate for the health and well-being of an individual and of his/her family, including food, clothing, housing and medical care and necessary social services. It gives special emphasis to motherhood and childhood, entitling them special care and assistance. It has protected the right freely to participate in the cultural life of the community.

The International Convention on Economic, Social and Cultural Rights (ICESCR) and International Convention on Civil and Political Rights (ICCPR) are also based on the principles of human dignity, equality, nondiscrimination, freedom, liberty and justice. Among all principles, these conventions have given emphasis to the inherent dignity of the human person. The nations that have ratified these treaties are bound through state obligations. They have to make amendments or laws according to the treaty's spirit. In cases of the failure of the nation, the victim can invoke justice through the Human Rights Committee.

In addition, the Convention on the Elimination of All Forms of Discrimination Against Women (CEDAW), 1979, is very significant. Article 2 of this convention has made the state parties to formulate a policy of eliminating discrimination against women. According to article 2(e) and 2(f), the state parties need to undertake all appropriate measures to eliminate discrimination against women by any person, organization or enterprise and to take all appropriate measures, including legislation, to modify or abolish existing laws, regulations, customs and practices which constitute discrimination against women. Nepal ratified this convention on 22April 1991. Since then, Nepal has been submitting its country report to the CEDAW committee. Nepal submitted its third and fourth periodic review reports to the CEDAW committee in 2010. Accordingly, the CEDAW committee is concerned about the persistence of harmful traditional practices in Nepal and has recommended that the government take steps to eliminate such harmful traditions in society. This recommendation is thus also applicable to eliminating *Chhaupadi*. The recommendations are as follows:

(a) Put in place without delay a comprehensive strategy, with concrete goals and timetables, to eliminate patriarchal attitudes and stereotypes that discriminate against women, in accordance with articles 2 (f) and 5 (a) of the Convention;
(b) Strengthen its awareness-raising and educational efforts, targeted at both women and men, with the involvement of civil society and community and religious leaders, to eliminate harmful traditional practices, and collaborate with the media to enhance a positive, non-stereotypical and non-discriminatory portrayal of women;
(c) Promptly enact the draft law on harmful social practices; ensure that it covers all forms of such practices; ensure full implementation of the law without delay; and monitor its effective implementation (CEDAW, 2011, p. 4).

Thus, it is important that although the *Chhaupadi* practice is committed by non-state actors, the state is nonetheless obliged to respect, actively protect and fulfill the civil, political, economic, social and cultural rights of every human being. In this context, the state is held to comply with the principle of due diligence under international law. According to the UN Special Rapporteur on Violence Against Women Rashida Manjoo, the standard of due diligence means that the state is not held responsible for the acts of others but it is held responsible for its own failure to prevent, investigate, prosecute or compensate for the commission of the act. Thus, under the obligation of due diligence, states are required to undertake effective investigations, prosecution and sanctions, guaranteeing de jure and de facto access to adequate and effective judicial remedies, ensuring comprehensive reparations, identifying certain groups as being at particular risk and eliminating prejudices and (customary) practices based on the idea of inferiority or superiority of certain members of society. "States may also be responsible for private acts if they fail to act with due diligence to prevent violations of rights or to investigate and punish acts of violence, and for providing compensation"(Manjoo, 2011).

It is important to note that the provisions of international human rights instruments have been used time and again by the Supreme Court of Nepal to safeguard the individual rights provided by international conventions. Accordingly, the petition filed in Supreme Court against the practice of *Chhaupadi* in Nepalese society was analyzed from national and international obligations of state and directions were given by the Supreme Court.

III. Findings of a Study

1. Method

The most popular nine daily newspapers—the *Kathmandu Post, Rajdhani, Gorkhapatra, Kantipur Daily, Annapurna Post, Nagarik,* the *Himalayan Times, Naya Patrika, Republica*—were selected as information sources for this study. These are the popular newspaper dailies that have high circulation and largest networks of reporters spread over Nepal. These daily newspapers are studied considering resource availability and time available for the study. Researchers used the library of Kathmandu School of Law, Bhaktapur, Nepal, for the research. The news published from 2010 to 2013 was reviewed by the authors. This was judged to be a time- and cost-effective means for developing some understanding of *Chhaupadi* in Nepal within the resource limits of authors.

2. Results

a. The Incidence of Chhaupadi According to Year

Since time immemorial, the *Chhaupadi* tradition has been practiced in mid-western and far-western parts of Nepal. This practice has been deeply rooted in the social and cultural tradition in society. The study showed that there have been reported cases of violence. The incidence is shown in Figure 30.1.

It is therefore found that in 2010, 2011 and 2012, there are many cases reporting incidences of *Chhaupadi*-related violence. In 2012, there is the highest incidence reported, and in 2013, there was one reported case of violence. It shows though the tradition is deeply rooted in the society, in the recent years it has been slowly changing, especially due to awareness programmes conducted in the affected districts in Nepal, and people are slowly being aware about the negative effect of the *Chhaupadi* tradition in society.

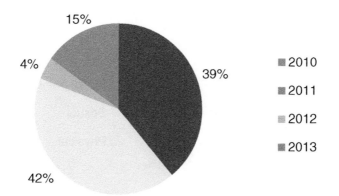

Figure 30.1 The incidence of *Chhaupadi* according to year. (*N*=27).

b. The Chhaupadi-Affected Area in Nepal

This practice is deeply entrenched in blind beliefs, and superstition especially prevailed in the western region of Nepal. The western part of Nepal, especially the villages of the districts Dadeldhura, Bajura, Baitadi, Bajhang, Mahendranagar, Accham, Dailekh, Doti, Jajarkot and Nepalgunj, are found to be affected by this tradition. The news reporting shows that there is massive reporting on *Chhaupadi* in the Accham district and there were ten such incidents. It is followed by Dailekh, Doti and Dadeldhura with three incidents each, Bajura with two incidents and one incident each in the other districts. Thus, in the mid-western and far-western regions, we still find these practices of *Chhaupadi* are prevalent, and it has differently affected various districts.

c. Violence Against the Chhau (women during menstruation)

The *Chhaupadi* practice is a tradition practiced forages in the western region of Nepal. It relates with the concept of "purity" and "impurity" from a religious aspect. So based on this belief, during the time of menstruation, knowingly or unknowingly, women and girls are physically, psychologically, socially and culturally coerced and threatened to follow this practice strictly. These practices thus directly or indirectly inflict violence upon women. The violence faced by women in the practice of *Chhaupadi* being reported by the newspaper in the stipulated time of study is shown below in the Figure 30.2.

- *Socio-Cultural violence*: *Chhaupadi* tradition rests on the social cultural belief of the society. Among the 27 reported cases, 22 were found to be cases of socio-cultural violence. Firstly, during the time of menstruation, women are forbidden to enter their home and are kept at *Chhaupadi Goth* for the period from four days minimum to fourteen days maximum. During that time, *Chhau* (women) are prohibited from showering, combing their hair or wearing vermillion powder (red powder worn by married women on their foreheads—or tika —either as a makeup accessory or vermillion powder that men and women wear on their foreheads after worshipping at a temple). Further, they are not allowed to walk on the regular route and also use the regular water tap. Girl students who go to school during the time of menstruation are expelled from school. Further, families supporting the girls and not keeping them in *Chhaupadi Goth* are socially ostracized.
- *Sexual and reproductive violence*: The practice of *Chhaupadi* has sexually exploited the women. Menstruation in women is a biological phenomenon, and it is a matter of right to privacy. However, the women are forced to reveal their menstrual status. Further, the practice is found

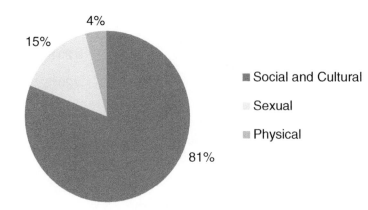

Figure 30.2 Violence against women during *Chhaupadi* (*N*=27).

to adversely affect the sexual and reproductive organs. During the time of menstruation of girls, they are found to have highly infected in sexual organs, and it is found that there is a high number of cases of prolapsed uterus in the women in the *Chhaupadi* practicing area. In addition, there are cases of giving birth to babies in *Chhaupadi Goth* without the help of other women or a doctor or nurse in the village. This has resulted in maternal and infant death too. It was even found the girls were being raped inside the *Chhaupadi Goth*. There were four incidents reported of sexual and reproductive violence. Thus, the social and cultural restriction on women during the time of menstruation has resulted sexual and reproductive violence to women.

- *Physical violence*: The *Chhaupadi* tradition is sometimes found to influence the society to physically torture the people who do not practice it strictly. A nineteen-year-old girl, after delivering her baby in the cowshed, stepped out of the *Goth*. Afterwards, she was severely beaten up with nettles by other women in the village for leaving the *Chhaupadi* hut.
- *Consequences on victim:* The tradition of *Chhaupadi* is based on old beliefs and superstitions practiced in the society. It forces women to live outside the house during the time of menstruation. For that purpose, a *Chhau Goth* is made, which is very congested and even compared to the sheds of the animals. Being ostracized and isolated during the time of menstruation, the women living in *Chhau Goth* face different problems. The practice of *Chhaupadi* can have serious physical, emotional, financial and social consequences in the life of women. These are shown in Figure 30.3.
- *Physical effects*: The *Chhaupadi* tradition is performed through social and cultural beliefs and adversely affects the physical condition of women. In following this tradition, it is found the women are victims of poor health, poor hygiene, disease and, in extreme cases, death. The conditions of the *chhau* sheds are horrific, subjecting women to cold extremities and dangerous risk of various infectious diseases, resulting in the death of women. It is found in the study that there were three incidents where women died due to excessive cold temperatures in *Chhau Goth*. Further, in one case, a woman died of suffocation. Likewise, there are cases of deaths of women due to snakebite, diarrhea, improper nutrition and clothing, epileptic stroke and the like.
- *Social effects*: The *Chhaupadi* system is strongly embedded in the social structure and cultural patterns in the affected area. The study shows there are cases of social ostracism towards families that deny continuing the practice of *Chhaupadi*. For instance, a family from Chhatiwan VDC-7 in Doti district has had to face ostracism from the community for not following *Chhaupadi*, as they kept their daughters inside the house during the time of menstruation. Thus, we find strict disobeying of *Chhaupadi* practices not only affects an individual but also has consequences for the social life of the whole family.

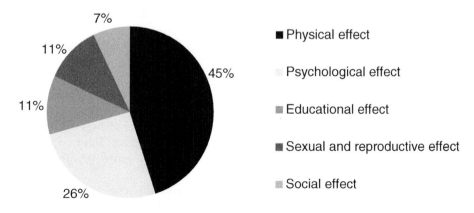

Figure 30.3 The effect of practice of *Chhaupadi* towards women (*N*=27).

- *Psychological effects*: It is found the *Chhaupadi* tradition has deeply affected the psychology of the women practicing it. Further, the women claim there are no facilities inside the hut, and during the nighttime when they are alone in the hut, the women pass the night mostly awake in fear and anxiety.

- *Sexual and reproductive effects*: It is found due to the unhygienic and unprotective system of *Chhaupadi,* the girls suffer from reproductive-related disease and sexual violence. The study report shows that in the far-western region, there are cases of high uterine prolapse in the women who practice *Chhaupadi*. Further, in one case it was found while staying in a *Chhau Goth*, a sixteen-year-old girl was raped by a local man.

- *Education effects*: It is found that during the stay at a *Chhau Goth*, villagers do not allow girl students to go to school for five days (during menstruation). It was reported in Doti district that campus students were compelled to take different routes for college during menstruation, violating the right of education of the children. Further, it was even reported in the same district that twenty-nine girls were expelled from school for attending the school at the time of menstruation. Thus, girls in these rural villages, due to *Chhaupadi*, have poor attendance and low grades at school and even are transferred or expelled.

However, it is estimated that the impact is far more grave then perceived since the recorded data is only from newspapers and not from complete, independent, comprehensive research.

In the legal perspective, these effects on the women due to *Chhaupadi* violate the range of basic rights guaranteed by the constitution and legal instruments in the country. The major rights violated during the practice of *Chhaupadi* tradition are:

1. *Right to freedom:* In the *Chhaupadi* tradition, *Chhau* women are bound and kept within the four walls of a small hut. They are prohibited to enter their own house. Even they are bound to walk different routes during the time of menstruation. This violates the right to freedom of women as provided in Article 17 of constitution of Nepal 2072.

2. *Right regarding clean environment:* During the time of *Chhaupadi*, the women are bound to live in *Chhau Goth*, which is very congested and unhygienic. In the time of winter, its temperature goes down to the extent that the women die. Sometimes due to its surroundings, the women suffer from infections and diseases. Thus, it violates the right of women to live in a healthy environment as provided in Article 30 by the constitution of Nepal 2072.

3. *Right to life and health:* Women are suffering from mental problems and fear. Further, there is the chance of attack by wild animals and snakebite to the women living in a *Chhau Goth*. The report shows that reproductive tract infections, proneness to pneumonia, malnutrition and many cases of fall of the uterus among the women practicing *Chhaupadi* tradition violate their right to life and health (article 35).

4. *Rights of women and children:* Women are provided special rights in the constitution in Article 38 and 40. However, we find that during *Chhaupadi,* women and girls are being discriminated against due to the biological phenomena in their body, and their reproductive rights are entangled in the social and cultural practices. Thus, the rights provided to women and girls by the constitution are violated.

5. *Right to children:* Menstruation generally starts at the beginning of the teenage years. So we find all most all girls facing ostracization during the time of menstruation. This type of tradition, which inflicts social and psychological violence upon children, is generally prohibited by the constitution in Article 39.

6. *Right of social justice*: During menstruation, women are generally restricted in their freedom, movement and behaviors on the basis of social belief and cultural tradition. Thus, it is against

the spirit of Article 42 of the constitution, which provides for the right of women to social justice.

7. *Right to privacy:* Menstruation is a biological phenomenon, and it is a matter of privacy. However, in the *Chhaupadi* tradition, privacy is totally ignored and this biological process is seen from social, cultural and religious aspects in the society, which is in contravention of Article 28.

8. *Right to religion:* During menstruation, women cannot go to temple, worship gods or perform any religious ceremonies. It is believed if they do so, they will be later punished by the gods. Thus, it even violates the right to religion during the time of menstruation.

9. *Right against exploitation:* The constitution of Nepal prohibits any kind of exploitation. However, the practice of *Chhaupadi* shows that women are physically, socially and sexually exploited by society in the name of culture.

10. *Right to education:* The right to education is specifically ensured by the constitution in Article 31. But it is found there is general belief in the society that if women during menstruation study books, the goddess Saraswati, the goddess of learning, would be angry and punish them. There are different discriminatory behaviors done to the girls in school who are menstruating. This kind of behavior definitely violates the educational rights of girls and women protected under the constitution.

11. *Right to housing:* Women during the time of menstruation are forbidden to enter their homes. They are forced to live in the special huts during the time of menstruation and spend the nights there. This type of tradition categorically violates the right of women to housing as provided under Article 37.

12. *Right to food:* Women during menstruation are not given nutritious food and not allowed to touch other food such as milk, etc. This violates the basic rights of women to food, including to have healthy and nutritious food for living a better and healthy life.

13. *Right to equality and to live with dignity:* Women during menstruation are treated as untouchables in the society. They are not allowed to touch things such as cattle, men, crops, gods and goddesses. The impurity concept leads them to stay far from their home and family, especially when they are in great need and support of their family, thus creating an environment of untouchability among the family members. Further, they are not allowed to enter their house and are kept far away from the house in the *Chhau Goth*. Thus, it violates the right to equality and non-discrimination of women as ensured by the constitution in Article 18 and 16.

14. *Right to religion and to participate in cultural practice:* During menstruation, women are not allowed to participate in cultural and religious affairs in the society. It is believed if they participate in such programmes the gods and goddess would be angry. In addition, the women are also prohibited to wear certain things which are culturally and religiously important. Thus, it violates the cultural and religious rights of the women.

The guarantee of these rights under the constitution makes possible that if there is any case of *Chhaupadi* practice which is creating problems for women in society, there is opportunity for the victim to get remedy directly by filing a petition with the Supreme Court for constitutional remedy. However, due to lack of knowledge and awareness about law and women rights, so far, no case of *Chhaupadi* victimization has been reported to any agencies. Therefore, in Nepal, it is in fact not the legal lacunas that actually entertain these sorts of practices. Rather, these practices are still continuing because of unawareness of existing laws to protect oneself from such harmful traditions. There are profound blind beliefs and superstitions among the people. Thus, at first, such belief in the society must be broken through education and awareness. It can be seen that the governmental and other non-government bodies and concerned stakeholders are working together to fight against these ill practices.

Accordingly, in this research paper, the reported cases of awareness programmes raised in the country against the *Chhaupadi* tradition are also studied.

Binita Pandey et al.

d. Positive Initiatives by Government of Nepal

I. DATE OF THE AWARENESS PROGRAMMES YEAR WISE

The study shows during the first two-year of study i.e. 2010 and 2011 AD, there were no cases reported about raising awareness programmes in the *Chhaupadi*-prevalent area. However, we find there are some awareness programmes conducted by the government, NGOs and INGOs in the year 2012 and 2013.

These data show that the government and concerned stakeholders have started to carry out activities to eliminate the *Chhaupadi* tradition and are moving towards fulfilling their promises to end all violence against women from Nepal. Further, these reports show that Nepal is trying its best to fulfill its international obligations and human rights commitments and protect the rights of women from harmful traditions practiced in the society.

II. AREA IN WHICH THE AWARENESS PROGRAMMES WERE IMPLEMENTED

The news showed the government has acknowledged the problem of *Chhaupadi* in different districts in Nepal. Consequently, in the districts of the mid-western and far-western regions in Accham, Baitadi, Bajura, Dadeldhura, Dailekh and Mahendranagar, it is found that awareness programmes are being launched by the government, NGOs, INGOs and concerned stakeholders.

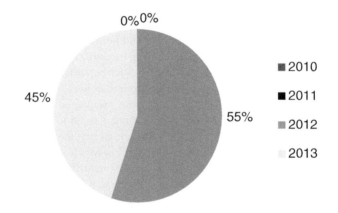

Figure 30.4 The number of incidents of awareness conducted in *Chhaupadi*-affected areas according to the year (N=11).

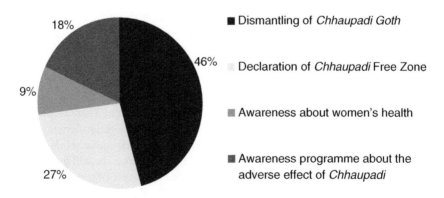

Figure 30.5 The types of awareness programme conducted in the *Chhaupadi*-affected areas (N=11).

338

III. THE AWARENESS PROGRAMMES

The existing practices cannot be eliminated unless the people are aware of them. The enactment of law is ineffective if the people are not aware about the existing problem and don't act to curb it. Thus, there has been some initiation from the government, NGOs and INGOs in Nepal to create awareness in the *Chhaupadi*-prone areas. The awareness campaign during a 4-year time period is shown in Figure 30.5.

Discussion and Conclusion

The study illustrates that government agencies and non-government organizations have been actively working for the abolishment of these practices. There were eleven reports on awareness campaigns in different districts. Protection of women from *Chhaupadi* practices is possible only when the society is given reproductive health education, and it has been possible with the awareness programmes initiated by the people of these regions. Accordingly, there have been massive discussions and programmes among the people and concerned stakeholders about the practices that violate the rights of women and girls in some districts. In addition, there is much news which illustrates the intervention of government and non-government organizations in the society, as they have lobbied to dismantle *Chhau Goths* where *Chhaupadi* are kept and encouraged the local societies to keep the women at home with safe and hygienic lifestyles during their menstruation. Thus, in recent news, we find more news on awareness campaigns raised in districts rather than the victimization of women due to *Chhaupadi* tradition. We can thus say that with the change in the circumstances, increasing literacy and intervention from the government and non-government organizations, the *Chhaupadi* practices in the mid-western and far-western regions are slowly changing the culture and tradition and heading towards providing respectable lives for women.

However, there were three news reports illustrating ineffectiveness of awareness programmes. For instance, despite many types of awareness programmes being organized in Dailekh district, the prevalence of superstitious beliefs related to *Chhaupadi* in the society remains, and there is the practice of ostracization of women during menstruation to *Chhaupadi goth*. Likewise, it is found in Achham district that the allocated budget to eliminate the *Chhaupadi* system in the area is ineffective, and 97 percent of women are still found living in *Chhaupadi Goth* during menstruation. Thus, we can say that we have made some positive efforts in the past yet, there is a lot to do in the future.

Equal rights of men and women are inalienable, interrelated, interdependent and inherent rights. These rights cannot be curtailed in the name of cultural practice. It is clear that the practice of menstruation and consequent belief in untouchability creates an obstruction to the development of women's personality. A woman does not become an evil force or untouchable during the time of menstruation, as it is purely a biological process. However, during the time of menstruation and childbirth, women are suffering from social and cultural violence. Along with these practices, women are deprived of the right to an adequate standard of living, including the right to housing, right to food, right to health, right against exploitation, right to human inherent dignity, right to non-discrimination, right to participate in cultural practice, right to freedom etc. This has resulted on severe consequences for women. Many women suffered fear and anxiety; some were attacked by wild animals inside the hut and some were bitten by snakes and died. Further, the severe cold in winter has also taken the lives of women. Moreover, there are cases of sexual violence like rape, and it is even found that while living in *Chhaupadi Goth*, women suffer from various diseases like diarrhea, fever etc.

Despite these consequences, the women are reluctant to report these incidents to authorities for getting proper remedy. It is because they have been brought up in such a society where the people believe menstruation is unnatural and women also are forced to believe this.

The twenty-first century has brought a consciousness among a limited demography that such practice is in fact not good. This change of belief can only be attributed to an increase in the level of education. However, the movement of elimination of this practice lacks an integrated attempt from all sectors, so the practice prevails in the majority. It is absolutely necessary to break the belief system through the realization that a culture, if harmful, is no culture. "No harm no culture" means that *Chhaupadi* can never be taken as a culture. The grotesque condition one lives in when experiencing the menstruation cycle can only be justified in the in realm of injustice.

Nevertheless, the government of Nepal has now conducted awareness programmes in these affected areas. The newspaper reporting also shows that slowly, there have been some changes in the villages to dismantle the *Chhaupadi Goth* and keep the women in their own houses. Further, there are some villages which are declared *Chhaupadi*-free zones. However, it is found still there is practice of *Chhaupadi* in the mid-western and far-western parts of Nepal. In addition, there is rampant practice of treating women as "untouchable" (i.e. *nachune* in local words) all over Nepal in Hindu communities. This makes it a bigger challenge to combat the *Chhaupadi* tradition also to change the mentality of people. Hence, it is important to create awareness about this ill practice not only in the *Chhaupadi*-affected area but also in other parts of Nepal and to make them aware about menstruation as a natural phenomenon and a matter of privacy. Thus, the writers suggest, the religious belief and cultural affairs associated with it should be properly discussed in the country to uproot it from the mentality of people. For that, government, non-governmental organizations and concerned stakeholders should work together. There are some events of success; however, more must be done.

References

Amgain, B. (2011). *Social dimension of Chhaupadi system: A study from Achham District, far West Nepal.* Kathmandu, Nepal: MMRA.

CEDAW. (2011). *Concluding observations of the committee on the elimination of discrimination against women*, 49th session, p. 4.

Chhaupadi Tradition Elimination Guideline.(2007).

DilbahadurBishwakarma and other vs. Council of Ministers and others.(2005). WPN 48.

Ethics in Action, *5*(5), October 2011, Published by Asian Human Right Commission (AHRC).

Gautam, J. (2011). *Untouchability during menstruation Chhaupadi custom.* Retrieved from http://feminismnwomen rights.blogspot.com/2011/04/untouchability-during-menstruation-and.html.

Ghimire, L.V. (2005). Unclean and unseen. *Student BMJ, 13*, 177–220.

Government of Nepal, Independent Report prepared by the National Women's Commission of Nepal to supplement the Combined 4th and 5th Periodic Report Submitted to the CEDAW Committee, 2012.

Khadka, N. (2014). Chhaupadi Pratha: Women's condition and suffering. Unpublished Thesis submitted for the partial fulfillment of the requirement for Degree of Master of Arts in Anthropology to the Tribhuvan University, Nepal. Retrieved from http://107.170.122.150:8080/xmlui/bitstream/handle/123456789/286/Thesis%20of%20Nirajan%20Khadka.%20new.pdf?sequence=1&isAllowed=y.

Manjoo, R. (2011). Report of the Special Rapporteur on violence against women, its causes and consequences, 14th session.

National Women Commission (NWC). (2008). Gender base disaggregated report.

Nepal's Monthly Monitoring and Annual Performance Review Worksheet, 2009–2010.

Raut, N., & Tandon, S. (2011). Historic custom of Chhaupadi isolation of girls & women during menstruation & after birth—Dangers for health, survival. Retrieved from www.wunrn.com/news/2011/03_11/03_21/032111_nepal.htm

United Nations Populations Fund.(2009). Fallen wombs, broken lives: Responding to uterine prolapse in Nepal. Retrieved from www.unfpa.org/public/News/pid/3282.

UN Resident and Humanitarian Coordinator (UNRCHC), Nepal. (2011). *Chhaupadi in the far-West*, Issue no 01, April 2011.

Volunteer Summer Nepal. (n.d.). *Chhaupadi Goth.* Retrieved from http://volunteersummernepal.org/chaupadi-pratha-seclusion-during-mensuration.

31

ROHINGYAS IN MYANMAR AND BANGLADESH

An Examination of Collective and Secondary Victimization

S. Manikandan

Introduction

The Rohingyas have been facing discrimination, violence and persecution from the Myanmar government for decades, and the issues with regard to the Rohingya got heated from 2016. In 2016, around 300 members who belong to Rohingya militant groups attacked the border police check post in Rakhine state and killed nine police officers, according to state media. These attacks triggered the Myanmar military to take strict action against the Rohingyas, because of which around 87,000 Rohingyas fled to Bangladesh (Dussich, 2018). At the end of 2016, discrimination, violence and persecution against the Rohingya Muslims increased, and it intensified in the middle of 2017. In the end of August 2017, it was reported by Myanmar's state media that ARSA (Arakan Rohingya Salvation Army) insurgents killed 12 border officers while a series of attacks targeting more than 20 police outposts and an army base in Rakhine state took place (Dussich, 2018). Due to the attack by ARSA, the Myanmar military counter-attacked, which they called 'clearance operations', attacking Rohingya Muslims brutally, including burning down villages, mass killings (including children below 5 years and sexual abuse including rape), which led to mass fleeing of about 509,000 Rohingyas to Cox's Bazaar in Bangladesh (Dussich, 2018). It was also alleged that Myanmar military forces randomly fired on fleeing Rohingya and planted land mines near the border area from where Rohingyas used to cross the border to reach Bangladesh (Albert, 2018).

The Rohingya crisis was at the peak in the month of September 2017. According to Medecins Sans Frontieres (MSF), around 6,700 Rohingyas, which also included 730 children under the age of 5, were killed brutally without any mercy after the violence broke out and intensified. Some Rohingya refugees said that the Myanmar military attacked and killed Rohingyas house by house (*BBC News* [Asia], n.d.). Even the government of Myanmar claimed that 'clearance operations', which was only against the militant groups, ended on 5 September, but BBC correspondents got evidence that the clearance operations by the Myanmar government continued after that also (*BBC News* [Asia], n.d.).

According to Human Rights Watch, which conducted an in-depth satellite imagery analysis, has stated that after August 2017, around 288 villages were totally or partially destroyed by fire in northern Rakhine state, and Human Rights Watch also pointed out that Maundaw township was the most damaged area in Rakhine state because of Myanmar military atrocities (*BBC News* [Asia], n.d.).

It was stated by the UNHCR that the Rohingya Muslims are the most persecuted minority in the world, and according to the UNHCR, it was estimated that around 687,000 Rohingyas have arrived since August 2017 (*BBC News* [Asia], n.d.). The UN also stated that the Rohingya issue is the "world's fastest growing refugee crisis", because when Rohingyas flee from Myanmar, they enter Bangladesh, which is not able to handle such a huge population of refugees, while other neighboring countries are afraid to take them as refugees because of many factors. Apart from providing asylum, there are many other aspects like providing emergency aid, which includes food, safe drinking water, shelter, sanitation facilities, medical or healthcare service and other such aids.

Initially the government of Bangladesh was able to handle the Rohingya refugee crisis situation by providing them emergency aid and all such facilities, but when the arrival of Rohingya refugees increased day by day, the government of Bangladesh was unable to handle it, even though international communities started helping these refugees. Due to this unhandled crisis situation, on September 2017, Bangladesh's Parliament unanimously passed a resolution insisting the United Nations and the international community to take strong diplomatic action against the Myanmar government to take back Rohingya people and also ensure their safe rehabilitation and provide citizenship rights (Abedin eiffel, 2017). Even after Myanmar and Bangladesh signed a pact with respect to the repatriation of the Rohingyas who had fled from Rakhine state, the repatriation work was not carried out, which shows that the Myanmar government is not interested in taking back the Rohingyas (Holmes O & Agencies, 2017).

On World Refugee Day (20 June 2018), it was estimated that there are more than 900,000 Rohingya refugees in the Cox's Bazaar district of Bangladesh, who are more vulnerable because of the monsoon, and Amnesty International called on the international community to increase international assistance urgently to safeguard this vulnerable population (Amnesty International, 2018). According to the United Nations, it was estimated that more than 200,000 Rohingya refugees are in danger zones of landslides and floods due to the monsoon season. In addition, more than 28,000 Rohingyas have been seriously affected by this critical weather condition, and around 3,000 shelters have been damaged due to 133 landslides (Amnesty International, 2018).

The Rohingyas have been victimized in various ways in Myanmar as well as Bangladesh as refugees. However, the refugees are not considered as ideal victims. Even though they are victims of abuse of power and are collectively victimized in many ways, few studies on them from a victimological perspective have been done. Apart from research on crime victimization, there is a greater need for criminologists and victimologists to study collective victimization and victims of abuses from international perspectives. Rohingyas are one of the most persecuted minorities in the world, and there is a greater need to study them and the collective victimization they face by the Myanmar armed forces. To fill the gap in analysis on victimization of refugees and the victimization of Rohingyas and also with an aspiration to contribute substantially to the field, I tried marrying refugee studies with victimology in this chapter.

This chapter is divided into three parts. The first part deals with the introduction to Rohingya Muslims and their historical background. Part two deals with victimization of Rohingyas inside Myanmar and secondary victimization faced by them as refugees in Bangladesh. The third part examines the phases of Rohingyas victimization in Myanmar and Bangladesh and policy recommendations.

I. Historical Background of Rohingya

The Rohingya ethnic minorities residing in the North Rakhine state of Myanmar have been facing torture at the hands of the state, and they are considered Bengali immigrants who are fleeing from their own land and seeking asylum in other countries of the world. In the three townships of the North Rakhine state of Myanmar—Maungdaw, Buthidaung and Ratheduang—there have been more than a million Rohingyas residing for many decades (Equal Rights Trust, Institute of Human Rights and Peace Studies, 2014). These Rohingyas are considered illegal immigrants, accused by the Myanmar government of being foreigners from the neighboring state of Bangladesh, and they are called 'Bengalis' with the motive of questioning their ethnicity; they are not considered as part of the indigenous population of Myanmar (Siddiqui, 2017). But if we try to look back at the history of Myanmar, we can find traces of Rohingyas staying in the North Rakhine state for decades.

1. Pre-Colonial History of Rohingya

The word 'Rohingya' was derived from 'Roang'/'Rohang'/'Roshang' (the old name of Arakan, now called as Rakhine), which is a corrupt Arabic term 'Raham' (blessing, mercy) meaning the land of god's blessing (Yunus, 1994). There are traces that in the eighth century, these Rohingyas were dwelling in an independent kingdom in Arakan which is now Rakhine state in Myanmar (Al-Mahmood, 2016). Till the beginning of the eighth century, these Rohingya had no contact with the Islamic religion, and it was between the 9th and 14th centuries, through the Arabs, who came for the trading purposes, that the people of Arakan state came into close contact with Islam (Al-Mahmood, 2016). During the trade activities, Arabs also carried out missionary activities by spreading Islam and, in the process, a huge number of people were converted to Islam (Islam, 2013). Moreover, many of the Arab traders married local women, brought up their families in Arakan and permanently settled. Because of conversions to Islam, marriages and migration, the Muslim population of Arakan state increased in the subsequent century (Islam, 2013). In 1404, Narameikhala, the Arakan king himself, admired Islam and adopted the Muslim name Solaiman Shah, and till that time, the Arakan state had been ruled only by a non-Muslim king (Islam, 2013). During the fall of Muslim rule in Arakan, Bodawpaya, a Burmese king of Ava, invaded Arakan and strongly gained control over Arakan in 1784, which made hundreds of thousands of Rohingya flee to Bengal as refugees (Al-Mahmood, 2016).

2. Colonial History of Rohingya

In 1824, the British East India Company captured Myanmar (then Burma), and the whole of Burma including Arakan came under the rule of British India. Due to the annexure of Burma with British India, a lot of migration took place between Arakan state and Bengal; especially construction workers were migrated to Burma from Bengal and other parts of British India for infrastructure projects. During colonial rule, the British addressed that there were conflicts between diverse communities in Burma, and they were not interested in national integration because those conflicts between diverse communities were used to continue their colonial rule with its policy of "divide and rule" (Islam, 2013). During the Second World War in 1942, the British promised the Rohingya that they would provide them a separate land in exchange for support in the war. During the war, the Rohingyas supported the British while Myanmar's nationalists supported the Japanese, and after the war, the British rewarded the Rohingya with higher prestigious posts in government (Abdelkader, 2017).

3. Post-Colonial History of Rohingya

In 1948, Myanmar (then Burma) got independence from the British, and the Rohingya were not given a separate state as the British promised. Before the independence of Burma, the nationalist leader General Aung San called all ethnic groups for a conference at Pang Long and agreed that regional autonomy shall be given to all states after ten years of independence. However, no autonomy to the state was provided, and Burma adopted a unitary character in its constitution after the death of the nationalist leader General Aung San (Abdelkader, 2017). After the independence of Myanmar, *U Nu* became the first prime minister, and the post-independence period in Myanmar witnessed a lot of ethnic conflict among many groups. Rohingya Muslims supporting the British during the pre-independence period and the betrayal of the British made them feel alienated as well as insecure in Independent Burma. The new Myanmar government dismissed many Rohingya Muslims from their posts in government that had been offered to them during the British period. The government made full efforts to decrease the Muslim majority in Arakan state by transmigrating Buddhist Burmese from other parts of Burma (Islam, 2013). Against the act of government, some Rohingya showed resistance, which was led by armed groups called Mujahids, but the resistance slowly died (Al-Mahmood, 2016).

Burma's first president, Sao Shwe Thaike, declared in 1959 that the "Muslims of Arakan (Rohingya) certainly belong to the indigenous races of Burma", and in 1960, Rohingyas were given voting rights to participate in the electoral process (Green, MacManus, & Venning, 2015, p. 2). On 2 March 1962, General Ne Win, the then-army chief, and his Burma Socialist Programme Party seized all powers; the constitution was abolished and the parliament was dissolved. Moreover, all powers of the state—legislative, judiciary and executive—were under the control of the Revolutionary Council (RC), which was headed by him. During his regime, discrimination against ethnic minorities including Rohingya Muslims was very high. The businesses of Muslims were completely taken over by the government, and the Revolutionary Council ordered Arakan divisional authorities to restrict the movement of the Muslims (Yunus, 1994).

In 1978, the Arakan state government, under the direct guidance of the Council of State (the highest executive body of the state), carried out the Muslim ethnic cleansing operation named King Dragon Operation or Nagarnin with the objective to intimidate and compel the Rohingya Muslims to leave Arakan state (Yunus, 1994). During the operation, Muslims of Arakan were arrested, both men and women, even young and old people, while women were raped freely in the detention camps, tortured and killed. Due to the increase in violence, around 300,000 Rohingya Muslims fled to Bangladesh to safeguard their lives. In 1979, with the help of UNHCR, a bilateral agreement was signed between Myanmar and Bangladesh, through which Myanmar took back the Rohingyas (Yunus, 1994). In 1982, the new citizenship law came into existence, which denied citizenship to the Rohingya by excluding them from the country's list of 135 national races. They were not considered as indigenous races and were called "illegal migrants" (Green, MacManus, & Venning, 2015, p.1).

4. The Historical Timeline of Rohingya

Year	Description
1785	Last Rakhine Kingdom annexed by Burmese King Bodawpaya.
1824–26	First Anglo-Burmese war; Arakan (Rakhine) state is annexed to British India.
1942–43	Pro-British Muslims and pro-Japanese Rakhine clash; massacres on both sides. Muslims flee north and Rakhine people move south, contributing to segregation.
1948	Burma gains independence from Britain, U Nu becomes first prime minister.
1959	Burma's first president, Sao Shwe Thaike, declares, "Muslims of Arakan certainly belong to the indigenous races of Burma".
1960	Rohingya vote in elections.
1962	Ne Win leads military coup; leads to increasing discrimination of ethnic minorities.
1974	Rakhine granted statehood.
1977–1978	Nationwide crackdown on 'illegal immigration'; 200,000 Rohingya flee to Bangladesh. Most return to Burma the following year.
1982	Citizenship law excludes Rohingya from country's list of 135 national races and strips Rohingya of citizenship.
1989	Burma renamed Myanmar; Arakan state renamed Rakhine state; new citizenship scrutiny cards issued to Myanmar nationals, excluding most Rohingya.
1990	Elections held, Rohingya and Kaman parties run; several Rohingya representatives elected.
1991–1992	Military operation Pyi Thaya in northern Rakhine state; 250,000 people flee to Bangladesh.

Year	Description
1992	NaSaKa military/border security force established in northern Rakhine state, notorious for abuses.
1993–1995	Rohingya who fled during operation Pyi Thaya repatriated under UNHCR's watch; Border Region Immigration Control restricts marriages of Rohingya in Maungdaw township; Myanmar stops issuing birth certificates to Rohingya children.
1997	Head of Sittwe Immigration Office restricts Rohingya travelling outside their township.
2001	Twenty-eight mosques and Islamic schools destroyed in and around Maungdaw township.
2005	Maungdaw Township Peace and Development Council restricts Rohingya marriages and birth rate.
2008	Rohingyas granted temporary registration cards and permitted to vote in widely discredited Myanmar constitution referendum.
2008–2009	Government spotchecks Rohingya homes and restricts movement.
2010	Myanmar elections, Rohingya allowed to vote.
2012	Violence erupts in Rakhine state between Buddhists and Muslims.
2014	March: Rakhine nationalists attack international NGO offices in Sittwe; April: Rohingya excluded from April nationwide census.
2015	February: Parliament grants temporary white card holders (mostly Rohingya) the right to vote in planned constitutional amendment; days later, the president reverses the decision and declares white cards invalid; May: boat crisis in Andaman Sea reported in the international press; June: UNHCR estimates over 150,000 people have fled from the Myanmar/Bangladesh border area since January 2012; August: Rohingya representative in northern Rakhine state, U Shwe Maung, is barred from re-election.

*Source: Countdown to annihilation: Genocide in Myanmar. *Report by International State Crime Initiative.*

II. Victimization of Rohingyas Inside Myanmar and Bangladesh

1. Collective Victimization and Persecution Faced by Rohingyas in Myanmar

The governance model says that the state should act as an *enabler* that provides the legal and regulatory framework and political order as well as acting as a *resource provider*. However, in the case of Rohingyas, the Myanmar government acted in a completely opposite manner and denied citizenship to Rohingyas and killed, victimized, persecuted and finally compelled the Rohingyas to flee from Rakhine state of Myanmar.

A lot of discrimination has been faced by Rohingyas, among which was the stripping of their citizenship under the 1982 Citizenship Act. It is very unusual that the Myanmar government itself promotes discrimination, harassment, violence and terror against the Rohingyas by having well-documented discriminatory state policies (Green, MacManus, & Venning, 2015, p. 70). The report by the international State Crime Initiative (2015) has revealed that the government of Myanmar started its institutionalized discrimination against Rohingyas 25 years ago when the businesses of Rohingya Muslims were slowly and systematically attacked by the government and Rohingya people were removed from administrative positions like civil services. The report also observed that the major discrimination is only because Rohingyas were Muslims, and over the period of time, the discrimination against Rohingya Muslims was so intense that they have become dehumanized. In the 1990s, the Myanmar military attacked and destroyed mosques in the town centers in the process of de-Islamification, from which it is very clear that the major discrimination against Rohingyas is only because they are Muslims.

Following are the discriminations which have been faced by Rohingyas in Myanmar:

- Myanmar army and local police have frequently forced Rohingyas into labor, and they were killed if they refused (Lowenstein, 2015).
- The two-child policy which is implemented in the Rakhine state is discriminatory in nature because it is implemented only for Rohingyas.
- State policy of restriction on marriage against Rohingyas, in which Rohingyas have to apply for permission to get married and the application is very abusive, is only applicable to Rohingyas.
- Policy restrictions on freedom of movement in which Rohingyas are not allowed to travel within or between townships without any permission authorized by local/regional authority and also, it is very difficult to obtain authorizations. This policy is discriminatory and in violation of their human rights to liberty of movement, nondiscrimination and equality before the law (Fortify Rights International (Organization), 2014, p. 33).
- There is much other discrimination like having separate wards in hospitals for Rohingyas, restricting their higher education and the preaching of ill about Rohingyas by monks.

Rohingyas are not considered citizens of Myanmar. Instead, they are termed foreigners in their own land. In 1982, the Burma citizenship law divided citizens into three categories—(1) citizens, (2) associate citizens and (3) neutral citizens. They were given three color-coded cards—pink, blue and green, respectively (Mathieson, 2009; Ullah, 2011). However, the Rohingyas were officially stripped of their citizenship, and the government refused to recognize them as an ethnic minority. In 1959, Burma's first president, Sao Shwe Thaike, declared that Muslims (Rohingya Muslims) of Arakan state belong to the indigenous races of Burma, and in 1960, Rohingya Muslims were granted voting rights. But then in 1982, they were completely stripped of their citizenship (Green, MacManus, & Venning, 2015, p. 7).

According to Section 6, 1982 Law, 'associate citizenship' was for those whose citizenship applications were being processed at the time, while "neutral citizenship" was given to those who were not the citizens but could establish that they and their predecessors lived in the country prior to independence, which could make their stay in Myanmar legal. But the lack of documentation to prove that their ancestors lived in the country for decades forced the Rohingyas to flee to other parts of the world, especially Bangladesh. Those who qualified under the 1948 law could no longer qualify under the new law. Thus, they would be considered associate citizens provided they applied for citizenship in 1948 (Mathieson, 2009). Where application for neutral citizenship is concerned, the refugees had to prove that their ancestral line was settled in Burma prior to independence. Thus, the Rohingyas could no longer enjoy the citizenship of their own homeland, leading to the onset of state-sponsored violence and discrimination.

The forced migration of Rohingyas started in 1942 when Japan invaded Burma and Britain retreated, forcing Rohingyas to flee to East Bengal (Ullah, 2005, 2008). In 1962, after Burma regained independence, a military coup produced a Socialist party known as the Burma Socialist Party, which would last 60 years. During their rule, the Rohingyas were killed, raped and abused, and their social and political organizations were dismantled by the Burmese army. When the national census in 1977 came to Myanmar for the total count of the citizens, the military very smartly excluded Rohingyas, as a result of which the Rohingyas had to leave for Bangladesh in 1978, the number being no less than 200,000. The Citizenship Act of 1982 again excluded considering Rohingyas the citizens of Myanmar, leading to around one million Rohingyas being homeless owing to being denied group citizenship rights. The act officially recognizes 135 'national races' that qualify for citizenship. As the Rohingyas were not recognized, they were denied the benefit of citizenship on account of what the Burmese government has described as "no indigenous ancestry" (Abdelkader, 2013). As non-citizens, the Rohingyas can only possess foreign registration cards, and to add to their horror, the schools and employers refuse to accept the cards. Hence, their rights as non-citizens under international law are also not guaranteed. Their right to marry, own property, move freely and have access to health care, employment and higher education is curbed by the government to build a mono-religious nation.

Violence against Rohingyas that took place specially in June and October 2012 displaced around 147,000 people, about 138,000 of them Rohingya who are living in vast detention camps on the outskirts of Sittwe, whereas others were living in more isolated camps and villages in and around Sittwe, Pauk, Mrauk U, Minbya and Myebon (Green, MacManus, & Venning, 2015). They were again excluded from the 2014 census and were denied the right to vote or stand for elections in 2015. According to Human Rights Watch (2000), there were six main periods when the Rohingyas had to leave for Bangladesh: late 1700s, early 1800s, 1940s, 1978 and 1991 (about 300,000), and the most recent movement was in 2012. According to a World Health Organization report (March 2018), currently there are around 1.3 million Rohingya refugees in Bangladesh, and WHO has appealed to international communities to contribute generously to supply proper and timely medical services to this highly vulnerable population, as currently the monsoon was approaching and there was a high risk of many crises, including natural calamities like flooding, landslides etc.

2. A Phase of Revictimization: Problems Faced by Rohingyas as Refugees

Bangladesh witnessed an influx of several millions of Rohingyas escaping the violence from Myanmar. More than 620,000 have crossed the border since August 2017, with camps drastically growing up in the Southern Cox's Bazar region (Holmes O & Agencies, 2017). The Rohingyas are blamed for drug-related and violent crimes happening in Cox's Bazar, because of which their movement and access to basic needs were restricted in 2012 following attacks on Buddhist communities in South-eastern Bangladesh (Ganguly & Miliate, 2015). The officials of Bangladesh decided to move the refugees from Cox's Bazar to Thengar Char, which flooded in a high tide in 2015 (Independent, January 2017). Such inhumane acts were planned by the Government of Bangladesh to execute the Rohingyas. Bangladesh is unable to form national policies for refugees and refuses to take help from the United Nations regarding the same. Recently Myanmar and Bangladesh signed an initial deal to deport the hundreds of thousands of Rohingyas who fled the Rakhine State. The signing took place between Myanmar's democratic leader, Aung San Suu Kyi, and the foreign minister of Bangladesh, Abul Hassan Mahmood Ali, in Myanmar's capital, Naypyidaw, leading to a peaceful situation (Holmes O & Agencies, 2017). But there is a high risk of revictimization, as there was no discussion about the safety and granting of citizenship to Rohingya refugees.

Though Bangladesh lacks resources to fulfill its own needs, it has accommodated around one million Rohingyas refugees on a humanitarian basis, but the living conditions of the camps of Cox's Bazaar are horrible. Most of the refugees are children, who are more vulnerable. Overcrowded camps make them frustrated because of lack of resources; poor sanitary conditions make it very difficult for women and girls; and there's difficulty in supplying fresh and clean drinking water to them as well (*Gulf News*, 2017). In many of the camps in Bangladesh, there is a prevalence of acute malnutrition among children, indicated by low weight for height because of the parents being unable to earn money to fulfill even their basic needs and the poor quality of the rations being given in the camps (Prodip, 2017).

One of the major problems among Rohingya refugees is child marriages. In the pursuit of obtaining Bangladeshi citizenship and of throwing away the economic burden of a girl child, most of the parents get their girl child married to any Bangladeshi citizen, which leads to three impacts on girls: dangers to health for both the young mother and the child, problems of social integration and the risk of experiencing abuse within marriage. It is also found that most girls in Rohingya refugee camps are married between the ages of 12 and 16 years, and they give birth to their first child between 14 and 18 years (Prodip, 2017).

United Nations refugee protection officials have warned that Rohingya people who fled from Myanmar and took refuge in Bangladesh are more vulnerable and at high risk of being "re-victimized even in exile" unless careful action is taken. "Without proper support, they also face risks such as child labor, gender-based violence and trafficking," said Shinji Kubo, UNHCR Representative in Bangladesh (UN News, 2017, p. 4).

The International Rescue Committee (IRC) and Relief International (RI) carried out a multisector assessment between September 29 and October 3, 2017, with an objective of understanding the needs and problems of Rohingya refugees who fled from Myanmar. The three main needs were money, household goods and non-food and food items. One-third of the surveyed population, because of lack of food, opt for less preferred and less expensive foods, reducing the number of meals taken per day and adults skipping food in order to feed their small children. Nearly one-third of families surveyed reported that open defecation and cleanliness are among the major concerns. Nearly half of all pregnant women do not receive any medical care for their pregnancies, and many of the families with pregnant women do not know where to seek medical care. It is also found that gender-based violence (GBV) is a major concern in the area (Morris, Chopyak, Gray, & Mamun, 2007).

One of the major victimizations faced by refugee girls is trafficking for sexual exploitation. Similarly, young teenage girls from Rohingya refugee camps are being trafficked for sexual exploitation in Bangladesh, while most of the traffickers are old Rohingya women themselves. In the name of offering jobs in Dhaka as domestic workers, kitchen staff and hotel employees, Rohingya girls are being trafficked into forced sex work and sometimes sold to foreigners. Some of the trafficked girls also say that they don't have any option other than sex work due to their poverty (*BBC News*, 2018).

Bangladesh Police in Cox's Bazar have tightened security in Rohingya refugee camps following increases in crime, including the killing of a refugee leader. According to Bangladesh Police in Cox's Bazar, around 106 cases were filed against 186 Rohingya people, half of which were murder and firearms cases and half drug related (*The Irrawaddy*, 2018).

III. Phases of Victimization

From the data analysis, I have constituted three phases of victimization of Rohingyas:

- **Phase 1:** Violence, persecution and collective victimization of Rohingyas in Myanmar.
- **Phase 2:** Victimization and problems faced during migrating from Myanmar to Bangladesh.
- **Phase 3:** Victimization due to the refugee camp situation and problems associated with the refugee camp.

i. Phase 1: Violence and persecution by the Myanmar army

1. *Rape and sexual assault:* The Myanmar army has raped and sexually assaulted many of the Rohingya women and girls. They detained many of the women and girls to rape, raped them and later killed them. There are some cases where the women and girls were kept in custody for a long time only to provide sexual services. It is also evident from that analysis that many school-going children were taken into custody and brutally raped.
2. *Mass killing:* The army has killed many people by randomly opening fire and also beheaded many people. There are a number of instances where they have killed children and elderly people as well.
3. *Destruction of property:* The army has been involved in the mass destruction of property as well, mostly burning the houses of Rohingya people.

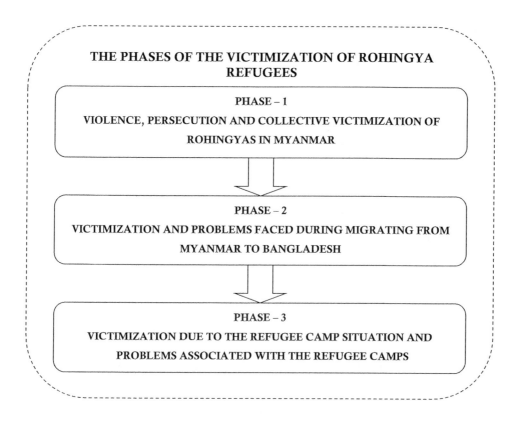

THE PHASES OF THE VICTIMIZATION OF ROHINGYA REFUGEES

PHASE – 1

VIOLENCE, PERSECUTION AND COLLECTIVE VICTIMIZATION OF ROHINGYAS IN MYANMAR

PHASE – 2

VICTIMIZATION AND PROBLEMS FACED DURING MIGRATING FROM MYANMAR TO BANGLADESH

PHASE – 3

VICTIMIZATION DUE TO THE REFUGEE CAMP SITUATION AND PROBLEMS ASSOCIATED WITH THE REFUGEE CAMPS

ii. Phase 2: Victimization and problems faced during migrating from Myanmar to Bangladesh

1. *Physical victimization:* They are forced to leave their villages and walk all the way from their village to the Myanmar seashore, which itself is a physical victimization. It is even more difficult for children, elderly people, women and physically challenged persons, who are very weak and more vulnerable.

2. *Violence and abuses by the army:* During the time of displacement also, the army randomly opened fire on many Rohingyas, due to which many people were injured, while others were killed in the attack. While crossing the army check post, Rohingyas were abused in the guise of checking.

3. *Hunger:* During the time of displacement, they didn't have much food, and they ate whatever was available at that time, but many times they had to stay hungry.

4. *Abuse by boat owners:* To reach Bangladesh, the Rohingyas used boats, but the boat owners abused the Rohingyas by demanding much more money than required. Sometimes their jewelry and valuables were stolen. People who didn't have money were asked for sexual favors. Sometimes the Rohingyas were left in the shallow water near the Bangladesh seashore.

iii. Phase 3: Victimization due to the refugee camp situation and problems associated with the refugee camp

1. *Issues with medical facilities:* The medical facilities provided in the refugee camps are very basic in nature and are insufficient to treat severe health issues. In medical centers, not enough doctors

are available, and if there is any kind of severe health issue, refugees have to go to the city for their treatment, which was not possible.

2.   *Overcrowding:* Overcrowding is one of the major issues Rohingya refugees are facing currently, and because of overcrowding, the refugees face issues like insufficiency of food items, insufficiency of water, hygiene issues and health issues, overusage of toilets and bathrooms etc.

3.   *Lack of water:* In the refugee camps, water is not available sufficiently. Even though the NGOs and Bangladesh government have installed a good number of tube wells, many of them have failed to work, because of which the refugees are facing a lot of problems.

4.   *Issues pertaining to food items:* Food items provided in the refugee camps are not enough, because of which many refugees are not able to have proper food. The food items lack nutrition, owing to which there is malnutrition among the children in the refugee camps as well.

5.   *Livelihood issues:* Most of the refugees are unemployed and do not have any kind of past earnings as well, and they are unable to fulfill their needs pertaining to, and the food that they do get doesn't include vegetables, meat and eggs.

6.   *Poor sanitation:* Sanitation is also a major problem in the refugee camps, as toilets and bathrooms are overused and not maintained properly. Because of this, the refugees often face health issues and hygiene-related issues.

7.   *Education:* There are only primary schools available in the refugee camps. There are no schools providing secondary education in the refugee camps. In these primary schools, there are no class divisions, and teaching is only based on age. Moreover, in these schools, only Burmese, Bengali and English language are taught, and no other subjects are taught.

8.   *Psychological trauma:* Psychological trauma is very common among the refugees, and during the interviews; the researcher has witnessed the participants crying with great deep pain while narrating the incidents.

9.   *Gender-based violence:* The refugees regularly face gender-based violence in the refugee camps.

iv. Policy Recommendations

Based on the broad literature review, analysis of the data and findings of this research study, the researcher came up with certain recommendations from various perspectives, which are as follows:

1. Short-Term Policy Recommendations

1.   Though the issues of overcrowding cannot be solved, other issues which have risen because of overcrowding can be controlled. In cases of hygiene-related issues or overusage of bathrooms and toilets, the matter can be taken care of by employing some Rohingya refugees with minimum wage to take care of cleaning the bathrooms and toilets on a daily basis.

2.   NGOs and the government of Bangladesh should initiate minimum wage employment programmes to provide employment and earning opportunities to the Rohingya refugees. They can be employed in refugee camp development and in farmland cultivation, as 70% of Bangladesh's land is arable. This will be beneficial for both Rohingya refugees and the Bangladesh government.

2. Long-Term Policy Recommendations

1.   Organizations and academics working in the field of victimology, like the World Society of Victimology (WSV), South Asian Society of Criminology and Victimology (SASCV) and Indian

Society of Victimology (ISV), should recognize the need for research in the area of collective victimization and should negotiate with international communities to grant victimhood status to the refugees, as they are more victimized but not recognized and hence called 'ideal victims'.

2. The United Nations should set up a task force to find out the facts and evidence of mass killing, persecution and violence against the Rohingyas and provide justice to them by initiating a criminal case against the Myanmar government in the International Court of Justice or the International Criminal Court.

3. The United Nations should put pressure on the international community to take strong diplomatic action against the Myanmar government to take back these Rohingyas and also provide them citizenship rights with full freedom.

4. Before starting any kind of repatriation process, the UN should send a task force to ensure safety and security of these Rohingyas in the Rakhine state of Myanmar. In the repatriation and rehabilitation process, the UN should act as a guardian to protect these affected Rohingyas from further victimization. The researcher has already cautioned that there are chances of a fourth phase of victimization which may arise during the process of repatriation and rehabilitation.

5. Future researchers can construct a victimization survey specially focused on the refugee population based on the phases of victimization explored in this study and also can conduct a wide range of quantitative research to establish welfare policies for the refugee population.

6. As per the governance model, non-governmental organizations and civil society play a major role in the formation of welfare policies for common people. So it is recommended that major international non-government organizations (like Amnesty International, Human Rights Watch, Genocide Watch) along with the UN should put pressure on the Myanmar government to provide citizenship and freedom to these affected Rohingyas instead of only focusing on relief work.

Conclusion

This chapter has explored various kinds of victimization faced by the Rohingyas in Myanmar and in Bangladesh as refugees. The chapter also explored issues associated with refugee camps and camp situations due to which these Rohingyas are directly or indirectly victimized. Also, I visited Bangladesh Rohingya Refugee Camps in 2018 and found that many Rohingya refugees are not interested to go back to Myanmar because they are afraid of violence and persecution by the Myanmar army, and also psychological trauma has caused them to not want to go back to Myanmar. On the other hand, some Rohingya refugees are still interested to go back to Myanmar, as they say that it is their country and they cannot live away from their home state (Rakhine) of Myanmar.

The Rohingya refugees are currently facing many issues in the camps, and one of the major issues is overcrowding. This overcrowding could be avoided if some other South Asian nations help these refugees by providing space in their respective countries. Notably, India has denied space for the Rohingya refugees, viewing them *intoto* as associates of terrorist groups. I think that the solution for this issue will only come when each and every one in this world changes his/her mentality of generalizing about the whole group or society based on the actions of a few.

The Rohingya refugee crisis is one of the major issues in the South East Asian and South Asian countries. Notably these refugees are still not repatriated to their country. Also, many talks on repatriation work between Bangladesh and Myanmar have failed because the UN has raised the question of safety and security of these refugees. The UN officials even doubt that after the repatriation process there are chances of revictimization of these Rohingyas.

I feel that there is a strong need for a regional-level response, and international pressure should be put on the Myanmar government to solve the Rohingya refugee crisis. This can only be achieved by strong regional cooperation among the South East Asian and South Asian countries, and through negotiation and mitigation, a process can be initiated to solve this Rohingya refugee crisis.

References

Abdelkader, E. (2013). The Rohingya Muslims in Myanmar: Past, present and future. *Oregon Review of International Law, 15*(3).

Abdelkader, E. (2017, September 21). The history of the persecution of Myanmar's Rohingya. *The Conversation.* Retrieved from http://theconversation.com/the-history-of-the-persecution-of-myanmars-rohingya-84040.

Abedin eiffel. (2017, September 11). Parliament passes resolution urging UN to mount pressure on Myanmar. *dhakatribune* [dhaka].

Albert. (2018, April 20). What forces are fueling Myanmar's Rohingya crisis? Retrieved from www.cfr.org/backgrounder/rohingya-crisis.

Al-Mahmood. (2016, December 23). Timeline: A short history of Myanmar's Rohingya minority. *The Wall Street Journal.*

Amnesty International. (2018, June 20). Bangladesh: International assistance urgently needed for Rohingya refugees. *Amnesty International News.*

BBC News. (2018, March 21). Rohingya teenagers trafficked for sex in Bangladesh. Retrieved from www.bbc.com/news/world-asia-43469043.

BBC News (Asia). (n.d.). Myanmar Rohingya: What you need to know about the crisis. Retrieved from www.bbc.com/news/world-asia-41566561.

Dussich, J.P. (2018). The ongoing genocidal crisis of the Rohingya minority in Myanmar. *Journal of Victimology and Victim Justice, 1*(1), 4–24. doi: 10.1177/2516606918764998.

Equal Rights Trust. Institute of Human Rights and Peace Studies. (2014). *Equal only in name: The human rights of stateless Rohingya in Thailand.* London: Institute of Human Rights and Peace Studies.

Fortify Rights International (Organization). (2014). *Policies of persecution: Ending abusive state policies against Rohingya Muslims in Myanmar.* Bangkok, Thailand.

Ganguly, S. & Miliate, B. (2015, October 14). Refugees and neighbours: Rohingya in Bangladesh. *The Diplomat.*

Green, P., MacManus, T., & de la Cour Venning, A. (2015). *Countdown to annihilation: Genocide in Myanmar.* London: International State Crime Initiative.

Gulf News. (2017, September 29). The many challenges facing the Rohingya.

Holmes, O., & Agencies. (2017, November 23). Myanmar signs pact with Bangladesh over Rohingya repatriation. *The Guardian.*

The Irrawaddy. (2018, February 2). Bangladesh tightens security in Rohingya camps.

Islam, N. (2013, May 27). Brief history of Rohingya. *RVision (Rohingya Vision).*

Lowenstein, A. K. (2015). *Persecution of the Rohingya Muslims: Is genocide occurring in Myanmar's Rakhine State? A legal analysis.* Yale, MI: International Human Rights Clinic, Yale Law School for Fortify Rights.

Mathieson, D. (2009). *Perilous plight: Burma's Rohingya take to the seas.* New York: Human Rights Watch.

Morris, B., Chopyak, E., Gray, A., & Mamun, K. (2007, October 29). October 2017 Assessment Report: Undocumented Myanmar nationals influx to cox's bazar, Bangladesh (Rep.). Retrieved from www.rescue.org/press-release/report-reveals-dire-needs-rohingya-refugees.

Prodip, M.A. (2017). Health and educational status of Rohingya refugee children in Bangladesh. *Journal of Population and Social Studies, 25*(2), 135–146. doi: 10.25133/jpssv25n2.005.

Siddiqui. (2017). *The Rohingya: The latest massacre in a violence-filled history.* Retrieved from Al Jazeera Centre for Studies website http://studies.aljazeera.net/mritems/Documents/2017/10/1/5c4d6de9786047a1b2895fbe0948a77b_100.pdf.

Ullah, A. K. M. A. (2005). Destiny of the trafficked in women and girls: Some theoretical and critical issues. *Empowerment, 12*, 75–84.

Ullah, A. K. M. A. (2008). The price of migration from Bangladesh to distant lands: Narratives of recent tragedies. *Asian Profile, 36*, 639–646.

Ullah, A.A. (2011). Rohingya refugees to Bangladesh: Historical exclusions and contemporary marginalization. *Journal of Immigrant & Refugee Studies, 9*(2), 139–161. doi: 10.1080/15562948.2011.567149.

UN News. (2017, May 4). Myanmar: Displaced Rohingya at risk of re-victimization warns un refugee agency. Retrieved from https://news.un.org/en/story/2017/05/556532-myanmar-displaced-rohingya-risk-re-victimization-warns-un-refugee-agency.

Yunus. (1994). *A history of Arakan: Past and present* (1st ed.). Retrieved from www.netipr.org/policy/downloads/19940101_Dr-Yunus-History-Of-Arakan.pdf.

CONCLUSION

South Asian Criminology in a Crossroad

K. Jaishankar

Though the eight nations of South Asia have their individual problems of crime and victimization, some of the tribulations are connected with history. Except Bhutan and Nepal, the British colonized all the other six nations of South Asia, and many of the problems are related to colonization and its aftermath. Notably, countries like Pakistan and Bangladesh were born only after 1947. While some of the nations like Sri Lanka and Maldives are Islands, most of the South Asian nations (excluding Afghanistan) are landlocked and part of the Indian subcontinent.

Issues like Kashmir ownership of India and Pakistan are still unresolved. Even after a decade of Sri Lankan civil war (where the army vanquished the LTTE), the problems of the nation are still burning. Maldives, Nepal, Bangladesh and Pakistan have their own political problems. Countries like Pakistan face terrorism as a hydra-headed monster. In 2011, Osama Bin Laden, the most wanted terrorist, was killed in a covert operation by US Navy Seals in Abbotabad, Pakistan. Except Bhutan, the Country of Happiness, the seven nations of South Asia, Afghanistan, Bangladesh, Sri Lanka, India, Maldives, Pakistan and Nepal are not happy. The internal and external problems of these countries are colossal, and most of them are irresolvable due its historical vestiges.

The above-said problems are academically examined by several universities of South Asia in their political science, sociology, psychology and history departments. Notably, South Asian criminology does not have a distinct identity like American criminology or British criminology, as there are not many departments of criminology/criminal justice in the universities of the South Asian region. Criminology as an independent field of study was introduced in 1959 in India at the University of Sagar, Madhya Pradesh, based on the recommendations of UNESCO in cooperation with the International Society of Criminology. The Indian Society of Criminology (ISC-www.isc70.org) was established in 1970 to advance the discipline of criminology in India. The South Asian Society of Criminology and Victimology (SASCV-www.sascv.org) was established by me in 2009 to advance the discipline in the South Asian region.

Criminology as an academic discipline is offered in bachelor's and master's programmes at various colleges and universities of Pakistan. The Pakistan Society of Criminology (PSC-www.pscriminol ogy.com) was established in the year 2008 by a few academics and law enforcement officers. The birth of academic criminology in Bangladesh can be traced back to the opening of a master's of social science in criminology and criminal justice programme at the Dhaka University in 2010. Notably, there are no independent departments of criminology/criminal justice in Maldives, Nepal, Bhutan and Afghanistan.

Even though the growth of criminology is in its nascent stages, there is no dearth of scholarship. The *Indian Journal of Criminology* is a flagship journal of the Indian Society of Criminology that was established in 1973 and has published several notable studies. The *International Journal of Criminal Justice Sciences*, the flagship journal of the South Asian Society of Criminology and Victimology (SASCV), is a forerunner in taking South Asian criminological researches to the international academics. Also, the *Pakistan Journal of Criminology*, the flagship journal of the Pakistan Society of Criminology, even though recently established, has published significant studies and contributed to the field of criminology in the South Asian region. The Bangladesh Society of Criminology and Sri Lankan Society of Criminology are newcomers, and they are on the threshold of making effective contributions to South Asian criminology.

In spite of the significant contributions of South Asian criminologists and others, South Asian criminology is still marginalized. Moosavi (2018a, p. 3) laments "criminology is dominated by Western scholars, literature and perspectives. This Western centrism of criminology means that non-Western criminological scholarship has largely been marginalised or ignored". Unfortunately, not only the Western world ignores scholarship on South Asian criminology, but the Southern and the Asian world does also. While there are notable calls for Southern criminology (Carrington et al., 2016) and Asian criminology (Liu, 2009), still these perspectives are limited. Even though these perspectives claim to be holistic, Southern criminology largely concentrates on the Asia-Pacific region (Australia and New Zealand), and Asian criminology concentrates on a few areas of the East Asian region (China, South Korea, Taiwan, Hong Kong, Thailand and Japan), largely ignoring the eight countries of the South Asian region.

Moosavi (2018b, P. 7) further highlights:

> It is also evident in the *Handbook of Asian Criminology* (Liu et al., 2013), in which there is a disproportionate focus on East Asia. For instance, there are more contributors to this collection who are based in East Asia compared to the combined total of contributors from South Asia, Southeast Asia, the Middle East and Central Asia. . . . it is clear that Asian criminology is dominated by East Asian criminologists, which may mean it would be more accurate to speak of 'East Asian Criminology' rather than 'Asian Criminology'.
>
> In the *Palgrave Handbook of Criminology and the Global South* (Carrington et al., 2018), the latest manifestation of Southern Criminology, almost half of the 79 contributors are based in Australian institutions. This is reflective of the way in which Southern criminology is dominated by Australian criminologists in a way that may mean Southern criminology may be better described as 'Australian Criminology'.

This academic parochialism is not helping the growth of criminology in the South Asian region, and I feel that South Asian criminology should be distinct and separate from the other criminologies, as I believe that both Southern and Asian criminologies will not be academically inclusive. Also, the criminological problems of the South Asian region are unique and regional in nature, which will not be understood by other regions of Asia or the Asia-Pacific. I am not going to reiterate on decolonizing criminology, as it is heavily discussed (Moosavi, 2018a), but would be wary if Southern and Asian criminologies would colonize South Asian criminology.

I sincerely hope that South Asian criminology will take root and that the countries in the South Asian region will consider starting more criminology/criminal justice departments in their universities and colleges. Also, the profession of criminology should be recognized by the governments by enacting a similar law that regulates the practice of the criminology profession in the Philippines (Musico, 2018). South Asian criminologists should publish frequently in South Asian and Western journals, especially the open-access ones like the *International Journal of Criminal Justice Sciences* (www. ijcjs.com), which will reach wider audiences.

I believe that this *Routledge Handbook of South Asian Criminology* is a great start for bringing out the scholarship of South Asian criminology holistically. While I took great care to be inclusive of chapter authors from all the South Asian nations, still it was difficult for me to get authors from all the eight nations of South Asia. I tried to balance it by getting a minimum of two authors or chapters from each region to a maximum of eight chapters. Also, some Western authors have significantly contributed to this book. I hope as a reader of the book you have enjoyed it contents. If there are any errors, please bring it to my notice, and I would be glad to rectify them in the future editions.

References

Carrington, K., Hogg, R., Scott, J., & Sozzo, M. (2018). Criminology, southern theory and cognitive justice. In K. Carrington, R. Hogg, J. Scott & M. Sozzo (Eds.), *The Palgrave handbook of criminology and the global south* (pp. 3–17). London: Palgrave Macmillan.

Carrington, K., Sozzo, M., & Hogg, R. (2016). Southern criminology. *British Journal of Criminology, 56*,1–20.

Liu, J. (2009). Asian criminology—Challenges, opportunities, and directions. *Asian Journal of Criminology, 4,* 1–9.

Liu, J., Hebenton, B., & Jou, S. (2013). Progress of Asian criminology. In J. Liu, B. Hebenton & S. Jou (Eds.), *Handbook of Asian criminology* (pp. 1–7). Springer-Verlag.

Moosavi, L. (2018a). Decolonising criminology: Syed Hussein Alatas on crimes. *Critical Criminology.* https://doi.org/10.1007/s10612-018-9396-9.

Moosavi, L. (2018b). A friendly critique of "Asian Criminology" and "Southern Criminology". *The British Journal of Criminology, 59*(2), 257–275.

Musico, J. (November 16, 2018). Duterte inks law regulating criminology profession. Retrieved from www.pna.gov.ph/articles/1054054.

INDEX

Note: Page numbers for figures are in *italic* type, page numbers for tables are in **bold** type and page numbers followed by 'n' signify endnotes.

Clarke, G. 46
Clarke, R. 130
classicism 161
CNN Freedom Project 190
Coalition to Stop the Use of Child Soldiers 187
Coast Guard Act 1994 (Bangladesh) 23
Code of Rules (1860; India) 47
Codes of Criminal Procedure: Bangladesh 24; India
  47–51, 278; Pakistan 73; Sri Lanka 86–90
Cold War 177
collective victimization (Rohingyas) 341–352
colonial period 353; Bhutan 36; Maldives 54;
  Rohingyas and 343; *see also* British India
Colonial Police Act of 1861 (Bangladesh) 21
Committee Against Torture 111
Committee on Economic, Social and Cultural
  Rights 257
communal riots, India 134–136, 154
Communism, Afghanistan 176–177, 183
Communist Party of Maoist Nepal (CPNM) 68, 229,
  232n1
Community Service Center (CSC; Nepal) 226–227
Company's Courts (India) 46–47
compensation, right to (Nepal) 315–316
Comprehensive Peace Agreement (CPA; Nepal) 68,
  220–221, 232n1
concurrent governance 188
confessions: Nepal 67–68; Sri Lanka 87–88
Congress Party (India) 135
Connor, K. 19n3
constitutions: of Afghanistan 178; of Bhutan 31–37;
  of India 48–49, 106, 257–259; of Maldives 55–56;
  of Nepal 62–67, 309, 330–333; of Pakistan 70,
  73–75, 79; of Sri Lanka 87, 90–92
contemporary India, homicide in 148–157
control model, for prisons 24
Convention on Children's Rights 278
Convention on the Elimination of All Forms of
  Discrimination Against Women (CEDAW) 111,
  297–298, 302, 327, 332
conviction rates: Nepal 63; Pakistan 78–80
Cooperation for Peace and Unity (CPAU) 180
Cooray (1926; Sri Lanka) 87
Cornwallis (Lord) 45, 50
corrections *see* jails; prisons/corrections
corrective justice 263
corrective regimes 16
corruption: Afghanistan 13–14, 174, 178–180;
  Bangladesh 25–26, 267; Bhutan 32–35; Pakistan
  77–78; trafficking and 166, 169
Council of Europe 253n3
Council of Ulama (Pakistan) 70
counter-trafficking 7
Court of *Diwan-e-mulzim* (India) 43
Court of *Fauzdar* (India) 43
courts: Afghanistan 174; Bangladesh 21–24; Bhutan
  290–291; India 41–47; Nepal 315; *see also* High
  Courts; Magistrate Courts; Supreme Courts

Cowen, T. 269
Cox's Bazaar, Bangladesh 341–342, 347–348
CPA (Comprehensive Peace Agreement; Nepal) 68,
  220–221, 232n1
CPAU (Cooperation for Peace and Unity) 180
CPNM (Communist Party of Maoist Nepal) 68, 229,
  232n1
CPNUML (Nepal Communist Party of United
  Marxist and Leninist) 227–229
CPOST (Chicago Project on Security and Terrorism)
  215–217
Crescent region 237, 320
crime and criminal justice processes: Afghanistan
  11–20; Bangladesh 21–29; Bhutan 30–38; India
  39–51; Maldives 52–60, 54; *Manusmriti* (Manu's
  code) and 101–103; Nepal 61–69; Pakistan 70–84;
  Sri Lanka 85–93
crime and justice policies: Bangladesh 263–270;
  Bhutan 281–293; human trafficking and 247–254;
  India 255–260, 271–280; Nirbhaya incident
  and 271–280; transgender rights and 255–260;
  transitional justice and 263–270; young offenders
  and 281–293
"Crime in India" (National Crime Records Bureau
  [NCRB]) 154
Crime Investigation Department (CID; Nepal) 62
crime statistics: Bangladesh 27–28, 322–323; Bhutan
  30–31, 282–286; India 154–156, 278; Maldives
  52–53; Nepal 221; Pakistan 77–80
Criminal Codes (1976; Afghanistan) 16
criminalization, Afghanistan 176–181
"Criminalize Torture" 66
criminal law-enforcement model 181
Criminal Laws (Amendment) Act, 2013 (India)
  258–259
Criminal Procedure Codes: Bangladesh 24; India
  258–259; Sri Lanka 87–89
Criminal Tribes Act of 1871 (India) 256
criminological theory 161–173
cruelty 126
CSC (Community Service Center; Nepal)
  226–227
culpable homicide 153
cultural atavism 302
curfew rule, Bhutan 284
custodial deaths, Bangladesh 25
*Cutting the Fuse: The Explosion of Global Suicide
  Terrorism and How to Stop It* (Pape) 215
CVICT 64
CWIN (Child Workers in Nepal) 308
cybercrime: Bangladesh 28; Bhutan 33, 36–37;
  Maldives 53–55; Pakistan 78

Daily Star 320
Dakshinapatha 122
Dalits 106, 111
danda 98–99, 103, 123, 149
dandaniti 42